Lecture Notes in Computer Science 13061

More information about this subseries at http://www.springer.com/series/7410

Branislav Bošanský · Cleotilde Gonzalez ·
Stefan Rass · Arunesh Sinha (Eds.)

Decision and Game Theory for Security

12th International Conference, GameSec 2021
Virtual Event, October 25–27, 2021
Proceedings

 Springer

Editors
Branislav Bošanský 🆔
Czech Technical University
Prague, Czech Republic

Stefan Rass 🆔
Johannes Kepler University Linz
Linz, Austria

University of Klagenfurt
Klagenfurt, Austria

Cleotilde Gonzalez 🆔
Carnegie Mellon University
Pittsburgh, PA, USA

Arunesh Sinha
Singapore Management University
Singapore, Singapore

ISSN 0302-9743   ISSN 1611-3349   (electronic)
Lecture Notes in Computer Science
ISBN 978-3-030-90369-5   ISBN 978-3-030-90370-1   (eBook)
https://doi.org/10.1007/978-3-030-90370-1

LNCS Sublibrary: SL4 – Security and Cryptology

This Springer imprint is published by the registered company Springer Nature Switzerland AG
The registered company address is: Gewerbestrasse 11, 6330 Cham, Switzerland

Preface

More than a year since the COVID-19 pandemic has substantially changed our lives, we are more than ever relying on having a stable and secure internet connection to learn, work, and talk to our loved ones. The pandemic forced people to change their behavior and do many more tasks online for the first time, leaving them, however, more vulnerable to online threats. To protect vulnerable users, we need to know and understand possible threats and then we can determine the best protective strategies. Game theory provides established mathematical foundations for such security problems and game-theoretic algorithms are used to find the optimal behavior for current and future problems in security.

Importantly, it has become clear that game-theoretic algorithms must not ignore the patterns of human behavior. To be effective, comprehensive security solutions need to address the human factor, humans' understanding, adherence, and trust of security mechanisms. GameSec 2021 tried to raise awareness of the behavioral aspects of decision and game theory relevant to security models. Invited speakers with eminent international reputations highlighted several aspects of human behavior of relevance for this community.

This volume contains the papers presented at GameSec 2021, the 12th Conference on Decision and Game Theory for Security held during October 25–27, 2021. While the plan was to host GameSec 2021 in Prague, Czech Republic, due to the COVID-19 pandemic and travelling restrictions, the conference was held only virtually. The GameSec conference series was inaugurated in 2010 in Berlin, Germany. Over 12 years, GameSec has become widely recognized as an important venue for interdisciplinary security research. The previous conferences were held in College Park (USA, 2011), Budapest (Hungary, 2012), Fort Worth (USA, 2013), Los Angeles (USA, 2014), London (UK, 2015), New York (USA, 2016), Vienna (Austria, 2017), Seattle (USA, 2018), Stockholm (Sweden, 2019), and College Park (USA/virtual conference, 2020).

As in the past years, the 2021 edition of GameSec featured a number of high-quality novel contributions. The conference program included 20 full paper presentations that were selected from 37 submissions. The program contained papers on traditional GameSec topics such as game-theoretic models of various security problems, as well as an increasing number of papers at the intersection of AI, machine learning, and security.

Several organizations supported GameSec 2021. We are particularly grateful to the Artificial Intelligence Center at the Czech Technical University in Prague, Springer, Blindspot, and a partner conference CyberSec&AI Connected.

We hope that readers will find this volume a useful resource for their security and game theory research.

October 2021

Branislav Bošanský
Cleotilde Gonzalez
Stefan Rass
Arunesh Sinha

Organization

General Chairs

Branislav Bošanský   Czech Technical University in Prague, Czech Republic
Cleotilde Gonzalez   Carnegie Mellon University, USA

Steering Board

Tansu Alpcan   University of Melbourne, Australia
John S. Baras   University of Maryland, USA
Tamer Başar   University of Illinois Urbana-Champaign, USA
Anthony Ephremides   University of Maryland, USA
Radha Poovendran   University of Washington, USA
Milind Tambe   Harvard University, USA

Advisory Board

Fei Fang   Carnegie Mellon University, USA
Tiffany Bao   Arizona State University, USA
Branislav Bošanský   Czech Technical University in Prague, Czech Republic
Stefan Rass   Johannes Kepler University Linz/University
     of Klagenfurt, Austria
Manos Panaousis   University of Greenwich, UK
Quanyan Zhu   New York University, USA

Technical Program Committee Chairs

Stefan Rass   Johannes Kepler University Linz/University
     of Klagenfurt, Austria
Arunesh Sinha   Singapore Management University, Singapore

Publicity Chair

Charles Kamhoua   Army Research Laboratory, USA

Web Chair

Petr Benda   Czech Technical University in Prague, Czech Republic

Technical Program Committee

Habtamu Abie	Norwegian Computing Center, Norway
Palvi Aggarwal	Carnegie Mellon University, USA
Bo An	Nanyang Technological University, Singapore
Tansu Alpcan	University of Melbourne, Australia
Parinaz Naghizadeh Ardabili	Ohio State University, USA
Noam Ben Asher	Cyber Security and Information Systems, Information Analysis Center, USA
Konstantin Avratchenkov	Inria Sophia Antipolis, France
Carlos Barreto	Vanderbilt University, USA
Svetlana Boudko	Norwegian Computing Center, Norway
Edward Cranford	Carnegie Mellon University, USA
Andrew Clark	Worcester Polytechnic Institute, USA
Kimberly Ferguson-Walter	Department of Defense, USA
Sunny James Fugate	Naval Information Warfare Center, USA
Robert Gutzwiller	Arizona State University, USA
Jens Grossklags	Technical University of Munich, Germany
Yezekael Hayel	University of Avignon, France
Ashish Hota	Indian Institute of Technology, Kharagpur, India
Hideaki Ishii	Tokyo Institute of Technology, Japan
Albert Jiang	Trinity University, USA
Eduard A. Jorswieck	TU Dresden, Germany
Mohammad Mahdi Khalili	University of Delaware, USA
Charles Kamhoua	Air Force Research Lab, USA
Murat Kantarcioglu	University of Texas at Dallas, USA
Christopher Kiekintveld	University of Texas at El Paso, USA
Sandra König	Austrian Institute of Technology, Austria
Aron Laszka	Vanderbilt University, USA
Yee Wei Law	University of South Australia, Australia
Christian Lebiere	Carnegie Mellon University, USA
M. Hossein Manshaei	Isfahan University of Technology, Iran
Damian Marriott	Defence Science and Technology Group, Australia
Katerina Mitrokotsa	Chalmers University of Technology, Sweden
Shana Moothedath	University of Washington, USA
Mehrdad Nojoumian	Florida Atlantic University, USA
Thanh Nguyen	University of Oregon, USA
Fernando Ordonez	Universidad de Chile, Chile
Miroslav Pajic	Duke University, USA
Sakshyam Panda	University of Surrey, UK
David Pym	University College London, UK
Bhaskar Ramasubramanian	University of Washington, USA
George Theodorakopoulos	Cardiff University, UK

Jayneel Vora   University of California, Davis, USA
Quanyan Zhu   New York University, USA
Jun Zhuang   SUNY Buffalo, USA

Contents

Theoretical Foundations in Equilibrium Computation

Computing Nash Equilibria in Multiplayer DAG-Structured Stochastic Games with Persistent Imperfect Information

Sam Ganzfried[(✉)]

Ganzfried Research, Miami Beach, FL, USA
http://www.ganzfriedresearch.com/

Abstract. Many important real-world settings contain multiple players interacting over an unknown duration with probabilistic state transitions, and are naturally modeled as stochastic games. Prior research on algorithms for stochastic games has focused on two-player zero-sum games, games with perfect information, and games with imperfect-information that is local and does not extend between game states. We present an algorithm for approximating Nash equilibrium in multiplayer general-sum stochastic games with persistent imperfect information that extends throughout game play. We experiment on a 4-player imperfect-information naval strategic planning scenario. Using a new procedure, we are able to demonstrate that our algorithm computes a strategy that closely approximates Nash equilibrium in this game.

Keywords: Stochastic game · Imperfect information · Nash equilibrium

1 Introduction

Many important problems involve multiple agents behaving strategically. In particular, there have been recent applications of game-theoretic algorithms to important problems in national security. These game models and algorithms have differing levels of complexity. Typically these games have two players, and algorithms compute a Stackelberg equilibrium for a model where the "defender" acts as the leader and the "attacker" as the follower; the goal is to compute an optimal mixed strategy to commit to for the defender, assuming that the attacker will play a best response [13,14]. Algorithms have been developed for both zero sum and non-zero-sum games. Computing Stackelberg equilibrium is easier than Nash equilibrium; for example, for two-player normal-form general-sum games, optimal Stackelberg strategies can be computed in polynomial time [4], while computing Nash equilibrium is PPAD-hard, and widely conjectured that no polynomial-time algorithms exist [3,5]. For many realistic scenarios, models are much more complex than even computing Nash equilibrium

© Springer Nature Switzerland AG 2021
B. Bošanský et al. (Eds.): GameSec 2021, LNCS 13061, pp. 3–16, 2021.
https://doi.org/10.1007/978-3-030-90370-1_1

in two-player general-sum simultaneous-move games. Many realistic problems in national security involve more than two agents, sequential actions, imperfect information, probabilistic events, and/or repeated interactions of unknown duration. While some approaches have been developed for models containing a subset of these complexities, we are not aware of any algorithms for solving models that contain all of them. We present an algorithm for solving a model for a naval strategic planning problem that involves all of these challenges. The model was constructed in consultation with a domain expert, and therefore we have strong reason to believe is realistic. Our model is a 4-player imperfect-information stochastic game. Our model builds on a closely related 4-player perfect-information game model [7]. The imperfect information adds a significant additional challenge not modeled by the prior work, which requires development of new algorithms.

The only prior research we are aware of for computing Nash equilibrium in multiplayer imperfect-information stochastic games are approaches that were applied to solve a 3-player poker tournament [8,9]. However, that setting had a property that made it significantly simpler than the general imperfect-information setting. In the poker tournament, the players were dealt a uniform-random poker hand at each game state (which is known privately to only the player), and these private hands did not persist to other states. This allowed them to devise algorithms that operated by essentially solving each state independently without considering effects of the solutions of one state on the private information beliefs at other states (though the algorithms must use value estimations for the transitions to other states). However, these approaches would not work for settings where the private information persists throughout game states, which is often the case in realistic problems. We refer to the case where the imperfect information does not extend beyond the current state a game with *local imperfect information*, and the setting where the imperfect information persists throughout the game—either remaining the same or changing dynamically—as *persistent imperfect information*.

As prior work has shown, the best existing algorithm for multiplayer stochastic games with perfect information and with local imperfect information is a parallel version of an algorithm that combines policy iteration with fictitious play, called *PI-FP* [7,9]. This algorithm has been demonstrated to quickly converge to provably very close approximations of Nash equilibrium for a 3-player imperfect-information poker tournament and a 4-player perfect information naval planning problem. PI-FP essentially involves solving each state independently (assuming value estimates for payoffs of the other states) using fictitious play, and then using a procedure analogous to policy iteration (an algorithm for solving single-agent Markov decision processes) to update these value estimates for all states. The parallel version of the algorithm, *Parallel PI-FP*, achieves a linear speedup by doing the state equilibrium computations for multiple states concurrently. While this algorithm has proven to be very successful for these settings, unfortunately it cannot be applied directly to the setting for persistent imperfect information, since it does not account for the private information extending between states.

We observe that our planning problem has the special structure that the game states form a directed acyclic graph (DAG). This allows us to devise a new algorithm that solves each game state sequentially, computes updated type distributions from the state equilibrium strategies at that state, and uses these updated type distributions for solving successive states within the current algorithm iteration. We refer to this new algorithm as *Sequential Topological PI-FP*. Unfortunately this algorithm cannot be parallelized to obtain the linear speedup of Parallel PI-FP; however, we are still able to obtain efficient speed in practice for our problem.

2 Imperfect-Information Naval Strategic Planning Problem

We will first review the perfect-information naval strategic planning problem that has been previously studied [7], and then describe the differences for the imperfect-information version. The game is based on a freedom of navigation scenario in the South China Sea where a set of *blue* players attempts to navigate freely, while a set of *red* players attempt to obstruct this from occurring. In our model there is a single blue player and several different red players which have different capabilities (we will specifically focus on the setting where there are three different red players). If a blue player and a subset of the red players happen to navigate to the same location, then a confrontation will ensue, which we call a Hostility Game.

In a Hostility Game, each player can initially select from a number of available actions (which is between 7 and 10 for each player). Certain actions for the blue player are *countered* by certain actions of each of the red players, while others are not. Depending on whether the selected actions constitute a counter, there is some probability that the blue player *wins* the confrontation, some probability that the red players win, and some probability that the game repeats. Furthermore, each action of each player has an associated *hostility level*. Initially the game starts in a state of zero hostility, and if it is repeated then the overall hostility level increases by the sum of the hostilities of the selected actions. If the overall hostility level reaches a certain threshold (300), then the game goes into *kinetic mode* and all players achieve a very low payoff (negative 200). If the game ends in a win for the blue player, then the blue player receives a payoff of 100 and the red players receive negative 100 (and vice versa for a red win). The game repeats until either the blue/red players win or the game enters kinetic mode. The game model and parameters were constructed from discussions with a domain expert.

Definition 1. *A perfect-information hostility game is a tuple $G = (N, M, c, b^D, b^U, r^D, r^U, \pi, h, K, \pi^K)$, where*

- *N is the set of players. For our initial model we will assume player 1 is a blue player and players 2–4 are red players (P2 is a Warship, P3 is a Security ship, and P4 is an Auxiliary vessel).*

- $M = \{M_i\}$ is the set of actions, or moves, where M_i is the set of moves available to player i
- For $m_i \in M_i$, $c(M_i)$ gives a set of blue moves that are counter moves of m_i
- For each blue player move and red player, a probability of blue success/red failure given that the move is defended against (i.e., countered), denoted as b^D
- Probability that a move is a blue success/red failure given the move is Undefended against, denoted as b^U
- Probability for a red success/blue failure given the move is defended against, r^D
- Probability for a red success/blue failure given the move is undefended against, r^U
- Real valued payoff for success for each player, π_i
- Real-valued hostility level for each move $h(m_i)$
- Positive real-valued kinetic hostility threshold K
- Real-valued payoffs for each player when game goes into Kinetic mode, π_i^K

We model hostility game G as a (4-player) stochastic game with a collection of stage games $\{G_n\}$, where n corresponds to the cumulative sum of hostility levels of actions played so far. The game has $K + 3$ states: $G_0, \ldots, G_K$, with two additional terminal states B and R for blue and red victories. Depending on whether the blue move is countered, there is a probabilistic outcome for whether the blue player or red player (or neither) will outright win. The game will then transition into terminal states B or R with these probabilities, and then will be over with final payoffs. Otherwise, the game transitions into $G_{n'}$ where n' is the new sum of the hostility levels. If the game reaches G_K, the players obtain the kinetic payoff π_i^K. Thus, the game starts at initial state G_0 and after a finite number of time steps will eventually reach one of the terminal states (B, R, G_K).

So far, we have described the Perfect-Information Hostility Game (PIHG), which was previously considered. In the real world, often players have some private information that they know but the other players do not. For example, in poker this can be one's private cards, or in an auction one's private valuation for an item. We consider a modification to the PIHG where each player has private information that corresponds to its "strength," or amount of resources it has available. We assume each player has a private type t_i from a discrete set T_i, where larger values of t_i correspond to increased strength. We assume that the players know only the value of their own type, while each player knows that the other players' private types are drawn from a public distribution. We assume that each player is drawn a private type t_i from the public distribution at the outset of the game, and that this type persists throughout the game's duration. Thus, the game model of the Imperfect-Information Hostility Game (IIHG) is a 4-player imperfect-information stochastic game.

The values of the type parameters affect the probabilities of each player's success during a confrontation, with larger values leading to greater success probabilities. For example, suppose there is an encounter between a blue ship of type t_b and red ship of type t_r, and suppose that blue player plays an action a_b that is a counter-move to red's action a_r. Then for the PIHG the probability of a blue success would be $p = b^D(a_b)$. In the IIHG we now have that the probability of a blue success will be $p' = p^{\frac{t_r}{t_b}}$. The other success/failure probabilities are computed analogously. Note that for $t_b = t_r$ we have $p' = p$ and the payoffs are the same as for the PIHG. If $t_r > t_b$ then $p' < p$, and similarly if $t_b < t_r$ then $p' > p$.

3   Algorithm

We first review the prior algorithm PI-FP, which has been successfully applied to solve PIHG. For standard PI-FP, we first initialize values for each player i at each state G_j, $v_i(G_j)$. For example, we can initialize them naïvely to all be zero or random, or use a more intelligent domain-specific heuristic if one is available. Next, we compute a Nash equilibrium in each game state G_j, assuming that the payoff is given by $v_i(G_{j'})$ for the transitions to states $G_{j'} \neq G_j$ (while it is given by the standard game parameters for the terminal payoffs). For Parallel PI-FP these computations are done in parallel, achieving a linear speedup in k, the number of available cores. The two main algorithms for approximating Nash equilibrium in multiplayer imperfect-information games are fictitious play [1,12] and counterfactual regret minimization [15]. We opt to use fictitious play due to recent results showing that it leads to closer equilibrium approximation in a variety of multiplayer game classes [6]. Note that fictitious play is guaranteed to converge to Nash equilibrium in two-player zero-sum games and certain other game classes, but not in general multiplayer games. While specific counterexamples can be constructed for which it fails to converge in multiplayer games, experiments have shown it to converge consistently in a range of realistic games [6]. It has also been shown to converge to equilibrium within the context of PI-FP [7,9].

After these game-state equilibrium strategies have been computed using fictitious play, we have now obtained strategies s_{ij} for each player i at each state G_j. We next need to update the values $v_i(G_j)$ given these new strategies. This is accomplished using procedures analogous to algorithms for solving Markov decision processes, *policy iteration* and *value iteration*. Value iteration would correspond to performing an essentially local update, where the values are now assigned to the new Nash equilibrium strategy values at that state, which assumed the prior round values for the adjacent states. Policy iteration would involve finding values $v_i(G_j)$ for all players and states that are consistent globally with the new strategies, which can be accomplished by solving a system of linear equations. These procedures both produce new values for all players at all states, which are then used to re-solve each state G_j again using fictitious play. While various termination criteria can be used for both the inner loop (fictitious play) and outer loop (value updating) portions of the algorithm, we will generally specify a fixed number of iterations in advance to run each, as neither is guaranteed to achieve convergence. When value iteration is used for the inner loop the algorithm is called VI-FP, and for policy iteration PI-FP. For the three-player poker tournament experiments, both VI-FP and PI-FP converged to strategies that constituted an ϵ-equilibrium for very small ϵ [8,9], with PI-FP converging faster than VI-FP. However for the perfect information hostility game experiments, all versions of VI-FP failed to converge to equilibrium while all versions of PI-FP did [7]. So for our experiments we will build on PI-FP, which has been demonstrated to have superior performance.

Our main metric for evaluation will be to compute the ϵ, which measures the degree of Nash equilibrium approximation. The value of ϵ denotes the largest amount that a player can gain by deviating from the strategy profile. In exact Nash equilibrium $\epsilon = 0$, and so naturally our goal is to produce strategies with as small value of ϵ as possible. We say that the computed strategies constitute an ϵ-equilibrium. Formally, for a given candidate strategy profile σ^*, define

$$\epsilon(\sigma^*) = \max_i \max_{\sigma_i \in \Sigma_i} \left[u_i(\sigma_i, \sigma_{-i}^*) - u_i(\sigma_i^*, \sigma_{-i}^*) \right].$$

Now suppose we try to apply standard PI-FP, or Parallel PI-FP, to solve the imperfect-information hostility game (Algorithm 1). Initially we assume that the type probabilities are distributed according to the public prior distribution. For our experiments, we will assume that the prior distribution is uniform over $\{1, \ldots, |T_i|\}$ for each player i. We will also assume that the type distribution initially agrees with the prior for all stage games G_j, in addition to the initial state G_0. We next solve all stage games G_j as before, assuming the types are distributed according to the prior at each game. After solving these games, we must then update the type distributions to make them consistent with the strategies that have just been computed. This can be accomplished by traversing through the states in order $G_0, G_1, \ldots, G_K$ and computing the updated type distribution at each state using Bayes' rule, assuming the type distributions already computed for the preceding states and transitions determined by the computed strategies. After the type distributions are updated at all states to be consistent with the strategies, we can then perform a similar value update step for policy iteration as before by solving the induced system of equations. We continue to repeat these three steps until termination: strategy computation, type distribution update, value update. This modified procedure for solving imperfect-information stochastic games with persistent imperfect-information is given in Algorithm 2.

Algorithm 1. Parallel PI-FP [7]

Inputs: Stopping condition C_S for stage game solving, stopping condition C_V for value updating, number of cores d

$V^0 = \text{initializeValues}()$
$i = 0$
while C_V not met **do**
$\quad i = i + 1$
$\quad$ **while** C_S not met for each stage game **do**
$\quad\quad$ Run fictitious play on each stage game on d cores (solving d stage games simultaneously) to obtain S^i
$\quad V^i = \text{evaluateStrategies}(S^i)$
return S^i

Algorithm 2. Parallel PI-FP for persistent imperfect-information

---

Inputs: Stopping condition C_S for stage game solving, stopping condition C_V for value updating, number of cores d

$V^0 = $ initializeValues()
$T^0 = $ initializeTypes()
$i = 0$
while C_V not met **do**
    $i = i + 1$
    while C_S not met for each stage game **do**
        Run fictitious play on each stage game with input type distribution according to T^i on d cores (solving d stage games simultaneously) to obtain S^i
        $T^i = $ updated types for all states consistent with S^i
        $V^i = $ evaluateStrategies(S^i, T^i)
    return S^i

Since the type-updating step can be performed efficiently by traversing the game states and applying Bayes' rule, Algorithm 2 can be performed as efficiently as Algorithm 1, and can obtain the same linear speedup from parallelization. However, there is unfortunately a major problem with Algorithm 2. When we are solving a given stage game G_j, we are assuming the players have types according to T_i, which are consistent with strategies for the states preceding G_j for the strategies under S_{i-1}, but not for the strategies that are being newly computed (in parallel) for those states at timestep i. So the algorithm would be essentially using stale type distributions that are consistent with old strategies when computing the current strategy at a given state. So the algorithm can still be run, and it may converge; but it will likely obtain poor performance due to the assumption of incorrect type distributions for the game solving.

Fortunately, we can create a new algorithm that correctly accounts for the updated types based on an observation about the structure of the imperfect-information hostility game. In particular, we observe that the game can only transition between states G_i to G_j for $i < j$, since we assume that the hostility levels for all actions are positive and therefore the cumulative hostility can only increase. Thus the states $\{G_i\}$ form a directed acyclic graph (DAG) with a natural topological ordering which is just $G_0, G_1, \ldots, G_K$, where states can only transition to other states that come later in the ordering. This allows us to solve each game state sequentially, compute updated type distributions from the state equilibrium strategies by applying Bayes' rule, and use these updated type distributions for solving successive states within the current algorithm iteration.

Algorithm 3 presents our new algorithm, Sequential Topological PI-FP (ST-PIFP) for solving DAG-structured stochastic games with persistent imperfect information. The algorithm solves each game state sequentially according to the topological ordering, using updated type distributions that have been computed applying Bayes' rule given the strategies and type distributions already computed for the preceding states (for state G_0 we assume the original prior type distributions). Then policy iteration is performed to update all game state values globally as before. Note that unfortunately this algorithm is sequential and does not benefit from the linear speedup that the parallel algorithms do. There is an inherent tradeoff in that Algorithm 2 will run significantly faster, but Algorithm 3 will be significantly more accurate. If Algorithm 3 can be run within the time constraints then it is clearly the preferable choice; however if this is not possible, then Algorithm 2 can still be run as a last resort.

Algorithm 3. Sequential Topological PI-FP (ST-PIFP)

Inputs: Stopping condition C_S for stage game solving, stopping condition C_V for value updating

    V^0 = initializeValues()
    T^0 = initializeTypes()
    $i = 0$
    while C_V not met **do**
        $i = i + 1$
        for $j = 0$ to $K - 1$ **do**
            T_j^i = updated types for state G_j by applying Bayes' rule assuming the types and strategies for all preceding states.
            while C_S not met for stage game G_j **do**
                Run fictitious play stage game G_j with input type distribution according to T_j^i to obtain S_j^i
        V^i = evaluateStrategies(S^i, T^i)
    return S^i

Note that a DAG-structured stochastic game is different from an *extensive-form game tree*, which is a common representation for modeling imperfect-information games. In a game tree each node can have only one parent node, and therefore there can only be at most one path from one node to another. However, this is not the case in a DAG-structured stochastic game; e.g., we can have a path $G_1 \rightarrow G_3 \rightarrow G_6$ as well as just $G_1 \rightarrow G_6$, while a tree can only have at most one of those paths. Thus, existing algorithms for solving extensive-form imperfect-information games are not applicable to DAG-structured stochastic games.

So far, we have been assuming that there is a single value for each player for each state. However, in reality the value depends on both the state and on the type distributions of the players. Using the terminology from the partially observable Markov decision processes (POMDP) community, there is a separate value for each *belief state*. While it is intractable to use a model where a separate value is computed for every possible type distribution (there are infinitely many possible distributions for each state), we can still obtain an improvement by associating a separate value depending on each state and assignment of specific types to each player (not distributions of types). It turns out that, assuming the type spaces are small, we can accomplish this with a relatively small modification to Algorithm 3. Previously, there were $|N|K$ values (one for each player i for each non-terminal state G_j), where $|N|$ is the number of players and K is the number of non-terminal states. Assuming that there are $|T_i|$ possible types for each player, our new model will have $K \prod_i |T_i|$ states. If all the $|T_i|$ are equal, then there will be $|N|K|T_i|^{|N|}$ values. While the number of states is exponential in the number of players, we are primarily interested in games with a small number of players. In our experiments we will be using $|T_i| = 2$ and $|N| = 4$ so there would be $64K$ total values.

Our new algorithm for the setting with type-dependent values in given in Algorithm 4. It has a few small differences from Algorithm 3. First, when running fictitious play to solve the stage games, we now consider the type-dependent game values for transitions to other states. And second, we must now solve a different system of equations for each of the $\prod_i |T_i|$ type combinations. As the bottleneck step of this algorithm is still the game-solving step, this algorithm still takes roughly the same amount of time as Algorithm 3 despite the increased complexity of the value updates.

Algorithm 4. ST-PIFP for type-dependent values (ST-PIFP-TDV)

Inputs: Stopping condition C_S for stage game solving, stopping condition C_V for value updating

$V^0 =$ initializeValues()
$T^0 =$ initializeTypes()
$i = 0$
while C_V not met **do**
    $i = i + 1$
    for $j = 0$ to $K - 1$ **do**
        $T_j^i =$ updated types for state G_j by applying Bayes' rule assuming the types and strategies for all preceding states.
        while C_S not met for stage game G_j **do**
            Run fictitious play stage game G_j with input type distribution according to T_j^i to obtain S_j^i
        for each combination t of types for each player **do**
            $V_t^i =$ evaluateStrategies(S^i, T^i)
    return S^i

To summarize, for multiplayer stochastic games with perfect information (e.g., the perfect-information hostility game) or with local imperfect information (e.g., the poker tournament), the best approach is Parallel PI-FP. This algorithm is applicable even if the game can have potentially infinite cycles and duration (which was the case for the poker tournament). For multiplayer DAG-structured stochastic games with persistent imperfect information, the best approach is Sequential Topological PI-FP, and in particular the new variant for type-dependent values (ST-PIFP-TDV). We can still apply Parallel PI-FP to these games, but will have worse performance.

4   Procedure for Computing Degree of Nash Equilibrium Approximation

In order to evaluate the strategies computed from our algorithm, we need a procedure to compute the degree of Nash equilibrium approximation, ϵ. For perfect-information stochastic games it turns out that there is a relatively straightforward approach for accomplishing this, based on the observation that the problem of computing a best response for a player is equivalent to solving a Markov decision process (MDP). We can construct and solve a corresponding MDP for each player, and compute the maximum that a player can obtain by deviating from our computed strategies for the initial state G_0. This approach is depicted in Algorithm 6. It applies a standard version of policy iteration, described in Algorithm 5. Note that while this version of policy iteration is for positive bounded models, we can still apply it straightforwardly to our model which includes negative payoff values, since we do not encounter the problematic situation of potentially infinite cycles of negative rewards. It turns out that Algorithm 6 can also be applied straightforwardly to stochastic games with local imperfect information. This algorithm was applied to compute the degree of equilibrium approximation in the prior experiments described on the perfect-information hostility game and 3-player imperfect-information poker tournament.

Algorithm 5. Policy iteration for positive bounded models with expected total-reward criterion [11]

---

1. Set $n = 0$ and initialize the policy π^0 so it has nonnegative expected reward.
2. Let v^n be the solution to the system of equations

$$v(i) = r(i) + \sum_j p_{ij}^{\pi^n} v(j)$$

   where $p_{ij}^{\pi^n}$ is the probability of moving from state i to state j under policy π^n. If there are multiple solutions, let v^n be the minimal nonnegative solution.
3. For each state s with action space $A(s)$, set

$$\pi^{n+1}(s) \in \operatorname*{argmax}_{a \in A(s)} \sum_j p_{ij}^a v^n(j),$$

   breaking ties so $\pi^{n+1}(s) = \pi^n(s)$ whenever possible.
4. If $\pi^{n+1}(s) = \pi^n(s)$ for all s, stop and set $\pi^* = \pi^n$. Otherwise increment n by 1 and return to Step 2.

Unfortunately, Algorithm 6 can no longer be applied for stochastic games with persistent imperfect information. For these games, computing the best response for each player is equivalent to solving a partially observable Markov decision processes (POMDP), which is significantly more challenging than solving an MDP. It turns out that computing the optimal policy for a finite-horizon

---

Algorithm 6. *Ex post* check procedure

Create MDP M from the strategy profile s^*
Run Algorithm 5 on M (using initial policy $\pi^0 = s^*$) to get π^*
return $\max_{i \in N} \left[v_i^{\pi_i^*, s_{-i}^*}(G_0) - v_i^{s_i^*, s_{-i}^*}(G_0) \right]$

POMDP is PSPACE-complete [10]. The main algorithms are inefficient and typically require an amount of time that is exponential in the problem size [2]. Common approaches involve transforming the initial POMDP to an MDP with continuous (infinite) state space, where each state of the MDP corresponds to a *belief state* of the POMDP; then this infinite MDP is solved using a version of value iteration where a separate value is associated with each belief state.

Due to the problem's intractability, we devised a new procedure for our setting that exploits domain-specific information to find optimal policies in the POMDPs which correspond to computing a best response. The algorithm is based on a recursive procedure, presented in Algorithm 7. The inputs to the procedure are a player i, a type t_i for player i, a set of type *distributions* $\{\tau_j\}$ for the other players $j \neq i$, the strategies computed by our game-solving algorithm $\{s_j^*\}$, a game state G_h, and a time horizon t. The procedure outputs the optimal value in the *belief state* for player i when he has type t_i and the opponents have type distribution $\{\tau_j\}$ at hostility state G_h for the POMDP defined by the strategies $\{s_j^*\}$, assuming that a time horizon of t remains. For simplicity of presentation we assume that $T_i = 2$ for each player (which is what we will use for our experiments), where τ_j denotes the probability that player j has type 1, and $1 - \tau_j$ the probability of type 2. The algorithm recursively calls itself for updated belief states corresponding to new hostility states that can be transitioned to with horizon $t - 1$. As the base case for $t = 0$ we consider only the attainable terminal payoffs from the current state with no additional transitions to new states permitted.

For the case where the prior type distribution is uniform (all values equal to $\frac{1}{|T_i|}$, which is what we use in our experiments), we apply Algorithm 7 as follows. For each player i and each type $t_i \in T_i$ we apply Algorithm 7, assuming that each opposing player has type t_j with probability $\tau_j = \frac{1}{|T_j|}$, using the initial game state G_0 and time horizon t. Call the result V_{t_i}. Then the optimal value for player i is $V_i = \frac{\sum_{t_i} V_{t_i}}{|T_i|}$. We repeatedly compute V_i for $t = 0, 1, 2 \ldots$ until it (hopefully) converges. We can then compare the converged values of V_i for each player to the expected payoff for the player under the computed strategy profile, $V_i^* = u_i(s^*)$. We then define $\epsilon_i = V_i - V_i^*$, and $\epsilon = \max_i \epsilon_i$. We were able to apply several implementation enhancements to improve the efficiency of Algorithm 7 for the Imperfect-Information Hostility Game. These included precomputing tables of coefficients for transition and terminal payoff probabilities and type indices, only iterating over future states with $h' > h$, and ignoring states $G_{h'}$ with extremely small transition probability from G_h (e.g., below 0.01).

Algorithm 7. ComputeValue($i, t_i, \{\tau_j\}, \{s_j^*\}, G_h, t$)

Inputs: player i, type t_i for player i, type distributions for opposing players $\{\tau_j\}$, strategies for opposing players $\{s_j^*\}$, hostility state G_h, time horizon t

max-payoff $= -\infty$

for each action a_i for player i **do**

    payoff $= 0$

    sum $= 0$

    for every possible combination of $\alpha_k = \prod_j \gamma_j$, where $\gamma_j \in \{\tau_j, (1 - \tau_j)\}$ **do**

        for every possible terminal outcome o, with payoff $u_i(o)$ **do**

            payoff $+= \alpha_k \cdot u_i(o) \cdot$ probability outcome o is attained when player i takes action a_i and other players follow $\{s_j^*\}$

            sum is incremented by same excluding $u_i(o)$ factor

    if $t \geq 1$ **then**

        for every possible hostility state $G_{h'} \neq G_h$ **do**

            $p' =$ total probability we will transition to state $G_{h'}$ when player i takes action a_i and opposing players have type distribution $\{\tau_j\}$ and follow strategies $\{s_j^*\}$

            $\{\tau_j'\} =$ new type distributions computed using Bayes' rule assuming player i takes action a_i and the game transitions to state $G_{h'}$

            payoff $+= p' \cdot$ ComputeValue($i, t_i, \{\tau_j'\}, \{s_j^*\}, G_{h'}, t - 1$)

            sum $+= p'$

    payoff $=$ payoff / sum

    if payoff $>$ max-payoff **then**

        max-payoff $=$ payoff

return max-payoff

---

5 Experiments

We ran Algorithm 3 (ST-PIFP) and Algorithm 4 (ST-PIFP-TDV) using 10,000 iterations of fictitious play each for 25 iterations on a single core on a laptop. Each iteration of ST-PIFP took around 20 min, while each iteration of ST-PIFP-TDV took around 23 min (using $K = 300$). So as predicted, the added complexity of including type-dependent values only led to a small increase in runtime because the running time of the bottleneck game-solving step remained the same. All of our game parameters were the same as for the previously-considered perfect-information version (e.g., 1 blue and 3 red players each with 7–10 actions available, payoffs of $+100/-100$ for a win/loss and -200 for Kinetic mode, fixed action hostilities and success probabilities which are modified to incorporate the players' types), except we used a smaller version with $K = 150$ to obtain convergence with Algorithm 7. (For $K = 300$ the algorithm converged for the first few strategy iterations but took too long to converge for later strategy iterations due to the greater degree of randomization in the later strategies, leading them to have weight on a larger number of transition sequences that must be considered.) We assume each player has $|T_i| = 2$ available types, which are initially uniform random according to the public prior, and we initialize all values for both algorithms to be zero.

Results for both algorithms after 10 iterations for $K = 150$ are given in Table 1. For each algorithm, we report V_i^A—the expected payoffs for player i under the computed strategies—as well as V_i^O—the optimal payoff according to Algorithm 7. The numbers in parentheses indicate the values for each type, which are averaged to obtain the value. We see that for ST-PIFP we have $(\epsilon_1, \epsilon_2, \epsilon_3, \epsilon_4) = (4.008, 1.126, 5.472, 0.228)$, giving $\epsilon = \max_i \epsilon_i = 5.472$, while for ST-PIFP-TDV we have $(\epsilon_1, \epsilon_2, \epsilon_3, \epsilon_4) = (0.064, 0.903, 0.538, 0.450)$, giving $\epsilon = \max_i \epsilon_i = 0.903$. Note that the smallest payoff magnitude in the game is 100 and these values correspond to approximately 5% and 1% of that quantity respectively. We expect that the ϵ would quickly converge to 0 with more strategy iterations even for larger games, as in the experiments on PIHG. The results indicate that utilizing type-dependent values does in fact lead to better strategies. As expected we observe that higher type values produce greater expected payoff. Interestingly we observe that the overall payoffs of the strategies for all red players are identical (for both algorithms), yet they differ for each type.

Table 1. V_i^A is the expected payoff to player i under the strategies computed by the algorithm given in the column, and V_i^O is the optimal payoff to player i according to Algorithm 7. Numbers in parentheses are the values given types 1 and 2 (which are averaged to produce the indicated value).

	ST-PIFP	ST-PIFP-TDV
V_1^A	$-94.642 \ (-98.271, -91.034)$	$-92.840 \ (-96.103, -89.576)$
V_1^O	$-90.634 \ (-97.034, -84.234)$	$-92.776 \ (-96.099, -89.454)$
V_2^A	$4.915 \ (-23.778, 33.608)$	$9.681 \ (-20.949, 40.311)$
V_2^O	$6.041 \ (-22.383, 34.465)$	$10.584 \ (19.807, 40.974)$
V_3^A	$4.915 \ (-9.961, 19.791)$	$9.681 \ (-1.916, 21.278)$
V_3^O	$10.387 \ (-3.405, 24.180)$	$10.219 \ (-2.035, 22.474)$
V_4^A	$4.915 \ (-7.620, 17.450)$	$9.681 \ (-2.512, 21.874)$
V_4^O	$5.143 \ (-7.529, 17.815)$	$10.131 \ (-1.105, 21.366)$

6 Conclusion

We presented new algorithms for computing Nash equilibrium in DAG-structured stochastic games with persistent imperfect information, which we applied to closely approximate Nash equilibrium strategies in a realistic naval planning problem devised by a domain expert. We evaluated the computed strategies with a new domain-specific procedure for solving the induced POMDP. In the future we would like to create a generalized approach that works for a broader class of games beyond those with a DAG-structured state space—ideally to all stochastic games including those with infinite cycles. We would also like to improve Algorithm 7 to more efficiently solve the induced POMDP for strategy evaluation. We expect our approaches to be broadly applicable to multiplayer imperfect-information stochastic games beyond the specific game considered.

Acknowledgments. We would like to acknowledge Arctan, Inc., and in particular Conner Laughlin and Charles Morefield.

References

1. Brown, G.W.: Iterative solutions of games by fictitious play. In: Koopmans, T.C. (ed.) Activity Analysis of Production and Allocation, pp. 374–376. Wiley, Hoboken (1951)
2. Cassandra, A.R., Kaelbling, L.P., Littman, M.L.: Acting optimally in partially observable stochastic domains. In: Proceedings of the AAAI Conference on Artificial Intelligence (AAAI) (1994)
3. Chen, X., Deng, X.: Settling the complexity of 2-player Nash equilibrium. In: Proceedings of the Annual Symposium on Foundations of Computer Science (FOCS) (2006)
4. Conitzer, V., Sandholm, T.: Computing the optimal strategy to commit to. In: Proceedings of the ACM Conference on Electronic Commerce (ACM-EC), Ann Arbor, MI (2006)
5. Daskalakis, C., Goldberg, P., Papadimitriou, C.: The complexity of computing a Nash equilibrium. SIAM J. Comput. **1**(39), 195–259 (2009)
6. Ganzfried, S.: Fictitious play outperforms counterfactual regret minimization (2020). arXiv:2001.11165
7. Ganzfried, S., Laughlin, C., Morefield, C.: Parallel algorithm for Nash equilibrium in multiplayer stochastic games with application to naval strategic planning. In: Taylor, M.E., Yu, Y., Elkind, E., Gao, Y. (eds.) DAI 2020. LNCS (LNAI), vol. 12547, pp. 1–13. Springer, Cham (2020). https://doi.org/10.1007/978-3-030-64096-5_1
8. Ganzfried, S., Sandholm, T.: Computing an approximate jam/fold equilibrium for 3-player no-limit Texas Hold'em tournaments. In: Proceedings of the International Conference on Autonomous Agents and Multi-Agent Systems (AAMAS) (2008)
9. Ganzfried, S., Sandholm, T.: Computing equilibria in multiplayer stochastic games of imperfect information. In: Proceedings of the 21st International Joint Conference on Artificial Intelligence (IJCAI) (2009)
10. Papadimitriou, C.H., Tsitsiklis, J.N.: The complexity of Markov decision processes. Math. Oper. Res. **12**(3), 441–450 (1987)
11. Puterman, M.L.: Markov Decision Processes: Discrete Stochastic Dynamic Programming. Wiley, Hoboken (2005)
12. Robinson, J.: An iterative method of solving a game. Ann. Math. **54**, 296–301 (1951)
13. Vorobeychik, Y., An, B., Tambe, M., Singh, S.: Computing solutions in infinite-horizon discounted adversarial patrolling games. In: International Conference on Automated Planning and Scheduling (ICAPS) (2014)
14. Vorobeychik, Y., Singh, S.: Computing Stackelberg equilibria in discounted stochastic games. In: Proceedings of the AAAI Conference on Artificial Intelligence (AAAI) (2012)
15. Zinkevich, M., Bowling, M., Johanson, M., Piccione, C.: Regret minimization in games with incomplete information. In: Proceedings of the Annual Conference on Neural Information Processing Systems (NIPS) (2007)

Two Algorithms for Computing Exact and Approximate Nash Equilibria in Bimatrix Games

Jianzong Pi[1]($\boxtimes$)(iD), Joseph L. Heyman[2](iD), and Abhishek Gupta[1](iD)

[1] The Ohio State University, Columbus, OH 43210, USA
{pi.35,gupta.706}@osu.edu
[2] United States Military Academy, West Point, NY 10996, USA
joseph.heyman@westpoint.edu

Abstract. In this paper, we first devise two algorithms to determine whether or not a bimatrix game has a strategically equivalent zero-sum game. If so, we propose an algorithm that computes the strategically equivalent zero-sum game. If a given bimatrix game is not strategically equivalent to a zero-sum game, we then propose an approach to compute a zero-sum game whose saddle-point equilibrium can be mapped to a well-supported approximate Nash equilibrium of the original game. We conduct extensive numerical simulation to establish the efficacy of the two algorithms.

1 Introduction

Non-cooperative game theory has become a popular method for modeling strategic interactions between decision makers, commonly referred to as "players". While originally applied to strategic interactions in games and economics, game theory is now gaining popularity in the fields of social and political sciences. Today, it is not uncommon to find game theory applied in diverse fields such as traffic engineering [10,13,24], online advertising [4,5], cyber-security [8,21], and many others.

While game theory has been a widely used modeling technique, efficient computation of a solution to a game has been difficult. In 1950, John Nash defined Nash equilibrium (NE) as a solution concept in non-cooperative games, in which each player's expected payoff is maximized with the knowledge of other players' strategies. Moreover, each player will receive less expected payoff if he/she deviates from the NE. Nash proved that there exists an equilibrium in every finite-action finite-player non-cooperative game [18] using Brouwer's Fixed Point

The second author was fully supported by the United States Military Academy and the Army Advanced Civil Schooling (ACS) program. The views expressed in this work are those of the authors and do not reflect the official policy or position of the Department of the Army, Department of Defense, or the U.S. Government.
The third author gratefully acknowledges support from NSF Grant 1565487.

© Springer Nature Switzerland AG 2021
B. Bošanský et al. (Eds.): GameSec 2021, LNCS 13061, pp. 17–36, 2021.
https://doi.org/10.1007/978-3-030-90370-1_2

Theorem. However, there is currently no known efficient algorithm for computing NE in general non zero-sum games, and it has remained an open problem for over 70 years. In a series of works, [6,7], Daskalakis et al. showed that finite games with more than three players is Polynomial Parity Arguments on Directed graphs (PPAD)-complete. While the computation of NE may seem simpler in two player games, Chen et al. showed the hardness results for this case a short time later [3].

With these hardness results established, one could hope to come up with an efficient algorithm to compute an approximate NE, which is also referred to as an ε-NE in two player games. For an ε-NE solution, any deviations from the ε-NE can gain either player at most an additional payoff of ε. In [16], Lipton et al. proposed a quasipolynomial time algorithm for computing an approximate NE for any fixed ε. The current "best" polynomial time algorithm for a fixed ε is due to [22], where Tsaknakis and Spirakis proposed an algorithm for $\varepsilon = 0.3393$. However, computation of ε-NE is still PPAD-complete if ε is inversely polynomial in the size of the game [2].

A more demanding notion of an approximate solution is the ε-well supported approximate Nash equilibrium (ε-WSNE) [6]. In an ε-WSNE, players only place positive probability on strategies that have a payoff within ε of the pure best response. ε-WSNE is a more restrictive approximation than ε-NE, as every ε-WSNE is an ε-NE, while the converse is not true [6].

There is significantly less literature studying ε-WSNE compared to ε-NE. For the case of ε-WSNE, the first and most well-known polynomial time algorithm for a fixed ε is $\frac{2}{3}$-WSNE as published in [15]. Fearney et al. [9] made improvement to the previous algorithm, which resulted in $\varepsilon = \frac{2}{3} - 0.005913759$. For random bimatrix games, Panagopoulo and Spirakis [20] found that the uniform mixed strategy profile is, with high probability, a $\sqrt{\frac{3 \ln n}{n}}$-WSNE.

In our work, we first devise an efficient algorithm for computing strategically equivalent zero-sum games using simple algebraic manipulations. Then, we propose a polynomial time algorithm for computing an ε-WSNE. To determine the latter algorithm, we define a certain affine game transformation to that leads to a simple linear program that outputs a zero-sum game that is "close" to the original nonzero-sum game. We show that any NE of this zero-sum game is an ε-WSNE of the original game.

1.1   Notation

In this paper, all vectors are column vectors and are written in bold font. We denote $\mathbf{1}_n$ and $\mathbf{0}_n$ as the ones and zeros vector of length n and denote e_j, $j \in \{1, 2, ..., n\}$, as a vector with 1 at the jth position and 0's elsewhere. We denote $\Delta_n \subset \mathbb{R}^n$ as the set of probability distributions over $\{1, ..., n\}$, i.e., $\Delta_n = \{\mathbf{p} \mid p_i \geq 0, \forall i \in \{1, ..., n\}, \sum_{i=1}^{n} p_i = 1\}$. For a matrix $A \in \mathbb{R}^{m \times n}$, we use $a_{i,j}$ to denote the entry on i-th row and j-th column of A. Moreover, we define $A_{(i)}$ as the i-th row of A, and $A^{(j)}$ as the j-th column of A. We define the max norm of matrix A as $\|A\|_{\max} = \max_{i,j} |a_{i,j}|$. Define $\texttt{ColSpan}(A)$ as the subspace spanned by the columns of matrix A. We define $\mathcal{D}_n \subseteq \mathbb{R}^{n \times n}$ as the set of all diagonal matrices with n rows and n columns with positive diagonal entries. For a diagonal matrix $D \in \mathcal{D}_n$, we use d_j to denote the (j,j)-th element in matrix D and note that $d_j > 0$ for all $j \in \{1, \dots, n\}$.

1.2   Outline of the Paper

In Sect. 2, we begin by introducing some preliminary concepts related to this paper. In Sect. 3, we propose necessary and sufficient conditions of existence of a strategically equivalent zero-sum game, then we devise an algorithm that efficiently computes the strategically equivalent zero-sum game and provide a complexity analysis. We will also run an experiment evaluate the performance. Then, in Sect. 4, we propose another efficient algorithm to compute approximate Nash equilibrium if the conditions in Sect. 3 are not satisfied. The auxiliary theorems for the proof in Sect. 3 are provided in Appendix A.

2   Preliminaries

In this section, we recall the definitions of Nash equilibrium and approximate Nash equilibrium. We focus on bimatrix games (2-player games) in this paper. Every bimatrix game can be defined by a tuple (m, n, A, B), where player 1 has m actions, player 2 has n actions, and $A, B \in \mathbb{R}^{m \times n}$ are the payoff matrices of player 1 and 2. Both players can choose to use pure strategies, that is, they can choose a single action from its own set of pure strategies denoted by $S_1 = \{1, \dots, m\}$ and $S_2 = \{1, \dots, n\}$. If the players play pure strategies $(i, j) \in S_1 \times S_2$, player 1 and player 2 will receive payoffs $a_{i,j}$ and $b_{i,j}$, respectively. Players may also play mixed strategies in bimatrix games. Player 1 and player 2 can choose probability distributions $\mathbf{p} \in \Delta_m$ over S_1 and $\mathbf{q} \in \Delta_n$ over S_2. Then, player 1 has expected payoff $\mathbf{p}^\mathsf{T} A \mathbf{q}$ and player 2 has expected payoff $\mathbf{p}^\mathsf{T} B \mathbf{q}$.

We state the definition of best response condition and best response correspondence in order to define Nash equilibrium. The best response is the mixed strategy that gives the best outcome for one player, given the mixed strategy of the other player. This is made precise in the following definition.

Definition 1 (Best response condition [18]). *Let* $\mathbf{p}$ *and* $\mathbf{q}$ *be mixed strategies of player 1 and player 2. Then* $\mathbf{p}$ *is a best response to* $\mathbf{q}$ *if and only if for all* $i \in S_1$,

$$p_i > 0 \implies (A\mathbf{q})_i = u = \max_{k \in S_1} (A\mathbf{q})_k,$$

and $\mathbf{q}$ *is a best response to* $\mathbf{p}$ *if and only if for all* $j \in S_2$,

$$q_j > 0 \implies (B^\mathsf{T}\mathbf{p})_j = v = \max_{k \in S_2} (B^\mathsf{T}\mathbf{p})_k.$$

Definition 2 (Best response correspondence). *For the payoff matrices A and B, define the best response correspondences $\Gamma_A : \Delta_n \rightrightarrows \Delta_m$ and $\Gamma_B : \Delta_m \rightrightarrows \Delta_n$ as*

$$\Gamma_A(\mathbf{q}) = \{\mathbf{p} \in \Delta_m : \mathbf{p}^{\mathsf{T}} A \mathbf{q} = \max_i [A\mathbf{q}]_i\},$$
$$\Gamma_B(\mathbf{p}) = \{\mathbf{q} \in \Delta_n : \mathbf{p}^{\mathsf{T}} B \mathbf{q} = \max_j [\mathbf{p}^{\mathsf{T}} B]_j\}.$$

When each player's mixed strategy is a best response to the other player's strategy, their strategies form a Nash Equilibrium. This is made precise in the following definition.

Definition 3 (Nash equilibrium [18]). *A pair $(\mathbf{p}, \mathbf{q})$ of mixed strategies is a Nash Equilibrium (NE) if and only if $\mathbf{p} \in \Gamma_A(\mathbf{q})$ and $\mathbf{q} \in \Gamma_B(\mathbf{p})$.*

In zero-sum games, we usually call the Nash equilibrium between two players as a saddle point equilibrium (SPE).

2.1   Strategically Equivalent Games

We focus on a bimatrix game (m, n, A, B) as defined above. We define the Nash equilibrium correspondence as $\Phi(A, B) : \mathbb{R}^{m \times n} \times \mathbb{R}^{m \times n} \rightrightarrows \Delta_m \times \Delta_n$. It was proved in [18] that every bimatrix game with a finite set of pure strategies has at least one NE in mixed strategies. Thus, the image $\Phi(A, B)$ is nonempty for any $(A, B) \in \mathbb{R}^{m \times n} \times \mathbb{R}^{m \times n}$. We say two games are strategically equivalent when both games have the same set of players, the same set of strategies, and the same set of NE. An equivalent definition of strategic equivalence based on the preference ordering for all mixed strategies $\mathbf{p} \in \Delta_m$ and $\mathbf{q} \in \Delta_n$ was given by Moulin and Vial [17], which is stated below.

Definition 4 (Strategically equivalence). *Two bimatrix games (m, n, A, B) and $(m, n, \bar{A}, \bar{B})$ are strategically equivalent if and only if for any $\bar{\mathbf{p}}, \mathbf{p} \in \Delta_m$ and $\bar{\mathbf{q}}, \mathbf{q} \in \Delta_n$, we have*

$$\bar{\mathbf{p}}^T A \mathbf{q} \geq \mathbf{p}^T A \mathbf{q} \iff \bar{\mathbf{p}}^T \bar{A} \mathbf{q} \geq \mathbf{p}^T \bar{A} \mathbf{q},$$
$$\mathbf{p}^T B \bar{\mathbf{q}} \geq \mathbf{p}^T B \mathbf{q} \iff \mathbf{p}^T \bar{B} \bar{\mathbf{q}} \geq \mathbf{p}^T \bar{B} \mathbf{q}.$$

Proving that two games are strategically equivalent in Definition 4 is difficult since all $\bar{\mathbf{p}}, \mathbf{p} \in \Delta_m$ and $\bar{\mathbf{q}}, \mathbf{q} \in \Delta_n$ need to be checked to satisfy the above conditions. However, there are several classes of transformations such that strategically equivalence is naturally conserved. Positive affine transformations (PAT) ensure the strategically equivalence of two games; that is, if two games have a PAT correspondence, then they are strategically equivalent. We define the PAT correspondence Υ as follows:

Definition 5 (PAT Correspondence [11]). *The game $(m, n, \bar{A}, \bar{B})$ is a PAT of (m, n, A, B) if and only if there exists $\alpha_1, \alpha_2 \in \mathbb{R}_{>0}$, $\mathbf{u} \in \mathbb{R}^n$, and $\mathbf{v} \in \mathbb{R}^m$*

such that $\bar{A} = \alpha_1 A + \mathbf{1}_m \mathbf{u}^T$ and $\bar{B} = \alpha_2 B + \mathbf{v} \mathbf{1}_n^T$. The map $\Upsilon : \mathbb{R}^{m \times n} \times \mathbb{R}^{m \times n} \rightrightarrows$ $\mathbb{R}^{m \times n} \times \mathbb{R}^{m \times n}$ is a PAT correspondence if

$$\Upsilon(A, B) = \{(\bar{A}, \bar{B}) \in \mathbb{R}^{m \times n} \times \mathbb{R}^{m \times n} : (\bar{A}, \bar{B}) \text{ is a PAT of } (A, B)\}.$$

It is obvious that PAT preserves the preference orderings given in Definition 4. Thus, two games are strategically equivalent if the two games have a PAT correspondence. Moreover, [17] also showed that the converse also holds. With the results above, we have the following lemma.

Lemma 1 ([17]). *Two games* (m, n, A, B) *and* $(m, n, \bar{A}, \bar{B})$ *are strategically equivalent if and only if* $(\bar{A}, \bar{B}) \in \Upsilon(A, B)$.

We say two games are strategically equivalent via a PAT if they have a PAT correspondence. In a special case where $\alpha_1 = \alpha_2 = 1$, we say that those two games are strategically equivalent via a 1-PAT.

2.2 Approximate Nash Equilibrium

While [18] showed that NE exists in all finite games, it remains an open problem to find an algorithm to compute NE efficiently in general bimatrix games [6]. On the other hand, there exists some efficient algorithms to compute approximate NE.

Definition 6 (ε-well-supported Nash Equilibrium). *We refer to the pair of strategies* $(\tilde{\mathbf{p}}, \tilde{\mathbf{q}})$ *as an epsilon-well-supported Nash Equilibrium (ε-WSNE) of game* (m, n, A, B) *if and only if:*

$$\text{for all } i \in S_1, k \in S_1, \; \tilde{p}_i > 0 \implies (A\tilde{\mathbf{q}})_i \geq (A\tilde{\mathbf{q}})_k - \varepsilon,$$
$$\text{for all } j \in S_2, l \in S_2 \; \tilde{q}_j > 0 \implies (B^\mathsf{T}\tilde{\mathbf{p}})_j \geq (B^\mathsf{T}\tilde{\mathbf{p}})_l - \varepsilon.$$

We also define the ε-approximation of payoff matrices as follows.

Definition 7. *For matrices* $\tilde{A}, R \in \mathbb{R}^{m \times n}$, $\tilde{A}$ *is an ε-approximation of R if* $\tilde{A} = R + E$, *where* $\varepsilon \geq \|E\|_{max}$.

Inspired by [14, Theorem 1], we have the following lemma on the connection between the approximation of the payoff matrices in a game and approximate Nash equilibrium of that game.

Lemma 2. *Given the game* $(m, n, \tilde{A}, \tilde{B})$, *let* $\tilde{A}$ *be an $\tilde{\varepsilon}_1$-approximation of R and* $\tilde{B}$ *be an $\tilde{\varepsilon}_2$-approximation of C. If* $(\tilde{\mathbf{p}}, \tilde{\mathbf{q}})$ *is an NE of the game* $(m, n, \tilde{A}, \tilde{B})$, *then* $(\tilde{\mathbf{p}}, \tilde{\mathbf{q}})$ *is a $2\tilde{\varepsilon}$-WSNE of the game* (m, n, R, C), *where* $\tilde{\varepsilon} = \max\{\tilde{\varepsilon}_1, \tilde{\varepsilon}_2\}$.

Proof. Applying Definitions 1 and 7, let $\tilde{A} = R + E$, where $\|E\|_{max} \leq \tilde{\varepsilon}$. For player 1 we have that:

$$\text{For all } i, k \in S_1, \; \bar{p}_i > 0 \implies (\tilde{A}\bar{\mathbf{q}})_i \geq (\tilde{A}\bar{\mathbf{q}})_k,$$
$$\iff (R\bar{\mathbf{q}} + E\bar{\mathbf{q}})_i \geq (R\bar{\mathbf{q}} + E\bar{\mathbf{q}})_k,$$
$$\iff (R\bar{\mathbf{q}})_i \geq (R\bar{\mathbf{q}})_k + (E\bar{\mathbf{q}})_k - (E\bar{\mathbf{q}})_i.$$

Since $\varepsilon_1 \geq \max_{i,j}|e_{i,j}|$ and $\bar{\mathbf{q}} \in \Delta_m$,

$$\text{For all } i, k \in S_1, \ (E\bar{\mathbf{q}})_k - (E\bar{\mathbf{q}})_i \geq -2\varepsilon_1.$$

Therefore,

$$\text{For all } i, k \in S_1, \ \bar{p}_i > 0 \implies (R\bar{\mathbf{q}})_i \geq (R\bar{\mathbf{q}})_k - 2\varepsilon_1.$$

The proof for player 2 is similar and thus omitted.   □

In [14] the authors show that additive transformations have no effect on the set of WSNE. Formally, we have the following lemma.

Lemma 3. *Consider the games (m, n, A, B) and (m, n, R, C) which are strategically equivalent via 1-PAT. The strategy pair $(\tilde{\mathbf{p}}, \tilde{\mathbf{q}})$ is an $\tilde{\varepsilon}$-WSNE of the game (m, n, A, B) if and only if $(\tilde{\mathbf{p}}, \tilde{\mathbf{q}})$ is an $\tilde{\varepsilon}$-WSNE of the game (m, n, R, C).*

Proof. Suppose $(\tilde{\mathbf{p}}, \tilde{\mathbf{q}})$ is an $\tilde{\varepsilon}$-WSNE of the game (m, n, R, C). Applying Definition 6 for player 1, we have that:

$$\text{For all } i, k \in S_1, \ \tilde{\mathbf{p}}_i > 0 \implies (R\tilde{\mathbf{q}})_i \geq (R\tilde{\mathbf{q}})_k - \tilde{\varepsilon},$$
$$\iff (A\tilde{\mathbf{q}})_i + (\mathbf{1}_m\mathbf{u}^\mathsf{T}\tilde{\mathbf{q}})_i \geq (A\tilde{\mathbf{q}})_k + (\mathbf{1}_m\mathbf{u}^\mathsf{T}\tilde{\mathbf{q}})_k - \tilde{\varepsilon},$$
$$\iff (A\tilde{\mathbf{q}})_i \geq (A\tilde{\mathbf{q}})_k - \tilde{\varepsilon}.$$

The final step of this proof relies on the fact that $(\mathbf{1}_m\mathbf{u}^\mathsf{T}\tilde{\mathbf{q}})_i = (\mathbf{1}_m\mathbf{u}^\mathsf{T}\tilde{\mathbf{q}})_k$ for any $i, k \in S_1$. The proof for player 2 is similar and thus omitted.   □

In the next section, we will introduce an efficient algorithm to compute Nash equilibria for general bi-matrix games.

3   A Fast Algorithm to Compute Strategically Equivalent Zero-Sum Games

In this section, we devise an algorithm that determines a strategically equivalent zero-sum game $(m, n, \bar{A}, \bar{B})$ given a non-zero-sum game (m, n, A, B) with $(\bar{A}, \bar{B}) \in \Upsilon(A, B)$ (and $\bar{A} + \bar{B} = 0$). This section is based on Chapter 3 of the second author's PhD dissertation [12].

We first introduce some notations. Define the set $\mathcal{M}_{m \times n} \subseteq \mathbb{R}^{m \times n}$ as

$$\mathcal{M}_{m \times n}(\mathbb{R}) =$$
$$\left\{ M \in \mathbb{R}^{m \times n} \mid \text{there exists } \mathbf{u} \in \mathbb{R}^n, \mathbf{v} \in \mathbb{R}^m \text{ s.t. } M = \mathbf{1}_m\mathbf{u}^\mathsf{T} + \mathbf{v}\mathbf{1}_n^\mathsf{T} \right\}.$$

Note that $\mathcal{M}_{m \times n}(\mathbb{R})$ is a linear space over field $\mathbb{R}$, hence $\mathcal{M}_{m \times n}(\mathbb{R})$ is closed under addition and scalar multiplication. Moreover, for matrix $\bar{A} \in \mathbb{R}^{m \times n}$, we define the set $\mathcal{WZ}(\bar{A})$ as

$$\mathcal{WZ}(\bar{A}) := \left\{ (\mathbf{w}, \mathbf{z}) \in \mathbb{R}^m \times \mathbb{R}^n \mid \mathbf{w}^\mathsf{T}\bar{A}\mathbf{z} \neq 0, \mathbf{1}_m^\mathsf{T}\mathbf{w} = \mathbf{1}_n^\mathsf{T}\mathbf{z} = 0 \right\}.$$

Then, given a nonzero-sum game (m, n, A, B), the following theorem provides a necessary and sufficient condition to the existence of strategic equivalent zero-sum game to the original game.

Theorem 1. *Consider a nonzero-sum game* (m, n, A, B), *where* $A, B \notin \mathcal{M}_{m \times n}(\mathbb{R})$. *The nonzero-sum game* (m, n, A, B) *is strategically equivalent to a zero-sum game* $(m, n, \bar{A}, \bar{B})$ *(where* $\bar{B} = -\bar{A}$) *if and only if the following conditions are satisfied:*

1. *For any* $(\mathbf{w}, \mathbf{z}) \in \mathbb{R}^m \times \mathbb{R}^n$ *such that* $\mathbf{1}_m^\top \mathbf{w} = \mathbf{1}_n^\top \mathbf{z} = 0$, *and* $\mathbf{w}^\top B \mathbf{z} \neq 0$,

$$\gamma := -\frac{\mathbf{w}^\top A \mathbf{z}}{\mathbf{w}^\top B \mathbf{z}} > 0.$$

2. $M := A + \gamma B \in \mathcal{M}_{m \times n}(\mathbb{R})$.

Proof. We start by proving the reverse direction. Suppose the two conditions are satisfied. Note that as $M = A + \gamma B \in \mathcal{M}_{m \times n}(\mathbb{R})$, $\texttt{rank}(M) \leq 2$. Next, we consider the three cases when $\texttt{rank}(M)$ is 2, 1 and 0.

1. **Case 1:** $\texttt{rank}(M) = 2$. We can write M as a summation of 2 rank-1 matrices, so $\mathbf{1}_m \in \texttt{ColSpan}(M)$ and $\mathbf{1}_n \in \texttt{ColSpan}(M^\top)$. Hence, there exists $\mathbf{x}_1 \in \mathbb{R}^n$ such that $M\mathbf{x}_1 = \mathbf{1}_m$. Moreover, there exists $\mathbf{y}_1 \in \mathbb{R}^m$ such that $\mathbf{y}_1^\top M \neq \mathbf{0}_m$ and $\mathbf{1}_m^\top \mathbf{y}_1 \neq 0$. Let $w_1 = \mathbf{y}_1^\top M \mathbf{x}_1 \neq 0$ and let $\hat{\mathbf{u}} := (w_1^{-1} \mathbf{y}_1^\top M)^\top$. Then, $w_1^{-1} M \mathbf{x}_1 \mathbf{y}_1^\top M = M - \mathbf{1}_m \hat{\mathbf{u}}^\top$. By applying Wedderburn rank reduction formula [23, p.69], we have

$$M_2 = M - w_1^{-1} M \mathbf{x}_1 \mathbf{y}_1^\top M = M - \mathbf{1}_m \hat{\mathbf{u}}^\top.$$

   Next, we show the existence of $\hat{\mathbf{v}} \in \mathbb{R}^m$ such that $M_2 = \hat{\mathbf{v}} \mathbf{1}_n^\top$. Indeed, $M \in \mathcal{M}_{m \times n}(\mathbb{R})$ and $\mathbf{1}_m \hat{\mathbf{u}}^\top \in \mathcal{M}_{m \times n}(\mathbb{R})$. As $\mathcal{M}_{m \times n}(\mathbb{R})$ is closed under addition, we have $M_2 \in \mathcal{M}_{m \times n}(\mathbb{R})$. In addition, by Wedderburn [23, p. 69], $\texttt{rank}(M_2) = 1$. By Theorem 6, $\mathbf{1}_m \notin \texttt{ColSpan}(M_2)$ implies there exists $\hat{\mathbf{v}} \in \mathbb{R}^m$ such that $M_2 = \hat{\mathbf{v}} \mathbf{1}_n^\top$. Finally, letting $\bar{A} := A - \mathbf{1}_m \hat{\mathbf{u}}^\top$ and $\bar{B} := \gamma B - M_2$, we have

$$\bar{A} + \bar{B} = A + \gamma B - \mathbf{1}_m \hat{\mathbf{u}}^\top - M_2 = 0_{m \times n}.$$

   Since $\gamma > 0$, we conclude that $(m, n, \bar{A}, \bar{B})$ is strategically equivalent to (m, n, A, B) via a PAT.

2. **Case 2:** $\texttt{rank}(M) = 1$. As $\texttt{rank}(M) = 1$, either $\mathbf{1}_m \in \texttt{ColSpan}(M)$ or $\mathbf{1}_n \in \texttt{ColSpan}(M^\top)$. We first assume $\mathbf{1}_m \in \texttt{ColSpan}(M)$. Let $M = \mathbf{1}_m \hat{\mathbf{u}}^\top$. Then we can let $\bar{A} = A - M$, and $\bar{B} = \gamma B$ and we have $\bar{A} + \bar{B} = 0_{m \times n}$.
   The proof of the case $\mathbf{1}_n \in \texttt{ColSpan}(M^\top)$ is similar and therefore omitted. Hence, we have found $\bar{A}, \bar{B}$ such that (m, n, A, B) is strategically equivalent to $(m, n, \bar{A}, \bar{B})$ via a PAT.

3. **Case 3:** $\texttt{rank}(M) = 0$. Let $\bar{A} = A$ and $\bar{B} = \gamma B$. Since $M = A + \gamma B = 0_{m \times n}$, $(m, n, \bar{A}, \bar{B})$ is zero-sum and strategically equivalent to (m, n, A, B) via a PAT.

Next, we prove the forward direction and assume that the nonzero-sum game (m, n, A, B) is strategically equivalent to a zero-sum game $(m, n, \bar{A}, \bar{B})$ via PAT. Since $B \notin \mathcal{M}_{m \times n}(\mathbb{R})$, Theorem 7 in Appendix A implies $\mathcal{WZ}(B) \neq \emptyset$. Pick $(\mathbf{w}, \mathbf{z}) \in \mathcal{WZ}(B)$, we have the following

(a) $\mathbf{w}^\mathsf{T} A\mathbf{z} = \alpha_1 \mathbf{w}^\mathsf{T} \bar{A}\mathbf{z} + \mathbf{w}^\mathsf{T} \mathbf{1}_m \mathbf{u}^\mathsf{T} \mathbf{z} = \alpha_1 \mathbf{w}^\mathsf{T} \bar{A}\mathbf{z}$,
(b) $\mathbf{w}^\mathsf{T} B\mathbf{z} = -\alpha_2 \mathbf{w}^\mathsf{T} \bar{A}\mathbf{z} + \mathbf{w}^\mathsf{T} \mathbf{v} \mathbf{1}_n^\mathsf{T} \mathbf{z} = -\alpha_2 \mathbf{w}^\mathsf{T} \bar{A}\mathbf{z}$.

Since $(\mathbf{w}, \mathbf{z}) \in \mathcal{WZ}(B)$, $\mathbf{w}^\mathsf{T} B\mathbf{z} \neq 0$, hence γ is well-defined. As $\alpha_1 > 0$ and $\alpha_2 > 0$, we conclude that

$$\gamma = -\frac{\mathbf{w}^T A\mathbf{z}}{\mathbf{w}^T B\mathbf{z}} = \frac{\alpha_1 \mathbf{w}^\mathsf{T} \bar{A}\mathbf{z}}{\alpha_2 \mathbf{w}^\mathsf{T} \bar{A}\mathbf{z}} = \frac{\alpha_1}{\alpha_2} > 0.$$

Note it is straightforward to show that $\mathcal{WZ}(A) = \mathcal{WZ}(\bar{A}) = \mathcal{WZ}(\bar{B})$. The fact that $M := A + \gamma B$ is in $\mathcal{M}_{m \times n}(\mathbb{R})$ follows from simple algebraic manipulations. The proof is thus complete. □

To turn the above theorem into a fast algorithm, we need to solve two specific problems. The first one is to determine whether or not the payoff matrices are in $\mathcal{M}_{m \times n}(\mathbb{R})$ and the second one is to compute $(\mathbf{w}, \mathbf{z}) \in \mathcal{WZ}(B)$. In the next section, we derive two results that immediately yield linear time algorithms to solve these two problems.

3.1   Algorithmic Implications for Matrices in $\mathcal{M}_{m \times n}(\mathbb{R})$

We first derive a fast approach to determine whether or not a matrix is in $\mathcal{M}_{m \times n}(\mathbb{R})$ in the next theorem.

Theorem 2. *Given a matrix $F \in \mathbb{R}^{m \times n}$, select any $(i, j) \in \{1 \ldots m\} \times \{1 \ldots n\}$ and let*

$$\bar{F} := \mathbf{1}_m F_{(i)} + (F^{(j)} - \mathbf{1}_m f_{i,j})\mathbf{1}_n^\mathsf{T}. \tag{1}$$

Then F is in $\mathcal{M}_{m \times n}(\mathbb{R})$ if and only if $F = \bar{F}$.

Proof. To begin with, notice that $\mathbf{1}_m F_{(i)} \in \mathcal{M}_{m \times n}(\mathbb{R})$ and $(F^{(j)} - \mathbf{1}_m f_{i,j})\mathbf{1}_n^\mathsf{T} \in \mathcal{M}_{m \times n}(\mathbb{R})$. Let $\hat{F} := F - \bar{F} = F - \mathbf{1}_m F_{(i)} - (F^{(j)} - \mathbf{1}_m f_{i,j})\mathbf{1}_n^\mathsf{T}$, then $\hat{F} \in \mathcal{M}_{m \times n}(\mathbb{R})$ if and only if $F \in \mathcal{M}_{m \times n}(\mathbb{R})$, as $\mathcal{M}_{m \times n}(\mathbb{R})$ is closed under addition. We will show that $\hat{F}$ is in $\mathcal{M}_{m \times n}(\mathbb{R})$ if and only if $F = \mathbf{0}_{m \times n}$. We have that

$$
\begin{aligned}
\hat{F} &= F - \mathbf{1}_m F_{(i)} - (F^{(j)} - \mathbf{1}_m f_{i,j})\mathbf{1}_n^\mathsf{T} \\
&= \begin{bmatrix} f_{1,1} - f_{i,1} - f_{1,j} + f_{i,j}, & \cdots & f_{1,n} - f_{i,n} - f_{1,j} + f_{i,j} \\ f_{2,1} - f_{i,1} - f_{2,j} + f_{i,j}, & \cdots & f_{2,n} - f_{i,n} - f_{2,j} + f_{i,j} \\ \vdots & \ddots & \vdots \\ f_{m,1} - f_{i,1} - f_{m,j} + f_{i,j}, & \cdots & f_{m,n} - f_{i,n} - f_{m,j} + f_{i,j} \end{bmatrix}.
\end{aligned}
$$

In this form, it is clear that $\hat{F}_{(i)} = \mathbf{0}_n^\mathsf{T}$ and $\hat{F}^{(j)} = \mathbf{0}_m$. Since $\hat{F}_{(i)} = \mathbf{0}_n^\mathsf{T}$ and $\hat{F}^{(j)} = \mathbf{0}_m$, from Lemma 6 $\hat{F}$ is in $\mathcal{M}_{m \times n}(\mathbb{R})$ if and only if $\hat{F} = \mathbf{0}_{m \times n}$. □

The matrix $\hat{F}$ constructed in Theorem 2 depends on which indices (i, j) were used to construct it, and the proper notation should be $\hat{F}(i, j)$. However,

---

Algorithm 1. Algorithm for determining if a matrix is in $\mathcal{M}_{m \times n}(\mathbb{R})$

1: **function** IsMatrixInM(F)
2:    Select any $(i,j) \in \{1 \ldots m\} \times \{1 \ldots n\}$
3:    **for** $s \leftarrow 1, m$ **do**
4:        $R_{(s)} \leftarrow F_{(i)}$
5:    **end for**
6:    **for** $t \leftarrow 1, n$ **do**
7:        $C^{(t)} \leftarrow F^{(j)} - \mathbf{1}_m f_{i,j}$
8:    **end for**
9:    $\hat{F} \leftarrow F - R - C$
10:    MatrixInM$\leftarrow 1$
11:    **for** $l \leftarrow 1, m$ **do**
12:        **for** $k \leftarrow 1, n$ **do**
13:            **if** $\hat{f}_{l,k} \neq 0$ **then**
14:                MatrixInM$\leftarrow 0$
15:                **break**
16:            **end if**
17:        **end for**
18:        **if** MatrixInM$= 0$ **then**
19:            **break**
20:        **end if**
21:    **end for**
22:    **return** (MatrixInM)
23: **end function**

---

since in all of our results that require similar notation the selection of (i,j) is arbitrary, in an abuse of notation we drop (i,j) and simply use $\hat{F}$. An algorithm for determining if a matrix is in $\mathcal{M}_{m \times n}(\mathbb{Q})$ is shown in Algorithm 1.

We now turn our attention to an efficient manner to calculate $\mathbf{z} \in \{\mathbf{z} \in \mathbb{R}^n \mid \mathbf{1}_n^\mathsf{T} \mathbf{z} = 0\}$ and $\mathbf{w} \in \{\mathbf{w} \in \mathbb{R}^m \mid \mathbf{1}_m^\mathsf{T} \mathbf{w} = 0\}$ such that $(\mathbf{w}, \mathbf{z}) \in \mathcal{WZ}(F)$. This is used to compute a candidate parameter γ in Theorem 1. The next corollary derives a computationally efficient method for computing $\mathbf{z}$ and $\mathbf{w}$ for $F \notin \mathcal{M}_{m \times n}(\mathbb{R})$.

Corollary 1. *Given matrix $F \in \mathbb{R}^{m \times n}$, $F \notin \mathcal{M}_{m \times n}(\mathbb{R})$, construct $\hat{F}$ as in Theorem 2. Choose any (l, k) such that $\hat{f}_{l,k} \neq 0$, let $\mathbf{w} = \mathbf{e}_l - \mathbf{e}_i$, and $\mathbf{z} = \mathbf{e}_k - \mathbf{e}_j$. Then $\mathbf{z} \in \{\mathbf{z} \in \mathbb{R}^n \mid \mathbf{1}_n^\mathsf{T} \mathbf{z} = 0\}$, $\mathbf{w} \in \{\mathbf{w} \in \mathbb{R}^m \mid \mathbf{1}_m^\mathsf{T} \mathbf{w} = 0\}$, and*

$$\mathbf{w}^\mathsf{T} F \mathbf{z} = \mathbf{w}^\mathsf{T} \hat{F} \mathbf{z} = \hat{f}_{l,k} \neq 0.$$

Proof. Clearly $\mathbf{w}$ and $\mathbf{z}$ are constructed such that $\mathbf{z} \in \{\mathbf{z} \in \mathbb{R}^n \mid \mathbf{1}_n^\mathsf{T} \mathbf{z} = 0\}$, $\mathbf{w} \in \{\mathbf{w} \in \mathbb{R}^m \mid \mathbf{1}_m^\mathsf{T} \mathbf{w} = 0\}$. From Theorem 2 we have that:

$$\hat{F} = F - \mathbf{1}_m F_{(i)} - (F^{(j)} - \mathbf{1}_m f_{i,j}) \mathbf{1}_n^\mathsf{T}.$$

Then we have:

$$\mathbf{w}^\mathsf{T} \hat{F} \mathbf{z} = \mathbf{w}^\mathsf{T} F \mathbf{z} - \mathbf{w}^\mathsf{T} \mathbf{1}_m F_{(i)} \mathbf{z} - \mathbf{w}^\mathsf{T} (F^{(j)} - \mathbf{1}_m f_{i,j}) \mathbf{1}_n^\mathsf{T} \mathbf{z} = \mathbf{w}^\mathsf{T} F \mathbf{z}.$$

Since $\hat{F}$ was constructed such that $\hat{F}_{(i)} = \mathbf{0}_n^\mathsf{T}$ and $\hat{F}^{(j)} = \mathbf{0}_m$, we have that:

$$\begin{aligned}
\mathbf{w}^\mathsf{T}\hat{F}\mathbf{z} &= (\mathbf{e}_l - \mathbf{e}_i)^\mathsf{T}\hat{F}(\mathbf{e}_k - \mathbf{e}_j) \\
&= (\mathbf{e}_l - \mathbf{e}_i)^\mathsf{T}(\hat{F}\mathbf{e}_k - \hat{F}\mathbf{e}_j) \\
&= (\mathbf{e}_l - \mathbf{e}_i)^\mathsf{T}(\hat{F}\mathbf{e}_k - \mathbf{0}_m) \\
&= \mathbf{e}_l^\mathsf{T}\hat{F}\mathbf{e}_k - \mathbf{e}_i^\mathsf{T}\hat{F}\mathbf{e}_k \\
&= \mathbf{e}_l^\mathsf{T}\hat{F}\mathbf{e}_k - \mathbf{0}_n^\mathsf{T}\mathbf{e}_k \\
&= \mathbf{e}_l^\mathsf{T}\hat{F}\mathbf{e}_k \\
&= \hat{f}_{l,k}.
\end{aligned}$$

Finally, $\hat{f}_{l,k}$ was selected such that $\hat{f}_{l,k} \neq 0$. This completes the proof. □

3.2   A Simple Example: Rock-Paper-Scissors

Consider the game matrix given in Fig. 1a and let us represent this game as $(m, n, A, -A)$. This is the classic Rock-Paper-Scissors (R-P-S) with well known NE strategies $\mathbf{p}^* = \mathbf{q}^* = [\frac{1}{3}, \frac{1}{3}, \frac{1}{3}]^\mathsf{T}$. The game in Fig. 1b is a positive affine transformation of $(m, n, C, -C)$. Let us represent this game as (m, n, A, B). Clearly, (m, n, A, B) is neither zero-sum nor constant-sum. However, by applying the process outlined above one can obtain the game in Fig. 1c, which is a zero-sum game and strategically equivalent to (m, n, A, B).

	R	P	S
R	0,0	−1,1	1,−1
P	1,−1	0,0	−1,1
S	−1,1	1,−1	0,0

(a) R-P-S

	R	P	S
R	−5,8	−6,10	10,6
P	−1,−5	−2,−3	2,−1
S	−9,13	2,9	6,11

(b) A PAT of R-P-S

	R	P	S
R	−16,16	−20,20	−12,12
P	−12,12	−16,16	−20,20
S	−20,20	−12,12	−16,16

(c) Zero-Sum Game equivalent to (b)

Fig. 1. (a) The classic zero-sum game Rock-Paper-Scissors. (b) A nonzero-sum game that is strategically equivalent to Rock-Paper-Scissors through a PAT. (c) A zero-sum game that is strategically equivalent to the PAT of Rock-Paper-Scissors.

By letting $\mathbf{w} = [-1, 1, 0]^\mathsf{T}$, $\mathbf{z} = [-1, 0, 1]^\mathsf{T}$, we have $\gamma = -\frac{\mathbf{w}^\mathsf{T}A\mathbf{z}}{\mathbf{w}^\mathsf{T}B\mathbf{z}} = -\frac{-12}{6} = 2$. Then let $(i, j) = (1, 1)$ to obtain the strategically zero-sum game:

$$\bar{A} = A - \mathbf{1}_m \begin{bmatrix} 11 & 14 & 22 \end{bmatrix}, \qquad \bar{B} = 2B - \begin{bmatrix} 0 \\ -22 \\ 6 \end{bmatrix} \mathbf{1}_n^\mathsf{T}.$$

The result of these calculations is the zero-sum game $(m, n, \bar{A}, \bar{B})$ which is displayed in Fig. 1c and, as expected, has the NE strategies $\mathbf{p}^* = \mathbf{q}^* = [\frac{1}{3}, \frac{1}{3}, \frac{1}{3}]^\mathsf{T}$.

Algorithm 2. Condensed algorithm for solving a strategically rank-0 game

---

1: **procedure** SHORTSER0(A, B)
2:     **if** A and/or $B \in \mathcal{M}_{m \times n}(\mathbb{Q})$ **then**
3:         Calculate pure strategy NE and **exit**
4:     **else**
5:         $\gamma \leftarrow -\frac{\mathbf{w}^{\mathsf{T}} A \mathbf{z}}{\mathbf{w}^{\mathsf{T}} B \mathbf{z}}$
6:         **if** $\gamma < 0$ **then**
7:             Not strategically equivalent via PAT. **exit**
8:         **else**
9:             $M \leftarrow A + \gamma B$
10:            **if** M not in $\mathcal{M}_{m \times n}(\mathbb{Q})$ **then**
11:                Not strategically equivalent via PAT. **exit**
12:            **else**
13:                choose $(i, j) \in (m \times n)$
14:    . $\bar{A} \leftarrow A - \mathbf{1}_m M_{(i)}$
15:                $\bar{B} \leftarrow \gamma B - (M^{(j)} - \mathbf{1}_m m_{i,j}) \mathbf{1}_n^{\mathsf{T}}$
16:                Solve $(m, n, \bar{A}, \bar{B})$ via LP
17:            **end if**
18:        **end if**
19:    **end if**
20: **end procedure**

3.3 Algorithm and Simulations

We have shown that given the game (m, n, A, B), one can determine if the game is strategically equivalent to the zero-sum game $(m, n, \bar{A}, \bar{B})$ through a PAT. If so, then it is possible to construct a rank-0 game which is strategically equivalent to the original game. One can then efficiently solve the strategically equivalent zero-sum game via linear programming. We state the key steps in our algorithm below and show that both the determination of strategic equivalence and the computation of the strategically equivalent zero-sum game can be done in time $\mathcal{O}(mn)$.

The analytical results and discussions throughout this paper apply to real bimatrix games, with $(A, B) \in \mathbb{R}^{m \times n} \times \mathbb{R}^{m \times n}$. However, for computational reasons, when discussing the algorithmic implementations we focus on rational bimatrix games, with $(A, B) \in \mathbb{Q}^{m \times n} \times \mathbb{Q}^{m \times n}$.

Theorem 3. *The SER0 algorithm determines if a game (m, n, A, B) is strategically equivalent to a rank-0 game and returns the strategically equivalent zero-sum game in time $\mathcal{O}(mn)$.*

We now turn our attention to the computational complexity of Algorithm 2. First, testing whether or not a matrix is in $\mathcal{M}_{m \times n}(\mathbb{R})$ is equivalent to implementing (1) and then comparing two matrices F and $\bar{F}$. Both these operations take time $\mathcal{O}(mn)$. Next, for any matrix $F \in \mathcal{M}_{m \times n}(\mathbb{R})$, calculating $\mathbf{w}^{\mathsf{T}} F \mathbf{z}$ takes time $\mathcal{O}(m^2) + \mathcal{O}(n) < \mathcal{O}(mn)$ for $m \leq n$. So, calculating γ can be done in time

$\mathcal{O}(mn)$ if one has candidate vectors $(\mathbf{w}, \mathbf{z})$. Corollary 1 gives an algorithm for determining such $(\mathbf{w}, \mathbf{z})$ that runs in time $\mathcal{O}(mn)$.

Forming the D matrix takes mn multiplications and mn additions, and therefore has time $\mathcal{O}(mn)$. Finally, calculating $\bar{A}, \bar{B}$ for the case $\texttt{rank}(M) = 2$ consists of scalar-matrix multiplication, vector outer product, and matrix subtraction. Therefore, it has time $\mathcal{O}(mn)$. This shows that overall the algorithm can both identify whether a game is strategically equivalent to a zero-sum game through a PAT and, if so, can determine the equivalent game in time $\mathcal{O}(mn)$.

3.4 Numerical Results

To evaluate the performance of the SER0 algorithm we ran the following experiment. We fixed m at $m = 1000$ and varied n with $n \in [2000, 10000]$. Each entry in the payoff matrices are uniformly distributed. We ran SER0 on 1000 different game instances for each value of n.

All experiments were conducted on a standard desktop computer running Windows 7 with 16 GB of RAM and an Intel Xeon E5-1603 processor with 4 cores running at 2.8 GHz.

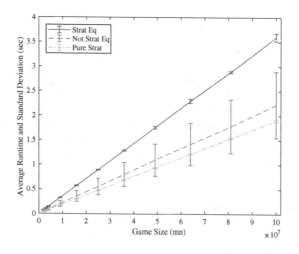

Fig. 2. Average running time and standard deviation of the SER0 algorithm for strategically equivalent games, games that are not strategically equivalent, and games that are guaranteed to have at least one pure strategy NE. For each value of mn, we ran the algorithm on 1000 such games.

For each set of experiments, we created instances (m, n, A, B) that were strategically equivalent to a zero-sum game $(m, n, \bar{A}, \bar{B})$. In all cases tested, the SER0 algorithm correctly identified the games as strategically zero-sum and calculated the equivalent game $(m, n, \bar{A}, \bar{B})$. As expected, one can observe from Fig. 2 that there is a clear linear relationship between the runtime of SER0 and the size of the game instance. In addition, for very large games of size (1000×10000) SER0 found the equivalent game in an average time of 3.6 s.

We then created games which were guaranteed to have a pure strategy NE. In other words, at least one of A or B were in $\mathcal{M}_{m \times n}(\mathbb{Q})$. Again, the SER0 algorithm correctly identified all of these cases as having a pure strategy NE. Again, we observe that SER0's runtime is linear in this case. As expected, this case is much faster than the strategically equivalent case as there is no need to calculate $\bar{A}, \bar{B}, M$ nor test for $M \in \mathcal{M}_{m \times n}(\mathbb{Q})$.

Finally, we conducted experiments on games that were not strategically equivalent to a zero-sum game via a PAT. Similar to the other two cases, the SER0 algorithm correctly identified these games as not strategically equivalent to a zero-sum game. As Fig. 2 show, this case also exhibits a linear relationship between runtime and the game size, although with a much higher standard deviation compared to the other two sets of experiments. This higher standard deviation is readily explainable by examining the SER0 algorithm. When testing whether or not a game is strategically equivalent, the test can return a negative result if either $\gamma \leq 0$ or $M \notin \mathcal{M}_{m \times n}(\mathbb{Q})$. For cases of $\gamma \leq 0$, the algorithm terminates and returns a negative result in much less time than it takes to calculate the M matrix and test for $M \in \mathcal{M}_{m \times n}(\mathbb{Q})$.

4 Approximate Nash Equilibrium Through an Affine Transformation

Thus far we have introduced sufficient and necessary conditions of the existence of strategically equivalent zero-sum games via PAT. Then, we proposed an algorithm to compute a Nash equilibrium in time $\mathcal{O}(mn)$, given that the conditions in Theorem 1 hold. Now, we introduce another algorithm that efficiently computes an approximate Nash equilibrium when conditions in Theorem 1 are not satisfied.

There are two key insights that drive the second algorithm. Given a bimatrix game (m, n, A, B), we can determine a strategically equivalent (not necessarily zero-sum) game (m, n, R, C) via PAT. Let $E = R + C$. Consider the zero-sum game $(m, n, \tilde{A}, \tilde{B})$, where $\tilde{A} = R - \frac{1}{2}E$ and $\tilde{B} = C - \frac{1}{2}E$. One may want the zero-sum game $(m, n, \tilde{A}, \tilde{B})$ to be, in some sense, 'close' to (m, n, R, C). One approach is to determine matrices R and C to reduce the max norm of E, by which the error of the approximate NE can be controlled.

The second insight is about the nature of the game transformation itself. From Definition 4, we conclude that when the two games are strategically equivalent, then for every player, the best response correspondence is the same in both games. We identify an affine game transformations below that bijectively transforms the best response correspondence. In other words, the best response correspondence of each player in the transformed game can be bijectively mapped to the best response correspondence of the original game.

Theorem 4. *Let $D_1 \in \mathcal{D}_n$ and $D_2 \in \mathcal{D}_m$ be positive definite diagonal matrices and consider the two games (m, n, A, B) and (m, n, AD_1, D_2B). We have*

$$\Gamma_A(\mathbf{q}) = \Gamma_{AD_1}\left(\frac{D_1^{-1}\mathbf{q}}{\mathbf{1}_n^\mathsf{T}(D_1^{-1}\mathbf{q})}\right), \qquad \Gamma_B(\mathbf{p}) = \Gamma_{D_2B}\left(\frac{D_2^{-1}\mathbf{p}}{\mathbf{1}_m^\mathsf{T}(D_2^{-1}\mathbf{p})}\right).$$

Proof. Since D_1 is positive definite diagonal matrix, we have $\mathbf{1}_n^\mathsf{T}(D_1^{-1}\mathbf{q}) > 0$. This yields

$$\mathbf{p} \in \Gamma_A(\mathbf{q}) \iff \mathbf{p}^\mathsf{T}A\mathbf{q} = \max_i[A\mathbf{q}]_i,$$

$$\iff \frac{\mathbf{p}^\mathsf{T}AD_1D_1^{-1}\mathbf{q}}{\mathbf{1}_n^\mathsf{T}(D_1^{-1}\mathbf{q})} = \max_i\left[\frac{AD_1D_1^{-1}\mathbf{q}}{\mathbf{1}_n^\mathsf{T}(D_1^{-1}\mathbf{q})}\right]_i,$$

$$\iff \mathbf{p} \in \Gamma_{AD_1}\left(\frac{D_1^{-1}\mathbf{q}}{\mathbf{1}_n^\mathsf{T}(D_1^{-1}\mathbf{q})}\right).$$

Hence the first equation is proved. The proof of the second equation is similar and therefore omitted. □

While the affine game transformation described above is simple and a straightforward extension of PAT, we are unable to find any reference in the literature on such an affine transformation. We next show that the Nash equilibria and approximate Nash equilibria of the transformed game can be mapped to that of the original game.

Lemma 4. *Consider games (m, n, A, B) and (m, n, AD_1, D_2B), where D_1, D_2 are diagonal, positive definite matrices. Let $\tilde{\mathbf{p}}^* = \frac{D_2^{-1}\mathbf{p}^*}{\mathbf{1}_m^\mathsf{T}(D_2^{-1}\mathbf{p}^*)}$, $\tilde{\mathbf{q}}^* = \frac{D_1^{-1}\mathbf{q}^*}{\mathbf{1}_n^\mathsf{T}(D_1^{-1}\mathbf{q}^*)}$. Then,*

(a) *$(\mathbf{p}^*, \mathbf{q}^*)$ is an ε-WSNE of the game (m, n, A, B) if and only if the strategy pair $(\tilde{\mathbf{p}}^*, \tilde{\mathbf{q}}^*)$ is an $\tilde{\varepsilon}$-WSNE of the game (m, n, AD_1, D_2B), where $\varepsilon = \tilde{\varepsilon}/\max\{\|D_1\|_{max}, \|D_2\|_{max}\}$*
(b) *$(\mathbf{p}^*, \mathbf{q}^*)$ is a NE of the game (m, n, A, B) if and only if the strategy pair $(\tilde{\mathbf{p}}^*, \tilde{\mathbf{q}}^*)$ is a NE of the game (m, n, AD_1, D_2B).*

Proof. We start by proving (a). Suppose $(\tilde{\mathbf{p}}^*, \tilde{\mathbf{q}}^*)$ is an $\tilde{\varepsilon}$-WSNE of the game (m, n, AD_1, D_2B). From Definition 6 we have

$$\forall i, k \in S_1, \tilde{\mathbf{p}}_i^* > 0 \implies (AD_1\tilde{\mathbf{q}}^*)_i \geq (AD_1\tilde{\mathbf{q}}^*)_k - \tilde{\varepsilon}.$$

Denote $d_{2,j}$ as the (j, j)th entry of matrix D_2. Since $d_{2,j} > 0 \; \forall j \in S_1$, we have $\tilde{\mathbf{p}}_i^* > 0 \iff \left(\frac{D_2\tilde{\mathbf{p}}^*}{\mathbf{1}_m^\mathsf{T}(D_2\tilde{\mathbf{p}}^*)}\right)_i = \tilde{\mathbf{p}}_i^* > 0$. This yields

$$(AD_1\tilde{\mathbf{q}}^*)_i \geq (AD_1\tilde{\mathbf{q}}^*)_k - \tilde{\varepsilon}$$

$$\implies \left(\frac{AD_1D_1^{-1}\mathbf{q}^*}{\mathbf{1}_n^\mathsf{T}(D_1^{-1}\mathbf{q}^*)}\right)_i \geq \left(\frac{AD_1D_1^{-1}\mathbf{q}^*}{\mathbf{1}_n^\mathsf{T}(D_1^{-1}\mathbf{q}^*)}\right)_k - \frac{\tilde{\varepsilon}}{\mathbf{1}_n^\mathsf{T}(D_1^{-1}\mathbf{q}^*)},$$

$$\iff (AD_1D_1^{-1}\mathbf{q}^*)_i \geq (AD_1D_1^{-1}\mathbf{q}^*)_k - \varepsilon,$$

$$\iff (A\mathbf{q}^*)_i \geq (A\mathbf{q}^*)_k - \varepsilon.$$

The proof of the other player is similar and thus omitted. The proof of (b) is straightforward by setting $\varepsilon = 0$.   □

4.1   Approximate Nash Equilibrium

We have shown in Lemma 2 that additive transformations only affect ε of the set of WSNE. Lemma 4 shows the set of NE is preserved via affine transformations. Now we establish a connection (in terms of approximate WSNE) between a bimatrix game and the approximated zero-sum game.

Theorem 5. *Let* $D_1 \in \mathcal{D}_n$, $D_2 \in \mathcal{D}_m$, $\mathbf{u} \in \mathbb{R}^n$, $\mathbf{v} \in \mathbb{R}^m$. *Consider games* (m, n, A, B) *and* $(m, n, R - \frac{1}{2}E, C - \frac{1}{2}E)$, *where* $R = AD_1 - \mathbf{1}_m \mathbf{u}^T$, $C = D_2 B - \mathbf{v}\mathbf{1}_n^T$, $E = R + C$, *and define* $\tilde{\varepsilon} := \|E\|_{max}$. *Let*

$$\mathbf{p}^* = \frac{D_2 \tilde{\mathbf{p}}^*}{\mathbf{1}_m^T (D_2 \tilde{\mathbf{p}}^*)}, \qquad \mathbf{q}^* = \frac{D_1 \tilde{\mathbf{q}}^*}{\mathbf{1}_n^T (D_1 \tilde{\mathbf{q}}^*)}, \qquad \varepsilon = \frac{\tilde{\varepsilon}}{\max\{\|D_1\|_{max}, \|D_2\|_{max}\}}.$$

If $(\tilde{\mathbf{p}}^*, \tilde{\mathbf{q}}^*)$ *is a saddle point equilibrium of the zero-sum game* $(m, n, R - \frac{1}{2}E, C - \frac{1}{2}E)$, *then the strategy pair* $(\mathbf{p}^*, \mathbf{q}^*)$ *is a* ε-WSNE *of the game* (m, n, A, B).

Proof. Suppose $(\tilde{\mathbf{p}}^*, \tilde{\mathbf{q}}^*)$ is a saddle point equilibrium of the game $(m, n, R - \frac{1}{2}E, C - \frac{1}{2}E)$. From Lemma 2 we have $(\tilde{\mathbf{p}}^*, \tilde{\mathbf{q}}^*)$ is an $\tilde{\varepsilon}$-WSNE of game (m, n, R, C). From Lemma 3, $(\tilde{\mathbf{p}}^*, \tilde{\mathbf{q}}^*)$ is an $\tilde{\varepsilon}$-WSNE of game $(m, n, AD_1, D_2 B)$. Finally, Lemma 4 implies that $(\mathbf{p}^*, \mathbf{q}^*)$ is a ε-WSNE of the original game (m, n, A, B).   □

4.2   Algorithmic Implementation

In the sequel, we formulate an optimization problem to compute $D_1 \in \mathcal{D}_n$, $D_2 \in \mathcal{D}_m$, $\mathbf{u} \in \mathbb{R}^n$, $\mathbf{v} \in \mathbb{R}^m$ given (A, B). This problem is equivalent to minimizing the max norm of the matrix $E = R + C = AD_1 - \mathbf{1}_m \mathbf{u}^T + D_2 B - \mathbf{v}\mathbf{1}_n^T$, which is formulated as the optimization problem:

$$\min_{\mathbf{u}, \mathbf{v}, D_1, D_2} \quad \|AD_1 - \mathbf{1}_m \mathbf{u}^T + D_2 B - \mathbf{v}\mathbf{1}_n^T\|_{max} \tag{CP1}$$
$$\text{s.t.} \quad \mathbf{u} \in \mathbb{R}^n, \mathbf{v} \in \mathbb{R}^m, D_1 \succeq I_n, D_2 \succeq I_m, D_1 \in \mathcal{D}_n, D_2 \in \mathcal{D}_m.$$

It is well known (see, for example [1, pg. 150]) that problems similar to CP1 can be equivalently written in the epigraph form as:

$$\min_{\mathbf{u}, \mathbf{v}, D_1, D_2, t} \quad t$$
$$\text{s.t.} \quad -d_{1,j} a_{i,j} - d_{2,i} b_{i,j} - t + u_j + v_i \leq 0, \qquad i = 1, \ldots, m, j = 1, \ldots, n$$
$$d_{1,j} a_{i,j} + d_{2,i} b_{i,j} - t - u_j - v_i \leq 0, \qquad i = 1, \ldots, m, j = 1, \ldots, n$$
$$\mathbf{u} \in \mathbb{R}^n, \mathbf{v} \in \mathbb{R}^m, d_{1,j} \geq 1, d_{2,i} \geq 1, t \geq 0. \tag{LP1}$$

Algorithm 3 . Algorithm for computing ε-Nash equilibrium of the game (m, n, A, B).

1: **procedure** APPROXIMATENE(m, n, A, B)
2:     Solve LP1 to get $D_1, D_2, \mathbf{u}, \mathbf{v}, \tilde{\varepsilon}$
3:     $R \leftarrow AD_1 - \mathbf{1}_m \mathbf{u}^{\mathsf{T}}$, $C \leftarrow D_2 B - \mathbf{v}\mathbf{1}_n^{\mathsf{T}}$, $E \leftarrow R + C$
4:     Calculate saddle point equilibrium $(\tilde{\mathbf{p}}^*, \tilde{\mathbf{q}}^*)$ of $(m, n, R - \frac{1}{2}E, C - \frac{1}{2}E)$
5:     Set $\mathbf{p}^* \leftarrow \frac{D_2 \tilde{\mathbf{p}}^*}{\mathbf{1}_m^{\mathsf{T}}(D_2 \tilde{\mathbf{p}}^*)}$, $\mathbf{q}^* \leftarrow \frac{D_1 \tilde{\mathbf{q}}^*}{\mathbf{1}_n^{\mathsf{T}}(D_1 \tilde{\mathbf{q}}^*)}$, $\varepsilon \leftarrow \tilde{\varepsilon} / \max\{\|D_1\|_{max}, \|D_2\|_{max}\}$
6: **end procedure**

The program in LP1 is a linear program and can be solved in polynomial time. Thus, what we have shown is that given a nonzero-sum game (m, n, A, B), we can, in polynomial time, find the zero-sum game $(m, n, R - \frac{1}{2}E, C - \frac{1}{2}E)$ such that $\tilde{\varepsilon} = \|E\|_{max}$ is minimized. Then, by Theorem 5, we can compute an ε-WSNE of game (m, n, A, B) by calculating the saddle point equilibrium $(\tilde{\mathbf{p}}^*, \tilde{\mathbf{q}}^*)$ of the zero-sum game. As a result, the Algorithm 3 finds an ε-WSNE of (m, n, A, B) in polynomial time using two calls of a linear program.

4.3 Numerical Simulation

To evaluate the performance of Algorithm 3, we ran an experiment to evaluate the theoretical and actual error ε. We generated games with square payoff matrices with $n \in [5, 50]$. The payoff values are independent and identically distributed, with uniform distribution in the set $[0, 1]$. We generated 10,000 different pairs of payoff matrices on each value of n.

For each game (m, n, A, B), we first ran Algorithm 3 to get an approximate WSNE $(\tilde{\mathbf{p}}, \tilde{\mathbf{q}})$. Then, we ran Lemke-Howson Algorithm to compute the exact Nash equilibrium $(\mathbf{p}, \mathbf{q})$. Finally, we computed the exact and theoretical ε. For each game size, we calculated the mean and variance of ε. In all cases tested, the actual error of $(\tilde{\mathbf{p}}, \tilde{\mathbf{q}})$ is less than the theoretical ε, as shown in Figs. 3 and 4.

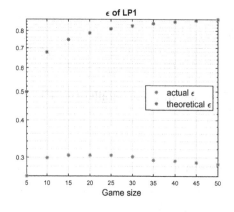
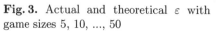
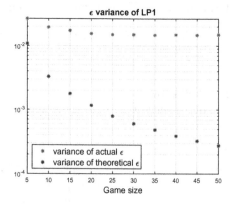

Fig. 3. Actual and theoretical ε with game sizes 5, 10, ..., 50

Fig. 4. Actual and theoretical variance of ε with game sizes 5, 10, ..., 50

5   Conclusion

In this paper, we proposed two algorithms to determine a strategically equivalent zero-sum game given a nonzero-sum game. In this process, we proposed a new result on best response bijection, by which we can compute the NE of a bimatrix game by computation of the fixed point of the transformed function. The algorithms to determine the strategically equivalent zero-sum games run in polynomial time in the size of the game. Consequently, we showed that a class of nonzero-sum games can be solved in polynomial time. In the cases where our second algorithm does not output a strategically equivalent zero-sum game, we show that it is a new algorithm for computing an ε-WSNE in polynomial time. Finally, we conducted numerical studies to show the efficacy of our algorithms.

For the future, we will extend the algorithm to dynamic nonzero-sum Markov games and dynamic games with asymmetric information. We will also evaluate the performance of our algorithm on different classes of games on GAMUT[19], compare the runtime with classic algorithms and evaluate ε from our algorithm. Moreover, given a bimatrix game that is not equivalent to a zero-sum game, is there a wider class of linear transformations (e.g. D_1 and D_2 being positive definite Stieltjes matrices) that can outperform the affine transformation in performance in a certain class of games?

A   Some Auxiliary Results on $\mathcal{M}_{m \times n}(\mathbb{R})$

This appendix is based on Appendix A.1.1 of [12].

Theorem 6. *For matrix $M \in \mathbb{R}^{m \times n}$ with $\mathbf{rank}(M) = r$. Let $M_1 = M$, and*

$$M_{k+1} := M_k - w_k^{-1} M_k \mathbf{x}_k \mathbf{y}_k^\mathsf{T} M_k, \qquad k \in \{1, \ldots, r\}. \tag{2}$$

Define rank 1 matrices $W_k := \mathbf{v}_k \mathbf{u}_k^\mathsf{T} = w_k^{-1} M_k \mathbf{x}_k \mathbf{y}_k^\mathsf{T} M_k$. Then, for any $j > k$, $\mathbf{v}_k \notin ColSpan(M_j)$ and $\mathbf{u}_k \notin ColSpan(M_j^\mathsf{T})$.

Proof. By (2), we have $M_{k+1} = M - \sum_{i=1}^k W_i = \sum_{i=k+1}^r W_i$. Then, [23, p. 69] implies $\mathbf{rank}(M_{k+1}) = \mathbf{rank}(M_k) - 1$. Hence the result is proved.   □

Theorem 7. *If a matrix $A \in \mathbb{R}^{m \times n}$ and $A \notin \mathcal{M}_{m \times n}(\mathbb{R})$, then $\mathcal{WZ}(A) \neq \emptyset$*

Proof. We can write $A = M + \sum_{i=1}^k \mathbf{v}_i \mathbf{u}_i^\mathsf{T}$, where

(a) $k = \mathbf{rank}(A) - \mathbf{rank}(M)$,
(b) $M = \mathbf{1}_m \mathbf{u}_o^\mathsf{T} + \mathbf{v}_0 \mathbf{1}_n^\mathsf{T} \in \mathcal{M}_{m \times n}(\mathbb{R})$, so $\mathbf{rank}(M) \leq 2$,
(c) For any $i \in \{1, \ldots, k\}$, $\mathbf{v}_i \notin ColSpan(M)$ and $\mathbf{u}_i \notin ColSpan(M^\mathsf{T})$,
(d) $\{\mathbf{v}_i\}_{i=1}^k$ and $\{\mathbf{u}_i\}_{i=1}^k$ are linearly independent.

Let $\mathbf{w}_0 = \mathbf{1}_m$ and $\mathbf{z}_0 = \mathbf{1}_n$, and construct orthogonal vectors such that

$$\mathbf{w}_i = \mathbf{v}_i - \sum_{j=0}^{i} \frac{\mathbf{v}_i^\mathsf{T}\mathbf{w}_j}{\mathbf{w}_j^\mathsf{T}\mathbf{w}_j}\mathbf{w}_j \qquad \forall i \in \{1,\ldots,k\}$$

$$\mathbf{z}_i = \mathbf{u}_i - \sum_{j=0}^{i} \frac{\mathbf{u}_i^\mathsf{T}\mathbf{z}_j}{\mathbf{z}_j^\mathsf{T}\mathbf{z}_j}\mathbf{z}_j \qquad \forall i \in \{1,\ldots,k\}$$

$$\mathbf{1}_m^\mathsf{T}\mathbf{w}_i = \mathbf{1}_n^\mathsf{T}\mathbf{z}_i = 0 \qquad \forall i \in \{1,\ldots,k\}$$

$$\mathbf{w}_i^\mathsf{T}\mathbf{v}_j = \mathbf{u}_j^\mathsf{T}\mathbf{z}_i = 0 \qquad \forall j < i$$

$$\mathbf{w}_i^\mathsf{T}\mathbf{v}_i \neq 0 \text{ and } \mathbf{u}_i^\mathsf{T}\mathbf{z}_i \neq 0 \qquad \forall i \in \{1,\ldots,k\}$$

After the iteration, we have that

$$\mathbf{w}_k^\mathsf{T}A\mathbf{z}_k = \mathbf{w}_k^\mathsf{T}M\mathbf{z}_k + \mathbf{w}_k^\mathsf{T}\sum_{i=1}^{k}\mathbf{v}_i\mathbf{u}_i^\mathsf{T}\mathbf{z}_k = \mathbf{w}_k^\mathsf{T}M\mathbf{z}_k + \mathbf{w}_k^\mathsf{T}\sum_{i=1}^{k-1}\mathbf{v}_i\mathbf{u}_i^\mathsf{T}\mathbf{z}_k + \mathbf{w}_k^\mathsf{T}\mathbf{v}_k\mathbf{u}_k^\mathsf{T}\mathbf{z}_k$$

$$= \mathbf{w}_k^\mathsf{T}\mathbf{v}_k\mathbf{u}_k^\mathsf{T}\mathbf{z}_k \neq 0.$$

The last step is because $\mathbf{w}_i^\mathsf{T}\mathbf{v}_j = \mathbf{u}_j^\mathsf{T}\mathbf{z}_i = 0$ for any $j < i$. □

Lemma 5. *For any matrix $M \in \mathcal{M}_{m \times n}(\mathbb{R})$:*

1. *If $\mathtt{rank}(M) = 2$, then $\mathbf{1}_m \in \mathtt{ColSpan}(M)$ and $\mathbf{1}_n \in \mathtt{ColSpan}(M^\mathsf{T})$. In addition, for all $\mathbf{x}, \mathbf{y}$ such that $M\mathbf{x} = \mathbf{1}_m, M^\mathsf{T}\mathbf{y} = \mathbf{1}_n, \mathbf{1}_n^\mathsf{T}\mathbf{x} = 0, \mathbf{1}_m^\mathsf{T}\mathbf{y} = 0$.*
2. *If $\mathtt{rank}(M) = 1$, then either $\mathbf{1}_m \in \mathtt{ColSpan}(M)$, or $\mathbf{1}_n \in \mathtt{ColSpan}(M^\mathsf{T})$ or both $\mathbf{1}_m \in \mathtt{ColSpan}(M)$ and $\mathbf{1}_n \in \mathtt{ColSpan}(M^\mathsf{T})$.*

Proof. For Claim 1, $\mathbf{1}_m \in \mathtt{ColSpan}(M)$ and $\mathbf{1}_n \in \mathtt{ColSpan}(M^\mathsf{T})$ follows directly from $\mathtt{rank}(M) = 2$. In addition, $M \in \mathcal{M}_{m \times n}(\mathbb{R})$ and $\mathtt{rank}(M) = 2$ implies that there exists $\mathbf{v} \neq \mathbf{0}_n$ and $\mathbf{u} \neq \mathbf{0}_m$ such that $M = \mathbf{1}_m\mathbf{u}^\mathsf{T} + \mathbf{v}\mathbf{1}_n^\mathsf{T}$. Also since $\mathtt{rank}(M) = 2$, we have that for all $a \in \mathbb{R}$, $\mathbf{v} \neq a\mathbf{1}_m$ since $\mathbf{v}$ and $\mathbf{1}_m$ must be linearly independent. Then, for all $\mathbf{x}$ such that $M\mathbf{x} = \mathbf{1}_m$ we have that:

$$M\mathbf{x} = \mathbf{1}_m\mathbf{u}^\mathsf{T}\mathbf{x} + \mathbf{v}\mathbf{1}_n^\mathsf{T}\mathbf{x} = \mathbf{1}_m = (\mathbf{u}^\mathsf{T}\mathbf{x})\mathbf{1}_m + (\mathbf{1}_n^\mathsf{T}\mathbf{x})\mathbf{v} = \mathbf{1}_m.$$

This implies $(\mathbf{1}_n^\mathsf{T}\mathbf{x})\mathbf{v} = (1 - \mathbf{u}^\mathsf{T}\mathbf{x})\mathbf{1}_m$. Further, $\mathbf{v} \neq a\mathbf{1}_m$ implies that the equation above is satisfied if and only if $\mathbf{1}_n^\mathsf{T}\mathbf{x} = 0$ and $\mathbf{u}^\mathsf{T}\mathbf{x} = 1$. To prove that for all $\mathbf{y}$ such that $M^\mathsf{T}\mathbf{y} = \mathbf{1}_n$, $\mathbf{1}_m^\mathsf{T}\mathbf{y} = 0$ apply the same technique to M^T.

Claim 2 follows directly from $\mathtt{rank}(M) = 1$. □

Lemma 6. *For any matrix $F \in \mathbb{R}^{m \times n}$, if there exists i, j such that $F_{(i)} = \mathbf{0}_n^\mathsf{T}$ and $F^{(j)} = \mathbf{0}_m$ then $F \in \mathcal{M}_{m \times n}(\mathbb{R})$ if and only if $F = \mathbf{0}_{m \times n}$.*

Proof. Clearly $F = \mathbf{0}_{m \times n}$ implies that $F \in \mathcal{M}_{m \times n}(\mathbb{R})$ and that for all i, j $F_{(i)} = \mathbf{0}_n^\mathsf{T}$ and $F^{(j)} = \mathbf{0}_m$. Now, consider the forward direction and suppose that $F \in \mathcal{M}_{m \times n}(\mathbb{R})$. Then from the definition of $\mathcal{M}_{m \times n}(\mathbb{R})$, we have that $\mathtt{rank}(F) \leq 2$. We will show that $\mathtt{rank}(F) = 0$. $F_{(i)} = \mathbf{0}_n^\mathsf{T}$ implies that $\mathbf{1}_m \notin \mathtt{ColSpan}(M)$ and $F^{(j)} = \mathbf{0}_m$ implies that $\mathbf{1}_n \notin \mathtt{ColSpan}(M^\mathsf{T})$. Then, by Lemma 5 $\mathtt{rank}(F) \neq 1, 2$. Therefore, $\mathtt{rank}(F) = 0$ and $F = \mathbf{0}_{m \times n}$. □

References

1. Boyd, S., Vandenberghe, L.: Convex Optimization. Cambridge University Press, Cambridge (2004)
2. Chen, X., Deng, X., Teng, S.H.: Computing Nash equilibria: approximation and smoothed complexity. In: 47th Annual IEEE Symposium on Foundations of Computer Science, FOCS 2006, pp. 603–612. IEEE (2006)
3. Chen, X., Deng, X., Teng, S.H.: Settling the complexity of computing two-player Nash equilibria. J. ACM (JACM) **56**(3), 14 (2009)
4. Choi, W.J., Sayedi, A.: Learning in online advertising. Mark. Sci. **38**(4), 584–608 (2019)
5. Dalessandro, B., Perlich, C., Stitelman, O., Provost, F.: Causally motivated attribution for online advertising. In: Proceedings of the Sixth International Workshop on Data Mining for Online Advertising and Internet Economy, pp. 1–9 (2012)
6. Daskalakis, C., Goldberg, P.W., Papadimitriou, C.H.: The complexity of computing a Nash equilibrium. SIAM J. Comput. **39**(1), 195–259 (2009)
7. Daskalakis, C., Papadimitriou, C.H.: Three-player games are hard. In: Electronic Colloquium on Computational Complexity, vol. 139, pp. 81–87 (2005)
8. Do, C.T., et al.: Game theory for cyber security and privacy. ACM Comput. Surv. (CSUR) **50**(2), 1–37 (2017)
9. Fearnley, J., Goldberg, P.W., Savani, R., Sørensen, T.B.: Approximate well-supported Nash equilibria below two-thirds. Algorithmica **76**(2), 297–319 (2016)
10. Gong, J., Liao, J., Wang, J., Qi, Q., Zhang, L.: Reducing the oscillations between overlay routing and traffic engineering by repeated game theory. In: 2013 19th Asia-Pacific Conference on Communications (APCC), pp. 591–596. IEEE (2013)
11. Heyman, J.L., Gupta, A.: Rank reduction in bimatrix games. arXiv:190400457. Submitted to International Journal of Game Theory
12. Heyman, J.L.: On the computation of strategically equivalent games. Ph.D. dissertation, The Ohio State University, Columbus (2019). http://rave.ohiolink.edu/etdc/view?acc_num=osu1561984858706805
13. Jiang, W., Zhang-Shen, R., Rexford, J., Chiang, M.: Cooperative content distribution and traffic engineering in an ISP network. In: Proceedings of the Eleventh International Joint Conference on Measurement and Modeling of Computer Systems, pp. 239–250 (2009)
14. Kontogiannis, S.C., Spirakis, P.G.: Efficient algorithms for constant well supported approximate equilibria in bimatrix games. In: Arge, L., Cachin, C., Jurdziński, T., Tarlecki, A. (eds.) ICALP 2007. LNCS, vol. 4596, pp. 595–606. Springer, Heidelberg (2007). https://doi.org/10.1007/978-3-540-73420-8_52
15. Kontogiannis, S.C., Spirakis, P.G.: Well supported approximate equilibria in bimatrix games. Algorithmica **57**(4), 653–667 (2010)
16. Lipton, R.J., Markakis, E., Mehta, A.: Playing large games using simple strategies. In: Proceedings of the 4th ACM Conference on Electronic Commerce, pp. 36–41. ACM (2003)
17. Moulin, H., Vial, J.P.: Strategically zero-sum games: the class of games whose completely mixed equilibria cannot be improved upon. Int. J. Game Theory **7**(3–4), 201–221 (1978)
18. Nash, J.: Non-cooperative games. Ann. Math. 286–295 (1951)
19. Nudelman, E., Wortman, J., Shoham, Y., Leyton-Brown, K.: Run the GAMUT: a comprehensive approach to evaluating game-theoretic algorithms. In: AAMAS, vol. 4, pp. 880–887 (2004)

20. Panagopoulou, P.N., Spirakis, P.G.: Random bimatrix games are asymptotically easy to solve (a simple proof). Theory Comput. Syst. **54**(3), 479–490 (2014)
21. Shiva, S., Roy, S., Dasgupta, D.: Game theory for cyber security. In: Proceedings of the Sixth Annual Workshop on Cyber Security and Information Intelligence Research, pp. 1–4 (2010)
22. Tsaknakis, H., Spirakis, P.G.: An optimization approach for approximate Nash equilibria. Internet Math. **5**(4), 365–382 (2008)
23. Wedderburn, J.H.M.: Lectures on Matrices, vol. 17. American Mathematical Society (1934)
24. Zhao, Y., Wang, S., Xu, S., Wang, X., Gao, X., Qiao, C.: Load balance vs energy efficiency in traffic engineering: a game theoretical perspective. In: 2013 Proceedings IEEE INFOCOM, pp. 530–534. IEEE (2013)

Separable Network Games with Compact Strategy Sets

Tomáš Kroupa$^{(\boxtimes)}$ ⬤, Sara Vannucci ⬤, and Tomáš Votroubek ⬤

Artificial Intelligence Center, Department of Computer Science, Faculty of Electrical
Engineering, Czech Technical University in Prague, Prague, Czech Republic
{tomas.kroupa,vanucsar,votroto1}@fel.cvut.cz
https://aic.fel.cvut.cz/

Abstract. A separable network game is a multiplayer finite strategic
game in which each player interacts only with adjacent players in a simple undirected graph. The utility of each player results from the aggregation of utilities in the corresponding two-player games. In our contribution, we extend this model to infinite games whose strategy sets are
compact subsets of the Euclidean space. We show that Nash equilibria
of a zero-sum continuous network game can be characterized as optimal
solutions to a specific infinite-dimensional linear optimization problem.
In particular, when the utility functions are multivariate polynomials,
this optimization formulation enables us to approximate the equilibria
using a hierarchy of semidefinite relaxations. We present a security game
over a complete bipartite graph in which the nodes are attackers and
defenders, who compete for control over given targets.

Keywords: Separable network game · Continuous game · Polynomial
game

1 Introduction

In this paper we extend separable network games (or, equivalently, polymatrix
games) [5,7] to the case when strategy sets are compact. A polymatrix game
is given by an undirected graph in which edges correspond to general-sum two-
player games, every player chooses a single strategy to play in all the games
corresponding to neighboring edges, and the player's payoff is the sum of payoffs in all these games. We will confine to the case in which the total sum of
utilities is zero (or, equivalently, constant). One direct way to obtain a zero-sum
polymatrix game is to create a polymatrix game in which all two-player games
are zero-sum; such games are investigated in [8]. In particular, the authors of
[8] proved that polymatrix games with zero-sum pairwise games can be reduced

---

This material is based upon work supported by, or in part by, the Army Research
Laboratory and the Army Research Office under grant number W911NF-20-1-0197.
The authors acknowledge the support by the project *Research Center for Informatics*
(CZ.02.1.01/0.0/0.0/16_019/0000765).

ⓒ Springer Nature Switzerland AG 2021
B. Bošanský et al. (Eds.): GameSec 2021, LNCS 13061, pp. 37–56, 2021.
https://doi.org/10.1007/978-3-030-90370-1_3

to two-person zero-sum games, which implies that mixed Nash equilibria can be computed efficiently by linear programming. We refer the reader to [19] and [6] for further results regarding the computability of Nash equilibria in polymatrix games. Both papers set limits for future research in this direction. In particular, if we drop the zero-sum hypothesis, finding a Nash equilibrium becomes PPAD-complete, even if we assume that all pairwise games are strictly competitive ([6, Theorem 1.2]). Some recent papers discuss other features of polymatrix games. Namely a connection between zero-sum polymatrix games and Hamiltonian dynamics is established in [2]. The dynamics of fictitious play in zero-sum separable network games is investigated in [11].

We will consider a generalization of polymatrix games with general-sum pairwise games [7] obtained by allowing strategy spaces to be infinite. In this way, we are able to capture situations in which players can distribute their capacities or resources in a continuous way across multiple targets to achieve control over them. The targets can be battlefields, inspection sites, exit points etc. We shall call the games which arise in this way network games. In Sect. 2 we observe, as a direct consequence of [12], that every network game with continuous utility functions has a Nash equilibrium in mixed strategies. In particular, we prove that in case of zero-sum continuous network games, Nash equilibria can be characterized as optimal solutions to a linear optimization problem; see Theorem 2. Most properties of two-person zero-sum games fail for zero-sum network games; we mention them briefly at the end of the section.

In Sect. 3 we formulate a generalization of the game over a complete bipartite graph discussed in [7, Example 1]. We assume that there is a finite set of targets together with a partition such that an attacker can attack any target, whereas a defender protects only the targets in a unique block of the partition. Thus every target is under the authority of a unique defender. Moreover, we assume that both attackers and defenders have capacities to be distributed among the targets. Any such distribution of resources is identified with a pure strategy. The resilience of each target toward the attack is given by an efficiency function. These functions determine the utility functions of the players. The pairwise games between attackers and defenders are general-sum, but the global game is constant-sum. Further, we consider a particular case of this game in which the efficiency functions, and consequently the utility functions, are discontinuous. We identify a Nash equilibrium of this game under the assumption that every target is defended with the same capacity. This Nash equilibrium is given by "uniform strategies", i.e. every attacker/defender distributes uniformly their attacking/defending capacities over the targets.

In Sect. 4 we discuss polynomial zero-sum network games. In such a game every utility function is a multivariate polynomial and, moreover, we assume that the strategy sets are basic-semialgebraic (the solution sets of finitely many polynomial inequalities). Finitely supported Nash equilibria are guaranteed to exist in such games. We show how to approximate the equilibria by an appropriate reformulation of the original optimization formulation (6a–6d). Our approach is based on the powerful techniques of global polynomial optimization and generalized moment problems; see [13,15]. Specifically, we formulate a hierarchy of semidefinite relaxations (25) of the problem (24) to find a Nash equilibrium using the characterization of moment sequences and Putinar's theorem. We conclude with examples of polynomial network games showing approximate computations of equilibria using the above approach.

2   Network Games

Let the player set be $N = \{1, \ldots, n\}$ for some integer $n \geq 1$. We will always assume that the strategy space S_i of each player $i \in N$ is a nonempty compact subset of $\mathbb{R}^{m_i}$, where m_i is a positive integer. In the class of games considered in this paper, each player is identified with a node of an undirected graph (N, E) without loops. The presence of an edge $\{i, j\} \in E$ means that players i and j engage in a two-person general-sum strategic game in which the utility function of player i is a function

$$u_{ij} \colon S_i \times S_j \to \mathbb{R} \tag{1}$$

and, analogously, the utility function of player j is a function

$$u_{ji} \colon S_j \times S_i \to \mathbb{R}. \tag{2}$$

We will always assume that functions u_{ij} and u_{ji} are at least integrable so that every expected utility appearing below is correctly defined. Let

$$\mathbf{S} = S_1 \times \cdots \times S_n.$$

A profile of pure strategies is a vector $\mathbf{x} = (x_1, \ldots, x_n) \in \mathbf{S}$. A player i typically takes part in more pairwise games. Therefore, there should be a mechanism that determines how player's strategy choice is propagated through the graph. We suppose that when player i picks a strategy $x_i \in S_i$, the same strategy is implemented in all two-person games played with the adjacent players in the graph (N, E). Thus, the aggregated utility of player i is computed as

$$u_i(\mathbf{x}) = \sum_{\substack{j \in N \\ \{i,j\} \in E}} u_{ij}(x_i, x_j), \qquad \mathbf{x} \in \mathbf{S}. \tag{3}$$

The resulting n-person game

$$\mathcal{G} = (N, (S_i)_{i \in N}, (u_i)_{i \in N}) \tag{4}$$

is called a *separable network game with compact strategy sets*. Throughout the paper we refer to game (4) as "network game" for short. We say that $\mathcal{G}$ is

- a *polymatrix game* when all strategy sets S_i are finite;
- *zero-sum* if $\sum_{i \in N} u_i(\mathbf{x}) = 0$ for all $\mathbf{x} \in \mathbf{S}$;
- *continuous* if each utility function u_i is continuous.

The class of network games most studied in literature is the class of zero-sum polymatrix games. The "global" zero-sum assumption makes such finite games computationally tractable; see [2,7,11] for further details.

Remark 1. One can ask what happens when a player is allowed to employ different strategies in the corresponding bilateral games. Then formula (3) could not be used, and the set

$$\underset{\substack{j \in N \\ \{i,j\} \in E}}{\times} S_i$$

would have to be considered instead of S_i as the strategy space of player i. Although this is an interesting alternative, in this paper we confine to the usual setup of network games explained above. △

Example 1. Let $N = \{1, 2, 3, 4\}$ and the graph (N, E) be the cycle on Fig. 1. This is the smallest example of a network game such that each player interacts only with a strict subset of other players. For example, the utility function of player 3 is $u_3(x_1, x_2, x_3, x_4) = u_{31}(x_3, x_1) + u_{34}(x_3, x_4)$. The zero-sum condition for this game can be formulated as $u_3 = -u_1 - u_2 - u_4$. △

Fig. 1. A network game with 4 players and 4 pairwise games

A mixed strategy of player i can be an arbitrary Borel probability measure μ_i over S_i; see [4] for mathematical details. Note that this general framework allows us to consider mixed strategies whose support is uncountably infinite, which is inevitable for the coherent treatment of games over compact strategy sets. We refer an interested reader to [1] and references therein for the discussion of this setting.

By $\mathcal{P}_i$ we denote the space of all mixed strategies of player $i \in N$. Let

$$\mathcal{P} = \mathcal{P}_1 \times \cdots \times \mathcal{P}_n$$

and let $\boldsymbol{\mu} = (\mu_1, \ldots, \mu_n) \in \mathcal{P}$ be a profile of mixed strategies. For the sake of brevity, we use $\boldsymbol{\mu}$ in place of the corresponding product probability measure in the definitions below involving integrals. The expected utility of player $i \in N$ is the function $U_i \colon \mathcal{P} \to \mathbb{R}$ such that $U_i(\boldsymbol{\mu}) = \int_{\mathbf{S}} u_i \, d\boldsymbol{\mu}$, where u_i is given by the formula (3). Define

$$\mathbf{S}_{-i} = \underset{\substack{j \in N \\ j \neq i}}{\times} S_j \quad \text{and} \quad \mathcal{P}_{-i} = \underset{\substack{j \in N \\ j \neq i}}{\times} \mathcal{P}_j.$$

For every $\boldsymbol{\mu} \in \mathcal{P}$ and each player $i \in N$, by $\boldsymbol{\mu}_{-i}$ we denote the restriction of $\boldsymbol{\mu}$ onto $\mathcal{P}_{-i}$. The value of expected utility of player i in a strategy profile $(x_i, \boldsymbol{\mu}_{-i}) \in S_i \times \mathcal{P}_{-i}$ is denoted by

$$U_i(x_i, \boldsymbol{\mu}_{-i}) = \int_{\mathbf{S}_{-i}} u_i(x_i, .) \, d\boldsymbol{\mu}_{-i}. \tag{5}$$

Definition 1. *A profile of mixed strategies $\boldsymbol{\mu}^* \in \mathcal{P}$ is a Nash equilibrium in a network game $\mathcal{G}$, if $U_i(\mu_i, \boldsymbol{\mu}^*_{-i}) \leq U_i(\boldsymbol{\mu}^*)$, for all $i \in N$ and every $\mu_i \in \mathcal{P}_i$.*

If $\mathcal{G}$ is a continuous network game, Nash equilibria exists in $\mathcal{G}$ as a direct consequence of Glicksberg's theorem [12], which applies to the broader class of multiplayer general-sum continuous games.

Theorem 1 ([12]). *Every continuous network game $\mathcal{G}$ has a Nash equilibrium $\boldsymbol{\mu}^* \in \mathcal{P}$ in mixed strategies.*

Moreover, mixed strategy profile $\boldsymbol{\mu}^*$ is a Nash equilibrium if, and only if,

$$U_i(\boldsymbol{\mu}^*) = \max_{x_i \in S_i} U_i(x_i, \boldsymbol{\mu}^*_{-i}), \qquad i \in N.$$

We will show that the Nash equilibra in a zero-sum continuous network game allow for a certain optimization-based characterization. Specifically, we consider the following infinite-dimensional linear optimization problem, which is a generalization of [7, LP 1]:

$$\underset{\boldsymbol{\mu}, \mathbf{w}}{\text{minimize}} \quad w_1 + \cdots + w_n \tag{6a}$$

$$\text{subject to} \quad w_i \geq U_i(x_i, \boldsymbol{\mu}_{-i}) \qquad \forall i \in N \; \forall x_i \in S_i \tag{6b}$$

$$\boldsymbol{\mu} = (\mu_1, \ldots, \mu_n) \in \mathcal{P} \tag{6c}$$

$$\mathbf{w} = (w_1, \ldots, w_n) \in \mathbb{R}^n \tag{6d}$$

Theorem 2. *For every profile of mixed strategies $\boldsymbol{\mu}^* \in \mathcal{P}$ in a zero-sum continuous network game $\mathcal{G}$, the following are equivalent.*

1. $\boldsymbol{\mu}^*$ *is a Nash equilibrium of game $\mathcal{G}$.*
2. $(\boldsymbol{\mu}^*, \mathbf{w}^*)$ *is an optimal solution to (6a–6d), where*

$$w_i^* = \max_{x_i \in S_i} U_i(x_i, \boldsymbol{\mu}^*_{-i}), \qquad i \in N. \tag{7}$$

Proof. First, observe that the maxima in (7) exist by compactness of S_i and continuity of function $U_i(., \boldsymbol{\mu}_{-i}) \colon S_i \to \mathbb{R}$. We need to show that the feasible set of problem 6a–6d is nonempty. Let $\boldsymbol{\mu}^* \in \mathcal{P}$ be any Nash equilibrium of game $\mathcal{G}$ (which exists by Theorem 1) and let $\mathbf{w}^*$ be the vector with coordinates (7). Then $(\boldsymbol{\mu}^*, \mathbf{w}^*) \in \mathcal{P} \times \mathbb{R}^n$ belongs to the feasible set of problem (6a–6d).

We claim that any feasible point $(\boldsymbol{\mu}, \mathbf{w}) \in \mathcal{P} \times \mathbb{R}^n$ satisfies the inequality

$$\sum_{i \in N} w_i \geq 0, \tag{8}$$

that is, the objective function of (6a–6d) is bounded from below by zero. From constraint (6b) and since $U_i(., \boldsymbol{\mu}_{-i})$ is an affine function, we get

$$\sum_{i \in N} w_i \geq \sum_{i \in N} \max_{x_i \in S_i} U_i(x_i, \boldsymbol{\mu}_{-i}) = \sum_{i \in N} \max_{\nu_i \in \mathcal{P}_i} U_i(\nu_i, \boldsymbol{\mu}_{-i}). \qquad (9)$$

Since the maxima in the last expression above are separated into different summands, it follows that

$$\sum_{i \in N} \max_{\nu_i \in \mathcal{P}_i} U_i(\nu_i, \boldsymbol{\mu}_{-i}) = \max_{\nu \in \mathcal{P}} \sum_{i \in N} U_i(\nu_i, \boldsymbol{\mu}_{-i}) \geq \sum_{i \in N} U_i(\boldsymbol{\mu}) = 0, \qquad (10)$$

which proves (8).

Assume now that $\boldsymbol{\mu}^*$ is a Nash equilibrium of $\mathcal{G}$ and let $\mathbf{w}^*$ be given by (7). This implies that

$$U_i(\boldsymbol{\mu}^*) = \max_{x_i \in S_i} U_i(x_i, \boldsymbol{\mu}^*_{-i}) = w_i^*$$

for all $i \in N$. Then $(\boldsymbol{\mu}^*, \mathbf{w}^*)$ is optimal for (6a–6d) by (8) since $w_1^* + \cdots + w_n^* = 0$ by the zero-sum property.

Conversely, assume that $(\boldsymbol{\mu}^*, \mathbf{w}^*)$ is an optimal solution to (6a–6d). The preceding part of the proof shows that the optimal value of problem (6a–6d) is zero. Hence, $w_i^* = 0$ for each $i \in N$. Then every inequality in (9)–(10) becomes an equality, which implies that

$$U_i(\boldsymbol{\mu}^*) = \max_{x_i \in S_i} U_i(x_i, \boldsymbol{\mu}^*_{-i}).$$

Therefore $\boldsymbol{\mu}^*$ is a Nash equilibrium.   □

In case of zero-sum polymatrix games, the problem (6a–6d) becomes a linear program, which can be solved directly [7]. However, the fully general optimization problem formulated in (6a–6d) explicitly involves Borel probability measures and continuous functions, which are not effectively computable. This seemingly abstract formulation will be refined in Sect. 4, where some instances of this problem are solved using the tools of polynomial optimization [15].

Remark 2 (Properties of zero-sum network games). Every zero-sum polymatrix game in sense of [7, Definition 1] is a continuous network game. Indeed, every strategy space S_i in a polymatrix game is finite, so it can be viewed as a compact set in $\mathbb{R}$, and therefore all utility functions u_i are trivially continuous. As in the case of zero-sum polymatrix games (and, clearly, two-person zero-sum games) we proved that Nash equilibria correspond to optimal solutions to a certain linear program. However, there are certain properties of two-person zero-sum games which fail for polymatrix games; consequently, such properties fail for the network games considered herein. We refer the interested reader to [7, Section 3] for the details. In particular, we recall that in a polymatrix game:

- Players may get different payoffs from playing equilibrium strategies.
- Equilibrium strategies are not necessarily max-min strategies.
- Equilibrium strategies are not necessarily exchangeable.

We also remark that any network game can be transformed into a pairwise constant-sum game. This derives from the fact that the payoff preserving transformation of polymatrix games [7, Section 4] can be straightforwardly generalized to infinite strategy sets.   △

3   Example: Security Game

In this section we introduce an interesting subclass of network games, which is motivated by the example of a security game discussed in [7]. For the reader's convenience, we will spell out the details of that example.

Example 2 ([7, Example 1]). Let

$$N = \{1, \ldots, m, m+1, \ldots, n\}$$

be the player set, where each player $i \leq m$ is an *evader* and every player $j > m$ is an *inspector*. There is a finite set $E \neq \emptyset$ of exit points through which evaders try to escape. Each evader may pick whichever exit point and, at the same time, every inspector is able to block only those exit points in their authority. Therefore, we can write $E = E_{m+1} \cup \cdots \cup E_n$, where the sets on the right-hand side are nonempty and mutually disjoint. The strategy sets are

$$S_i = \begin{cases} E & i \leq m, \\ E_i & i > m, \end{cases} \quad \text{for all } i \in N.$$

The underlying graph is a complete bipartite graph over N in which two nodes are connected by an edge $\{i, j\}$ precisely when i is an evader and j is an inspector. This yields a polymatrix game whose pairwise games between such i and j are defined as follows:

- If the evader's exit point is not inspected, the evader wins one point, otherwise nothing:

$$u_{ij}(e_i, e_j) = \begin{cases} 1 - \delta(e_i, e_j) & e_i \in E_j, \\ 0 & e_i \notin E_j, \end{cases} \quad \text{for all } (e_i, e_j) \in E \times E_j,$$

  where δ is the Kronecker delta.
- An inspector obtains one point for the evader whose exit point is blocked:

$$u_{ji}(e_j, e_i) = \delta(e_j, e_i), \quad \text{for all } (e_j, e_i) \in E_j \times E.$$

This implies that the utility of each evader i is $u_i(\mathbf{e}) = 1 - \delta(e_i, e_{k(i)})$, where $\mathbf{e} = (e_1, \ldots, e_n)$ and $k(i)$ is the unique inspector in charge of $E_{k(i)}$ such that $e_i \in E_{k(i)}$. The utility of inspector j is simply the total number of evaders caught, $u_j(\mathbf{e}) = |\{i = 1, \ldots, m \mid e_i = e_j\}|$. Hence,

$$\sum_{i=1}^{m} u_i(\mathbf{e}) + \sum_{j=m+1}^{n} u_j(\mathbf{e}) = \text{evaders escaped} + \text{evaders blocked} = m,$$

which means that the resulting polymatrix game is constant-sum.   △

We extend the game from Example 2 to the setting when players can allocate a certain amount of their resources in an effort to defend/attack given targets. We confine to the discussion of solution in pure strategies.

Specifically, let $N_A = \{1, \ldots, m\}$ be the set of *attackers* for some integer $m \geq 1$ and by $N_D = \{m + 1, \ldots, n\}$ we denote the set of *defenders*, where $n \geq m + 1$. Put $N = N_A \cup N_D$ and let (N, E) be the complete bipartite graph whose two partitions are N_A and N_D. This means that in the graph (N, E) there is an undirected edge $\{i, j\}$ for each pair $(i, j) \in N_A \times N_D$, and there are no other edges in (N, E). See Fig. 2 for an example.

Fig. 2. The complete bipartite graph of a security game with 3 attackers and 2 defenders

Further, we assume that there is a finite set $T \neq \emptyset$ of *targets* such that for each target $t \in T$ there exists precisely one defender $j \in N_D$ who is in charge of t. Thus, we can write

$$T = T_{m+1} \cup \cdots \cup T_n, \tag{11}$$

where $T_j \neq \emptyset$ is the set of targets protected by defender $j \in N_D$ and $T_j \cap T_k = \emptyset$, whenever $j, k \in N_D$ are not equal. The attackers and the defenders fight for control over the targets—see Fig. 3.

The players' strategies are defined in the following way. We associate with each attacker $i \in N_A$ their attack capacity $a_i > 0$ that shall be distributed among all the targets in T. Analogously, any defender $j \in N_D$ can deploy the amount $d_j > 0$ of their total resources to protect the targets in their control, i.e. the targets in the block T_j. Then, each player decides the ratios of their attack/defend capacity to be distributed across the corresponding targets. Although the resources needed to attack maybe different from those involved in the defense, we assume that only their relative proportions are relevant. This means that we can model each strategy space as a finite-dimensional simplex Δ_I^c for some finite set $I \neq \emptyset$ and $c > 0$, where

$$\Delta_I^c = \left\{ \mathbf{x} \in \mathbb{R}_+^I \;\middle|\; \sum_{i \in I} x_i = c \right\}$$

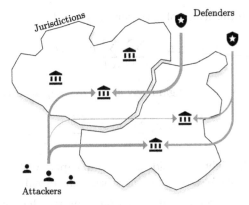

Fig. 3. An attacker can attack any target, but each defender can only protect targets within their jurisdiction.

and $\mathbb{R}_+ = \{x \in \mathbb{R} \mid x \geq 0\}$. The strategy space of each attacker/defender is thus

$$
S_i = \begin{cases} \Delta_T^{a_i} & i \in N_A, \\ \Delta_{T_i}^{d_i} & i \in N_D. \end{cases}
$$

The resilience of each target $t \in T_j$ towards the attack is measured by an *efficiency function* $e_t \colon \mathbb{R}_+^2 \to \mathbb{R}$. Let $\mathbf{x}_i = (x_{it})_{t \in T} \in S_i$ and $\mathbf{y}_j = (y_{jt})_{t \in T_j} \in S_j$ be strategies of attacker and defender, respectively. The bilateral game associated with target $t \in T_j$ is evaluated using function e_t. The higher the values of $e_t(x_{it}, y_{jt})$, the greater is the actual resilience of target $t \in T_j$ towards the attack by attacker i, in case that this target is protected by defender j.

Finally, the pairwise games between each pair $(i, j) \in N_A \times N_D$ are defined as follows. The utility function of defender j is

$$
u_{ji}(\mathbf{y}_j, \mathbf{x}_i) = \sum_{t \in T_j} e_t(x_{it}, y_{jt}) \tag{12}
$$

and the utility function of attacker i is

$$
u_{ij}(\mathbf{x}_i, \mathbf{y}_j) = -u_{ji}(\mathbf{y}_j, \mathbf{x}_i) + \sum_{t \in T_j} x_{it}, \tag{13}
$$

for all $\mathbf{x}_i \in S_i$ and $\mathbf{y}_j \in S_j$. Let a generic strategy profile in this game be denoted by

$$
\mathbf{z} = (\mathbf{x}_1, \ldots, \mathbf{x}_m, \mathbf{y}_{m+1}, \ldots, \mathbf{y}_n) \in \bigtimes_{i=1}^n S_i. \tag{14}
$$

Then the total utility of defender j equals

$$
u_j(\mathbf{z}) = \sum_{i \in N_A} \sum_{t \in T_j} e_t(x_{it}, y_{jt}),
$$

and, similarly, the total utility of attacker i is given by

$$u_i(\mathbf{z}) = a_i - \sum_{j \in N_D} \sum_{t \in T_j} e_t(x_{it}, y_{jt}).$$

The resulting n-person network game $(N, (S_i)_{i \in N}, (u_i)_{i \in N})$ is constant-sum since

$$\sum_{i \in N_A} u_i + \sum_{j \in N_D} u_j = \sum_{i \in N_A} a_i,$$

where the sum on the right-hand side is the total capacity of all attackers. Hence, we can make this game into a zero-sum network game by subtracting the constant $\frac{\sum_{i \in N_A} a_i}{n}$ from every player's utility function. Observe that the pairwise games between $i \in N_A$ and $j \in N_D$ are not constant-sum as

$$u_{ij}(\mathbf{x}_i, \mathbf{y}_j) + u_{ji}(\mathbf{y}_j, \mathbf{x}_i) = \sum_{t \in T_j} x_{it},$$

where $\mathbf{x}_i \in S_i$ and $\mathbf{y}_j \in S_j$.

Remark 3. By assumption (11) each target is protected only by one defender. However, there are typically more attackers focusing on the target which is in the authority of the defender. This does not mean that the resources of defender are split into the bilateral games involving the defender and the attackers over the same target. The defender is simply rewarded for detecting the attackers and blocking their hostile action. This is analogous to the interpretation of Example 2, since an inspector can block more evaders trying to escape via the same exit. Accordingly, the resources of defender can be viewed as detection devices, sensors, or any other facilities which can be strategically distributed in order to prevent intrusion into secured areas.   △

3.1   Security Game with the Tullock Function

In this section we adopt a particular form for the efficiency functions e_t associated with targets $t \in T$. Namely each efficiency function is given by

$$e_t(x, y) = \begin{cases} \frac{y}{x+y} & x, y > 0, \\ 1/2 & x = y = 0, \end{cases} \tag{15}$$

where $x, y \geq 0$ are the attack and defense capacities allocated to target $t \in T_j$ as a strategy choice in the two-player game between $i \in N_A$ and $j \in N_D$, respectively. Function (15) is an instance of the Tullock rent-seeking contest success function for a special choice of parameters, whose general variant is used in the lottery Blotto game [16] or in the rent-seeking game [3]. Since function (15) has a discontinuity at point $(0,0)$, the resulting security game defined by the formulas (12)–(13) is not continuous.

We will show that, despite the lack of continuity of this game, there exists a pure Nash equilibrium in case that the ratio between the defense capacity d_j and the size of T_j is the same for all the defenders $j \in N_D$. Specifically, suppose that

$$\frac{d_j}{|T_j|} = \frac{d_k}{|T_k|} \quad \text{for all } j, k \in N_D. \tag{16}$$

This assumption is reasonable in the following scenario, for example. Suppose that an external autority establishes how the set of all targets is divided into blocks T_j and decides that the defenders have a total capacity d to be distributed among them. It is reasonable to assume that the defenders would agree on having every target $t \in T$ defended with the same capacity, i.e. each defender is assigned defending capacity d_j such that (16) holds. Note that the assumption is valid also in the mirror scenario in which an external autority assigns each defender their defending capacity d_j and leave to the defenders the task to distribute the targets among themselves, i.e. determining the blocks T_j.

We will show that under the assumption (16) the uniform strategy profile forms a Nash equilibrium. Let

$$\mathbf{z}^* = (\mathbf{x}_1^*, \ldots, \mathbf{x}_m^*, \mathbf{y}_{m+1}^*, \ldots, \mathbf{y}_n^*)$$

be a strategy profile such that

$$\mathbf{x}_i^* = \tfrac{1}{|T|}(a_i, \ldots, a_i) \in \Delta_T^{a_i}, \quad \text{for each } i \in N_A,$$

and

$$\mathbf{y}_j^* = \tfrac{1}{|T_j|}(d_j, \ldots, d_j) \in \Delta_{T_j}^{d_j}, \quad \text{for each } j \in N_D.$$

First, we prove that the choice $\mathbf{y}_j^*$ is optimal for each defender $j \in N_D$, that is,

$$u_j(\mathbf{y}_j, \mathbf{z}_{-j}^*) \leq u_j(\mathbf{z}^*), \quad \text{for all } \mathbf{y}_j \in \Delta_{T_j}^{d_j}. \tag{17}$$

Our goal is to maximize a differentiable function $f \colon \Delta_{T_j}^{d_j} \to \mathbb{R}_+$ defined by

$$f(\mathbf{y}_j) = u_j(\mathbf{y}_j, \mathbf{z}_{-j}^*) = \sum_{i \in N_A} \sum_{t \in T_j} \frac{y_{jt}}{\frac{a_i}{|T|} + y_{jt}} = \sum_{t \in T_j} \sum_{i \in N_A} \frac{y_{jt}}{\frac{a_i}{|T|} + y_{jt}}.$$

Its partial derivative with respect to variable y_{jt} is

$$\frac{\partial u_j}{\partial y_{jt}}(\mathbf{y}_j) = \sum_{i \in N_A} \frac{\frac{a_i}{|T|}}{(\frac{a_i}{|T|} + y_{jt})^2}, \quad t \in T_j.$$

Since the Hessian of f is a diagonal matrix whose diagonal entries

$$-\sum_{i \in N_A} \frac{2\frac{a_i}{|T|}}{(\frac{a_i}{|T|} + y_{jt})^3}$$

are negative whenever $y_{jt} \geq 0$, the function f is strictly concave over $\Delta_{T_j}^{d_j}$.

The optimality conditions for the problem with a single linear equality constraint

$$\underset{\mathbf{y}_j \in \mathbb{R}^{|T_j|}}{\text{maximize}} \quad f(\mathbf{y}_j)$$

$$\text{subject to} \quad \sum_{t \in T_j} y_{jt} = d_j$$

are

$$\sum_{i \in N_A} \frac{\frac{a_i}{|T|}}{\left(\frac{a_i}{|T|} + y_{jt}\right)^2} = \lambda, \qquad t \in T_j, \tag{18}$$

for some real $\lambda > 0$.

If $y_{jt'} > y_{jt}$ for some $t, t' \in T_j$, then

$$\lambda = \sum_{i \in N_A} \frac{\frac{a_i}{|T|}}{\left(\frac{a_i}{|T|} + y_{jt}\right)^2} > \sum_{i \in N_A} \frac{\frac{a_i}{|T|}}{\left(\frac{a_i}{|T|} + y_{jt'}\right)^2} = \lambda,$$

a contradiction. This implies that any $\mathbf{y}_j \in \mathbb{R}^{|T_j|}$ solving (18) satisfies $y_{jt} = y_{jt'}$ for all $t, t' \in T_j$. The only way how to guarantee that such $\mathbf{y}_j$ belongs to $\Delta_{T_j}^{d_j}$ is letting $y_{jt} = \frac{d_j}{|T_j|}$ for all $t \in T_j$. This proves (17).

In order to show that uniform strategy vector $\mathbf{x}_i^*$ is optimal for attacker $i \in N_A$, we proceed analogously. In this case the system of Eqs. (18) becomes

$$\frac{\frac{d_{j(t)}}{|T_{j(t)}|}}{\left(\frac{d_{j(t)}}{|T_{j(t)}|} + x_{it}\right)^2} = \lambda, \qquad t \in T, \tag{19}$$

where $j(t) \in N_D$ is the unique defender in charge of target t. By the assumption (16), the only solution to (19) belonging to $\Delta_T^{a_i}$ is $\mathbf{x}_i^*$. In conclusion, the profile of pure uniform strategies $\mathbf{z}^*$ is an equilibrium of the security game in which the additional assumption (16) holds.

4   Polynomial Network Games

In this section, we make three additional assumptions about the strategy spaces and the utility functions of a network game $\mathcal{G}$ defined by (4).

1. Every compact strategy space $S_i \subseteq \mathbb{R}^{m_i}$ is a *basic semi-algebraic set*; that is,

$$S_i = \{\mathbf{x} \in \mathbb{R}^{m_i} \mid g_{ik}(\mathbf{x}) \geq 0, \ k \in K_i\}, \tag{20}$$

where each g_{ik} is a real polynomial in m_i variables and $K_i \neq \emptyset$ is a finite index set. By compactness of S_i, there exists a real number $a \geq 0$ such that

$$S_i \subseteq \{\mathbf{x} \in \mathbb{R}^{m_i} \mid \|\mathbf{x}\|^2 \leq a\},$$

where $\|.\|$ is the Euclidean norm. This means that the quadratic constraint

$$a - \|\mathbf{x}\|^2 \geq 0$$

is redundant in the presentation (20) of S_i. However, we will always assume that $g_{ik}(\mathbf{x}) = a - \|\mathbf{x}\|^2$ for some $k \in K_i$. This assumption guarantees that the quadratic module (23) defined below is Archimedean, which makes it possible to use powerful certificates of positivity for polynomials such as the Putinar's theorem (Theorem 3).

2. In every two-player game involving players $i, j \in N$, the utility functions u_{ij} and u_{ji} of player i and j, respectively, are real polynomials in $m_i + m_j$ indeterminates. Therefore, each utility function u_i given by (3) is a real polynomial in $m_1 + \cdots + m_n$ indeterminates.

3. The game $\mathcal{G}$ is zero-sum.

The three assumptions define a *polynomial zero-sum network game* $\mathcal{G}$. We remark that the first assumption is very mild—many sets important for applications are in fact the solution sets of finitely many polynomial inequalities. In particular, a compact semi-algebraic set is not necessarily convex or connected. Moreover, Glicksberg's theorem (Theorem 1) can be significantly strengthened for polynomial games—each polynomial game has Nash equilibria in which every player mixes only among finitely many pure strategies; see [9] or [20] for further details. In the rest of this section, we explain how to compute such equilibria using Theorem 2, the techniques of polynomial optimization, and their dual counterparts, the generalized moment problems [15]. It is worth emphasizing that two highly related papers [17] and [14] focus on two-player zero-sum polynomial games, but their results cannot be directly adapted to our setting.

4.1 Moment-Based Formulation

Let $\mathcal{G}$ be a polynomial zero-sum network game. The crucial observation is that the constraints of optimization problem (6a–6d) depend on the profile of mixed strategies $\boldsymbol{\mu}_{-i}$ only through the expected utilities (5). Since the utility functions are polynomials by the assumption, such integrals are exactly moments of the corresponding mixed strategies. By $\mathbb{N}$ we denote the set of nonnegative integers $\{0, 1, 2, \dots\}$. For each player $i \in N$ and a multi-index

$$\boldsymbol{\alpha} = (\alpha_1, \dots, \alpha_{m_i}) \in \mathbb{N}^{m_i},$$

define the monomial

$$\mathbf{x}^{\boldsymbol{\alpha}} = x_1^{\alpha_1} \cdots x_{m_i}^{\alpha_{m_i}}.$$

The $\boldsymbol{\alpha}$-th *moment* of a mixed strategy $\mu_i \in \mathcal{P}_i$ is the real number

$$\mu_i'(\boldsymbol{\alpha}) = \int_{S_i} \mathbf{x}^{\boldsymbol{\alpha}} \, d\mu_i.$$

The infinite sequence $\boldsymbol{\mu}_i' = (\mu_i'(\boldsymbol{\alpha}))_{\boldsymbol{\alpha} \in \mathbb{N}^{m_i}}$ is the *moment sequence* and μ_i is called a *representing measure*. A modified version of the classical moment problem is to characterize those real sequences $\mathbf{y} = (y_\alpha)_{\alpha \in \mathbb{N}^{m_i}}$ which are moment sequences, that is, $\mathbf{y} = \boldsymbol{\mu}'_i$ for some mixed strategy μ_i on S_i.

For any $d \in \mathbb{N}$, put

$$\mathbb{N}_d^{m_i} = \{\boldsymbol{\alpha} \in \mathbb{N}^{m_i} \mid |\boldsymbol{\alpha}| \leq d\},$$

where

$$|\boldsymbol{\alpha}| = \alpha_1 + \cdots + \alpha_{m_i}.$$

Let $\mathbf{y} = (y_\alpha)_{\alpha \in \mathbb{N}^{m_i}}$ be a real sequence and $d \in \mathbb{N}$. The *moment matrix of order* d is the matrix $M_d(\mathbf{y})$ with rows indexed by $\boldsymbol{\alpha} \in \mathbb{N}_d^{m_i}$ and columns indexed by $\boldsymbol{\beta} \in \mathbb{N}_d^{m_i}$ such that

$$(M_d(\mathbf{y}))_{\alpha\beta} = y_{\alpha+\beta}.$$

Any polynomial g_{ik} from the representation (20) of S_i can be written as

$$g_{ik}(\mathbf{x}) = \sum_\gamma c_\gamma \mathbf{x}^\gamma$$

for some real coefficients c_γ, where only finitely many of them are nonzero. The *localizing matrix of order* d is the matrix $M_d(g_{ik}, \mathbf{y})$ with rows indexed by $\boldsymbol{\alpha} \in \mathbb{N}_d^{m_i}$ and columns indexed by $\boldsymbol{\beta} \in \mathbb{N}_d^{m_i}$, where

$$(M_d(g_{ik}, \mathbf{y}))_{\alpha\beta} = \sum_\gamma c_\gamma y_{\alpha+\beta+\gamma}.$$

When a real symmetric matrix A is positive semidefinite, we write $A \succeq 0$. Moment sequences are characterized by positive semidefinitness of moment and localizing matrices; see [15, Theorem 2.44(b)]. Specifically, a real sequence $\mathbf{y} = (y_\alpha)_{\alpha \in \mathbb{N}^{m_i}}$ with $y_0 = 1$ is a moment sequence with a representing probability measure supported by S_i if, and only if,

$$\begin{aligned} M_d(\mathbf{y}) &\succeq 0 \quad \forall d \in \mathbb{N} \\ M_d(g_{ik}, \mathbf{y}) &\succeq 0 \quad \forall d \in \mathbb{N}, \forall k \in K_i. \end{aligned} \tag{21}$$

Example 3. Let $N = \{1, 2, 3\}$, the graph (N, E) be complete, and $S_i = [0, 1]$ for $i \in N$. The utility function (3) of player $i \in N$ is the polynomial

$$u_i(\mathbf{x}) = u_{ij}(x_i, x_j) + u_{ik}(x_i, x_k) = \sum_\alpha \left(c_\alpha(ij) x_j^{\alpha_j} + c_\alpha(ik) x_k^{\alpha_k} \right) x_i^{\alpha_i},$$

for some real coefficients $c_\alpha(ij)$ and $c_\alpha(ik)$. If $\boldsymbol{\mu}_{-i} \in \mathcal{P}_{-i}$, then a tedious but direct verification shows that $U_i(x_i, \boldsymbol{\mu}_{-i})$ given by (5) is a polynomial in the single indeterminate x_i:

$$U_i(x_i, \boldsymbol{\mu}_{-i}) = \sum_\alpha \left(c_\alpha(ij) \mu'_j(\alpha_j) + c_\alpha(ik) \mu'_k(\alpha_k) \right) x_i^{\alpha_i}. \tag{22}$$

We can represent the strategy set $[0,1]$ as $\{x \in \mathbb{R} \mid x - x^2 \geq 0\}$. Then, the problem (6a–6d) can be reformulated as follows:

$$\underset{y_1, y_2, y_3, w}{\text{minimize}} \quad w_1 + w_2 + w_3$$

$$\begin{aligned}
\text{subject to} \quad & w_i - U_i(x_i, \boldsymbol{\mu}_{-i}) \geq 0 && \forall x_i \in S_i,\ \forall i \in N \\
& \mathbf{y}_i = (y_{i,\alpha})_{\alpha \in \mathbb{N}} \text{ is a real sequence and } y_{i,0} = 1, && \forall i \in N \\
& M_d(\mathbf{y}_i) \succeq 0 && \forall d \in \mathbb{N},\ \forall i \in N \\
& M_d(x - x^2, \mathbf{y}_i) \succeq 0 && \forall d \in \mathbb{N},\ \forall i \in N \\
& \mathbf{w} = (w_1, \ldots, w_3) \in \mathbb{R}^3 \\
& \mathbf{y}_i \text{ has a representing measure } \mu_i && \forall i \in N
\end{aligned}$$

Observe that the first constraint says that the polynomial on the left-hand side is nonnegative over $[0,1]$. △

4.2 Nonnegative Polynomials Using Sums of Squares

Our next goal is to find a condition that expresses the nonnegativity of polynomials on S_i such that the condition can be verified by an algorithm. A polynomial $p(\mathbf{x})$ is a *sum of squares (SOS)* if there exist polynomials $q_0(\mathbf{x}), \ldots, q_m(\mathbf{x})$ such that

$$p(\mathbf{x}) = q_0^2(\mathbf{x}) + \cdots + q_m^2(\mathbf{x}).$$

It is obvious that any SOS polynomial is a nonnegative function, but the converse fails—there are nonnegative polynomials which are not SOS.

We recall that each strategy set S_i has the representation (20) as a basic semi-algebraic set. The *quadratic module* generated by the set $\{g_{ik} \mid k \in K_i\}$ is

$$Q(S_i) = \left\{ s_0 + \sum_{k \in K_i} g_{ik} s_k \mid s_0, s_k \text{ are SOS polynomials, } \forall k \in K_i \right\}. \qquad (23)$$

Theorem 3 (Putinar's Positivstellensatz [18]). *If a polynomial $p(\mathbf{x})$ is strictly positive on S_i, then $p(\mathbf{x}) \in Q(S_i)$.*

While we seek a certificate for nonnegative polynomials rather than strictly positive ones, we are solving the problem numerically, in which case the difference is irrelevant. The problem whether $p(\mathbf{x}) \in Q(S_i)$ can be effectively tested, unlike nonnegativity of polynomials, which is very hard to decide.

Specifically, we can formulate the sum of squares condition using semidefinite constraints. Let

$$[\mathbf{x}]_d = (\mathbf{x}^\alpha)_{\alpha \in \mathbb{N}_d^{m_i}}.$$

The monomials $\mathbf{x}^\alpha$ form a basis of the linear space of polynomials with degree at most d. Hence, any such polynomial $p(\mathbf{x})$ can be expressed as

$$p(\mathbf{x}) = \sum_{|\alpha| \leq d} c_\alpha \mathbf{x}^\alpha = \mathbf{c}^T [\mathbf{x}]_d,$$

where $\mathbf{c} = (c_\alpha)_{\alpha \in \mathbb{N}_d^{m_i}}$ is a coefficient vector.

By [15, Proposition 2.1], a polynomial $p(\mathbf{x})$ of degree at most $2d$ is SOS if, and only if, there exists a positive semidefinite matrix G such that $p(\mathbf{x}) = [\mathbf{x}]_d^T G [\mathbf{x}]_d$. We can therefore formulate the problem of checking whether such $p(\mathbf{x})$ is SOS as the semidefinite feasibility problem for a matrix G indexed by β and γ:

$$\sum_{\beta+\gamma=\alpha} G_{\beta\gamma} = c_\alpha \quad \forall \alpha, |\alpha| \leq 2d,$$

$$G \succeq 0.$$

Moreover, testing the membership of $p(\mathbf{x})$ in $Q(S_i)$ can be formulated via a single semidefinite program; see [15, Chapter 2.4.2] for details. Now, we consider the reformulation of the initial problem (6a–6d), where $\bar{u}_i(\mathbf{y}_{-i})$ denotes the polynomial in variables $\mathbf{x}_i$ and $\mathbf{y}_{-i}$ is substituted for the corresponding moments analogously to (22).

$$
\begin{aligned}
&\underset{\mathbf{y}_1,\ldots,\mathbf{y}_n,\mathbf{w}}{\text{minimize}} && w_1 + \cdots + w_n \\
&\text{subject to} && w_i - \bar{u}_i(\mathbf{y}_{-i}) \in Q(S_i) && \forall i \in N \\
& && \mathbf{y}_i = (y_{i,\alpha})_{\alpha \in \mathbb{N}^{m_i}} \text{ and } y_{i,0} = 1 && \forall i \in N \\
& && M_d(\mathbf{y}_i) \succeq 0 && \forall i \in N \\
& && M_d(g_{ik}, \mathbf{y}_i) \succeq 0 && \forall d \in \mathbb{N}, \forall k \in K_i, \forall i \in N \\
& && \mathbf{w} = (w_1,\ldots,w_n) \in \mathbb{R}^n
\end{aligned}
\qquad (24)
$$

4.3   Hierarchy of Semidefinite Relaxations

The last optimization problem above still raises several questions. First, there is no obvious way how to bound the degrees of polynomials in $Q(S_i)$; second, it is not clear what to do with the infinitely many constraints on moment matrices. Although we cannot solve the problem directly, we use an approach inspired by Lasserre's hierarchy of relaxations [15, Chapter 6] and provide a numerical method for approximating the solution.

We consider the quadratic module $Q_h(S_i)$ truncated to a degree h:

$$
Q_h(S_i) = \{s_0 + \sum_{k \in K_i} g_{ik} s_k \mid s_0, s_k \text{ SOS polynomials,} \\
\deg(g_{ik}s_k) \leq h, \forall k \in K_i, \\
\deg(s_0) \leq h\}.
$$

Instead of requiring that the constraints hold for all moments, the h-th program in a hierarchy only constrains the moment/localizing matrices of order h. Moreover, we consider only truncated moment sequences $\hat{\mathbf{y}}_i$, which are just finite-dimensional real vectors. The h-th level of the hierarchy is the following semidefinite program:

$$\begin{aligned}
\underset{\hat{y}_1,\ldots,\hat{y}_n,\mathbf{w}}{\text{minimize}} \quad & w_1 + \cdots + w_n \\
\text{subject to} \quad & w_i - \bar{u}_i(\hat{\mathbf{y}}_{-i}) \in Q_{2h}(S_i) && \forall i \in N \\
& \hat{\mathbf{y}}_i = (y_{i,\alpha})_{\alpha \in \mathbb{N}_{2h}^{m_i}} \text{ and } y_{i,0} = 1 && \forall i \in N \\
& M_h(\hat{\mathbf{y}}_i) \succeq 0 && \forall i \in N \\
& M_h(g_{ik}, \hat{\mathbf{y}}_i) \succeq 0 && \forall k \in K_i, \forall i \in N \\
& \mathbf{w} = (w_1, \ldots, w_n) \in \mathbb{R}^n
\end{aligned} \qquad (25)$$

It is difficult to find the smallest h for which the hierarchy of such semidefinite programs converges in practice. We therefore iteratively solve each level of the hierarchy until all sequences $\hat{\mathbf{y}}_i$ have a representing atomic measure. We then fix the moments in the constraints

$$w_i - \bar{u}_i(\hat{\mathbf{y}}_{-i}) \in Q_{2h}(S_i)$$

and verify that their duals are atomic, thereby certifying the optimality of all the bounds and consequently the best response condition.

Since the program (25) finds only the optimal payoffs to each player and the corresponding truncated moment vectors, we need to do additional processing to extract the representing equilibrium strategies. The recovery of a measure from its moments is a classical problem for which several algorithms exist. We employed [15, Algorithm 6.9], which is based on the decomposition of the moment matrix obtained from the converged solution for the hierarchy.

4.4 Examples

In the remaining part of this paper we show several examples of polynomial games. Their equilibria are recovered by the method explained in the previous section. We implemented the hierarchy of programs (25) in Julia using JuMP [10] and the SumOfSquares.jl package [21]. We solved the semidefinite programs using Mosek on a laptop with a 3.1 GHz dual-core CPU. Our code is available on GitHub at https://github.com/votroto/PolyNets.jl.

Example 4 (Two-player zero-sum polynomial game). Since polynomial network games are a generalization of polynomial games, we can use the same framework to solve them. Let there be a polynomial game with the player set $N = \{1, 2\}$ and each strategy set S_i be

$$S_i = \{x \in \mathbb{R} \mid -x^2 + 1 \geq 0\}.$$

The utility functions are given by

$$u_1(x_1, x_2) = 2x_1 x_2^2 - x_1^2 - x_2 = -u_2(x_1, x_2).$$

A pure Nash equilibrium is achieved when Player 1 plays $x_1 = 0.4$ and Player 2 plays $x_2 = 0.63$. The optimal payoffs to each player are $\mathbf{w} = (-0.47, 0.47)$. This problem was solved at order 4 of the hierarchy. Due to the low number of variables the problem required only 44 constraints and it was solved within 10 ms. $\triangle$

Example 5 (Three-player game with a complete graph). This example is a concrete instance of Example 3. We consider a polynomial network game with the player set $N = \{1, 2, 3\}$. Each strategy set S_i is equal to

$$S_i = \{x \in \mathbb{R} \mid -x^2 + 1 \geq 0\}$$

and the utility functions are

$$u_1(x_1, x_2, x_3) = -2x_1x_2^2 - 2x_1^2 + 5x_1x_2 - 4x_1x_3 - x_2 - 2x_3,$$
$$u_2(x_1, x_2, x_3) = 2x_1x_2^2 - 2x_2x_3^2 - 2x_1^2 - 5x_1x_2 - 2x_2^2 + 5x_2x_3 + x_2,$$
$$u_3(x_1, x_2, x_3) = 2x_2x_3^2 + 4x_1^2 + 4x_1x_3 + 2x_2^2 - 5x_2x_3 + 2x_3.$$

A partially mixed Nash equilibrium is this strategy profile:

$$x_1 = -0.06$$
$$x_2 = 0.35$$
$$x_3 = \begin{cases} 1 & 72\% \\ -1 & 28\% \end{cases}$$

The corresponding utilities are $\mathbf{w} = (-1.22, 0.26, 0.97)$. This problem converged at order 4, resulting in 96 constraints. The solve time was around 10 ms.   △

Example 6 (Polynomial security game). We consider a polynomial security game with attackers $N_A = \{1, 2\}$, defenders $N_D = \{3, 4\}$, and targets $T_3 = \{t_1, t_2\}$ and $T_4 = \{t_3, t_4\}$. The capacities of attackers are $a_1 = 0.5$, $a_2 = 0.8$, and the defenders' capacities are $d_3 = d_4 = 1$. The efficiency functions are:

$$e_{t1}(x, y) = (1 - y^2) \cdot 0.7x^2$$
$$e_{t2}(x, y) = (y^2 - 2y + 1) \cdot (1.4x - 0.7x^2)$$
$$e_{t3}(x, y) = (1 - y^2) \cdot (1.8x - 0.9x^2)$$
$$e_{t4}(x, y) = (y^2 - 2y + 1) \cdot 0.9x^2$$

Our algorithm returns the partially mixed strategy profile at order 6:

$$(x_{1,t_1}, x_{1,t_2}, x_{1,t_3}, x_{1,t_4}) = (0.29, 0.0, 0.0, 0.21)$$
$$(x_{2,t_1}, x_{2,t_2}, x_{2,t_3}, x_{2,t_4}) = (0.36, 0.13, 0.04, 0.24)$$
$$(y_{1,t_1}, y_{1,t_2}) = \begin{cases} (0.33, 0.67) & 46\% \\ (0.69, 0.31) & 54\% \end{cases}$$
$$(y_{2,t_2}, y_{2,t_4}) = \begin{cases} (0.46, 0.54) & 2\% \\ (0.08, 0.92) & 6\% \\ (0.91, 0.09) & 92\% \end{cases}$$

The payoffs to each player are $\mathbf{w} = (0.1, 0.3, -0.17, -0.23)$. While the payoffs converged at order 4 already and took only 3 s to solve, the corresponding strategies could only be extracted at order 6, which took 6 min to solve. Due to the high dimensionality of the utility functions and the fast growth of the hierarchy, the resulting SDP contained over 25 thousand constraints.   △

The payoffs computed by this method depend only on the solver used and are generally of high quality; the corresponding measures, on the other hand, are less accurate. For example, the strategy in the last example yields a loss of only 0.16 instead of 0.17. This problem is inherent to the sum-of-squares optimization.

5 Conclusions

We introduced separable network games in which players are able to select their strategies continuously. In future research we will focus on the problem of finding another solutions for the security game discussed in Sect. 3.1 and relaxing the assumption (16). We presented a method to find equilibria for polynomial network games in Sect. 4, which is based on solving the hierarchy of semidefinite programs (25). The convergence was experimentally verified on selected examples. However, to prove that the hierarchy in fact converges is an interesting open problem for further research.

References

1. Adam, L., Horčík, R., Kasl, T., Kroupa, T.: Double oracle algorithm for computing equilibria in continuous games. In: Proceedings of the AAAI Conference on Artificial Intelligence, pp. 5070–5077 (2021)
2. Bailey, J.-P., Piliouras, G.: Multi-agent learning in network zero-sum games is a Hamiltonian system. In: Proceedings of the 18th International Conference on Autonomous Agents and MultiAgent Systems, AAMAS, Montreal, QC, Canada, pp. 233–241. International Foundation for Autonomous Agents and Multiagent Systems (2019)
3. Baye, M.-R., Kovenock, D., de Vries, C.-G.: The solution to the tullock rent-seeking game when $R > 2$: mixed-strategy equilibria and mean dissipation rates. Public Choice **81**(3), 363–80 (1994). https://doi.org/10.1007/BF01053238
4. Billingsley, P.: Probability and Measure, 3rd edn. Sons Inc., New York (1995)
5. Bregman, L.M., Fokin, I.N.: On separable non-cooperative zero-sum games. Optimization **44**(1), 69–84 (1998). https://doi.org/10.1080/02331939808844400
6. Cai, Y., Daskalkis, C.: On minmax theorems for multiplayer games. In: Proceedings of the Twenty-Second Annual ACM-SIAM Symposium on Discrete Algorithms, San Francisco, California, pp. 217–234. Society for Industrial and Applied Mathematics (2011). https://doi.org/10.1137/1.9781611973082.20
7. Cai, Y., Candogan, O., Daskalakis, C., Papadimitriou, C.: Zero-sum polymatrix games: a generalization of minmax. Math. Oper. Res. **41**(2), 648–655 (2016). https://doi.org/10.1287/moor.2015.0745
8. Daskalakis, C., Papadimitriou, C.H.: On a network generalization of the minmax theorem. In: Albers, S., Marchetti-Spaccamela, A., Matias, Y., Nikoletseas, S., Thomas, W. (eds.) ICALP 2009, Part II. LNCS, vol. 5556, pp. 423–434. Springer, Heidelberg (2009). https://doi.org/10.1007/978-3-642-02930-1_35
9. Dresher, W., Karlin, S., Shapley, L.-S.: Polynomial games. Contributions to the Theory of Games. Ann. Math. Stud. **1**, 161–180 (1950). https://doi.org/10.7249/P100
10. Dunning, I., Huchette, J., Lubin, M.: JuMP: a modeling language for mathematical optimization. SIAM Rev. **59**(2), 295–320 (2017)

11. Ewerhart, C., Valkanova, K.: Fictitious play in networks. Games Econom. Behav. **123**, 182–206 (2020). https://doi.org/10.1016/j.geb.2020.06.006
12. Glicksberg, I.-L.: A further generalization of the Kakutani fixed point theorem, with application to Nash equilibrium points. In: Proceedings of the American Mathematical Society, pp. 170–174 (1952). https://doi.org/10.1090/S0002-9939-1952-0046638-5
13. Henrion, D., Korda, M., Lasserre J.B.: Moment-SOS Hierarchy. The Lectures in Probability, Statistics, Computational Geometry, Control And Nonlinear PDEs, vol. 4 (2020). https://doi.org/10.1142/q0252
14. Laraki, R., Lasserre, J.B.: Semidefinite programming for min-max problems and games. Math. Program. **131**(1–2), 305–332 (2012)
15. Lasserre, J.B.: An Introduction to Polynomial and Semi-algebraic Optimization, vol. 52. Cambridge University Press, Cambridge (2015). https://doi.org/10.1017/CBO9781107447226
16. Osorio, A.: The lottery blotto game. Econ. Lett. **120**(2), 164–66 (2013). https://doi.org/10.1016/j.econlet.2013.04.012
17. Parrilo, P.: Polynomial games and sum of squares optimization. In: 2006 45th IEEE Conference on Decision and Control, pp. 2855–2860 (2006)
18. Putinar, M.: Positive polynomials on compact semi-algebraic sets. Indiana Univ. Math. J. **42**, 969–984 (1993). https://doi.org/10.1016/S0764-4442(99)80251-1
19. Rubinstein, A.: Inapproximability of Nash equilibrium. In: Proceedings of the Forty-Seventh Annual ACM Symposium on Theory of Computing, Portlan, Oregon, USA, pp. 409–418. Association for Computing Machinery (2015). https://doi.org/10.1145/2746539.2746578
20. Stein, N.-D., Ozdaglar, A., Parrilo, P.-A.: Separable and low-rank continuous games. Int. J. Game Theory **37**(4), 475–504 (2008)
21. Weisser, T., Legat, B., Coey, C., Kapelevich, L., Vielma, J.-P.: Polynomial and moment optimization in Julia and JuMP. JuliaCon (2019). https://pretalx.com/juliacon2019/talk/QZBKAU

Machine Learning and Game Theory

Countering Attacker Data Manipulation in Security Games

Andrew R. Butler[1(✉)], Thanh H. Nguyen[1], and Arunesh Sinha[2]

[1] University of Oregon, Eugene, USA
{arbutler,thanhhng}@cs.uoregon.edu
[2] Singapore Management University, Singapore, Singapore
aruneshs@smu.edu.sg

Abstract. Defending against attackers with unknown behavior is an important area of research in security games. A well-established approach is to utilize historical attack data to create a behavioral model of the attacker. However, this presents a vulnerability: a clever attacker may change its own behavior during learning, leading to an inaccurate model and ineffective defender strategies. In this paper, we investigate how a wary defender can defend against such deceptive attacker. We provide four main contributions. First, we develop a new technique to estimate attacker true behavior despite data manipulation by the clever adversary. Second, we extend this technique to be viable even when the defender has access to a minimal amount of historical data. Third, we utilize a maximin approach to optimize the defender's strategy against the worst-case within the estimate uncertainty. Finally, we demonstrate the effectiveness of our counter-deception methods by performing extensive experiments, showing clear gain for the defender and loss for the deceptive attacker.

1 Introduction

Learning adversary behavior from historical attack data is a firmly established methodology in adversarial settings, both in academic literature [15,19], and in real world applications such as wildlife security [4,24]. Herein lies a vulnerability: a clever attacker may modify its own behavior in order to conceal information or mislead the defender. This deceptive behavior can influence the defender's learning process, creating future gainful opportunities for the attacker. Indeed, such deception has received considerable attention in security games literature [6, 18,28]. However, robustness of the defender to the adversary's deceit is much less explored.

In this work, we investigate the defender's counteraction against attacker deception in a Stackelberg security game setting. Our work builds upon the *partial behavior deception* model [16] in which the defender models the behavior of the entire attacker population using a single Quantal Response (QR) [14] model of which the parameter $\lambda \in \mathbb{R}$ is learned from past attack data. Among the attackers, however, there is a rational attacker who can cause harm to the defender by

© Springer Nature Switzerland AG 2021
B. Bošanský et al. (Eds.): GameSec 2021, LNCS 13061, pp. 59–79, 2021.
https://doi.org/10.1007/978-3-030-90370-1_4

manipulating part of attack data. Such manipulation makes the defender learn a wrong λ, leading to an ineffective defender strategy. Addressing the attacker deception is still an open problem, which is the focus of our paper.

As our *first contribution*, we develop a new technique to estimate the true behavior of the non-deceptive attackers (represented by a parameter value λ^{true} of QR), given the perturbed training data. Our technique leverages the Karush-Kuhn-Tucker conditions of the rational attacker's optimization to formally express the relation between true behavior of non-deceptive attackers (λ^{true}) and learning outcome (λ^{learnt}) forced by the deceptive attacker. Based on this relation, we find that there is an interval of possible values for λ^{true} which leads to the same deception outcome λ^{learnt}. Moreover, bounds of this interval are increasing in λ^{learnt}. We thus propose a binary-search based method which uses λ^{learnt} to guide the search for these bounds within an ϵ-error.

As our *second contribution*, we extend our first contribution, perhaps surprisingly, to apply in scenarios with small number of attacks. The core issue is that the empirical attack distribution induced by limited attack samples may be far different from the true attack distribution induced by λ^{true}, making it challenging to characterize the relation between the true behavior and the deceptive outcome. We overcome this challenge by re-formulating the attack sampling process as choosing random *seeds* $\mathbf{u}$ drawn from the uniform distribution on $[0, 1]$ followed by a deterministic computation on $\mathbf{u}$.

We first prove that given any fixed $\mathbf{u}$, all mathematical results (from our first contribution) hold for small number of attacks. As the random seed chosen by nature is unknown, we then leverage the above result to perform binary search for *multiple* random seeds and construct a new interval spanning all found intervals as our final estimate for the range of λ^{true}.

As our *third contribution*, we propose a maximin approach to optimize the defender strategy against the worst case within the uncertainty interval for λ^{true}. We formulate this maximin problem as a multiple non-linear programs, each corresponds to a particular optimal attack choice of the deceptive attacker. *Finally*, via extensive experiments, we show that, even when optimizing against a wide uncertainty interval of λ^{true}, our algorithm gives significantly higher utility for the defender, and less benefit for the deceptive attacker.

2   Related Work

Adversarial Learning. Adversarial learning is a field within machine learning that has become increasingly popular [9, 12, 13, 23, 29]. The attacker deception here is analogous to a *causative attack* (or poisoning attack) in adversarial learning [9]. A significant difference between our work and adversarial learning is that we seek to maximize defender utility *through* predicting the attacker's behavior, whereas in adversarial learning, the end goal is prediction accuracy.

Attacker Behavior Inference. Learning the behavior of bounded rational attackers is crucial, and a major area of interest in security games. Various models including QR have been explored [10,20,22,27,28]. As this learning is used to create a defender strategy, the training attack pool is vulnerable to manipulation by a clever attacker. This paper focuses on addressing this challenge in security games. Our work overlaps with settings in which one or more players has limited information [1].

Deception in Security Games. Historically, most work has focused on deception from the defender side [7,30]. In this scenario, the defender typically exploits information asymmetry to fool the attacker (e.g. in network security, concealing some system characteristics). More recently, research has investigated deception from the attacker side [6,18,28] in SSGs, and the follower side in general Stackelberg games [5]. Much of this work concentrates on a single attacker whose payoff values are unknown to the defender. The attacker-deception model we utilize [16], on the other hand, describes a realistic scenario in which the defender must contend with multiple attackers of *unknown* behavior.

3 Preliminaries

3.1 Stackelberg Security Games (SSGs)

In SSGs [24], the *defender* must protect a set of T targets from one or more *attackers*. The defender has a limited number ($K < T$) of *resources* that each can be allocated to protect a single target. A pure strategy of the defender is defined as a one-to-one allocation of resources to targets. A mixed defense strategy, x, is a probability distribution over these pure strategies. For the purposes of this paper, we consider no scheduling constraints to the defender's strategy, meaning that a mixed strategy can be compactly represented as a coverage probability vector, given by $\mathbf{x} = \{x_1, x_2, \ldots, x_T\}$ where $x_i \in [0, 1]$ represents the probability that target i is protected by the defender and $\sum_i x_i \leq K$. We denote by $\mathbf{X}$ the set of all feasible defense strategies. In SSGs, the attacker is fully aware of the defender's mixed strategy and chooses a target to attack based on this knowledge.

An attack on target i gives each player a reward or a penalty, depending on whether the defender is currently protecting target i. If i is unprotected, the attacker gains reward R_i^a and the defender receives penalty P_i^d. Conversely, if target i is protected, the attacker takes penalty $P_i^a < R_i^a$ and the defender gains reward $R_i^d > P_i^d$. Given coverage probability x_i, the expected utilities for the defender and the attacker for an attack on target i can be formulated as follows:

$$U_i^d(x_i) = x_i R_i^d + (1 - x_i) P_i^d$$
$$U_i^a(x_i) = x_i P_i^a + (1 - x_i) R_i^a$$

Quantal Response Behavior Model (QR). QR is an well-known model describing attacker behavior in SSGs [14,27]. Intuitively, QR provides a mechanism by which higher expected utility targets are attacked more frequently. Essentially, the probability of attacking target i is given as follows:

$$q_i(\mathbf{x}; \lambda) = \left(e^{\lambda U_i^a(x_i)}\right) \Big/ \left(\sum_j e^{\lambda U_j^a(x_j)}\right) \tag{1}$$

3.2   Partial Behavior Deception Model

Our work on developing an optimal counter-deception strategy for the defender is built upon the partial behavior deception model introduced by [16]. In this model, multiple attackers are present, who have the same payoffs but different attack behavior due to different rationality levels. Among these attackers, there is a rational attacker who intends to play deceptively to mislead the defender. The defender, on the other hand, is aware of the attackers' payoffs but is uncertain about the behavior of the attackers. The defender thus attempts to build a behavior model, i.e., the QR model, to predict the attack distribution of the entire attacker population. Real-world applications such as wildlife conservation also use this single-behavior-modeling approach as park rangers usually cannot differentiate data collected, such as poaching signs, among multiple sources [10].

Two-Phase Learning-Planning of Defender. This model describes a *one-shot two-phase learning-planning* problem for the defender, consisting of a learning phase and a planning phase. This is the typical security game model used in literature [24,27]. Essentially, in the learning phase, the defender uses training attack data to estimate the parameter λ of QR using the Maximum Likelihood Estimation method (MLE), as formulated below:

$$\lambda^{\text{learnt}} \in \operatorname*{argmax}_{\lambda} \sum_m \sum_i z_i^m \log q_i(\mathbf{x}^m; \lambda) \tag{2}$$

where x_i^m is the defender's coverage probability at target i and step m and z_i^m is the corresponding number of attacks.

During the planning phase, the defender utilizes the learned λ^{learnt} value to optimize his defense against such an attacker. The optimal strategy, $\mathbf{x}^*$, is given by:

$$\mathbf{x}^* \in \operatorname*{argmax}_{\mathbf{x} \in \mathbf{X}} \sum_i q_i(\mathbf{x}; \lambda^{\text{learnt}}) U_i^d(x_i) \tag{3}$$

Behavior Deception of Attacker. [16] Since the (naive) defender uses the entire learning dataset to construct a single attacker model, a clever attacker might change its own behavior during the learning phase in order to benefit during the planning phase[1]. It is naturally assumed that only perfectly rational attackers

---

[1] In this paper, we focus on the one-shot game which only consists of a learning phase and planning phase—a commonly-used security game model in literature. Therefore, the deceptive attacker can simply play perfectly rationally in the planning phase after deceiving the defender in the learning phase. This model can also serve as the basis for repeated security games which involve multiple learning-planning rounds where the attacker plays deceptively in all rounds except the last round.

display such deceptive behavior. Therefore, the partial behavior deception model centers on a single perfectly rational deceptive attacker, amongst the bounded rational attackers, that can alter some fraction of the training dataset. The bounded rational attackers attack non-deceptively according to a fixed unknown QR parameter λ^{true}. Essentially, the deceptive attacker wants to find the best perturbation of the training data to maximize its utility in the planning phase, denoted by $U^a(\mathbf{x}^*(\mathbf{z}))$, as follows:

$$(\texttt{DecAlter}) : \max_{\mathbf{z}=\{z_i^m\}} U^a(\mathbf{x}^*(\mathbf{z})) \tag{4}$$

$$\text{s.t. } z_i^m \geq n_i^m, \forall m, i \tag{5}$$

$$\sum_i z_i^m \leq (f+1) \cdot \sum_i n_i^m, \forall m. \tag{6}$$

where $\mathbf{x}^*(\mathbf{z})$ is the defender's strategy determined based on his learning-planning method in (2–3). In addition, n_i^m is the number of attacks by the non-deceptive attackers and $f \in \mathbb{R}$ is the ratio of deceptive attacks to non-deceptive attacks at each step m. Constraints (5–6) guarantee that the deceptive attacker can only control its own attacks. We denote by $\mathbf{z} = \{z_i^m\}$ the deception outcome of the deceptive attacker, which includes the non-deceptive attacks ($\mathbf{n} = \{n_i^m\}$). The defender learns a (deceptive) parameter λ^{learnt} using $\mathbf{z}$.

3.3 Cognitive Hierarchy Approach

In order to determine a counter-deception strategy for the defender, a possible approach is to compute a fixed point equilibrium of the deception game in which each player reasons about its opponent's strategy recursively till infinity. However, finding a fixed point equilibrium in our game is extremely challenging. This is because the defender has no information (or prior) about the behavior of the non-deceptive attackers. As a result, the defender has to relate the equilibrium outcome for every possible true behavior of these non-deceptive attackers to the observed (manipulated) attacks. This task is challenging (as well as impractical) given that the behavior space of attackers is infinite.

In real world settings, cognitive hierarchy models have been proven more effective than equilibrium based approaches at realistically modeling player behavior [2,3,8]. This is because human players do not exhibit infinite level strategic reasoning. Cognitive hierarchy theory states that players in games can be divided into different *levels* of thinkers, each assuming that no players are on levels above them [26]. In a mixed attacker deception setting, we can model the levels as follows:

- Level 1: The rational attacker plays truthfully. The defender follows the two-stage learning-planning approach to compute a defense strategy.
- Level 2: The rational attacker plays deceptively, assuming the defender is at level 1. The level 2 defender, on the other hand, attempts to counter the attacker deception, assuming the attackers are at levels 0, 1, or 2.

– Level $l > 2$: The strategic reasoning is similar to level 2. Specifically, the attacker assumes the defender is at level $l - 1$ while the defender assumes the attackers are at any one of the levels *up to and including* l.

Previous work has shown that distributions of human players in normal form games mostly consist of lower level players [26]. The aforementioned partial behavior deception model focuses on the deception by a level 2 attacker [16]. Our paper studies the counter-deception by a level 2 defender.

4   Finding Non-deceptive Attacker Behavior

In order to determine an effective defense strategy, we begin our analysis by characterizing the space of *possible* attack behavior (described by QR) of the non-deceptive attackers, given the perturbed data **z**. Recall that the non-deceptive attackers respond according to a fixed λ^{true}, unknown to the defender. Instead, the defender obtains a learning outcome λ^{learnt} given perturbed training data. Our goal is to estimate the possible values of λ^{true} given observed learning outcome λ^{learnt}.

4.1   Characterizing Deceptive Attacker's Behavior

We first analyze the deception possibilities for the deceptive attacker *given any value* λ^{true} of the non-deceptive attackers. The results we establish here help us in our goal of estimating λ^{true}. For analysis sake, we assume that the number of attacks is large enough such that the sampled attacks is close to the actual attack probability distributions. We will relax this assumption later. Mathematically, we assume:

$$\left(n_i^m \right) / \left(\sum_j n_j^m \right) \approx q_i^m(\mathbf{x}^m, \lambda^{\text{true}}), \forall m \tag{7}$$

where n_i^m refers to the number of attacks committed by the *non-deceptive* attacker at target i. As shown in (DecAlter), the objective utility function of the deceptive attacker depends on the strategy of the defender, which in turn is governed by the training data $\{z_i^m\}$, and the training data contains attacks by the non-deceptive attacker too ($\{n_i^m\}$). Thus, the outcome of λ^{learnt} depends on the behavior of the non-deceptive attacker λ^{true} (or $\{n_i^m\}$). We thus also use the notion $\text{DecAlter}(\lambda^{\text{true}}) = \lambda^{\text{learnt}}$ to represent the dependence of the learning result (*altered* by deception) on λ^{true}.

For this portion of our analysis, we relax the domain of **z** to be continuous. This allows our proofs to be simpler and more concise. In practice, this value is limited to discrete integers; fractional attacks are nonsensical. Later, we will extend the methods to the discrete **z** case, and show why they still apply. We exploit the KKT condition for the optimality of the deceptive λ^{learnt} as the outcome of the defender's learning, formulated in optimization (2). Essentially, λ^{learnt} has to satisfy the following KKT condition:

$$\sum_m \left[\sum_i z_i^m\right]\left[\frac{\sum_i z_i^m U_i^a(x_i^m)}{\sum_i z_i^m} - \underbrace{\sum_i q_i(\mathbf{x}^m; \lambda^{\text{learnt}}) U_i^a(x_i^m) U^a}_{\text{Attacker utility}}\right] = 0$$

where $U^a(\mathbf{x}^m; \lambda^{\text{learnt}})$ is the attacker's expected utility when the defender plays $\mathbf{x}^m$ and the attacker plays according to λ^{learnt}. In our theoretical analysis, we leverage the following important monotonicity property of this utility function:

Observation 1 ([17]) $U^a(\mathbf{x}^m, \lambda)$ *is an increasing function of* λ *for any given strategy* $\mathbf{x}^m$.

Let's assume, WLOG, the attacker's utilities at each target has the following order: $U_1^a(x_1^m) \le U_2^a(x_2^m) \le \cdots \le U_T^a(x_T^m)$ for all m. Observation 1 aids us in showing that all feasible (not necessarily optimal) deceptive λ values form an interval $[\lambda_{\min}^{\text{learnt}}, \lambda_{\max}^{\text{learnt}}]$ with $\lambda_{\min}^{\text{learnt}}, \lambda_{\max}^{\text{learnt}}$ specified as follows:

Theorem 1 (Characterization of Deception Space). *Given* λ^{true} *and the attack ratio* f, *the space of deceptive parameters inducible by the deceptive attacker forms an interval* $[\lambda_{\min}^{learnt}, \lambda_{\max}^{learnt}]$, *where* $\lambda_{\max}^{learnt}$ *is the unique solution of:*

$$\sum_{m,j} n_j^m \left[U^a(\mathbf{x}^m; \lambda^{true}) + fU_T^a(x_T^m) - (f+1)U^a(\mathbf{x}^m, \lambda_{\max}^{learnt})\right] = 0$$

and $\lambda_{\min}^{learnt}$ *is the unique solution of:*

$$\sum_{m,j} n_j^m \left[U^a(\mathbf{x}^m; \lambda^{true}) + fU_1^a(x_1^m) - (f+1)U^a(\mathbf{x}^m, \lambda_{\min}^{learnt})\right] = 0$$

All formal proofs are in the appendix. Essentially, Theorem 1 states that given some true behavior of the non-deceptive attacker λ^{true}, the deceptive attacker can force the deceptive λ to be any value in $[\lambda_{\min}^{\text{learnt}}, \lambda_{\max}^{\text{learnt}}]$. Further, the deceptive attacker cannot make the defender learn any λ outside of this range. Based on Theorem 1, we present the following corollaries which characterize the monotonicity of $\lambda_{\min}^{\text{learnt}}$ and $\lambda_{\max}^{\text{learnt}}$, as well as the monotonicity of the optimal deception $\lambda^{\text{learnt}} = \texttt{DecAlter}(\lambda^{\text{true}}) \in [\lambda_{\min}^{\text{learnt}}, \lambda_{\max}^{\text{learnt}}]$ with respect to the non-deceptive attacker behavior λ^{true}.

Corollary 1. *Consider two different behavior parameters,* $\lambda_1^{true} \le \lambda_2^{true}$. *Denote by* $[\lambda_{\min,1}^{learnt}, \lambda_{\max,1}^{learnt}]$ *and* $[\lambda_{\min,2}^{learnt}, \lambda_{\max,2}^{learnt}]$ *the corresponding deceptive parameter ranges, we have:* $\lambda_{\max,1}^{learnt} \le \lambda_{\max,2}^{learnt}$ *and* $\lambda_{\min,1}^{learnt} \le \lambda_{\min,2}^{learnt}$.

Based on Corollary 1, we obtain Corollary 2 showing the monotonicity relation between λ^{learnt} and λ^{true}.

Corollary 2. *Consider two different behavior parameters,* $\lambda_1^{true} \ne \lambda_2^{true}$. *Then, we have:*

$$\lambda_1^{true} \le \lambda_2^{true} \implies \texttt{DecAlter}(\lambda_1^{true}) \le \texttt{DecAlter}(\lambda_2^{true}) \tag{8}$$

$$\texttt{DecAlter}(\lambda_1^{true}) < \texttt{DecAlter}(\lambda_2^{true}) \implies \lambda_1^{true} < \lambda_2^{true} \tag{9}$$

Corollary 3. *Consider two different behavior parameters $\lambda_1^{true} \leq \lambda_2^{true}$. If the corresponding optimal deception solutions:* $\mathtt{DecAlter}(\lambda_1^{true}) = \mathtt{DecAlter}(\lambda_2^{true})$, *then for any $\lambda^{true} \in [\lambda_1^{true}, \lambda_2^{true}]$, we also have its optimal deception solution:* $\mathtt{DecAlter}(\lambda^{true}) = \mathtt{DecAlter}(\lambda_1^{true})$.

4.2 RaBiS: Characterizing Behavior of Non-deceptive Attacker

In this section, we attempt to find the range of possible values for λ^{true}, which is unknown to the defender, as only the deceptively altered $\mathtt{QR}$ parameter λ^{learnt} is observed. We leverage the results of Corollaries 2 and 3 for this analysis.

Lemma 1. *Given some learned λ^{learnt}, there exists an interval $[\lambda_{min}^{true}, \lambda_{max}^{true}]$ such that all values $\lambda^{true} \in [\lambda_{min}^{true}, \lambda_{max}^{true}]$ leads to the same outcome λ^{learnt}. In addition, both bounds λ_{min}^{true} and λ_{max}^{true} are increasing in λ^{learnt}.*

Based on the above result, we propose a binary-search based approach, RaBiS (**Ra**nge-finding **Bi**nary **S**earch), to find the interval $[\lambda_{min}^{true}, \lambda_{max}^{true}]$ within an ϵ-error in a polynomial time for arbitrary small $\epsilon > 0$. RaBiS consists of two binary searches: the first binary search is to find the upper bound λ_{max}^{true} and the second binary search is to find the lower bound λ_{min}^{true}. Both binary searches maintain a pair of bounds for binary search (lb, ub). While in theory the range of λ^{true} is $[0, \infty)$, in practice, a limited range of $[0, M]$, where M is a very large constant, ensures that the attacker's $\mathtt{QR}$ behavior with $\lambda^{true} = M$ is close enough to $\lambda^{true} = \infty$. Therefore, in our algorithm, we initialize $lb = 0$ and $ub = M$.

At each iteration, we examine the mid-value $r = (lb + ub)/2$ by comparing the deception calculation $\lambda' = \mathtt{DecAlter}(r)$ with the actual deception outcome computed by the defender, λ^{learnt}. In particular, in the binary search for finding λ_{max}^{true}, if $\lambda' \leq \lambda^{learnt}$, there must be a $\lambda_{max}^{true} \in [r, ub]$ such that $\mathtt{DecAlter}(\lambda_{max}^{true}) = \lambda^{learnt}$ and any $\lambda > \lambda^{true}$ implies $\mathtt{DecAlter}(\lambda) > \lambda^{learnt}$. Thus, in order to find λ_{max}^{true}, we update the lower bound $lb = r$. Conversely, if $\lambda' > \lambda^{learnt}$, it means all $\lambda^{true} \in [r, ub]$ will lead to a deceptive parameter value strictly greater than λ^{learnt}. Therefore, we update the upper bound $ub = r$. This process stops when $ub - lb < \epsilon$. The binary search process for finding λ_{min}^{true} is similar.

4.3 Principled Approach for Low-Data Challenge

Thus far, our analysis of the range of the non-deceptive attacker λ^{true} was performed under the approximation assumption of Eq. 7. However, in practice, this assumption may not hold true. This is because the attacker may conduct a limited number of attacks, which leads to a substantial difference between the empirical attack distribution and the true attack distribution, that is:

$$(n_i^m)/\left(\sum_j n_j^m\right) \neq q_i^m(\mathbf{x}^m; \lambda^{true}), \forall m$$

To address this challenge, we first investigate the generation of limited attack samples from the true distribution under a *static random seed*. We show that

Fig. 1. Attack generation by transforming uniform dist.

our previous theoretical results for the ideal scenario still hold in this "limited-attack" scenario. We then leverage this result for a static random seed to address the general case of *unknown* random seed.

Sampling by Transformation. Sample generation from certain parameterized distributions can be split into a two step process by using a transformation of known distributions [11,21]. We show that such split generation is possible for our problem. Let u be a real valued random variable that is distributed uniformly between 0 and 1. Given a defense strategy, $\mathbf{x}^m$, and QR parameter λ, we define the function f_λ such that $P\big(f_\lambda(u) = i\big) = q_i(\mathbf{x}^m; \lambda)$. Note that f_λ is a deterministic function dependent on λ, which we define explicitly next. For any given $\mathbf{x}^m$, partition the interval $[0, 1]$ according to the attack probabilities $q_i(\mathbf{x}^m; \lambda)$ specified by QR with parameter λ, with the following partition boundary points: $S(0; \lambda) = 0$, $S(i; \lambda) = \sum_{j=1}^{i} q_j(\mathbf{x}^m; \lambda)$, and $S(T; \lambda) = 1$. Figure 1 is an example when the number of targets is $T = 3$. Given this division, we define $f_\lambda(u) = i$ when $u \in [S(i-1; \lambda), S(i; \lambda)]$; it can be readily verified that $P\big(f_\lambda(u) = i\big) = q_i(\mathbf{x}^m; \lambda)$. In the case of $N > 1$ attacks, we can view the attack generation process as N samples of u to get $\mathbf{u} = \{u_1, \ldots, u_N\}$ and then applying f_λ to each of those samples to obtain the targets attacked.

Static Random Seed Generation. For our problem with parameter λ^{true}, after separating the randomness (u) and the effect of the parameter ($f_{\lambda^{\text{true}}}$) in attack generation, the main idea of a static random seed is to assume that the N uniformly sampled values $\mathbf{u}$ are the same for any value of λ^{true} that we consider in the binary search for $\lambda_{\min}^{\text{true}}$ or $\lambda_{\max}^{\text{true}}$. By controlling the randomness, we establish a deterministic baseline to compare the empirical distribution arising from the different λ^{true} that we consider. A big advantage of controlling randomness is that it allows us to carry over all the previous proofs to a low data setting, as described next.

Let $E(\mathbf{u}, \lambda^{\text{true}})$ be the empirical distribution when attacks are computed using $f_{\lambda^{\text{true}}}$ and the generated N samples $\mathbf{u}$. We can define the attacker expected utility w.r.t. this distribution, denoted by $U^a(\mathbf{x}^m; E(\mathbf{u}, \lambda^{\text{true}}))$, exactly analogously to how $U^a(\mathbf{x}^m; \lambda^{\text{true}})$ is defined w.r.t. the true distribution. We obtain Lemma 2 which is analogous to Observation 1.

Lemma 2. *For a fixed seed, $\mathbf{u}$, the attacker expected utility computed based on the corresponding empirical distribution, $U^a(\mathbf{x}^m; E(\mathbf{u}, \lambda^{true}))$, is an increasing function of λ^{true}.*

In all results previously (including corollaries), we only used the Observation 1 property of $U^a(\mathbf{x}^m; \lambda^{\text{true}})$. With the result above, we can replace

$U^a(\mathbf{x}^m; \lambda^{\text{true}})$ by $U^a(\mathbf{x}^m; E(\mathbf{u}, \lambda^{\text{true}}))$ and all proofs still go through. Hence, our Theorem 1 holds with respect to $U^a(\mathbf{x}^m; E(\mathbf{u}, \lambda^{\text{true}}))$ (which replaces $U^a(\mathbf{x}^m; \lambda^{\text{true}})$ in the equations presented in Theorem 1). This result shows that for a fixed random seed $\mathbf{u}$ we can recover all previous results.

Extension to Unknown Random Seed. The random seed used (by nature) in the generation of the training data is not known to the defender. To overcome this challenge, we extend our binary search to consider multiple random seeds. For each random seed, we run RaBiS to obtain an interval of possible values for λ^{true}. Taking a worst-case approach, we consider the smallest interval that spans all of these ranges as the uncertainty set containing all possible values of λ^{true}.

5   Maximin to Optimize Defender Utility

After finding the range $[\lambda_{\min}^{\text{true}}, \lambda_{\max}^{\text{true}}]$, the defender must optimize its strategy accordingly. Essentially, the defender is aware that there are attacks not only from a rational (deceptive) attacker (who will act optimally in the defender's planning phase) but also from bounded rational attackers (whose λ^{true} can be any value within $[\lambda_{\min}^{\text{true}}, \lambda_{\max}^{\text{true}}]$). In order to overcome the uncertainty about the behavior of these attackers, we take a maximin approach where the defender seeks to *maximize* its utility against the *worst* possible (for the defender) λ value within the calculated range. In practice, to deal with the computational challenge due to an infinite number of possible values in $[\lambda_{\min}^{\text{true}}, \lambda_{\max}^{\text{true}}]$, we break down this range into a set of possible discrete values $\{\lambda_{\min}^{\text{true}}, \lambda^1, \lambda^2, \ldots, \lambda_{\max}^{\text{true}}\}$. Furthermore, since the rational attacker will choose an optimal target to attack in the planning phase, we decompose our defense problem into multiple non-linear programs, each corresponds to a particular optimal target to attacker for the rational attacker. In particular, our non-linear program corresponding to an optimal target j can be formulated as follows:

$$\max_{\mathbf{x}} f \cdot U_j^d(x_j) + U_{\text{worst-case}}^d \tag{10}$$

$$\text{s.t. } U_j^a(x_j) \geq U_i^a(x_i), \forall i \tag{11}$$

$$U_{\text{worst-case}}^d \leq \sum_i q_i(\mathbf{x}; \lambda) U_i^d(x_i), \tag{12}$$

$$\forall \lambda \in \{\lambda_{\min}^{\text{true}}, \lambda^1, \lambda^2, \ldots, \lambda_{\max}^{\text{true}}\}$$

$$\sum_i x_i \leq K, x_i \in [0, 1], \forall i \tag{13}$$

The objective (Line 10) balances optimization against the fully rational attacker, $U_j^d(x_j)$, and the worst possible bounded rational attacker, $U_{\text{worst-case}}^d$, with multiplier f corresponding to the ratio of deceptive to non-deceptive attacks. Constraint (11) ensures that the target chosen by the fully rational attacker, j, is indeed the highest-utility target. Constraint (12) effectively iterates through the λ range, setting $U_{\text{worst-case}}^d$ equal to the lowest defender utility value among all possible lambdas. In a zero sum game, these lines could be replaced by simply setting $\lambda = \lambda_{\max}^{\text{true}}$. Lastly, constraint (13) provides logical bounds to the defender's strategy: the total coverage percentage of all targets cannot exceed the number of resources, and all targets have coverage probability between 0 and 1.

6   Experiments

In our experiments, we analyze: (i) the defender's utility gain by addressing deception, and (ii) the loss of utility for the devious attacker. The training data includes attacks from both the fully rational deceptive attacker and a boundedly rational attacker whose behavior is described by QR. We use 5 defender training strategies ($M = 5$) each with 50 non-deceptive attacks ($\sum_i n_i^m = 50$) sampled from the QR distribution with λ^{true} of the bounded rational attacker. Each data point is averaged over 200+ games, generated using GAMUT (http://gamut. stanford.edu). For our trials, we vary (i) the true non-deceptive lambda λ^{true} value and (ii) the fraction f of attacks done by the devious adversary. Due to limited space, we will only highlight important results. Additional results are included in our appendix. All utility results are statistically significant under bootstrap-t ($\alpha = 0.05$) [25].

Figures 2a and 2b display the defender's utility in two cases: (i) Addressed— the defender addresses the attacker's deception using our counter-deception algorithm; and (ii) Unaddressed—the defender simply does not take the attacker's deception into account. In these two figures, the y-axis represents the defender's expected utility on average. Both figures show that the defender can significantly increase his utility for playing our maximin counter-deception strategy. In Fig. 2b we observe that, when deception is unaddressed, the defender's utility decreases exponentially as the deceptive attack ratio increases. On the other hand, when the defender *does* address deception, the slope is far more gradual. Figure 2b shows how defender utility increases as the non-deceptive λ^{true} value does. This effect tapers off on the upper end of the spectrum. This result is expected because the non-deceptive attacker gets more rational as λ^{true} increases, leading to less changes in the defender's maximin strategy. Furthermore, in Fig. 2b, the lowest utility point for the defender is when λ^{true} gets to zero. This makes sense: as the non-deceptive attackers become completely non-strategic (*i.e.*, $\lambda^{\text{true}} = 0$), the non-deceptive attackers will have less influence on the training data, or equivalently, the deceptive attacker has more power to manipulate the data.

Naturally, we observe an opposite trend in the attacker-utility graphs shown in Figs. 2c and 2d. That is, the utility of the attacker reduces substantially when the defender addresses the attacker deception. Figure 2c shows that when the defender plays our maximin strategy, the attacker's utility actually decreases w.r.t. the percentage of attacks controlled by the deceptive attacker. This result appears to be counter-intuitive at first glance. However, it's logical: our maximin algorithm knows the attack ratio so it tailors more of the defense strategy towards a fully rational attacker (the actual rationality of the deceptive attacker).

Lastly, we analyze runtime performance of both portions of the algorithm in Fig. 3. For the binary search, runtime is high across the board due to the

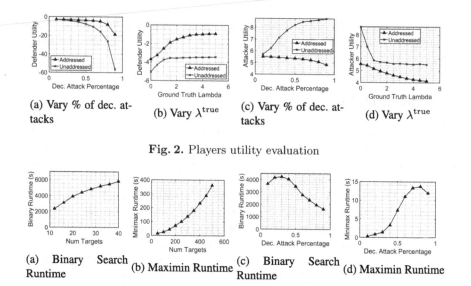

(a) Vary % of dec. attacks

(b) Vary λ^{true}

(c) Vary % of dec. attacks

(d) Vary λ^{true}

Fig. 2. Players utility evaluation

(a) Binary Search Runtime

(b) Maximin Runtime

(c) Binary Search Runtime

(d) Maximin Runtime

Fig. 3. Runtime evaluation

sheer number of partial deception games (DecAlter) solved in each search. However, this runtime scales linearly w.r.t. the number of targets (Fig. 3a), implying that the algorithm can be scaled to large games. Furthermore, when varying the attack percentage (Fig. 3c), we see that the runtime peaks with a percentage around 0.3. This peak is shifted compared to the runtime for solving (DecAlter) only, which peaks around 0.5 [16]. This is because the range, $[\lambda^{true}_{min}, \lambda^{true}_{max}]$ increases as the deceptive attack percentage does, meaning the total search time decreases as RaBiS exits earlier.

Figure 3b shows how the maximin runtime increases w.r.t. the number of targets. This is expected since the number of non-linear programs involved is equal to the number of targets. The maximin optimization can scale to large games: 500 target games are solved in less than 10 minutes. Observe that we examine a larger spread of targets here than for the binary search portion of the algorithm; the binary search runtime is orders of magnitude higher, reaching our 100 min cut-off with far fewer targets. Figure 3d shows that maximin runtime initially increases as the percentage of attacks that are deceptive does, reflecting the wider range of possible values for λ^{true}. At higher values this effect diminishes and runtime ends up decreasing at the 0.9 marker, indicating that it is easier to optimize a strategy against mostly rational attacks.

7   Conclusion

We successfully addressed attacker deception in security games, showing both theoretically and experimentally the value of our approach. Through mathematical analysis we explored the characteristics of deception and defense and developed effective countermeasures: RaBiS allowed the defender to see through the deceptively altered historical attack data, after which a maximin approach yielded a robust strategy. Our experiments showed the wary defender receiving much higher utility than its naive counterpart.

Acknowledgement. This work was supported by ARO grant W911NF-20-1-0344 from the US Army Research Office.

A   Appendix

A.1   Proof of Theorem 1

In order to prove this theorem, we introduce a series of Lemmas (3–6). For the sake of analysis, we denote by:

$$y_i^m = \frac{z_i^m}{\sum_j z_j^m} \qquad\qquad c^m = \frac{1}{\sum_j z_j^m}$$

Intuitively, y_i^m is the empirical attack distribution estimated from the perturbed training data $\hat{\mathcal{D}} = \{x_i^m, z_i^m\}$ and c^m is the normalization term. Also, $\{y_i^m, c^m\}$ and $\{z_i^m\}$ are interchangeable. That is, given $\{y_i^m, c^m\}$, we can determine $z_i^m = \frac{y_i^m}{c^m}$. We first present the Lemma 1 which determines the deception capability of the deceptive attacker:

Lemma 3. *Given the true behavior λ^{true} of the non-deceptive attackers and the attack ratio f, the deceptive space for the deceptive attacker is specified as follows:*

$$\sum_m \frac{1}{c^m}\left[\sum_i y_i^m U_i^a(x_i^m) - U^a(\mathbf{x}^m, \lambda)\right] = 0 \tag{14}$$

$$\frac{y_i^m}{c^m} \geq n_i^m, \forall m, i \tag{15}$$

$$c^m \geq \frac{1}{(f+1)\sum_i n_i^m}, \forall m \tag{16}$$

$$y_i^m \in [0,1], \sum_i y_i^m = 1, \forall m, i \tag{17}$$

That is, any deceptive λ that the defender learns has to be a part of a feasible solution (λ, y_i^m, c^m) of the system (14–17). Conversely, given any feasible (λ, y_i^m, c^m) satisfying (14–17), the deceptive attacker can make the defender learn λ by inducing the following perturbed data:

$$z_i^m = \frac{y_i^m}{c^m}$$

Proof. Equation (14) is simply the KKT condition presented in the previous section with y_i^m and c^m substituted in. Similarly, the constraints (15–16) correspond to the constraints for the deception capability of the deceptive attacker in (5–6). Finally, the constraint (17) follows from the definition of y_i^m and ensures that $\sum_i \frac{z_i^m}{\sum_j z_j^m} = 1$ and $\frac{z_i^m}{\sum_j z_j^m} \leq 1$.

According to Lemma 3, we now can prove Theorem 1 based on the characterization of the feasible solution domain of λ for the system (14–17). We denote
by:

$$\mathcal{F}(\lambda, \{y_i^m, c^m\}) = \sum_m \frac{1}{c^m} \left[\sum_i y_i^m U_i^a(x_i^m) - U^a(\mathbf{x}^m, \lambda) \right]$$

the LHS of (14). In addition, we denote by $\mathbf{S} = \{(y_i^m, c^m) : \text{conditions (15–17)}$
are satisfied$\}$ the feasible region of (y_i^m, c^m) which satisfy the conditions (15–17).
In the following, we provide Lemmas 4 and 5 which specify the range of $\mathcal{F}$ as a
function of λ. Essentially, if the value of $\mathcal{F}$ contains the point zero, then λ is a
feasible solution of the system (14–17). We will use this property to characterize
the feasible region of λ.

Lemma 4. *Assume that, WLOG, $U_1^a(x_1^m) \leq U_2^a(x_2^m) \leq \cdots \leq U_T^a(x_T^m)$ for all
m. Given a λ, the optimal solution to*

$$\mathcal{F}^{\max}(\lambda) = \max_{\{y_i^m, c^m\} \in \mathbf{S}} \mathcal{F}(\lambda, \{y_i^m, c^m\}) \tag{18}$$

is determined as follows:

$$c^m = \frac{1}{(f+1) \sum_i n_i^m} \tag{19}$$

$$y_i^m = n_i^m c^m, \quad \text{when } i < T \tag{20}$$

$$y_i^m = 1 - c^m \sum_{i=1}^{T-1} n_i^m \quad \text{when } i = T \tag{21}$$

Proof. First, $\mathcal{F}(\lambda, \{y_i^m, c^m\})$ can be reformulated as:

$$\sum_m \frac{1}{c^m} \left[U_T^a(x_T^m) + \sum_{i=1}^{T-1} y_i^m [U_i^a(x_i^m) - U_T^a(x_T^m)] - U^a(\mathbf{x}^m, \lambda) \right]$$

Under our assumption that $U_1^a(x_1^m) \leq U_2^a(x_2^m) \leq \cdots \leq U_T^a(x_T^m)$, we know that
$[U_i^a(x_i^m) - U_T^a(x_T^m)]$ is a strictly non-positive term for all i. Thus, maximizing $\mathcal{F}$
involves minimizing y_i^m when $i < T$. From constraint (15), the minimum y_i^m for
all i is $n_i^m c^m$. This gives us $y_i^m = n_i^m c^m$ when $i < T$. From constraint (17), we
know that this leaves us with $y_i^m = 1 - c^m \sum_{i=1}^{T-1} n_i^m$ when $i = T$.

Finally, given this specification of $\{y_i^m\}$, the optimization problem (18) is
reduced to:

$$\max_{c^m} \sum_m \sum_{i<T} n_i^m [U_i^a(x_i^m) - U_T^a(x_T^m)] + \frac{U_T^a(x_T^m) - U^a(\mathbf{x}^m, \lambda)}{c^m}$$

$$\text{s.t. } c^m \geq \frac{1}{(f+1) \sum_i n_i^m} \text{ and } c^m \leq \frac{1}{\sum_i n_i^m}, \forall m$$

in which the objective function comprises of two terms: the first term does not depend on $\{c^m\}$ and the second term is a decreasing function of c^m (since $U_T^a(x_T^m) - U^a(\mathbf{x}^m, \lambda) > 0$). Therefore, it is maximized when c^m is minimized, which is $c^m = \frac{1}{(f+1)\sum_i n_i^m}$, concluding the proof.

Lemma 5. *Assume that, WLOG, $U_1^a(x_1^m) \leq U_2^a(x_2^m) \leq \cdots \leq U_T^a(x_T^m)$ for all m. Given a λ, the optimal solution to*

$$\mathcal{F}^{\min}(\lambda) = \min_{\{y_i^m, c^m\} \in \mathbf{S}} \mathcal{F}(\lambda, \{y_i^m, c^m\}) \tag{22}$$

is determined as follows:

$$c^m = \frac{1}{(f+1)\sum_i n_i^m} \tag{23}$$

$$y_i^m = n_i^m c^m, \quad when\ i > 1 \tag{24}$$

$$y_i^m = 1 - c^m \sum_{i=2}^{T} n_i^m \quad when\ i = 1 \tag{25}$$

The proof of Lemma 5 is similar. Finally, using Lemmas (4–5) and the approximation in Eq. 7, we obtain:

$$\mathcal{F}^{\max}(\lambda) = \sum_m \left[\sum_j n_j^m\right] \left[U^a(\mathbf{x}^m, \lambda^{\text{true}})\right.$$
$$\left. + fU_T^a(x_T^m) - (f+1)U^a(\mathbf{x}^m, \lambda)\right] \tag{26}$$

$$\mathcal{F}^{\min}(\lambda) = \sum_m \left[\sum_j n_j^m\right] \left[U^a(\mathbf{x}^m, \lambda^{\text{true}})\right.$$
$$\left. + fU_1^a(x_1^m) - (f+1)U^a(\mathbf{x}^m, \lambda)\right] \tag{27}$$

Observe that, given λ, $\mathcal{F}(\lambda, \cdot)$ is continuous in $\{y_i^m, c^m\}$. Therefore, given a λ', if $\mathcal{F}^{\max}(\lambda') \geq 0 \geq \mathcal{F}^{\min}(\lambda')$, there must exist $\{y_i^m, c^m\} \in \mathbf{S}$ such that $\mathcal{F}(\lambda', \{y_i^m, c^m\}) = 0$. In other words, λ' is a part of a feasible solution for (14–17). Conversely, if $\mathcal{F}^{\max}(\lambda') < 0$ or $\mathcal{F}^{\min}(\lambda') > 0$, it means λ' is not feasible for (14–17). Moreover, using Observation 1, we can infer that both $\mathcal{F}^{\max}$ and $\mathcal{F}^{\min}$ are continuous and decreasing in λ. We obtain Lemma 6 which states that feasible solutions of (14–17) form an interval.

Lemma 6. *Let us assume $\lambda_1 < \lambda_2$ are two feasible solutions of (14–17). Then any $\lambda \in [\lambda_1, \lambda_2]$ is also a feasible solution of the system.*

Proof. Since λ_1 and λ_2 are feasible solutions of (14–17), we obtain the inequalities:

$$\mathcal{F}^{\max}(\lambda_1) \geq 0 \geq \mathcal{F}^{\min}(\lambda_1)$$
$$\mathcal{F}^{\min}(\lambda_2) \geq 0 \geq \mathcal{F}^{\min}(\lambda_2)$$

For any $\lambda \in [\lambda_1, \lambda_2]$, since $\mathcal{F}^{\max}$ and $\mathcal{F}^{\min}$ are decreasing functions in λ, the following inequality holds true:

$$\mathcal{F}^{\max}(\lambda) \geq \mathcal{F}^{\max}(\lambda_2) \geq 0 \geq \mathcal{F}^{\min}(\lambda_1) \geq \mathcal{F}^{\min}(\lambda)$$

which implies that λ is also a feasible solution for (14–17), concluding the proof.

Lemma 7 specifies the interval $[\lambda_{\min}^{learnt}, \lambda_{\max}^{learnt}]$ of feasible λ values for (14–17).

Lemma 7. *There exist* $\lambda_{\max}^{learnt} \geq \lambda_{\min}^{learnt}$ *such that:*

$$\mathcal{F}^{\max}(\lambda_{\max}^{learnt}) = \mathcal{F}^{\min}(\lambda_{\min}^{learnt}) = 0,$$

which means $\lambda_{\min}^{learnt}$ *and* $\lambda_{\max}^{learnt}$ *are feasible solutions for (14–17) and any* $\lambda \notin [\lambda_{\min}^{learnt}, \lambda_{\max}^{learnt}]$ *is not a feasible solution for (14–17).*

Proof. As noted before, $\mathcal{F}^{\max}(\lambda)$ is a continuous and decreasing function in λ. On the other hand, we have:

$$\mathcal{F}^{\max}(\lambda = +\infty) = \sum_m \left[\sum_j n_j^m \right] \left[U^a(\mathbf{x}^m, \lambda^{\text{true}}) - U_T^a(x_T^m) \right] \leq 0$$

$$\mathcal{F}^{\max}(\lambda = -\infty) = \sum_m \left[\sum_j n_j^m \right] \left[U^a(\mathbf{x}^m, \lambda^{\text{true}}) \right.$$
$$\left. + f U_T^a(x_T^m) - (f+1) U_1^a(x_1^m)) \right] \geq 0$$

for all λ^{true} since $U^a(\mathbf{x}^m, \lambda^{\text{true}} = +\infty) = U_T^a(x_T^m)$ and $U^a(\mathbf{x}^m, \lambda^{\text{true}} = -\infty) = U_1^a(x_1^m)$ is the highest and lowest expected utilities for the attacker among all targets , respectively, and by Observation 1, $U^a(\mathbf{x}^m, \lambda^{\text{true}})$ is increasing in λ^{true}. Since $\mathcal{F}^{\max}(\lambda)$ is continuous, there must exist a value of $\lambda_{\max}^{learnt} \in (-\infty, +\infty)$ such that $\mathcal{F}^{\max}(\lambda_{\max}^{learnt}) = 0$. The proof for $\lambda_{\min}^{learnt}$ is similar.

Finally, for any $\lambda < \lambda_{\min}^{learnt}$, we have $\mathcal{F}^{\min}(\lambda) > \mathcal{F}^{\min}(\lambda_{\min}^{learnt}) = 0$ since $\mathcal{F}^{\min}$ is decreasing in λ. Similarly, for any $\lambda > \lambda_{\max}^{learnt}$, we have $\mathcal{F}^{\max}(\lambda) < \mathcal{F}^{\max}(\lambda_{\max}^{learnt}) = 0$. Both imply that λ is not feasible, concluding our proof.

By combining Lemmas 3, 6, and 7, we obtain Theorem 1.

Proof of Corollary 1

Proof. Corollary 1 is deduced based on the monotonicity property of the attacker's utility (Observation 1). When $\lambda_1^{\text{true}} \leq \lambda_2^{\text{true}}$, we have $U^a(\mathbf{x}^m; \lambda_1^{\text{true}}) \leq U^a(\mathbf{x}^m; \lambda_2^{\text{true}})$ for all m. Based on the relationship between $U^a(\mathbf{x}^m; \lambda^{\text{true}})$ and $U^a(\mathbf{x}^m; \lambda_{\max}^{\text{learnt}})$ presented in Theorem 1, we readily obtain $\lambda_{\max,1}^{\text{learnt}} \leq \lambda_{\max,2}^{\text{learnt}}$. Similarly, we have: $\lambda_{\min,1}^{\text{learnt}} \leq \lambda_{\min,2}^{\text{learnt}}$.

Proof of Corollary 2

Proof. We first prove (8). Let's consider the true behavior parameters $\lambda_1^{\text{true}} \leq \lambda_2^{\text{true}}$. Based on Corollary 1, the corresponding optimal deception solutions have to belong to the deception ranges: $\texttt{DecAlter}(\lambda_1^{\text{true}}) \in [\lambda_{\min,1}^{\text{learnt}}, \lambda_{\max,1}^{\text{learnt}}]$ and $\texttt{DecAlter}(\lambda_2^{\text{true}}) \in [\lambda_{\min,2}^{\text{learnt}}, \lambda_{\max,2}^{\text{learnt}}]$ where $\lambda_{\min,1}^{\text{learnt}} \leq \lambda_{\min,2}^{\text{learnt}}$ and $\lambda_{\max,1}^{\text{learnt}} \leq \lambda_{\max,2}^{\text{learnt}}$. We have two cases:

The first case is when the deception ranges do not overlap, i.e., $(\lambda_{\max}^1 < \lambda_{\min}^2)$. In this case, it is apparent that $\texttt{DecAlter}(\lambda_1^{\text{true}}) < \texttt{DecAlter}(\lambda_2^{\text{true}})$.

The other case is when the ranges overlap (i.e., $\lambda_1^{max} \geq \lambda_2^{min}$). If the optimal deceptive value for one or both does not belong to the overlap, i.e., $\texttt{DecAlter}(\lambda_1^{\text{true}}) < \lambda_{\min,2}^{\text{learnt}}$ and/or $\texttt{DecAlter}(\lambda_2^{\text{true}}) > \lambda_{\max,1}^{\text{learnt}}$), the result is clearly the same as in our previous case ($\texttt{DecAlter}(\lambda_1^{\text{true}}) < \texttt{DecAlter}(\lambda_2^{\text{true}})$). On the other hand, if both values fall within the overlap, that is $\lambda_{\min,2}^{\text{learnt}} \leq \texttt{DecAlter}(\lambda_1^{\text{true}}), \texttt{DecAlter}(\lambda_2^{\text{true}}) \leq \lambda_{\max,1}^{\text{learnt}}$, both will take on the same value ($\texttt{DecAlter}(\lambda_1^{\text{true}}) = \texttt{DecAlter}(\lambda_2^{\text{true}})$). This is true because both deceptive values $\texttt{DecAlter}(\lambda_1^{\text{true}})$ and $\texttt{DecAlter}(\lambda_2^{\text{true}})$ are being optimized to maximize the same objective: the utility of the deceptive attacker (as shown in $\texttt{DecAlter}$).

Finally, (9) can be easily deduced based on (8). Let's consider $\texttt{DecAlter}(\lambda_1^{\text{true}}) < \texttt{DecAlter}(\lambda_2^{\text{true}})$. We can prove $\lambda_1^{\text{true}} < \lambda_2^{\text{true}}$ by contradiction. That is, we assume $\lambda_1^{\text{true}} \geq \lambda_2^{\text{true}}$. According to (8), it means $\texttt{DecAlter}(\lambda_1^{\text{true}}) \geq \texttt{DecAlter}(\lambda_2^{\text{true}})$, which is a contradiction.

Proof of Corollary 3

Proof. Corollary 3 is a direct result of Corollary 2. Indeed, since $\lambda_1^{\text{true}} \leq \lambda^{\text{true}} \leq \lambda_2^{\text{true}}$, we obtain the inequality among optimal deception solutions $\texttt{DecAlter}(\lambda_1^{\text{true}}) \leq \texttt{DecAlter}(\lambda^{\text{true}}) \leq \texttt{DecAlter}(\lambda_2^{\text{true}})$ as a result of Corollary 2. Therefore if $\texttt{DecAlter}(\lambda_1^{\text{true}}) = \texttt{DecAlter}(\lambda_2^{\text{true}})$, we obtain the optimal deception solution: $\texttt{DecAlter}(\lambda^{\text{true}}) = \texttt{DecAlter}(\lambda_1^{\text{true}})$.

Proof of Lemma 1

Proof. Corollary 2 says that the deception outcome $\lambda^{\text{learnt}} = \texttt{DecAlter}(\lambda^{\text{true}})$ is an increasing (not strict) function of λ^{true}, and additionally using Corollary 3, we can say that given some deception outcome λ^{learnt}, there exists (unknown) $\lambda_{\min}^{\text{true}}, \lambda_{\max}^{\text{true}}$ such that any $\lambda^{\text{true}} \in [\lambda_{\min}^{\text{true}}, \lambda_{\max}^{\text{true}}]$ leads to the same outcome $\lambda^{\text{learnt}} = \texttt{DecAlter}(\lambda^{\text{true}})$. Any λ outside of the range $[\lambda_{\min}^{\text{true}}, \lambda_{\max}^{\text{true}}]$ cannot lead to the deception outcome λ^{learnt}. Corollary 2 further implies that $\lambda_{\min}^{\text{true}}$ and $\lambda_{\max}^{\text{true}}$ are increasing functions of λ^{learnt}.

Proof of Lemma 2

Proof. Assume WLOG, $U_1^a(x_1^m) \leq U_2^a(x_2^m) \leq \cdots \leq U_T^a(x_T^m)$. We claim that $S(i, \lambda^{\text{true}}) = \sum_{j=1}^{i} q_j(\mathbf{x}^m; \lambda^{\text{true}})$ for $T > i \geq 1$ is decreasing (not strictly) in λ^{true}, or in other words, the upper bound of the ith segment is decreasing (not strictly) for all i except $i = T$. This means that for any single fixed u value, increasing λ^{true} implies that $f_{\lambda^{\text{true}}}(u)$ is also increasing (or stays same) because the upper bound of the interval that u lies in shifts downwards as λ^{true} increases. $f_{\lambda^{\text{true}}}(u)$ increasing means a higher value target is chosen for attack. Thus, for fixed u, a higher λ^{true} implies that the empirical distribution places more (or equal) attacks on higher utility targets and hence $U^a(\mathbf{x}^m, E(u; \lambda^{\text{true}}))$ increases (not strictly) with λ^{true}. Finally, to prove our claim at the start of the proof, we show that the derivative of $S(i, \lambda^{\text{true}})$ is non-positive everywhere. Indeed, its derivative is computed as follows:

$$\sum_{j=1}^{i} q_j(\mathbf{x}^m; \lambda^{\text{true}}) U_j^a(x_j^m) - S(i, \lambda^{\text{true}}) U^a(\mathbf{x}^m; \lambda^{\text{true}})$$

$$= S(i, \lambda^{\text{true}}) \left[\sum_{j=1}^{i} \frac{q_j(\mathbf{x}^m; \lambda^{\text{true}})}{S(i, \lambda^{\text{true}})} U_j^a(x_j^m) - U^a(\mathbf{x}^m; \lambda^{\text{true}}) \right] \qquad (28)$$

decomposing the attacker utility function $U^a(\mathbf{x}^m; \lambda^{\text{true}})$, as follows:

$$S(i, \lambda^{\text{true}}) \sum_{j=1}^{i} \frac{q_j(\mathbf{x}^m; \lambda^{\text{true}})}{S(i, \lambda^{\text{true}})} U_j^a(x_j^m) +$$

$$\left(\sum_{j=i+1}^{T} q_j(\mathbf{x}^m; \lambda^{\text{true}}) \right) \sum_{j=i+1}^{T} \frac{q_j(\mathbf{x}^m; \lambda^{\text{true}})}{\sum_{j=i+1}^{T} q_j(\mathbf{x}^m; \lambda^{\text{true}})} U_j^a(x_j^m)$$

As we know that $U_1^a(x_1^m) \leq U_2^a(x_2^m) \ldots \leq U_T^a(x_T^m)$, the following inequality holds:

$$\sum_{j=i+1}^{T} \frac{q_j(\mathbf{x}^m; \lambda^{\text{true}})}{\sum_{j=i+1}^{T} q_j(\mathbf{x}^m; \lambda^{\text{true}})} U_j^a(x_j^m) \geq U_i^a(x_i^m) \geq \sum_{j=1}^{i} \frac{q_j(\mathbf{x}^m; \lambda^{\text{true}})}{S(i, \lambda^{\text{true}})} U_j^a(x_j^m)$$

Using this we get:

$$U^a(\mathbf{x}^m; \lambda^{\text{true}}) \geq \left(S(i, \lambda^{\text{true}}) + \sum_{j=i+1}^{T} q_j(\mathbf{x}^m; \lambda^{\text{true}}) \right) \sum_{j=1}^{i} \frac{q_j(\mathbf{x}^m; \lambda^{\text{true}})}{S(i, \lambda^{\text{true}})} U_j^a(x_j^m)$$

$$= 1 \cdot \sum_{j=1}^{i} \frac{q_j(\mathbf{x}^m; \lambda^{\text{true}})}{S(i, \lambda^{\text{true}})} U_j^a(x_j^m)$$

Using the above in the derivative Eq. 28, we get that the derivative of $S(i, \lambda^{\text{true}})$ is non-positive, hence it is decreasing w.r.t. λ, concluding our proof.

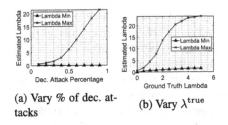

(a) Vary % of dec. attacks

(b) Vary λ^{true}

Fig. 4. Lambda range evaluation with 20 targets

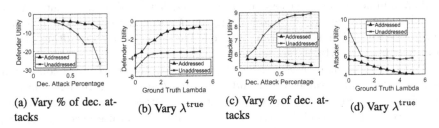

(a) Vary % of dec. attacks

(b) Vary λ^{true}

(c) Vary % of dec. attacks

(d) Vary λ^{true}

Fig. 5. Utility evaluation with 30 targets

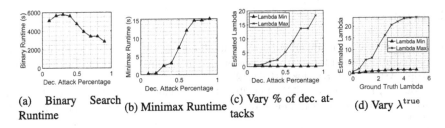

(a) Binary Search Runtime

(b) Minimax Runtime

(c) Vary % of dec. attacks

(d) Vary λ^{true}

Fig. 6. Runtime and λ evaluation with 30 targets

Supplemental Experiments. First, in Fig. 4, we examine the range $[\lambda_{\min}^{\text{true}}, \lambda_{\max}^{\text{true}}]$ that the defender learns. Figure 4a shows that the range increases w.r.t. the percentage of attacks controlled by the deceptive attacker. This is intuitive, as more manipulation gives more power to the deceptive attacker. Figure 4b displays how this range also increases with the ground truth λ^{true} value of the non-deceptive attackers. As λ^{true} increases, the deceptive attacker produces a larger uncertainty range.

Lastly, Figs. 6 through 5 are for 30-target games, and each corresponds to a previously discussed 20-target figure. We observe the same trends in both cases.

Experimental Details. All experiments were run on the same HPC cluster, on instances using dual E5-2690v4 processors (28 cores). Each process was allocated 16000 megabytes of RAM. Instances run Red Hat Enterprise Linux Server, version 7.8. The Matlab version used was R2018b.

All experiments used the L-Infinity norm with a value of 2 as a *rejection threshold* for non-deceptive attack samples. This is done to prevent outlying samples from compromising the binary search. Values between .5 and 5 for this metric were tested, along with the same value ranges for the L1 and L2 norms. This norm and value were shown to produce the best results, without drastically increasing the runtime of the algorithm.

Additionally, all experiments used a value of 0.05 as a *tolerance multiplier within the binary search itself.* This prevents the inherent inaccuracy of discrete attack samples from ruining binary search. For the sake of consistency, an initial random number generation seed of 1 was used across all experiments. After defender strategy generation and solving (`DecAlter`), the binary search is run 10 times, each with a different random seed. The superset of all resulting ranges forms our final uncertainty set for λ^{true}.

The trials shown in Figs. 4a, 2a, 2c, 3, 6c, 5a, 5c, and 6 were conducted using a true lambda value of 0.4 and a resource/target ratio of 0.2. Those in Figs. 4b, 2b, 2d, 6d, 5d, and 5d utilized a deceptive attack percentage of 0.3, and a resource/target ratio of 0.2. Experiments in Figs. 3 and use deceptive attack percentage of 0.1, a true lambda value of 0.4, and a resource/target ratio of 0.2.

References

1. Albarran, S.E., Clempner, J.B.: A Stackelberg security Markov game based on partial information for strategic decision making against unexpected attacks. Eng. Appl. Artif. Intell. **81**, 408–419 (2019)
2. Brown, A.L., Camerer, C.F., Lovallo, D.: To review or not to review? Limited strategic thinking at the movie box office. Am. Econ. J. Microecon. **4**(2), 1–26 (2012)
3. Camerer, C.F., Ho, T.H., Chong, J.K.: A cognitive hierarchy model of games*. Q. J. Econ. **119**(3), 861–898 (2004). https://doi.org/10.1162/0033553041502225
4. Fang, F., et al.: Deploying paws: field optimization of the protection assistant for wildlife security. In: IAAI 2016 (2016)
5. Gan, J., Guo, Q., Tran-Thanh, L., An, B., Wooldridge, M.: Manipulating a learning defender and ways to counteract. In: NIPS 2019 (2019)
6. Gan, J., Xu, H., Guo, Q., Tran-Thanh, L., Rabinovich, Z., Wooldridge, M.: Imitative follower deception in Stackelberg games. In: EC 2019 (2019)
7. Guo, Q., An, B., Bosansky, B., Kiekintveld, C.: Comparing strategic secrecy and Stackelberg commitment in security games. In: IJCAI (2017)
8. Hortaçsu, A., Luco, F., Puller, S.L., Zhu, D.: Does strategic ability affect efficiency? Evidence from electricity markets. AER **109**(12), 4302–4342 (2019)
9. Huang, L., Joseph, A.D., Nelson, B., Rubinstein, B.I., Tygar, J.D.: Adversarial machine learning. In: AISec (2011)
10. Kar, D., et al.: Cloudy with a chance of poaching: adversary behavior modeling and forecasting with real-world poaching data. In: AAMAS 2017 (2017)
11. Kingma, D.P.: Auto-encoding variational bayes. In: ICLR (2014)
12. Lowd, D., Meek, C.: Adversarial learning. In: ACM SIGKDD (2005)
13. Madry, A., Makelov, A., Schmidt, L., Tsipras, D., Vladu, A.: Towards deep learning models resistant to adversarial attacks (2017)

14. McKelvey, R.D., Palfrey, T.R.: Quantal response equilibria for normal form games. In: Games and Economic Behavior (1995)
15. Nguyen, T.H., et al.: Capture: a new predictive anti-poaching tool for wildlife protection. In: AAMAS 2016, pp. 767–775 (2016)
16. Nguyen, T.H., Sinha, A., He, H.: Partial adversarial behavior deception in security games. In: IJCAI (2020)
17. Nguyen, T.H., Vu, N., Yadav, A., Nguyen, U.: Decoding the imitation security game: handling attacker imitative behavior deception. In: 24th European Conference on Artificial Intelligence (2020)
18. Nguyen, T.H., Wang, Y., Sinha, A., Wellman, M.P.: Deception in finitely repeated security games. In: AAAI 2019 (2019)
19. Peng, B., Shen, W., Tang, P., Zuo, S.: Learning optimal strategies to commit to. In: 33th AAAI Conference on Artificial Intelligence (2019)
20. Perrault, A., Wilder, B., Ewing, E., Mate, A., Dilkina, B., Tambe, M.: Decision-focused learning of adversary behavior in security games. CoRR abs/1903.00958 (2019). http://arxiv.org/abs/1903.00958
21. Price, R.: A useful theorem for nonlinear devices having Gaussian inputs. IEEE Trans. Inf. Theory **4**, 69–72 (1958)
22. Sinha, A., Kar, D., Tambe, M.: Learning adversary behavior in security games: a PAC model perspective. In: AAMAS 2016 (2016)
23. Song, Y., et al.: Vital: visual tracking via adversarial learning. In: IEEE CVPR (2018)
24. Tambe, M.: Security and Game Theory: Algorithms, Deployed Systems, Lessons Learned. Cambridge University Press, Cambridge (2011)
25. Wilcox, R.: Applying Contemporary Statistical Techniques. Academic Press, Cambridge (2002)
26. Wright, J.R., Leyton-Brown, K.: Level-0 meta-models for predicting human behavior in games. In: EC 2014. ACM (2014). https://doi.org/10.1145/2600057.2602907
27. Yang, R., Kiekintveld, C., Ordonez, F., Tambe, M., John, R.: Improving resource allocation strategy against human adversaries in security games. In: IJCAI (2011)
28. Zhang, J., Wang, Y., Zhuang, J.: Modeling multi-target defender-attacker games with quantal response attack strategies. Reliab. Eng. Syst. Saf. **205** (2021)
29. Zhang, X., Zhu, X., Lessard, L.: Online data poisoning attack (2019)
30. Zhuang, J., Bier, V.M., Alagoz, O.: Modeling secrecy and deception in a multi-period attacker-defender signaling game. Eur. J. Oper. Res. **203**, 409–418 (2010)

Scalable Optimal Classifiers for Adversarial Settings Under Uncertainty

Benjamin Roussillon$^{(\boxtimes)}$ and Patrick Loiseau

Univ. Grenoble Alpes, Inria, CNRS, Grenoble INP, LIG, Grenoble, France
`benjamin.roussillon@inria.fr`

Abstract. We consider the problem of finding optimal classifiers in an adversarial setting where the class-1 data is generated by an attacker whose objective is not known to the defender—an aspect that is key to realistic applications but has so far been overlooked in the literature. To model this situation, we propose a Bayesian game framework where the defender chooses a classifier with no *a priori* restriction on the set of possible classifiers. The key difficulty in the proposed framework is that the set of possible classifiers is exponential in the set of possible data, which is itself exponential in the number of features used for classification. To counter this, we first show that Bayesian Nash equilibria can be characterized completely via functional threshold classifiers with a small number of parameters. We then show that this low-dimensional characterization enables us to develop a training method to compute provably approximately optimal classifiers in a scalable manner; and to develop a learning algorithm for the online setting with low regret (both independent of the dimension of the set of possible data). We illustrate our results through simulations.

1 Introduction

Detecting attacks such as spam, malware, or fraud is a key part of security. This task is usually approached as a *binary classification* problem where the defender classifies incoming data (login pattern, text features, or other data depending on the application) as legitimate (non-attack, modeled as class 0) or malicious (attack, modeled as class 1) [8,47].

It is well known that using standard classification algorithms for this task leads to poor performance because attackers are able to avoid detection by adjusting the data that they generate while crafting their attacks [36,45,46,51]. There is a vast literature on adversarial classification (see Sect. 1.1), but these works often propose ad-hoc defense methods optimized against specific attacks without fully modeling the attacker's adaptiveness. This leads to an arms race between attack and defense papers.

This work was supported by the French National Research Agency through the "Investissements d'avenir" program (ANR-15-IDEX-02) and through grant ANR-16-TERC0012; by the DGA; by the Alexander von Humboldt Foundation.

B. Bošanský et al. (Eds.): GameSec 2021, LNCS 13061, pp. 80–97, 2021.
https://doi.org/10.1007/978-3-030-90370-1_5

To better take into account the interaction between attacker and defender, several game-theoretic models of adversarial classification have emerged over the last decade (see Sect. 1.1). Most of them, however, have two crucial limitations. First, they restrict the possible classifiers to a specific set of known parameterized classifiers and assume that the defender only selects those parameters. Second, they assume complete information about the attacker's objective,[1] which is often too strong in practice [50].

In a recent paper, Dritsoula et al. [15] propose a model where the defender can select *any* classifier (i.e., function from the set of data to $\{0, 1\}$). A key difficulty lies in the exponential size of the resulting set of classifiers. The authors show that it is possible to restrict it to a small set of *threshold* classifiers on a function that appears in the attacker's payoff. The classifiers identified, however, have no parameter and their solution method is ad-hoc for the restrictive model chosen—with complete information and simplistic payoffs—, hence it cannot extend to more realistic scenarios. In realistic adversarial classification scenarios with uncertainty on the attacker's payoff, this leaves open the questions: *What classifiers should the defender use at equilibrium? And how to compute optimal classifiers in a scalable manner?*

In this paper, we answer both questions through the following contributions:

1. We introduce structural extensions to the model of [15] where the defender can choose any function from a set of data $\mathcal{V}$ to $\{0, 1\}$ as a classifier: we model the uncertainty of the defender on the attacker's payoff as a Bayesian game and use generalized payoffs (see Sect. 2.3).
2. We characterize the equilibrium of the game and exhibit a set of optimal threshold classifiers depending on a small number of parameters (in number independent of $|\mathcal{V}|$). Our method first uses a classical technique in resource allocation games (see Sect. 1.1) to establish a link between a mixed strategy on the set of classifiers and a 'random classifier' that assigns a probability in $[0, 1]$ to every data vector $v \in \mathcal{V}$. The set $\mathcal{V}$, however, is still exponentially large—this is the key challenge in our work. We then show that the 'random classifier' used by the defender at equilibrium has a specific form described with a small number of parameters, and that finding it is equivalent to maximizing a piecewise linear function of the previously mentioned parameters. This low-dimensional characterization has many interesting consequences: it enables using classical stochastic programming and online optimization techniques for efficient learning both online and offline in our game.
3. We show that our parametric expression of equilibrium classifiers allows the defender to train parameters on a labeled dataset with access to only limited information. In particular, our training method, which leverages classical stochastic programming techniques combined with our low-dimensional characterization, produces error bounds independent of $|\mathcal{V}|$ and does not require knowledge of the non-attack distribution. This gives much desired scalability since $|\mathcal{V}|$ is exponential in the number of features and might be large.

---

[1] with the exception [20], but which considers regression.

4. We illustrate our results through numerical simulations on different games, in particular a credit card fraud game built from the distributions in the publicly available real-world dataset [48] introduced in [12].

5. We also show that our parametric expression of equilibrium classifiers allows the defender to learn in an online setting—where they update the classifier and receive feedback from the classification at each time step—with very little regret (in particular, independent of $|\mathcal{V}|$). Additional illustrations for this setting are provided in [32].

Our results provide a basis for designing provably robust classifiers for adversarial classification problems. Our characterization of equilibrium strategies also emphasizes the potential of randomized operating point methods from [31]: our final classification algorithm can be seen as a randomized operating point on a non-trivial class of optimal threshold classifiers (see discussion below Theorem 1). Interestingly, we find that the set of optimal randomized defenses is of low pseudo-dimension. This highlights recent results by Cullina et al. [11]: in our model, facing adversaries simplifies the learning process as worst-case attacks are predictable while classical learning is chaotic (see discussion below Proposition 1). This is further supported by our finding that the set of optimal threshold classifiers is of VC dimension 1 [43]; hence our result could be interpreted in hindsight as showing that a reduction to classifiers of VC dimension 1 would come at no loss to the defender. Yet, we emphasize that there is no reason *a priori* why this set would be sufficient, it is a consequence of our results.

Due to space constraints, proofs and additional illustration are presented as supplementary material in [32].

1.1   Related Work

Adversarial Learning: The literature on adversarial learning usually studies two types of attacks: 'poisoning attacks', where the attacker can alter the training set to tamper the classifier's training [2,13,18,21,27,52]; and 'evasion attacks', where the attacker tries to reverse engineer a fixed classifier to find a negative instance of minimal cost [29,33,35]. This literature, however, does not fully model the attacker's adaptiveness, which often leads to an arms race. In recent years, the adversarial learning research focused on evasion attacks called adversarial examples that affect deep learning algorithms beyond attack detection applications [19,37,38]. These works, however, follow the same pattern. [11] extend PAC theory to adversarial settings and show that fundamental learning bounds can be extended to this setting and that the adversarial VC dimension can be either larger or smaller than the standard one.

Game-Theoretic Models of Adversarial Classification: A number of game-theoretic models of adversarial classification have been proposed, with various utility functions and hypotheses on the attacker's capabilities. Most of them, however, restrict a priori the possible classifiers: [52,53] rely on kernel methods; [23] assumes that the defender uses a single type of classifier (though unspecified in the model); [13] focuses on naive Bayes classifiers (and only compute one-stage best responses); [5,6] constrain the classifier to a specific form and look for the (pure) equilibrium value of the parameters; [28] uses a different model but also restrict to linear classifiers; [14] restricts the defender to a set of adversarially trained classifiers of different strengths; [29] uses a more general classifier, but restricts for most results to a family of classifiers constructed on a given basis (their model of the attacker is also more constrained than ours); and [31] abstracts away the classifier through a ROC curve (attacker and defender only select thresholds). In contrast, the objective of our work is to derive the optimal form of the classifiers so we do not make any restriction a priori on the classifiers used.

At the exception of [29,31], the aforementioned papers build deterministic classifiers while recent papers tend to advocate for randomization: [7] introduces random strategies on top of [5] while [39] highlights the importance of randomized attacks and [40] of randomized defenses (albeit without being able to characterize the equilibrium). In our work, we completely characterize the equilibrium and naturally find that it must involve randomized attack and defense strategies.

It is important to understand that these works consider two main types of model. [5,6,40] study *adversarial learning* problems where the learning problem is defined even without attackers (e.g., image recognition), whereas [13,23,28, 29,31,52,53] study *adversarial classification* where the learning problem is to detect attacks and exists only because there are attackers (e.g., spam filtering). These models lead to different attack methods and defenses. Our work belongs to the second category, of adversarial classification problems.

Security Games: Our game has similarities with *security resource allocation* games [1,3,4,9,16,24,34,42] used in applications such as airport security [41]. These works consider a defender with limited resources (e.g. guards) to be allocated to the defense of critical targets. In these settings, problems are at a relatively low scale and are usually entirely described via loss in case of attack of an undefended target. The challenge is the management of the limited amount of resources, which produces NP-hard problems [26] preventing these models to be transferred to very large scale settings. Our work studies a similar setting applied to classification, where targets would correspond to attack vectors in $\mathcal{V}$. In contrast to the security games literature, we do not impose limited resources (the defender self-restricts its detection to limit false alarm costs whereas in security games resources lead to hard constraints on the possible strategies), which eliminates the combinatorial issue. We are then able to provide a very different characterization of the solutions with applicability to classification as well as to scale to very large sets $\mathcal{V}$ that is never studied in classical security games and is the major challenge in our model.

Exponential Zero-Sum Games: Our game reparametrization with 'randomized classifiers' to reduce the dimension of the set of classifiers from $2^{|\mathcal{V}|}$ to $|\mathcal{V}|$ borrows ideas classical in security games. This technique is also studied for more generic zero-sum games [22]; but with objectives and limitations similar to security games.

2 Model

In this section we present our game-theoretic model. We introduce utility functions from the defender's viewpoint as we focus on optimal classifiers. We then introduce the probability of detection function as a tool to reduce complexity and discuss the model's assumptions and applicability.

2.1 Setting and Notation

Consider the following situation. A defender receives data samples that can be either attacks (class 1) or non-attacks (class 0) and wants to predict the class of incoming data. We assume that a data example is represented by a feature vector v that belongs to the same set $\mathcal{V}$ regardless of the class. This vector is typically a simplified representation of the actual attack/non-attack (e.g., spam/non-spam) in a feature space used to perform the classification. We assume that the probability that a data example is an attack, denoted p_a, is fixed.

Vectors corresponding to non-attacks follow a fixed probability distribution P_0 on $\mathcal{V}$ whereas vectors corresponding to attacks are generated by attackers. Attackers choose the vector they generate to maximize a utility function (see below) depending on the classification of the defender. To model the uncertainty of the defender, we assume that strategic attackers are endowed with a type $i \in \{1, \ldots, m\}$ that encodes their utility. The defender does not know the type of the attacker but holds a prior $(p_i)_{i \in \{1,\ldots,m\}}$ on the possible types.

The defender chooses a classifier in $\mathcal{C} = 2^{\mathcal{V}}$, that maps a vector to a predicted class. The defender maximizes a utility function balancing costs/gains in different cases as follows. A *false negative* incurs a loss $U_i^u(v)$ when facing a type-i attacker. A *true positive* incurs a gain $U_i^d(v)$ when facing a type-i attacker. A *false positive* incurs a false alarm cost $C_{\text{fa}}(v)$. A *true negative* incurs no cost. The attacker's gain is the opposite of the defender's for each classification outcome.

Summarizing the above discussion, the utilities of the attacker and defender, when the attacker is of type i, are defined as follows:

$$U_i^A(v, c) = U_i^u(v)\mathbb{1}_{c(v)=0} - U_i^d(v)\mathbb{1}_{c(v)=1}, \tag{1}$$
$$U_i^D(v, c) = -p_a U_i^A(v, c) - (1 - p_a) \sum_{v' \in \mathcal{V}} C_{\text{fa}}(v')P_0(v')\mathbb{1}_{c(v')=1}.$$

We assume that $\mathcal{V}$ is finite and all functions of v are arbitrary. Our main result, however, extends to $\mathcal{V}$ compact (details in [32] due to space constraints).

The above primitives define a Bayesian game that we denote by $\mathcal{G}$. Note that we assume that all parameters of the game including p_a, P_0, and the utility functions (but not the attacker's type) are known to both players. (We will discuss later how to relax this assumption.) As we will see, in this game, equilibria exist only in mixed strategy (intuitively, both players have an incentive to be unpredictable). For the defender, a mixed strategy β is a probability distribution on $\mathcal{C}$. A mixed strategy of the attacker is a function $\alpha : \{1, \ldots, m\} \rightarrow \Delta(\mathcal{V})$ such that for all $i \in \{1, \ldots, m\}$, α_i is a probability distribution over $\mathcal{V}$ chosen by a type-i attacker. Throughout the paper, we will use the standard solution concept of Bayesian Nash equilibrium, which intuitively prescribes that no player can gain from unilateral deviation.

Definition 1. (α^*, β^*) is a Bayesian Nash equilibrium (BNE) of the game $\mathcal{G}$ if and only if, for all α, β,

$$\sum_{i \in \{1, \ldots, m\}} p_i U_i^D(\alpha^*, \beta^*) \geq \sum_{i \in \{1, \ldots, m\}} p_i U_i^D(\alpha^*, \beta), \text{ and} \tag{2a}$$

$$\sum_{i \in \{1, \ldots, m\}} p_i U_i^A(\alpha^*, \beta^*) \geq \sum_{i \in \{1, \ldots, m\}} p_i U_i^A(\alpha, \beta^*). \tag{2b}$$

The defender's utility depends on the attacker they face. With the belief the defender holds on the probability of each attacker type, it is natural that the defender tries to maximize their average utility. The equilibrium is also described with the average utility of the different attacker types, but as the actions of different attacker types are unrelated it is equivalent to each type maximizing its own utility.

Finally, for all $i \in \{1, \ldots, m\}$, we define $\underline{G}_i = \max_{v \in \mathcal{V}} \left(-U_i^d(v) \right)$ and $\overline{G}_i = \max_{v \in \mathcal{V}} \left(U_i^u(v) \right)$, which respectively represent the minimum possible gain of the attacker (even if all vectors are always detected they can gain this quantity) and their maximum possible gain. Note that all results in our paper assume knowledge of these bounds (even when knowledge of utilities is limited). While finding these intervals is challenging if the utilities are arbitrary, they are easy to find in many applications from reasonable monotonicity assumptions on the utilities, as they simply represent the most damage an undetected/detected attack can cause.

2.2   Preliminary: Reduction of Dimensionality

A first difficulty of the model we study is the exponential size of $\mathcal{C}$ in $\mathcal{V}$. This issue is commonly found in resource allocation games (similar reparametrizations are found in other games such as dueling algorithms) and circumvented through the use of a probability of allocation function: only the probability that an abstract resource is allocated to a target is considered thus ignoring the actual allocation and removing combinatorial complexity (assuming that one can compute this function at equilibrium). In our case, in the spirit of [15], we define a probability of detection π, for any strategy β of the defender, as $\pi^\beta(v) = \sum_{c \in \mathcal{C}} \beta_c \mathbb{1}_{c(v)=1}$.

This transformation exploits the fact that, as long as a vector is detected, the actual classifier used for the detection is not important. Thus, with this probability of detection function, we can rewrite the payoffs independently of classifiers:

$$U_i^A(\alpha, \beta) = \sum_{v \in \mathcal{V}} \alpha_v^i \left[U_i^u(v) - \pi^\beta(v) \cdot \left(U_i^u(v) + U_i^d(v) \right) \right];$$

$$U_i^D(\alpha, \beta) = -p_a U_i^A(\alpha, \beta) - (1 - p_a) \sum_{v \in \mathcal{V}} C_{\text{fa}}(v) P_0(v) \pi^\beta(v). \tag{3}$$

Any probability of detection function can be attained through simple threshold classifiers crafted for this function. To see this, consider the set of threshold classifier $c(v) = \mathbb{1}_{\pi^\beta(v) \geq t}$ for some $t \in [0, 1]$. Then, picking a random threshold uniformly on $[0, 1]$ defines a strategy achieving detection probability $\pi^\beta(\cdot)$.

2.3   Model Discussion

The main motivating scenarios for our model are detection of malicious behaviors such as spam (in emails, social media, etc.), fraud (e.g., bank or click fraud), or illegal intrusion. In such scenarios, the attacker is the spammer, fraudster or intruder while the non-attacker represents a normal user (e.g., non-spam message). The vector v is a representation of the observed behavior on which the classification is done. For spam filtering, it can be a simplified representation of the messages obtained by extracting features such as number of characteristic words. The distribution P_0 represents the distribution over those features for normal messages (not chosen with any adversarial objective). In our basic model, we assume that it is known by both players. It is reasonable in applications where it can be estimated from observation of a large number of easily obtainable messages (e.g., in social medias they are public). We relax it in Sect. 3.2 and Sect. 4 where we show that the defender can learn well without a priori knowledge of P_0, p_a and p_i.

In our model the defender is uncertain of its own utility as soon as they have uncertainty regarding the attacker they face. Although not the most classical setting, it is meaningful and well studied in Bayesian games (see [17]). It is well justified in our case. For instance, if a fraudster manages to get access to sensitive information or to an account, the amount of harm may differ depending on the skills and resources of the fraudster. In these fraud settings it makes sense that the attacker's gain is the defender's loss or a fraction of it (e.g. a bank must reimburse its clients or pay higher insurance fees if it is victim of fraud). We note here that our model is still valid for this last case as we rely on zero-sum min-max properties which are robust to small changes such as multiplying factors.

The interaction between classifier and attacker is often modeled as a Stackelberg game where the attacker observes and reacts to the defender's strategy. We focus on the (Bayesian) Nash equilibrium which makes sense if the attacker cannot have perfect information about the defender's strategy. More generally though, we will see that in our game the defender's strategy at BNE must be min-max; hence, any strategy of the defender in a Stackelberg equilibrium would have the same property. We use the Stackelberg model in the online setting where there would be a bigger difference. Note that this min-max property also yields robustness.

Our payoff function generalizes that of [15] in a practically important way. In their model, a reward $R(v)$ is granted to an attack with vector v regardless of the outcome and a fixed detection cost c_d is paid if the attack is detected. This is unreasonable in many applications such as bank fraud. In our model, the utility in case of detected and undetected attacks are arbitrary unrelated functions of v (which is equivalent to letting the detection cost c_d depend on v). This alone breaks the ad-hoc method of [15] to compute the equilibrium. We also generalize to a Bayesian game (The complete information game is the case where $m = 1$), and consider training and online learning problems of practical importance.

3 BNE Characterization and Computation

In this section, we first characterize the equilibrium entirely and exhibit a class of threshold classifiers which are sufficient to define an optimal classifier. Leveraging this characterization, we then show how to compute approximately optimal strategies through training with limited knowledge.

3.1 Equilibrium Characterization

Finding a Bayesian Nash equilibrium is often hard in general games. A key property is that our game is essentially zero-sum and can be reduced to a min-max problem. Compiling this with the action space reduction via the probability of detection we are able to completely characterize the BNE.

Using the payoffs defined in (1), we can see that adding the false alarm term to the payoff of the attacker gives an equivalent Bayesian zero-sum game (as this term is independent from the action of the attacker this addition does not change their strategy). This transformation does not change the defender's payoff. This implies that at equilibrium they maximize their minimum average gain and gives the following lemma (whose proof can be found in [32]):

Lemma 1. *Let* (α^*, β^*) *be a BNE. Then*

$$\beta^* \in arg \max_{\beta} \min_{\alpha} \sum_i p_i U_i^D(\alpha, \beta). \tag{4}$$

Computing the min-max strategies of Lemma 1 can be done via a classical transformation to a linear program, but this "naive" program would be of size exponential in $|\mathcal{V}|$. Even by expressing it in terms of π^β, the program would remain of size $|\mathcal{V}|$, which may be too large. Instead, we will leverage the min-max property to show that the equilibrium can be described compactly using a small number of parameters $G = (G_1, \cdots, G_m)$ that can be interpreted as the utility of the attacker for each type. Formally, we define:

Definition 2 (Optimal probability of detection). *For any* $G \in [\underline{G}_1, \overline{G}_1] \times \dots \times [\underline{G}_m, \overline{G}_m]$, *let*

$$\pi_G(v) = \max \left\{ 0, \max_i \left\{ \frac{U_i^u(v) - G_i}{U_i^u(v) + U_i^d(v)} \right\} \right\}, \ \forall v \in \mathcal{V}. \tag{5}$$

As we will see, this quantity is the unique probability of detection that guarantees attacker utility below G while minimizing the false alarms, so it plays a key role in the BNE strategy. In particular, it allows us to express the strategy of the defender as the maximum of a concave function of G:

Definition 3 (Minimum gain function U^D) *For all* $\boldsymbol{G} \in [\underline{\boldsymbol{G}}_1, \overline{\boldsymbol{G}}_1] \times \ldots \times [\underline{\boldsymbol{G}}_m, \overline{\boldsymbol{G}}_m]$, *let* $U^D(\boldsymbol{G}) = -p_a \sum_i p_i G_i - (1 - p_a) \sum_{v \in \mathcal{V}} C_{fa}(v) P_0(v) \pi_G(v)$.

This function represents the minimum utility of the defender assuming they use a probability of detection function $\pi_G(\cdot)$ for some $\boldsymbol{G}$. It allows us to state our parametrization result which is the main tool we use to prove all our core results.

Proposition 1. *For any* $\boldsymbol{G}_{\max} \in arg\, max_{\boldsymbol{G} \in [\underline{\boldsymbol{G}}_1, \overline{\boldsymbol{G}}_1] \times \ldots \times [\underline{\boldsymbol{G}}_m, \overline{\boldsymbol{G}}_m]}(U^D(\boldsymbol{G}))$, *any strategy of the defender that yields a probability of detection function* $\pi_{\boldsymbol{G}_{\max}}(v)$ *for all* $v \in \mathcal{V}$ *is a min-max strategy and* $\max_\beta \min_\alpha \sum_i p_i U_i^D(\alpha, \beta) = U^D(\boldsymbol{G}_{\max})$.

A proof of Proposition 1 can be found in [32]. The proof relies on the min-max property of the problem which implies that the defender must maximize their minimum gain. We show that for a given utility profile $\boldsymbol{G}$, the minimum gain of the defender as defined in (4) is at least $U^D(\boldsymbol{G})$. However, the key difficulty is that not all utility profiles $\boldsymbol{G} \in [\underline{\boldsymbol{G}}_1, \overline{\boldsymbol{G}}_1] \times \ldots \times [\underline{\boldsymbol{G}}_m, \overline{\boldsymbol{G}}_m]$ are feasible and the set of feasible utility profiles needs not be convex due to our Bayesian game and arbitrary functions; hence $U^D(\boldsymbol{G})$ could be meaningless. Our proof bypasses this difficulty by showing that $\pi_{\boldsymbol{G}_{\max}}(\cdot)$ is a min-max strategy in any case and shows as a corollary that $\boldsymbol{G}_{\max}$ is a feasible utility profile.

Proposition 1 states that in order to find the equilibrium strategy, the defender should only find m parameters $(G_1, \cdots, G_m)$, corresponding to the maximum utility that it should let each attacker type gain. From those parameters, the probability of detection function is naturally defined. This has multiple consequences.

First, from this characterization we deduce that one does not need to know all the parameters of the problem to find a good strategy. Finding "good enough" parameters for the utility of the different attacker types allows the defender to fully define its strategy. This is the main tool allowing us to define strategies which can generalize to unknown vectors in Sect. 3.2. In particular, in Theorem 2 we prove that near-optimal (and even optimal with high probability) classifiers can be computed by training the model on a labeled dataset with very limited information. Note that this is a key difference between our work and security games where the probability of allocation is computed directly using a linear program. There, the lack of a simple expression for the allocation probability prevents the definition of strategies that can generalize. It is also worth noting that unlike linear programs, our method can be generalized to a continuous vector set—we refer to [32] for details about that.

Second, the result from Proposition 1 shows that the presence of strategic adversaries *simplifies* learning in our problem. Indeed, the class of real valued functions $\{\pi_G\}$ which contains the optimal strategy is of low pseudo-dimension (e.g., if there exist v_1 (resp. v_0) of class 1 (resp 0) with $U^u(v_0) > U^u(v_1)$ and $U^d(v_0) < U^d(v_1)$, these two points cannot be shattered). This can be explained by the predictable aspect of adversaries acting according to their best-response. On the contrary, when facing non-strategic adversaries the optimal strategy would be a cost-sensitive adaptation of the naive Bayes classifier, which can potentially be any arbitrary function of $2^{\mathcal{V}}$ (since we make no assumption on P_0). This is noteworthy as such a possibility was hinted at by Cullina et al. [11] who show that, for adversaries who can modify vectors in some neighborhood, the adversarial VC dimension can be either lower or higher than the standard one— i.e., the complexity can either increase or decrease in the presence of adversaries. In our adversarial classification model, the complexity drastically decreases. This suggests that classifiers relying on simply adapting classical training might be inefficient as they do not take into account the fundamental complexity differences between classical and adversarial learning.

With Proposition 1 describing the probability of detection function at equilibrium, we can deduce a characterization in terms of threshold classifiers.

Definition 4 (Generalized threshold classifiers). *For all $G \in \mathbb{R}^m$, define*

$$\mathcal{C}_G^T = \{c \in \mathcal{C} : c(v) = \mathbb{1}_{\pi_G(v) \geq t}, \forall v \in \mathcal{V} \text{ for some } t \in [0, 1]\}.$$

Theorem 1. *There exists $G \in \mathbb{R}^m$ such that the defender can achieve equilibrium payoff using only classifiers from $\mathcal{C}_G^T$.*

This theorem settles our first main question: "which classifiers should the defender use at the equilibrium?". These are threshold classifiers on a nonstandard function with threshold t representing a probability of detection. A threshold t can be interpreted as classifying a vector as an attack if, even when being detected with probability t, at least one type of attacker gains at least G_i on average. Interestingly, $\mathcal{C}_G^T$ has a VC dimension of only 1 as the set comprised of v_1 (resp. v_0) of class 1 (resp. 0) with $\pi_G(v_1) < \pi_G(v_0)$ cannot be shattered. This strengthens our previous remark on the complexity of adversarial classification. Efficient randomized classification for adversarial settings does not require high capacity classifiers but rather classifiers tailored to the players payoffs. Then, our threshold classifiers may be linear classifier if payoffs are linear as the condition $\pi_G(v) \geq t$ can be rewritten as $\max_i \{U_i^u(v) - G_i - t(U_i^u(v) + U_i^d(v))\} \geq 0$. Thus, in the linear setting, our threshold classifiers correspond to the defender picking a linear classifier for each type of attacker and outputting class 1 if at least one of the linear classifiers outputs it. In general however, linear classifiers may perform sub optimally.

The fact that the defender uses specifically threshold classifiers is noteworthy as there is already a literature on the choice of threshold and on this choice in an adversarial setting as in [31]. However, the random choice of the threshold in our setting is surprisingly simple – it is a threshold on the probability of detection and choosing a threshold uniformly over $[0, 1]$ gives the desired strategy. This emphasizes that randomization is necessary to defend against an adversary but also that the choice of the set of classifiers to use is crucial to obtain good results.

Having characterized the equilibrium, we must now answer our second main question "How can the defender compute optimal strategies in a scalable manner?". Before presenting a scalable training procedure exploiting our equilibrium parametrization to compute an approximate equilibrium (Sect. 3.2), let us notice that the equilibrium characterization naively leads to a linear programming solution polynomial in $|\mathcal{V}|$ to compute an exact equilibrium as function U^D is piecewise linear. This is presented in Proposition 2; note that a similar program could be obtained without our equilibrium characterization. We give in [32] a linear program that allows computing the attacker's strategy in time polynomial in $|\mathcal{V}|$.

Proposition 2. *Maximizing $U^D(\mathbf{G})$ is equivalent to solving the linear program:*

$$\underset{\pi,G}{maximize} \; -p_a \sum_{i=1}^{m} p_i G_i - (1-p_a) \sum_{v \in \mathcal{V}} C_{fa}(v) P_0(v) \pi_v$$
$$subject \; to: G_i \geq U_i^u(v) - \pi_v(U_i^u(v) + U_i^d(v)), \forall i, \forall v$$
$$\pi_v \leq 1, \forall v.$$

3.2   Scalable Approximate Computation

Our previous results allow computing the equilibrium in time polynomial in $|\mathcal{V}|$. Yet, two major challenges remain: (i) $|\mathcal{V}|$ may be too large, in particular it grows exponentially with the number of features k; and (ii) computing the equilibrium requires knowledge of all parameters of the game and in particular of P_0, which can be hard to evaluate. In this section, we propose a training method that solves both issues by leveraging stochastic programming techniques. To do so, we first express $U^D(\mathbf{G})$ as an expected value as follows: $U^D(\mathbf{G}) = E[U^D(\mathbf{G}, \xi)]$ where $U^D(\mathbf{G}, \xi) = G_i$ with probability $p_a p_i$ and $U^D(\mathbf{G}, \xi) = C_{fa}(v)\pi_G(v)$ with probability $(1-p_a)P_0(v)$ for all $v \in \mathcal{V}$. Leveraging the specific form of this stochastic function, we apply a stochastic programming technique called sample average approximation (SAA) [25,30,44,49] to obtain our training method, Algorithm 1.

Algorithm 1. Sample average approximation

Sample $\xi_1 \ldots, \xi_N$
Define $\tilde{U}^D(\mathbf{G}) = 1/N \sum_{i=1}^{N} U^D(\mathbf{G}, \xi_i)$
Maximize $\tilde{U}^D(\mathbf{G})$ on $[\underline{G}_1, \overline{G}_1] \times \ldots \times [\underline{G}_m, \overline{G}_m]$

The maximization step in Algorithm 1 can be done exactly through a linear program in the spirit of Proposition 2, in time polynomial in N since $\tilde{U}^D(\mathbf{G})$ is piecewise linear. Thus the complexity of this algorithm depends only on the sample size and not on the problem dimension. Additionally, very little information is required: the defender only needs to have access to N samples, which may correspond to a labeled dataset, as well as to the parameters $C_{fa}(v)$, $U_i^u(v)$, $U_i^d(v)$ for those samples, and $\underline{G}_i$, $\overline{G}_i$. Yet the following theorem shows that Algorithm 1 outputs an very good approximation of the defender's min-max strategy.

Theorem 2. *Let $\hat{S}$ be the set of maximizers of $\tilde{U}^D(\mathbf{G})$ from Algorithm 1 and $p_N = Pr[\hat{S} \subseteq arg\; max U^D(\mathbf{G})]$. We have*

$$\limsup_{N \to \infty} \frac{1}{N} \log(1-p_N) < 0.$$

A proof of Theorem 2 can be found in [32]. It relies on a strong result for sample average approximation (Theorem 15 of [44]), which fully exploits the structure of our problem as it requires the optimized stochastic function to be piecewise linear and to depend on random variables with finite support (extensions to continuous supports are possible under mild assumptions). This result is then enabled by the polyhedral structure of the problem.

Theorem 2 states that Algorithm 1 will find an exact maximum of $U^D(G)$ with probability exponentially close to one (where the randomness is in the draw of the training set from unknown P_0, p_a and p_i). Then, from Theorem 1, this immediately gives an exact min-max strategy of the defender. The rate of the exponential convergence of p_N to 1 is not given by Theorem 2. It is possible to state a stronger result that gives the rate if the problem is "well conditioned"—which roughly means that arg max $U^D(G)$ is a singleton and the function is not flat around the optimum—, but this is not guaranteed in any instance of our game, and such a result is anyways impractical because it depends on the true optimal value. From the high-probability result of Theorem 2, it is easy to derive that the output of Algorithm 1 is exponentially close to the true optimum since the function is bounded; although the exponential rate may be arbitrarily low if the problem is not well conditioned. In that case, though, worst case bounds show convergence of expected value at least in $N^{-1/2}$ and depending only on $Var[U^D(G_{\max}, \xi)]$ [44].

Theorem 2 combined with Theorem 1 shows that using SAA on top of our equilibrium characterization solves the key difficulties of our problem: we are able to compute an exact min-max strategy for the defender with high probability from a labeled training set without knowledge of P_0, p_a and p_i. It is remarkable that we do not need to estimate P_0 from the training set, this is automatically done within the stochastic approximation procedure. Other stochastic approximation algorithms (e.g., as stochastic gradient descent) could be used but without strong convexity property (which is our case since our function is piecewise linear), they only have convergence guarantees in $N^{-1/2}$.

3.3 Numerical Illustration

We performed numerical experiments on different games to illustrate various aspects of our results. In particular, we performed experiments on controlled artificial setups to illustrate the convergence of our training method, the (in)dependence on the number of features, and the form of the equilibrium with multiple attacker types. Due to space constraints, the results are deferred to [32], along with details on the experimental setup for reproducibility (all our code will be made public upon acceptance). We present here the results for a game defined with a real feature distribution from a credit card fraud dataset [48], to illustrate the form of the equilibrium for simple payoffs.

The dataset [48] contains transactions made by European cardholders in September 2013. A data vector is composed of 31 features: the amount of the transaction (in €) denoted A, the time since the first transaction in the dataset, whether the transaction was malicious (i.e., the label), and 28 anonymized features coming from a PCA. We instantiate our game with this static data set by replacing each attack in the data set by an abstract adaptative attack in our model. For simplicity, we focus only on the amount of the transaction and consider a single attacker type with the following gains: $U^u(v) = A$, $U^d(v) = 0$, and $C_{\mathrm{fa}}(v) = \ell \times A$ for a given $\ell > 0$. This models an attacker that gains the transaction's amount if successful (and the bank loses it), but gains nothing if detected. On the other hand, when a valid transaction is blocked, the bank pays a fraction ℓ of the transaction as false alarm cost. This choice of utility functions is meant to illustrate the equilibrium in a reasonable and simple scenario and not to represent a practical ready-to-implement setting. In the dataset, the fraction of attacks is $p_a = 0.00172$, the maximum transaction is $25,691.16€$ with an average of $88.35€$. There are $N = 284,807$ transactions in total.

Figure 1 represents the histogram of valid transaction amounts in $[0, 700]$ (where the majority of transactions occur) and the probability of detection function π_G obtained through our training for different values of ℓ (G_ℓ denotes the parameter trained on the dataset with false alarm cost factor ℓ). When ℓ is small, the defender classifies "aggressively" as fraud by accepting a high false alarm rate. When ℓ increases, the probability of detection functions show that the defender flags as fraud less often. For example, transactions of $700€$ are flagged with probability ~ 0.9 by the most aggressive strategy ($\ell = 0.006$) but only with probability ~ 0.1 for the least aggressive strategy ($\ell = 0.074$).

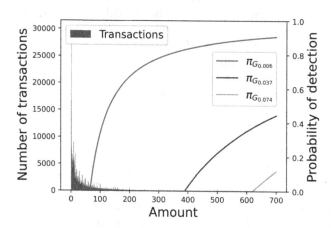

Fig. 1. Empirical distribution of transaction amounts and representation of defender min-max strategies for various l.

The results presented here are computed through our training method in Algorithm 1 and may not be exact. We evaluate the quality of our approximation on games based on artificial distributions (as we only have access to the empirical distribution). The results suggest that the approximation is good even for much smaller training sets as hinted by the theoretical guarantee. Computation times (not exceeding 15 min) can be found in [32].

4 Online Learning

In the previous section, we showed how the defender can compute an approximate min-max strategy from a training set. Yet, such historical data is not always available. We now show how our low-dimensional characterization of the min-max strategy also allows the defender to learn a good strategy *on-line*, without a priori knowledge of P_0, p_a and p_i, while incurring low loss as captured by the regret.

We consider the following setting. At each time step $t = 1, \ldots, T$, the defender chooses a probability of detection function π_t and receives a vector v_t that is classified as an attack with probability $\pi_t(v_t)$. They incur a loss $l(v_t)$ that is $C_{\text{fa}}(v_t)$ in case of false positive and 0 in case of true negative if facing a non-attacker; and $-U_i^d(v_t)$ and $U_i^u(v_t)$ in case of true positive and false negative respectively when facing a type i attacker. We assume that after classification, the defender can observe the type of attack (for convenience, we denote by type $i = 0$ non-attacks) and that they can compute $C_{\text{fa}}(v_t)$ and $U_i^u(v_t), U_i^d(v_t)$ for all i. Finally, as in [10], we assume that attackers act according to best responses to π_t in a Stackelberg fashion, i.e., if the defender faces an attacker of type i at time t we have $v_t \in \arg\max_v \{U_i^u(v)(1 - \pi_t(v)) - U_i^d(v)\pi_t(v)\}$. The defender seeks to minimize the Stackelberg regret:

Definition 5 (Stackelberg regret). *The Stackelberg regret for a sequence of vectors $(v_1, \ldots, v_T)$ is:* $R(T) = \sum_{t=1}^T E_{\pi_t}[l(v_t)] - \min_\pi \sum_{t=1}^T E_\pi[l(v_t)]$.

The notion of Stackelberg regret implies that the sequence of vectors depends on the probabilities of detection used. In particular, $\min_\pi \sum_t E_\pi[l(v_t)]$ must be computed using the best response of the attacker to π. It is also key to remember that in our setting, the unknown quantities are P_0, p_a and p_i. The attacker's strategy is assumed to be known as it is best-response to the utilities U_i^u, U_i^d.

It is possible to achieve low regret in T using naively the online gradient descent algorithm of [54]—see [32]—to learn π directly. This gives, however, a bound on the Stackelberg regret of

$$R(T) \leq \frac{D^2\sqrt{T}}{2} + \left(\sqrt{T} - \frac{1}{2}\right)L^2, \tag{6}$$

with $L = \max(\max_v\{C_{\text{fa}}(v)\}, \max_{v,i}\{|U_i^u(v)+U_i^d(v)|\})$ (maximum gradient) and $D^2 = |\mathcal{V}|$ (maximum L_2 distance between two π functions)—see a proof in [32]. This bound is meaningless if the number of features k is large as $|\mathcal{V}| = \Omega(2^k)$. The full strategy π also may not fit into memory.

Building on our characterization of the min-max strategy, we parametrize the defender's strategy by G to propose an alternate learning scheme as Algorithm 2 (where $\Pi_{\mathcal{S}}$ denotes the euclidean projection on a set $\mathcal{S}$).

Algorithm 2. Efficient online gradient descent

Choose $G_1 \in [\underline{G}_1, \overline{G}_1] \times \dots \times [\underline{G}_m, \overline{G}_m]$ arbitrarily
  for $t = 1, \dots, T$ **do**
    Predict π_{G_t} and receive vector v_t and type i
    if v_t came from a non-attacker **then**
      grad $\in \partial(\pi_{G_t}(v_t)C_{\text{fa}}(v_t))$
    else if v_t came from an attacker of type i **then**
      grad $= e_i$ (i^{th} vector of the canonical base of $\mathbb{R}^m$)
    $G_{t+1} = \Pi_{[\underline{G}_1,\overline{G}_1]\times\dots\times[\underline{G}_m,\overline{G}_m]}(G_t - \frac{1}{\sqrt{t}}\text{grad})$

Algorithm 2 exploits the fact that each attacker best responds to the defender's strategy, hence only strategies of the form $\pi_G(\cdot)$ are worth using. Thus, instead of learning directly π, the defender learns the parameters G. Note that this implies that the defender must be able to evaluate the bounds on the attackers' gain they can impose. Algorithm 2 presents two major advantages: *First*, the defender's strategy is compactly represented with a small number m of parameters, independent of $|\mathcal{V}|$. *Second*, we get a much better regret bound:

Theorem 3. *Algorithm 2 gives Stackelberg regret bound* (6) *with* $L = \max\{1, \max_{v,i}\{\frac{C_{fa}(v)}{U_i^d(v)+U_i^u(v)}\}\}$ *and* $D = ||\overline{G} - \underline{G}||_2$.

Theorem 3 is proved in [32]; the proof leverages our characterization of the min-max strategy with parameters G. The result formalizes the intuition that learning G rather than π allows a much smaller regret (D is now independent in $|\mathcal{V}|$). Parameter L^2 now represents the change in false alarm cost one can expect at worst when changing parameters G; which is different from L^2 in the naive procedure that corresponded to a gradient wrt π. We performed numerical experiments that illustrate the result of Theorem 3 (in particular the independence in $|\mathcal{V}|$) in [32]. In addition, we observe that G_t converges towards $G_{\max}$.

5 Concluding Remarks

We provided a low-dimensional characterization of the min-max strategy in adversarial classification games with general payoffs and showed that this characterization enables efficient training and online learning in practice. Our characterization also allows extending our results to continuous (compact) sets of data $\mathcal{V}$—see the details in [32].

We considered here only strategic attackers. It is possible to extend the model to include non-strategic attackers that follow fixed strategy, through a redefinition of the false alarm cost that preserves the game structure and allows all our results to be transferred. This can model attacks that are the result of a fixed algorithm. Attacks that are the result of an adaptive algorithm are outside the scope of the current work, but we note that for a wide class of adaptive algorithm this may be modeled in the long run through a utility function.

In the paper, we considered only strategic attackers maximizing their utility. It is possible, however, to extend the model to include non-strategic attackers that follow fixed strategy, through a redefinition of the false alarm cost that preserves the game structure and allows all our results to be transferred. This can be useful for instance to model attacks that are the result of a fixed algorithm. Modeling attacks that are the result of an adaptive algorithm may be more complex and is outside the scope of the current work, but we note that for a wide class of adaptive algorithm this may be well modeled in the long run through a utility function. (e.g. when attacks are the results of a fixed algorithms) in the analysis with minimal changes assuming that the benefits of detecting non-strategic attackers never outweighs the false alarm costs. This allows modeling non-strategic attackers by considering the difference between the previous two quantities as false alarm cost (which is then strictly positive). Non-strategic attackers with shifting strategies are, however, beyond the scope of this paper.

References

1. Balcan, M.-F., Blum, A., Haghtalab, N., Procaccia, A.D.: Commitment without regrets: online learning in Stackelberg security games. In: Proceedings of EC, pp. 61–78 (2015)
2. Barreno, M., Nelson, B., Joseph, A.D., Tygar, J.D.: The security of machine learning. Mach. Learn. **81**(2), 121–148 (2010). https://doi.org/10.1007/s10994-010-5188-5
3. Bošanský, B., Lisý, V., Jakob, M., Pěchouček, M.: Computing time-dependent policies for patrolling games with mobile targets. In: Proceedings of AAMAS, pp. 989–996 (2011)
4. Brown, M., Sinha, A., Schlenker, A., Tambe, M.: One size does not fit all: a game-theoretic approach for dynamically and effectively screening for threats. In: Proceedings of the Thirtieth AAAI Conference on Artificial Intelligence, pp. 425–431 (2016)
5. Brückner, M., Kanzow, C., Scheffer, T.: Static prediction games for adversarial learning problems. J. Mach. Learn. Res. **13**, 2617–2654 (2012)
6. Brückner, M., Scheffer, T.: Stackelberg games for adversarial prediction problems. In: Proceedings of ACM SIGKDD, pp. 547–555 (2011)
7. Bulò, S.R., Biggio, B., Pillai, I., Pelillo, M., Roli, F.: Randomized prediction games for adversarial machine learning. IEEE Trans. Neural Netw. Learn. Syst. **28**(11), 2466–2478 (2016)
8. Caruana, G., Li, M.: A survey of emerging approaches to spam filtering. ACM Comput. Surv. **44**(2), 9:1-9:27 (2012)
9. Chen, L., Leneutre, J.: A game theoretical framework on intrusion detection in heterogeneous networks. IEEE Trans. Inf. Forensics Secur. **4**(2), 165–178 (2009)
10. Chen, Y., Liu, Y., Podimata, C.: Learning strategy-aware linear classifiers. In: Proceedings of NIPS (2020)
11. Cullina, D., Bhagoji, A.N., Mittal, P.: PAC-learning in the presence of adversaries. In: Advances in Neural Information Processing Systems (NIPS), vol. 31, pp. 230–241 (2018)
12. Pozzolo, A.D., Caelen, O., Johnson, R.A., Bontempi, G.: Calibrating probability with undersampling for unbalanced classification. In: 2015 IEEE Symposium Series on Computational Intelligence, pp. 159–166. IEEE (2015)

13. Dalvi, N., Domingos, P., Mausam, Sanghai, S., Verma, D.: Adversarial classification. In: Proceedings of ACM KDD, pp. 99–108 (2004)
14. Dasgupta, P., Collins, J.B., McCarrick, M.: Improving costs and robustness of machine learning classifiers against adversarial attacks via self play of repeated Bayesian games. In: The Thirty-Third International Flairs Conference (2020)
15. Dritsoula, L., Loiseau, P., Musacchio, J.: A game-theoretic analysis of adversarial classification. IEEE Trans. Inf. Forensics Secur. **12**(12), 3094–3109 (2017)
16. Fang, F., Jiang, A.X., Tambe, M.: Optimal patrol strategy for protecting moving targets with multiple mobile resources. In: Proceedings of AAMAS, pp. 957–964 (2013)
17. Forges, F.: Chapter 6 Repeated games of incomplete information: non-zero-sum. In: Aumann, R., Hart, S. (eds.) Handbook of Game Theory with Economic Applications, vol. 1, pp. 155–177. Elsevier (1992)
18. Globerson, A., Roweis, S.: Nightmare at test time: robust learning by feature deletion. In: Proceedings of ICML (2006)
19. Goodfellow, I., Shlens, J., Szegedy, C.: Explaining and harnessing adversarial examples. In: ICLR (2015). arXiv:1412.6572
20. Großhans, M., Sawade, C., Brückner, M., Scheffer, T.: Bayesian games for adversarial regression problems. In: Proceedings of ICML, pp. III-55-III-63 (2013)
21. Huang, L., Joseph, A.D., Nelson, B., Rubinstein, B.I.P., Tygar, J.D.: Adversarial machine learning. In: Proceedings of ACM AISec, pp. 43–58 (2011)
22. Immorlica, N., Kalai, A.T., Lucier, B., Moitra, A., Postlewaite, A., Tennenholtz, M.: Dueling algorithms. In: Proceedings of STOC, pp. 215–224 (2011)
23. Kantarcioglu, M., Xi, B., Clifton, C.: Classifier evaluation and attribute selection against active adversaries. Data Min. Knowl. Disc. **22**(1), 291–335 (2011). https://doi.org/10.1007/s10618-010-0197-3
24. Kiekintveld, C., Jain, M., Tsai, J., Pita, J., Ordóñez, F., Tambe, M.: Computing optimal randomized resource allocations for massive security games. In: Proceedings of AAMAS, pp. 689–696 (2009)
25. Kim, S., Pasupathy, R., Henderson, S.G.: A guide to sample average approximation. In: Fu, M.C. (ed.) Handbook of Simulation Optimization. ISORMS, vol. 216, pp. 207–243. Springer, New York (2015). https://doi.org/10.1007/978-1-4939-1384-8_8
26. Korzhyk, D., Conitzer, V., Parr, R.: Complexity of computing optimal Stackelberg strategies in security resource allocation games. In: Proceedings of AAAI, pp. 805–810 (2010)
27. Laskov, P., Lippmann, R.: Machine learning in adversarial environments. Mach. Learn. **81**(2), 115–119 (2010). https://doi.org/10.1007/s10994-010-5207-6
28. Li, B., Vorobeychik, Y.: Feature cross-substitution in adversarial classification. In: Proceedings of NIPS, pp. 2087–2095 (2014)
29. Li, B., Vorobeychik, Y.: Scalable optimization of randomized operational decisions in adversarial classification settings. In: Proceedings of AISTATS (2015)
30. Linderoth, J., Shapiro, A., Wright, S.: The empirical behavior of sampling methods for stochastic programming. Ann. Oper. Res. **142**(1), 215–241 (2006). https://doi.org/10.1007/s10479-006-6169-8
31. Lisý, V., Kessl, R., Pevný, T.: Randomized operating point selection in adversarial classification. In: Calders, T., Esposito, F., Hüllermeier, E., Meo, R. (eds.) ECML PKDD 2014. LNCS (LNAI), vol. 8725, pp. 240–255. Springer, Heidelberg (2014). https://doi.org/10.1007/978-3-662-44851-9_16
32. Loiseau, P., Roussillon, B.: Scalable optimal classifiers for adversarial settings under uncertainty (2021)

33. Lowd, D., Meek, C.: Adversarial learning. In: Proceedings of ACM KDD, pp. 641–647 (2005)
34. Marecki, J., Tesauro, G., Segal, R.: Playing repeated Stackelberg games with unknown opponents. In: Proceedings of AAMAS, pp. 821–828 (2012)
35. Nelson, B., et al.: Near optimal evasion of convex-inducing classifiers. In: Proceedings of AISTATS (2010)
36. Nelson, B., et al.: Misleading learners: co-opting your spam filter. In: Yu, P.S., Tsai, J.J.P. (eds.) Machine Learning in Cyber Trust: Security, Privacy, and Reliability, pp. 17–51. Springer, Boston (2009). https://doi.org/10.1007/978-0-387-88735-7_2
37. Papernot, N., McDaniel, P., Sinha, A., Wellman, M.: Towards the science of security and privacy in machine learning. In: Proceedings of IEEE EuroS&P, April 2018
38. Papernot, N., McDaniel, P., Wu, X., Jha, S., Swami, A.: Distillation as a defense to adversarial perturbations against deep neural networks. In: Proceedings of IEEE S&P, May 2016
39. Perdomo, J.C., Singer, Y.: Robust attacks against multiple classifiers, CoRR (2019)
40. Pinot, R., Ettedgui, R., Rizk, G., Chevaleyre, Y., Atif, J.: Randomization matters. how to defend against strong adversarial attacks. In: Proceedings of ICML (2020)
41. Pita, J., et al.: Using game theory for Los Angeles airport security. AI Mag. **30**, 43–57 (2009)
42. Schlenker, A., et al.: Deceiving cyber adversaries: a game theoretic approach. In: Proceedings of AAMAS, pp. 892–900 (2018)
43. Shalev-Shwartz, S., Ben-David, S.: Understanding Machine Learning: From Theory to Algorithms. Cambridge University Press, Cambridge (2014)
44. Shapiro, A.: Monte Carlo sampling methods. Handbooks Oper. Res. Manag. Sci. **10**, 353–425 (2003)
45. Sommer, R., Paxson, V.: Outside the closed world: on using machine learning for network intrusion detection. In: Proceedings of IEEE S&P (2010)
46. Thomas, K., McCoy, D., Grier, C., Kolcz, A., Paxson, V.: Trafficking fraudulent accounts: the role of the underground market in twitter spam and abuse. In: Proceedings of USENIX Security, pp. 195–210 (2013)
47. Tsai, J.J.P., Yu, P.S. (eds.): Machine Learning in Cyber Trust: Security, Privacy, and Reliability. Springer, Heidelberg (2009). https://doi.org/10.1007/978-0-387-88735-7
48. ULB. Credit card fraud detection (2013). https://www.kaggle.com/mlg-ulb/creditcardfraud/version/3
49. Verweij, B., Ahmed, S., Kleywegt, A.J., Nemhauser, G., Shapiro, A.: The sample average approximation method applied to stochastic routing problems: a computational study. Comput. Optim. Appl. **24**(2–3), 289–333 (2003). https://doi.org/10.1023/A:1021814225969
50. Vorobeychik, Y., Kantarcioglu, M.: Adversarial Machine Learning. Synthesis Lectures on Artificial Intelligence and Machine Learning. Morgan & Claypool (2018)
51. Wang, G., Wang, T., Zheng, H., Zhao, B.Y.: Man vs. machine: practical adversarial detection of malicious crowdsourcing workers. In: Proceedings of USENIX Security, pp. 239–254 (2014)
52. Zhou, Y., Kantarcioglu, M.: Adversarial learning with Bayesian hierarchical mixtures of experts. In: Proceedings of SIAM SDM, pp. 929–937 (2014)
53. Zhou, Y., Kantarcioglu, M., Thuraisingham, B., Xi, B.: Adversarial support vector machine learning. In: Proceedings of KDD, pp. 1059–1067 (2012)
54. Zinkevich, M.: Online convex programming and generalized infinitesimal gradient ascent. In: Proceedings of ICML, pp. 928–936 (2003)

Learning Generative Deception Strategies in Combinatorial Masking Games

Junlin Wu[1]($\boxtimes$), Charles Kamhoua[2], Murat Kantarcioglu[3],
and Yevgeniy Vorobeychik[1]

[1] Washington University, Saint Louis, MO 63130, USA
{junlin.wu,yvorobeychik}@wustl.edu
[2] Army Research Laboratory, Adelphi, MD 20783, USA
charles.a.kamhoua.civ@mail.mil
[3] University of Texas, Dallas, TX 75080, USA
muratk@utdallas.edu

Abstract. Deception is a crucial tool in the cyberdefence repertoire, enabling defenders to leverage their informational advantage to reduce the likelihood of successful attacks. One way deception can be employed is through obscuring, or masking, some of the information about how systems are configured, increasing attacker's uncertainty about their targets. We present a novel game-theoretic model of the resulting defender-attacker interaction, where the defender chooses a subset of attributes to mask, while the attacker responds by choosing an exploit to execute. The strategies of both players have combinatorial structure with complex informational dependencies, and therefore even representing these strategies is not trivial. First, we show that the problem of computing an equilibrium of the resulting zero-sum defender-attacker game can be represented as a linear program with a combinatorial number of system configuration variables and constraints, and develop a constraint generation approach for solving this problem. Next, we present a novel highly scalable approach for approximately solving such games by representing the strategies of both players as neural networks. The key idea is to represent the defender's mixed strategy using a deep neural network generator, and then using alternating gradient-descent-ascent algorithm, analogous to the training of Generative Adversarial Networks. Our experiments, as well as a case study, demonstrate the efficacy of the proposed approach.

Keywords: Deception games · Masking strategies · Generative adversarial networks

1 Introduction

The use of deception in cyber defense has a long tradition. Honeynets are perhaps the most popular examples [8,21,26], but numerous other ideas, such as adding fake information or changing observable configurations of machines or networks have also been explored [2,23–25,28]. While many such studies have either

B. Bošanský et al. (Eds.): GameSec 2021, LNCS 13061, pp. 98–117, 2021.
https://doi.org/10.1007/978-3-030-90370-1_6

focused on lower-level implementation issues or qualitative analysis, there has emerged a robust literature that formally models deception as a game-theoretic interaction between a defender and an attacker [11, 12, 15, 18, 20, 24, 25, 28, 31].

While game-theoretic models of deception are fundamentally appealing, as they aspire to use deploy such tools even while accounting for highly sophisticated adversaries who carefully reason about it, approaches are typically either highly stylized and qualitative [4, 12, 19], or use game representations that do not scale well with dimensionality of system configuration space [11, 24, 28]. For example, Schlenker et al. [24] represent the set of possible system attributes and possible deceptions (which, in this work, involve observable characteristics of the systems) by enumerating all possibilities. This representation, however, is exponential in the number of system attributes, and real systems may have hundreds of these. Furthermore, much of recent work on deception presumes that the attacker's decision amounts to the choice of a target system to attack. In real cybersecurity encounters, attacks are launched via exploits, and once an exploit is developed, it can in principle be used nearly indiscriminately against *any machine which has the vulnerable operating system, applications, required open ports, and so on.* To the extent that exploit deployment against a particular organizational network is automated, *all* vulnerable machines can be targeted simultaneously.

We build on the insight offered by Shi et al. [25], who represent systems that are to be defended using a collection (vector) of features. Deception in their model entails modifications to individual features, subject to linear constraints. Unlike this, and much of other prior work, however, we turn our attention to a relatively underinvestigated means for deception through *masking*, rather than changing true system attributes. As shown recently, masking can be just as effective as changing features [9], but is in practice often easier to implement.

Specifically, we introduce a *combinatorial masking game (CMG)*, in which a defender controls a collection of potentially vulnerable computers, each characterized by a vector of features (e.g., OS type and version, applications installed and their versions, etc.). The defender (whom we call Alice) chooses a subset of features to mask for each machine. The attacker (whom we name Bob), in turn, observes the non-masked features of all machines, as well as which features are masked and which are not, and in response chooses an exploit to execute against the *entire collection of defender's computers*. Consequently, all of the computers which contain the exploited vulnerability are viewed as successfully compromised, and the attacker gains (while the defender loses) the total value of these (which is, in general, a function of their *true* features).

The game above is a zero-sum Bayesian game, and we seek its Bayes-Nash equilibrium which characterizes both the mixed strategies of the defender (i.e., the randomized deception strategy) and of the attacker. Our first step is to derive a linear programming (LP) formulation of the Bayes-Nash equilibrium solution of this game. Unfortunately, the resulting LP is even intractable to represent as we increase the number of features, since the strategies of both players are combinatorial in size. Our solution is to represent the strategies of both players as neural networks. This is straightforward for the attacker, as he chooses among a set of exploits, which we explicitly enumerate. For the defender, however, we need to represent a probability distribution over all possible masking strategies—a set combinatorial in the feature space dimension. Adding a constraint generation procedure helps, but the approach still fails to scale beyond tiny problem instances. Our solution is to represent these as *generative neural networks*, akin to the generator in Generative Adversarial Networks (GANs) [10]. Since both strategies are now differentiable, we develop a gradient descent-ascent algorithm for learning these (resulting in an approximate Bayes-Nash equilibrium), which is inspired by the algorithm used for training GANs (although the specifics of the training process, such as the loss function, are quite different).

Finally, we evaluate the proposed approach experimentally. First, we show that our approach is near-optimal (compared to linear programming) on small problem instances, with significantly better scalability. Next, we compare it with three baselines: random masking, unconditional masking, (independent of actual device configuration), and a heuristic greedy approach for masking. We show that while random masking is extremely fast, it typically results in solutions that are much worse for the defender. Greedy heuristic yields better solutions, but our approach still offers a significant improvement over this approach, and is in fact also much more scalable. Proposed approach also yields better solutions than unconditional masking. We close with a case study of a synthetic example that illustrates the nature of our solutions.

2   Related Work

One of the most common concrete instantiations of deception are honeypots and honeynets [8,21,26]. One of the main ideas behind honeypots is to detect and investigate cyber threats, taking advantage of the information asymmetry that favors the defender, who knows which of their machines are real and which are honeypots, in contrast to the attackers who, at least in theory, do not. This idea has a number of variations, such as adding "honey" (fake) accounts and fake data [1,3,13].

One of the early abstractions of cyber deception was proposed by Cohen, who studied it as a problem of guiding attackers through a benign part of an attack graph [5–7]. A further formalization of this idea was to investigate how deception can impact the evolution of the attacker's beliefs [9,12].

One of the earliest game-theoretic modeling approaches to deception was through *signaling games*, in which a defender (sender) has a type that they may deceptively communicate (signal) to an attacker (receiver) [4,19]. However, these models were relatively abstract and simplistic. An alternative paradigm of security games, in which the interactions between a defender, who protects a set of targets, and an attacker, who chooses the best target to attack, provided a higher-resolution game-theoretic modeling framework for studying strategic security interactions [27]. This framework then gave birth to some of the most recent investigations of deceptive signaling in security, leveraging the defender's informational advantage about which targets have been chosen to be protected (which is only observed by the attacker after they choose the target to attack) [22, 29, 30].

Several recent game-theoretic models for deception provide the core intellectual precedent for our work. Schlenker et al. [24] introduced the idea of observable configurations as the defender's strategy space, with the attacker choosing a target to attack after reasoning about the posterior distribution of actual, given observable, configurations. The key technical limitation in that work is the requirement of fully enumerating the entire configuration space (both actual and observed) in the model. Shi et al. [25] address this limitation by proposing a factored (feature-based) representation of these, but the game-theoretic model they use involves a myopic bounded-rational attacker who does not explicitly reason about deception. We build on both of these, using both a feature-based representation of the problem that enables us to take algorithmic advantage of problem structure, but at the same time model attackers as fully rational—that is, fully reasoning about deception.

Our approach of using generative neural networks to represent defender's mixed strategies is partly inspired by Generative Adversarial Networks (GANs) [10] and conditional GANs [17], as well as the use of such representations in fictious play algorithms for solving games [14]. Our key idea is to use conditional GANs that are a function of a true configuration to learn an implicit mixed strategy for the defender. This is also quite unlike Kamra et al., who learn unconditional generative model as a randomized *best response* to a fixed memory of actions by the other players.

3   Deception Through Attribute Masking

Consider a defender (Alice) in charge of security for an organizational network comprised of a collection of m devices. Each device is characterized by a feature vector of attributes $x = (x_i)_{i \in [n]}$, where $[n]$ denotes the set $\{1, \ldots, n\}$. Each attribute, x_i, in turn, can take on one of a finite collection of values, i.e., $x_i \in X_i \subseteq \{-1, 1, \ldots, V\}$, where the attribute value of -1 corresponds to a default configuration (e.g., application is not installed, port is not open) or to "N/A" (e.g., a version number of an application that is not installed), and V the largest possible attribute value. When there are multiple devices on the network, we represent each device by x^k. However, we will omit this superscript when it is either not relevant, or not important.

This defender faces an attacker (Bob) who aspires to compromise as many of these devices as he can. More precisely, let $v(x)$ be the value to the attacker successfully compromising a device with configuration x; we assume that $v(x)$ is also the loss to the defender in the event of compromise. If S is a set of devices the attacker successfully compromises, the resulting utility of the attacker (and loss to the defender) is then $\sum_{k \in S} v(x^k)$.

The means that the attacker uses for his ends is to choose an exploit e from a collection of actionable exploits E. The set E can be alternatively viewed as a collection of exploitable vulnerabilities, and the attacker chooses one of these to develop a custom exploit for, leveraging any additional information about the target network. We assume that the attacker chooses only a single exploit from this collection. Each exploit $e \in E$ is associated with a set of configurations that the exploit requires to successfully execute. We assume that this set, which we denote by X^e, can be specified as a conjunction of required sets for each attribute, that is, $X^e = \{X_1^e, \ldots, X_n^e\}$, where $X_i^e = [a_{i1}, \ldots, a_{il_i}] \subseteq X_i$. The interpretation is that the value of each attribute x_i must be in the set X_i^e in order for the exploit e to successfully execute. For example, an exploit may target all versions of a Chrome browser between versions 75 and 85 installed on Windows 10 versions 1500-1900, as long as ports 23 and 25 are open. Note that the values of most attributes may not be relevant to attack execution, in which case $X_i^e = X_i$. We use notation $x \in X^e$ to mean that configuration x satisfies the requirements of the exploit e and, consequently, the device with this configuration can be compromised by e.

Once an exploit e is chosen by Bob, *all* the devices on Alice's network which can be successfully attacked by it are compromised. The gain to Bob, and loss to Alice, is then $\sum_{k=1}^{m} v(x^k)\delta(x^k \in X^e)$, where $\delta(\cdot)$ is an indicator function which is 1 if the condition is True and 0 otherwise.

To deal with this predicament, Alice (the defender) can mask a subset of configuration attributes of her devices. Let $y^k \in \{0, 1\}^n$ denote this mask applied to device k, where $y_i^k = 0$ means attribute i of device k is suppressed (not observable) and $y_i^k = 1$ means that it can be observed (by Bob, the attacker, as well as, potentially others). Thus, we only allow suppression of attributes, but not changing their observed values as done in prior work [24,25]. In addition, and crucially, we assume that the masked attributes cannot be easily inferred from the observed ones (except by the attacker computing a posterior, as discussed below). Of course, masking is costly for a number of reasons. For example, information about attributes can be important to broadcast to ensure proper implementation choices and application compatibility. We let $c(y^k)$ denote the cost of choosing a mask y^k for a device k. We assume that the total masking cost is additive over devices, that is, $c(y^1, \ldots, y^m) = \sum_k c(y^k)$.

Given a true configuration x^k and a mask y^k for a device k, the attacker observes two things: 1) the mask y^k (inability to see the particular attributes of the device gives it away) and 2) the true values of the *observable* attributes, which we denote by $\tilde{x}^k = x^k \odot y^k$, where $\odot$ is a Hadamard product. Indeed, note that $\tilde{x}^k$ actually captures all of the relevant information, since in our notation above, $\tilde{x}_i^k = 0$ necessarily implies that attribute i is not observed (since observed values do not include 0 in our problem encoding). This notation will prove convenient below.

The game which we described above, which we call a *Combinatorial Masking Game (CMG)*, constitutes a Bayesian game in which (x^k) (the actual configurations of the devices) is private information of the defender, while the attacker observes $(\tilde{x}^k)$, observable features after masks y^k have been applied to all devices k. Let $p(x^1, \ldots, x^m)$ be the prior distribution over device configurations on the network, which is common knowledge to both Alice and Bob. As noted above, the utility (after all uncertainty is resolved) of both players depends *only* on the configurations x^k of the defender's devices and the exploit chosen by the attacker e, but *not Alice's masking choices* y^k, which serve solely as a means of deception. Since this is a Bayesian game, the defender's mixed strategy is a probability distribution over masks y^k conditional on actual configurations x^k. Letting $\mathbf{y}$ and $\mathbf{x}$ be the vectors that concatenate the masks chosen by the defender for all devices and the actual device features, respectively, we formally denote her mixed strategy by $q(\mathbf{y}; \mathbf{x}) = \Pr\{\mathbf{y}|\mathbf{x}\}$. The attacker's mixed strategy, in turn, is the probability of choosing an exploit e given his observation of the devices $\tilde{x}^k$, which we concatenate into a vector $\tilde{\mathbf{x}}$. Formally, we denote this by $z(e; \tilde{\mathbf{x}}) = \Pr\{e|\tilde{\mathbf{x}}\}$.

We denote by $u(q, z)$ the expected utility of the attacker choosing a mixed strategy z while the defender chooses q. Our goal is to compute a (mixed-strategy) Bayes-Nash equilibrium (BNE) of this zero-sum game. In our setting, a strategy profile (q^*, z^*) is a BNE if

$$q^* \in \arg\min_{q}\left(u(q, z^*) + \mathbb{E}_{\mathbf{y} \sim q}[c(\mathbf{y})]\right) \text{ and } z^* \in \arg\max_{z} u(q^*, z).$$

Note that since this game is strategically zero-sum, the BNE strategy q^* of Alice is also her Stackelberg equilibrium strategy [16].

4   Computing Equilibrium Deception Strategies

Recall that our goal is to compute a BNE of the game presented in Sect. 3. We begin our discussion of BNE computation in *CMGs* by considering a single device in the charge of the defender. In Sect. 5 we extend the approach to an arbitrary collection of such devices. Since we are dealing with a single device, we omit the superscripts k throughout this section.

Central to our task will be to derive the precise expressions for the best responses of both the attacker and defender. These expressions will subsequently naturally lead to a linear programming representation of our problem, which in turn yields the first (but highly intractable) solution approach. We begin by deriving an expression for the attacker's best response problem.

4.1   Computing the Attacker's Best Response

Consider a defender who plays a mixed strategy $q(y; x)$, where x is the true feature vector for the (single) device, while y is the associated mask, and $\tilde{x}$ is the feature vector for the device observed by the attacker. We now derive an expression for the attacker's best response to this strategy.

The first step is to obtain the attacker's posterior distribution over the device configuration x given observation $\tilde{x}$ (where we explicitly use both $\tilde{x}$ and y as observations for clarity):

$$b(x; \tilde{x}, y) \equiv \Pr\{x|\tilde{x}, y\} = \frac{\Pr\{\tilde{x}, y|x\}p(x)}{p(\tilde{x}, y)},$$

where $p(\tilde{x}, y) = \sum_x \Pr\{\tilde{x}, y | x\} p(x)$. Now, note that

$$\Pr\{\tilde{x}, y | x\} = \Pr\{\tilde{x} | y, x\} \Pr\{y | x\} = \Pr\{\tilde{x} | y, x\} q(y; x) = \delta(\tilde{x} = x \odot y) q(y; x).$$

Based on the definition of $\tilde{x}$, if $\tilde{x} = x \odot y$, then $\Pr\{\tilde{x} | y, x\} = 1$, and otherwise, it is 0. Thus, we can represent $\Pr\{\tilde{x} | y, x\}$ using the indicator function $\delta(Cond)$ where $\delta(Cond) = 1$ if $Cond$ is true, and 0 otherwise.

Since a successful attack on the device with configuration x yields the attacker a value $v(x)$ which is lost to the defender, the utility of the attacker for deploying exploit e after observing $(\tilde{x}, y)$ is

$$u_a(e, \tilde{x}, y, q) = \sum_x v(x) b(x; \tilde{x}, y) \delta(x \in X^e)$$

$$= \frac{1}{p(\tilde{x}, y)} \sum_x v(x) q(y; x) p(x) \delta(x \in X^e) \delta(\tilde{x} = x \odot y).$$

Next, recall that $z(e; \tilde{x})$ represents the attacker's mixed strategy, that is, the probability distribution over exploits e chosen. Moreover, it is important to keep in mind that $\tilde{x}$ is (implicitly) a function of y, which is observed by the attacker, as well as x, which is not. The attacker's optimal utility is then

$$u_a^*(\tilde{x}, y, q) = \max_z \sum_e z(e; \tilde{x}) u_a(e, \tilde{x}, y, q), \tag{1}$$

that is, this is the maximum utility that the attacker achieves by choosing an optimal exploit to deploy against the defender's device.

Finally, we will use a mathematical trick to rewrite the attacker's best response condition in a form that will prove more convenient. Note that mathematically, it makes no difference if we optimize z separately for each $(\tilde{x}, y)$, or simultaneously over all $(\tilde{x}, y)$ where we maximize *expected utility* with respect to the prior distribution $p(\tilde{x}, y)$ over configurations. Thus, for the attacker, the maximization problem in Eq. (1) is equivalent to

$$u_a^*(q) = \max_z \sum_{\tilde{x}, y} p(\tilde{x}, y) u_a^*(\tilde{x}, y, q) \tag{2a}$$

$$= \max_z \sum_{\tilde{x}, y} \sum_e z(e; \tilde{x}) \sum_x v(x) q(y; x) p(x) \delta(x \in X^e) \delta(\tilde{x} = x \odot y) \tag{2b}$$

$$= \max_z \sum_x p(x) \sum_y q(y; x) \sum_e z(e; \tilde{x}) v(x) \delta(x \in X^e), \tag{2c}$$

where $\delta(\tilde{x} = x \odot y)$ and the sum over $\tilde{x}$ are no longer necessary, since we are already summing over x and y and the terms where $\tilde{x} \neq x \odot y$ will yield 0.

4.2   Computing the Defender's Best Response

We now turn to deriving a similar expression for the defender's best response to an attacker's mixed strategy $z(e; \tilde{x})$.

For the defender, who knows x, chooses y, and faces an attack e, the utility is

$$u_d(e, y; x) = -(v(x)\delta(x \in X^e) + c(y)).$$

Since the defender actually chooses a randomized strategy $q(y; x)$ and aims to maximize the utility over all such strategies q in response to the attacker's mixed strategy $z(e; \tilde{x})$, the optimal expected utility for the defender is

$$u_d^*(z; x) = -\min_q \sum_y q(y; x) \left(\sum_e z(e; \tilde{x}) v(x) \delta(x \in X^e) + c(y) \right). \tag{3}$$

Moreover, maximizing the defender's utility for a given x is equivalent to maximizing the expected utility with respect to the prior distribution $p(x)$. Thus, we can redefine the defender's ex ante utility as follows:

$$u_d^*(z) = -\min_q \sum_x p(x) u_d^*(z; x) \tag{4a}$$

$$= -\min_q \sum_x p(x) \sum_y q(y; x) \left(\sum_e z(e; \tilde{x}) v(x) \delta(x \in X^e) + c(y) \right) \tag{4b}$$

4.3 Computing Equilibrium Deception

Recall that the pair of strategies (q, z) constitute a (Bayes-)Nash equilibrium iff they jointly satisfy Eqs. (2c) and (4b). Since this game is zero-sum, BNE deception strategy and Bayes-Stackelberg equilibrium deception coincide, and we consequently focus on computing a BNE deception strategy for the defender (the attacker's equilibrium strategy ultimately serves as a means to that end).

We can rewrite the BNE of the deception game as the following minimax problem:

$$\min_q \max_z \ \sum_x p(x) \sum_y q(y; x) \left(\sum_e z(e; \tilde{x}) v(x) \delta(x \in X^e) + c(y) \right). \tag{5}$$

This, in turn, can be represented as the following linear program (LP):

$$\min_{q \geq 0, u_a^*} \ u_a^* + \sum_x p(x) \sum_y q(y; x) c(y) \tag{6a}$$

$$\text{s.t. :} \tag{6b}$$

$$u_a^* \geq \sum_x p(x) \sum_y q(y; x) \left(\sum_e z(e; \tilde{x}) v(x) \delta(x \in X^e) \right) \quad \forall \, z(e; \tilde{x}) \tag{6c}$$

$$\sum_y q(y; x) = 1 \quad \forall \, x \tag{6d}$$

$$\sum_e z(e; \tilde{x}) = 1 \quad \forall \, \tilde{x}, y. \tag{6e}$$

Note that here, the Constraints (6c) are for all possible attack strategies (i.e., functions of $\tilde{x}$). However, since there is always a pure strategy best response, we can restrict this to consider only *deterministic* attack strategies. Nevertheless, the set of constraints is exponential in possible $\tilde{x}$, in addition to the fact that the number of variables in this LP is exponential (ranging over the entire domains of x and y). Consequently, even though we can use standard tools, such as CPLEX, to solve this LP in principle, scalability will be severely limited.

Algorithm 1: Constraint generation algorithm for solving the linear programming.

Input: Exploits set $E = \{e_1, e_2, \cdots\}$; $p(x)$; cost function c
Output: Optimal utility for defender and attacker; defender's optimal strategy $q(y; x)$; attacker's optimal strategy $z(e; \tilde{x})$.
Initialization: randomly generate some attacker's strategy $\{z(e; \tilde{x})\}$ set Z;
$err \leftarrow \infty$; tolerance ϵ;
while $err > \epsilon$ **do**

    1. Solve defender's LP:

$$\min_{q \geq 0, u_a^*} \quad u_a^* + \sum_x p(x) \sum_y q(y; x) c(y)$$

    s.t. :

$$u_a^* \geq \sum_x p(x) \sum_y q(y; x) \left(\sum_e z(e; \tilde{x}) v(x) \delta(x \in X^e) \right) \quad \forall\, z(e; \tilde{x}) \in Z$$

$$\sum_y q(y; x) = 1 \quad \forall\, x.$$

    2. Fix $q(y; x)$ from defender's LP solution and solve the attacker's LP:

$$\max_{z \in \{0,1\}} \quad \sum_x p(x) \sum_y q(y; x) \left(\sum_e z(e; \tilde{x}) v(x) \delta(x \in X^e) \right)$$

    s.t. :

$$\sum_e z(e; \tilde{x}) = 1 \quad \forall\, \tilde{x}, y.$$

    3. Add attacker's LP solution $\{z(e; \tilde{x})\}$ to Z
    4. Calculate $err \leftarrow$ Abs(defender's LP obj - $\sum_x p(x) \sum_y q(y; x) c(y)$ - attacker's LP obj)
end

To partially address the scalability challenge, we can use constraint generation to avoid explicitly enumerating Constraints (6c) corresponding to possible attacks. Algorithm 1 formalizes this approach, which at the high level proceeds as follows. We start with a small set of constraints (attacker strategies), solve the resulting relaxed LP, then compute the attacker's best response, which is added to the LP, and the process is then repeated until convergence. Note that although we still need to enumerate the attacker strategies in computing the best response, we avoid the key bottleneck, which is *space* complexity (having to explicitly represent the LP with all of the constraints in memory is a greater bottleneck than enumeration of these).

Although using constraint generation can significantly reduce the size of the LPs we have to store in memory, it will still scale poorly in the dimensionality n of the feature representation space of the devices. Next, we describe our approach for entirely side-stepping the scalability challenge by representing the defender and attacker mixed strategies as neural networks, and then solving the game using a gradient-based method.

4.4   Scalable Approximation of Equilibrium Deception Through Generative Adversarial Masking

To solve *CMGs* at scale, we now propose a novel gradient-based learning method inspired by generative adversarial networks (GANs), which we term *generative adversarial masking (GAM)*. The key idea is to first represent the strategies of both players using deep neural networks, and then leverage an alternating gradient descent-ascent algorithm with the defender's expected loss as the objective.

To begin, we rewrite Eq. (5) in a manner that will prove especially convenient. Specifically, note that this expression is equivalent to first taking the expectation with respect to $x \sim p(x)$ (i.e., x distributed according to the prior distribution $p(x)$), and then taking the expectation with respect to $y \sim q(y; x)$, where the distribution is actually defined by the defender's mixed strategy, and conditional on x. We thus rewrite Eq. (5) as follows:

$$\min_q \max_z \quad \mathbb{E}_{x \sim p(x)} \mathbb{E}_{y \sim q(y;x)} \left(\sum_e z(e; \tilde{x}) v(x) \delta(x \in X^e) + c(y) \right). \tag{9}$$

Now, suppose we represent the attacker's strategy $z(e; \tilde{x})$ as a deep neural network with parameters θ, i.e., $z(e; \tilde{x}; \theta)$. Of course, we need to ensure that this is a valid probability distribution over E, but that is straightforward to implement by adding a softmax layer, just as in standard classification problems. The strategy of the attacker is then simply a parametric function, with parameters θ, that takes $\tilde{x}$ as input and outputs a distribution over e, as desired.

The representational idea above does not, however, work for the defender, as it is inherently intractable to *explicitly* represent an arbitrary probability distribution over y (since the number of outputs becomes exponential). Instead, we propose to use a *conditional generative neural network (CGNN)* (or simply *generator*) as an *implicit* representation of this distribution, as is done in GANs. A CGNN takes two inputs: 1) the conditioning input x (which in our case is the true device configuration), and 2) a random variable $r \in [0, 1]^n$, which we assume is distributed uniformly at random. We write the resulting CGNN representation as (deep neural network) $Q(x, r; \beta)$, where β are the neural network parameters. For a given input (x, r), the CGNN *deterministically* outputs y; consequently, since r is generated stochastically, Q induces a probability distribution over y conditional on x. Moreover, since r is a valid probability distribution, so is Q. By optimizing its parameters β, we can now optimize the probability distribution Q. Since $y \in \{0,1\}^n$, we use sigmoid layer as the last layer of $Q(x, r; \beta)$ neural network and binarize y every k iterations (k is a hyperparameter determined through experiment trials), as well as the last iteration using 0.5 as the threshold to ensure the neural network can be properly trained and the final output y generated by Q is a binary vector.

Rewriting everything using both the CGNN Q and the neural network for representing the attacker's best response z, we obtain

$$\min_{\beta \geq 0} \max_{\theta \geq 0} \quad \mathbb{E}_{x \sim p(x)} \mathbb{E}_{y \sim Q(x,r;\beta)} \left(\sum_e z(e; \tilde{x}; \theta) v(x) \delta(x \in X^e) + c(y) \right).$$

The final useful observation is that the sole source of stochasticity in y is the randomness of generated uniform random r, with $y = Q(x, r; \beta)$. Consequently, we can rewrite as follows:

$$\min_{\beta \geq 0} \max_{\theta \geq 0} \quad \mathbb{E}_{x \sim p(x)} \mathbb{E}_{r \sim U^n} \left(\sum_e z(e; x \odot Q(x, r; \beta); \theta) v(x) \delta(x \in X^e) + c(Q(x, r; \beta)) \right),$$

where U^n is a uniform distribution over $[0, 1]^n$. Observe that now both expectations are unconditional, and so the order no longer matters.

To obtain the final algorithm for learning β and θ, we simply approximate the expectations using finite samples of x and r, and alternate gradient descent (for updating β and gradient ascent (for updating θ) until convergence. Algorithm 2 presents the complete learning procedure.

5   Extension to Multiple Devices

In this section we extend the single-device approach presented in Sect. 4 to a setting where the defender controls the security for multiple devices. Suppose that the defender has m devices on the network whose configurations follow the distribution $\mathbf{x} = (x^1, \cdots, x^m) \sim p(\mathbf{x})$. The defender chooses the masking strategy $\mathbf{y} = (y^1, \cdots, y^m) \sim q(\mathbf{y}; \mathbf{x})$. The attacker observes $\tilde{\mathbf{x}} = (\tilde{x}^1, \cdots, \tilde{x}^m)$ and chooses an exploit $e \in E$, which will target *all of the devices on the defender's network*, affecting a subset of them that are vulnerable to the chosen exploit. The attacker and defender's optimal utility functions, after fixing the strategy of the counterpart, become

$$u_a^*(q) = \max_z \sum_{\mathbf{x}} p(\mathbf{x}) \sum_{\mathbf{y}} q(\mathbf{y}; \mathbf{x}) \sum_e z(e; \tilde{\mathbf{x}}) \sum_k v(x^k) \delta(x^k \in X^e)$$

$$u_d^*(z) = -\min_q \sum_{\mathbf{x}} p(\mathbf{x}) \sum_{\mathbf{y}} q(\mathbf{y}; \mathbf{x}) \left(\sum_e z(e; \tilde{\mathbf{x}}) \sum_k v(x^k) \delta(x^k \in X^e) + c(\mathbf{y}) \right).$$

Algorithm 2: The *GAM* gradient descent-ascent algorithm for training N_Q and N_z neural networks. N_Q represents the neural network for $q(y; x)$ and N_z represents the neural network for $z(e; \tilde{x})$.

Input: Exploits set $E = \{e_1, e_2, \cdots\}$; $p(x)$; cost function c; number of samples k

Output: Optimal utility for attacker; optimal utility for defender; $(y^{(i)}, x^{(i)})$ which embeds the defender's optimal strategy $q(y; x)$; the attacker's optimal strategy $z(e; \tilde{x})$.

Initialization;

Sample $\{(x^{(1)}, r^{(1)}), \cdots, (x^{(k)}, r^{(k)})\}$ where $r \sim U^n$ and $x \sim p(x)$;

for *number of training iterations* **do**

    for *number of N_z training* **do**

        Update N_z by using gradient descent-ascent to maximize the objective

        $\nabla_{\theta_z} \frac{1}{k} \sum_{i=1}^{k} (\sum_e N_z(e; x^{(i)} \odot N_Q(x^{(i)}, r^{(i)}; \beta_Q); \theta_z) v(x^{(i)}) \delta(x^{(i)} \in X^e))$;

    end

    Update N_Q by using gradient descent-ascent to minimize the objective

    $\nabla_{\beta_Q} \frac{1}{k} \sum_{i=1}^{k} (\sum_e N_z(e; x^{(i)} \odot N_Q(x^{(i)}, r^{(i)}; \beta_Q); \theta_z) v(x^{(i)}) \delta(x^{(i)} \in X^e) + c(N_Q(x^{(i)}, r^{(i)}; \beta_Q)))$;

end

The corresponding min-max problem becomes:

$$\min_q \max_z \quad \sum_{\mathbf{x}} p(\mathbf{x}) \sum_{\mathbf{y}} q(\mathbf{y}; \mathbf{x}) \left(\sum_e z(e; \tilde{\mathbf{x}}) \sum_k v(x^k) \delta(x^k \in X^e) + c(\mathbf{y}) \right).$$

This can be solved using a straightforward variation of Algorithm 2, with the strategy representations and loss function modified as above.

6   Experiments

6.1   Near-Optimality of Generative Adversarial Masking

Our first goal is to evaluate the quality of solutions produced by the proposed *GAM* approach. The only reliable way to do this is to compare to optimal solutions, but as we noted earlier, our lone approach for computing optimal solutions to combinatorial masking games is the LP with constraint generation (*LP+CG*), which scales poorly. Our first set of experiments, therefore, is focused on small-scale problem instances in order to evaluate how close to optimal the *GAM* solutions are. For these experiments, we let $x \in \{-1, 1\}^n$ and $p(x)$ is a uniform distribution. We let $c(y) = \sum_i 0.01(1 - y_i)$, while $v(x) = \frac{1}{2} \sum_i (x_i + 1)$ (that is, the number of features that are 1). We draw 5000 samples of x and r in *GAM* algorithm training. All results are averages of 100 draws of actual device configurations $\mathbf{x}$ (observable to the defender). For each dimension n in this experiment we pre-generated 2 exploits (specified in Table 1) for all of the runs; these constructed a prior (and not randomly generated) in order to avoid trivial solutions. The *GAM* is trained on GPU NVIDA GeForce GTX 1050 Ti using Pytorch and Cuda. Linear programs are solved using CPLEX with tolerance set to 10^{-5}. Recall that n denotes the number of device features while m is the number of devices.

Table 1. Comparison between *LP+CG* and *GAM*.

n	m	Exploit Requirements*	defender loss		run time (seconds)	
			LP+CG	*GAM* (mean)	*LP+CG*	*GAM*
2	2	$[-1, 1], [1, -1]$	1.52	1.57 ± 0.07	1.9	1.7
4	1	$[-1, 1, -1, -1], [1, -1, 1, 1]$	1.25	1.26 ± 0.03	1.3	1.7
5	1	$[-1, 1, 1, -1, -1], [-1, -1, 1, -1, 1]$	0.88	0.90 ± 0.04	5.6	1.9
6	1	$[-1, 1, 1, -1, -1, -1], [-1, -1, 1, -1, 1, -1]$	1.01	1.04 ± 0.06	64	1.9

* Note that we use a simpler representation here than above: 1 represents that the configuration has to be 1, while -1 means the associated feature does not matter.

The results are presented in Table 1, and show that the *GAM* approach yields near-optimal solutions. Moreover, even at this scale we can already observe a dramatic advantage it has in scalability: even when $n = 6$, the *LP+CG* method clocks in at 64 s, whereas the running time of *GAM* is nearly unchanged (1.7–1.9 s) between $n = 2$ and $n = 6$.

6.2   Systematic Large-Scale Experiments

Experiment Setup. Our next goal is to investigate the efficacy of the *GAM* approach to solving combinatorial masking games at scale, in comparison to several baselines. Throughout, we let $c(y) = \sum_i c(1 - y_i)$, where c is a constant we systematically vary in the experiments.

The feature vector x^k for each device on the defender's network is constructed i.i.d. according to the following model. The first three dimensions correspond to the Operating System installed, for which we have three options: Windows, Linux, or Mac OS. The next three dimensions correspond to the associated versions of each of these installed, and we constrain that exactly one OS is installed, and only one version of it. The last 50% of the features correspond to ports (which may be either open, -1, or closed, 1); we constrain that at least one port is open on each device. The remaining features correspond to applications (binary, corresponding to installed, or not) and their associated versions, with the constraint that an installed application has only a single version. The features corresponding to versions are -1 if the associated OS/application is not installed, and integers between 1 and V otherwise, where V is set to either 1 (i.e., binary attributes) or 3 as specified in the experiments below. Aside from the constraints above, each x^k is generated uniformly at random (i.e., we randomly choose which OS and applications are installed, which versions of these, and which ports are open). We set $v(x) = 1 + [$the number of installed applications$]$.

We construct the set of exploits (the size of which we systematically vary) as follows. Each exploit $e \in E$ either targets a contiguous sequence of versions of a particular OS, or a contiguous sequence of versions of both an OS and an application. In either case, a particular target port is required to be open for the exploit to succeed. All choices above are made uniformly at random. For each experimental setting, we tune the parameters of *GAM* through a pre-testing phase. In all cases, *GAM* takes 10^4 samples of x and r, and the results provided are averages of 10^3 runs. In the experiments we use GPU NVIDIA TITAN Xp, GeForce RTX 2080Ti, and GeForce GTX 1080Ti using Pytorch and Cuda.

Baseline Approaches. We compare *GAM* to the following three baselines:

Random Masking. This is a simple baseline in which the mask is chosen uniformly at random from $\{0,1\}^n$ for any $\mathbf{x}$. Since the run time of this is negligible, we do not report it below.

Unconditional Masking. A natural baseline is to use a simpler mixed strategy for the defender $q(\mathbf{y}; \mathbf{x})$ which is independent of $\mathbf{x}$, i.e., $q_{unc}(\mathbf{y})$. We can still apply a simplified version of the *GAM* approach to compute the associated distribution.

Greedy Masking. Greedy search generates the mask y by iteratively minimizing the expected marginal loss. We initialize y as not masking any configurations. In each step, we decide whether to mask an (additional) attribute that has not yet been masked, choosing an attribute that yields than greatest reduction in expected loss to the defender (and stopping if this is negative). Note that here we also assume that the masking strategy y is independent of x. Even in this case, greedy masking is time consuming, since in order to evaluate the marginal impact of masking we need to execute the attacker's best response, which itself entails training the best response neural network z.

Results. We begin by comparing *GAM* with the *unconditional masking* baseline in which $q_{unc}(\mathbf{y})$ does not depend on the true state $\mathbf{x}$ (in game-theoretic language, this would correspond to a *pooling strategy*, which is uninformative as regards to the true device attributes). In this experiment, we consider a single device, fix $c = 0.05$ and set $V = 3$, and further simplify by considering a single possible version for each OS and application.

The results are shown in Fig. 1. We can observe that *GAM* is significantly better than unconditional masking over a range of n, with the difference often above 25%. This demonstrates that a simple *pooling* strategy is inadequate, and it is critical to condition the mixed strategy of the defender on the true state of the devices.

Next, we run four sets of experiments and compare to our *GAM* approach to the remaining two baselines (random and greedy masking) in terms of both defender loss and running time.

In the first experiment, we systematically vary n, with the number of exploits matching the dimension. We keep $m = 1$, and set cost $c = 0.01$. We set $V = 3$. Figure 2 (left) shows that *GAM* significantly outperforms the two baselines in terms of defender loss, particularly as we increase the number of attributes

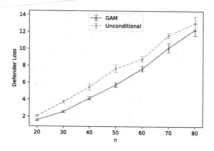

Fig. 1. Comparison of defender loss between *GAM* and *Unconditional Masking*.

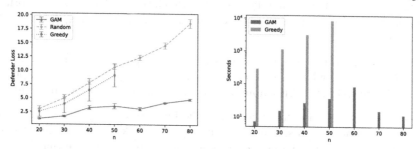

Fig. 2. Experiment 1 results: efficacy and scalability as a function of n.

n. Interestingly, Greedy is only slightly better than Random, and it fails to scale beyond $n = 50$. Figure 2 (right) compares the running time between *GAM* and Greedy, demonstrating that while *GAM* is remarkably scalable, with little difference in running time between $n = 20$ and $n = 80$, Greedy is significantly slower, and fails to scale well with n.

In Experiment 2, we fix $n = 20$, $m = 1$, $c = 0.01$, and $V = 3$, and systematically vary the number of exploits. Figure 3 shows again that *GAM* significantly outperforms both baselines in terms of defender's loss, and Greedy in terms of running time. It is interesting to note that the defender's loss in all three approaches appears to depend only weakly on the number of exploits available. This demonstrates the value of deception: although increasing the number of exploits also increases the likelihood that at least one can successfully attack the defender's device, deception serves to make it difficult for the attacker to choose the correct one.

Experiment 3 now systematically varies the relative cost c of masking, keeping $n = 20$, $m = 1$, $V = 1$, and $|E| = 20$. Figure 4 presents the results. As we can expect, defender's loss increases as we increase c (as masking becomes more expensive), but *GAM* remains significantly better than the baselines. Running time (Fig. 4, right) again shows a significant advantage of *GAM* over Greedy.

Finally, in Experiment 4 we study the impact of the number of devices m. We set $n = 20$, $c = 0.01$, $V = 1$, and $|E| = 20$ for this experiment. As shown in Fig. 5 (left), the defender's loss scales roughly linearly (as one would expect) with the

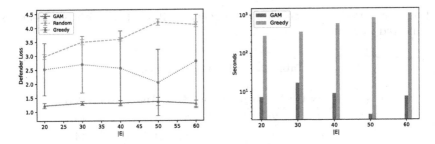

Fig. 3. Experiment 2 results: efficacy and scalability as a function of $|E|$.

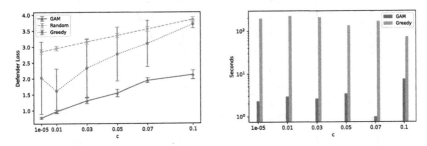

Fig. 4. Experiment 3 results: efficacy and scalability as a function of c.

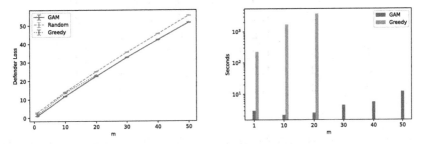

Fig. 5. Experiment 4 results: efficacy and scalability as a function of m.

number of devices, with GAM still offering the best solution. Scalability results (Fig. 5, right) show again that GAM scales much better than Greedy. While Greedy could not run for high values of m, the number of devices m appears to have relatively limited impact on the running time for GAM, which grows from ~ 3 s to ~ 12 s as m increases from 1 to 50.

7 Case Study

We now use a case study to delve more deeply into the nature of masking and attack strategies obtains as solutions to the CGM. We consider a single device, and use the same $v(x)$ and $c(y)$ as above, with $c = 0.01$. We let $n = 20$, generating x as described in Sect. 6.2, and generate 19 exploits with requirements documented in Table 2.

Table 2. Exploit requirements.

Exploit #	System	System Version	App	App Version	Port
1	0	2, 3	3	1	19
2	0	2	8	1, 2, 3	14
3	0	2, 3			17
4	1	2, 3	3	1, 2	14
5	1	1	4	1, 2	12
6	1	1, 2, 3	4	3	17
7	1	1, 2, 3	5	1, 2, 3	14
8	1	3	5	3	19
9	1	2	6	1	12
10	1	1, 2	7	2	11
11	1	2, 3	7	1, 2, 3	17
12	1	3			16
13	2	2, 3	3	1, 2	12
14	2	2, 3	5	1, 2	11
15	2	1, 2	5	3	12
16	2	1, 2	6	1, 2, 3	12
17	2	1, 2, 3	8	1, 2, 3	18
18	2	1, 2, 3	9	1, 2, 3	13
19	2	1, 2, 3			10

Figure 6 visualizes the BNE masking strategy, with the support (masks chosen with positive probability) as columns, and device attributes as rows. Red corresponds to attributes chosen to be masked, while blue encodes a decision not to mask an attribute. We can glean several insights from this figure. First, note that we always mask OS information. This is because all exploits have specific OS requirements. Moreover, exploits 3, 12, and 19 *only* have an OS requirement (i.e., they exploit the OS vulnerabilities, rather then application vulnerabilities). The masking strategy also always masks application 5, because there are 4 exploits available targeting this application (exploits 7, 8, 14, 15), the most of any applications, and these become obvious choices if application 5 is known to be installed. Note, moreover, we never mask whether port 15 is open, as no exploits target it.

Finally, we study the attacker's mixed strategy by computing the *average* probability of choosing each exploit over all possible attacker observations. Table 3 shows the results for exploits with a non-negligible probability of being chosen. Note that one exploit (19) is chosen an overwhelming fraction of the

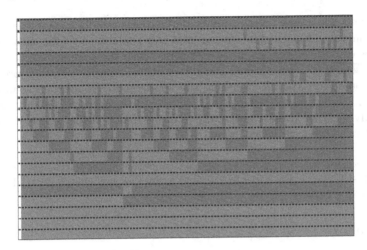

Fig. 6. Visualization of the support of the masking strategy computed by *GAM* in the case study. Red encodes a decision to mask an attribute, while blue encodes a decision not to mask. (Color figure online)

Table 3. Attacker's strategy.

Exploit #	Avg Pctg	System	System Version	App	App Version	Port
19	85.7%	2	1, 2, 3			10
7	5.3%	1	1, 2, 3	5	1, 2, 3	14
18	5.3%	2	1, 2, 3	9	1, 2, 3	13
3	2.2%	0	2, 3			17
17	1.5%	2	1, 2, 3	8	1, 2, 3	18
Sum	100.0%					

time, and only 5 are chosen with any frequency. All 5 exploits chosen have relatively weak requirements: 19 and 3 only require a particular OS and port (these exploits have the weakest requirements of all), while 7, 17, and 18 can exploit any extant version of their targeted application.

8   Conclusion

This paper studies a form of cyber deception in which a defender can only mask a subset of observable device attributes, while the attacker chooses one of a collection of exploits to deploy against the defender's network. The strategic interaction can be viewed as a combinatorial signaling game in which the defender's privacy information (a vector of attributes, or features, about their devices) is partially and strategically leaked to the adversary, with the express goal of deception in order to make it difficult for the adversary to carefully target exploits against the network. The adversary, in turn, reasons about such deception to choose an exploit that maximizes their expected posterior utility. Solving this game exactly for a Bayes-Nash equilibrium becomes rapidly intractable for even a small number of attributes. We address this challenge by first encoding the strategies of both players as neural networks, with the defender's mixed strategy represented by a conditional generative neural network. We then propose a gradient-based approach for learning the approximate equilibrium solutions of the game. Our experiments show that the proposed approach is highly effective and highly scalable, while a case study confirms that it yields intuitive solutions to realistic cybersecurity encounters.

Acknowledgments. This work was partially supported by the National Science Foundation (IIS-1905558 and ECCS-2020289) and Army Research Office (W911NF1910241 and W911NF1810208).

References

1. Abay, N.C., Akcora, C.G., Zhou, Y., Kantarcioglu, M., Thuraisingham, B.: Using deep learning to generate relational honeydata. In: Al-Shaer, E., Wei, J., Hamlen, K.W., Wang, C. (eds.) Autonomous Cyber Deception, pp. 3–19. Springer, Cham (2019). https://doi.org/10.1007/978-3-030-02110-8_1
2. Albanese, M., Battista, E., Jajodia, S.: Deceiving attackers by creating a virtual attack surface. In: Jajodia, S., Subrahmanian, V.S.S., Swarup, V., Wang, C. (eds.) Cyber Deception, pp. 169–201. Springer, Cham (2016). https://doi.org/10.1007/978-3-319-32699-3_8
3. Bercovitch, M., Renford, M., Hasson, L., Shabtai, A., Rokach, L., Elovici, Y.: HoneyGen: an automated honeytokens generator. In: IEEE International Conference on Intelligence and Security Informatics, pp. 131–136 (2011)
4. Carroll, T., Grosu, D.: A game theoretic investigation of deception in network security. Secur. Commun. Netw. **4**(10), 1162–1172 (2011)
5. Cohen, F., Lambert, D., Preston, C., Berry, N., Stewart, C., Thomas, E.: A framework for deception, working paper, Fred Cohen & Associates (2001)
6. Cohen, F., Marin, I., Sappington, J., Stewart, C., Thomas, E.: Red teaming experiments with deception technologies, working paper, Fred Cohen & Associates (2001)
7. Cohen, F., Koike, D.: Leading attackers through attack graphs with deceptions. Comput. Secur. **22**(5), 402–411 (2003)
8. Dagon, D., et al.: HoneyStat: local worm detection using honeypots. In: Jonsson, E., Valdes, A., Almgren, M. (eds.) RAID 2004. LNCS, vol. 3224, pp. 39–58. Springer, Heidelberg (2004). https://doi.org/10.1007/978-3-540-30143-1_3
9. Estornell, A., Das, S., Vorobeychik, Y.: Deception through half-truths. In: AAAI Conference on Artificial Intelligence, pp. 10110–10117 (2020)
10. Goodfellow, I., et al.: Generative adversarial nets. In: Neural Information Processing Systems (2014)
11. Guo, Q., An, B., Bosansky, B., Kiekintveld, C.: Comparing strategic secrecy and Stackelberg commitment in security games. In: International Joint Conference on Artificial Intelligence, pp. 3691–3699 (2017)
12. Horak, K., Zhu, Q., Bosansky, B.: Manipulating adversary's belief: a dynamic game approach to deception by design for proactive network security. In: Rass, S., An, B., Kiekintveld, C., Fang, F., Schauer, S. (eds.) GameSec 2017. LNCS, vol. 10575, pp. 273–294. Springer, Heidelberg (2017). https://doi.org/10.1007/978-3-319-68711-7_15

13. Juels, A., Rivest, R.L.: Honeywords: making password-cracking detectable. In: ACM SIGSAC Conference on Computer & Communications security, pp. 145–160 (2013)
14. Kamra, N., Gupta, U., Wang, K., Fang, F., Liu, Y., Tambe, M.: DeepFP for finding Nash equilibrium in continuous action spaces. In: Alpcan, T., Vorobeychik, Y., Baras, J.S., Dán, G. (eds.) GameSec 2019. LNCS, vol. 11836, pp. 238–258. Springer, Cham (2019). https://doi.org/10.1007/978-3-030-32430-8_15
15. Kiekintveld, C., Lisý, V., Píbil, R.: Game-theoretic foundations for the strategic use of honeypots in network security. In: Jajodia, S., Shakarian, P., Subrahmanian, V.S., Swarup, V., Wang, C. (eds.) Cyber Warfare. AIS, vol. 56, pp. 81–101. Springer, Cham (2015). https://doi.org/10.1007/978-3-319-14039-1_5
16. Korzhyk, D., Yin, Z., Kiekintveld, C., Conitzer, V., Tambe, M.: Stackelberg vs. Nash in security games: an extended investigation of interchangeability, equivalence, and uniqueness. J. Artif. Intell. Res. **41**, 297–327 (2011)
17. Mirza, M., Osindero, S.: Conditional generative adversarial nets. arXiv preprint arXiv:1411.1784 (2014)
18. Nguyen, T., Wang, Y., Sinha, A., Wellman, M.: Deception in finitely repeated security games. In: AAAI Conference on Artificial Intelligence (2019)
19. Pawlick, J., Zhu, Q.: Deception by design: evidence-based signaling games for network defense. In: Workshop on the Economics of Information Security (2015)
20. Píbil, R., Lisý, V., Kiekintveld, C., Bošanský, B., Pěchouček, M.: Game theoretic model of strategic honeypot selection in computer networks. In: Grossklags, J., Walrand, J. (eds.) GameSec 2012. LNCS, vol. 7638, pp. 201–220. Springer, Heidelberg (2012). https://doi.org/10.1007/978-3-642-34266-0_12
21. Provos, N.: Honeyd-a virtual honeypot daemon. In: DFN-CERT Workshop (2003)
22. Rabinovich, Z., Jiang, A.X., Jain, M., Xu, H.: Information disclosure as a means to security. In: International Conference on Autonomous Agents and Multiagent Systems, pp. 645–653 (2015)
23. Rowe, N.C.: Deception in defense of computer systems from cyber attack. In: Cyber Warfare and Cyber Terrorism, pp. 97–104 (2007)
24. Schlenker, A., et al.: Deceiving cyber adversaries: a game theoretic approach. In: International Conference on Autonomous Agents and Multiagent Systems (2018)
25. Shi, Z.R., et al.: Learning and planning in the feature deception problem. In: Conference on Decision and Game Theory for Security (2020)
26. Spitzner, L.: Honeypots: Tracking Hackers. Addison-Wesley, Reading (2003)
27. Tambe, M.: Security and Game Theory: Algorithms, Deployed Systems, Lessons Learned. Cambridge University Press, Cambridge (2011)
28. Wang, W., Zeng, B.: A two-stage deception game for network defense. In: Bushnell, L., Poovendran, R., Başar, T. (eds.) GameSec 2018. LNCS, vol. 11199, pp. 569–582. Springer, Cham (2018). https://doi.org/10.1007/978-3-030-01554-1_33
29. Xu, H., Rabinovich, Z., Dughmi, S., Tambe, M.: Exploring information asymmetry in two-stage security games. In: AAAI Conference on Artificial Intelligence (2015)
30. Yan, C., Xu, H., Vorobeychik, Y., Li, B., Fabbri, D., Malin, B.A.: To warn or not to warn: online signaling in audit games. In: IEEE International Conference on Data Engineering, pp. 481–492 (2020)
31. Yin, Y., An, B., Vorobeychik, Y., Zhuang, J.: Optimal deceptive strategies in security games: a preliminary study. In: AAAI Symposium on Applied Computational Game Theory (2014)

Network Games with Strategic Machine Learning

Kun Jin[1](✉) (iD), Tongxin Yin[1](✉) (iD), Charles A. Kamhoua[2](✉) (iD),
and Mingyan Liu[1](✉) (iD)

[1] University of Michigan, Ann Arbor, MI 48109, USA
{kunj,tyin,mingyan}@umich.edu
[2] US Army Research Laboratory, Adelphi, MD 20783, USA
charles.a.kamhoua.civ@mail.mil

Abstract. In this paper, we study the strategic machine learning problem with a planner (decision maker) and multiple agents. The planner is the first-mover, who designs, publishes, and commits to a decision rule. The agents then best-respond by manipulating their input features to obtain a desirable decision outcome so as to maximize their utilities. Earlier works in strategic machine learning assume that every agent's strategic action is independent of others'. By contrast, we consider a different case where agents are connected in a network and can either benefit from their neighbors' positive decision outcomes from the planner or benefit from their neighbors' actions. We study the Stackelberg equilibrium in this new setting and highlight the similarities and differences between this model and the literature on network/graphical games and strategic machine learning.

Keywords: Stackelberg game · Strategic machine learning · Mechanism design

1 Introduction

In this paper, we study a strategic machine learning problem with a planner (decision maker) and multiple, interdependent agents. This is modeled as a sequential (two-stage) game of the Stackelberg type but with a crucial difference: the planner is the first-mover, who designs, publishes, and commits to a decision rule (e.g., a classifier); the agents simultaneously best-respond to not only the decision rule by the planner but also to other agents' actions (because of the dependencies), by manipulating their input features to obtain a desirable decision outcome so as to maximize their utilities.

The interdependence among the agents is a key difference between the problem studied in this paper and strategic machine learning problems commonly found in the literature, see e.g., [2,6,8,9,11,13,14], where one or more agents strategically, and independent from other agents, choose actions to manipulate their features in response to the published machine learning decision rule while

B. Bošanský et al. (Eds.): GameSec 2021, LNCS 13061, pp. 118–137, 2021.
https://doi.org/10.1007/978-3-030-90370-1_7

the planner seeks to design the optimal decision rule in anticipation of the agents' manipulation.

This difference means that the commonly studied problem with independent agents is typically modeled as a Stackelberg game between the planner as the first mover and the agents the second movers, who each independently best responds to the planner's decision rules. By contrast, our problem is modeled as *modified* Stackelberg game, where the agents not only best respond to the planner's decision rules but also simultaneously best respond to each other in a manner similar to that in a network game.

The literature on network and graphical games, see e.g., [1,12,15–20,22–24], studies the strategic interactions between agents whose dependencies are captured through an underlying network/graph, typically represented using a weighted adjacency matrix. Most of this literature is simply concerned with the interactions among agents in the absence of a planner. The addition of a planner in a network game is often studied within the context of intervention [5] and mechanism design [15–17,19,21].

One major difference between this literature on network game intervention and the study presented in this paper is that we consider agents with multi-dimensional actions. This is motivated by the fact that most of the machine learning models take multi-dimensional feature inputs. This modeling choice also substantially broadens the class of games such a model can represent. Network games with multi-dimensional actions have been studied in [20,23,24], but without a planner; consequently the focus in these studies is on characterizing the Nash equilibrium of a strategic one-shot game, rather than a sequential (Stackelberg) game we study in this paper. Under the same motivation, we will also choose to use typical machine learning decision rules like linear regression and classification for the planner.

There are several types of planners in terms of their objectives found in the strategic classification literature, e.g., a selfish player whose utility is directly tied to the classification outcomes [8,9,14], or a social planner with a welfare objective who uses the decision rule as an incentive mechanism to elicit desirable actions from agents [6,11]. Our work follows this second type of model and considers a number of social objectives for the planner.

To the best of our knowledge, our work is the first that applies machine learning decision rules as incentive mechanisms over a set of interdependent agents. This work extends existing research in both (intervention in) network games (to multi-dimensional actions) and strategic machine learning (to interdependent agents), as the above literature review illustrates; it also explores the intersection of these two areas.

The main contributions in our work are summarized as follows. Firstly, we develop two different types of game models for network games with strategic machine learning, where the agents are interdependent on their decision outcomes (resp. actions) in the first (resp. second). Secondly, we study the Stackelberg equilibrium in the games where the planner chooses to use linear mechanisms or linear threshold mechanisms [6] and determine how the planner can find the optimal decision rule. Last but not least, we offer insight on some unique properties of this problem through a comparison between our work and prior work in network and graphical games and in strategic machine learning, respectively.

The remainder of this paper is organized as follows. In Sect. 2, we introduce our network game models with strategic machine learning. Then we study the Stackelberg equilibrium and the optimal decision rule when the planner chooses linear mechanisms in Sect. 3. Section 4 demonstrates the Stackelberg equilibrium and the optimal decision rule when the planner chooses linear threshold mechanisms. Section 5 shows our numerical experiment results. We make the comparisons between our work and the previous works in Sect. 6 and conclude this paper in Sect. 7.

2   Game Model

We consider a Stackelberg game with a planner (alternately referred to as the mechanism designer or decision maker), the first mover, and N agents, the simultaneous second movers. The planner publishes a decision rule and then the agents simultaneously best respond.

The agents, denoted by $a_i, i = 1, \ldots, N$, have interdependent utilities, with dependencies represented by a directed weighted graph and a corresponding adjacency matrix $G \in \mathbf{R}^{N \times N}$, where $G \geq 0 \Leftrightarrow g_{ij} \geq 0, \forall i, j = 1, 2, \ldots, N$. We denote by $\mathcal{N}_i = \{j | j \neq i, g_{ij} > 0\}$ the set of agent indices of a_i's neighbors on the graph. The planner's decision rule is given by $f : \mathbf{R}^K \mapsto \mathbf{R}$, and the a_i's strategic action $\boldsymbol{x}^{(i)} \in \mathbf{R}^M$. Since the decision rule maps a set of features to the real line, we will also sometimes refer to f as a "scoring mechanism". We will study this as a perfect information game, where f is public knowledge, as are the agents' utility functions and the matrix G.

Below we define two different types of interdependent strategic machine learning games given by different utility functions.

2.1   Interdependent in Decision Outcomes (Type 1)

In this first type of utility function, we assume an agent's decision outcome is based on certain *observable* features of the agents rather than directly based on actions. This is very common in machine learning algorithms, where one's actions (e.g., effort in preparing for an exam) determine one's features (e.g., scores on an exam) that form the input to the algorithm. We will further assume that the network effect is through each agent's decision outcome (e.g., one may derive satisfaction from not only one's own positive decision outcome but from one's friends' positive outcome, etc.

With this in mind, we will use a mapping matrix $P \in \mathbf{R}^{K \times M}$, where $rank(P) = K < M, P \geq 0$ that maps action $\boldsymbol{x}^{(i)}$ to observable features $\boldsymbol{z}^{(i)} \in \mathbf{R}^K$, in the form $\boldsymbol{z}^{(i)} = P\boldsymbol{x}^{(i)}$. The observable features $\boldsymbol{z}^{(i)}$ are then used as inputs to the decision rule f.

The utility functions of the agents are given by the following:

$$u^{(i)}(\boldsymbol{x}^{(i)}, \boldsymbol{x}^{(-i)}) = f(\boldsymbol{z}^{(i)}) + \sum_{j \in \mathcal{N}_i} g_{ij} \cdot f(\boldsymbol{z}^{(i)}) \cdot f(\boldsymbol{z}^{(j)}) - \frac{1}{2}||\boldsymbol{x}^{(i)}||_2^2, \qquad (1)$$

where the decision outcome $f(\boldsymbol{z}^{(i)})$ represents the *standalone marginal benefit* a_i receives from the decision, $\sum_{j \in \mathcal{N}_i} g_{ij} \cdot f(\boldsymbol{z}^{(i)}) \cdot f(\boldsymbol{z}^{(j)})$ captures the network effect, and $-\frac{1}{2}||\boldsymbol{x}^{(i)}||^2$ is the *action cost*. When $G \geq 0$, for two neighbors a_i, a_j such that $f(\boldsymbol{z}^{(i)}) > 0, f(\boldsymbol{z}^{(j)}) > 0$, there is a positive externality between them.

For a given decision rule f, a_i best responds to f and other agents' actions, where we use $(\boldsymbol{x}^{(i)})^* \in \mathbf{R}^M$ to denote the best response action, and

$$(\boldsymbol{x}^{(i)})^* = \arg\max_{\boldsymbol{x}^{(i)}} u^{(i)}(\boldsymbol{x}^{(i)}, \boldsymbol{x}^{(-i)}). \qquad (2)$$

The planner uses backward induction to determine a decision rule f that induces the best responses $(\boldsymbol{x}^{(i)})^*, i = 1, \ldots, N$, which can maximize the following social welfare objective

$$U(f) = \sum_{i=1}^{N} \boldsymbol{q}^T (\boldsymbol{x}^{(i)})^*, \qquad (3)$$

where $\boldsymbol{q} \geq 0$. We can think of $\boldsymbol{q}^T \boldsymbol{x}^{(i)}$ as the social value (quality) improvement of a_i, and the planner is trying to maximize the sum of all agents' social value improvements. This type of social objective function models the scenario where each dimension of action has its social value and every agent has the same marginal contribution on the same dimension. For example, in a school admissions exam setting, the action dimensions may include a student's amount of effort or amount of cheating spent on a certain subject. In this case, we could view $\boldsymbol{q}^T \boldsymbol{x}^{(i)}$ as the quality of the student, and the planner's objective is to maximize the average quality by judiciously selecting the decision rule f. This type of planner objective is also used in [6].

2.2   Interdependent in Observable Features (Type 2)

In the second type of utility function, we assume the agent's utility only depends on its own decision outcome and action cost, but its observable features depend not only on its own actions but its neighbors' actions. In other words, in this utility type, the externality or network effect is through actions impacting features, rather than through the end decision outcomes. Continuing the same example used earlier, this model captures the scenario where one's test score is a function of one's own effort in exam preparation as well as one's friends' effort, e.g., perhaps through group studies, etc., but that one's utility is only a function of the individual decision one receives (e.g., whether one gets a certificate based on the exam outcome).

Specifically, we define the projection matrix P similarly, but now the observable features $\boldsymbol{z}^{(i)}$ are given by:

$$z^{(i)} = P(\boldsymbol{x}^{(i)} + \sum_{j \in \mathcal{N}_i} g_{ij}\boldsymbol{x}^{(j)}), \tag{4}$$

and the utility function of a_i is given by:

$$u^{(i)}(\boldsymbol{x}^{(i)}, \boldsymbol{x}^{(-i)}) = b_i(f(\boldsymbol{z}^{(i)})) - \boldsymbol{c}^T\boldsymbol{x}^{(i)}, \tag{5}$$

where b_i is a twice differentiable, strictly increasing, and strictly concave function, and it models the *benefit term* for a_i. Graph neural network models in [7,10] use similar feature aggregation methods in Eq. (4).

We will use the same objective function for the planner as given in Eq. (3). The agents' best responses are also similarly defined as in Eq. (2).

3   Equilibrium Analysis–Linear Mechanisms

In this section, we study the Stackelberg equilibrium when the planner uses a *linear mechanism* for each of the models in Sect. 2.

We begin with the following definitions.

Definition 1. *Monotone Decision Rules: A decision rule f is monotone if $f(\boldsymbol{z})$ is weakly increasing in every element of $\boldsymbol{z}$.*

Definition 2. *Cosine Similarity: the cosine similarity of two vectors $\boldsymbol{x}, \boldsymbol{y} \in \mathbf{R}^K$ is defined as*

$$s_{cos}(\boldsymbol{x}, \boldsymbol{y}) = \frac{\boldsymbol{x}^T \boldsymbol{y}}{||\boldsymbol{x}||_2 \cdot ||\boldsymbol{y}||_2}. \tag{6}$$

For example, $s_{cos}(\boldsymbol{x}, \boldsymbol{y}) = 1, 0, -1$ means that $\boldsymbol{x}$ and $\boldsymbol{y}$ are pointing in the same direction, are orthogonal to each other and are pointing in opposite directions respectively.

Now we introduce the definition of linear mechanisms.

Definition 3. *Linear Mechanisms: We say decision rule f is a linear mechanism if $f(\boldsymbol{z}) = \boldsymbol{w}^T\boldsymbol{z}$.*

The linear mechanisms have the same form as the weighted sum functions in regression problems. They are typical end products of algorithms like linear regression. This type of mechanism and the corresponding strategic manipulations are also studied in [4,6,11]. We will focus on monotone linear mechanisms where $\boldsymbol{w} \geq 0$.

In the remainder of this section, we will provide Stackelberg equilibrium analysis on each of the models introduced in Sect. 2. For each model, we will first derive agents' best responses to given a linear mechanism and then discuss the optimal linear mechanism for the planner.

3.1   Type 1 Model Analysis

We begin with the best responses.

Lemma 1. *When the planner chooses a linear mechanism* $f(z) = w^T z$, *agent* $a^{(i)}$ *will choose a best response action* x_i^* *such that*

$$s_{cos}(P^T w, (x^{(i)})^*) = 1. \tag{7}$$

In other words, the best response action $(x^{(i)})^*$ and the vector $P^T w$ are pointing in the same direction. We note that Lemma 1 captures the direction of agents' best responses, which only depends on decision rule f, while the magnitude of best response actions depends on both the network topology G and f.

Proposition 1. *When the planner chooses a linear mechanism* $f(z) = w^T z$, *agent* $a^{(i)}$ *will choose a best response action* x_i^* *such that*

$$(x^{(i)})^* = (\alpha^{(i)})^* \cdot \frac{P^T w}{||P^T w||}, \tag{8}$$

where $(\alpha^{(i)})^*$ *satisfy*

$$\alpha^* = ((\alpha^{(i)})^*)_{i=1}^N = ||P^T w||(I - ||P^T w||^2 G)^{-1} \mathbf{1},$$

if $I - ||P^T w||^2 G$ *is positive definite. This* α^* *is also the unique NE for the agents given* f.

We next discuss the optimal linear mechanism for the planner. We assume that the planner can choose from linear mechanisms such that w satisfies $||P^T w|| \leq r$, which captures some type of reward constraint in the real world. Such constraints are related to the projection matrix P since observable features may have very different scales.

Proposition 2. *If* $(I - r^2 G) \succ 0$, *then the* w *vector in the optimal linear mechanism satisfies* $||P^T w|| = r, s_{cos}(w, Pq) = 1$.

Interestingly, if $(I - r^2 G) \succ 0$, the optimal linear mechanism in the Type 1 model only depends on the planner's objective and the projection matrix P, but is independent of the adjacency matrix G. The first reason is that f alone determines the best response directions. The second reason is although the best response magnitude depends on both f and G, the planner's objective is monotonically increasing in $||P^T w||$ and thus is determined by r instead of G.

3.2   Type 2 Model Analysis

Lemma 2. *Given* $f = w^T z$, *the best response of* $a_i, \forall i$ *satisfies*

$$\begin{cases} (x^{(i)})_k^* \geq 0, \text{ if } \frac{(P^T w)_k}{c_k} = \max_l \frac{(P^T w)_l}{c_l}, \\ (x^{(i)})_k^* = 0, \text{ otherwise} \end{cases} \tag{9}$$

In other words, the agent will choose the action dimension k with the highest return to cost ratio $\frac{(P^T w)_k}{c_k}$. Without loss of generality, we assume that the agents choose the dimension in favor of the planner when breaking ties.

Proposition 3. *The best response action for $a^{(i)}$ is*

$$(\boldsymbol{x}^{(i)})^* = (\alpha^{(i)})^* \cdot \boldsymbol{e}_k, \tag{10}$$

where $k = \arg\max_l \frac{(P^T w)_l}{c_l}$ (without loss of generality, we assume k is unique), and $\boldsymbol{e}_k$ is the k-th orthogonal basis. The magnitude vector $\boldsymbol{\alpha}^* = ((\alpha^{(i)})^*)_{i=1}^N$ is the solution to the following Linear Complementary Problem

$$\boldsymbol{v} - (I + G)\boldsymbol{\alpha} = -\boldsymbol{t},$$
$$\boldsymbol{v} \geq 0, \boldsymbol{\alpha} \geq 0, \boldsymbol{v}^T \boldsymbol{\alpha} = 0, \tag{11}$$

where $\boldsymbol{t}$ satisfies $b_i'(t_i) = \frac{c_k}{(P^T w)_k}$.

When $I + G$ is a P-matrix, there is a unique NE for the agents given f. Moreover, if $I + G$ is invertible and $(I + G)^{-1} \boldsymbol{t} \geq 0$, we have $\boldsymbol{\alpha}^* = (I + G)^{-1} \boldsymbol{t}$.

We note that the best response direction (dimension) only depends on f, but the manipulation magnitude depends on both G and f.

The planner can design an optimal linear mechanism following the two steps below.

1. Find out the action dimensions that can be incentivized with f in the agents' best responses;
2. Iterate through every incentivizable dimension and use the best responses in Eq. (10) to see which one can maximize the planner's objective.

Similar to the type 1 model, we assume that the planner has some resource restrictions and can only choose from linear mechanisms where $\|w\|_1 \leq 1$. It's not hard to prove that $\|w\|_1 = 1$ is achieved since the magnitude of agents' best responses is monotonically increasing in every dimension of w. However, finding the action dimensions that can be incentivized is not trivial.

The definition of *substitutability* of an action dimension in [11] gives a necessary condition for an action dimension to be *incentivizable*, i.e., having positive magnitude in a best response. Below we define the substitutability of an action dimension in our type 2 model.

Definition 4. *Substitutability: We use κ_k to denote the substitutability of action dimension k in $\boldsymbol{x}$, formally*

$$\kappa_k := \min_{\boldsymbol{y} \in \mathbf{R}^M, \boldsymbol{y} \geq 0} \frac{\boldsymbol{c}^T \boldsymbol{y}}{c_k}, \quad s.t. \ P\boldsymbol{y} - \boldsymbol{p}_k \geq 0. \tag{12}$$

The vector $\boldsymbol{p}_k := (p_{lk})_{l=1}^K$ is the l-th column vector of matrix P. We denote the set of linear mechanisms that can incentivize dimension k action as

$$\mathcal{L}_k := \left\{ w \mid \frac{(P^T w)_r}{c_r} \leq \frac{w^T \boldsymbol{p}_k}{c_k} \right\}. \tag{13}$$

Every $\boldsymbol{w} \in \mathcal{L}_k$ can incentivize best responses in dimension k because

$$\frac{(P^T\boldsymbol{w})_r}{c_r} \leq \frac{\boldsymbol{w}^T\boldsymbol{p}_k}{c_k} \Leftrightarrow \frac{\partial f}{\partial x_r} \cdot \frac{1}{c_r} \leq \frac{\partial f}{\partial x_k} \cdot \frac{1}{c_k}.$$

Lemma 3. *If $\kappa_k = 1$, then there exists a linear mechanism that can incentivize it, i.e., $\mathcal{L}_k$ is non-empty. Moreover, the linear mechanism can be found in polynomial time.*

Lemma 4. *If $\kappa_k < 1$, then $(\boldsymbol{x}^{(i)})_k^* = 0$ for any choice of $\boldsymbol{w} \geq 0$, i.e., $\mathcal{L}_k$ is empty.*

Intuitively, if $\kappa_k < 1$, the agent can always find a "cheaper" combination of actions that result in the same observable features and thus the action dimension k will have magnitude 0 in best responses. Please see an intuitive example in the appendix.

4   Equilibrium Analysis–Linear Threshold Mechanisms

In this section, we study the Stackelberg equilibrium when the planner uses a *linear threshold mechanism* for each of the models introduced in Sect. 2.

Definition 5. *Linear threshold mechanism: A linear threshold mechanism has the following form*

$$f(\boldsymbol{z}) = \mathbf{1}(\boldsymbol{w}^T\boldsymbol{z} \geq \tau). \tag{14}$$

The linear threshold mechanisms have the same form as the separating hyperplanes in binary classification problems. They are typical end products of algorithms like linear SVM and linear logistic regression. This type of mechanism and the corresponding strategic manipulations are also studied in [3,6,9]. Similar to the previous section, we will focus on monotone linear threshold mechanisms where $\boldsymbol{w} \geq 0$.

4.1   Type 1 Model Analysis

We can see that if the planner scales $||\boldsymbol{w}||_2$ and τ simultaneously, f remains the same. Therefore, we assume that the planner chooses $\boldsymbol{w}$ such that $||P^T\boldsymbol{w}||_2 = 1$.

We start with the agent's best responses.

Lemma 5. *For a given $f = \mathbf{1}(\boldsymbol{w}^T\boldsymbol{z} \geq \tau)$, if $(\boldsymbol{x}^{(i)})^* \neq 0$, we have*

$$s_{cos}(\boldsymbol{x}^{(i)}, P^T\boldsymbol{w}) = 1, \quad \boldsymbol{w}^T P(\boldsymbol{x}^{(i)})^* = \tau. \tag{15}$$

Using Lemma 5, we can write out the agents' best responses given $f = \mathbf{1}(\boldsymbol{w}^T\boldsymbol{z} \geq \tau)$ as follows

$$(\boldsymbol{x}^{(i)})^* = \begin{cases} \tau P^T\boldsymbol{w} & \text{if } 1 + \sum_{j \in \mathcal{N}_i} g_{ij}\mathbf{1}((\boldsymbol{x}^{(j)})^* \neq 0) \geq \frac{1}{2}\tau^2 \\ 0 & \text{o.w.} \end{cases} \tag{16}$$

It is true that both the all 0 NE and non-zero NE exist in the second stage of the game. We assume that the agents will choose to play the non-zero NE where most agents manipulate. This is also the NE that makes all agents who manipulate better off than the all 0 NE.

Lemma 6. *When $G \geq 0$, each agent's decision outcome and the number of agents getting decision outcome 1 are both weakly decreasing in τ.*

Intuitively, when the threshold τ is lower, more agents can have a profitable manipulation action. Moreover, once some agents manipulate to get decision outcomes of 1, the benefit for their neighbors to get decision outcomes of 1 also increases. There is a cascading effect here: the more agents get decision outcomes of 1, the more are incentivized to invest in their actions and get decision outcomes of 1.

The agent with the highest weighted in-degree $\max_i 1 + \sum_{j \in \mathcal{N}_i} g_{ij}$ value can help the planner find an upper bound value $\bar{\tau}$ of the threshold, where

$$\bar{\tau} = \sqrt{2 \cdot (\max_i 1 + \sum_{j \in \mathcal{N}_i} g_{ij})}. \tag{17}$$

A threshold $\tau > \bar{\tau}$ will make manipulation too costly for every agent and thus no social value improvement is incentivized. Similarly, the planner can find a lower bound $\underline{\tau} = \sqrt{2}$, and any threshold $\tau \in [0, \sqrt{2}]$ can incentivize all agents but are dominated by $\sqrt{2}$ due to the magnitude of the best response actions.

Proposition 4. *The planner's optimal choice of $\boldsymbol{w}$ satisfies $s_{cos}(\boldsymbol{w}, P\boldsymbol{q}) = 1$ (without loss of generality, $\|P^T \boldsymbol{w}\| = 1$). Moreover, the planner can scan the choice of threshold in interval $[\sqrt{2}, \bar{\tau}]$ with a small step size ϵ. This will give the planner an approximate solution with the following performance lower bound*

$$\frac{U(\tilde{f})}{\max_f U(f)} > 1 - \frac{\epsilon}{\sqrt{2}}. \tag{18}$$

4.2 Type 2 Model Analysis

We consider a simplified version where the $b_i(\cdot)$ is the same for every agent and assume $b_i(1) = 1$. Then we know that the $a^{(i)}$ is willing to flip the decision outcome if $\exists \, \boldsymbol{x}^{(j)}, j = 1, \ldots, N, \text{s.t.}, f(\boldsymbol{z}^{(i)}) = 1, \boldsymbol{c}^T \boldsymbol{x}^{(i)} \leq 1$. We can see that free-riding issue exists. Sometimes agents can be caught up in bad NEs where no one is incentivized to manipulate.

To avoid playing the bad NE, a subset of agents S who form a clique with the corresponding sub-graph's adjacency matrix G_S can negotiate to play a better NE than the all 0 NE.

We characterize the agents' best responses in that better NE with the following proposition.

Proposition 5. *For a given* $f = \mathbf{1}(\boldsymbol{w}^T\boldsymbol{z} \geq \tau)$, *if* $(\boldsymbol{x}^{(i)})^* \neq \boldsymbol{0}$, *we have*

$$(\boldsymbol{x}^{(i)})^* = (\beta_S^{(i)})^* \cdot \boldsymbol{e}_k, \tag{19}$$

where $k = \arg\max\limits_{l} \frac{(P^T\boldsymbol{w})_l}{c_l}$. *The magnitude is determined by*

$$(I_{|S|} + G_S)\boldsymbol{\beta}_S^* = \frac{\tau}{(P^T\boldsymbol{w})_k} \cdot \mathbf{1}_{|S|} \Leftrightarrow \boldsymbol{\beta}_S^* = \frac{\tau}{(P^T\boldsymbol{w})_k} \cdot (I_{|S|} + G_S)^{-1}\mathbf{1}_{|S|}, \tag{20}$$

the individual rationality requires

$$\frac{\tau}{(P^T\boldsymbol{w})_k} \cdot (I_{|S|} + G_S)^{-1}\mathbf{1}_{|S|} - \frac{1}{c_k}\mathbf{1}_{|S|} \geq 0. \tag{21}$$

When the agents don't form a clique, they might not agree on involving everyone in the subset. Below is an example of this claim.

Example 1. Let's consider a simple three-agent, single action dimension game given $f = \mathbf{1}(x^{(i)} \geq 1)$. The adjacency matrix is $G = \begin{bmatrix} 0 & 0.3 & 0 \\ 0.3 & 0 & 0.3 \\ 0 & 0.3 & 0 \end{bmatrix}$ where $a^{(1)}$ and $a^{(3)}$ are both connected to $a^{(2)}$ but have no mutual dependence.

When all agents best respond together, we have

$$\boldsymbol{x}^* = (I + G)^{-1}\mathbf{1} = [0.854, 0.488, 0.854]^T,$$

and when $a^{(3)}$ is not involved, we have

$$\begin{bmatrix} (x(1))^* \\ (x(2))^* \end{bmatrix} = \begin{bmatrix} 1 & 0.3 \\ 0.3 & 1 \end{bmatrix}^{-1} \begin{bmatrix} 1 \\ 1 \end{bmatrix} = \begin{bmatrix} 0.769 \\ 0.769 \end{bmatrix}.$$

Clearly $a^{(2)}$ wants to involve $a^{(3)}$ but $a^{(1)}$ doesn't.

When an agent is involved in multiple cliques, we assume that it will choose the one that can result in the highest utility. But finding the best clique might be impractical in some cases, and we will focus on the special case where the network consists of several fully connected components, i.e., the maximum cliques have no intersections.

Then given the above mentioned conditions, the planner can design the optimal linear threshold mechanism in polynomial time as follows:

- Step 1: Find the set $\mathcal{I}$ of all action dimension k such that $\kappa_k = 1$.
- Step 2: Choose an element k to remove from $\mathcal{I}$, find a $\boldsymbol{w} \in \mathcal{L}_k$ for f.
- Step 3: Compute the NE best responses according to Eq. (19) and (20).
- Step 4: Based on the NE best responses, find the highest τ such that individual rationality in Eq. (21) hold for all agents in the network.
- Step 5: Update the optimal objective value with the current objective value, and find agents that reach equality in Eq. (21), which we call *peripheral agents* who faces the highest action costs.
- Step 6: Remove peripheral agents from the network and go back to Step 3 until all subsets become empty. If all subsets are empty, go to Step 7.
- Step 7: Go back to Step 2 if $\mathcal{I}$ is non-empty, otherwise end the process.

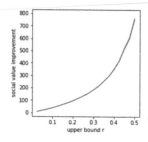
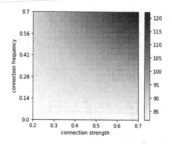

Fig. 1. Type 1 $U^*(f)$ in r.   **Fig. 2.** Type 1 $U^*(f)$ over G.

5   Numerical Results

We present some numerical results in this section. We explore four different classes of games (Type1, Type2) × (linear mechanism, linear threshold mechanism) discussed in Sects. 3 and 4. In each class of games, we generate synthetic data samples and study how the network structure influences the Stackelberg equilibria.

The synthetic data samples are generated using the following parameters. We set $N = 50$. In generating a random symmetric G, the diagonal elements are set to 0 based on Sect. 2. We use a Bernoulli distribution with parameter $F_{conn} \in [0,1]$ to determine if an edge exists (connection frequency) between a pair of agents. If an edge exists between $a^{(i)}$ and $a^{(j)}$, we then draw the value of g_{ij} from a uniform distribution on the interval $[S_{low}, S_{high}]$. We also set $M = 5$ and $K = 8$ and draw the values of elements p_{ij} in the projection matrix P from a uniform distribution on the interval $[0,1]$ where we guarantee $rank(P) = M$. The values of q_k in $\boldsymbol{q}$ are arbitrarily drawn from $[0,1]$.

5.1   Type 1 Model, Linear Mechanism

We show how the equilibrium social value improvement $U^*(f)$ changes with (1) the magnitude upper bound r on $||P^T \boldsymbol{w}|| \leq r$ in Fig. 1, and (2) the network topology controlled by the connection frequency F_{conn} and the connection strengths S_{low}, S_{high} in G shown in Fig. 2.

We see from Fig. 1 that $U^*(f)$ is monotonically increasing in r as we proved in Proposition 2. In Fig. 2, the darker the cells, the higher the value of $U^*(f)$. We observe that $U^*(f)$ increases in both the connection frequency F_{conn} and the average connection strength S_{avg} (normalized by N), where $S_{low} = S_{avg} - 0.2, S_{high} = S_{avg} + 0.2$. This shows that under the Type 1 model, stronger network connections improve agents' incentive to manipulate as well as increase the equilibrium action magnitude; this thus helps the planner to achieve higher objective values.

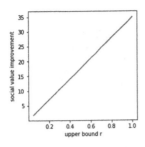

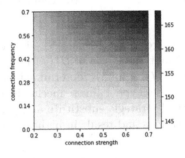

Fig. 3. Type 2 $U^*(f)$ in r.   **Fig. 4.** Type 2 $U^*(f)$ over G.

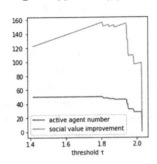

Fig. 5. Type 1 $U^*(f), |S_\tau^+|$.   **Fig. 6.** Type 1 $U^*(f)$ over G.

5.2   Type 2 Model, Linear Mechanism

In this case we use logarithm functions for the benefit terms $b_i(t) = \gamma^{(i)}\ln(t)$. Experiments show that having heterogeneous or homogeneous $\gamma^{(i)}$ results in similar findings; we thus present our numerical results by arbitrarily choosing $\gamma^{(i)} = 1$ for all agents. Again, we examine $U^*(f)$'s change with (1) the magnitude upper bound r on $\|w\|_1 \leq r$ in Fig. 3, and (2) the network topology G in Fig. 4.

Similar to the Type 1 model, Fig. 3 shows that $U^*(f)$ is monotonically increasing in r. But different from Type 1 model, Fig. 4 shows that $U^*(f)$ is decreasing in the connection frequency and average connection strengths in G. This is because when the connectivity increases in G, the agents have higher levels of strategic substitute received from the network, and thus free-riding becomes more significant and the planner's objective decreases.

5.3   Type 1 Model, Linear Threshold Mechanism

We examine (1) how $U^*(f)$ and the number of active agents $|S_\tau^+|$ change with the choice of τ in Fig. 5, and (2) how $U^*(f)$ changes in the connection frequency and average connection strength of G in Fig. 6.

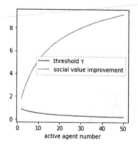 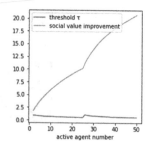 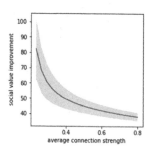

Fig. 7. Type 2 threshold, single component.

Fig. 8. Type 2 threshold, two components.

Fig. 9. Type 2 threshold, $U^*(f)$ over G.

We see from Fig. 5 that $|S_\tau^+|$ is weakly decreasing in τ as we proved in Lemma 6, but the curve of $U^*(f)$ has multiple local maximum points. This is because $U^*(f)$ is jointly determined by τ, G and $|S_\tau^+|$. In Fig. 6, we see that similar to the Type 1 linear mechanism games, network connectivity increases the effect of strategic substitute and thus can incentivize more agents to invest in their actions and result in higher planner objective values.

5.4 Type 2 Model, Linear Threshold Mechanism

To be consistent with our analytical results, we choose to use G with one or more fully connected components that have no mutual connections with other components for our data samples in this part. Figure 7 shows that when the network is fully connected, then both $U^*(f)$ and the threshold τ are decreasing in $|S_\tau^+|$. But as shown in Fig. 8, when we have more than one connected component in the network, τ is no longer decreasing in $|S_\tau^+|$. We note that having the highest $U^*(f)$ at the NE with the most active agents is in general not true, which we can use a simple example with three agents where $g_{12} = g_{21} = g_{31} = g_{32} = 0.01, g_{13} = g_{23} = 1.5$ to show this. Figure 9 shows that $U^*(f)$ is decreasing in the average connection strength and the reason is due to free-riding similar to the Type 2 linear mechanism games.

6 Discussion

6.1 Comparisons with Previous Works

Since our game (its agents) is positioned over a network, it would be interesting to compare in what ways this game is similar to or different from the commonly studied network games, some of which we reviewed earlier. Below we summarize the main differences in the solutions we obtained, compared to that of conventional network games:

1. Compared to previous network games literature with multi-dimensional agent actions, our work embeds this game within a Stackelberg setting, with the

introduction of a planner who uses decision rules to incentivize agents to take certain actions. Similar to previous work on network games, the agents' equilibrium actions still depend on the network structure. However, in our setting the equilibrium actions also depend on the decision rules imposed by the planner.

2. Our model assumes the planner only sees observable features z, which are incomplete or noisy versions of the true features x. Specifically, the projection matrix P itself maps high dimensional actions to lower dimensional observable features, making it impossible for the planner to recover the true action profile only from the observable features.

3. The free-riding issue is frequently studied in the network games literature. Our analysis shows how this issue is more complex depending on whether agents are coupled through their respective decision outcomes (Type 1) or through their respective actions (Type 2). In particular, free-riding exists in Type 2 models, but not Type 1 models. That it exists in Type 2 models has a similar reason to what happens in a conventional network game: each agent's actions have externalities on their neighbors in that when an agent increases its investment, its neighbors could invest less and still get the same decision outcome, effectively making their actions strategic substitutes. This results in free-riding. What happens in the Type 1 models is more interesting as the externalities function through the agents' decision outcomes, not directly through their actions. First of all, in Type 1 models with linear threshold mechanisms free-riding cannot happen; this is because the externality from a neighbor's outcome only exists when an agent itself gets a positive decision outcome. In the case of Type 1 model with a linear mechanism, a neighbor's higher decision outcome actually incentivizes the agent to exert higher effort (so as to also obtain a higher decision outcome). This effectively makes agents' actions strategic complements, thus ruling out free-riding.

7   Conclusion

In this paper, we studied strategic machine learning problems where agents are interdependent in their best responses. We established two Stackelberg game models where the planner publishes the decision rules in the first stage and the agents best respond to the decision rule and other agents in the second round. We focused on two types of commonly used decision rules in the games, the linear mechanisms, and linear threshold mechanisms. Then in both types of games, we analyzed the Stackelberg equilibrium and how the planner can find the optimal decision rules. Last but not least, we compared our work and previous works in strategic machine learning, as well as previous works in network games and graphical games.

A   Proof of Lemma 1

Proof. First of all, we have from Sect. 2 that $z^{(i)} = Px^{(i)}$, and thus $w^T z^{(i)} = w^T P x^{(i)}$.

We can see that any manipulation action $\boldsymbol{x}^{(i)}$ that violate lemma 1 will be strictly dominated by its projection onto $P^T\boldsymbol{w}$. This is because the action cost increases but the decision outcome $f(\boldsymbol{z}^{(i)})$ remains the same and thus the utility strictly decreases. Therefore, any best response should satisfy Lemma 1.

B   Proof of Proposition 1

Proof. We can rewrite utility function of a_i as follows

$$u_i = \boldsymbol{w}^T P \boldsymbol{x}^{(i)} + \boldsymbol{w}^T P \boldsymbol{x}^{(i)} \cdot \sum_{j \in \mathcal{N}_i} g_{ij} \boldsymbol{w}^T P \boldsymbol{x}^{(j)} - \frac{1}{2}||\boldsymbol{x}^{(i)}||^2.$$

From Lemma 1, we can denote $(\boldsymbol{x}^{(i)})^* = \alpha_i \frac{P^T \boldsymbol{w}}{||P^T \boldsymbol{w}||}$, and then

$$u_i = ||P^T \boldsymbol{w}||\alpha_i + ||P^T \boldsymbol{w}||^2 \alpha_i \sum_{j \in \mathcal{N}_i} g_{ij}\alpha_j - \frac{1}{2}\alpha_i^2,$$

and thus from the first order derivatives

$$\frac{\partial u_i}{\partial \alpha_i} = -\alpha_i + ||P^T \boldsymbol{w}|| + ||P^T \boldsymbol{w}||^2 \sum_{j \in \mathcal{N}_i} g_{ij}\alpha_j,$$

we know that the agents have a unique Nash equilibrium

$$\boldsymbol{\alpha}^* = ||P^T \boldsymbol{w}||(I - ||P^T \boldsymbol{w}||^2 G)^{-1}\mathbf{1},$$

if $I - ||P^T \boldsymbol{w}||^2 G$ is positive definite.

C   Proof of Proposition 2

Proof. Since $G \succ \mathbf{0}$ and $(I - r^2 G) \succ \mathbf{0}$, we can write out its eigendecomposition as $G = V \Lambda V^T$, where $\Lambda = \mathbf{diag}(\boldsymbol{\lambda})$, $\lambda_1 \geq \lambda_2 \geq \cdots \geq \lambda_N > 0$, and we denote $\tilde{\lambda}_i := (1 - l^2\lambda_i)^{-1} > 0, \tilde{\Lambda} := \mathbf{diag}(\tilde{\boldsymbol{\lambda}}), l = ||P^T \boldsymbol{w}|| \leq r$, then

$$\boldsymbol{\alpha}^* = l \cdot V \tilde{\Lambda} V^T \mathbf{1}.$$

For the planner, it's equivalent to maximize

$$\sum_{i=1}^{N} \boldsymbol{q}^T \boldsymbol{x}_i^* = \mathbf{1}^T \boldsymbol{\alpha}^* \cdot \frac{\boldsymbol{q}^T (P^T \boldsymbol{w})}{||P^T \boldsymbol{w}||} = \mathbf{1}^T V \tilde{\Lambda} V^T \mathbf{1} \cdot \boldsymbol{q}^T (P^T \boldsymbol{w}),$$

which is monotonically increasing in l (since both $\mathbf{1}^T V \tilde{\Lambda} V^T \mathbf{1}$ and $\boldsymbol{q}^T (P^T \boldsymbol{w})$ are positive and monotonically increasing in l) and thus the planner's optimal linear mechanism satisfies $||P^T \boldsymbol{w}|| = l = r$.

Then since the first term is independent of the $\boldsymbol{w}$, we need to choose $\boldsymbol{w}$ that maximizes $\boldsymbol{w}^T (P\boldsymbol{q})$. When they have cosine similarity 1, the objective is maximized.

D   Proof of Lemma 2

Proof. We have

$$f(\boldsymbol{z}^{(i)}) = \boldsymbol{w}^T P(\boldsymbol{x}^{(i)} + \sum_{j \in \mathcal{N}_i} g_{ij}\boldsymbol{x}^{(j)}) = (P^T\boldsymbol{w})^T\boldsymbol{x}^{(i)} + (P^T\boldsymbol{w})^T \sum_{j \in \mathcal{N}_i} g_{ij}\boldsymbol{x}^{(j)},$$

where the second part remains the same when a_i's neighbors' actions are fixed. For an arbitrary $\boldsymbol{x}^{(i)} \geq 0, s_{cos}(\hat{\boldsymbol{x}}^{(i)}, \boldsymbol{e}_k) \neq 1$, we can show that it is strictly dominated.

Since $s_{cos}(\hat{\boldsymbol{x}}^{(i)}, \boldsymbol{e}_k) \neq 1$, there exist a dimension t, such that $\frac{(P^T\boldsymbol{w})_t}{c_t} < \frac{(P^T\boldsymbol{w})_k}{c_k}$, and $(\boldsymbol{x}^{(i)})_t > 0$. We consider

$$(\boldsymbol{x}^{(i)})' = \boldsymbol{x}^{(i)} - (\boldsymbol{x}^{(i)})_t\boldsymbol{e}_t + \frac{(\boldsymbol{x}^{(i)})_t c_k}{c_t}(\boldsymbol{x}^{(i)})_k,$$

then it's not hard to see that the action cost remains the same

$$\boldsymbol{c}^T\boldsymbol{x}^{(i)} = \sum_{k=1}^{K} c_k(\boldsymbol{x}^{(i)})_k = \boldsymbol{c}^T(\boldsymbol{x}^{(i)})',$$

and $(\boldsymbol{x}^{(i)})'$ achieves a higher decision outcome since

$$\sum_{k=1}^{K}(P^T\boldsymbol{w})_k(\boldsymbol{x}^{(i)})'_k > \sum_{k=1}^{K}(P^T\boldsymbol{w})_k(\boldsymbol{x}^{(i)})'_k.$$

This means that $(\boldsymbol{x}^{(i)})'$ strictly dominates $\boldsymbol{x}^{(i)}$. Similarly, any dimension other than k is suboptimal investment for a rational agent and thus any best response should satisfy Lemma 2. ∎

E   Proof of Proposition 3

Proof. The direction of $(\boldsymbol{x}^{(i)})^*$ follows Lemma 2, it remains to show the expression of $\boldsymbol{\alpha}^*$ and the uniqueness claim.

We can rewrite the utility functions as follows

$$u^{(i)}(\alpha^{(i)}, \boldsymbol{\alpha}^{(-i)}) = b_i((P^T\boldsymbol{w})_k[\alpha^{(i)} + \sum_{j \in \mathcal{N}_i} g_{ij}\alpha^{(j)}]) - c_k\alpha^{(i)}. \qquad (22)$$

The first order derivatives are

$$\frac{\partial u^{(i)}}{\partial \alpha^{(i)}} = (P^T\boldsymbol{w})_k b'_i(\alpha^{(i)} + \sum_{j \in \mathcal{N}_i} g_{ij}\alpha^{(j)}) - c_k,$$

and thus solving for them gives us the LCP in Eq. (11).

The uniqueness result follows Theorem 1 of [19]. ∎

F   Proof of Lemma 3

Proof. Consider the following linear program

$$\text{maximize}_{w \in \mathbf{R}^K} \quad \frac{w^T p_k}{c_k}$$
$$\text{subject to} \quad \frac{(P^T w)_r}{c_r} \leq 1, \forall r \tag{23}$$
$$w \geq 0$$

If the optimal objective value in Eq. (23) is no less than 1, then $\mathcal{L}_k$ is non-empty. The dual problem of Eq. (23) is

$$\text{minimize}_{y \in \mathbf{R}^M} \quad y^T c$$
$$\text{subject to} \quad Py \geq p_k \tag{24}$$
$$y \geq 0$$

We can rewrite the constraints in Eq. (24) as follows

$$[Py]_t \geq (p_k)_t \Leftrightarrow \sum_{r=1}^M p_{tr} y_r \geq p_{tk}, \tag{25}$$

and thus we know from the definition of κ_k that Eq. (24) has optimal objective value 1. By duality, the optimal objective value in Eq. (23) is also 1 which shows that $\mathcal{L}_k$ is non-empty. Moreover, the linear program in Eq. (23) can be solved in polynomial time, which concludes the proof.

G   Proof of Lemma 4

Proof. We denote $\tilde{y}$ as the solution to the optimization problem in Eq. (12), i.e., $\tilde{y}^T c = \kappa_k < e_k^T c$ and $\tilde{z} = P\tilde{y} \geq p_k, \tilde{y} \geq 0$.

This is equivalent to say that comparing the two action profiles $\tilde{y}$ and e_k, we know that $\tilde{y}$ achieves a weakly higher benefit $f(\tilde{z}) \geq f(p_k)$ while having a strictly lower cost $\tilde{y}^T c = \kappa_k < e_k^T c$. Since $b^{(i)}(\cdot)$ is strictly increasing, we know $u^{(i)}(\tilde{z}) > u^{(i)}(e_k)$, indicating that any action profile $x^{(i)}$ s.t., $x^{(i)} = l > 0$ is strictly dominated by $x^{(i)} - l \cdot e_k + l \cdot \tilde{z}$ which completes the proof.

H   Proof of Lemma 5

Proof. First of all, we show that $w^T P(x^{(i)})^* = \tau$. If $w^T P(x^{(i)})^* < \tau$ and $(x^{(i)})^* \neq 0$, then the decision outcome is $f(z^{(i)}) = 0$ and the action cost is $\frac{1}{2}\|(x^{(i)})^*\|_2^2 > 0$, which means $(x^{(i)})^*$ is strictly dominated by 0. On the other hand, if $w^T P(x^{(i)})^* > \tau$, we can see that action $\hat{x}^{(i)} = \frac{\tau}{w^T P(x^{(i)})^*}$ also results in $f(z^{(i)}) = 1$ and lowers the action cost, and thus strictly dominates $(x^{(i)})^*$.

Then we show that $s_{cos}(\boldsymbol{x}^{(i)}, P^T\boldsymbol{w}) = 1$. We can write out the agent's optimization problem as follows

$$\text{minimize } \|\boldsymbol{x}^{(i)}\|_2^2$$
$$\text{subject to } \boldsymbol{w}^T P \boldsymbol{x}^{(i)} = \tau,$$

which clearly gives us $s_{cos}(\boldsymbol{x}^{(i)}, P^T\boldsymbol{w}) = 1$, since following the normal vector of the hyperplane is the shortest path to reach the hyperplane.

I   Proof of Lemma 6

Proof. Given $f = \mathbf{1}(\boldsymbol{w}^T\boldsymbol{z} \geq \tau)$, we denote the set of active agents (agents getting decision outcome 1 and thus non-zero action) as S_τ^+ and the set of inactive agents as S_τ^-, where obviously $S_\tau^+ \bigcup S_\tau^- = \{a_1, \ldots, a_N\}, S_\tau^+ \bigcap S_\tau^- = \emptyset$.

Then we consider an alternative threshold $\tilde{\tau}$ s.t., $\tilde{\tau} > \tau$, and if $a_i \in S_{\tilde{\tau}}^+$, we have from Eq. (16) that

$$1 + \sum_{j \in \mathcal{N}_i} g_{ij} \mathbf{1}((\boldsymbol{x}^{(j)})_{\tilde{\tau}}^* \neq \mathbf{0}) \geq \frac{1}{2}\tilde{\tau}^2 > \frac{1}{2}\tau^2,$$

where we add a subscript to the equilibrium action to indicate the corresponding decision rule. This shows that it is profitable for all $a_i \in S_{\tilde{\tau}}^+$ to jointly manipulate, which is a sufficient condition to conclude joint manipulation is profitable for all $a_i \in S_{\tilde{\tau}}^+$ at a lower threshold τ. In other words, $a_i \in S_{\tilde{\tau}}^+ \Rightarrow a_i \in S_\tau^+$ if $\tilde{\tau} > \tau$, and thus $S_{\tilde{\tau}}^+ \subseteq S_\tau^+$ if $\tilde{\tau} > \tau$. Equivalently, $a_i \in S_\tau^- \Leftrightarrow a_i \notin S_\tau^+ \Rightarrow a_i \notin S_{\tilde{\tau}}^+ \Leftrightarrow a_i \in S_{\tilde{\tau}}^-$ if $\tilde{\tau} > \tau$, and thus $S_{\tilde{\tau}}^- \supseteq S_\tau^-$ if $\tilde{\tau} > \tau$.

J   Proof of Proposition 4

Proof. We first show that $\boldsymbol{w}$ such that $s_{cos}(\boldsymbol{w}, P\boldsymbol{q}) = 1$ (weakly) dominates all other $\boldsymbol{v}$ such that $s_{cos}(\boldsymbol{v}, P\boldsymbol{q}) < 1$ in the linear threshold mechanism.

For an arbitrary linear threshold mechanism $f_0(\boldsymbol{z}) = \mathbf{1}(\boldsymbol{v}^T\boldsymbol{z} \geq \tau_0)$ such that $s_{cos}(\boldsymbol{v}, P\boldsymbol{q}) < 1$, the agents' best responses are

$$(\boldsymbol{x}^{(i)})^* = \begin{cases} \tau_0 P^T \boldsymbol{v} & \text{if } 1 + \sum_{j \in \mathcal{N}_i} g_{ij} \mathbf{1}((\boldsymbol{x}^{(j)})^* \neq \mathbf{0}) \geq \frac{1}{2}\tau_0^2 \\ \mathbf{0} & \text{o.w.} \end{cases}$$

Then let $\boldsymbol{w}$ be such that $s_{cos}(\boldsymbol{w}, P\boldsymbol{q}) = 1$, $\|P^T\boldsymbol{w}\|_2 = \|P^T\boldsymbol{v}\|_2$, then $f(\boldsymbol{z}) = \mathbf{1}(\boldsymbol{w}^T\boldsymbol{z} \geq \tau_0)$ is a (weakly) better option for the planner. This is because agents' best responses become

$$(\boldsymbol{x}^{(i)})^* = \begin{cases} \tau_0 P^T \boldsymbol{w} & \text{if } 1 + \sum_{j \in \mathcal{N}_i} g_{ij} \mathbf{1}((\boldsymbol{x}^{(j)})^* \neq \mathbf{0}) \geq \frac{1}{2}\tau_0^2 \\ \mathbf{0} & \text{o.w.} \end{cases}$$

and thus $U(f) \geq U(f_0)$ since $\boldsymbol{w}^T(P\boldsymbol{q}) > \boldsymbol{v}^T(P\boldsymbol{q})$.

Next, we show the performance lower bound part in Eq. (18). Suppose the planner's optimal choice of threshold is τ^*, then during the scanning, there exist

τ_0 such that $\tau_0 \in (\tau^* - \epsilon, \tau^*]$. We denote the number of agents incentivized to manipulate at threshold τ as N_τ. From Lemma 6, we know that $N \geq N_{tau_0} \geq N_{\tau^*}$, and then

$$\frac{U(f_{\tau_0})}{\max_f U(f)} = \frac{U(f_{\tau_0})}{U(f_{\tau^*})} \geq \frac{N_{\tau_0}\tau_0}{N_{\tau^*}\tau^*} \geq \frac{\tau_0}{\tau^*} > 1 - \frac{\epsilon}{\tau^*} \geq 1 - \frac{\epsilon}{\sqrt{2}},$$

which completes the proof.

K   Proof of Proposition 5

Proof. We begin by showing that $s_{cos}((\boldsymbol{x}^{(i)})^*, \boldsymbol{e}_k) = 1$. This part is similar to the proof of Lemma 2. For $\forall \boldsymbol{x}^{(i)}, \text{s.t.} s_{cos}(\boldsymbol{x}^{(i)}, \boldsymbol{e}_k) < 1, \boldsymbol{w}^T P \boldsymbol{x}^{(i)} = \tau$, we can show that

$$(\boldsymbol{x}^{(i)})' = \boldsymbol{x}^{(i)} - (\boldsymbol{x}^{(i)})_t \boldsymbol{e}_t + \frac{(\boldsymbol{x}^{(i)})_t c_k}{c_t}(\boldsymbol{x}^{(i)})_k,$$

keeps the same action cost and satisfies $\boldsymbol{w}^T P(\boldsymbol{x}^{(i)})' > \boldsymbol{w}^T P\boldsymbol{x}^{(i)}$. We denote

$$\tau' := \boldsymbol{w}^T P((\boldsymbol{x}^{(i)})' + \sum_{j \in \mathcal{N}_i} g_{ij}\boldsymbol{x}^{(j)}), \quad \eta := \boldsymbol{w}^T P \sum_{j \in \mathcal{N}_i} g_{ij}\boldsymbol{x}^{(j)}, \quad \gamma := \frac{\tau - \eta}{\tau' - \eta} < 1.$$

Then the agent can choose the action $\gamma(\boldsymbol{x}^{(i)})'$ to increase it's utility and still gets decision outcome of 1. Therefore, any dimension other than k is suboptimal investment for a rational agent.

Then we need to show the expression of $\boldsymbol{\beta}^*$. For every agent in S, they need $f(\boldsymbol{z}^{(i)}) = 1$, which is equivalent to

$$\boldsymbol{w}^T P(\boldsymbol{x}^{(i)} + \sum_{j \in \mathcal{N}_i} g_{ij}\boldsymbol{x}^{(j)}) = \tau, \forall i \ \Leftrightarrow \ (P^T\boldsymbol{w})_k \cdot (\beta_S^{(i)} + \sum_{j \in \mathcal{N}_i} g_{ij}\beta_S^{(j)}) = \tau, \forall i,$$

which is equivalent to

$$(I + G_S)\boldsymbol{\beta} = \frac{\tau}{(P^T\boldsymbol{w})_k} \cdot \mathbf{1} \ \Leftrightarrow \ \boldsymbol{\beta} = \frac{\tau}{(P^T\boldsymbol{w})_k}(I + G_S)^{-1}\mathbf{1}.$$

For the individual rationality part, the cost cannot exceed 1, which requires $(\beta_S^{(i)})^* \leq \frac{1}{c_k}, \forall i$.

References

1. Bramoullé, Y., Kranton, R., D'amours, M.: Strategic interaction and networks. Am. Econ. Rev. **104**(3), 898–930 (2014)
2. Brückner, M., Kanzow, C., Scheffer, T.: Static prediction games for adversarial learning problems. J. Mach. Learn. Res. **13**, 2617–2654 (2012)
3. Chen, Y., Wang, J., Liu, Y.: Strategic classification with a light touch: Learning classifiers that incentivize constructive adaptation (2021)

4. Chen, Y., Podimata, C., Procaccia, A.: Strategyproof linear regression in high dimensions, pp. 9–26 (2018). https://doi.org/10.1145/3219166.3219175
5. Galeotti, A., Golub, B., Goyal, S.: Targeting interventions in networks. SSRN Electron. J. (2017). https://doi.org/10.2139/ssrn.3054353
6. Haghtalab, N., Immorlica, N., Lucier, B., Wang, J.: Maximizing welfare with incentive-aware evaluation mechanisms, pp. 160–166 (2020). https://doi.org/10.24963/ijcai.2020/23
7. Hamilton, W., Ying, R., Leskovec, J.: Inductive representation learning on large graphs (2017)
8. Hardt, M., Megiddo, N., Papadimitriou, C., Wootters, M.: Strategic classification, pp. 111–122 (2016). https://doi.org/10.1145/2840728.2840730
9. Hu, L., Immorlica, N., Vaughan, J.: The disparate effects of strategic manipulation, pp. 259–268 (2019). https://doi.org/10.1145/3287560.3287597
10. Kipf, T., Welling, M.: Semi-supervised classification with graph convolutional networks (2016)
11. Kleinberg, J., Raghavan, M.: How do classifiers induce agents to invest effort strategically? ACM Trans. Econ. Comput. 8, 1–23 (2020). https://doi.org/10.1145/3417742
12. La, R.J.: Interdependent security with strategic agents and cascades of infection. IEEE/ACM Trans. Netw. 24(3), 1378–1391 (2016)
13. Miller, J., Milli, S., Hardt, M.: Strategic classification is causal modeling in disguise. In: III, H.D., Singh, A. (eds.) Proceedings of the 37th International Conference on Machine Learning. Proceedings of Machine Learning Research, vol. 119, pp. 6917–6926. PMLR (2020)
14. Milli, S., Miller, J., Dragan, A., Hardt, M.: The social cost of strategic classification, pp. 230–239 (2019). https://doi.org/10.1145/3287560.3287576
15. Naghizadeh, P., Liu, M.: Budget balance or voluntary participation? Incentivizing investments in interdependent security games (2014). https://doi.org/10.1109/ALLERTON.2014.7028578
16. Naghizadeh, P., Liu, M.: Exit equilibrium: towards understanding voluntary participation in security games, pp. 1–9 (2016). https://doi.org/10.1109/INFOCOM.2016.7524353
17. Naghizadeh, P., Liu, M.: Opting out of incentive mechanisms: a study of security as a non-excludable public good. IEEE Trans. Inf. Foren. Secur. 11, 2790–2803 (2016). https://doi.org/10.1109/TIFS.2016.2599005
18. Naghizadeh, P., Liu, M.: On the uniqueness and stability of equilibria of network games. In: 2017 55th Annual Allerton Conference on Communication, Control, and Computing (Allerton), pp. 280–286. IEEE (2017)
19. Naghizadeh, P., Liu, M.: Provision of public goods on networks: on existence, uniqueness, and centralities. IEEE Trans. Netw. Sci. Eng. 5(3), 225–236 (2018)
20. Parise, F., Ozdaglar, A.: A variational inequality framework for network games: existence, uniqueness, convergence and sensitivity analysis. Games Econ. Behav. 114, 47–82 (2019)
21. Park, J., Schaar, M.: Intervention mechanism design for networks with selfish users (2010)
22. Rebille, Y., Richefort, L.: Equilibrium uniqueness in network games with strategic substitutes (2012)
23. Scutari, G., Facchinei, F., Pang, J.S., Palomar, D.P.: Real and complex monotone communication games. IEEE Trans. Inf. Theory 60(7), 4197–4231 (2014)
24. Scutari, G., Palomar, D.P., Barbarossa, S.: Asynchronous iterative water-filling for Gaussian frequency-selective interference channels. IEEE Trans. Inf. Theory 54(7), 2868–2878 (2008)

No Time to Lie: Bounds on the Learning Rate of a Defender for Inferring Attacker Target Preferences

Mark Bilinski[1], Joseph diVita[1], Kimberly Ferguson-Walter[2],
Sunny Fugate[1], Ryan Gabrys[1(✉)], Justin Mauger[1], and Brian Souza[1]

[1] Naval Information Warfare Center Pacific, San Diego, CA, USA
{bilinski,divita,fugate,gabrys,jmauger,bsouza}@spawar.navy.mil
[2] Laboratory for Advanced Cybersecurity Research, Laurel, MD, USA
kimberly.j.ferguson-walter.civ@mail.mil

Abstract. Prior work has explored the use of defensive cyber deception to manipulate the information available to attackers and to proactively misinform on behalf of both real and decoy systems. Such approaches can provide advantages to defenders by detecting inadvertent attacker interactions with decoy systems, by delaying attacker forward progress, by decreasing or eliminating attacker payoffs in multi-round interactions, and by predicting and interfering with (or incentivizing) likely attacker actions (probe, attack, and walk-away). In this work, we extend our prior model by examining the ability of a defender to learn an attacker's preferences through observations of their interactions with targeted systems. Knowledge of an attacker's preferences can be used to guide defensive systems, particularly those which present deceptive features to an attacker. Prior work did not distinguish between targets other than as real or decoy and only modeled an attacker's behaviors as it related to their costs for probing or attacking defended systems. While this was able to predict an attacker's likelihood of continuing their interactions or walking away from the game, it did not inform a defender as to an attacker's likely future actions as expressed through preferences for various defended systems. In this paper, we first present a theoretical model in which lower and upper bounds on the number of observations needed for a defender to learn an attacker's preferences is expressed. We then present empirical results in the form of simulated interactions between an attacker with fixed preferences and a learning defender. Lastly we discuss how these bounds can be used to inform an adaptive deceptive defense in which a defender can leverage their knowledge of attacker preferences to more optimally interfere with an attacker's future actions.

1 Introduction

Skilled cyber defenders are in short supply and new successful cyber attacks continue to be breaking news. While cybersecurity has begun to take its proper place as a priority throughout industry and government, provable cybersecurity solutions are still a rarity. Many techniques and technologies rely on flashy

© Springer Nature Switzerland AG 2021
B. Bošanský et al. (Eds.): GameSec 2021, LNCS 13061, pp. 138–157, 2021.
https://doi.org/10.1007/978-3-030-90370-1_8

marketing to sell what is claimed to be a good idea. While it is easy to demonstrate failure of a prior cybersecurity practice or posture, it is very difficult to provide scientific evidence of the effectiveness of a new defense. This has resulted in widespread use of myriad techniques and technologies which claim a security benefit (and which may truly resolve a known security deficit) but for which few counterarguments can be made due to lack of falsifiability of security claims [1]. Scientific contributions that can mathematically or empirically demonstrate the effectiveness of or the bounds on a defensive technique are in critical need for the advancement of cybersecurity.

Our efforts towards provable cybersecurity focus on cyber deception. Various cyber deception techniques have been introduced [13,14] and their benefits discussed [15] throughout academic literature. However, application of these technologies in operational computer networks is not yet commonplace. This is perhaps due to several open questions that remain about how to best utilize deception and how to balance deceptive defense with other cyber defensive goals and strategies. For example, traditional computer security practices often focus on quick detection and ejection of malicious activity. However, with cyber deception, ejection is often delayed, and increased interaction with the malicious actor promoted in order to gain some sort of advantage for the defender. This advantage could be delaying the attacker from their goal, steering them to a specific location, or learning their tactics, techniques, and procedures (TTPs) or preferences in order to build attacker profiles or deploy personalized defenses [16]. However, how long should defenders allow the interaction to continue? While defenders can gain knowledge about the attacker through continued interaction, there is also a risk of them revealing information to the attacker. This work addresses the fundamental question of determining the minimum number of interactions that will provide defenders with necessary and sufficient knowledge of an attacker's preferences to make informed defensive decisions.

2   Related Work

Deception is an important tactic that has been extensively studied in the field of cybersecurity [9]. Early works modeled the interactions between an attacker and defender using tools from game theory under the scenario where a defender attempts to deceive an attacker through the use of honeypots [10]—usually under a single-round framework. Under this setup, a defender first chooses a defense, which in this case is a particular arrangement of honeypots, and then afterwards the attacker, who is unaware of this arrangement, will choose to attack some subset of the network resources.

However, in many real-world security scenarios, the exchanges between an attacker and a defender are better modeled as multi-round interactive Stackelberg games. Furthermore, a defender typically does not know about the characteristics or goals of an attacker at the start of these interactions. In order for a defender to employ deception for this setup, they first need to learn the attacker's preferences.

In [11], the authors consider algorithms for the setup where a defender has no prior knowledge about either the game payoffs or the attacker's behavior. In [12], no-regret algorithms were developed to mitigate the effects of this uncertainty. Unlike many previous works, the focus of [7] was on the case where the behavior of the adversary population is not necessarily homogenous. Based upon a study, their work demonstrates that individuals can be naturally grouped into multiple distinct categories that share similar behaviors.

A theoretical analysis of the learnability of a bounded rational attacker was undertaken in [3]. For the Subjective Utility Quantal Response (SUQR) model, the authors found that a surprisingly small number of defender strategies suffice to learn the model. In [2], a similar model was applied to the cyber scenario where the goal is for a defender to learn the preferences of an attacker for a set of features that exist across a collection of machines or targets in the environment. There, the authors provide an expression on the number of samples sufficient to learn the attacker's score function within a certain multiplicative factor of the true score function. In addition, the authors propose an approximation algorithm for finding the optimal defender strategy and present simulations to validate their results.

Our work is most closely related to [2]. In the following, we provide expressions for the number of samples both necessary and sufficient to learn the attacker's score function. The number of samples that are sufficient has been studied to some extent in previous work, with assumptions about the structure of targets in the environment. In this work, we derive an expression that removes these assumptions about the structure of the targets in the environment, and it replaces it with the assumption the targets are randomly designed. We believe this assumption is relevant in cyber scenarios where the defender has no prior knowledge of the attacker and therefore stages machines/targets accordingly. We also derive a lower bound on the number of samples necessary for a defender to accurately estimate an attacker's score function. To the best of the author's knowledge, ours is the first result towards this effort, and such information can be used to determine the degree of uncertainty a defender will have regarding the aims/goals of an attacker. This uncertainty can then be used to formulate future informed defender strategies.

One of our main theoretical result shows that given a set of m features (where each feature can represent a service hosted, software or operating system versions, ports open) the defender can learn the attacker's score function provided a surprisingly small set of samples for a wide range of parameters. In particular, we show that the number of samples can be much less than $\mathcal{O}(\log m)$ in many cases. This result is verified via extensive simulation results using both a least squares approach as well as gradient descent. In addition, we consider the case of an attacker whose preferences change, and we show that with certain parameters it is possible for a defender to accurately recover an attacker's preferences as they evolve over time.

3 Model

The model we study, which we now review, is similar to the one from [2] and is known as the Feature Deception Problem (FDP). We assume that we have the setup of an attacker and a defender. The defender in this scenario is capable of presenting N targets to the attacker and we characterize each target by a set of m features or configuration options. Suppose that for target $i \in [N]$, the attacker observes the configuration $\mathbf{x}^{(i)} = (x_1^{(i)}, \ldots, x_m^{(i)}) \in \mathbb{R}_+^m$, so that $\mathbf{x}^{(i)}$ is a vector consisting of m positive real numbers. We assume that in this environment, the attacker will attack target i with probability

$$\frac{f(\mathbf{x}^{(i)})}{\sum_{j \in [N]} f(\mathbf{x}^{(j)})}. \tag{1}$$

We note that this model corresponds to the Luce model [4] from quantum choice theory and is a special case of the logit quantal response model. This model is a generalization of rationality models considered in several other works such as [5,6]. Similar to [2,3], we assume in this work that the attacker's reward function is given by

$$f(\mathbf{x}^{(i)}) = \exp\left(\sum_{j \in [m]} w_j x_j^{(i)}\right), \tag{2}$$

which corresponds to a neural network with parameter $\mathbf{w} = (w_1, w_2, \ldots, w_m) \in \mathbb{R}_+^m$, which has been used in the context of modeling attacker preferences in past work in cybersecurity [7]. The vector $\mathbf{w}$ from the previous equation represents the preferences of an attacker since according to (1) and (2) it determines which machine(s) the attacker is more likely to attack.

A critical step in generating an appropriate defender strategy is to determine the effect to which the defender can learn the function f. As will be discussed soon, we will see that the defender's ability to learn this information is dependent on two variables:

1. The amount of time that the attacker and defender interact, and
2. The configuration of the targets presented to the attacker.

For 1., the longer the period of time the defender is allowed to observe the attacker for, the better the estimate for f will be. For 2., we will see that our ability to accurately quantify f will be dependent on the structure of the feature matrix $A^{(F)}$ whose rows consist of the vectors $\mathbf{x}^{(i)}$, $i \in [N]$.

Let $\widetilde{f}$ denote the approximation to f, which is formed after M observations of the attacker. Note that the function f is completely determined by the vector $\mathbf{w}$. We therefore characterize the similarity between $\widetilde{f}$ and f by the 2-norm of the difference $\mathbf{w} - \widetilde{\mathbf{w}}$ where $\widetilde{f}(\mathbf{x}) = \exp\left(\widetilde{\mathbf{w}}^T \mathbf{x}\right)$. We say that $\widetilde{f}$ is ε-close if

$$\left\|\widetilde{\mathbf{w}} - \mathbf{w}\right\|_2 \leqslant \varepsilon.$$

Thus, under this setup, the goal for the defender will be to determine, given a set of N targets that the defender determines, the reward function for the attacker.

In a sense, one can think of each target generated by the defender as a sampling of the distribution of the function f.

The contributions of this work are the following. First, using Eq. (2) along with a fixed set of chosen targets $\{\mathbf{x}^{(1)}, \ldots, \mathbf{x}^{(N)}\}$, in Sect. 4 we will present necessary conditions on M as well as the feature matrix

$$A^{(F)} = \left(\mathbf{x}^{(i)}\right)_{i=1,\ldots,N}$$

(consisting of N rows) to guarantee that $\widetilde{f}$ is ε-close to f. In Sect. 5, we present an upper bound on the number of observations needed for the setup where the features for each of the targets are chosen randomly. Afterwards, in Sect. 6 we give simulation results that verify our results using two different techniques for the defender and where we also consider the setup where the preferences of the attacker, represented by the vector $\mathbf{w}$, are allowed to evolve over time.

We note that our setup is similar to previous work in terms of the model. However, the aim in this work is different than in previous work. In particular, our notion of similarity is different than the one used previously (and in particular necessarily more general since we do not restrict the range of our features to be between 0 and 1). Furthermore, unlike [2], we provide **both** upper and lower bounds on our conditions, which provides a more robust framework in which to base our choice of deceptive strategies. The upper bound represents a worst-case scenario in which an attacker may attempt to hide their preferences to subvert a defender's ability to learn. As will be described in more detail in Sect. 5, our upper bound is derived using a probabilistic construction of the feature matrix $A^{(F)}$, which may be useful for two reasons. First, the result shows that we can learn the attacker's preferences with high probability given a sufficient number of rounds using the simple strategy of randomly generating the features on each of the targets presented to an attacker. Secondly, even in the case of an attacker who randomly targets systems according to their preferences, this is no worse than a defender that arranges the targets and target features uniformly at random. In such a worst-case scenario our result implies an upper bound on the number of observations necessary for a defender to infer attacker preferences with no prior knowledge of the attacker.

4   Lower Bound on the Number of Observations

In this section, we derive our lower bound on the number of observations necessary to accurately estimate the attacker's preferences. We first introduce some notation before proceeding. Denote

$$P_i := \frac{f(\mathbf{x}^{(i)})}{\sum_{j \in [N]} f(\mathbf{x}^{(j)})}, \tag{3}$$

and let

$$\widetilde{P}_i := \frac{\widetilde{f}(\mathbf{x}^{(i)})}{\sum_{j \in [N]} \widetilde{f}(\mathbf{x}^{(j)})}.$$

We say that a distribution $P = (P_i)_{i \in [N]}$ is ζ-similar to $\widetilde{P} = (\widetilde{P}_i)_{i \in [N]}$ if $\forall i \in [N]$

$$\left| P_i - \widetilde{P}_i \right| \leqslant \zeta. \tag{4}$$

The main result of the section appears as Theorem 1. Our approach to deriving this result contains two steps. First, in Lemma 1, we determine (with high probability) the minimum number of rounds necessary to produce an accurate estimate $(\widetilde{P}_1, \widetilde{P}_2, \ldots, \widetilde{P}_N)$ for the distribution $(P_1, P_2, \ldots, P_N)$ defined in (3). Lemma 2 then provides a lower bound for the distance between $\mathbf{w}$ and any estimate $\widetilde{\mathbf{w}}$ for $\mathbf{w}$ provided the distribution $(\widetilde{P}_1, \widetilde{P}_2, \ldots, \widetilde{P}_N)$. Afterwards, by combining the results from the previous two lemmas, our lower bound is stated in Theorem 1.

Lemma 1. *Suppose we wish to generate an estimate $\widetilde{P}$ which is ζ-similar to P with probability $1 - \Delta$. Then, the number of observations required is at least M where*

$$M \geqslant \frac{\frac{1}{2}(1 - \beta)^{\beta - 1}}{(1 + \beta)^{\beta + 1} - (1 - \beta)^{\beta - 1}},$$

$0 < \zeta < \frac{1}{2N}$ *and* $\beta = N\zeta$.

Proof. We assume in the following for simplicity that N is divisible by two. Under our setup let Ω be a finite sample space and suppose that $P = (P_1, \ldots, P_N) = (\frac{1}{N}, \frac{1}{N}, \ldots, \frac{1}{N})$, $\widetilde{P} = (\widetilde{P}_1, \ldots, \widetilde{P}_N)$ are distributions on Ω so that P represents the uniform distribution. Let $E \in \Omega^M$ be a sequence of M independent events. Then, from Pinsker's inequality, we have

$$\left| \widetilde{P}_E - P_E \right| \leqslant \sqrt{M D_{KL}(P \| \widetilde{P})},$$

where D_{KL} denotes the Kullback-Leibler divergence. From (4), we have

$$D_{KL}(P \| \widetilde{P}) = \sum_{i \in [N]} \widetilde{P}_i \log \frac{\widetilde{P}_i}{P_i}$$

$$\overset{(a)}{\leqslant} \frac{N}{2}\left(\frac{1}{N} + \zeta\right) \log\left(1 + N\zeta\right) + \frac{N}{2}\left(\frac{1}{N} - \zeta\right) \log\left(1 - N\zeta\right)$$

$$= \frac{1}{2}\left(\log(1 + N\zeta) + \log(1 - N\zeta)\right) + \frac{1}{2}\left(\log(1 + N\zeta)^{N\zeta} - \log(1 - N\zeta)^{N\zeta}\right)$$

$$\overset{(b)}{=} \frac{1}{2}\log\left((1 - \beta^2)\left(\frac{1 + \beta}{1 - \beta}\right)^{\beta}\right)$$

$$\overset{(c)}{\leqslant} \frac{1}{2}\left((1 - \beta^2)\left(\frac{1 + \beta}{1 - \beta}\right)^{\beta} - 1\right),$$

$$= \frac{1}{2}\left(\frac{(1 + \beta)^{\beta + 1}}{(1 - \beta)^{\beta - 1}} - 1\right). \tag{5}$$

Inequality (a) follows from the fact that for any $0 < x_1, x_2 < \frac{1}{2N}$, $(\frac{1}{N} - x_1)$ $\log\left(\frac{1}{N} - x_1\right) + (\frac{1}{N} - x_2) \log\left(\frac{1}{N} - x_2\right) \leqslant \left(\frac{1}{N} - (x_1 + x_2)\right) \log\left(\frac{1}{N} - (x_1 + x_2)\right)$, which implies that $\sum_{i\in[N]} \widetilde{P}_i \log \frac{\widetilde{P}_i}{P_i}$ is maximized when $\widetilde{P}_i = \frac{1}{N} \pm \zeta$. Line (b) follows by substituting $\beta = N\zeta$ and for (c) we have used the identity that $\log x \leqslant x - 1$.

Let $R : \Omega^M \to \{0,1\}$ be a decision rule where given an event $E' \in \Omega^M$, $R(E') = 1$ if E' is the result of M observations under the distribution $\widetilde{P}$ and otherwise $R(E') = 0$. Suppose that the probability R is correct is at least $1 - \Delta$. Then it follows that

$$\Pr\Big(R(E') = 0 | E' \sim P\Big) - \Pr\Big(R(E') = 0 | E' \sim \widetilde{P}\Big) \geqslant 1 - 2\Delta.$$

Letting E' be the event that $R(E') = 0$, then according to (5) if $\beta = N\zeta$, we have

$$\left| \Pr\Big(R(E') = 0 | E' \sim P\Big) - \Pr\Big(R(E') = 0 | E' \sim \widetilde{P}\Big) \right| \leqslant \sqrt{\frac{M}{2}\left(\frac{(1+\beta)^{\beta+1}}{(1-\beta)^{\beta-1}} - 1\right)}$$

$$= \sqrt{\frac{M}{2}\left(\frac{(1+\beta)^{\beta+1} - (1-\beta)^{\beta-1}}{(1-\beta)^{\beta-1}}\right)}.$$

If $M < \frac{\frac{1}{2}(1-\beta)^{\beta-1}}{(1+\beta)^{\beta+1} - (1-\beta)^{\beta-1}}$, the previous expression is at most $\frac{1}{2}$, which implies a contradiction.

The next lemma relates ε-close functions to ζ-similar distributions.

Lemma 2. *There exists two ζ-similar distributions $P, \widetilde{P}$ where*

$$\varepsilon = \left\|\widetilde{\mathbf{w}} - \mathbf{w}\right\|_2 > \frac{\sqrt{m}\beta}{(1+\beta)\sigma_{\max}},$$

where $\beta = N\zeta$, $m = N$ and $\sigma_{\max}$ represents the largest singular value of the feature matrix $A^{(F)} := \left(\mathbf{x}^{(i)}\right)_{i\in[N]}$, whose rows are equal to $\mathbf{x}^{(1)}, \ldots, \mathbf{x}^{(N)}$, and $A^{(F)}$ has full rank.

Proof. Suppose that $f(\mathbf{x}) = \exp\Big(\mathbf{w}^T\mathbf{x}\Big)$ and that our estimate for $f(\mathbf{x})$ is $\widetilde{f}(\mathbf{x}) = \exp\Big(\widetilde{\mathbf{w}}^T\mathbf{x}\Big)$. In order to derive our lower bound on M, we assume that the quantity $\sum_{j\in[N]} f(\mathbf{x}^{(j)})$ is known and in particular that $\sum_{j\in[N]} f(\widetilde{\mathbf{x}}^{(j)}) = \sum_{j\in[N]} f(\mathbf{x}^{(j)})$. We also assume that $m = N$. Notice that

$$\log\left(\frac{\widetilde{P}_i}{P_i}\right) = \log\left(\frac{\widetilde{f}(\mathbf{z})}{f(\mathbf{z})}\right) = \left(\widetilde{\mathbf{w}}^T - \mathbf{w}^T\right)\mathbf{z},$$

where $\mathbf{z} \in \mathbb{R}^m$. Since we assume that f and $\widetilde{f}$ have the form (2), it follows that $\widetilde{\mathbf{w}}^T - \mathbf{w}^T$ is such that

$$A^{(F)}\left(\widetilde{\mathbf{w}}^T - \mathbf{w}^T\right) = \begin{bmatrix} \log(\widetilde{P_1}/P_1) \\ \log(\widetilde{P_2}/P_2) \\ \vdots \\ \log(\widetilde{P_m}/P_m) \end{bmatrix}.$$

For shorthand, let $\mathbf{b} = \begin{bmatrix} \log(\widetilde{P_1}/P_1) \\ \log(\widetilde{P_2}/P_2) \\ \vdots \\ \log(\widetilde{P_m}/P_m) \end{bmatrix}$. Suppose P is the uniform distribution

and that for $i \in [N/2]$, $\widetilde{P_i} = P_i + \zeta$ and when $i \in \{N/2+1, \ldots, N\}$, we have $\widetilde{P_i} = P_i - \zeta$. Let $(A^{(F)})^{-1} = A^{(-F)}$. Since $A^{(F)}$ by assumption has full column rank, then $||A^{(-F)}\mathbf{b}||_2 \geqslant \frac{1}{\sigma_{\max}}||\mathbf{b}||_2$. Thus, we have

$$\left\|\widetilde{\mathbf{w}}^T - \mathbf{w}^T\right\|_2 \geqslant \left\|A^{(-F)}\mathbf{b}\right\|_2 \geqslant \frac{1}{\sigma_{\max}}\sqrt{\frac{m}{2}\log^2\left(1+\beta\right) + \frac{m}{2}\log^2\left(1-\beta\right)}$$

$$\overset{(a)}{\geqslant} \frac{1}{\sigma_{\max}}\sqrt{\frac{m}{2}\left(\frac{\beta}{1+\beta}\right)^2 + \frac{m}{2}\left(\frac{-\beta}{1-\beta}\right)^2}$$

$$> \sqrt{m}\frac{\beta}{(1+\beta)\sigma_{\max}},$$

where (a) follows from the fact that $\log x \geqslant 1 - \frac{1}{x}$.

As a result of the previous two lemmas, we arrive at our lower bound on M.

Theorem 1. *If $||\widetilde{\mathbf{w}} - \mathbf{w}||_2 \leqslant \varepsilon$ holds with probability $1 - \Delta$, then*

$$M \geqslant \frac{\frac{1}{2}(1-\gamma)^{\gamma-1}}{(1+\gamma)^{\gamma+1} - (1-\gamma)^{\gamma-1}},$$

where $\gamma = \frac{\varepsilon\sigma_{\max}/\sqrt{m}}{1-\varepsilon\sigma_{\max}/\sqrt{m}}$ and $m = N$.

Proof. If $||\widetilde{\mathbf{w}} - \mathbf{w}||_2 \leqslant \varepsilon$, then from Lemma 2 it follows that $\beta \leqslant \frac{\varepsilon\sigma_{\max}/\sqrt{m}}{1-\varepsilon\sigma_{\max}/\sqrt{m}}$, which according to Lemma 1 implies the desired result.

One potential application of Theorem 1 is that it can be used as part of an adaptive defense strategy whereby initially (due to a lack of knowledge about the attacker) a defender may choose to employ random defense tactics that are effective across a number of potential attacker types. The catalogue of appropriate actions available to a human or automated defender depends on what information is known about the attacker and the defended network and computing environments. As the defender gains more knowledge about the attacker the defender may choose to combine or replace a set of random defense tactics with ones that are specifically suited to a specific attacker. For example, a proactive defender may deploy pre-configured honeypots and decoys on their network to distract attackers from critical assets and delay attacker forward progress. However, as it becomes more probable that the defender can determine the attacker's preferences according to Theorem 1, adaptive deceptive defenses can be personalized to react to the specific ongoing attack by changing the appearance or behavior of the honeypots or decoys, thus optimizing the defense against the attacker currently present.

5   Upper Bound on the Number of Observations

Next, we turn to discussing upper bounds. Recall that our aim is to consider the setup where the defender has no prior knowledge of the attacker. To account for this scenario, we assume that each of the N targets $\boldsymbol{x}^{(i)}$ are generated randomly according to the normal distribution $\mathcal{N}(\log m, \frac{1}{2})$. In order to guarantee that with high probability the feature matrix, whose i-th row is equal to $\boldsymbol{x}^{(i)}$, has full rank we will require that the number of targets N is such that $N = m \log m$, which implies that the number of targets generated under this approach only differs from the dimension of $\mathbf{w}$ by a factor of roughly $\log m$.

Let $P = (P_1, \ldots, P_N)$ be as defined in (3) and assume that $\widehat{P} = \left(\widehat{P}_1, \ldots, \widehat{P}_N \right)$ is the observed distribution. In other words $\widehat{P} = (\widehat{P}_1, \ldots, \widehat{P}_N)$ indicates the frequency the attacker attacks target $i \in [N]$ for a sufficient number of rounds which will be specified in Theorem 2. As will be discussed in more detail later, we will take linear combinations of the rows of the random feature matrix and show that with high probability we can recover an accurate estimate $\widetilde{\mathbf{w}}$ for $\mathbf{w}$ given a sufficient number of observations with high probability.

In the following, we assume that for each $i \in [N]$, $P_i > \delta$, where δ is some small positive constant. In practice, this is equivalent to guaranteeing that the targets are chosen in a manner that the attacker chooses to attack each target with non-negligible probability. We proceed in a similar manner as the previous section by first bounding the difference between $\widehat{P}$ and P. To avoid unnecessary notation, we will say that P is **well-behaved** if for each $i \in [N]$, $P_i > \delta$.

Our main result in this section appears as Theorem 2. In order to prove this result, we first show that if the number of observations M is large enough, then we can accurately infer the distribution $P = (P_1, \ldots, P_N)$ given the observed frequencies $\widehat{P} = \left(\widehat{P}_1, \ldots, \widehat{P}_N \right)$. Lemma 4 establishes some useful properties of randomly generated matrices that are used in the proof of Lemma 5. Lemma 5 shows that given $\widehat{P}$, which is similar to P, we can recover an accurate estimate estimate $\widetilde{\mathbf{w}}$ for $\mathbf{w}$. Finally, Theorem 2 results from combining the statements in Lemma 3 and 5.

Our first result follows from a straightforward application of a Chernoff bound.

Lemma 3. *Let $\zeta > 0$ be a small positive constant. If $M > \frac{12}{\zeta^2 \delta} \log m$, then for all $i \in [N]$, we have that the following holds*

$$\widehat{P}_i \leqslant (1 + \zeta) P_i, \tag{6}$$

and

$$\widehat{P}_i \geqslant (1 - \zeta) P_i, \tag{7}$$

with high probability provided that P is well-behaved.

Proof. Using the assumption that P is well-behaved along with a standard Chernoff bound we have

$$\Pr\left(\widehat{P}_i M \leqslant (1 - \zeta) P_i M\right) \leqslant \exp(-\zeta^2 P_i M/2) < \exp\left(-\zeta^2 \delta M/2\right) < m^{-6},$$

which implies the probability that (7) holds with probability at least $1 - m^{-6}$. Similarly,

$$\Pr\left(\widehat{P}_i M \geqslant (1 + \zeta) P_i M\right) \leqslant \exp\left(-\zeta^2 P_i M/3\right) < \exp\left(-\zeta^2 \delta M/3\right) < m^{-4},$$

which implies the probability that (6) holds with probability $1 - m^{-4}$. Combining these facts gives the statement in the lemma.

The following claim will be used in Lemma 5 and its proof appears in the appendix.

Lemma 4. *Suppose A_1, A_2 are $m \log m \times m$ matrices whose entries are independent and identically distributed according to the normal distribution $\mathcal{N}\left(\log m, \frac{1}{2}\right)$. Then the following holds:*

1. *With high probability, each entry $a_{i,j}$ of A_1 is non-negative.*
2. *With high probability, the smallest singular value for $A_1 - A_2$ is at least $\sqrt{m \log m} - \sqrt{m} - \log m$.*

The next lemma details how to recover an estimate $\widetilde{w}$ for w using the previous claim and its preceeding lemma. For a matrix M consisting of n rows and a set of integers $\mathcal{I} \subseteq [n]$ let $M_{\mathcal{I}}$ be the matrix which is the result of removing from M the rows outside the index set $\mathcal{I}$. In order to maintain the flow of the section, the proof of this result also appears in the appendix.

Lemma 5. *Suppose $\widehat{P} = (\widehat{P}_1, \ldots, \widehat{P}_N)$ is such that for any $i \in [N]$, we have $(1 - \zeta) P_i < \widehat{P}_i < (1 + \zeta) P_i$. Then, there exists an estimate $\widetilde{w}$ for w, where*

$$\|w - \widetilde{w}\|_2 \leqslant \frac{\sqrt{m \log \frac{1+\zeta}{1-\zeta}}}{\sqrt{m \log m} - \sqrt{m} - \log m},$$

with high probability.

We now arrive at a statement of our upper bound which follows by combining the previous lemma with Lemma 3.

Theorem 2. *Suppose the observed distribution P is well-behaved and that $\sigma = \sqrt{m \log m} - \sqrt{m} - \log m$. Then, with high probability, given M observations where*

$$M < \frac{12}{\delta} \left(\frac{1 + \exp(\varepsilon^2 \sigma^2 / m)}{\exp(\varepsilon^2 \sigma^2 / m) - 1} \right)^2 \log m,$$

we can derive an estimate $\widetilde{\mathbf{w}}$ for $\mathbf{w}$ such that

$$||\mathbf{w} - \widetilde{\mathbf{w}}||_2 \leqslant \varepsilon.$$

Proof. According to the previous lemma, if $||\mathbf{w} - \widetilde{\mathbf{w}}||_2 = \varepsilon$, then $\frac{\sqrt{m \log \frac{1+\zeta}{1-\zeta}}}{\sqrt{m \log m} - \sqrt{m} - \log m} \leqslant \epsilon$. As in the lemma statement, let $\sigma = \sqrt{m \log m} - \sqrt{m} - \log m$ so that $\frac{\sqrt{m \log \frac{1+\zeta}{1-\zeta}}}{\sigma} \leqslant \epsilon$, which after some manipulation implies $\zeta \leqslant \frac{\exp(\varepsilon^2 \sigma^2 / m) - 1}{1 + \exp(\varepsilon^2 \sigma^2 / m)}$. Substituting ζ into Lemma 3 gives the desired result.

The following corollary shows that under certain conditions it is possible with high probability to generate an estimate $\widehat{\mathbf{w}}$ for $\mathbf{w}$ provided the smallest singular value of the matrix $A^{(F)}$ is large enough.

Corollary 1. *Suppose the observed distribution $\widehat{P}$ is well-behaved and that $\sigma \varepsilon \geqslant \sqrt{m}$. Then, with high probability, given M observations where*

$$M = \mathcal{O}\left(\frac{12}{\delta} \log m \right),$$

we can derive an estimate $\widetilde{\mathbf{w}}$ for $\mathbf{w}$ such that

$$||\mathbf{w} - \widetilde{\mathbf{w}}||_2 \leqslant \varepsilon.$$

These bounds can provide direct guidance to adaptive deception systems as to when sufficient observations of an attacker have been collected to infer (and act on) knowledge of attacker preferences. These preferences can then be used to change the configuration of the defensive deception to better match the attacker preferences, thus making them more effective at delaying their progress or luring them away from real assets.

In the next section, we present simulations in light of our upper and lower bounds. In particular, we show that it is possible in many cases to produce an accurate estimate for $\mathbf{w}$ using far fewer samples than the number advertised in Theorem 2.

6   Simulation Results

In the following we verify through simulation how quickly and accurately a defender is able to learn the attackers preferences as a function of the number of samples or observations. Our setup is identical to the one described in Sect. 3. There are N targets and each target is characterized by m features. The attacker will attack target i with probability P_i, which is given in (3). For this model, both the attacker preferences, represented by the vector $\mathbf{w}$, and the target features, represented by the vectors $\boldsymbol{x}^{(i)}$, were randomly generated vectors whose entries each have values between 0 and 1.

We consider two approaches that the defender can use to learn the parameter $\mathbf{w}$. The first method, linear least squares (LLS), is similar to the approach discussed in the proof of Lemma 5. Afterwards, we discuss the gradient descent (GD) method.

The goal of both approaches is to generate an estimate $\widehat{\mathbf{w}}$ provided a set of observations which we represent using the vector $\boldsymbol{a} = (a_1, a_2, \ldots, a_N)$. For $i \in [N]$, a_i represents the number of times the attacker is observed to attack target i. Recall that $\boldsymbol{x}^{(i)}$ represents the configuration vector for target $i \in [N]$ and that the i-th row of $A^{(F)} \in \mathbb{R}_+^{m \times N}$ is equal to $\boldsymbol{x}^{(i)}$ for $i \in [N]$.

For the LLS method, we first form two matrices $X_1 \in \mathbb{R}_+^{m \times (N-1)}$ and $X_2 \in \mathbb{R}_+^{m \times (N-1)}$ where X_1 is equal to the first $N-1$ rows of $A^{(F)}$ and X_2 is equal to the last $N-1$ rows of $A^{(F)}$. Next, we generate the vector $\boldsymbol{q} = (q_1, q_2, \ldots, q_N)$ where $q_i = \frac{a_i}{\sum_{j=1}^{N} a_i} \in [0,1]$ represents the observed frequency with which target i was attacked. Then, we generate $\widetilde{\mathbf{w}}$ according to the LLS approach by solving the following over-determined system of equations:

$$(X_1 - X_2)\,\widehat{\mathbf{w}} = \begin{bmatrix} \log\left(\frac{q_1}{q_2}\right) \\ \log\left(\frac{q_2}{q_3}\right) \\ \vdots \\ \log\left(\frac{q_{N-1}}{q_N}\right) \end{bmatrix}. \tag{8}$$

For the GD approach, we assume as before that we have access to the observation vector $\boldsymbol{a} = (a_1, a_2, \ldots, a_N)$. The function which we seek to minimize is the following:

$$F(\widehat{\mathbf{w}}, a) = \sum_{i=1}^{N} \left(\frac{\exp\left(\widehat{\mathbf{w}}^T \boldsymbol{x}^{(i)}\right)}{\sum_{j=1}^{N} \exp\left(\widehat{\mathbf{w}}^T \boldsymbol{x}^{(i)}\right)} - \frac{a_i}{\sum_{j=1}^{N} a_j} \right)^2. \tag{9}$$

The idea is that we want to minimize the mean squared error of the estimate $\widehat{\mathbf{w}}$ for $\mathbf{w}$ provided the observations $a_1, a_2, \ldots, a_N$ and this estimate is updated incrementally. Let $\widetilde{\mathbf{w}}^{(k+1)}$ denote our estimate for $\mathbf{w}$ after the k-th iteration. Then,

$$\widehat{\mathbf{w}}^{(k+1)} = \widehat{\mathbf{w}}^{(k)} - \alpha \nabla F(\widehat{\mathbf{w}}^{(k)}, a),$$

where $\nabla F(\widehat{\mathbf{w}}^{(k)}, \mathbf{a})$ is the gradient and α dictates how much we update our estimate after each iteration. For each of the simulations presented in this section, the value of α was fixed at 0.9.

For each of the plots presented below, we allowed the defender to observe between 10^2 and 10^{23} attacks (or observations) in order to better understand the relationship between the accuracy of the estimate for $\mathbf{w}$ and the number of observations. As expected, for most of the cases observed, the larger the number of observations, the more accurate the estimate for $\mathbf{w}$.

Figure 1 is showing the result of running both the LLS and the GD techniques. Gradient descent was run for 5000 iterations. The figure contains 3 plots; the one on the left was run for the $(N = 6, m = 3)$ setup (the case where there are 6 targets and 3 features), the center plot was for $(N = 8, m = 4)$, and the one on the right had $(N = 10, m = 5)$. The line labeled "Lower Bound" on the left/center/middle plots is displaying Theorem 1 for the case where $m = 3/4/5$, respectively. We note that despite the fact that the bound from Theorem 1 assumes the number of machines is equal to the number of features, it appears to provide an accurate prediction for the LLS technique for all the parameters which were examined. The line labeled "Upper Bound" on the left/center/middle plots is displaying the upper bound from Theorem 2.

As can be seen in Fig. 1, the two techniques seem to provide similar results for the case where $(N = 6, m = 3)$, but that for the other two plots the estimate for $\mathbf{w}$ generated by gradient descent doesn't improve beyond roughly 10^{11} observations.

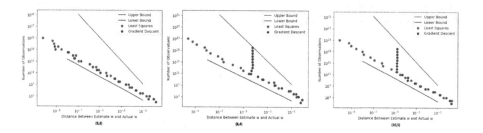

Fig. 1. LLS and GD with 5,000 iterations

Figures 2 and 3 illustrate the result of running the GD method with a larger number of iterations. In Fig. 2 the GD method is run for 10,000 iterations in Fig. 3 the GD method is run for 20,000 iterations. Notice that as the number of iterations increases, the performance of GD more closely mimics the performance of LLS, and we no longer see the performance of GD stalling once the number of iterations is increased to 20,000. In fact, when the number of iterations is increased to 20,000, Figs. 2 and 3 show that GD actually outperforms LLS for most of the data points for the $(N = 6, m = 3)$ setup.

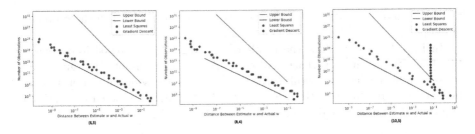

Fig. 2. LLS and GD with 10,000 iterations

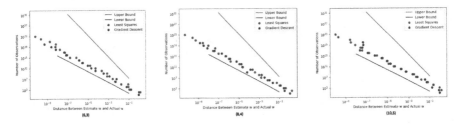

Fig. 3. LLS and GD with 20,000 iterations

While LLS in general appears to be the more accurate of the two methods for the parameters under consideration, one of the advantages of the GD technique is that it can be applied to the setup where an attacker may adaptively change their preferences over time. This may occur in situations where an attacker becomes aware that their preferences are being learned, where an attacker attempts to mislead an adaptive defense by diluting their presented preferences by adjusting their behavior, or where an attacker's interaction with a system are so extended that their preferences have changed over time. In the 2020 Mandiant M-Trends report, the global median dwell time, defined as the duration between the start of a cyber intrusion and it being identified, decreased to 56 days [17]. However, this amount of time is still quite significant, and means we must consider that attackers can gradually change their preferences over the course of an intrusion. Moreover, for intrusions where the cyber attacker is taking direction from another source, whether for cyber crime, hacktivism, or nationally-backed professionals, their preferences may appear to change instantaneously. But this isn't likely to happen with high frequency.

In order to account for such scenarios, we considered the setup where the $\mathbf{w}$ vector is perturbed by the quantity ρ after a certain amount of time to reflect the changing attacker preferences. More concretely, suppose that the current attacker preference vector is equal to $\mathbf{w}$ and that a perturbation is triggered. Then the updated attacker preference vector would be

$$\mathbf{w}(1 - \rho) + \mathbf{x}'\rho,$$

where $\mathbf{x}'$ is a randomly generated vector (whose entries each have value between 0 and 1) that has the same length as $\mathbf{w}$. As a starting point, we only considered the case where $\rho = .001$, and we varied the frequency with which these updates are applied.

In Figs. 4, 5, 6 we show the result of running GD for 10,000 iterations. In Fig. 4, we trigger a perturbation after every 10 iterations of GD. Our results seem to indicate that under this setup, the estimate for **w** doesn't improve much beyond 10^{-1} in this case (in other words the two norm between our estimate and the true value of **w** doesn't get smaller than 10^{-1}).

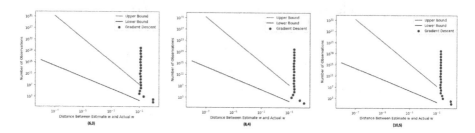

Fig. 4. Perturbations every 10 iterations

Figure 5 is illustrating the case where the perturbations were introduced after every $1,000$ iterations of GD. As expected, the estimate for **w** produced under this setting is much more accurate than the estimate generated in Fig. 4 and given enough observations we can track **w** to within an accuracy of 10^{-3}. Notice also that as the number of observations increases we see that the accuracy of **w** has an oscillating behavior where the estimate for **w** will alternate between getting better and worse, which is what one would expect as a result of the perturbations which are being introduced at regular intervals.

In Fig. 6, we see that the results for GD closely mimic the setup where no perturbations were used at all for the cases where $(N = 6, m = 3)$ and $(N = 10, m = 5)$. In particular, we see that the oscillating behavior which was observed in Fig. 5 is less likely, which is is most likely a result of the fact that the perturbations were small enough to not influence the behavior of the gradient descent method.

In summary, the following trends can be observed from our simulation results for the setting where a defender is attempting to learn the preferences of an attacker with high accuracy:

1. For the case where LLS is used and where the attacker preferences are static, the number of observations required to estimate **w** is much less than the upper bound provided in Theorem 2. From Corollary 1, this indicates that for many cases if the attacker preference vector **w** has dimension m, then the number of observations required by a defender is much less than $\mathcal{O}(\log m)$.
2. Given enough iterations, the GD and LLS methods give highly accurate results and their performance is competitive under many of the parameters considered.

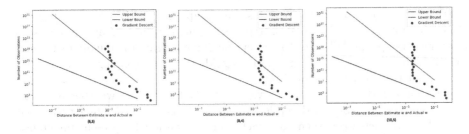

Fig. 5. Perturbations every 1,000 iterations

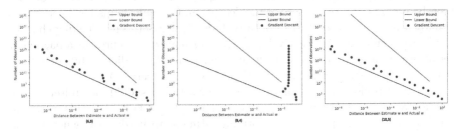

Fig. 6. Perturbations every 100,000 iterations

3. When the attacker preferences are static, the accuracy of the estimate for GD and LLS appears to deviate from the lower bound in Theorem 1 by less than a few orders of magnitude for most of the simulations.
4. For the case where the attacker preferences are adaptive, GD can achieve a high degree of accuracy provided we allow enough time to transpire between changes to the attacker's preferences.

7   Conclusion

In this paper we have pinpointed the upper and lower bounds for the number of observations required to infer attacker preferences under the Subjective Utility Quantal Response model. We have also validated our results in simulation and shown that for many parameters of interest, the number of observations needed to learn the score function of an attacker scales at most logarithmically with the dimension of the feature space.

Future work will consider the problem from the point of view of *both* the attacker and defender. While knowledge of attacker preferences provides a defender with the key distributional information needed to guide the deployment of interesting decoys and effective deception features, estimates of attacker learning can help determine how long a defender can maintain a persistent configuration of the deceptive facade to gain the most benefit from learning an attacker's preferences. In particular, we will consider the following question: how many observations does the attacker require to learn the truth about the network topology and how does this match up against the ideal strategy for defender interactions? The presented deception may eventually become stale and lose its appeal. Whether the deception is reconfigured manually or through artificial intelligence, this work begins to guide when those changes should occur and what those changes should be.

Extending this work further, we are also interested in whether an aware attacker may use counter-deception to present false or misleading preferences to a learning defender. Such an attacker may intentionally present preferences which are distributionally different from their true preferences. This may be done as a ruse to cajole a defender into changing a system's presented deception and thereby giving away the nature of the deception. One solution is for defenders to employ solutions that can affect both real and false assets when making changes or apparent changes. Alternatively, an attacker may wish to present a particular set of preferences to prevent a defender from correctly predicting future actions (such as future exploitation of a particular system or service).

Lastly, it is clear that neither defender nor attacker should indefinitely maintain a stationary strategy for offense or defense. We believe that this work and related work takes steps towards informing future adaptive defenses when attackers are both dynamic and tenacious. As a final note, while the model and simulation presented primarily concerns an attacker's preferences and a defender's ability to observe such preferences, a similar model may apply equally well when an attacker makes repeated observations of a defender's preferences of the defense of one system over another. This unfortunate yet inevitable circumstance should give defenders making use of static preferences pause and to use such models to enable a more dynamic and less easily learned defensive strategy.

Acknowledgement. This work was partially funded by Cyber Technologies, C5ISREW Directorate, Office of the Under Secretary of Defense Research and Engineering as well as the Laboratory for Advanced Cybersecurity Research.

A   Proof of Lemma 4

The first statement follows from a standard concentration inequality. In particular, if a variable $X \sim \mathcal{N}(\log m, \frac{1}{2}) = \mathcal{N}(\mu, \sigma^2)$ it follows that

$$\Pr(X \geqslant \mu + \sigma x) \leqslant \frac{1}{2\pi x} \exp(-x^2/2),$$

which implies $\Pr(X \geqslant \log m + \log m) \leqslant \frac{1}{2\pi \log m} \exp(-(\log m)^2/2) = \frac{1}{2\pi \log m} m^{-\frac{\log m}{2}} < m^{-\frac{\log m}{2}}$ so that by symmetry $\Pr(X < 0) \leqslant \frac{1}{2\pi \log m} \exp(-(\log m)^2/2) < m^{-\log m/2}$. Therefore, applying a union bound, this implies $\Pr(a_{i,j} < 0)$ for any i, j is at most

$$m^{-\frac{\log m}{2}} m^2 \log m,$$

which implies the desired result.

For the second statement in the claim, first note that the matrix $A_1 - A_2$ is comprised of elements from the standard normal distribution $\mathcal{N}(0,1)$, since each element is the difference of two elements $\sim \mathcal{N}(\log m, \frac{1}{2})$. It is well-known that the smallest singular value of a random $\mathcal{N}(0,1)$ matrix satisfies $\Pr(\sigma_{min} \leqslant \sqrt{m \log m} - \sqrt{m} - t) \leqslant \exp(-t^2/2)$ for $t > 0$ (see [8] for instance), which implies

$$\Pr(\sigma_{min} \leqslant \sqrt{m \log m} - \sqrt{m} - \log m) \leqslant \exp\left(-(\log m)^2/2\right),$$

which implies the second statement of the claim.

B   Proof of Lemma 5

Proof. Define $\mathbf{b} \in \mathbb{R}^{N-1}$ so that

$$\mathbf{b} = \begin{bmatrix} \log(\widehat{P}_1/\widehat{P}_2) \\ \log(\widehat{P}_2/\widehat{P}_3) \\ \vdots \\ \log(\widehat{P}_{N-1}/\widehat{P}_N) \end{bmatrix}.$$

Define $A^{(1)}, A^{(2)}$ so that

$$A^{(1)} = \begin{bmatrix} \mathbf{x}^{(1)} \\ \mathbf{x}^{(2)} \\ \vdots \\ \mathbf{x}^{(N-1)} \end{bmatrix}, \quad A^{(2)} = \begin{bmatrix} \mathbf{x}^{(2)} \\ \mathbf{x}^{(3)} \\ \vdots \\ \mathbf{x}^{(N)} \end{bmatrix}.$$

Then it follows from (1) and (2) that if $\widehat{P} = P$, we can write

$$\left(A^{(1)} - A^{(2)}\right)\mathbf{w} = \mathbf{b},$$

where the entries of $A^{(1)}, A^{(2)}$ are $\sim \mathcal{N}(\log m, \frac{1}{2})$. Note that according to Claim 4, since with high probability the smallest singular value of $A^{(1)} - A^{(2)}$ is greater than zero, it follows that there are m linearly independent rows in $A^{(1)} - A^{(2)}$. Let $\mathcal{I} = \{k_{i_1}, k_{i_2}, \ldots, k_{i_m}\}$ denote the indices of these linearly independent rows. Assuming $\widehat{P} = P$, we can solve for $\mathbf{w}$ as follows

$$\mathbf{w} = \left(A^{(1)} - A^{(2)}\right)_{\mathcal{I}}^{-1} \cdot \mathbf{b}_{\mathcal{I}}.$$

Then, using the same logic for the case where $\widehat{P}$ may not be equal to P, we have

$$\|\mathbf{w} - \widetilde{\mathbf{w}}\|_2 = \left\|\left(A^{(1)} - A^{(2)}\right)_{\mathcal{I}}^{-1}\left(\widetilde{\mathbf{b}}_{\mathcal{I}} - \mathbf{b}_{\mathcal{I}}\right)\right\|_2 \leqslant \left\|\left(A^{(1)} - A^{(2)}\right)_{\mathcal{I}}^{-1}\right\|_2 \left\|\widetilde{\mathbf{b}}_{\mathcal{I}} - \mathbf{b}_{\mathcal{I}}\right\|_2,$$

where

$$
\widetilde{\mathbf{b}}_{\mathcal{I}} - \mathbf{b}_{\mathcal{I}} =
\begin{bmatrix}
\log\left(\dfrac{\widehat{P}_{k_{i_1}} P_{k_{i_1}+1}}{\widehat{P}_{k_{i_1}+1} P_{k_{i_1}}} \right) \\[2ex]
\log\left(\dfrac{\widehat{P}_{k_{i_2}} P_{k_{i_2}+1}}{\widehat{P}_{k_{i_2}+1} P_{k_{i_2}}} \right) \\[2ex]
\vdots \\[2ex]
\log\left(\dfrac{\widehat{P}_{k_{i_m}} P_{k_{i_m}+1}}{\widehat{P}_{k_{i_m}+1} P_{k_{i_m}}} \right)
\end{bmatrix}
$$

Since $(1 - \zeta)P_i < \widehat{P}_i < (1 + \zeta)P_i$, it follows that $\|\widetilde{\mathbf{b}}\|_2 \leqslant \sqrt{m \log \frac{1+\zeta}{1-\zeta}}$ and so $\|\mathbf{w} - \widetilde{\mathbf{w}}\|_2 \leqslant \frac{1}{\sigma_{\min}} \sqrt{m \log \frac{1+\zeta}{1-\zeta}}$. Since $\sigma_{\min} \geqslant \sqrt{m \log m} - \sqrt{m} - \log m$ with high probability the result follows.

References

1. Herley, C.: Unfalsifiability of security claims. Proc. Natl. Acad. Sci. **113**(23), 6415–6420 (2016)
2. Shi, Z.R., et al.: Learning and planning in the feature deception problem. In: Decision and Game Theory for Security, College Park, MD (2020)
3. Haghtalab, N., Fang, F., Nguyen, T.H., Sinha, A., Procaccia, A.D., Tambe, M.: Three strategies to success: learning adversary models in security games. In: International Joint Conference on Artificial Intelligence (IJCAI) (2016)
4. Luce, R.D.: Individual Choice Behavior: A Theoretical Analysis, Courier Corporation (2005)
5. McFadden, D.L.: Quantal choice analysis: a survey. Ann. Econ. Soc. Meas. **5**(4), 363–390 (1976)
6. Nguyen, T., Yang, R., Azaria, A., Kraus, S., Tambe, M.: Analyzing the effectiveness of adversary modeling in security games. In: Proceedings of the 27th AAAI Conference on Artificial Intelligence (AAAI), pp. 718–724 (2013)
7. Abbasi, Y., et al.: Know your adversary: insights for a better adversarial behavioral model. In: CogSci (2016)
8. Rudelson, M., Vershynin, R.: Smallest singular value of a random rectangular matrix. Commun. Pure Appl. Math. **62**(12), 1707–1739 (2009)
9. Pawlick, J., Colbert, E., Zhu, Q.: A game-theoretic taxonomy and survey of defensive deception for cybersecurity and privacy. ACM Comput. Surv. **52**(4), 1–28 (2019)
10. Mairh, A., Barik, D., Verma, K., Jena, D.: Honeypot in network security: a survey. In: Proceedings of the 2011 International Conference on Communication, Computing and Security, pp. 600–605 (2011)
11. Xu, H., Tran-Thanh, L., Jennings, N.R.: Playing repeated security games with no prior knowledge. In: Proceedings of the 2016 International Conference on Autonomous Agents and Multiagent Systems, pp. 104–112 (2016)
12. Balcan, M.F., Blum, A., Haghtalab, N., Procaccia, A.D.: Commitment without regrets: online learning in stackelberg security games. In: Proceedings of the Sixteenth ACM Conference on Economics and Computation, pp. 61–78 (2015)

13. Heckman, K.E., Stech, F.J., Thomas, R.K., Schmoker, B., Tsow, A.W.: Cyber Denial, Deception and Counter Deception: A Framework for Supporting Active Cyber Defense. Springer, Heidelberg (2015). https://doi.org/10.1007/978-3-319-25133-2
14. Rowe, N.C., Rrushi, J.: Introduction to Cyberdeception. Springer, Heidelberg (2016). https://doi.org/10.1007/978-3-319-41187-3
15. Ferguson-Walter, K.J., Major, M.M., Johnson, C.K., Muhleman, D.H.: Examining the efficacy of decoy-based and psychological cyber deception. In: USENIX Security Symposium (2021)
16. Cranford, E.A., Gonzalez, C., Aggarwal, P., Cooney, S., Tambe, M., Lebiere, C.: Toward personalized deceptive signaling for cyber defense using cognitive models. Top. Cogn. Sci. **12**(3), 992–1011 (2020)
17. Mandiant: M-Trends (2020). https://content.fireeye.com/m-trends/rpt-m-trends-2020. Accessed 20 July 2021

When Should You Defend Your Classifier?
– A Game-Theoretical Analysis of Countermeasures Against Adversarial Examples

Maximilian Samsinger[1]([✉]), Florian Merkle[1], Pascal Schöttle[1], and Tomas Pevny[2]

[1] Management Center Innsbruck, Universitätsstr. 15, Innsbruck, Austria
{maximilian.samsinger,florian.merkle,pascal.schoettle}@mci.edu
[2] Department of Computers and Engineering, Czech Technical University in Prague, Prague, Czech Republic
pevnak@protonmail.ch

Abstract. Adversarial machine learning, i.e., increasing the robustness of machine learning algorithms against so-called adversarial examples, is now an established field. Yet, newly proposed methods are evaluated and compared under unrealistic scenarios where costs for adversary and defender are not considered and either all samples or no samples are adversarially perturbed. We scrutinize these assumptions and propose the advanced adversarial classification game, which incorporates all relevant parameters of an adversary and a defender. Especially, we take into account economic factors on both sides and the fact that all so far proposed countermeasures against adversarial examples reduce accuracy on benign samples. Analyzing the scenario in detail, where both players have two pure strategies, we identify all best responses and conclude that in practical settings, the most influential factor might be the maximum amount of adversarial examples.

Keywords: Adversarial classification · Game theory · Correct classification rate

1 Introduction

Machine learning and especially deep convolutional neural networks have become the de facto standard in a variety of computer vision related tasks [11,12]. However, at least since 2004 the vulnerability of machine learning classifiers to carefully crafted attack points is known [5] and has gained a lot of attention in the

All authors are supported by the Austrian Science Fund (FWF) and the Czech Science Foundation (GACR) under grant no. I 4057-N31 ("Game Over Eva(sion)"). Tomas Pevny was additionally supported by Czech Ministry of Education 19-29680L and by the OP VVV project CZ.02.1.01/0.0/0.0/16_019/0000765 "Research Center for Informatics".

B. Bošanský et al. (Eds.): GameSec 2021, LNCS 13061, pp. 158–177, 2021.
https://doi.org/10.1007/978-3-030-90370-1_9

research community lately [1]. Generally, attacks against machine learning classifiers can be divided into poisoning and evasion attacks [1]. In the former, the adversary can already tamper with the training procedure, and in the latter, the adversary tries to evade the classifier at inference time. We deal with evasion attacks only in this paper, as especially the vulnerability of neural networks to so-called adversarial examples [22] caused a stir in the machine learning community. Adversarial examples are benign input points to which tiny, maliciously crafted perturbations are added. For humans, these perturbed images are often indistinguishable from their unmodified counterparts [14] but they trick a neural network into misclassification. In the light of modern applications, including, but not limited to, facial recognition, self-driving cars, or spam filtering, adversarial examples pose an obvious security concern.

Yet, to the best of our knowledge, most of the papers on either new attack methods or new countermeasures deal with unrealistic conditions: the cost of creating adversarial examples is disregarded; the cost of training or defending the model is not considered; and the proportion of adversarial examples to be expected, is either 100% or 0%, but nothing in between. Taking into account the observation that all countermeasures against adversarial examples proposed so far strictly decrease the accuracy on benign images, we argue that depending on the expected amount of adversarial examples faced, defending a neural network classifier by one of these countermeasures might not be worth it. As a motivating example, we use the clean and robust accuracies from the famous paper [14] to create Fig. 1. Here, we show the expected proportion of adversarial examples (x-axis) and an evaluation metric (formally introduced in Sect. 3.3) that balances the classifier's adversarial robustness against its accuracy on benign inputs (y-axis).

This shows that when expecting less then 17% adversarial examples, the undefended model (solid line) yields a higher correct classification rate than the defended model (dashed line) and thus, is favorable for the defender – assuming that misclassifying a benign or and adversarial example induce the same penalty.

Given this drawback of all so far proposed countermeasures against adversarial examples, we raise the question if a rationally acting defender would actually deploy these countermeasures when facing a rationally acting adversary. We do so by proposing a game-theoretical model and a thorough analysis of a minimal instantiation. Our contributions are as follows:

1. We propose the *Advanced Adversarial Classification Game* that captures all relevant properties in the competition between adversary and defender in adversarial machine learning. Our game can be instantiated with all possible defender and adversary strategies (meaning classification models on the defender's side and attack algorithms on the adversary's side).
2. We thoroughly analyse the game and identify situations where both players play pure (or mixed) strategies.
3. We define two new metrics, the correct classification rate (CCR) for the defender and the attack success rate (ASR) for the adversary, and show their role in the analysis of the game.

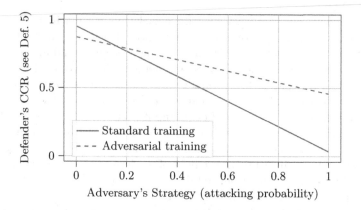

Fig. 1. Correct classification rate on CIFAR-10 test images based on the original data in [14], as mentioned in Sect. 2. We consider the "wide" architecture.

4. By starting with a rigorous mathematical formulation of an economic model and identifying all simplifications made, we justify the sufficiency and practical importance of CCR and ASR.

The remainder of the paper is structured as follows: In Sect. 2 we review the most relevant related work before introducing our game-theoretical model in Sect. 3. We instantiate this general model in Sect. 4 and analyze the case where both, defender and adversary have two possible strategies. We report best responses and Nash equilibria before ending with a discussion and conclusion.

2   Related Work

In the last couple of years, stronger and stronger attacks against machine learning classifiers were developed, e.g., [2,16,17], with basically everyday new papers appearing on this subject[1].

Naturally, with an increased interest in attacks, also an increasing number of countermeasures have been proposed. Already the seminal work that first identified the existence of adversarial examples [22] suggested to harden the underlying convolutional neural networks (CNN) against these adversarial examples by incorporating them into the training procedure. This method is by now commonly called *adversarial training*. It is one of the most prominent approaches in the research of CNNs that are robust against adversarial examples [14]. Another approach to avert the danger of adversarial examples is to try to detect them either inside the CNN itself [9], or by applying detection methods to every input object and sorting out adversarial examples before they even enter the neural network [23]. Here, one important observation is that all countermeasures against adversarial examples proposed so far strictly decrease the accuracy on

---

[1] More than 3500 papers can be found at: https://preview.tinyurl.com/yxenrc4k.

benign images. For example, adversarial training decreases clean accuracy from 95.2% to 87.3% in the "wide" model considered in [14] and from 95.6% to 90.0% with the approach proposed in [24]. Even the randomized defence mechanism proposed in [18] decreases the accuracy on benign inputs from 88% to 80%. (All results are for CIFAR-10.)

Most of the literature on attacks against machine learning classifiers and countermeasures against these assumes that an adversary will always attack and a defender will always (try to) defend, irrespective of whether it actually pays off to do so. As soon as we assume both, adversary and defender to act rationally, and only attack and defend when it pays off, we enter the realm of game theory. Game-theoretical analysis of adversarial machine learning dates back to 2004, when Dalvi et al. analyzed the security of a machine learning-based spam detector against a strategic adversary [5]. Here, the spam detector is a binary classifier and the adversary creates adversarial examples by perturbing some well chosen features of legitimate emails. The simultaneous move game is solved for a Nash equilibrium [15] by formulating the problem as a constrained optimization problem and solving this with a mixed linear program.

Following up on this, researchers have framed *adversarial classification* with zero-sum [8] and non zero-sum games [6] and as simultaneous move and sequential move (Stackelberg) games [3]. With the increasing interest of the machine learning community in deep neural networks, also the game-theoretical analysis of these machine learning frameworks [20], as well as their security properties [10,18] appeared. Interestingly, to the best of our knowledge, there is no work which that to incorporate costs on both the adversary's and the defender's side and the decreased accuracy on benign inputs, mentioned above, and then analyzes the optimal strategies of both players.

Probably closest to our work is Gilmer et al.'s paper titled "Motivating the Rules of the Game for Adversarial Example Research" [7]. Besides the title, it does not deal with game theory although many of its arguments follows game-theoretical considerations, such as the question who moves first, the adversary or the defender (like in a Stackelberg game), or allowing the adversary a strategy between never attacking and always attacking (as in a mixed strategy).

We adapt the following definitions from game theory literature, e.g., [13]:

Definition 1 (Mixed strategy). *A **mixed strategy** is a strategy, which assigns a positive probability to two or more pure strategies. A **fully** mixed strategy assigns a positive probability to all pure strategies.*

Definition 2 (Best response). *A defender's **best response** $s^* \in S$ to an adversary's strategy $r \in R$ satisfies $\text{Utility}^{\text{def}}(s^*, r) \geq \text{Utility}^{\text{def}}(s, r)$ for all $s \in S$. Likewise, an adversary's **best response** $r^* \in R$ to a defender's strategy $s \in S$ satisfies $\text{Utility}^{\text{adv}}(s, r^*) \geq \text{Utility}^{\text{adv}}(s, r)$ for all $r \in R$.*

Definition 3 (Nash equilibrium). *A **Nash equilibrium** is a strategy profile (s^*, r^*) where both strategies are mutual best responses. In a Nash equilibrium neither of the two actors has an incentive to unilaterally change her strategy. A game can have zero, one, or multiple Nash equilibria.*

3   The Advanced Adversarial Classification Game

This section introduces our game model. It starts by identifying and justifying costs of both parties, namely those of the adversary (cf. Sect. 3.1) and those of the defender (cf. Sect. 3.2). Once these costs are identified, we use them to formulate the game characterizing the interplay between the parties. As is usual in economic studies, we partition the utility into *initial costs* (I) that are mandatory and independent of the use of attack (or defence), *ongoing costs* (O), which scale with how many times the attack (or defence) is used, and *total reward*, TR, which is the reward and which is also assumed to be proportional to the number of usage. Hence, the utility of each actor is given by

$$\text{Utility}^k = -\text{I}^k - \text{O}^k + \text{TR}^k, \tag{1}$$

where $k \in \{\text{adv}, \text{def}\}$. As expected (and used later below), ongoing costs O and total reward TR can be represented by a single term for both adversary and defender. We started by denoting them separately in order to clearly communicate their origins and factors.

3.1   Adversary

The adversary's **action** set is defined by the attack methods she can use, her perturbation budget, and the fraction of samples she can attack. Each action has associated properties with regards to its cost structure and the attack success rate, depending on the model to be attacked (which is in turn the defender's chosen action).

Initial costs of an adversary, I^{adv}, may include gathering intelligence about the victim, stealing the targeted model, acquisition of suitable data to train a surrogate model, computational costs to train a surrogate model, hardware or software, and human capital. Notice that some costs occur even though no attack is carried out. For example, as soon as an adversary contemplates to attack a model, time is spent to investigate the options, get information on the target, or prototype an attack.

Ongoing costs of an adversary, O^{adv}, are mainly characterized by the computational costs of the attack to calculate perturbations. They depend on the attack method(s), but other factors might contribute such as a fee charged by the model provider per prediction, if the adversary does not own the model (or has trained a surrogate model).

Total rewards of an adversary, TR^{adv}, are the rewards the adversary obtains for attacking the defender's classifier. They can be positive when the target is successfully deceived, or negative for failed attacks. While often close to zero, negative rewards are conceivable, if every failed attack allows the defender to learn something about the adversary's strategies which helps them to detect the adversary more successfully.

3.2   Defender

The defender has many **actions** to choose from, where each action is a combination of choices with regard to the architecture of the model, the data used
to train the model, the training algorithm itself which can already implement
defence mechanisms such as adversarial training [14], and the inference mode [4].
Each unique combination of the above leads to a model, which is considered to
be a pure strategy. Hence, in the context of the defender, the terms model and
action are used interchangeably. Each of them has associated properties with
regard to its cost structure, its accuracy on clean inputs, and the robust accuracy on adversarial examples crafted with a given attack method and strength,
where the last two are adversary's actions.

The **initial costs** of the defender, I^{def}, include, but are not limited to, gathering and labeling training data, training the model (computational costs) and
human capital, e.g. hiring an expert to instantiate the classification pipeline.
Therefore some of them, such as the data acquisition, are mostly independent
of the defender's strategy, while others like the number of trained models or the
complexity of the training procedure clearly depend on them.

Ongoing costs of the defender, O^{def}, occur constantly per classified input.
They mainly correspond to the computational costs for inference of a specific
model. Ongoing costs for models in the same complexity class can be considered
equivalent, but some defences [19] recommend classifying each sample many
times (subjected to some randomness), which increases ongoing costs by orders
of magnitude.

Total reward of the defender. A rational defender will only train and deploy
the model when she can draw positive reward, TR^{def}, (not necessarily monetary) from its operation. As mentioned above, we assume these rewards to be
described on a per-sample basis, specifically for correct outputs only. Further,
it is reasonable to expect a negative reward, i.e. some penalty term, when the
model's output differs from the ground truth. The extent of this penalty might
differ from sample to sample and might be smaller for benign samples, but larger
for samples manipulated by the adversary.

Following the above considerations, we model the game as a non-zero-sum
game as both actions are clearly interdependent and one actor's positive reward
is not necessarily equal to the other actor's negative reward. We further choose
a simultaneous move game in which both actors decide on their strategy at the
same time without having certainty about the opponent's chosen strategy.

3.3   Cost of Pure Strategies

The defender classifies a finite number of samples $n \in \mathbb{N}$, out of which a fraction
$r_{max} \in [0, 1]$ is under the control of the adversary, which means she can attack
them by any method of her choice.[2] The adversary may use up to $M - 1$ different

---

[2] Note that this is already a simplification, since in practice none of the parties knows
how many samples the adversary can influence.

attacks (we refer to the j-th attack as attack j) and may also choose to leave a sample untouched (not to attack), which is denoted as attack M. The defender may choose one of N different models to classify samples (we refer to the i-th model as model i). The accuracy of the i-th model is given by acc_i and its robustness against the j-th attack is given by rob_{ij}.

For expressing the costs, it will be useful to introduce two metrics: Attack success rate (ASR) and Correct classification rate (CCR). The first quantifies how successful the j-th attack is against the i-th classifier, while the second quantifies the probability of correctly classifying samples with model i, taking into account that samples might be attacked by attack j with probability ρ. Though both quantities seem to be similar at first glance, we have shown below that they allow to compactly represent the strategies and play a pivotal role in the analysis of the game in Sect. 4.

Definition 4 (Attack Success Rate). *We define the attack success rate ASR of attack j against model i as*

$$\mathrm{ASR}_{ij} = 1 - \mathrm{rob}_{ij}. \tag{2}$$

Definition 5 (Correct Classification Rate). *We define the correct classification CCR rate of model i, where only a fraction $\rho \in [0, r_{\max}]$ of all samples are perturbed by the j-th adversarial attack.*

$$\mathrm{CCR}_{ij}(\rho) = (1 - \rho)\mathrm{acc}_i + \rho\,\mathrm{rob}_{ij} \tag{3}$$

Figure 1 shows the correct classification rate for the "wide" architecture in [14] with $r_{\max} = 1$. The lines of the two models intersect at $\approx 17\%$, clearly indicating that the defender should use the undefended model if the proportion of adversarial examples is below, and the defended model when the proportion is above.

Adversary. Below, we state and discuss our assumptions on the economic factors of the adversary which are based on adversarial machine learning literature.

(A1) The initial costs $I^{\mathrm{adv}} \geq 0$ are constant and non-negative. This corresponds to a case where all attacks are similar in nature. That is, all attacks require a similar level of intelligence on the victim's model, use the same surrogate model (if applicable) and demand the same hardware, software and development costs. Moreover, this assumes that the adversary has to instantiate each attack to assess its quality. This incurs the initial costs, even if the adversary does not create a single adversarial example.

(A2) Generating an adversarial example with attack j, where $j < M$, inflicts constant ongoing costs $O_j^{\mathrm{adv}} \geq 0$.

(A3) Successful attacks yield revenue $R_+^{\mathrm{adv}} \geq 0$, while unsuccessful attacks cost $R_-^{\mathrm{adv}} \geq 0$.

(A4) Attack $j < M$ against model i succeeds with probability $\mathrm{ASR}_{ij} = 1 - \mathrm{rob}_{ij}$ and fails with probability $1 - \mathrm{ASR}_{ij} = \mathrm{rob}_{ij}$.

(A5) Attack M corresponds to refraining from attacking. No adversarial examples are generated, ongoing costs $O_M^{adv} = 0$ are assumed to be equal to zero, though we assume an adversary has to pay the initial costs. Furthermore, ASR_{iM} is undefined and $CCR_{iM} \equiv acc_i$ for all models i.

With the above assumptions, we define the expected payoff (revenue) per sample (EPPS) of the adversary when using the j-th attack against the i-th model as:

$$EPPS_{ij}^{adv} = -O_j^{adv} - R_-^{adv}(1 - ASR_{ij}) + R_+^{adv}ASR_{ij}, \qquad (4)$$

where the minus in front of $R_-^{adv}(1 - ASR_{ij})$ indicates that adversary has to pay for failed attacks (or cannot get revenue, if R_-^{adv} is equal to zero). The total revenue (utility) of the adversary after perturbing nr_{max} samples is

$$U_{ij}^{adv} = \begin{cases} -I^{adv} + nr_{max}EPPS_{ij}^{adv} & \text{if } j < M \\ -I^{adv} & \text{if } j = M \end{cases}, \qquad (5)$$

where we have used assumption (A1) (initial costs are not influenced by strategy of any party) and (A5) (refraining from attacking does not cost anything).

Defender. Next, we state and discuss our assumptions on the economic factors of the defender, again based on the literature on adversarial machine learning.

(D1) The defender has to classify all $n \in \mathbb{N}$ samples. This models a situation, where the defender cannot distinguish between any sample a priori and therefore does not exclude any of them. Note that adversarial examples are indistinguishable from benign examples by definition.

(D2) The initial costs $I^{def} \geq 0$ are constant and do not depend on the defender's choice of model. This covers all cases, where the costs for training each model are either the same or are dominated by the costs for setting up the training pipeline.

(D3) Classifying a sample with the i-th model inflicts ongoing costs $O_i^{def} > 0$, which only depend on the model itself.

(D4) Defender rewards only depend on the correct classification rate. That is, correctly classifying a sample yields $R_+^{def} \geq 0$, while misclassifications incurs cost $R_-^{def} \geq 0$. In particular, errors on benign samples are as expensive as errors on adversarial examples.

Based on these assumptions we construct the utilities of the defender for the i-th model and the j-th attack. Remember that the adversary perturbs at most a fraction $r_{max} \in [0,1]$ of all samples. By choosing any attack $j < M$ the adversary generates nr_{max} adversarial examples. The expected payoff (revenue) per classified sample (EPPS) for the defender is given by

$$EPPS_{ij}^{def} = \begin{cases} -O_i^{def} - R_-^{def}(1 - CCR_{ij}(r_{max})) + R_+^{def}CCR_{ij}(r_{max}) & \text{if } j < M \\ -O_i^{def} - R_-^{def}(1 - acc_i) + R_+^{def}acc_i & \text{if } j = M \end{cases}, \qquad (6)$$

Table 1. Overview of Game parameters

Description			Fraction of samples that can be	
	Total number of samples to classify $n \in \mathbb{N}$		adversarially perturbed $r_{\max} \in [0,1]$	
	Accuracy values of all models $\mathrm{acc} \in [0,1]^N$		Robustness values of all models $\mathrm{rob} \in [0,1]^{N \times (M-1)}$	
	Defender's side		Adversary's side	
Positive reward	Correct classification	$R_+^{\mathrm{def}} \in [0,\infty)$	Successful attack	$R_+^{\mathrm{adv}} \in [0,\infty)$
Negative reward	Misclassification	$R_-^{\mathrm{def}} \in [0,\infty)$	Failed attack	$R_-^{\mathrm{adv}} \in [0,\infty)$
Initial costs		$I^{\mathrm{def}} \in [0,\infty)$		$I^{\mathrm{adv}} \in [0,\infty)$
Ongoing costs		$O^{\mathrm{def}} \in [0,\infty)^N$		$O^{\mathrm{adv}} \in [0,\infty)^{M-1}$
Choice parameter		$s \in \mathcal{S}$		$r \in \mathcal{R}$
Performance measure	Correct classification rate	$\mathrm{CCR}(r)^\dagger$	Attack success rate	$\mathrm{ASR}(s)^\dagger$
Expected payoff per sample	Classified	$\mathrm{EPPS}^{\mathrm{def}}(r)^\dagger$	Adversarially perturbed	$\mathrm{EPPS}^{\mathrm{adv}}(s)^\dagger$

$\dagger$: Note that these entries depend on the opponent's choice

where we have used assumption (D3) (classifying a sample incurs constant costs) and (D4) (reward depends only on correct classification rate). By assumption (A5) no adversarial examples are generated if $j = M$. By further incorporating assumption (D1) (defender has to classify all samples) and (D2) (initial costs are constant), we get the defender's utility

$$\mathbf{U}_{ij}^{\mathrm{def}} = -\mathrm{I}^{\mathrm{def}} + n\,\mathrm{EPPS}_{ij}^{\mathrm{def}}. \tag{7}$$

3.4   Utility of Mixed Strategies

Let $\mathcal{R} = \Delta^M$ and $\mathcal{S} = \Delta^N$ denote the strategy space[3] of the adversary and defender, respectively. Each strategy $r \in \mathcal{R}/s \in \mathcal{S}$ corresponds to a probability distribution, where the adversary/defender chooses action j/i with probability r_j/s_i, respectively.

The adversary's and defender's utility function are given by

$$\mathrm{Utility}^{\mathrm{adv}}(s,r) = \sum_{i=1}^{N} \sum_{j=1}^{M} s_i \mathbf{U}_{ij}^{\mathrm{adv}} r_j = s^T \mathbf{U}^{\mathrm{adv}} r$$

$$\mathrm{Utility}^{\mathrm{def}}(s,r) = \sum_{i=1}^{N} \sum_{j=1}^{M} s_i \mathbf{U}_{ij}^{\mathrm{def}} r_j = s^T \mathbf{U}^{\mathrm{def}} r,$$

respectively. For the analysis of the game, it is convenient to represent the utility functions as

$$\mathrm{Utility}^{\mathrm{adv}}(s,r) = -\mathrm{I}^{\mathrm{adv}} + n\,r_{\max}\,r^T\,\mathrm{EPPS}^{\mathrm{adv}}(s) \tag{8}$$

$$\mathrm{Utility}^{\mathrm{def}}(s,r) = -\mathrm{I}^{\mathrm{def}} + n\,s^T\,\mathrm{EPPS}^{\mathrm{def}}(r), \tag{9}$$

with the expected payoff per classified sample depending only their respective opponent's strategy $\mathrm{EPPS}^{\mathrm{adv}}(s) := (\mathrm{EPPS}^{\mathrm{adv}} s)^T$ and $\mathrm{EPPS}^{\mathrm{def}}(r) := \mathrm{EPPS}^{\mathrm{def}} r$.

---

[3] $\Delta^d = \{v \in [0,1]^d : v_1 + \cdots + v_d = 1\}$ is the $d-1$ dimensional probability simplex.

By this, the advanced adversarial classification game is fully described as a non-zero-sum normal form game with the adversary and defender as players, pure strategy sets $\{e_1^{\text{def}}, \ldots, e_N^{\text{def}}\}$ and $\{e_1^{\text{adv}}, \ldots, e_M^{\text{adv}}\}$, and utility functions Utility^{adv} and Utility^{def}, where $e_i^{\text{def}} \in \mathbb{R}^N$ and $e_j^{\text{adv}} \in \mathbb{R}^M$ are the i-th and j-th standard unit vectors, respectively. The mixed strategy sets are given by $\mathcal{R}$ and $\mathcal{S}$. All parameters of the game are shown in Table 1.

3.5 Expected Payouts for Mixed Strategies

In this subsection we introduce two performance measures for both players which depend only on non-choice parameters and their respective opponent's strategy. These performance measures are generalizations of the attack success rate (ASR) and correct classification rate (CCR) in Definitions 4 and 5.

Definition 6 (ASR for mixed strategies). *Given a defender's strategy $s \in \mathcal{S}$, we define the attack success rate of attack j as*

$$\text{ASR}_j(s) := s^T(\vec{1} - \text{rob}_{.j}) = 1 - \sum_{i=1}^{N} s_i \text{rob}_{ij}.$$

This is a direct extension of the attack success rate from Definition 4 to mixed strategies, since $\text{ASR}_j(e_i^{\text{def}}) = \text{ASR}_{ij}$. As the name implies, it quantifies the probability of a successful attack given a possibly mixed defender's strategy.

Definition 7 (CCR for mixed strategies). *We define the correct classification rate with respect to an adversary's strategy $r \in \mathcal{R}$ against model i as*

$$\text{CCR}_i(r; r_{\max}) := r^T \left(\text{CCR}_{ij}(r_{\max})\right)_{1 \leq j \leq M} = \sum_{j=1}^{M} r_j \text{CCR}_{ij}(r_{\max}),$$

where $\text{CCR}_{iM} \equiv \text{acc}_i$ by assumption (A5).

Similar to above, this generalizes the correct classification rate from Definition 5 to mixed strategies. Unlike the above, we place an additional restriction on the performance metric. Here, the proportion of adversarial examples is explicitly restricted to $r_{\max} \in [0, 1]$. For pure strategies of the adversary we get $\text{CCR}_i(e_j^{\text{adv}}; r_{\max}) = \text{CCR}_{ij}(r_{\max})$, the probability of correctly classifying a sample if the adversary chooses attack j.

Expected Payoff per Sample. Both performance measures allow us to concisely describe each entry of the EPPS-functions in Eq. (8) and (9)

$$\text{EPPS}_j^{\text{adv}}(s) = -O_j^{\text{adv}} - R_-^{\text{adv}}(1 - \text{ASR}_j(s)) + R_+^{\text{adv}}\text{ASR}_j(s)$$

$$= -O_j^{\text{adv}} - R_-^{\text{adv}} - (R_+^{\text{adv}} + R_-^{\text{adv}})\,\text{ASR}_j(s) \tag{10}$$

$$\text{EPPS}_i^{\text{def}}(r) = -O_i^{\text{def}} - R_-^{\text{def}}(1 - \text{CCR}_i(r; r_{\max})) + R_+^{\text{def}}\text{CCR}_i(r; r_{\max})$$

$$= -O_i^{\text{def}} - R_-^{\text{def}} + (R_+^{\text{def}} + R_-^{\text{def}})\,\text{CCR}_i(r; r_{\max}). \tag{11}$$

$\mathrm{EPPS}_j^{\mathrm{adv}}(s)$ corresponds to the expected payoff per adversarially perturbed sample for attack j given the strategy $s \in \mathcal{S}$. Similarly, $\mathrm{EPPS}_i^{\mathrm{def}}(r)$ corresponds to the expected payoff per classified sample given model i and strategy $r \in \mathcal{R}$.

4 Game Instantiation and Analysis

Below, we analyse the simplest realization of the game, where $N = 2$ and $M = 2$. The defender chooses from two classifiers (typically one of them trained as usual and the other using some form of adversarial training increasing robustness) and the adversary may attack or not. Hence their strategy spaces can be specified by a single scalar parameter $r = (r_1, 1-r_1)$ and $s = (s_1, 1-s_1)$ with $r_1, s_1 \in [0, 1]$ for the adversary and defender, respectively. By this, "not attacking", i.e., attack $M = 2$ is represented by the second entry $(1 - r_1)$. We further simplify the notation by writing rob_i instead of rob_{i1} and $\mathrm{ASR}(s)$ instead of $\mathrm{ASR}_1(s)$.

As a convention, motivated by experimental results of state of the art methods for adversarial training, we assume the first model (trained normally) to have higher accuracy on benign samples but lower on adversarial samples (robustness) compared to the second model. Furthermore, accuracy on attacked samples of both models is assumed to be lower than that on clean samples, since the adversary aims to cause a misclassification and not to help the defender. This means the accuracy and robustness are ordered as

$$\mathrm{acc}_1 > \mathrm{acc}_2 > \mathrm{rob}_2 > \mathrm{rob}_1. \qquad (12)$$

This order also makes sense from a game-theoretical point of view. If the first model would have both, higher accuracy and higher robustness, choosing this model would be a strictly dominant strategy and the defender will never use the second model, assuming equal ongoing costs as has been justified above. Contrary, if the first inequality would not hold, choosing model 2 would be strictly dominant. In order to simplify the equations in this section, we define

$$\Delta\mathrm{acc} := \mathrm{acc}_1 - \mathrm{acc}_2 > 0$$
$$\Delta\mathrm{rob} := \mathrm{rob}_2 - \mathrm{rob}_1 > 0$$

4.1 Best Response Analysis of the Adversary

Assuming a fixed strategy of the defender $s \in \mathcal{S}$, a best response of the adversary maximizes the utility $r^* \in \arg\max_{r \in \mathcal{R}} \mathrm{Utility}^{\mathrm{adv}}(s, r)$ defined in Eq. (8). Since the initial costs $\mathrm{I}^{\mathrm{adv}}$ are constant (by Assumption (A1)), the utility linearly increases in r, hence the maximization is trivial depending on the sign of her expected payout per sample, $\mathrm{EPPS}^{\mathrm{adv}}(s)$, as follows:

$$r_1^* \in \begin{cases} \{0\} & \text{iff } \mathrm{EPPS}^{\mathrm{adv}}(s) < 0 \\ \{1\} & \text{iff } \mathrm{EPPS}^{\mathrm{adv}}(s) > 0 \ . \\ [0, 1] & \text{iff } \mathrm{EPPS}^{\mathrm{adv}}(s) = 0 \end{cases} \qquad (13)$$

Table 2. All possible best responses $r^* = (r_1^*, 1 - r_1^*) \in \mathcal{R}$ of the adversary depending on the defender's strategy $s = (s_1, 1 - s_1) \in \mathcal{S}$. The first, second and third row summarize Case 1, 2, and 3, respectively. If the precondition does not hold, then the condition on $s \in \mathcal{S}$ cannot be satisfied.

Case	Best responses	Condition	Precondition
1	$r^* = (0, 1)$	$\mathrm{ASR}(s) < \mu^{\mathrm{adv}}$	$1 - \mu^{\mathrm{adv}} < \mathrm{rob}_2$
2	$r^* = (1, 0)$	$\mathrm{ASR}(s) > \mu^{\mathrm{adv}}$	$\mathrm{rob}_1 < 1 - \mu^{\mathrm{adv}}$
3	$r^* \in \mathcal{R}$	$\mathrm{ASR}(s) = \mu^{\mathrm{adv}}$	$\mathrm{rob}_1 \leq 1 - \mu^{\mathrm{adv}} \leq \mathrm{rob}_2$

The last line means that any $r^* \in \mathcal{R}$ is a best response. We refer to these cases as Case 1 (never attack), Case 2 (always attack), and Case 3 (indifferent) in that order. The definition of $\mathrm{EPPS}^{\mathrm{adv}}$ from Eq. (10) can be reformulated as

$$\mathrm{EPPS}^{\mathrm{adv}}(s) = \left(R_+^{\mathrm{adv}} + R_-^{\mathrm{adv}} \right) \left(\mathrm{ASR}(s) - \mu^{\mathrm{adv}} \right),$$

where

$$\mu^{\mathrm{adv}} := \frac{O^{\mathrm{adv}} + R_-^{\mathrm{adv}}}{R_+^{\mathrm{adv}} + R_-^{\mathrm{adv}}},$$

which leads to an alternative characterization of the best responses from Eq. (13)

$$r_1^* \in \begin{cases} \{0\} & \text{iff } \mathrm{ASR}(s) < \mu^{\mathrm{adv}} \\ \{1\} & \text{iff } \mathrm{ASR}(s) > \mu^{\mathrm{adv}} \\ [0, 1] & \text{iff } \mathrm{ASR}(s) = \mu^{\mathrm{adv}} \end{cases}. \tag{14}$$

The last Eq. (14) relates the attack success rate ASR to the economic factors of adversary rewards, as μ^{adv} is defined in terms of her rewards and ongoing costs. Assuming the penalty for a failed attack R_-^{adv} is negligible (presently, most crimes of this type are left unpunished due to lack of legislation, law enforcement, and forensic tools) and the reward R_+^{adv} dominates the ongoing costs, μ^{adv} is in practice going to be close to zero. In consequence this means that if there is a slight chance of an attack to succeed, every rational adversary will always attack.

We summarize our results in Table 2. We specify the case on the left-most column. The best responses for the given case are shown in the second column. For each case, we have a corresponding equivalent condition on the $\mathrm{ASR}(s)$, which is shown in the third column. The fourth and last column shows for each case if it is satisfiable at all by any $s \in \mathcal{S}$. These preconditions depend only on non-choice parameters in Table 1 and not on the defender's strategy itself.

4.2 Best Response Analysis of the Defender

For a given adversary strategy $r \in \mathcal{R}$, a best response of the defender maximizes the utility $s^* \in \arg\max_{s \in \mathcal{S}} \mathrm{Utility}^{\mathrm{def}}(s, r)$, see Eq. (9). This is equivalent to maximizing the expected payout per sample $s^T \mathrm{EPPS}^{\mathrm{def}}(r)$ as defined in Eq. (11), which we rewrite as

$$\mathrm{EPPS}_i^{\mathrm{def}}(r) = \left(R_+^{\mathrm{def}} + R_-^{\mathrm{def}} \right) \left(\mathrm{CCR}_i(r; r_{\max}) - \mu_i^{\mathrm{def}} \right), \tag{15}$$

where

$$\mathrm{CCR}_i(r; r_{\max}) = (1 - r_1 r_{\max})\mathrm{acc}_i + r_1 r_{\max}\, \mathrm{rob}_i$$

and

$$\mu_i^{\mathrm{def}} = \frac{O_i^{\mathrm{def}} + R_-^{\mathrm{def}}}{R_+^{\mathrm{def}} + R_-^{\mathrm{def}}}.$$

We observe that similarly to the adversary's case, the defender chooses a model i with maximal $\mathrm{CCR}_i(r; r_{\max}) - \mu_i^{\mathrm{def}}$. Here again the performance metric $\mathrm{CCR}_i(r; r_{\max})$ is related to the economic setting term μ_i^{def}. Importantly and unlike the adversary's case, the choice of the defender's strategy depends on $r_{\max}$, the maximal fraction of samples the adversary can influence. As will be seen below, this means that for some small $r_{\max}$ (which occurs in many practical situations), the defender will not have an incentive to use the robust classifier.

For the analysis of Nash equilibria in the next section, it is useful to analyze the difference $\mathrm{EPPS}_1^{\mathrm{def}} - \mathrm{EPPS}_2^{\mathrm{def}}$,

$$\Delta\mathrm{CCR}(r; r_{\max}) - \Delta\mu^{\mathrm{def}} = \frac{\mathrm{EPPS}_1^{\mathrm{def}}(r) - \mathrm{EPPS}_2^{\mathrm{def}}(r)}{R_+^{\mathrm{def}} + R_-^{\mathrm{def}}}, \qquad (16)$$

where

$$\Delta\mathrm{CCR}(r; r_{\max}) := \mathrm{CCR}_1(r; r_{\max}) - \mathrm{CCR}_2(r; r_{\max}), \text{ and}$$

$$\Delta\mu^{\mathrm{def}} := \mu_1^{\mathrm{def}} - \mu_2^{\mathrm{def}} = \frac{O_1^{\mathrm{def}} - O_2^{\mathrm{def}}}{R_+^{\mathrm{def}} + R_-^{\mathrm{def}}}.$$

Notice that in many practical situations, the difference in ongoing costs of two classifiers is almost zero (non-robust and robust versions differ mainly in training, not in the architecture of the model, which makes inference costs akin), therefore $\Delta\mu^{\mathrm{def}} \approx 0$. The best responses for the defender are given by

$$s_1^* \in \begin{cases} \{0\} & \text{iff } \Delta\mathrm{CCR}(r; r_{\max}) < \Delta\mu^{\mathrm{def}} \\ \{1\} & \text{iff } \Delta\mathrm{CCR}(r; r_{\max}) > \Delta\mu^{\mathrm{def}} \\ [0,1] & \text{iff } \Delta\mathrm{CCR}(r; r_{\max}) = \Delta\mu^{\mathrm{def}} \end{cases}. \qquad (17)$$

The last line means that any $s^* \in \mathcal{S}$ is a best response. We refer to these cases as Case A (always defend), Case B (never defend), and Case C (indifferent) in that order.

Defender's best responses are summarized in Table 3. The case is specified in the left-most column, the best responses for the given case are shown in the second column, and the corresponding equivalent condition on r is shown in the third column. The fourth and last column shows prerequisites for the given case that only depend on non-choice parameters.

4.3   (Fully) Mixed Nash Equilibria

In Subsect. 4.1 and 4.2 we discussed and listed all possible best responses for both adversary and defender. The results are summarized in Table 2 and 3. Now

Table 3. All possible best responses $s^* = (s_1^*, 1 - s_1^*) \in \mathcal{S}$ of the defender depending on the adversary's strategy $r = (r_1, 1 - r_1) \in \mathcal{R}$. The first, second and third row summarize Case A, B, and C, respectively. If the precondition does not hold true, then the condition on $r \in \mathcal{R}$ cannot be satisfied.

Case	Best responses	Condition	Precondition
A	$s^* = (0,1)$	$\Delta\mathrm{CCR}(r; r_{\max}) < \Delta\mu^{\mathrm{def}}$	$\frac{\Delta\mathrm{acc} - \Delta\mu^{\mathrm{def}}}{\Delta\mathrm{acc} + \Delta\mathrm{rob}} < r_{\max}$
B	$s^* = (1,0)$	$\Delta\mathrm{CCR}(r; r_{\max}) > \Delta\mu^{\mathrm{def}}$	$\Delta\mu^{\mathrm{def}} < \Delta\mathrm{acc}$
C	$s^* \in \mathcal{S}$	$\Delta\mathrm{CCR}(r; r_{\max}) = \Delta\mu^{\mathrm{def}}$	$0 \leq \frac{\Delta\mathrm{acc} - \Delta\mu^{\mathrm{def}}}{\Delta\mathrm{acc} + \Delta\mathrm{rob}} \leq r_{\max}$

we investigate if and when mixed strategy Nash equilibria exist at all. For this we consider Case 3 and Case C, that is

$$\mathrm{ASR}(s) = \mu^{\mathrm{adv}} \quad \text{and} \quad \Delta\mathrm{CCR}(r; r_{\max}) = \Delta\mu^{\mathrm{def}}$$

or, equivalently,

$$s_1 = \frac{\mathrm{rob}_2 - 1 + \mu^{\mathrm{adv}}}{\Delta\mathrm{rob}} \quad \text{and} \quad r_1 r_{\max} = \frac{\Delta\mathrm{acc} - \Delta\mu^{\mathrm{def}}}{\Delta\mathrm{acc} + \Delta\mathrm{rob}}, \tag{18}$$

respectively. Obviously, $s \in \mathcal{S}$ and $r \in \mathcal{R}$ are mixed strategies, and therefore $s_1, r_1 \in (0,1)$, if and only if

$$\mathrm{rob}_1 < 1 - \mu^{\mathrm{adv}} < \mathrm{rob}_2 \quad \text{and} \quad 0 < \frac{\Delta\mathrm{acc} - \Delta\mu^{\mathrm{def}}}{\Delta\mathrm{acc} + \Delta\mathrm{rob}} < r_{\max}, \tag{19}$$

respectively.

Theorem 1. *Let* $\mathrm{rob}_1 < 1 - \mu^{\mathrm{adv}} < \mathrm{rob}_2$ *and* $0 < \frac{\Delta\mathrm{acc} - \Delta\mu^{\mathrm{def}}}{\Delta\mathrm{acc} + \Delta\mathrm{rob}} < r_{\max}$. *Then the fully mixed strategy Nash equilibrium* (s^*, r^*) *given by*

$$s_1^* = \frac{\mathrm{rob}_2 - 1 + \mu^{\mathrm{adv}}}{\Delta\mathrm{rob}} \quad \text{and} \quad r_1^* r_{\max} = \frac{\Delta\mathrm{acc} - \Delta\mu^{\mathrm{def}}}{\Delta\mathrm{acc} + \Delta\mathrm{rob}}. \tag{20}$$

is unique.

Proof. Consider Tables 2 and 3. By the analysis above, s_1^* and r_1^* are given as in Eq. (18) and therefore the conditions for Case 3 and Case C are satisfied. That is all $r \in \mathcal{R}$ are a best response to s^* and all $s \in \mathcal{S}$ are a best response to r^*. Furthermore, the conditions in Eq. (19) are fulfilled and therefore both strategies are mixed strategies. In conclusion, (s^*, r^*) is a fully mixed strategy Nash equilibrium.

In order to prove uniqueness of the Nash equilibrium, we first assume there exists another Nash equilibrium $(\hat{s}, \hat{r})$. That is, either $\hat{s}_1 \neq s_1^*$ or $\hat{r}_1 \neq r_1^*$. We consider only the case $\hat{s} < s^*$, as all other cases are conducted analogously. Observe that

$$s \mapsto \mathrm{ASR}(s) = 1 - \mathrm{rob}_2 + s_1 \Delta\mathrm{rob}$$

strictly increases in s_1 and

$$r \mapsto \Delta\mathrm{CCR}(r; r_{\max}) = \Delta\mathrm{acc} - r_1 r_{\max}(\Delta\mathrm{acc} + \Delta\mathrm{rob})$$

strictly decreases in r_1. Since $\hat{s}$ and $\hat{r}$ are mutual best responses, we have

$$
\begin{aligned}
\hat{s}_1 < s_1^* &\implies \mathrm{ASR}(\hat{s}) < \mathrm{ASR}(s^*) = \mu^{\mathrm{adv}} \\
&\implies \hat{r} = (0,1) \\
&\implies \Delta\mathrm{CCR}(\hat{r}; r_{\max}) > \Delta\mathrm{CCR}(r^*; r_{\max}) = \mu^{\mathrm{adv}} \\
&\implies \hat{s} = (1,0) \implies \hat{s}_1 > s_1^*,
\end{aligned}
$$

which is a contradiction. All in all, (s^*, r^*) is a unique Nash equilibrium.   □

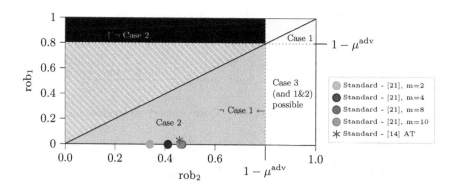

Fig. 2. Adversary's preferences with regards to rob_1 and rob_2 for μ^{adv}. Decreasing μ^{adv} shifts the horizontal and vertical lines (captioned "$1 - \mu^{\mathrm{adv}}$") up and right. This means that area of Case 2 (always attack) is getting bigger and the area Case 3 (mixed strategy is possible) is getting smaller. As discussed earlier, in practice $\mu^{\mathrm{adv}} \approx 0$. This would mean the adversary will always attack. Note that the area above the minor diagonal line is unreachable, because of the assumption in Eq. (12).

4.4   Results

In the previous section, we have identified best responses and their preconditions for both actors given the opponent's strategy (see Tables 2 and 3). They allow to identify the set of strategies available to each rationally behaving actor for the given economic factors.

We visualize the adversary's options in Fig. 2, where we can see that μ^{adv} (see lines captioned "$1 - \mu^{\mathrm{adv}}$") determines the areas, where the adversary will always attack (Case 2), never attack (Case 1), and where we cannot say without considering the defender's actions and she might play a mixed strategy (Case 3). Note that the area above minor diagonal is unreachable (by Eq. (12)). We can

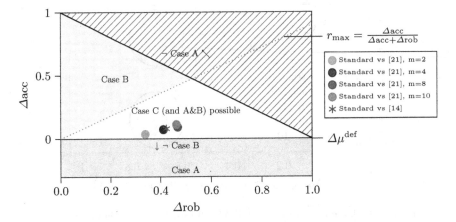

Fig. 3. Visualization of the defender cases with regards to Δacc and Δrob for $\Delta\mu^{\mathrm{def}} = 0$ and $r_{\max} = 0.45$. Note that lower (negative) $\Delta\mu^{\mathrm{def}}$ values shift the horizontal line that indicates the area where $\neg$ Case B downwards and the diagonal line that indicates $\neg$ Case A to the right.

observe that most area is covered by Case 2, which means that the adversary is incentivized to always attack, especially if a value of μ^{adv} is low, which happens if the costs for being caught R^{adv}_{-} and her ongoing cost O^{adv} are low and when the potential reward R^{adv}_{+} is high. Note that the black area, where neither Case 1, nor Case 2 (and thus also not Case 3) is true, does never fulfill the ordering in Eq. (12) and thus is undefined in our setting.

The same visualization for the defender is shown in Fig. 3 for a given $\Delta\mu^{\mathrm{def}} = 0$ and $r_{\max} = 0.45$. Reachable areas are Case B (between the solid and dotted line), where the defender will never defend, and Case C where possibly a mixed strategy occurs. Note, while the slope of the solid line is fixed (by the ordering in Eq. (12)), the slope of the dotted line depends only on the value of $r_{\max}$[4]. With decreasing value of $r_{\max}$, the slope will also decrease, which means that the defender will have less incentive to use the robust classifier (the area of Case B will increase). Therefore if the proportion of samples the adversary can influence (or attack) $r_{\max}$ is small, a rational defender might not have an incentive to use the robust model, regardless of the strategy of the adversary. The case, where the defender will always use the robust classifier is not considered, as it would correspond to a case when the robust model has lower costs than the non-robust, even though it might have a lower CCR (but such a pure strategy can be still a solution of Case C).

The solid diagonal line depicts the condition that Δacc + Δrob < 1, so all points to the right (the striped area) are not valid.[5] Further, the ordering

---

[4] An alternative formulation of the linear equation for the dotted line in Fig. 3 is: Δacc $= \frac{r_{\max}\Delta\mathrm{rob}}{1-r_{\max}}$ (for $\Delta\mu^{\mathrm{def}} = 0$).

[5] Note that Δacc + Δrob $= \mathrm{acc}_1 - (\mathrm{acc}_2 - \mathrm{rob}_2) - \mathrm{rob}_1 < \mathrm{acc}_1 \leq 1$, by Eq. (12).

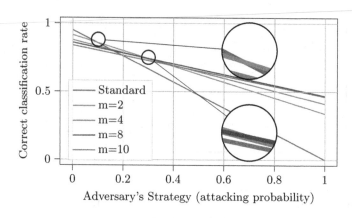

Fig. 4. Correct classification rate on CIFAR-10 based on the original data in [21].

(Eq. (12)) ensures that $acc_1 > acc_2$ and thus $\Delta acc > 0$. Therefore, all points below the horizontal line at $\Delta acc = 0$ are invalid. We include this area into the figure to illustrate when the defender would purely deploy the second model (Case A) without considering the adversary's strategy. This is only the case when $\Delta\mu^{def}$ is positive which in turn is only true if $O_1^{def} > O_2^{def}$, i.e. in our scenario, the defended model has lower ongoing costs than the undefended model.

Colored dots and a star in Fig. 2 and Fig. 3 illustrate the CIFAR-10 models proposed in [14] and [21], where the accuracy and robustness values are taken from corresponding publications. We see in Fig. 2 that for these values and the chosen μ^{adv}, an adversary would always attack, independent of the strategy the defender chooses (Case 1). Similarly in Fig. 3, we can see that for the given values and the chosen μ^{def} and r_{max}, the defender is always in Case C, meaning that she might use both models. Keep in mind that values of r_{max}, μ^{adv} and μ^{def} are arbitrarily chosen and the defender will play a model with higher CCR for that given attack rate (recall that the adversary will likely attack). Needless to say that our chosen value $r_{max} = 0.45$ is very high as it means that the adversary can influence up to 45% of samples. Realistically r_{max} will be much lower, even as low as one percent, which means that the defender might opt to use the non-robust model, although the adversary will always attack.

5   Discussion

First of all, we extend the analysis of the CCR, as already shown in Fig. 1 to the results reported in [21] in Fig. 4. Here, we can see that of all the countermeasures proposed (for CIFAR-10 data), only $m = 2$ and $m = 8$ would be considered by the defender, again depending on the strategy of the adversary. If the adversary would choose to attack in less than $\approx$10% of the cases or $r_{max} \leq 0.1$, the undefended model would be strictly preferable. The proposed ideal solution from [21], $m = 8$, is only optimal if the adversary chooses to attack with an probability of more than $\approx$30% (or if $r_{max} > 0.3$). In between, the countermeasure with $m = 2$

is the defender's optimal strategy and all other strategies ($m = 4, m = 10$) are strictly dominated and thus never optimal (under Assumption 3.3). A similar figure was also shown in [7], but with a completely different focus and lack of theoretical foundation. By analysing our advanced adversarial classification game with the help of ASR and CCR, we justify these figures by a solid theory and encourage researchers to incorporate this evaluation method when reporting results about new attack methods or countermeasures.

Then, as mentioned in Sect. 4.2, in many cases $\Delta\mu^{\text{def}} \approx 0$. This holds especially true, if we consider the setting where the defender can choose between any standard trained model (model $i = 1$) and its adversarially trained counterpart (model $i = 2$). Since the architecture of both models is identical, they incur the same ongoing costs to operate. By Table 3 the defender's best response is determined by the sign of $\Delta\text{CCR}(r; r_{\text{max}})$. This can be interpreted geometrically; $\Delta\text{CCR}(r; r_{\text{max}}) = 0$ (Case C), corresponds to an intersection of the functions

$$\rho \mapsto \text{CCR}_{11}(\rho) = (1 - \rho)\text{acc}_1 + \rho\,\text{rob}_{11}$$
$$\rho \mapsto \text{CCR}_{21}(\rho) = (1 - \rho)\text{acc}_2 + \rho\,\text{rob}_{21},$$

where $\rho = r_1 r_{\text{max}} \in [0, r_{\text{max}}]$. Visually, this intersection can be seen in Fig. 1 and Fig. 4. All ρ values before and after the point of intersection correspond to Case B and A respectively. Finally, if $r_{\text{max}} = 1$, then the condition of all cases A, B and C are satisfiable by some $r \in \mathcal{R}$.

Similarly, if μ^{adv} is close to zero, as motivated above, the adversary will always attack at her maximum. Thus, in such a situation, the defender will face a proportion r_{max} adversarial examples out of all samples.

Contrarily, the defender could also aim at increasing the value of μ^{adv}. This means, either increasing the ongoing costs (e.g., by specifically designed countermeasures), decreasing the positive reward, or increasing the negative reward (e.g., by law enforcement and legal frameworks that harm an adversary).

Furthermore, some of our simplifying assumptions might be object to discussion, such as that the adversary has to pay the initial costs, even when she does not attack, that misclassifying adversarial examples costs the defender exactly the same as misclassifying benign samples, that each successful adversarial example gives the same reward to the adversary, or that the ongoing costs of the adversary do not depend on the defender's strategy. Our intention was to advance the theory of adversarial classification games by a first simple cost/reward structure, and thus we leave the mentioned extensions for future work.

Finally, we want to mention that although interesting from a game-theoretical point of view, the situations where adversary and defender play a mixed strategy Nash equilibrium might not be particularly relevant in practice. First of all, as mentioned above, in practice it seems unrealistic to reach one of these states at all, and even if we reach such a state, these Nash equilibria are very unstable. Small changes to the defender's strategy lead to a pure strategy best response of the adversary. Small changes to the adversary's strategy lead to a pure strategy best response of the defender.

6   Conclusion

We started this paper with the question: when should you defend your classifier?

To answer this, we present the *advanced adversarial classification game* that captures all relevant aspects of the interplay between an adversary and a defender in adversarial machine learning. We introduce two new metrics, the attack success rate for the adversary and the correct classification rate for the defender, which enables us to capture both players' expected payoff when being faced with every, possibly mixed, opponent strategy. By analyzing in detail the most common case in the literature, where the adversary has one possible attack and the defender may choose to implement one countermeasure, we are able to identify pure and mixed strategy equilibria for our game.

By taking into consideration that in realistic scenarios both cost parameters, μ^{adv} and $\Delta\mu^{\mathrm{def}}$ will be close to zero, we can conclude that the most important parameter of the game is $r_{\max}$, i.e., the proportion of samples an adversary can perturb. As shown in Figs. 1 and 4, no rational defender would implement any of these proposed countermeasures if she would expect less than $\approx 17\%$, respectively $\approx 10\%$ adversarial examples. Putting this into an universal answer to the question we set out to answer, it means:

$$\text{Do not defend your classifier when } r_{\max} \leq \frac{\Delta \mathrm{acc}}{\Delta \mathrm{acc} + \Delta \mathrm{rob}}.$$

References

1. Biggio, B., Roli, F.: Wild patterns: ten years after the rise of adversarial machine learning. Pattern Recogn. **84**, 317–331 (2018)
2. Brendel, W., Rauber, J., Bethge, M.: Decision-based adversarial attacks: reliable attacks against black-box machine learning models. arXiv preprint arXiv:1712.04248 (2017)
3. Brückner, M., Scheffer, T.: Stackelberg games for adversarial prediction problems. In: Proceedings of the 17th ACM SIGKDD International Conference on Knowledge Discovery and Data Mining, pp. 547–555 (2011)
4. Cohen, J., Rosenfeld, E., Kolter, Z.: Certified adversarial robustness via randomized smoothing. In: International Conference on Machine Learning, pp. 1310–1320. PMLR (2019)
5. Dalvi, N., Domingos, P., Sanghai, S., Verma, D.: Adversarial classification. In: Proceedings of the Tenth ACM SIGKDD International Conference on Knowledge Discovery and Data Mining, pp. 99–108 (2004)
6. Dritsoula, L., Loiseau, P., Musacchio, J.: A game-theoretic analysis of adversarial classification. IEEE Trans. Inf. Forensics Secur. **12**(12), 3094–3109 (2017)
7. Gilmer, J., Adams, R.P., Goodfellow, I., Andersen, D., Dahl, G.E.: Motivating the rules of the game for adversarial example research. arxiv (2018). https://arxiv.org/abs/1807.06732
8. Globerson, A., Roweis, S.: Nightmare at test time: robust learning by feature deletion. In: Proceedings of the 23rd International Conference on Machine Learning, pp. 353–360 (2006)

9. Grosse, K., Papernot, N., Manoharan, P., Backes, M., McDaniel, P.: Adversarial examples for malware detection. In: Foley, S.N., Gollmann, D., Snekkenes, E. (eds.) ESORICS 2017. LNCS, vol. 10493, pp. 62–79. Springer, Cham (2017). https://doi.org/10.1007/978-3-319-66399-9_4
10. Großhans, M., Scheffer, T.: Solving prediction games with parallel batch gradient descent. In: Appice, A., Rodrigues, P.P., Santos Costa, V., Soares, C., Gama, J., Jorge, A. (eds.) ECML PKDD 2015. LNCS (LNAI), vol. 9284, pp. 152–167. Springer, Cham (2015). https://doi.org/10.1007/978-3-319-23528-8_10
11. He, K., Zhang, X., Ren, S., Sun, J.: Deep residual learning for image recognition. In: Proceedings of the IEEE Conference on Computer Vision and Pattern Recognition, pp. 770–778 (2016)
12. Krizhevsky, A., Sutskever, I., Hinton, G.E.: ImageNet classification with deep convolutional neural networks. In: Advances in Neural Information Processing Systems, pp. 1097–1105 (2012)
13. Leyton-Brown, K., Shoham, Y.: Essentials of game theory: a concise multidisciplinary introduction. Synth. Lect. Artif. Intell. Mach. Learn. **2**(1), 1–88 (2008)
14. Madry, A., Makelov, A., Schmidt, L., Tsipras, D., Vladu, A.: Towards deep learning models resistant to adversarial attacks. arXiv preprint arXiv:1706.06083 (2017)
15. Nash, J.: Non-cooperative games. Ann. Math. **54**, 286–295 (1951)
16. Papernot, N., McDaniel, P., Goodfellow, I.: Transferability in machine learning: from phenomena to black-box attacks using adversarial samples. arXiv preprint arXiv:1605.07277 (2016)
17. Papernot, N., McDaniel, P., Goodfellow, I., Jha, S., Celik, Z.B., Swami, A.: Practical black-box attacks against machine learning. In: Proceedings of the 2017 ACM on Asia conference on computer and communications security, pp. 506–519 (2017)
18. Pinot, R., Ettedgui, R., Rizk, G., Chevaleyre, Y., Atif, J.: Randomization matters how to defend against strong adversarial attacks. In: International Conference on Machine Learning, pp. 7717–7727. PMLR (2020)
19. Salman, H., et al.: Provably robust deep learning via adversarially trained smoothed classifiers. arXiv preprint arXiv:1906.04584 (2019)
20. Schuurmans, D., Zinkevich, M.A.: Deep learning games. In: Advances in Neural Information Processing Systems, pp. 1678–1686 (2016)
21. Shafahi, A., et al.: Adversarial training for free! In: Advances in Neural Information Processing Systems, pp. 3358–3369 (2019)
22. Szegedy, C., et al.: Intriguing properties of neural networks. In: International Conference on Learning Representations (ICLR) (2014)
23. Xu, W., Evans, D., Qi, Y.: Feature squeezing: detecting adversarial examples in deep neural networks. In: Network and Distributed System Security Symposium (2018)
24. Zhang, D., Zhang, T., Lu, Y., Zhu, Z., Dong, B.: You only propagate once: accelerating adversarial training via maximal principle. In: Advances in Neural Information Processing Systems, pp. 227–238 (2019)

Ransomware

A Mechanism Design Approach to Solve Ransomware Dilemmas

Iman Vakilinia[1(✉)], Mohammad Mahdi Khalili[2], and Ming Li[3]

[1] University of North Florida, Jacksonville, FL, USA
i.vakilinia@unf.edu
[2] University of Delaware, Newark, DE, USA
khalili@udel.edu
[3] University of Texas at Arlington, Arlington, TX, USA
ming.li@uta.edu

Abstract. Recently ransomware attacks have caused tremendous costs for businesses and society. Although cybersecurity researchers have developed best practices to protect computer systems from hackers, it is not expected that ransomware attacks will be prohibited in a near future mainly due to their complexity and profitability. Despite the wide research studies for developing the proactive approaches to protect the systems from ransomware attacks, facilitating the negotiation between attacker and victim after a successful attack has not been well investigated yet. As the attacker does not know the victim's true valuation for the data and the victim does not know the minimum ransom value that can satisfy the attacker, bargaining for ransom value can be time-consuming causing extra interruption cost for the victim. On the other hand, as there is no guarantee that the attacker will in turn release the decryption key after the payment of ransom, many victims are reluctant to pay the ransom and they accept the cost of data loss. Therefore, it is important to facilitate the negotiation between the attacker and victim to accelerate the release of data. To this end, first, we propose a mechanism to assist the negotiation for ransom value without a Trusted Third Party (TTP). We study the fair ransom value and investigate the development of a double-sided-blind auction mechanism to achieve the incentive-compatibility. In the second part, we propose a mechanism enforcing the victim and attacker to make the payment and release of decryption key without a TTP. To achieve this goal, we create a dynamic game and set incentives such that the subgame perfect equilibrium matches our design goal. We utilize smart-contract for the implementation of our proposed mechanisms to alleviate the TTP requirement.

Keywords: Ransomware · Mechanism design · Smart-contract

1 Introduction

Ransomware is a type of malware that uses cryptoviral extortion techniques to hold the victim's data hostage and demands a ransom for the decryption

© Springer Nature Switzerland AG 2021
B. Bošanský et al. (Eds.): GameSec 2021, LNCS 13061, pp. 181–194, 2021.
https://doi.org/10.1007/978-3-030-90370-1_10

key. At least 2,345 US companies, local governments, healthcare facilities, and schools were victims of ransomware in 2020 according to cyber-security company Emsisoft [1]. Emsisoft has also estimated that the true global cost of ransomware, including business interruption and ransom payments in 2020, was nearly a minimum of \$42bn and a maximum of \$170bn [2].

According to Sophos 2021 ransomware survey [3], the average total cost of recovery from a ransomware attack has more than doubled in a year, increasing from \$761,106 in 2020 to \$1.85 million in 2021. The findings also show that only 8% of organizations managed to get back all of their data after paying a ransom, with 29% getting back no more than half of their data [3]. On average, only 65% of the encrypted data was restored after the ransom was paid. It is estimated that the victims' average downtime is 21 days [4], and the average number of days it takes a business to fully recover from an attack is 287 days [1]. *Therefore, in many cases, business interruption costs are the largest source of losses.*

Despite the efforts for protecting cyber-systems from ransomware, it is not expected that these types of attacks can be stopped in near future mainly due to their complexity, profitability, and high number of attacks.

Considering the importance of solving the ransomware issues, in this paper, we study the game-theoretic solutions for accelerating the recovery process for the victim. To this end, we propose mechanisms to facilitate the negotiation between attacker and victim with the goal of decreasing the business interruption cost for the victim while satisfying the attacker. More specifically, we introduce and study two problems in the ransomware context which we name *ransomware-dilemma-1* and *ransomware-dilemma-2*.

In the *ransomware-dilemma-1*, the problem is how we can have a mechanism to assist ransom value negotiation without a Trusted Third Party (TTP). This is a challenging task due to the asymmetric nature of this game. As the attacker does not know the victim's true valuation for the data and the victim does not know the minimum value that can satisfy the attacker, such a bargaining between attacker and victim can be time-consuming causing extra interruption cost for the victim. To solve this dilemma, we model a game between attacker and victim and then analyze the *Shapley Value* of such a game to find a fair ransom value. Afterward, we study the development of a *double-sided-blind auction* mechanism to achieve *incentive-compatibility*.

In the *ransomware-dilemma-2*, the problem is how we can design a mechanism without a TTP in which the only equilibrium of the game is ransom payment and sharing the decryption key. This is also a challenging task, as when there is no TTP, if the victim pays the ransom first, then there is no guarantee that the attacker is going to reveal the decryption key. On the other hand, if the attacker releases the decryption key first, then there is no guarantee that the victim is going to pay the ransom. To solve this problem, we design a dynamic game such that the attacker's strategy for sharing the key becomes the only subgame perfect equilibrium.

Note that solving these dilemmas effectively decreases the business cost for the victim which is the main goal of this paper. This is due to the fact that having implementable mechanisms for these dilemmas accelerates and guarantees the process of releasing the decryption key.

The main contributions of this paper are the two parts, as described below:

- We define ransomware dilemmas and investigate the design of mechanisms to overcome such problems with the goal of decreasing the business interruption cost for the victims while satisfying the attacker.
- We propose smart-contract based solutions to alleviate the TTP requirement in the ransomware dilemmas.

The rest of the paper is organized as follows. The next section reviews major related research studies in the game-theoretic analysis of ransomware attacks. In Sect. 3, we introduce our system model. Details of our proposed mechanisms are described in Sect. 4. In Sect. 5, the smart-contract implementation of the proposed mechanisms has been discussed. Finally, we conclude our paper in Sect. 6.

2   Related Work

As ransomware threats are becoming a national security issue, governments have started to legislate requirements to improve the digital defense against ransomware. On the other hand, the Ransomware Task Force, a team of more than 60 experts from software companies, cybersecurity vendors, government agencies, non-profits, and academic institutions has been convened to develop a comprehensive framework for tackling ransomware threat [5].

The detection, prevention, and analysis of ransomware have been studied widely in the cybersecurity literature   [6,7]. Several works have studied ransomware attacks with the game-theoretic perspective. Laszka et al. [8] have developed a game-theoretic model for the ransomware attack with the focus on aspects of the adversarial interaction between organizations and ransomware attackers. In particular, this work emphasizes the modeling of security investment decisions for mitigation. More specifically, this research have studied the strategic decision for the level of backup effort as well as to pay a ransom or not.

Li and Liao [9] have investigated the best response strategy of the attacker and victim in a ransomware model that the attacker can gain profit by selling stolen data in addition to the ransom demand. Fang et al. [10] have modeled ransomware as Bayesian games and studied the conditions that ransom should be paid. Hernandez-Castro et al. [11] have studied the strategies criminals can employ to profit from ransomware. This research has also investigated the welfare costs to society of such strategies by providing the analysis of a survey on willingness to pay and accept for loss of files. Dey and Lahiri [12] have studied the externality affect of ransom payment by modeling an infinite-horizon multi-period game and investigated the role of policy maker to prohibit the ransom payment.

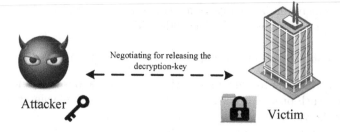

Fig. 1. Negotiation for releasing the decryption key

On the other hand, recently there are many research studies focusing on the development of smart-contract applications to facilitate parties' interactions by relieving the role of TTP. Green [13] has predicted the application of smart-contract in ransomware attacks in the near future. He discussed the concept of autonomous ransomware in which the ransomware does not require operators in the process of decryption key delivery. Karapapas *et al.* [14] have investigated the applications of smart-contract in the development of Ransomware-as-a-Service. Asgaonkar and Krishnamachari [15] have proposed a dual-deposit escrow smart-contract for cheat-proof delivery and payment for a digital good without a trusted mediator.

Considering the previous research studies, in this paper we take a mechanism design approach to facilitate the negotiation of attacker and victim with the goal of decreasing the business interruption cost for the victim while stimulating the attacker. Furthermore, we utilize smart-contract technology to implement our proposed mechanisms to release the TTP requirement for the negotiation. As far as the authors' knowledge this work is the first to propose a smart-contract solution for ransomware negotiation. It is worth mentioning that, our proposed mechanisms are applicable for other scenarios expecting the same outcome. For example, consider a scenario where a business has a task that can only be done by a specific worker, and the task owner and the worker want to reach an agreement without a TTP.

3   System Model

In this paper, the *attacker* is an entity that successfully executed ransomware and encrypted the victim's data. The *victim* is the true owner of the data taken hostage by the attacker. The only way that the victim can decrypt the data is to pay the attacker a satisfactory ransom to receive the decryption key. In our model, the attacker and victim negotiate for the release of decryption key as depicted in Fig. 1. Our model does not include the threat of data leakage.

Let $\mu > 0$ represent the minimum ransom value that the attacker expects to receive from the victim. In other words, the attacker will not share the decryption key, if the ransom value is less than μ. We assume that μ is drawn from the distribution $U(0, M)$, a uniform distribution in the interval $(0, M)$. Moreover, we assume that μ and M are unknown to the victim. Let $\delta > 0$ represent the valuation of the hostaged data for the victim. In other words, the victim does not pay a ransom of more than δ to receive the decryption key. We assume, the attacker does not know the true valuation of the data for the victim (i.e., δ).

Let r represent the ransom value that the victim pays to the attacker. Therefore, we have, $\mu < r < \delta$. We assume the players are rational such that they choose their strategies to maximize their payoffs. Therefore, the victim's goal is to minimize r while the attacker aims to maximize it. In our model, players are self-interested such that harming the other player does not provide extra benefit for a player.

The set of possible agreements for ransom value is $R = \{r \in \mathbb{R}^+ \mid \mu < r < \delta\}$. However, negotiating of such a value is time-consuming causing an extra business interruption cost for the victim. In other words the value of δ is decreasing over the time. Therefore, players would reach to an agreement sooner rather than later. We assume players would accept a *fair* ransom value which we investigate it in the next section.

For example, assume an attacker successfully executed a ransomware on a victim's system. The attacker expects to receive a ransom money which is more than "$100" (i.e., $\mu = 100$), and the value of decryption key for the victim is "$1000" (i.e., $\delta = 1000$)[1]. Players would agree on a fair ransom value between $100 < r < 1000$.

To facilitate the negotiation between the attacker and victim, we take a mechanism design approach by designing games between the attacker and victim. A mechanism can be specified by a game $g : \mathcal{M} \to \mathcal{X}$ where $\mathcal{M}$ is the set of possible input messages and $\mathcal{X}$ is the set of possible outputs of the mechanism. The design objective is to place a set of rules for the ransomware game for the attacker and victim to meet the requirements. However, as the attacker has the upper hand in the ransomware scenario by having the decryption key, the mechanisms should be carefully designed to incentivize the attacker to participate in such games. Currently, as there is no guarantee that the attacker will share the decryption key after the ransom payment, the victim is reluctant to make the ransom payment and might accept the cost of data loss which can be more than the ransom value. Therefore, the attacker would increase the chance of ransom payment by assuring the victim that he will indeed turn in the decryption key after the successful ransom payment. A naive solution is to apply a TTP to manage the ransom payment and release of the key. TTP receives the ransom money and decryption key from the victim and the attacker respectively, and hands them over afterward. However, having such a TTP is not feasible in ransomware scenarios, this is mainly due to the fact that working with an attacker is legally questionable.

To alleviate the TTP requirement, we utilize the *smart-contract*. The smart-contract acts as a mediator to rule the ransomware game's principles. Smart-contract is powered by blockchain technology. Blockchain technology has provided an agreeable platform for parties to make payments without a TTP.

---

[1] Note that quantification of μ and δ are out of the scope of this paper.

Blockchains are managed by a peer-to-peer network to manage a digital ledger. A smart-contract is a code in the blockchain that automatically enforces a contract between two parties without any help from a third party. Therefore, there is no need for an intermediary between contracting entities to enforce the contract.

4   Proposed Mechanisms

In this section, we study the design of mechanisms that can solve the ransomware dilemmas.

4.1   Ransomware-Dilemma-1

As the attacker does not know the true valuation of the data for the victim (i.e., δ), he is motivated to ask for more than whatever the victim is proposing as the ransom value. On the other hand, the victim would pay as little as possible for the ransom, and also she would receive the decryption key as soon as possible to decrease her business interruption cost. Even if the victim proposes a fair value for the ransom, the attacker might think that the victim is bluffing and the true value of the data is much more. The attacker might even demand a ransom value higher than δ resulting in the outcome of (No ransom payment, No key sharing). We are interested in the design of a mechanism ensuring the attacker that the proposed ransom value is a fair amount.

Therefore, first, we need to investigate what is the fair ransom value? and then we need to investigate an *incentive-compatibility* mechanism to achieve the fair ransom in the bargaining process.

For the sake of simplicity, at this point, let's assume the attacker will share the decryption key upon transferring the ransom. We study ransomware-dilemma-2 in the next subsection to satisfy this assumption.

We investigate one of the most widely used fair allocation methods which is *Shapley Value* [16].

Shapley Value- The *Shapley Value* deals with dividing the surplus among players in a coalition. Given the coalition (v, N), the *Shapley Value* for each player i is calculated as:

$$\phi_i(v) = \sum_{S \subseteq N \setminus \{i\}} \frac{|S|!(n - |S| - 1)!}{n!} [v(S \cup \{i\}) - v(S)] \qquad (1)$$

Note that once the attacker and victim make an agreement for the ransom, they make a coalition such that they agree to cooperate (i.e., Attacker by sharing the key, and victim by paying the ransom). In a coalitional game with transferable utility, an n-person game is given by the pair $G(N, v)$, where $N = \{1, 2, ..., n\}$ is the set of players and v is a real-valued payoff that the coalition's members can distribute among themselves. v is also called the characteristic function of the game, which returns a value for each subset of N. *Superadditivity* and *Convexity* of the game are defined as follows.

Superadditivity- A game $G(N, \text{v})$ is superadditive, if for all $S, T \subset N$ and $(S \cap T = \emptyset)$, then $\text{v}(S) + \text{v}(T) \leq \text{v}(S \cup T)$.

Convexity- A game $G(N, \text{v})$ is convex if for all $S, T \subset N$, then $\text{v}(S \cup T) \geq \text{v}(S) + \text{v}(T) - \text{v}(S \cap T)$.

While the characteristic function describes the payoff available to coalitions, it does not prescribe a way of distributing these payoffs. An allocation is a vector $x = (x_1, ..., x_n)$ assigning payoff to each player. In the ransomware game, we are looking for a fair allocation. We are looking for an allocation which is located in the *Core*.

Core- An allocation x is in the core of $G(N, \text{v})$ iff $x(N) = \text{v}(N)$ and for any $S \subseteq N$ we have $x(S) \geq \text{v}(S)$. In other words, the core is the set of x payoff allocations with the property that no coalition of agents can guarantee all of its members a payoff higher than what they currently receive under x.

Characteristic Function- Following Eq. (1), in order to find the *Shapley Value* for the ransomware game, we need to model the characteristic function. The attacker's strategy is to decide whether to accept or decline the ransom amount. If the attacker accepts the offer, then his payoff is $u_a = r$, and otherwise, his payoff is 0. On the other side, once the attacker accepts the offer and shares the decryption key then the utility of the victim player is $u_v = \delta - r$. In other words, when the attacker and victim cooperate, then the characteristic function of such a coalition is δ. Considering this fact, the characteristic function of this game can be represented as

$$\text{v}(S) = \begin{cases} \delta & |S| = 2 \\ 0 & \text{Otherwise} \end{cases} \tag{2}$$

In this setting, it is trivial that, there is no incentive for any subset of the members to separate and form smaller cooperation. In other words, this game is *Superadditive.*

Proposition 1. The *Shapley Value* allocation for the Ransomware game is located in the *Core.*

Proof. As the *Shapley Value* solution of a convex game is in the core [17], we investigate the convexity of the ransomware game. As in this game $\text{v}(S \cup T) = \text{v}(S) + \text{v}(T)$ and the value of $\text{v}(S \cap T) \geq 0$, thus the game is convex and its *Shapley Value* solution is in the core. □

Proposition 2. In the ransomware game, the *Shapley Values* for the attacker and victim are equal, and it is half of the benefit that the victim earns after decrpyting the data.

Proof. This can be easily verified by replacing the characteristic function of (2) in the *Shapley Value* formula (1).

$$\phi_i(\text{v}) = \frac{\delta}{2} \tag{3}$$

□

Enforcing Fair Bid for Ransom

Finding the fair ransom value, now we want to investigate how we can design a mechanism to achieve it? In other words, we need a mechanism to enforce the victim to proposes a fair ransom value, this is due to the fact that the attacker does not know the true valuation of the data.

Therefore, the victim's best response strategy should be the propose of $\frac{\delta}{2}$ for the ransom. This is a challenging task as the attacker does not aware of the true valuation of the data for the victim (i.e., δ). In other words, the proposed mechanism should be *incentive-compatible*. A mechanism is called *incentive-compatible* if every participant can achieve the best outcome for themselves just by acting according to their true preferences.

To this end, we utilize a double-sided-blind auction. In this auction, both attacker and victim submit sealed bids. The attacker submits his minimum acceptable value for the ransom (i.e., μ), and the victim submits the proposed ransom value (i.e., r_v). If $\mu < r_v$ then the ransom value is accepted as $r = r_v$, otherwise, the proposed ransom is rejected, and there will be no agreement. As can be seen in the following proposition, the best response strategy for the victim is to bid $r_v = \frac{\delta}{2}$ which is the fair ransom value. Note that, following our system model, we assume the victim does not know the attacker's minimum acceptable value.

Proposition 3. *In the proposed double-sided-blind auction, the best response strategy of the victim is to bid $r_v = \frac{\delta}{2}$.*

Proof. Let $\mathbb{E}[u_v]$ represent the expected payoff of victim, then we have:

$$\mathbb{E}[u_v] = Pr(\text{Win}|r_v) \cdot (\delta - r_v)$$
$$= Pr(\mu \leq r_v) \cdot (\delta - r_v)$$
$$= (\frac{r_v}{M}) \cdot (\delta - r_v)$$

The first order condition is

$$\frac{\partial((\frac{r_v}{M}) \cdot (\delta - r_v))}{\partial r_v} = 0$$
$$\frac{\delta - r_v^*}{M} - \frac{r_v^*}{M} = 0$$
$$r_v^* = \frac{\delta}{2}$$

As the second derivative of the expected gain is negative, r_v^* provides the maximum expected gain. □

In this mechanism, irrespective of the real value for μ and M, the best response strategy for the victim is to choose the fair ransom value as her bid. On the other hand, attacker's best response strategy is to submit true value for μ as well. This is because there is no incentive for the attacker to bid another value, as submitting the true value of μ results in the highest payoff for the attacker. The attacker does not accept the ransom value less than μ. If the attacker bids higher than true valuation $\mu < \mu'$ then there are two possible outcomes. If $r_v \geq \mu'$, then r_v is selected, and the attacker's payoff is same as what he can earn by submitting μ. On the other hand, if $r_v < \mu'$, then the attacker's payoff will be zero. Therefore, this mechanism satisfies the *incentive-compatibility* requirement.

Example. Assume an attacker successfully executed a ransomware in a victim's system. The attacker expects a ransom money which is at least $\mu = \$100$. In other words, the attacker does not share the decryption key, if the ransom is less than \$100. On the other hand, the value of decryption key for the victim is $\delta = \$1000$. The attacker does not know the value of δ and the victim does not know the value of μ. Following the proposed mechanism, attacker and victim participate in a double-sided-blind auction. The victim submits 500 as her bid since this value is the best response strategy for the victim, and the attacker submits 100 as his bid for the same reason. As $500 > 100$, the ransom value is set to be 500 which is the fair ransom value as discussed earlier.

Discussion. Although the *Shapley Value* for the ransom is $\delta/2$, it can be argued that if it is a fair value to pay to an attacker. Fairness is defined as impartial and just treatment or behavior without favoritism or discrimination. Despite the fact that the goal of this research study is to decrease the victim's cost, if the mechanism cannot satisfy the attacker then the victim endures more cost due to the loss of data or business interruption cost. Therefore, the proposed mechanism is designed to incentivize both victim and attacker.

4.2   Ransomware-Dilemma-2

As there is no guarantee that the attacker shares the decryption key once the victim has paid the ransom, how can we design a mechanism without a TTP to ensure the transferring of the legitimate decryption key to the victim after the successful ransom payment?

When there is no TTP, then we can model the ransomware-dilemma-2 as an extensive form game as depicted in Fig. 2. The victim's strategies are "Pay Ransom" or "Not Pay Ransom", and the attacker's strategies are "Share Key" and "Not Share Key". Although in this game, the best outcome is (Pay Ransom, Share Key), this outcome is not the only equilibrium. Many victims do not pay the ransom, as there is no guarantee that the attacker will, in turn, share the key, and in reality, many attackers do not share the key when they received the ransom since there is no incentive for doing so.

A TTP can mediate between parties. Receiving the ransom money and decryption key from the victim and the attacker respectively, and hands them over afterward. However, in reality, it is not easy to find such a TTP. Especially, entities would not work with the attacker as it is legally questionable. To alleviate the TTP requirement, we utilize the smart-contract. The smart-contract acts as a mediator to rule the ransomware game's principles. A smart-contract code is a self-enforcing code managed by a blockchain. Once the smart-contract code is deployed, then no parties can modify the code and its execution. Therefore, the

190   I. Vakilinia et al.

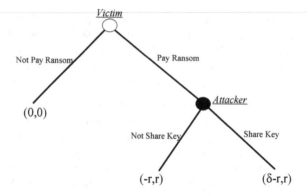

Fig. 2. Ransomware-dilemma-2 extensive form representation

precise execution of predefined rules in the smart-contract code is guaranteed
for the parties involved in the contract.

Now, we need to design the principles of the game to ensure that the game's
equilibrium is only "Pay Ransom" and "Share Key". To this end, we need to
provide incentives for the parties to stay in the game till both players achieve
their goal. Figure 3 shows the steps of the proposed game.

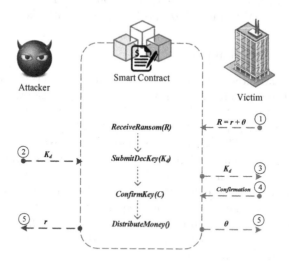

Fig. 3. The proposed solution for ransomware-dilemma-2

In this game, the victim is the first moving player. In the first step, the victim
deposits the amount of $R = r + \theta$ to the contract. Here, r is the ransom value and
θ acts as the *earnest-money* which will be refunded in the last step. The contract
checks the correctness of the deposit value, and if it is correct then moves to the
next step. In the next step, the attacker should submit the decryption key to

the contract. Once the decryption key is uploaded in the contract, then it is accessible to the victim. The victim downloads the decryption key and verifies its correctness. If it is correct, then the victim sends a confirmation signal to the contract. At this point, once the contract receives the approval signal from the victim, it deposits the amount of r to the attacker's address and returns the victim's earnest-money θ. The goal of having the earnest-money is to make sure that the victim will not leave the contract once she received the decryption key. Therefore, θ should be an attractive value in the case that the victim earns more profit by hurting the attacker. However, as in our system model, the players are self-interested and hurting the other player does not provide more benefit, any value larger than zero (i.e., $\theta > 0$) should do the work.

Proposition 4. The Subgame Perfect Equilibrium of the proposed mechanism is ("Pay Ransom, Share Key, Confirm").

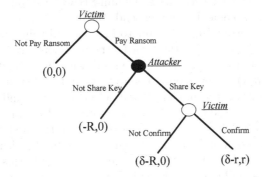

Fig. 4. Extensive form representation for the proposed ransom-key exchange mechanism

Proof. The extensive form of this game is shown in Fig. 4. As can be seen, following the *backward-induction*, the subgame perfect equilibrium of this game is ("Pay Ransom, Share Key, Confirm") (Note that $\delta - r > \delta - R$).   □

Example. Assume the ransom and earnest money values are set to be $r = \$1000$, and $\theta = \$1000$, respectively. The victim submits $R = \$2000$ to the smart-contract. The attacker verifies the correctness of submitted value to the smart-contract, and then submits the decryption key to the smart-contract. The victim receives the decryption key from the smart-contract and verifies it's correctness. If the decryption key is correct, then the victim submits a confirm signal to the smart-contract, and then the smart-contract sends $\$1000$ to the victim, and $\$1000$ to the attacker. Note that the smart-contract code is managed by a peer-to-peer network and cannot be modified once it is deployed in the blockchain. Therefore, the smart-contract assures the attacker and victim that no entity can interfere with the execution of the code.

5 Smart-Contract Implementation

In this section, we discuss the smart-contract implementation of the proposed mechanisms. We have used the Solidity language for the implementation of the smart-contract. We start with the implementation of a double-sided-blind auction as described in Sect. 4.1. As the transactions are transparent in the public blockchain, the smart-contract implementation of the sealed-bid auction is challenging mainly because storing bids in the blockchain can be read by the public.

To overcome this problem, the idea is to perform the bidding process in two stages. In the first stage, bidders submit their blinded-bids, and in the second stage, bidders reveal their bids.

For submitting the blinded-bid, the bidders send a *commitment* value of their bids. A commitment scheme has hiding and binding properties. Hiding requires that a commitment does not reveal any information about the committed value, and binding property guarantees that a commitment cannot be opened to another value. We have used the Ethereum-SHA3 hash function (Keccak256) as the commitment scheme. If a bidder sends the hash of the bid, the other player can still perform a brute force attempt to find the bid value when the range of possible bid value is small. In other words, the malicious user can compute the hashes of possible bid values and compare them with the submitted hash (a.k.a. rainbow table attack). To overcome this problem and make the scheme stronger, in our implementation, the bidder should select a secret random value (a.k.a. salt) and append it to the bid, and then compute the hash of the string.

Once the bidders submitted their blinded bids, in the next step, the bidders should reveal their committed values. Because of the binding feature of the commitment scheme, the bidders cannot forge another value in this step. Therefore, in the reveal phase, bidders send their bids together with the secret value. The smart-contract calculate the hash of bids and secret values and verify their correctness. Note that, we set a time interval for bidding and revealing phases such that bidders can only call these functions on their time windows.

The rest of the implementation of smart-contract code is straightforward. The program checks if the victim's bid is larger than the attacker's minimum acceptable value. If this is the case, then the victim should submit the ransom value in addition to the earnest-money as described in Sect. 4.2. Once the attacker verifies the successful transaction in the previous step, he sends the decryption key to the smart-contract. Afterward, the victim reads the decryption key and verifies its correctness. Finally, once the smart-contract receives the confirmation from the victim, deposits the ransom to the attacker's address, and returns the earnest-money to the victim.

On the Ethereum network, Gas is the unit that measures the amount of computational effort required to execute specific operations. We have used *remix*[2] to compile the smart-contract code. Table 1 demonstrates the gas cost for our

---

[2] https://remix.ethereum.org/.

implementation. The ether price on 6/26/2021 is \$1,785.35[3], and the gas cost is 6 Gwei[4] on average (1 ether = 10^9 Gwei).

Table 1. Gas cost for the Ransomware Smart-Contract

Operations	Gas units	Gas cost (USD)
Code Deployment Cost	446000	4.77
Bidding	42893	0.47
Revealing	47492	0.50
Key Delivery	20309	0.21

As can be seen, the cost of deployment and transaction fees are trivial and the proposed mechanisms are implementable. The smart-contract implementation is accessible to the public in the following GitHub repository.

https://github.com/imanvk/RansomwwareKeyNegotiation

6 Conclusion

Considering the massive business interruption loss caused by ransomware attacks, we have proposed mechanisms to facilitate the negotiation between attacker and victim for the release of the decryption key. First, we have studied the fair ransom value, and then we have proposed a double-sided-blind auction to achieve such a value in the bargaining process. Furthermore, we proposed a mechanism to ensure the decryption key delivery upon successful ransom payment. We have utilized smart-contract for the implementation of our proposed mechanisms to reveal the TTP requirement.

References

1. EMSISOFT (2021): The state of ransomware in the us: Report and statistics (2020). https://blog.emsisoft.com/en/37314/the-state-of-ransomware-in-the-us-report-and-statistics-2020/
2. EMSISOFT: The cost of ransomware in 2020. a country-by-country analysis (2020). https://blog.emsisoft.com/en/35583/report-the-cost-of-ransomware-in-2020-a-country-by-country-analysis/
3. SOPHOS: The state of ransomware (2021). https://secure2.sophos.com/en-us/medialibrary/pdfs/whitepaper/sophos-state-of-ransomware-2021-wp.pdf
4. COVEWARE: Ransomware payments fall as fewer companies pay data exfiltration extortion demands (2020). https://www.coveware.com/blog/ransomware-marketplace-report-q4-2020

---

[3] https://www.coindesk.com/price/ethereum.
[4] https://etherscan.io/gastracker.

5. Institute for Security and Technology. Combatting ransomware (2021). https://
   securityandtechnology.org/wp-content/uploads/2021/04/IST-Ransomware-Task-
   Force-Report.pdf
6. Dargahi, T., Dehghantanha, A., Bahrami, P.N., Conti, M., Bianchi, G., Benedetto,
   L.: A cyber-kill-chain based taxonomy of crypto-ransomware features. J. Comput.
   Virol. Hacking Tech. **15**(4), 277–305 (2019)
7. Al-rimy, B.A.S., Maarof, M.A., Shaid, S.Z.M.: Ransomware threat success factors,
   taxonomy, and countermeasures: a survey and research directions. Comput. Secur.
   74, 144–166 (2018)
8. Laszka, A., Farhang, S., Grossklags, J.: On the economics of ransomware. In: Rass,
   S., An, B., Kiekintveld, C., Fang, F., Schauer, S. (eds.) Decision and Game Theory for Security. GameSec 2017. LNCS, vol. 10575, pp. 397–417. Springer, Cham
   (2017). https://doi.org/10.1007/978-3-319-68711-7_21
9. Li, Z., Liao, Q.: Game theory of data-selling ransomware. J. Cyber Secur. Mob.
   65–96 (2021)
10. Fang, R., Xu, M., Zhao, P.: Should the ransomware be paid? arXiv preprint
    arXiv:2010.06700 (2020)
11. Hernandez-Castro, J., Cartwright, A., Cartwright, E.: An economic analysis of
    ransomware and its welfare consequences. R. Soc. Open Sci. **7**(3), 190023 (2020)
12. Dey, D., Lahiri, A.: Should we outlaw ransomware payments? In: Proceedings of
    the 54th Hawaii International Conference on System Sciences, p. 6609 (2021)
13. Green, M.: The future of ransomware (2017). https://blog.
    cryptographyengineering.com/2017/02/28/the-future-of-ransomware/
14. Karapapas, C., Pittaras, I., Fotiou, N., Polyzos, G.C.: Ransomware as a ser-
    vice using smart contracts and IPFS. In: 2020 IEEE International Conference on
    Blockchain and Cryptocurrency (ICBC), pp. 1–5. IEEE (2020)
15. Asgaonkar, A., Krishnamachari, B.: Solving the buyer and seller's dilemma: a dual-
    deposit escrow smart contract for provably cheat-proof delivery and payment for a
    digital good without a trusted mediator. In: 2019 IEEE International Conference
    on Blockchain and Cryptocurrency (ICBC), pp. 262–267. IEEE (2019)
16. Shapley, L.S.: A value for n-person games, Contributions to the Theory of Games,
    vol. 2, no. 28, pp. 307–317 (1953)
17. Shapley, L.S.: Cores of convex games. Int. J. Game Theory **1**(1), 11–26 (1971)

Winning the Ransomware Lottery

A Game-Theoretic Approach to Preventing Ransomware Attacks

Erick Galinkin[1,2]([envelope]) [ID]

[1] Rapid7, Boston, MA 02114, USA
erick_galinkin@rapid7.com
[2] Drexel University, Philadelphia, PA 19104, USA

Abstract. Ransomware is a growing threat to individuals and enterprises alike, constituting a major factor in cyber insurance and in the security planning of every organization. Although the game theoretic lens often frames the game as a competition between equals – a profit maximizing attacker and a loss minimizing defender – the reality of many situations is that ransomware organizations are not playing a noncooperative game, they are playing a lottery. The wanton behavior of attackers creates a situation where many victims are hit more than once by ransomware operators, sometimes even by the same group. If defenders wish to combat malware, they must then seek to remove the incentives of it. In this work, we construct an expected value model based on data from actual ransomware attacks and identify three variables: the value of payments, the cost of an attack, and the probability of payment. Using this model, we consider the potential to manipulate these variables to reduce the profit motive associated with ransomware attack. Based on the model, we present mitigations to encourage an environment that is hostile to ransomware operators. In particular, we find that off-site backups and government incentives for their adoption are the most fruitful avenue for combating ransomware.

Keywords: Security · Malware · Economics · Ransomware · Incentives · Backups

1 Introduction

Ransomware is a family of malware that encrypts files on a system and demands payment for the ability to decrypt these files. Although proof of concept ransomware has existed since at least 1996 [35], modern ransomware tactics result from CryptoLocker's revolutionary use of Bitcoin for payment [14]. This innovation has allowed ransomware actors to perpetrate increasingly sophisticated attacks, including the 2017 WannaCry attack [16] – an attack whose effects,

---

Funded in part by the Auerbach Berger Chair in Cybersecurity held by Spiros Mancoridis, at Drexel University.

B. Bošanský et al. (Eds.): GameSec 2021, LNCS 13061, pp. 195–207, 2021.
https://doi.org/10.1007/978-3-030-90370-1_11

according to ransomware payment tracker Ransomwhere[1] are still being felt today. We have seen a pivot in targeting, from the wanton use of exploit kits and watering hole attacks that largely affected end users to the current increase in enterprise victims [22] by way of malicious loaders and initial access brokers [12].

The threat of ransomware grows larger year after year, with a spate of recent attacks including on the Colonial pipeline [18] and the Kaseya supply chain attack [23] demonstrating the devastation and real-world impact of the issues. The Ransomware Task Force report [9] identifies the goal of disrupting the ransomware business model as an important goal. This goal is uniquely important, since ransomware is so often an attack of opportunity – akin to a mugging or kidnapping – and not the sort of highly-targeted attack that is often expected from sophisticated adversaries. We frame the problem in a new way, as the attacker is not playing a single game against a single defender. Rather, attackers seek to find vulnerable victims wherever they may be, and so instead of playing a game with attackers, we view the problem from the attacker point of view. To this end, we suggest that defenders should consider the problem of ransomware and ransomware payments in particular as analogous to an attacker playing a lottery instead of a strategic game between equals.

2   Related Work

In recent years, considerable research has been done on the game theory of ransomware payments. The earliest relevant work on the topic appears to be by Spyridopoulos et al. [27], who found a Nash equilibrium balancing potential costs of mitigation with the cost of a successful attack. Leveraging epidemiologically-inspired models of malware spread, this work considered the equilibria of available defender strategies. The game is constructed under a unified proliferation model, with infection, immunization, and disinfection rates that informed the strategies of the players. These player's payoffs were then computed for a set of strategies given the parameters controlled by the attacker and the defender – the infection rate, patch rate, removal rate, and the rate of both patching and removal. Spryidopoulos et al.'s work informed defenders how to approach ransomware worm attacks and defined the optimal strategy for the defender.

The work of Laszka et al. [13] was the first to consider the economics of ransomware using models that reflect the similarity of ransomware to kidnapping and ransom. They developed an economic model of the interaction between attackers and victim organizations, and studied that model to minimize the economic impact to those organizations. Primarily, the work focused on the cost-benefit of investing in backup solutions, a recommendation that is still widely regarded as the best way to prepare for ransomware attacks [9]. Laszka et al. also showed how coordinated backup investments can deter ransomware attackers in particular – a novel insight in the literature. Our work borrows from their recommendations and builds on this existing literature, but we differ in our approach to the game-theoretic model.

---

[1] https://ransomwhe.re/

Caporusso *et al.* [5] also built upon the kidnap and ransom literature, leveraging a negotiation model represented as an extensive-form game. This work dealt with ransomware in cases where renegotiation of the ransom is possible, a surprisingly common phenomenon that has been seen with some ransomware operators [17] – though other ransomware operators refuse to negotiate. Caporusso *et al.* identified the post-attack dynamics between the human victim and the human ransomware operator, acknowledging that there are substantial human factors outside of ransom negotiation to be made in the decision making process.

Cartwright *et al.* [6] grappled with the question of whether or not to pay a ransom at all. Their work largely built upon the earlier paper of Laszka *et al.* and framed the problem of ransomware under the lens of kidnap and ransom. It did so by building upon two existing kidnapping models, those of Selten [25], and Lapan and Sandler [11]. The Selten model informed the optimal ransom to be set by the attacker, while the model of Lapan and Sandler aided in deciding whether or not victims should take action to deter the kidnapping in the first place. In contrast to this work, we present a novel approach to the game and develop a model under a differing set of assumptions.

3 Probability and Lotteries

In common parlance, "lottery" typically refers to a form of gambling where a player purchases a ticket at some nominal cost with a fixed set of different numbers. Then, another set of numbers with the same size is drawn at random without replacement. After this draw, some reward that confers some amount of utility may be given depending on how many numbers in the randomly drawn set match the set on the purchased ticket.

Mathematically, we can formalize a lottery as follows: Let X be a set of prizes, $X = \{x_1, ..., x_n\}$, that confers some utility. From this set of prizes, we define a lottery $L = \{p_i, ..., p_n\}$ over the set of prizes such that for each $x_i \in X$, there is a corresponding $p_i \geq 0$, and $\sum_{i=1}^{n} p_i = 1$. There is also some cost $c \geq 0$ to enter the lottery. Then, for each of the prizes, there is some utility $u(x_i)$ that the agent derives from receiving that prize, and their expected utility over the lottery is then $\sum_{i=1}^{n} p_i u(x_i) - c$. In the ransomware context, a prize x corresponds to a payment to a ransomware operator, and p is the probability that a victim will pay that amount.

The optimal ransom value for x has been explored in other work [6] so we instead deal with the binary probability that a victim will pay or not pay, assuming that the optimal ransom value is set. In our ransomware lottery, we thus define 2 probabilities: p_{win}, when a victim pays a ransom and $p_{\mathrm{lose}} = 1 - p_{\mathrm{win}}$, when a victim does not. For simplicity in this initial model, we incorporate the probability that the attack is not successful into p_{lose}. There is, as mentioned, also some small cost c associated with launching the ransomware attack.

Conveniently for ransomware operators, c is quite small, and x_{win} can be quite large, as we discuss in Sect. 4. By contrast, $x_{\mathrm{lose}} = 0$, since there is no chance that ransomware operators will have to pay more than the cost to launch the attack – the victim will simply ignore the attack because they do not value the information which has been ransomed or have some mitigation such as those outlined in Sect. 5. In total, this means that the game played, from the perspective of ransomware operators, is as follows:

$$L = \{p_{\text{win}}, p_{\text{lose}}\}$$
$$X = \{x_{\text{win}}, 0\}$$

and therefore, the expected utility for a single successful attack is:

$$
\begin{aligned}
E[u(x)] &= \sum_{i=\{\text{win,lose}\}} p_i(x_i - c) \\
&= (p_{\text{win}}(x_{\text{win}} - c)) + (p_{\text{lose}}(0 - c)) \\
&= p_{\text{win}} x_{\text{win}} - (p_{\text{win}} c + p_{\text{lose}} c) \\
&= p_{\text{win}} x_{\text{win}} - c
\end{aligned}
\tag{1}
$$

Since $x_{\text{lose}} = 0$ and $p_{\text{lose}} = 1 - p_{\text{win}}$, for the sake of simplicity and readability, we use x and p in the remainder of the paper to represent the case when a victim pays. We can see from Eq. 1 that ransomware operators are incentivized to continue operating for as long as the value of $px > c$, since they will profit from each attack, on average. Research by Kaspersky Labs [10] shows that 56% of ransomware victims pay the ransom to restore access to their data. At this rate of payment, the cost of an average ransomware attack would need to be 1.7857 times – nearly double – the optimal payment to remove the incentive.

We can see that probabilistically, this is equivalent to betting on a biased coin flip. Since $E[u(x)]$ is a function of the random variable x, it is itself a random variable, which we denote Y. Given a cost to make a bet c, we flip a biased coin with win probability p and receive payout x at that rate. Let b be the amount of capital available to the bettor – our attacker – and let $b > c$. We initialize b_0 to be the amount of capital available before any bets are cast and b_i the available capital to the bettor at trial i. Then after the first trial, our possible values for b_1 are $b_1 = b_0 - c$ or $b_1 = b_0 - c + x$. Our expected value of b_1 is $(b_0 - c) + px$, as in Eq. 1.

By the linearity of expectation, our expected bank at trial k is:

$$b_k = b_0 + E[Y_k] = b_0 + k(px - c)$$

We can see that if $px > c$, then the expected value of each trial is positive, and so for the player making the bet,

$$\lim_{k \to \infty} E[Y_k] = k(px - c) = \infty \tag{2}$$

This suggests that any player who can participate in the game is highly incentivized to play as many rounds as possible, since the potential payoff is infinite. Note that this expected value only holds in an idealized world with infinite money and no law enforcement, so it does not capture the intricate relationships of the real world. It does, however, demonstrate that since the expectation is not finite, there is no optimal stopping time. Therefore, there is no incentive for any attacker to ever stop conducting ransomware attacks when $px - c$ is reasonably large.

To demonstrate this, we construct three simple simulations, shown in Fig. 1. We set our payout value $x = 170404$ and cost $c = 4200$ based on analysis in Sect. 4. Then, for three different values of p: 0.1, 0.3024, and 0.5, we run 1000 trials. With probability p, the player receives value $x - c$, and with probabiltiy $1 - p$, the player receives value $-c$. We can see that overall, the accumulated value is linear with respect to p, as we would expect from Eq. 1.

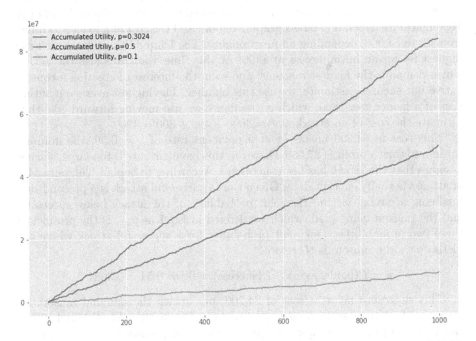

Fig. 1. Plot of simulation demonstrating accumulated utility at $p = 0.1$, $p = 0.3024$, and $p = 0.5$

4   Paying to Play

The cost of running a ransomware attack is very opaque and highly variable. Some cybercriminal organizations are sophisticated operations that develop their malware in-house [31]. These organizations have software development lifecycles, version control, testing, and pay staff to perform all of these functions. Other organizations simply purchase ransomware-as-a-service [15] (RaaS) or piece together their arsenal from so-called darknet markets. A 2017 study [30] found that prices ranged from $0.50 to $3,000 for ransomware products, at a median price of $10.50. In contrast to these prices, most RaaS providers take a percentage of the ransom, rather than providing an executable for a flat fee.

In order to infect an endpoint with ransomware, however, one needs to gain initial access. Furthermore, most ransomware operators leverage a loader – a small program designed to install another malware on a target system – to actually get the ransomware onto the endpoint. Nearly all ransomware variants [20] rely on phishing, commodity malware, exploit kits, and vulnerable services – particularly the remote desktop protocol – to deliver their malware. This factors in to the overall cost of operation, but is challenging to estimate, since cybercriminals are not forthcoming with this information. A technical report issued by Deloitte [1] found the cost of initial access to be between $70 and $400 per 1000 machines depending on geographic region, and the cost of a loader to range from $3 to $4,000, depending on functionality. The United States demanded the highest fee for an initial access at $400. At this time, the US is also the nation which demands the highest ransoms, and so in the interest of creating a conservative but accurate estimate, we use this number. The highest average monthly cost of a loader was $800, which is the figure we use moving forward. We thus estimate the cost of an attack at $c = 3000 + 400 + 800 = 4200$.

This cost of $4,200 means at at a payment rate of $p = 0.56$, the minimal ransom to turn a profit is $7,500. However, this payment rate is too large, since it assumes that the attack has been successful. According to Sophos [26], only 54% of attacks actually encrypt data. Given that a successful attack is a precondition for being a paying victim, the joint probability of the attack being successful and the ransom being paid, which we defined in Eq. 1 as p_{win} is the product of these two probabilities. Our joint probability for a successful attack where the victim pays the ransom is therefore:

$$p = P(\text{paid}|\text{success}) \cdot P(\text{success}) = 0.56 \cdot 0.54 = 0.3024$$

This suggests that at a cost of $4,200, per attack the minimal ransom an attacker must request to remain profitable is $13,888.89. As of March 2021, the average value of ransomware a payout for a compromised organization was $312,493 [8], around 22 times the minimal value needed to incentivize the attacks. We note that other estimates, such as those by Sophos [26] are a more modest $170,404 for mid-sized organizations in the United states, a value which is still around 12 times the minimum to create positive expected value for these attacks. We treat these as a "reasonable average range" in our subsequent analysis.

There are three variables in this problem that may disincentivize the perpetration of ransomware attacks:

1. Lowering the value of the payments
2. Increasing the cost of operating ransomware
3. Decreasing the probability of payment

We discuss the feasibility of using each of these three variables to disincentivize ransomware attacks in turn.

4.1 Lowering the Value of Payments

Today, there are few options for lowering the value of a payment. Since nearly all payments for ransomware are rendered in cryptocurrency, a steep decline in the value of cryptocurrency or the inability to exchange it for other goods or services would remove the effective value of a successful attack. To date, some proposals have been made to ban [7], or regulate cryptocurrencies [19,24], though the effect of these bans and proposed regulations on the price of cryptocurrency remains to be seen. Moreover, even if cryptocurrency were regulated into obsolescence, ransoms could be paid in gift cards or other hard to track currency equivalents. This suggests that lowering the value of payments is not a viable path for removing the incentive.

4.2 Increasing Costs

The onus for increasing costs falls on the ransomware developers and operators themselves, and so there is likely a cost ceiling. If the marketplace efficiencies of initial access brokers and ransomware-as-a-service were removed entirely, the cost of conducting an attack would be the cost of development plus the cost of deployment and maintenance of the infrastructure. This would require more technical skill and initial investment than relatively low-skill ransomware operators would be capable of, but after the initial investment, would likely cost less per-attack than the $3,000 high-end figure from [30]. This may, on balance, reduce the overall prevalence of malware attacks. However, this would also require the takedown of nearly all darknet marketplaces. Despite a number of high-profile takedowns, ransomware continues to flourish on these marketplaces. Thus, the options for increasing costs to operators are also limited.

4.3 Decreasing Payment Probability

Since the probability of payment is the one thing out of the control of the attackers, it stands to reason that it is where defenders can exercise the most control. In our model, decreasing the probability of a successful attack that gets paid linearly reduces the expected value of an attack. This means that organizations have two options available to them to reduce an attack's expected value. Decreasing the success of launched attacks will prevent the victim having to decide whether or not to pay the ransom in the first place. Assuming an attack is successful, decreasing the chance that the ransom is paid will also reduce the attacker's value.

Given our average payout value range of $x = [170, 404, 312493]$, the expected value of an attack at current payment rates is in the range $[47, 300.17, 170, 798.08]$. A 50% reduction in probability of payout to $p = 0.28$ against a cost of $c = 4200$, with attack success rates held equal yields an expected value range of $[21565.08, 43048.94]$ – an amount that a would-be ransomware operator could make as a software engineer in Europe [21] instead of perpetrating ransomware attacks. Given the financial motivation of most ransomware

operators [2], it stands to reason that a comparable salary is a perfectly substi-
tutable good for rational actors. To eliminate profit entirely, assuming current
attack success rates and sufficient economies of scale, payment probability would
need to decrease to 2.489% on the high-end of average payments and 4.564% on
the low-end of payments – a dramatic reduction from today's payment rates.

Despite that "break-even" probability, ransomware operators are likely to
turn to some other income stream before profits hit zero due to law enforcement activities surrounding cybercrime. In particular, the US Federal Bureau of
Investigations and the UK National Cyber Security Centre have pursued cybercriminals abroad [28], indicting and sanctioning ransomware operators. However,
in order to drastically reduce the payout rate of ransomware, organizations will
need to have a reason not to pay the ransoms.

5   Lowering the Stakes

In order to lower the probability of payment and create an environment where
attackers are not incentivized to continue launching ransomware attacks, victims
must be incentivized not to pay the ransom. An effective strategy for lowering
the probability of payment ultimately consists of one where the victim's options
for restoration are meaningfully less costly than paying the ransom. Considerable
work has been done on quantifying these differences and we point to the article
by Cluley [8] for details, as the specific rates will differ from organization to
organization. Since the use of ransomware is illegal, there are external, non-
financial mechanisms for reducing attacker incentives such as arrest, seizure of
assets, indictment, and sanctions. We do not address these mechanisms in our
framework and reserve their impact for future work.

In order to reduce attacker incentives, we consider the potential impact of
four commonly discussed strategies:

1. Decreasing Attack Success
2. Cyber Insurance
3. Use of Decrypters
4. Off-Site Backups

5.1   Decreasing Attack Success

Decreasing attack success is the goal of any organizational information security program. The success of attacks has myriad factors, ranging from human
factors such as insider threats and phishing to software vulnerabilities and mis-
configurations. Modern antivirus technologies can assist in catching the loaders
that often deliver the ransomware, and some endpoint security solutions can
even detect exploitation of vulnerabilities. In addition, training programs for
phishing emails and advising customers not to open attachments from unknown
senders are widely used to attempt to mitigate these attacks. A comprehensive
listing of ways to reduce an organization's attack surface is out of the scope of

this paper, but a 2020 report by Deloitte and the Financial Services Information Sharing and Analysis Center [4] showed that on average, 10% of an organization's information technology budget – approximately 0.2% of company revenue – is dedicated to cybersecurity. In light of the increasing threats associated with ransomware, this amount may not be sufficient to reduce the probability that an attack is successful.

The figure in Eq. 1 only holds for cases where a ransomware infection has been successful and does not account for failed attacks – only payments. Reducing the incidence of these attacks through other means such as the use of application allowlists, strong spam filters, protection of exposed ports and services, and other well-known security hygiene methods can serve to reduce the success of these attacks. Since the cost to an attacker is undertaken whether or not the attack is successful, the failure of these attacks will discourage these attackers. In order to isolate the influence of payment probability, our analysis assumed that all attacks are successful – a naive assumption that suggests the 1.5% payout probability derived in Sect. 4.3 is the probability of payment overall, not merely the conditional probability of payment given a successful attack.

5.2   Cyber Insurance

Cyber insurance is a strategy that is often mentioned as an organizational solution in the context of ransomware. This can help to protect businesses from the cost of ransomware attacks, covering the cost to restore encrypted data. However, in cases where cyber insurance alleviates the burden to victims, attackers are still paid, doing nothing to remove the incentives surrounding ransomware. Consequently, from an attacker incentive perspective, cyber insurance does nothing to alleviate the overall problem of ransomware.

5.3   Use of Decrypters

The use of decrypters is a significant way to allow victims to ignore the effects of ransomware. Although decrypters for some of the most popular strains of ransomware today are not available, organizations like No More Ransom![2] offers free decrypters for more than 150 families of ransomware. Widespread knowledge of these utilities and increased investment by security researchers on developing these utilities could allow victims to decrypt their own files without paying a ransom. Note that when decrypters become available or kill-switches as seen in WannaCry [16] shut down operations, ransomware operators will patch their malware [3] to continue operations.

5.4   Off-Site Backups

The most commonly proposed solution for organizations to avoid the impacts of ransomware and confidently be able to not pay a ransom is the use of off-site

---

[2] https://www.nomoreransom.org.

backups. An off-site backup can be used to restore systems to pre-ransomware configurations and tends to cost significantly less than paying the ransom. Research by Wood *et al.* [34] acknowledges the difficulties of backup deployments. Although they develop their recovery from a disaster preparedness perspective, their cost estimates show that both cloud-based and colocation for backups can allow for high uptime at a fraction of the cost associated with paying a ransom. Additionally, having a backup that allows for restoration reduces the cost to remediate possible residual traces of the attacker, reduces time to remediate, and mitigates much of the reputational damage associated with paying a ransom.

5.5   Impact of Mitigations

The aforementioned approaches may allow victims to choose not to pay, but as Cartwright *et al.* [6] demonstrate, victims will have different willingness to pay given some set ransom. This willingness to pay depends on the size of the ransom and therefore encourages the victim to mitigate the attack. When victims pay, they usually – though not always [26] – get their files back, a factor which discourages paying. However, there is some cost to deterrence, and if that is too high, the victim will instead accept their chances of being infected.

There are also factors at play external to the relationship between the cost of a ransom versus the cost of mitigation. For example, in the United States, ransom payments can be written off [33] as "ordinary, necessary, and reasonable" expenses for tax purposes. This factor actually incentivizes victims to pay, and discourages additional investments into mitigation. Wheeler and Martin [32] point out that in the current regulatory environment of the United States, there is a misalignment between public interests to discourage ransomware and private interests to recover data and resume operations at the lowest cost. We conclude then, that government and regulatory organizations interested in preventing ransomware should create financial incentives for organizations and individuals to invest in backups that allow for ransoms not to be paid. Further, policy solutions to change the tax incentives associated with paying ransoms could be pursued to improve the chance that companies will invest in security technologies.

6   Conclusion

Ransomware remains a significant problem in the world, and our analysis demonstrates why – there is effectively unlimited incentive to use ransomware. Since the cost is relatively low and the potential payouts are high, financially-motivated actors are encouraged to pursue this line of attack. Additionally, the victims of successful attacks are more likely to pay than not for a variety of factors, including the ability to write-off the ransom as a business expense.

If we wish to eliminate the threat of ransomware, we cannot attack the market itself, as the actors are aware that their actions are illegal but have accepted that risk. Instead, we must see that attackers are engaged in a simple game where they do not need to account for the strategies of their victims. Where defenders have power to affect ransomware is largely on the front of actually paying the ransoms.

We outlined a handful of commonly-discussed solutions and conclude that off-site backups remain the most effective way to ignore the impact of ransomware attacks. In order to encourage organizations to pursue these policies, we conclude that governmental and regulatory organizations will need to provide incentives for organizations to invest in these backup solutions. Short of encouraging these solutions and allowing victims not to pay ransoms, we can reasonably expect the ransomware threat to continue to grow.

The model used here leveraged a probabilistic model and expected utility theory to identify incentives and explore the security impacts of those incentives. In future work, we seek to explore a more realistic model of the risk behaviors these attackers and defenders exhibit based on their subjective beliefs. Furthermore, there are meaningful non-financial mechanisms such as those mentioned in Sect. 5, and inclusion of those mechanisms would require a more complex model. This could be done by representing uncertainty via cumulative prospect theory [29], as has been done in the economic literature. In particular, there is a significant amount of uncertainty on the part of attackers about whether or not an attack will be successful. Similarly, there is significant uncertainty for defenders about how, when, and where they will be attacked. By representing the choice under uncertainty more richly than in an expected utility model, we may better model the true behaviors of attackers and defenders.

References

1. Analytics, D.T.I.: Black-market ecosystem: Estimating the cost of "pwnership". Deloitte Technical report (2018). https://www2.deloitte.com/us/en/pages/risk/articles/vigilant-threat-studies-deloitte-us.html
2. Anderson, R.: Security Engineering: A Guide to Building Dependable Distributed Systems. John Wiley & Sons, Hoboken (2020)
3. Arghire, I.: "patched" wannacry ransomware has no kill-switch. Security-Week (2017). https://www.securityweek.com/patched-wannacry-ransomware-has-no-kill-switch
4. Bernard, J., Nicholson, M.: Reshaping the cybersecurity landscape. Deloitte Technical report (2020). https://www2.deloitte.com/us/en/insights/industry/financial-services/cybersecurity-maturity-financial-institutions-cyber-risk.html
5. Caporusso, N., Chea, S., Abukhaled, R.: A game-theoretical model of ransomware. In: Ahram, T.Z., Nicholson, D. (eds.) AHFE 2018. AISC, vol. 782, pp. 69–78. Springer, Cham (2019). https://doi.org/10.1007/978-3-319-94782-2_7
6. Cartwright, E., Hernandez Castro, J., Cartwright, A.: To pay or not: game theoretic models of ransomware. J. Cybersecur. 5(1), tyz009 (2019)
7. Clark, M.: What we know about china's cryptocurrency crackdown. Vox (2021). https://www.theverge.com/2021/6/23/22544367/china-crypto-crackdown-bitcoin-mining-sichuan-ban-hydro-cryptocurrency-trading
8. Cluley, G.: Average ransomware payouts shoot up 171% to over $300,000. Tripwire - The State of Security (2021). https://www.tripwire.com/state-of-security/featured/average-ransomware-payouts-shoot-up/

9. Force, R.T.: Combating ransomware (2021)
10. labs, K.: Consumer appetite versus action: the state of data privacy amid growing digital dependency. Kaspersky Consumer IT Security Risks Report 2021 (2021). https://media.kasperskydaily.com/wp-content/uploads/sites/92/2021/03/16090300/consumer-appetite-versus-action-report.pdf
11. Lapan, H.E., Sandler, T.: To bargain or not to bargain: that is the question. Am. Econ. Rev. **78**(2), 16–21 (1988)
12. Larson, S., Blackford, D., Garrett, G.: The first step: Initial access leads to ransomware. Proofpoint Threat Insight (2021). https://www.proofpoint.com/us/blog/threat-insight/first-step-initial-access-leads-ransomware
13. Laszka, A., Farhang, S., Grossklags, J.: On the economics of ransomware. In: Rass, S., An, B., Kiekintveld, C., Fang, F., Schauer, S. (eds.) Decision and Game Theory for Security. GameSec 2017. LNCS, vol. 10575, pp. 397–417. Springer, Cham (2017). https://doi.org/10.1007/978-3-319-68711-7_21
14. Liao, K., Zhao, Z., Doupé, A., Ahn, G.J.: Behind closed doors: measurement and analysis of cryptolocker ransoms in bitcoin. In: 2016 APWG Symposium on Electronic Crime Research (eCrime), pp. 1–13. IEEE (2016)
15. Meland, P.H., Bayoumy, Y.F.F., Sindre, G.: The ransomware-as-a-service economy within the darknet. Comput. Secur. **92**, 101762 (2020). https://doi.org/10.1016/j.cose.2020.101762, https://www.sciencedirect.com/science/article/pii/S0167404820300468
16. Mohurle, S., Patil, M.: A brief study of wannacry threat: ransomware attack 2017. Int. J. Adv. Res. Comput. Sci. **8**(5), 1938–1940 (2017)
17. Monroe, R.: How to negotiate with ransomware hackers. The New Yorker (2021). https://www.newyorker.com/magazine/2021/06/07/how-to-negotiate-with-ransomware-hackers
18. Morrison, S.: How a major oil pipeline got held for ransom. Vox (2021). https://www.vox.com/recode/22428774/ransomeware-pipeline-colonial-darkside-gas-prices
19. Nabilou, H.: How to regulate bitcoin? Decentralized regulation for a decentralized cryptocurrency. Int. J. Law Inf. Technol. **27**(3), 266–291 (2019)
20. Networks, P.A.: Ransomware threat report, 2021. Palo Alto Networks Technical report (2021). https://www.paloaltonetworks.com/resources/research/unit42-ransomware-threat-report-2021
21. Orosz, G.: The trimodal nature of software engineering salaries in the Netherlands and Europe. Pragmatic Engineer (2021). https://blog.pragmaticengineer.com/software-engineering-salaries-in-the-netherlands-and-europe/
22. O'Gorman, B., Wueest, C., O'Brien, D., Cleary, G.: Symantec internet security threat report. Symantec Corp., Mountain View, CA, USA, Technical report (2019)
23. Press, A.: Scale, details of massive Kaseya ransomware attack emerge. NPR (2021). https://www.npr.org/2021/07/05/1013117515/scale-details-of-massive-kaseya-ransomware-attack-emerge
24. Schaupp, L.C., Festa, M.: Cryptocurrency adoption and the road to regulation. In: Proceedings of the 19th Annual International Conference on Digital Government Research: Governance in the Data Age, pp. 1–9 (2018)
25. Selten, R.: Models of Strategic Rationality, vol. 2. Springer Science & Business Media, Heidelberg (2013)
26. Sophos: Sophos state of ransomware 2021. Sophos Technical report (2021). https://secure2.sophos.com/en-us/medialibrary/pdfs/whitepaper/sophos-state-of-ransomware-2021-wp.pdf

27. Spyridopoulos, T., Maraslis, K., Mylonas, A., Tryfonas, T., Oikonomou, G.: A game theoretical method for cost-benefit analysis of malware dissemination prevention. Inf. Secur. J. A Glob. Perspect. **24**(4–6), 164–176 (2015)

28. Tidy, J.: The ransomware surge ruining lives. BBC (2021). https://www.bbc.com/news/technology-56933733

29. Tversky, A., Kahneman, D.: Advances in prospect theory: cumulative representation of uncertainty. J. Risk Uncertain. **5**(4), 297–323 (1992)

30. Unit, C.B.T.A.: Dark web ransomware economy growing at an annual rate of 2,500%. Carbon Black Threat Research (2017). https://www.carbonblack.com/2017/10/11/dark-web-ransomware-economy-growing-annual-rate-2500/

31. U.S. Attorney's Office, Western District of Washington: High-level organizer of notorious hacking group fin7 sentenced to ten years in prison for scheme that compromised tens of millions of debit and credit cards (2021)

32. Wheeler, T., Martin, C.: Should ransomware payments be banned? The Brookings Institute Tech Stream (2021). https://www.brookings.edu/techstream/should-ransomware-payments-be-banned/

33. Wood, R.: Garmin hack's $10m ransom payment, $10m tax deduction. Forbes (2020). https://www.forbes.com/sites/robertwood/2020/07/27/garmin-hacks-10m-ransom-payment-10m-tax-deduction/?sh=4452ae4712c5

34. Wood, T., Cecchet, E., Ramakrishnan, K.K., Shenoy, P.J., van der Merwe, J.E., Venkataramani, A.: Disaster recovery as a cloud service: economic benefits & deployment challenges. HotCloud **10**, 8–15 (2010)

35. Young, A., Yung, M.: Cryptovirology: extortion-based security threats and countermeasures. In: Proceedings 1996 IEEE Symposium on Security and Privacy, pp. 129–140. IEEE (1996)

Combating Ransomware in Internet of Things: A Games-in-Games Approach for Cross-Layer Cyber Defense and Security Investment

Yuhan Zhao$^{(\boxtimes)}$, Yunfei Ge, and Quanyan Zhu

Department of Electrical and Computer Engineering, Tandon School of Engineering, New York University, Brooklyn, NY 11201, USA
{yhzhao,yg2047,qz494}@nyu.edu

Abstract. The recent surge in ransomware attacks has threatened many critical infrastructures such as oil pipeline systems, hospitals, and industrial Internet of Things (IoT). Ransomware is a cryptoviral extortion attack that involves two phases: the cyber infection of the malware and the financial transaction of the ransom payment. As the ransomware attackers are financially motivated, the protection of the infrastructure networked systems requires a cross-layer risk analysis that not only examines the vulnerability of the cyber system but also consolidates the economics of ransom payment. To this end, this paper establishes a two-player multi-phase and multi-stage game framework to model cyber and economic phases of a ransomware attack. We use a zero-sum Markov game to capture the multi-stage penetration of ransomware in the lateral movement. A sequential-move game is proposed to model the ransom payment interactions at the second phase. Two games are composed to form a multi-phase and multi-stage game-in-games (MPMS-GiG) that enables a holistic risk assessment of ransomware in networks and a cross-layer design of cyber defense and investment strategies to mitigate the attack. We provide a complete equilibrium characterization of ransomware game and design interdependent optimal strategies for cyber protection and ransom payment. We use prospect theory to analyze the impact of human factors on equilibrium strategies. Finally, we use a prototypical industrial IoT network as a case study to corroborate the results.

Keywords: Ransomware · Cybersecurity · Game theory · Security economics · Risk assessment · Prospect theory · Internet of Things

1 Introduction

Ransomware is a type of malware that infects particular network entities to demand ransom. It is in general classified into two categories: the locker ran-

This work is partially supported by grants SES-1541164, ECCS-1847056, CNS-2027884, and BCS-2122060 from National Science Foundation (NSF), DOE-NE grant 20-19829 and grant W911NF-19-1-0041 from Army Research Office (ARO).

B. Bošanský et al. (Eds.): GameSec 2021, LNCS 13061, pp. 208–228, 2021.
https://doi.org/10.1007/978-3-030-90370-1_12

somware and the crypto ransomware [23]. Once infected, the ransomware either locks the target device to deny any access or encrypts the target device data to disrupt normal functionality. [12,18]. Emerged in 1989 as a floppy disk Trojan, the ransomware has developed dramatically with time and has evolved into different families such as CryptoLocker [21], Petya [2], etc. It is becoming more prevalent nowadays with the fast advance of the Internet of Things (IoT) in various fields such as manufacturing and transportation [20,22]. The broad connections for IoT devices provide more security threats and vulnerabilities. Besides, the massive number of IoT devices increases the risk of getting infected by ransomware since any device could be the target. The consequence can be severe if critical devices such as medical equipment and generators are compromised. Indeed, the ransomware attack has caused significant economic losses in industrial domains. It is reported that there have been at least 150 ransomware attacks in manufacturing and 37 attacks in transportation industries in the third quarter of 2020 [7]. The estimated global damage from ransomware reaches $20 billion in 2021 [3]. A recent ransomware attack on the energy infrastructure company Colonial Pipeline this May alone has caused more than $2 million loss for the company [1]. The detriment of ransomware is no longer negligible.

A ransomware attack in general contains four stages: "code", "spread", "extract", and "monetize" [14], which can be summarized into cyber and economic phases. The cyber phase focuses on the multi-stage intrusion kill chain. An attacker first assembles the ransomware code and finds the initial entry point to deploy ransomware. Once entered, the ransomware penetrates over the network to compromise the target. After infecting the target, the ransomware extracts and processes the target's data to either lock it or encrypt important files. The economic phase refers to preliminary precautions and the "monetize" stage, which models the ransom payment interactions between the attacker and the victim.

As two indispensable components in the ransomware attack, the cyber and economic phases are naturally interdependent. A network defender can design effective cyber defense schemes by taking into account the risk of ransom payment. The defender's security investment and ransom payment strategy can benefit from the properly designed defense system. Therefore, a holistic and cross-layer defense-payment design framework can cost-effectively mitigate the cyber risks as well as reduce monetary losses. Traditional studies in ransomware treat the cyber and the economic phases separately. For the cyber phase, Intrusion Detection Systems (IDS) [6] have been widely studied in networks to detect malicious behaviors in cyberspace. However, they only provide monitoring information but no defense actions to mitigate the attack. Intrusion Response Systems (IRS) outperform IDS as they can conduct necessary actions to respond to malicious attacks [11], but the limited predefined actions confine their capability to cope with sophisticated attacks such as ransomware attacks. Practical methods, such as constantly updating the software and running network scans [24], fail to capture the complex behavior of the ransomware. Once compromised by ransomware, we may be discouraged by the fact that victims simply pay the ransom in many cases, and even the FBI once inadvertently mentioned paying the ransom if the network device is infected [5]. It is not until recently that several studies have been conducted to understand the economics of ransomware [4,9,15]. These works mainly focus on the mitigation strategy after the target is compromised. A cost-effective strategy to combat ransomware requires not only a post-infection solution but also a proper cyber defense and security investment strategy to minimize the ransomware risk across multiple phases.

To this end, in this work, we propose a two-player multi-phase multi-stage ransomware game to capture both the cyber and economic phases of a ransomware attack and provide a holistic consideration and design for cyber defense and ransom payment. In the cyber phase, we use a zero-sum Markov game to characterize the sophisticated and dynamic features of ransomware. The attacker (i.e., the ransomware) explores the network edge vulnerabilities and moves laterally to infect the target, while the defender aims to prevent the penetration by hardening specific connection links. The cyber Markov game serves as a risk assessment measure to help make security decisions in the sequel. The economic phase depicts the ransom payment interactions between two players. Once the target is infected, we use a sequential-move ransom-payment game to analyze the defender's optimal payment strategy and the optimal ransom demanded by the attacker. The cyber Markov game is composed with the ransom-payment game to form a multi-phase multi-stage games-in-games (MPMS-GiG) framework that enables a holistic risk assessment of the ransomware in IoT networks and a cross-layer design of cyber defense and ransom payment strategies to mitigate the attack. The interdependency between the two phases is captured by ransom demand, security investment, and security budget. Specifically, the defender invests in IoT network security to better deter the penetration of ransomware, resulting in a lower infection probability. The infection probability and the remaining budget then influence the following ransom payment interactions. By considering the interdependency between the two phases, we analyze and provide a cross-layer defense-payment strategy to better combat ransomware and protect IoT network security.

Another special feature of ransomware attack is human factors. In ransomware attacks, the victims are humans, who hold biased recognition concerning losses and risks, which can lead to different defense strategies compared with the perfectly rational one. This phenomenon is explained by prospect theory, and it is necessary to investigate its impact on the decision-making within the ransomware attack. Our framework also provides an analysis of how human factors affect the optimal attack/defense strategies.

The contribution of this paper is as follows. First, we propose an MPMS-GiG framework to capture both the cyber and economic phases in the ransomware attack. Second, we provide a complete characterization and analysis of the equilibrium solution of the ransomware game and design interdependent optimal cyber protection and ransom payment strategies. Third, we use sensitivity analysis and prospect theory to investigate how human factors play a role in combating ransomware attacks. Finally, we use a case study with a prototypical industrial Internet of Things (IoT) network to corroborate the results.

1.1 Related Work

The penetration process of ransomware in the cyber phase is commonly modeled by the lateral movement in Advanced Persistent Threats (APTs). Some works have adopted game theory to study the defense against lateral movement. Noureddine et al. in [17] have used a zero-sum game to model the lateral movement over enterprise networks, where the attacker seeks the shortest path to compromise the target and the defender responds by disconnecting available services of a potential victim node. Huang and Zhu in [10] have adopted a multi-stage Bayesian game to characterize the lateral movement with uncertainty in the infrastructure network. The equilibrium strategies are derived for network security enhancement. Although these works do not focus on ransomware, they share a similar penetration process as the cyber phase in ransomware attacks.

From the economic perspective, game theory has not been adopted to analyze ransomware until recently. Hernandez-Castro et al. in [9] provide an economic analysis of ransomware including the optimal pricing and bargaining strategies. They have also discussed several determinants of the victim's willingness to pay. Caporusso et al. in [4] have proposed a two-stage game to characterize the ransomware behavior after the target is compromised. Several cases are discussed based on the different parameters such as the attacker's cost. Laszka et al. in [15] have built a two-stage game-theoretic framework to study the ransomware ecosystem. They have studied the behavior of two target groups with different infection probabilities, including their optimal payment strategies and the attacker's optimal attack plan. Additionally, a backup strategy as a precaution to alleviate the ransomware attack has also been considered in their model. Cartwright et al. [5] have adapted two kidnapping game models and have applied them to the ransomware context. Theoretical results are discussed to understand the behavior of the attacker and the victim.

1.2 Organization of the Paper

The rest of the paper is organized as follows. Section 2 discusses the basic settings and formulates the ransomware problem. Section 3 analyzes the risk assessment outcome of the cyber Markov game and the equilibrium of the ransomware game. Section 4 studies the impact of the security budget and human factors on the equilibrium strategy with prospect theory. We use a case study in Sect. 5 to demonstrate the results and conclude the paper in Sect. 6.

2 Problem Formulation

In this section, we formulate the ransomware game as a two-player multi-phase multi-stage security game. The notations[1] are summarized in Table 1.

---

[1] The notations of the cyber Markov game are listed in Sect. 2.3 separately.

Table 1. List of notations in the ransomware game.

Symbol	Description
r_d, q_d	security investment and payment action
r_a, q_a	demanded ransom and attack action
U_d, U_a	defender's/attacker's payoff
c_f, c_s, δ	attack cost, overall and additional attack cost
θ	successful defense probability
λ	defender's untrusted level to the attacker
w	value of the target (defender's willingness to pay)
μ	defender's expected willingness to pay
B	defender's total security budget
$\hat{r}_d$	threshold investment to prevent the ransomware attack

2.1 Basic Settings

The ransomware game (RG) captures both cyber and economic phases in a ransomware attack and consists of two players, a defender (she) and an attacker (he). The defender operates a network with multiple connected entities and has a total security budget of $B > 0$. Her objective is to protect the target asset and to maximize the payoff by (a) investing the network security and (b) determining the payment strategy if the target is infected.

Let $w \in \mathbb{R}$ be the value of the target, which can also be interpreted as the defender's willingness to pay. We denote $\lambda \in [0, 1]$ as the defender's untrusted level to the attacker, which can be measured by the portion of people who choose not to pay the ransom in practice. Because of λ, we define the defender's expected willingness to pay as $\mu = (1 - \lambda)w$. We assume that $B > \mu$ so that the budget can cover the ransom if the target is infected by ransomware. Let $r_d \in [0, B]$ be the network security investment and $q_d \in \{0, 1\}$ be the defender's decision to pay ($q_d = 1$) or not to pay ($q_d = 0$) the ransom after infection. The objective of the attacker is to maximize the payoff using ransomware. He can either deploy ransomware ($q_a = 1$) or abandon the attack ($q_a = 0$). If the attacker decides to attack, he compromises some initial entry points to penetrate the network and searches for the target. The penetration process is modeled by the cyber Markov game in Sect. 2.3. Once the target is compromised, the attacker locks the target and determines the amount of ransom $r_a \in \mathbb{R}_+$. Note that the sum of the security investment and the ransom payment should not exceed the budget B, which we refer to as the budget constraint:

$$r_d + r_a \leq B. \tag{1}$$

2.2 Multi-phase Multi-stage Game Formulation

We formulate the RG as a two-phase three-stage game to capture the sequential interactions between the defender and the attacker, illustrated as follows.

Stage 1 *Initial Investment*: Defender invests r_d to improve the network security.

Stage 2 *Cyber Defense*: Two sub-stages due to attacker's binary action q_a.

Stage 2a The attacker decides whether to attack $q_a = 1$ or not $q_a = 0$. He receives a zero payoff if he abandons the attack and the game terminates. Otherwise, he enters Stage 2b.

Stage 2b The attacker deploys ransomware and starts the penetration, which is captured by the cyber Markov game. With probability θ, he fails to infect the target and receives a cost $c_f \in \mathbb{R}_+$; with probability $1 - \theta$, he compromises the target and demands the ransom r_a. The overall cost for a successful attack is $c_s = c_f + \delta$.

Stage 3 *Ransom Payment*: Two sub-stages due to defender's binary action q_d.

Stage 3a The defender decides whether to pay $q_d = 1$ or not $q_d = 0$. She receives a loss of $w + r_d$ if she does not pay and the game terminates. Otherwise, she enters Stage 3b. Note that the defender will not pay if the remaining budget is not sufficient to cover the ransom ($B - r_d < r_a$).

Stage 3b The defender pays the ransom but still faces the risk of target recovery failure: with probability λ, the attacker keeps locking the target and the defender loses both ransom and the target; with probability $1 - \lambda$, the attacker releases the target.

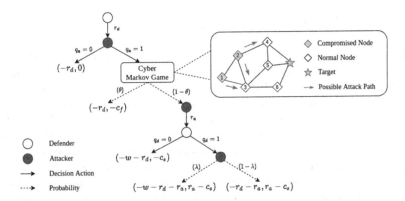

Fig. 1. Structure of the multi-phase and multi-stage game: A cyber Markov game is embedded in the ransom game.

2.3   Cyber Markov Game for Ransomware Penetration

In the cyber phase of the ransomware attack, the attacker penetrates the network and searches for attack paths to infect the target. The defender's security investment can increase the difficulty of ransomware penetration. We assume that after a maximum of K rounds search, if the attacker still cannot reach the target, a security update will be applied to the system and the attack fails. We model the attack-defense interactions in the penetration process under the security investment r_d as a finite horizon zero-sum Markov game (MG).

We consider a network (represented by a graph) $\mathcal{G} = (\mathcal{V}, \mathcal{E})$, where $\mathcal{V}$ is the node set and $\mathcal{E} = \{(u, v) | u, v \in \mathcal{V}, u \neq v\}$ represents the edge set. Each node in $\mathcal{V}$ represents an entity such as a controller, database, etc. An edge in $\mathcal{E}$ means that two entities are connected and can perform service exchange. We attach a label function $L^k \colon \mathcal{V} \mapsto \{0, 1\}$ to each node in $\mathcal{V}$ at time k, representing their operation status. For all $v \in \mathcal{V}$ at time k,

$$L^k(v) = \begin{cases} 1 & \text{if } v \text{ is compromised,} \\ 0 & \text{if } v \text{ is normal.} \end{cases}$$

At time $k = 0$, the attacker compromises the initial node v_0 and searches for the target $\hat{v}$. Hence $L^0(v) = 0, \forall v \in \mathcal{V} \backslash v_0$ and $L^0(v_0) = 1$. We define the cyber MG by the tuple $\langle \mathcal{S}, \mathcal{A}_\mathcal{M}, \mathcal{D}_\mathcal{M}, P, C, K \rangle$. Each component is discussed as follows.

- *State space $\mathcal{S}$:* The finite set $\mathcal{S}$ constitutes all possible labeled graph in K steps, i.e., $\mathcal{S} = \{(\mathcal{G}, L^k)\}_{k=0}^K$, where $\mathcal{G}$ is the underlying network and L^k contains all possible labels for all nodes $v \in \mathcal{V}$ at time k. We denote $\mathcal{S}^k$ as the subset of $\mathcal{S}$ at time k and write $s^k \in \mathcal{S}^k$ as a specific state.
- *Attacker's action space $\mathcal{A}_\mathcal{M}$:* The attacker (minimizer) attempts to attack a normal node through edge vulnerabilities for the next step penetration. Given the game state s^k, the attacker's action set is defined as

$$\mathcal{A}_\mathcal{M}(s^k) = \{(u, v) | (u, v) \in \mathcal{E}, L^k(u) = 1, L^k(v) = 0\}.$$

We write $a^k \in \mathcal{A}_\mathcal{M}(s^k)$ as a specific attacker's action at time k. In Fig. 1, the edges $\{(1, 3), (2, 3), (2, 4)\}$ form the attacker's action set $\mathcal{A}_\mathcal{M}$ in this example.
- *Defender's action space $\mathcal{D}_\mathcal{M}$:* The defender (maximizer) aims to mitigate the attack by hardening the service security over the selected edge. Thus, she shares the same action set as the attacker at time k, i.e., $\mathcal{D}_\mathcal{M}(s^k) = \mathcal{A}_\mathcal{M}(s^k)$.
- *Transition probability P:* We write the transition probability as $\Pr(s' | s, a, d)$ where s', s are current and future states and a, d are attacker's and defender's actions. If the attack $a^k = (u, v)$ succeeds, the label for node v is set to $L^{k+1}(v) = 1$ and the game state is updated accordingly. In our model, the defender combats the attacker by investing the edge security and increasing the attack cost of edge d^k. Thus, the defender's action will not influence the transition probability. Given s^k and a^k, we have

$$\Pr(s^{k+1} | s^k, a^k, d^k) = \Pr(s^{k+1} | s^k, a^k) = \begin{cases} \gamma(r_d, a^k) & s^{k+1} \neq s^k, \\ 1 - \gamma(r_d, a^k) & s^{k+1} = s^k, \end{cases}$$

where $\gamma(r_d, e) \in [0, 1], \forall e \in \mathcal{E}$ is the attack success probability through edge e, which captures the impact of the security investment r_d on that edge.

– *Immediate utility C:* Given the state s^k and the action pair (a^k, d^k), we have

$$C(s^k, a^k, d^k) = \begin{cases} C_d & \text{if } a^k = d^k, \\ C_e(a^k) - H(v) & \text{if } a^k \neq d^k, \end{cases}$$

where

- $C_d \in \mathbb{R}$ is cost for the attacker when the defender protect the same edge.
- $C_e(a^k) \in \mathbb{R}$ is cost of attacking through the chosen edge a^k without defense. Note that $C_d > C_e(e), \forall e \in \mathcal{E}$.
- $H(v) \in \mathbb{R}$ is the attractiveness of the next node v, which is given by

$$H(v) = \frac{n}{(\text{distance to } \hat{v})} + q \cdot (\# \text{ of possible paths to } \hat{v}),$$

where n and q are positive weights.

The attacker receives an additional terminal reward $-w$ when he compromises the target $\hat{v}$. Then, he stays in $\hat{v}$ till the game terminates.

– *Game horizon K:* The horizon K represents the maximum time span for the ransomware to exist in the network. A successful defense prevents the attacker from reaching the target $\hat{v}$ within K steps.

2.4 Solution Concept

Ransomware can be viewed as a special case of APT attacks. In APT attacks, the attacker usually acquires sufficient knowledge about the system with preliminary reconnaissance. Therefore, we assume that both players have complete information in the RG. We adopt sub-game perfect Nash equilibrium (SPNE) as the solution concept in the RG. The cyber MG generates the successful defense probability and the attack cost, which serve as risk assessment parameters to develop the SPNE of the RG. The complete information assumption is crucial to characterize the interdependency between cyber and economic phases.

3 Ransomware Game Analysis

In this section, we first discuss the risk assessment outcome of the cyber MG and then provide a complete equilibrium analysis of the RG.

3.1 Risk Assessment Outcome of the Cyber Markov Game

In the cyber MG, at each state s^k, we denote the strategy of player $i = \{$Attacker, Defender$\}$ as $\pi_i(s^k)$. To find the optimal strategies, we adopt the finite value iteration method [13] to solve the game computationally. Given the investment r_d, we denote the equilibria of the cyber MG $\pi_i^*(r_d)$. We mention that $\pi^*(r_d) = \{\pi_A^*(r_d), \pi_D^*(r_d)\}$ captures the successful defense probability $\theta \in [0, 1]$ and the attack cost $c_f \in \mathbb{R}_+$ given the investment $r_d \in [0, B]$. We define

$$\theta(r_d) = \frac{N_{\text{succ}}(r_d)}{N}, \quad c_f(r_d) = \mathbb{E}_{\pi^*(r_d)}\left[\sum_{k=1}^{K} C^k\right],$$

where N is the total simulated attacks and N_{succ} is the number of successful attacks[2], and C^k is the immediate utility he received at time k.

The average outcome in the cyber MG can serve as a risk assessment measure for the future security decision making. Although it is difficult to characterize $\theta(r_d)$ and $c_f(r_d)$ analytically, we can confirm their positive correlations with r_d. For the purpose of future analysis, we assume the differentiability and $\theta'(r_d) \geq 0$, $c'_f(r_d) \geq 0$. Indeed, these assumptions can be verified in our case study in Sect. 5. We also define the attacker's cost for a successful attack as $c_s(r_d) = c_f(r_d) + \delta$, where δ is the additional cost representing the cost of remote communication and manipulation to the target. Without causing confusions, we write θ and c_f for $\theta(r_d)$ and $c_f(r_d)$ in the rest of the paper.

3.2 Equilibria of the Ransomware Game

We use backward induction to analyze the SPNE of the RG. We use the subscript and the superscript to denote the players' payoffs under different actions and different stages respectively. For example, $U_d|_{q_d=1}^3$ represents the defender's payoff at stage 3 when she decides to pay the ransom.

At stage 3, the defender decides whether to pay ($q_d = 1$) or not to pay ($q_d = 0$) the ransom. We have two possibilities: the remaining budget is either sufficient ($B - r_d \geq r_a$) for the ransom or not sufficient ($B - r_d < r_a$). In the latter case, the defender's only option is not to pay and her payoff is $-w - r_d$. In the former case, the defender can decide whether to pay or not to pay. The payoff of not to pay is still $-w - r_d$. Thus, we have $U_d|_{q_d=0}^3 = -w - r_d$. If the defender decides to pay, then her expected payoff is

$$U_d|_{q_d=1}^3 = \lambda(-w - r_a - r_d) + (1 - \lambda)(-r_a - r_d) = -r_a - r_d - \lambda w.$$

Therefore, we conclude that the defender will choose to pay when the budget is sufficient and $U_d|_{q_d=1}^3 \geq U_d|_{q_d=0}^3$, which indicates the optimal payment action is

$$q_d^* = \begin{cases} 1 & B - r_d \geq r_a, (1 - \lambda)w \geq r_a, \\ 0 & \text{otherwise.} \end{cases} \tag{2}$$

Similarly, the attacker's payoffs at stage 3 for different cases are

$$U_a|_{q_d=0}^3 = -c_s, \quad U_a|_{q_d=1}^3 = r_a - c_s. \tag{3}$$

At stage 2, the attacker first decides whether to attack ($q_a = 1$) or not ($q_a = 0$) and then chooses the amount of ransom r_a if the attack is successful. The payoff of abandoning the attack is simply $U_a|_{q_a=0}^2 = 0$. If the attacker decides

---

[2] An attack is successful if the attacker compromises the target within K steps.

to attack, his expected payoff is related to the successful defense probability θ in the following cyber MG:

$$U_a|^2_{q_a=1} = \theta(-c_f) + (1-\theta)U_a|^2_{q_a=1,\text{succ}}.$$

$U_a|^2_{q_a=1,\text{succ}}$ either equals $U_a|^3_{q_d=1}$ or $U_a|^3_{q_d=0}$, depending on the defender's payment action at stage 3. From (3) we always have $U_a|^3_{q_d=1} \geq U_a|^3_{q_d=0}$. In order to maximize the payoff, the attacker would set the ransom value to encourage ransom payment of the defender. Hence, by considering (1), we have

$$r_a \leq \min\{B - r_d, (1-\lambda)w\} = \min\{B - r_d, \mu\}. \tag{4}$$

In this case, the payoff of the attacker choosing to attack is

$$U_a|^2_{q_a=1} = \theta(-c_f) + (1-\theta)(r_a - c_s). \tag{5}$$

In addition, to ensure that starting the attack is indeed a better strategy, the attacker needs $U_a|^2_{q_a=1} \geq U_a|^2_{q_a=0} = 0$, which yields

$$r_a \geq \frac{\theta c_f + (1-\theta)c_s}{1-\theta}. \tag{6}$$

We note that (4) and (6) form a closed set of r_a, which we denote as $\Omega = \{r_a \,|\, (4) \text{ and } (6) \text{ hold}\} \subseteq \mathbb{R}$. As long as Ω is not empty, the optimal strategies for the attacker and the defender are to start the ransomware attack and to pay the ransom, respectively. The optimal amount of ransom is

$$r_a^* = \arg\max_{r_a \in \Omega} U_a|^2_{q_a=1} = \min\{B - r_d, \mu\} \tag{7}$$

provided $\Omega \neq \varnothing$. Thus, the optimal attack strategy at stage 2 is

$$q_a^* = \begin{cases} 1 & \Omega \neq \varnothing, \\ 0 & \text{otherwise.} \end{cases} \tag{8}$$

The defender's utility is simply the defense investment $-r_d$ if the attack abandons the attack, i.e., $U_d|^2_{q_a=0} = -r_d$. According to the aforementioned analysis, if the attacker decides to attack, he sets the amount of ransom to encourage ransom payment. Therefore, the defender pays the ransom and faces the risk that the attacker does not release the target even after receiving the payment. We can write the expected utility as

$$U_d|^2_{q_a=1} = \theta(-r_d) + (1-\theta)U_d|^3_{q_d=1} = -r_d - (1-\theta)(r_a + \lambda w). \tag{9}$$

At stage 1, the defender determines the security investment r_d to maximize her payoff. If the attacker implements the attack, the defender and the attacker play the cyber MG under the enhanced network with defense investment r_d. Since the outcomes of the cyber MG (θ and c_f) depend on the r_d, the set Ω is also parameterized by r_d and we denote it as $\Omega(r_d)$. To further analyze the optimal security investment, we first focus on the structure of $\Omega(r_d)$ and arrive at the following proposition.

Proposition 1. *There exists $r_d \geq 0$ such that $\Omega(r_d) \neq \varnothing$ if $c_s < \mu$. Furthermore, there exists a unique threshold $\hat{r}_d \in [0, B]$ such that $\Omega(r_d) = \varnothing$ when $r_d > \hat{r}_d$.*

Proof. Let $f(r_d) = \frac{\theta c_f + (1-\theta)c_s}{1-\theta}$. Further let $g(r_d) = \min\{B - r_d, \mu\} - f(r_d)$. Then, $g(r_d)$ denotes the length of $\Omega(r_d)$ when it is positive. Using the assumptions in Sect. 3.1, we show that $f'(r_d) > 0$. Therefore, $g'(r_d) < 0$ except for the point $r_d = B - \mu$, which does not affects the monotonicity of $g(r_d)$. So $g(r_d)$ is decreasing in $r_d \geq 0$. Since $B > w$ and $c_s < \mu$, we have $g(0) = \mu - c_s > 0$. Therefore, there exists $r_d \geq 0$ such that $\Omega(r_d) \neq \varnothing$. It is clear that $f(0) > 0$ and $g(B) < 0$. With the continuity assumption of θ and c_f, there exists a unique $\hat{r}_d$ such that $g(\hat{r}_d) = 0$ and $g(r_d) < 0$ when $r_d > \hat{r}_d$.

Remark 1. The condition $c_s < \mu$ implies that the attacker always has the incentive to attack. We assume the condition always holds in the sequel.

Remark 2. $f(r_d)$ and $\hat{r}_d$ have straightforward but critical interpretations. From (6), $f(r_d)$ is the minimum ransom that the attacker has to demand if he decides to attack. Otherwise, he receives a negative payoff, which is worse than abandoning the attack. The monotonic property $f'(r_d) > 0$ indicates that the minimum ransom increases along with the improvement of network security level. $\hat{r}_d$ is the *threshold investment* such that the attacker cannot make any profit by attacking. It refers to the scenario where the maximum possible ransom is not sufficient to offset the attack cost. Note that $\hat{r}_d$ is a critical value in the sense of economics, which does not indicate the network is fully secured with $\theta(\hat{r}_d) = 1$. In practice, rational attackers will not attack in the first place if they cannot profit from it.

Proposition 1 indicates a *threshold strategy* for investing the network security. If the defender invests any amount larger than $\hat{r}_d$, we have $\Omega = \varnothing$ and the attacker's optimal strategy is to abandon the attack and receives a zero payoff, i.e., $U_a|^1_{r_d \geq \hat{r}_d} = 0$. Then the defender successfully secure the target with this investment. However, we note that the defender has no incentive to invest more than $\hat{r}_d$ because the attacker will not attack anyway. Therefore, in this case, $r_d^* = \hat{r}_d$ and the optimal payoff $U_d^*|_{r_d \geq \hat{r}_d} = -\hat{r}_d$. On the other hand, if the defender invests $\tilde{r}_d < \hat{r}_d$, the attacker has the incentive to attack. In this case, the defender's payoff is

$$U_d|^1_{r_d < \hat{r}_d} = U_d|^2_{q_a = 1} = -r_d - (1 - \theta)(r_a^* + \lambda w)$$

$$= \begin{cases} -r_d - (1 - \theta)w & 0 \leq r_d < B - \mu, \\ -\theta r_d - (1 - \theta)(B + \lambda w) & B - \mu \leq r_d < \hat{r}_d, \end{cases} \tag{10}$$

and the corresponding optimal security investment is

$$\tilde{r}_d^* = \arg \max_{0 \leq r_d < \hat{r}_d} U_d|^1_{r_d < \hat{r}_d}, \tag{11}$$

which is related to the property of the successful defense probability $\theta(r_d)$. We summarize the optimal investment strategy as follows:

$$r_d^* = \begin{cases} \hat{r}_d & U_d|_{r_d<\hat{r}_d}^1(\widetilde{r}_d^*) < -\hat{r}_d, \\ \widetilde{r}_d^* & U_d|_{r_d<\hat{r}_d}^1(\widetilde{r}_d^*) \geq -\hat{r}_d. \end{cases} \tag{12}$$

Proposition 2. *The RG possesses one of the equilibrium solutions below based on the relationship between* $-\hat{r}_d$ *and* $U_d|_{r_d<\hat{r}_d}^1(\widetilde{r}_d^*)$, *where* $\widetilde{r}_d^*$ *is defined in* (11):

(Eq_1) If $-\hat{r}_d \geq U_d|_{r_d<\hat{r}_d}^1(\widetilde{r}_d^*)$: $\langle r_d^* = \hat{r}_d, q_d^* = 1, r_a^* = \min\{B - \hat{r}_d, \mu\}, q_a^* = 0 \rangle$.
Optimal payoffs are $U_d^* = -\hat{r}_d$, $U_a^* = 0$.
(Eq_2) If $-\hat{r}_d < U_d|_{r_d<\hat{r}_d}^1(\widetilde{r}_d^*)$: $\langle r_d^* = \widetilde{r}_d^*, q_d^* = 1, r_a^* = \min\{B - r_d^*, \mu\}, q_a^* = 1 \rangle$.
Optimal payoffs are $U_d^* = U_d|_{r_d<\hat{r}_d}^1(\widetilde{r}_d^*)$, $U_a^* = (1-\theta)r_a^* - \theta c_f - (1-\theta)c_s$.

4 Sensitivity Analysis and Impact of Human Factors

In this section, we study the impact of the security budget and human factors on the equilibrium attack/defense strategy by using sensitivity analysis and prospect theory. As shown in Sect. 3.2, the equilibrium is closely related to the structure of the set Ω, which can vary for different cases shown in Fig. 2. These cases can be distinguished by the relationship between $\bar{r}_d = B - \mu$ and $\hat{r}_d$. We split the region $r_d \geq 0$ into three sub-regions: sub-region I refers to the interval $[0, \bar{r}_d)$; sub-region II is equal to $[\bar{r}_d, \hat{r}_d)$; sub-region III refers to $[\hat{r}_d, \infty)$. Three sub-regions coexist in Fig. 2a, and sub-region II vanishes in Fig. 2b.

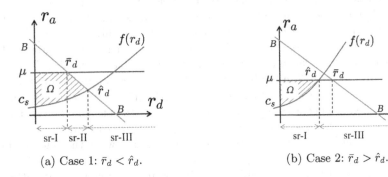

(a) Case 1: $\bar{r}_d < \hat{r}_d$.

(b) Case 2: $\bar{r}_d > \hat{r}_d$.

Fig. 2. Ω in two cases. $f(r_d)$ is defined in Proposition 1. As $\bar{r}_d$ increases, sub-region II gradually vanishes till $\bar{r}_d = \hat{r}_d$. Sub-region I remains $[0, \hat{r}_d)$ when $\bar{r}_d > \hat{r}_d$.

4.1 Impact of the Security Budget

The security budget B affects both on the optimal investment r_d^* and the defender's optimal utility U_d^*. We first note that large budget B barely affects r_d^* and U_d^* as observed in Fig. 2b. This is because Ω is no longer determined by

B and $\mathrm{d}U_d|^1_{r_d<\hat{r}_d}/\mathrm{d}B = 0$. In this scenario, the defender compares $U_d|^1_{r_d<\hat{r}_d}(\widetilde{r}^*_d)$ in sub-region I and $-\hat{r}_d$ to determine which equilibrium strategy to use. To look into $\widetilde{r}^*_d$, since $U_d|^1_{r_d<\hat{r}_d} = -r_d - (1-\theta)w$, we have

$$\frac{\mathrm{d}U_d|^1_{r_d<\hat{r}_d}}{\mathrm{d}r_d} = 0 \quad \Rightarrow \quad \theta' = \frac{1}{w}.$$

We call this value $\frac{1}{w}$ the *critical sensitivity threshold* as it determines whether the increment of security investment helps improve the defender's payoff or not. If the network defense is not sensitive enough to the security investment, i.e., $\theta'(r_d) \leq \frac{1}{w}$, the defender will suffer more loss as she invests more. This is because the investment in security cannot provide strong enough defense to suppress attack threats. Conversely, if the investment can bring sufficient security improvement, i.e., $\theta'(r_d) > \frac{1}{w}$, the defender can benefit more from more investment.

If we lower the budget B, we arrive at the scenario shown in Fig. 2a. The payoff $U_d|^1_{r_d<\hat{r}_d}$ and the effective defense threshold in sub-region I remains the same as in the cases of large budget B. While in sub-region II, we have $U_d|^1_{\hat{r}_d \leq r_d < \bar{r}_d} = -\theta r_d - (1-\theta)(B + \lambda w)$, and

$$\frac{\mathrm{d}U_d|^1_{\hat{r}_d \leq r_d < \bar{r}_d}}{\mathrm{d}r_d} = 0 \quad \Rightarrow \quad \theta' = \frac{\theta}{B + \lambda w - r_d} < \frac{1}{w},$$

which implies that the critical sensitivity threshold is reduced. This result means that the network defense becomes less sensitive to the investment. With the assumption that θ grows slower as the investment increases (verified in Sect. 5), the defender would spend more on the security investment.

The decrease in the critical sensitivity threshold reflects the interdependency between cyber and economic phases. Since the attacker knows the defender's budget, when the budget is sufficient, the attacker can always demand μ as the ransom. As the budget reduces, the attacker may not make any profit if he keeps demanding μ, because the defender may not be able to afford it. The less budget remains at stage 3 in the RG, the less the attacker can profit, and the less incentive he has to start the attack. In short, as the defender's budget reduces, the network defense becomes less sensitive to the investment, which incentivizes the defender to invest more rather than nothing to secure the target.

An interesting but counter-intuitive observation is that when the defender has a small budget, we have $\mathrm{d}U_d|^1_{\hat{r}_d \leq r_d < \bar{r}_d}/\mathrm{d}B = -(1-\theta) < 0$ and $\mathrm{d}(-\hat{r}_d)/\mathrm{d}B < 0$[3] in sub-region II and III, which implies that increasing the budget does not help improve the defender's payoff. This phenomenon has two reasons: the complete-information structure of the RG and the interdependency between the cyber and economic phases. The defender cannot invest much if she has a small budget, leading to a high probability of being compromised. Since the attacker knows the budget, he can always demand the remaining budget to make the most profit. For the defender, she either invests $\hat{r}_d$ to avoid the attack or invests some value less than $\hat{r}_d$ while facing the risk of being compromised. Her utility will go down

---

[3] See Appendix for the proof of $\mathrm{d}(-\hat{r}_d)/\mathrm{d}B < 0$.

in both ways if she increases her budget a bit. We name this phenomenon as the *budget dilemma*. We mention that the budget dilemma happens only when the budget is small. It disappears when the defender has a sufficient budget because her expected willingness to pay μ starts to dominate the attacker's ransom strategy.

To summarize, we arrive at the following insights. First, a sufficient budget corresponds to a fixed critical sensitivity threshold $\frac{1}{w}$. Conversely, a small budget reduces the threshold, which incentivizes the defender to invest more in network security. Second, the defender faces the budget dilemma for a small budget, but the dilemma disappears as the budget increases.

4.2 Impact of Human Factors and Prospect Theory

Humans have different cognitive preferences. In general, people are more averse to losses and less sensitive to gains; people inflate the belief for rare events and deflate for high-probability ones. Prospect theory captures human factors by

$$V(x) = \begin{cases} x^\beta & x \geq 0 \\ -\alpha(-x)^\beta & x < 0 \end{cases}, \qquad h(p) = \frac{p^\varsigma}{p^\varsigma + (1-p)^\varsigma}, \tag{13}$$

where $V(x)$ and $h(p)$ are biased utility and weighted probability, respectively, and α, β, ς are prospect parameters.

In the RG, we assume that the attacker is completely rational and the human factors are embodied in the defender's side (λ and w). Prospect theory provides a way to understand the impact of these human factors on the game equilibrium.

We denote the biased untrusted level λ and willingness to pay w as $\tilde{\lambda}$ and $\tilde{w}$. The biased expected willingness to pay becomes $\tilde{\mu} = (1 - \tilde{\lambda})\tilde{w}$. Note that $-w$ describes the defender's potential loss. From (13), the defender expects a larger loss $-\tilde{w} < -w$ during decision-making. The biased $\tilde{\mu}$ also depends on λ. For large λ (the defender barely trust the attacker), $\tilde{\lambda}$ is deflated and thus $\tilde{\mu} > \mu$. For small λ (the defender trusts the attacker), $\tilde{\lambda}$ is inflated and $1 - \tilde{\lambda}$ is deflated. The value of $\tilde{\mu}$ depends on specific values of $\tilde{w}$ and $\tilde{\lambda}$.

We first look into how human factors influence the critical investment $\hat{r}_d$. When the budget is sufficient (see Fig. 2b), an increased $\tilde{\mu}$ leads to an increased $\hat{r}_d$. This means that the defender has to invest more in network security to eliminate the attack risk if she has a higher expected willingness to pay. When the budget is small (see Fig. 2a), $\hat{r}_d$ is no longer affected by $\tilde{\mu}$ and thus remain unchanged. Therefore, human factors affect the critical investment $\hat{r}_d$ in a way such that $\hat{r}_d$ has a positive correlation in $\tilde{\mu}$ for only for sufficient budget B.

For the optimal investment r_d^*, the defender either takes $\hat{r}_d$ or some value between $[0, \hat{r}_d)$ as r_d^*, depending on which strategy yields a larger payoff. Note that $\tilde{w}$ reduces the critical sensitivity threshold, which implies that the defender's payoff can be further improved by more investment compared with the unbiased case. We conclude that if the defender's optimal investment $r_d^* \neq \hat{r}_d$ in the unbiased case, human factors will enhance r_d^*; if the defender takes $r_d^* = \hat{r}_d$ in the unbiased case, human factors affect r_d^* by following the variation trend of $\tilde{\mu}$.

As for the defender's optimal payoff U_d^*, we focus on the case where the untrusted level λ is small (e.g., $\lambda = 0.3$). From (10) we see that the defender's payoff in sub-region I is always decreasing because $\widetilde{w} > w$. Besides, $\widetilde{\lambda}$ is inflated, causing a decrease in the defender's payoff in sub-region II. In sub-region III, the defender's payoff becomes $-\hat{r}_d$, and it is influenced by $\widetilde{\mu}$. To conclude, for small λ, if the defender's optimal investment $r_d^* \neq \hat{r}_d$ in the unbiased case, her optimal payoff is always worsened by the inflated $\widetilde{w}$; if the defender takes $r_d^* = \hat{r}_d$ in the unbiased case, human factors affect U_d^* by following the variation trend of $\widetilde{\mu}$.

The rational attacker may profit from the defender's bias. From (7), the attacker demands ransom $r_a = \min\{B - r_d^*, \mu\}$. Therefore, when the budget B is sufficient while the security investment r_d^* is small such that $B - r_d^* \geq \mu$, the attacker demands $r_a = \mu$ and he can receive more profit if $\widetilde{\mu} > \mu$. However, as r_d^* increases, the attacker can only demand $r_a = B - r_d^*$. So human factors influence his payoff in the exact opposite way as r_d^*. Specifically, if we have $\widetilde{\mu} > \mu$, the attacker in fact receives a worse payoff compared with the unbiased case.

5   Case Studies and Discussion

In this section, we use a case study over a prototypical industrial IoT network to analyze the impact of ransomware attacks. We conduct simulations to evaluate the performance of the cyber MG defense mechanism, which serves as the cyber risk assessment for future security decision-making. We analyze the equilibrium strategy in the RG and discuss the influences of limited budget and prospect theory on the equilibrium strategy.

5.1   Model Implementation

Typically, industrial networks are segregated into several interconnected sub-level networks based on the usage [16,25]. We consider the following network with four layers shown in Fig. 3, where the massively interconnected devices are grouped by their functions for simplicity. Each entity can represent a set of agents with similar functions. The target asset in our case is the production unit (e.g., a robotic arm) which can generate profit. We consider a locker ransomware attack, where the infected target will be locked and lose all its functionality. The target value can be assessed by the real loss in production if the target is locked. Since the value can vary dramatically for different applications, we use a normalized value $w = 10$ to denote the target value. Other money-related values can be converted to have the same magnitude as the w. We also set the untrusted level $\lambda = 0.3$ based on empirical results of the ransomware attack.

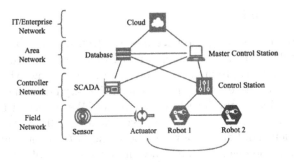

Fig. 3. A prototypical industrial IoT network consists of four network layers including IT/enterprise network, area network, controller network and field network. The target node of the attacker is Robot 2.

5.2 Outcome of Cyber Markov Game

In the cyber MG, we refer to the Common Vulnerability Scoring System (CVSS) [19] to describe the cost $C_e(e)$ of mounting an attack through edge $e \in \mathcal{E}$. CVSS provides a risk measurement of edge vulnerabilities. We convert the score into the same magnitude as w and simulates the MG under this setting.

The attacker establishes the initial foothold at the cloud in the IT network layer, penetrating through sub-level networks to infect the target. The defender invests $r_d \in [0, B]$ to change the transition probability $\gamma(r_d, e)$ in the cyber MG. In this case study, we assume that the influence of security investment is equivalent on each edge, i.e., $\gamma(r_d, e) = \widetilde{\gamma}(r_d), \forall e \in \mathcal{E}$. In our case, we select

$$\widetilde{\gamma}(r_d) = 1 - \sqrt{\frac{r_d}{\eta w}},$$

where η is the scaling factor to measure the effectiveness of the investment. To obtain the average results of the cyber MG, we choose $\eta = 2$ and sample 40 points of $(r_d/\eta w)$ at equal intervals between 0 and 1. We simulate the cyber MG for $N = 5000$ times under each r_d to evaluate the empirical successful defense probability $\theta(r_d)$ and the attack cost $c_f(r_d)$, which are shown in Fig. 4. The additional attack cost for a successful attack is set to $\delta = 0.5$.

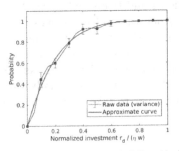

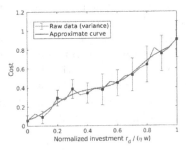

(a) Empirical defense probability $\theta(r_d)$.   (b) Empirical attack cost $c_f(r_d)$.

Fig. 4. Simulation outcome with variance and approximations of the cyber MG

5.3 Impact of Budget

Under the parameter setting, we have $\mu = 7$. Thus, we vary B from 9 to 16 to study how the defense strategy changes under different budgets.

The derivative of approximated θ function in Fig. 5 shows that the network defense is highly sensitive to the investment at the very beginning and gradually losses its sensitivity as the investment increases. We observe that the critical sensitivity threshold in Fig. 5 splits the investment $r_d \geq 0$ into two regions, and the r_d on the left-hand side is always above the critical sensitivity threshold. This implies that the defender can always improve her payoff by investing some value rather than nothing. Therefore, the zero investment strategy is ruled out.

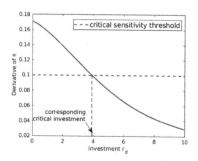

Fig. 5. Sensitivity of the network defense.

The optimal investment strategy r_d^* and the defender's optimal payoff in three sub-regions are shown in Fig. 6a and Fig. 6b respectively. The variation of $\hat{r}_d$ and $\bar{r}_d$ are also plotted in Fig. 6a. For a small budget of B, the length of sub-region I is short. The entire sub-region can be above the threshold. So the defender will not seek the optimal investment in this sub-region. For a better payoff, the defender will invest more. Thus, the optimal investment is $\hat{r}_d$ as shown in Fig. 6a.

As the budget improves, we see that the value of $\hat{r}_d$ also increases as discussed in Sect. 4.1. However, the network defense becomes less sensitive, which means that the defender may not be better off if she keeps investing $\hat{r}_d$. So she would consider the investment strategy in sub-region I and II instead of $\hat{r}_d$. As shown in Fig. 6a, the defender no longer invests $\hat{r}_d$ when the budget reaches $B = 10.5$. She starts to take some value in sub-region II as the optimal investment. Note that r_d^* is still not in sub-regions I because the size of sub-regions I is still small and the entire region is still above the critical sensitivity threshold. As we keep improving the budget, $\hat{r}_d$ keeps increasing and sub-region II gradually vanishes. As the budget reaches $B = 11.8$, the defender starts to take values in sub-region I as the optimal investment.

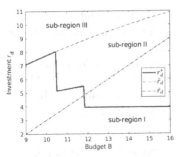
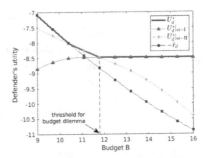

(a) Optimal investment strategy. Three sub-regions are split by $\hat{r}_d$ and $\bar{r}_d$.

(b) Defender's optimal payoff. We can also observe the udget dilemma.

Fig. 6. Defender's optimal investment strategy and optimal payoff.

We can observe the budget dilemma in Fig. 6b, where the defender's payoff is decreasing as the budget goes up when the budget is small. The decrements stop when $B = 11.8$ and remain unchanged with a larger budget, which coincides with the analysis that the budget dilemma disappears for a large budget. Note that in this case, we even do not need to arrive at the situation in Fig. 2b to suppress the budget dilemma, as the budget after $B = 11.8$ already stops influencing the optimal utility.

To conclude, when the defender has a small budget, she should invest $\hat{r}_d$ to eliminate the threat of attack. When the budget is sufficient, the defender can choose some other investment less than $\hat{r}_d$ to optimize her payoff. We note that the large budget offsets the defender's initiative to protect the target. This is because (a) network defense becomes less sensitive to the security investment and (b) paying the ransom becomes acceptable compared with the security expenditure. Therefore, the budget reflects the trade-off between the security investment and redeeming the target, which further implies the interdependency between cyber and economic phases in the ransomware attack.

5.4 Prospect Theory

To study the impact of human factors on $\hat{r}_d, r_d^*, U_d^*, r_a^*$, we discuss two cases with small budget $B = 14$ and large budget $B = 20$ respectively. We apply typical perspective parameters $\alpha = 2.25, \beta = 0.88, \zeta = 0.69$ in [8]. Under these parameters, the biased willingness to pay $\tilde{\mu} = 12.47 > \mu$, which implies human factors increases the μ. We mention that $B = 14$ a small budget for the biased case in this subsection, although it is large enough for the unbiased case. The results are summarized in Table 2

Followed by the analysis in Sect. 4.2, we observe that $\hat{r}_d$ remains unchanged for small budget in Table 2a, but increases for large budget because of inflated $\tilde{\mu}$, shown in Table 2b. Meanwhile, the biased $\tilde{w}$ reduces the critical sensitivity threshold regardless of the budget, which requires the defender to invest more to be better off. Thus, the optimal investment r_d^* increases compared with the unbiased case both in Table 2a–2b. Likewise, the inflated $\tilde{w}$ and $\tilde{\mu}$ can reduce the defender's optimal payoff U_d^* despite the budget. This shows that human factors in this case in fact worsen the defender's situation.

The attacker does not profit from the bias of the defender either. In both cases we study here, the defender selects r_d^* such that $B - r_d^* < \mu$. Therefore, the defender can only demand $r_a = B - r_d^*$. Since r_d^* is enlarged in both cases, the ransom r_a is also reduced, which is observed in Table 2a–2b.

Table 2. Impact of human factors under different budget scenarios.

	$\hat{r}_d$	r_d^*	U_d^*	r_a^*		$\hat{r}_d$	r_d^*	U_d^*	r_a^*
unbiased	10	3.93	−8.48	10.08	unbiased	11.9	3.93	−8.48	16.07
biased	10	6.6	−9.84	7.4	biased	12.3	6.55	−10.85	13.45
(a) Small budget $B = 14$.					(b) Large $B = 20$.				

6   Conclusion

In this paper, we have investigated the ransomware attack in networks by establishing an MPMS-GiG framework. The proposed framework captures both cyber and economic phases of the ransomware attack and provides a holistic analysis of the interdependency between them. The equilibrium characterizes the defense-payment strategy with budget constraints. The sensitivity analysis suggests that the network security investment is more effective to combat the ransomware attack when the defender has a small budget. It is also recommended to increase the investment to reduce the defender's overall loss under a small budget. We also observe the budget dilemma when the defender's budget is insufficient, which reflects the interdependency between cyber and economic phases in the ransomware attack. Human factors also contribute to the equilibrium attack/defense strategy. Being risk-averse can drop the defender's overall loss because she values the target more. It is also worth noting that the attacker gains less from a biased defender as she prefers to invest more in network security. Case studies show the equilibrium attack/defense strategy over a prototypical industrial IoT network and successfully corroborates the results in the paper.

For future work, we would consider the ransomware attack with incomplete information. For example, the attacker may not know exactly the defender's willingness to pay except for a prior distribution. Another direction would be to study cyber insurance and its impact on the equilibrium of ransomware attacks.

A   Proof in the Budget Dilemma

Recall that $\hat{r}_d$ is the root of $g(r_d, B) = B - r_d - f(r_d)$ for small B. Assume the differentiability of θ and c_f, it is easy to show that $f'(r_d) > 0$. Using the implicit function theorem, we can find a function $\hat{r}_d = h(B)$ in the neighborhood of $(B, \hat{r}_d)$ where $g(r_d, B) = 0$. Hence, we have $\frac{d\hat{r}_d}{dB} = -(-1 - f'(\hat{r}_d))^{-1} = \frac{1}{1+f'(\hat{r}_d)} > 0$. The defender's utility is $-\hat{r}_d$ if she chooses to invest $\hat{r}_d$. Thus, $\frac{d(-\hat{r}_d)}{dB} < 0$.

References

1. Colonial pipeline ransomware attack. Wikipedia. https://en.wikipedia.org/wiki/Colonial_Pipeline_ransomware_attack. Accessed 20 July 2021
2. Aidan, J.S., Verma, H.K., Awasthi, L.K.: Comprehensive survey on petya ransomware attack. In: 2017 International Conference on Next Generation Computing and Information Systems (ICNGCIS), pp. 122–125. IEEE (2017)
3. Braue, D.: Global ransomware damage costs predicted to exceed $265 billion by 2031 (2021). https://cybersecurityventures.com/global-ransomware-damage-costs-predicted-to-reach-250-billion-usd-by-2031/. Accessed 20 July 2021
4. Caporusso, N., Chea, S., Abukhaled, R.: A game-theoretical model of ransomware. In: Ahram, T.Z., Nicholson, D. (eds.) AHFE 2018. AISC, vol. 782, pp. 69–78. Springer, Cham (2019). https://doi.org/10.1007/978-3-319-94782-2_7
5. Cartwright, E., Hernandez Castro, J., Cartwright, A.: To pay or not: game theoretic models of ransomware. J. Cybersecur. 5(1), tyz009 (2019)
6. Di Pietro, R., Mancini, L.V.: Intrusion Detection Systems, vol. 38. Springer Science & Business Media, Heidelberg (2008)
7. Flores, R.: The impact of modern ransomware on manufacturing networks (2020). https://www.trendmicro.com/en_us/research/20/l/the-impact-of-modern-ransomware-on-manufacturing-networks.html. Accessed 20 July 2021
8. Fox, C.R., Poldrack, R.A.: Prospect theory and the brain. In: Neuroeconomics, pp. 145–173. Elsevier (2009)
9. Hernandez-Castro, J., Cartwright, E., Stepanova, A.: Economic analysis of ransomware. Available at SSRN 2937641 (2017)
10. Huang, L., Zhu, Q.: Adaptive strategic cyber defense for advanced persistent threats in critical infrastructure networks. ACM SIGMETRICS Perform. Eval. Rev. 46(2), 52–56 (2019)
11. Inayat, Z., Gani, A., Anuar, N.B., Khan, M.K., Anwar, S.: Intrusion response systems: foundations, design, and challenges. J. Netw. Comput. Appl. 62, 53–74 (2016)
12. Kalaimannan, E., John, S.K., DuBose, T., Pinto, A.: Influences on ransomware's evolution and predictions for the future challenges. J. Cyber Secur. Technol. 1(1), 23–31 (2017)
13. Kearns, M., Mansour, Y., Singh, S.: Fast planning in stochastic games. arXiv preprint arXiv:1301.3867 (2013)
14. Kivilevich, V.: Ransomware gangs are starting to look like ocean's 11 (2021). https://ke-la.com/ransomware-gangs-are-starting-to-look-like-oceans-11/. Accessed 20 July 2021
15. Laszka, A., Farhang, S., Grossklags, J.: On the economics of ransomware. In: Rass, S., An, B., Kiekintveld, C., Fang, F., Schauer, S. (eds.) Decision and Game Theory for Security. GameSec 2017. Lecture Notes in Computer Science, vol. 10575, pp. 397–417. Springer, Cham (2017). https://doi.org/10.1007/978-3-319-68711-7_21
16. Mayoral-Vilches, V., Pinzger, M., Rass, S., Dieber, B., Gil-Uriarte, E.: Can ros be used securely in industry? red teaming ros-industrial. arXiv preprint arXiv:2009.08211 (2020)

17. Noureddine, M.A., Fawaz, A., Sanders, W.H., Başar, T.: A game-theoretic approach to respond to attacker lateral movement. In: Zhu, Q., Alpcan, T., Panaousis, E., Tambe, M., Casey, W. (eds.) GameSec 2016. LNCS, vol. 9996, pp. 294–313. Springer, Cham (2016). https://doi.org/10.1007/978-3-319-47413-7_17
18. Richardson, R., North, M.M.: Ransomware: evolution, mitigation and prevention. Int. Manag. Rev. **13**(1), 10 (2017)
19. Scarfone, K., Mell, P.: An analysis of CVSS version 2 vulnerability scoring. In: 2009 3rd International Symposium on Empirical Software Engineering and Measurement, pp. 516–525. IEEE (2009)
20. Tonn, G., Kesan, J.P., Zhang, L., Czajkowski, J.: Cyber risk and insurance for transportation infrastructure. Transp. Policy **79**, 103–114 (2019)
21. Touchette, F.: The evolution of malware. Netw. Secur. **2016**(1), 11–14 (2016)
22. Tuptuk, N., Hailes, S.: Security of smart manufacturing systems. J. Manuf. Syst. **47**, 93–106 (2018)
23. Yaqoob, I., et al.: The rise of ransomware and emerging security challenges in the internet of things. Comput. Netw. **129**, 444–458 (2017)
24. Zahra, S.R., Chishti, M.A.: Ransomware and internet of things: a new security nightmare. In: 2019 9th International Conference on Cloud Computing, Data Science & Engineering (confluence), pp. 551–555. IEEE (2019)
25. Zhu, Q., Rass, S., Dieber, B., Vilches, V.M.: Cybersecurity in robotics: Challenges, quantitative modeling, and practice. arXiv preprint arXiv:2103.05789 (2021)

Cyber-physical Systems Security

A Game-Theoretic Framework for Controlled Islanding in the Presence of Adversaries

Luyao Niu[1(✉)], Dinuka Sahabandu[2], Andrew Clark[1], and Radha Poovendran[2]

[1] Department of Electrical and Computer Engineering, Worcester Polytechnic Institute, Worcester, MA 01609, USA
lniu@wpi.edu, aclark@wpi.edu
[2] Network Security Lab, Department of Electrical and Computer Engineering, University of Washington, Seattle, WA 98195-2500, USA
sdinuka@uw.edu, rp3@uw.edu

Abstract. Controlled islanding effectively mitigates cascading failures by partitioning the power system into a set of disjoint islands. In this paper, we study the controlled islanding problem of a power system under disturbances introduced by a malicious adversary. We formulate the interaction between the grid operator and adversary using a game-theoretic framework. The grid operator first computes a controlled islanding strategy, along with the power generation for the post-islanding system to guarantee stability. The adversary observes the strategies of the grid operator. The adversary then identifies critical substations of the power system to compromise and trips the transmission lines that are connected with compromised substations. For our game formulation, we propose a double oracle algorithm based approach that solves the best response for each player. We show that the best responses for the grid operator and adversary can be formulated as mixed integer linear programs. In addition, the best response of the adversary is equivalent to a submodular maximization problem under a cardinality constraint, which can be approximated up to a $(1 - \frac{1}{e})$ optimality bound in polynomial time. We compare the proposed approach with a baseline where the grid operator computes an islanding strategy by minimizing the power flow disruption without considering the possible response from the adversary. We evaluate both approaches using IEEE 9-bus, 14-bus, 30-bus, 39-bus, 57-bus, and 118-bus power system case study data. Our proposed approach achieves better performance than the baseline in about 44% of test cases, and on average it incurs about 12.27 MW less power flow disruption.

This work was supported by AFOSR grant FA9550-20-1-0074 and NSF grant CNS-1941670.
L. Niu, D. Sahabandu—Authors contributed equally to this work.

B. Bošanský et al. (Eds.): GameSec 2021, LNCS 13061, pp. 231–250, 2021.
https://doi.org/10.1007/978-3-030-90370-1_13

1   Introduction

The electric power system is a complex large-scale network that delivers electricity to customers. Modern power systems leverage Internet of Things (IoT) technologies and have integrated information and communication components [2], leading to the smart grid paradigm. However, incorporating cyber components exposes the power system to malicious cyber attacks [17,20]. For example, the service outage incurred by the Ukrainian electric company in 2015 was caused by malicious cyber attacks [16].

Cyber attacks impact power systems by biasing the decision of the power grid operator, masking physical outages, and/or causing malfunctions of system components [29]. These disturbances can potentially lead to *cascading failures*. In a cascading failure, the outage of one component, e.g., a transmission line, shifts the load to other connected components, making them overload and fail. Power systems are under increasing risks of cascading failures since they are operated close to their capacity limits so as to meet ever-increasing electricity demands. Cascading failures can cause catastrophic economic consequences; the 2003 North American blackout, for example, left more than 55 million people in dark and caused 10 billion dollars loss [21]. An intelligent adversary may therefore take advantage of cascading failures to cause severe damage to power systems using limited resources.

Controlled islanding has been demonstrated to be an effective countermeasure against cascading failures [33]. Controlled islanding determines a subset of transmission lines to be tripped to partition the power system into multiple subsystems, following a disturbance such as transmission line outage.

Various techniques [7,9,18,24,28,33] have been proposed for designing controlled islanding strategies with different criteria such as power flow disruption and power imbalance. To the best of our knowledge, however, there has been little study focusing on controlled islanding for power systems in the presence of malicious adversaries. Different from exogenous causes such as natural disasters and increasing load demand [32], intelligent adversaries can infer the islanding strategy of the grid operator and deliberately trip transmission lines to make the islands ineffective or even unstable. In the 2015 Ukrainian blackout, the adversaries compromised the substations and leveraged the strategies of the grid operator against the power system [16].

In this paper, we propose a game-theoretic model of controlled islanding to mitigate cascading failures in the presence of a malicious adversary. The adversary can compromise a subset of substations of the power system, and trip the transmission lines that are connected to the compromised substations. The grid operator aims at preventing cascading failure triggered by the adversary by implementing a controlled islanding strategy and designing corresponding post-islanding strategies. We make the following contributions:

- We model the interaction between the grid operator and adversary as a Stackelberg game, which we formulate as a mixed integer nonlinear program.

- We propose a double oracle algorithm based approach to solve for the strategies of the grid operator. The proposed approach iteratively computes the best response of each player.
- We analyze the best response for each player, and formulate it as a mixed integer linear program. In addition, we show the equivalence between the adversary's best response and a submodular function maximization problem with a cardinality constraint. A greedy algorithm can then be used to approximately compute the adversary's best response in polynomial time.
- We evaluate our proposed approach using IEEE 9-bus, 14-bus, 30-bus, 39-bus, 57-bus, and 118-bus power system case study data. We show that on average the power system performs better in 44% of the test cases and incurs 12.27 MW less power flow disruption when using the proposed approach, compared with a baseline that ignores the presence of an adversary.

The remainder of this paper is organized as follows. Related literature is reviewed in Sect. 2. Preliminary background on power system model and Stackelberg games is presented in Sect. 3. Section 4 gives the models for the adversary and grid operator, and maps the problem to a Stackelberg game. We present the solution approach in Sect. 5. Numerical evaluation results are presented in Sect. 6. We conclude the paper in Sect. 7.

2   Related Work

Computing controlled islanding strategies for power systems under large disturbances has been extensively studied. Typical approaches include slow coherency based islanding [33], ordered binary decision diagram (OBDD) methods [28], two-step spectral clustering technique [9], weak submodularity based controlled islanding [18], and mixed integer program based approaches [7,24]. These works study the controlled islanding by assuming the disturbance has been detected and fixed. When there exists an adversary who can intelligently adjust its strategy, the islanding strategies computed using the aforementioned contributions need to be adjusted also to incorporate the possible response from the adversary.

Malicious attacks targeting power system have been reported and studied. The malicious attacks can be roughly classified into two categories. The first category of attacks manipulates the grid topology via transmission line switching [6,22] and compromising substations [35]. Another category of attacks targets at the cyber components such as false data injection attack [8,31]. In this paper, we consider a malicious adversary that compromises substations using cyber attacks and trips transmission lines. Different from existing literature, the adversary model studied in this paper not only identifies the critical components in the power system, but also considers the possible corrective action taken by the grid operator. In addition, existing topological models may discard the power system dynamics to simplify the computations [11], while this paper takes the physical properties of power systems into consideration.

In this paper, we map the interaction between the grid operator and adversary to a Stackelberg game. Stackelberg games have been widely used to model real-world security applications such as airport protection [26]. To compute the

Stackelberg equilibrium [5] of the game in this paper, we propose a double oracle algorithm based approach [19]. Double oracle algorithm has been widely used to solve games of large-scale [3,13,14], due to the advantage that it avoids the enumeration over all possible strategies for the players.

3   Model and Preliminaries

3.1   Power System Model

A power system with B substations and L transmission lines can be described by a graph $\mathcal{G} = (\mathcal{B}, \mathcal{L})$, where $\mathcal{B} = \{1, \ldots, B\}$ is the set of substations and $\mathcal{L} \subseteq \mathcal{B} \times \mathcal{B}$ is the set of transmission lines. A transmission line $l = (i, j) \in \mathcal{L}$ if substations i and j are connected via l. We define the set of neighboring substations for each $i \in \mathcal{B}$ as $\mathcal{T}(i) = \{j : (i, j) \in \mathcal{L}\}$. The power injected to substation i is denoted as g_i, and the power drawn from substation i is denoted as d_i.

We consider DC power flow in the power system. The power flow $P_{i,j}$ through each transmission line (i, j) is calculated as

$$P_{i,j} = S_{i,j}(\theta_i - \theta_j), \ \forall (i, j) \in \mathcal{L} \tag{1}$$

where $S_{i,j}$ is the electrical susceptance of transmission line (i, j), and θ_i, θ_j are the voltage angles at substations i and j, respectively. Each substation $i \in \mathcal{B}$ respects the power flow conservation law given as

$$\sum_{j \in \mathcal{T}(i)} P_{j,i} + g_i - d_i = 0, \ \forall i \in \mathcal{B}. \tag{2}$$

Power generators exhibit varying behaviors following a large disturbance. Two generators are said to be *coherent* if their rotor angle deviations are within a certain tolerance [10]. To maintain the internal stability of the power system, the coherent generators need to be connected, while the non-coherent ones must be separated during islanding. In this paper, we assume that the set of power generators are classified into K coherent groups. Detailed techniques on computing coherent groups can be found in [4].

There are various metrics that have been proposed to measure the performance of power system when incurring disturbance. Typical metrics include power flow disruption [25,30] and power imbalance [28,34]. Minimum power flow disruption improves the transient stability of the system and reduces the risk of overloading transmission lines [12]. In this paper, we adopt power flow disruption as the performance metric, which is defined as

$$R(\mathcal{S}) = \sum_{(i,j) \in \mathcal{L}} (1 - z_{i,j}) \frac{|P_{i,j}| + |P_{j,i}|}{2}, \tag{3}$$

where $\mathcal{S} \subseteq \mathcal{L}$ represents the set of tripped transmission lines. Parameter $z_{i,j} = 1$ if $(i, j) \in \mathcal{L} \backslash \mathcal{S}$ and $z_{i,j} = 0$ if $(i, j) \in \mathcal{S}$.

3.2   Stackelberg Game

Game theory models the interaction among multiple players. Consider a game consisting of two players, denoted as Player 1 and Player 2. Players 1 and 2 have their action spaces $\mathcal{A}_1$ and $\mathcal{A}_2$, respectively. Each action of $\mathcal{A}_1$ and $\mathcal{A}_2$ is also known as the pure strategy for Player 1 and Player 2, respectively. A mixed strategy is a probability distribution over the action space. When Players 1 and 2 take strategies s_1 and s_2, respectively, they obtain utilities $U_1(s_1, s_2)$ and $U_2(s_1, s_2)$ during the interaction.

Two-player Stackelberg games model interactions with information asymmetry, where Player 1 moves first by committing to a strategy, and Player 2 observes the strategy committed by Player 1 and chooses its strategy to maximize $U_2(\cdot, \cdot)$. Player 1 and Player 2 are also known as the leader and follower, respectively.

The solution concept of Stackelberg game is called Stackelberg equilibrium. We say strategies s_1^* and s_2^* for Players 1 and 2 comprise a Stackelberg equilibrium if $s_1^* = \text{argmax}_{s_1} U(s_1, s_2^*)$, where $s_2^* \in \mathcal{BR}(s_1^*)$ and $\mathcal{BR}(s_1^*) = \text{argmax}_{s_2} \{U_2(s_1^*, s_2)\}$ is the best response taken by Player 2 to s_1^*.

4   Problem Formulation

4.1   Adversary Model

We consider a power system $\mathcal{G} = (\mathcal{B}, \mathcal{L})$. A malicious adversary aims at destabilizing the power system and maximizing the power flow disruption. To achieve this goal, the adversary has two capabilities: (i) the adversary can compromise at most C substations $\hat{\mathcal{B}} \subset \mathcal{B}$, and (ii) the adversary can trip the set of transmission lines that are connected with the compromised substations. These capabilities have been demonstrated by real-world adversaries. For instance, the adversary that initiated the attack against the Ukrainian electric system compromised the substations and thus gained control over field devices [16].

We assume the adversary has access to the following information. The adversary knows the grid topology $\mathcal{G} = (\mathcal{B}, \mathcal{L})$ and the power flow before it trips any transmission line. In addition, the adversary can observe the strategies taken by the grid operator (we will detail the model of grid operator in Sect. 4.2). We denote the information available to the adversary as $\mathcal{I}^a$. It has been reported that the adversary can harvest such information via cyber attacks [16].

In the following, we define the strategy for the adversary. A pure strategy for the adversary $\tau : \mathcal{I}^a \to 2^{\mathcal{B}} \times 2^{\mathcal{L}}$ maps from the information set of the adversary to a pair of compromised substations $\hat{\mathcal{B}}$ and tripped transmission lines $\hat{\mathcal{L}}$. A mixed strategy for the adversary $\tau : \mathcal{I}^a \to \Delta(2^{\mathcal{B}} \times 2^{\mathcal{L}})$ maps from the information set of the adversary to a pair of probability distributions over $2^{\mathcal{B}} \times 2^{\mathcal{L}}$, where $\Delta(\cdot)$ represents a probability distribution over some set. We define the set of proper adversary strategies as follows.

Definition 1. *We say strategy τ is proper if the following conditions hold: (i) $|\hat{\mathcal{B}}| \leq C$, and (ii) $\hat{\mathcal{L}} \subseteq \{(i,j) \in \mathcal{L} : i \in \hat{\mathcal{B}} \text{ or } j \in \hat{\mathcal{B}}\}$.*

The adversary computes its strategy τ as

$$\max_{\tau} R(\mathcal{S}) \tag{4a}$$

$$\text{subject to } \tau \text{ is proper} \tag{4b}$$

where $R(\mathcal{S})$ is defined in Eq. (3), $\mathcal{S} = \hat{\mathcal{L}} \cup \tilde{\mathcal{L}} \subseteq \mathcal{L}$, and $\tilde{\mathcal{L}}$ is the set of transmission lines tripped by the grid operator (we will introduce $\tilde{\mathcal{L}}$ later in Sect. 4.2).

4.2   Grid Operator Model

In this subsection, we present the model of the grid operator. The goal of the grid operator is to protect the power system $\mathcal{G} = (\mathcal{B}, \mathcal{L})$ when large disturbance is incurred. The grid operator has the following control capabilities. The grid operator can trip a subset of transmission lines $\tilde{\mathcal{L}} \subset \mathcal{L} \setminus \hat{\mathcal{L}}$ to partition the power system into a collection of subsystems $\{\mathcal{G}_k\}_{k=1}^K$, where $\mathcal{G}_k = (\mathcal{B}_k, \mathcal{L}_k)$, $\mathcal{B}_k \subset \mathcal{B}$, and $\mathcal{L}_k \subset \mathcal{L}$. A subsystem $\mathcal{G}_k$ is also known as an island. After the power system is partitioned into subsystems, the grid operator controls the power injection g_i from each generator at each generation substation $i \in \mathcal{B}$.

We assume that the grid operator knows the grid topology and has perfect observation over the power system so that it can monitor the parameters such as the voltage angle at each substation, the power flow at each transmission line, the power injection from the generators, and the power drawn by the load demands. Additionally, the grid operator can compute the set of generator coherent groups. We denote the information available to the grid operator as $\mathcal{I}^o$.

A pure strategy for the grid operator is defined as $\mu : \mathcal{I}^o \to 2^{\mathcal{L}} \times \mathbb{R}^N$ that maps from $\mathcal{I}^o$ to the set of possibly tripped transmission lines and the space of power generations. Note that here the set of open transmission lines are tripped by the grid operator, and is different from those tripped by the adversary. A mixed strategy for the grid operator is defined as $\mu : \mathcal{I}^o \to \Delta(2^{\mathcal{L}} \times \mathbb{R}^N)$. We define the set of proper strategies for the grid operator.

Definition 2. *A strategy μ for the grid operator is proper if the following conditions hold: (i) strategy μ partitions the power system into disjoint subsystems, i.e., $\mathcal{B}_k \cap \mathcal{B}_{k'} = \emptyset$ and $\mathcal{L}_k \cap \mathcal{L}_{k'} = \emptyset$, (ii) the generators belonging to the same coherent group are within the same subsystem, (iii) each subsystem $\mathcal{G}_k$ is connected, (iv) the post-islanding power generation and voltage angle are within the generation capacity for each generator and voltage angle bound for each substation, respectively, (v) the post-islanding power flow does not exceed the transmission capacities for all transmission lines, and (vi) the post-islanding power generation meets the load demand.*

4.3   Interaction Model Between the Grid Operator and Adversary

In this subsection, we present the interaction model between the grid operator and adversary. We denote the mixed strategy of the grid operator as $\mu : \mathcal{I}^o \to \Delta(2^{\mathcal{L}}, \mathbb{R}^N)$. The adversary observes strategy μ of the grid operator by intruding into the power network and learning the strategies of the grid operator, and then computes a proper strategy τ. Then the adversary executes its attack strategy τ so as to destabilize the power system and maximize the power flow disruption. Once the grid operator detects the disturbance caused by the adversary, it samples a pair $(\tilde{\mathcal{L}}, g)$ following strategy μ, and implements the sampled action to partition the system into a collection of subsystems.

There exists information asymmetry during the interaction between the grid operator and adversary. The adversary observes the strategy of the grid operator, while the grid operator has no information on the strategy of the adversary. This information asymmetry is captured by the Stackelberg game as described in Sect. 3.2. During this interaction, since the grid operator computes strategy μ first, it becomes the leader in the Stackelberg game. The adversary, who observes the leader's strategy, is the follower in this setting.

The problem investigated in this paper is stated as follows.

Problem 1. Consider a power system $\mathcal{G} = (\mathcal{B}, \mathcal{L})$. Synthesize a proper strategy μ for the grid operator that minimizes the power flow disruption, given that the adversary observes μ and computes its best response to μ, i.e.,

$$\min_{\mu} \ \mathbb{E}_{\mu}[R(\mathcal{S}(\mu, \tau))] \tag{5a}$$

$$\text{subject to } \mu \text{ is proper} \tag{5b}$$

$$\tau \in \mathcal{BR}(\mu) \tag{5c}$$

where $\mathbb{E}_{\mu}[\cdot]$ denotes the expectation with respect to μ and $\mathcal{S}(\mu, \tau) = \hat{\mathcal{L}} \cup \tilde{\mathcal{L}} \subseteq \mathcal{L}$ is the set of tripped transmission lines that is jointly determined by μ and τ.

Note that the interaction between the grid operator and adversary is zero-sum. We can thus establish the existence of Stackelberg equilibrium strategies μ and τ of the game in Eq. (5) using [5, Sect. 2].

5   Solution Approach

In this section, we present the solution approach to Problem 1. We prove that the sets of proper strategies μ and τ can be mapped to sets of mixed integer constraints. Then the optimization problem in Eq. (5) is formulated as a mixed integer nonlinear program. We propose a double oracle algorithm based approach to compute the Stackelberg equilibrium strategies. The proposed approach computes the best response of each player in each iteration. We show that the best responses for both players can be formulated as mixed integer linear programs.

5.1   Mixed Integer Nonlinear Bi-level Optimization Formulation

In this subsection, we first map the set of proper strategies μ and τ to a set of mixed integer constraints. We then rewrite Eq. (5) as a mixed integer nonlinear bi-level optimization problem.

We let y_i be a binary variable representing if substation $i \in \mathcal{B}$ is compromised by the adversary ($y_i = 1$) or not ($y_i = 0$). We then have the following constraints:

$$\sum_{i \in B} y_i \leq C, \quad y_i \in \{0, 1\}, \ \forall i \in B. \tag{6}$$

We define $z_{i,j}^a$ as an indicator function for each transmission line (i, j) to represent if transmission line (i, j) is tripped ($z_{i,j}^a = 0$) or not ($z_{i,j}^a = 1$) by the adversary. Note that the adversary can trip a transmission line (i, j) if and only if substation i or j is compromised. We formulate this property as

$$z_{i,j}^a \in \{0, 1\}, \ z_{i,j}^a = z_{j,i}^a, \ \forall (i, j) \in \mathcal{L} \tag{7a}$$

$$z_{i,j}^a + y_i + y_j \geq 1, \ \forall i \in B, \ \forall (i, j) \in \mathcal{L}. \tag{7b}$$

We denote y as the vector obtained by stacking y_i for all $i \in B$ and z^a as the vector obtained by stacking $z_{i,j}^a$ for all $(i, j) \in \mathcal{L}$. We characterize the relations given by Eq. (6) and (7) as follows.

Lemma 1. *The set of proper strategies for the adversary is equal to the set of feasible solutions (y, z^a) to Eq. (6) and (7).*

Proof. We prove the statement using Definition 1. Consider condition (i) in Definition 1. Since $y_i \in \{0, 1\}$ for all $i \in B$, we have that if y is feasible to Eq. (6), then at most C substations can be compromised. Consider condition (ii) in Definition 1. By Definition 1 and the definitions of z^a and y, we have that $z_{i,j}^a = 0$ only if $y_i + y_j \geq 1$. However, $y_i + y_j \geq 1$ does not necessarily imply that $z_{i,j}^a = 0$, i.e., the adversary can choose to not trip transmission line (i, j) even if substation i or j is compromised. In addition, $z_{i,j}^a = 1$ must hold if $y_i + y_j = 0$. Summarizing these three possible scenarios, we have that $z_{i,j}^a$, y_i, and y_j cannot be zero simultaneously, which is equivalent to Eq. (7b). Combining the arguments above yields the lemma.   □

Consider the set of proper strategies for the grid operator. Note that the pure strategy space for the grid operator grows exponentially with respect to the number of transmission lines L. To this end, we define a set of variables for each transmission line as a compact representation of the set of proper strategies.

Let $x_{i,k}$ be a binary indicator representing if substation i is included in subsystem k ($x_{i,k} = 1$) or not ($x_{i,k} = 0$) for all $i \in B$ and $k = 1, \ldots, K$. In addition, we let $w_{i,j,k}$ be an indicator, representing if transmission line $(i, j) \in \mathcal{L}$ is included ($w_{i,j,k} = 1$) in subsystem $\mathcal{G}_k = (\mathcal{B}_k, \mathcal{L}_k)$ or not ($w_{i,j,k} = 0$). For each transmission line (i, j), we define $z_{i,j}^o$ as an indicator representing if transmission line $(i, j) \in \mathcal{L}$ is tripped ($z_{i,j}^o = 0$) or not ($z_{i,j}^o = 1$) by the grid operator. We then formulate the constraints as

$$w_{i,j,k} \in \{0, 1\}, \ w_{i,j,k} \leq x_{i,k}, \ w_{i,j,k} \leq x_{j,k}, \ \forall (i, j) \in \mathcal{L}, \ \forall k = 1, \ldots, K \tag{8a}$$

$$z_{i,j}^o = \sum_{k=1}^{K} w_{i,j,k}, \ z_{i,j}^o \in \{0, 1\}, \ z_{i,j}^o = z_{j,i}^o, \ \forall (i, j) \in \mathcal{L} \tag{8b}$$

$$\sum_{k=1}^{K} x_{i,k} \leq 1, \ \forall i \in B \tag{8c}$$

$$x_{i,k} \in \{0,1\}, \ \forall i \in \mathcal{B}, \ \forall k = 1, \ldots, K \tag{8d}$$

$$z_{i,j}^o \leq z_{i,j}^a, \ \forall (i,j) \in \mathcal{L} \tag{8e}$$

Equation (8e) captures the fact that the grid operator takes islanding action after the adversary executes the malicious attack. Hence, the grid operator cannot open a transmission line that has been tripped by the adversary.

Given the generator coherent groups, we let indicator $v_{i,k} = 1$ if generation substation i is set as the reference generator and belongs to subsystem $\mathcal{G}_k$. Then using the coherent group, we can let

$$x_{j,k} = v_{i,k}, \ \forall i, j \in \mathcal{C}_k, \tag{9}$$

where $\mathcal{C}_k$ represents the k-th generator coherent group. In addition, each subsystem $\mathcal{G}_k$ is required to be connected. In order to incorporate this constraint, we define an auxiliary flow $f_{i,j,k}$ on each transmission line (i,j) of subsystem k. Then the auxiliary flow should respect the flow conservation law given as

$$0 \leq f_{i,j,k} \leq Z z_{i,j}^o, \ \forall (i,j) \in \mathcal{L} \tag{10a}$$

$$v_{i,k} \sum_{j \in \mathcal{B}} x_{j,k} - x_{i,k} + \sum_{j \in \mathcal{T}(i)} f_{j,i,k} = \sum_{j \in \mathcal{T}(i)} f_{i,j,k}, \ \forall i \in \mathcal{B}, k = 1, \ldots, K \tag{10b}$$

where Z is a sufficiently large positive constant. The first term of Eq. (10b) implies that $\sum_{j \in \mathcal{B}} x_{j,k}$ amount of auxiliary flow originates from the reference generator of subsystem $\mathcal{G}_k$. The second term of Eq. (10b) indicates that one unit of auxiliary flow is consumed at substation i. The remaining two terms of Eq. (10b) capture the incoming and outgoing auxiliary flows at substation i.

Relations given in Eq. (8) to Eq. (10) characterize the topological properties of each subsystem $\mathcal{G}_k$. In the following, we characterize the physical properties including the power flow and voltage angle in the power system after controlled islanding is implemented.

Each generator is constrained by its generation capacity modeled as

$$\underline{g}_i \leq g_i \leq \bar{g}_i, \ \forall i \in \mathcal{B} \tag{11}$$

where $\underline{g}_i$ and $\bar{g}_i$ are the minimum and maximum power generation capacities for generation substation i, respectively. We denote the post-islanding power flow on transmission line as $\tilde{P}_{i,j}$ and voltage angle of substation i as θ_i. By Eq. (1), we have that $S_{i,j}(\theta_i - \theta_j) - \tilde{P}_{i,j} = 0$ holds for all $(i,j) \in \mathcal{L}$. To incorporate the fact that the transmission line (i,j) can be tripped by the grid operator and adversary, we have that

$$-(1 - z_{i,j}^o z_{i,j}^a)Z \leq S_{i,j}(\theta_i - \theta_j) - \tilde{P}_{i,j} \leq (1 - z_{i,j}^o z_{i,j}^a)Z, \tag{12}$$

where Z is a sufficiently large positive constant. Taking the transmission line capacity and voltage angle bound into consideration, we have

$$\underline{P}_{i,j} z_{i,j}^o z_{i,j}^a \leq \tilde{P}_{i,j} \leq \bar{P}_{i,j} z_{i,j}^o z_{i,j}^a, \ \forall (i,j) \in \mathcal{L}, \ \underline{\theta}_i \leq \theta_i \leq \bar{\theta}_i, \ \forall i \in \mathcal{B}, \tag{13}$$

where $\bar{P}_{i,j}$ and $\underline{P}_{i,j}$ are the maximal and minimal power flow capacity for transmission line (i,j), and $\underline{\theta}_i$ and $\bar{\theta}_i$ are respectively the minimum and maximum voltage angle at substation i. Using Eq. (13), we observe that the only feasible power flow through a tripped transmission line is zero. By Eq. (2), the power balance at each substation i is modeled as

$$\sum_{j \in \mathcal{T}(i)} \tilde{P}_{j,i} + g_i - d_i = 0, \ \forall i \in \mathcal{B}. \tag{14}$$

We denote w, x, v, z^o, f, $\tilde{P}$, g, and θ as the vectors or matrices that are obtained by stacking $w_{i,j,k}$, $x_{i,k}$, $v_{i,k}$, $z^o_{i,j}$ $f_{i,j,k}$, $\tilde{P}_{i,j}$, g_i, and θ_i, respectively. We characterize Eq. (8) to (14) as follows.

Lemma 2. *If variables w, x, t, z^o, f, $\tilde{P}$, g, and θ are feasible to Eq. (8) to Eq. (14), then these variables represent a proper strategy for the grid operator as given in Definition 2.*

Proof. Consider variables w, x, t, z^o, f, $\tilde{P}$, g, and θ that are feasible to Eq. (8) to Eq. (14). We then verify that conditions (i)–(vi) in Definition 2 are satisfied.

Satisfaction of Condition (i). Suppose that Eq. (8) is satisfied while the subsystems $\mathcal{G}_k$ are not disjoint. Thus we have that there exists $k \neq k'$ such that $x_{i,k} = x_{i,k'} = 1$ holds for some $i \in \mathcal{B}$ or $w_{i,j,k} = w_{i,j,k'} = 1$ holds for some $(i,j) \in \mathcal{L}$. If $x_{i,k} = x_{i,k'} = 1$ holds for some $i \in \mathcal{B}$, then Eq. (8c) is violated. $w_{i,j,k} = w_{i,j,k'} = 1$ holds for some $(i,j) \in \mathcal{L}$, then Eq. (8b) implies that $z^o_{i,j} > 1$, which leads to contradiction. Thus, condition (i) of Definition 2 is satisfied.

Satisfaction of Condition (ii). Condition (ii) holds immediately by the definition of $x_{i,k}$, $v_{i,k}$, and Eq. (9).

Satisfaction of Condition (iii). Suppose f satisfies Eq. (10) while there exists some subsystem $\mathcal{G}_k$ that is not connected. Without loss of generality, we assume that substation i belonging to subsystem $\mathcal{G}_k$ is not connected with substations $j \in \mathcal{B}_k \backslash \{i\}$. If substation i is not the k-th reference generation substation, then Eq. (10b) becomes $-x_{i,k} = 0$, which contradicts our hypothesis that $x_{i,k} = 1$. If substation i is the k-th reference generation substation, then $v_{i,k} = 1$ and Eq. (10b) is rewritten as $\sum_{j \in \mathcal{B}} x_{j,k} - x_{i,k} = 0$, which leads contradiction since there exists $j \in \mathcal{B}_k \backslash \{i\}$ such that $x_{j,k} = 1$. Therefore, we can conclude that condition (iii) of Definition 2 is satisfied when Eq. (10) is satisfied.

Satisfaction of Condition (iv). Condition (iv) follows from Eq. (11) and (13).

Satisfaction of Condition (v). Consider Eq. (13) for a transmission line (i,j). If transmission line (i,j) is tripped by either the adversary or the grid operator, then Eq. (13) implies that $\tilde{P}_{i,j} = 0$, which satisfies the power flow equation. If transmission line (i,j) is tripped by neither the adversary nor the grid operator, then power flow $\tilde{P}_{i,j}$ satisfies Eq. (1). The transmission line capacity constraint then immediately follows from Eq. (13).

Satisfaction of Condition (vi). Condition (vi) of Definition 2 holds by the definitions of $\tilde{P}_{i,j}$, g_i, d_i, and Eq. (2). □

Lemma 1 and 2 imply that we can represent the pure strategy space using a collection of variables, whose size is polynomial in terms of B and L. Using these variables, we can rewrite optimization problem (5) as

$$\min_{w,x,z^o,f,\tilde{P},g,\theta} \mathbb{E}_\mu \left[\sum_{(i,j)\in\mathcal{L}} (1 - z_{i,j}^o z_{i,j}^a) \frac{|P_{i,j}| + |P_{j,i}|}{2} \right] \tag{15a}$$

subject to Eq. (8) to Eq. (14) $\tag{15b}$

$$(y, z^a) \in \text{argmax} \sum_{(i,j)\in\mathcal{L}} (1 - z_{i,j}^o z_{i,j}^a) \frac{|P_{i,j}| + |P_{j,i}|}{2} \tag{15c}$$

subject to Eq. (6) to Eq. (7) $\tag{15d}$

Equation (15a) to (15b) and Eq. (15c) to (15d) are known as the upper and lower level of bi-level optimization program (15), respectively. We remark that although $\tilde{P}$ and θ are set as decision variables in optimization program (15), they are inherently determined once the grid topology and power generation g are given. Therefore, the upper level of Eq. (15) is interpreted as computing the partitions of the power system using z^o as a corrective measure against the malicious attack. For the power system partition z^o, the grid operator needs to compute power generation g so that there exists some feasible post-islanding DC power flow $\tilde{P}_{i,j}$ satisfies conditions (iv)–(vi) in Definition 2.

5.2   Double Oracle Algorithm Based Approach

In this subsection, we present a double oracle algorithm based approach to solve Problem 1. The proposed approach alternatively solves the upper and lower level of optimization problem (15), and converges to the Stackelberg equilibrium.

Algorithm 1. Double Oracle Algorithm for Controlled Islanding

---

1: Initialize a set of actions $(\mathcal{Z}^o, G)$ for the grid operator, with each $(z^o, g) \in (\mathcal{Z}^o, G)$ being feasible to Eq. (8) to Eq. (14)
2: Initialize a set of actions $(Y, \mathcal{Z}^a)$ for the adversary, with each $(y, z^a) \in (\mathcal{Y}, \mathcal{Z}^a)$ being feasible to Eq. (6) to Eq. (7)
3: **while** not converge **do**
4:     Solve for (μ, τ) by constraining the grid operator and adversary to take actions from $(\mathcal{Z}^o, G)$ and $(\mathcal{Y}, \mathcal{Z}^a)$, respectively
5:     Compute (z^o, g), assuming the adversary takes strategy τ
6:     $(\mathcal{Z}^o, G) \leftarrow (\mathcal{Z}^o, G) \cup (z^o, g)$
7:     Solve for (y, z^a), assuming the grid operator takes strategy μ
8:     $(\mathcal{Y}, \mathcal{Z}^a) \leftarrow (\mathcal{Y}, \mathcal{Z}^a) \cup (y, z^a)$
9: **end while**
10: **return** (μ, τ)

Algorithm 1 presents the double oracle approach. It consists of four steps. The first step is presented in lines 1 to 2 of Algorithm 1. In this step, the algorithm initializes a set of pure strategies for the grid operator and adversary, respectively. The initialized pure strategies are proper. The second step corresponds to line 4 of Algorithm 1. In this step, the algorithm solves a mixed strategy μ for the grid operator and a pure strategy τ for the adversary. The reason that pure strategy is considered for the adversary is that it is the follower in the game, whose pure strategies suffice for best response calculation [5]. Note that here mixed strategy μ defines a probability distribution over $(\mathcal{Z}^o, G)$, rather than the full strategy space. Similarly, best response τ gives an action selected from $(\mathcal{Y}, \mathcal{Z}^a)$. Lines 5 to 6 correspond to the third step of Algorithm 1. This step computes a pure strategy for the grid operator over all the feasible strategies, given that the adversary plays strategy τ. The fourth step is presented in lines 7–8 of Algorithm 1, where the adversary computes its best response to mixed strategy μ. The second to the last step of Algorithm 1 are executed in an iterative manner. The iteration terminates when no pure strategies for the grid operator and adversary are included in line 6 and line 8. The worst-case number of iterations Algorithm 1 can take to converge is $(2^L - 1)$, which is identical to solving for the Stackelberg equilibrium using linear program [5]. However, implementing the linear program requires constructing the action spaces of dimensions 2^L for the grid operator and adversary and the corresponding constraints.

Given the current set of pure strategies $(\mathcal{Z}^o, G)$ and $(\mathcal{Y}, \mathcal{Z}^a)$ for the gird operator and adversary, respectively, line 4 of Algorithm 1 can be formulated as

$$\min_{\mu, \tau, r} \sum_{z^o \in \mathcal{Z}^o} \sum_{z^a \in \mathcal{Z}^a} \mu(z^o) \tau(z^a) \sum_{(i,j) \in \mathcal{L}} \frac{1 - z^o_{i,j} z^a_{i,j}}{2} (|P_{i,j}| + |P_{j,i}|) \quad (16a)$$

$$\text{subject to} \quad \sum_{z^o \in \mathcal{Z}^o} \mu(z^o) = 1 \quad (16b)$$

$$\mu(z^o) \in [0,1], \ \forall z^o \in \mathcal{Z}^o \quad (16c)$$

$$\sum_{z^a \in \mathcal{Z}^a} \tau(z^a) = 1 \quad (16d)$$

$$\tau(z^a) \in \{0,1\}, \ \forall z^a \in \mathcal{Z}^a \quad (16e)$$

$$0 \le r - \sum_{z^o \in \mathcal{Z}^o} \mu(z^o) \sum_{(i,j) \in \mathcal{L}} \frac{1 - z^o_{i,j} z^a_{i,j}}{2} (|P_{i,j}| + |P_{j,i}|)$$

$$\le (1 - \tau(z^a))Z, \ \forall z^a \in \mathcal{Z}^a \quad (16f)$$

$$r \ge 0 \quad (16g)$$

$$\text{Eq. (6) to Eq. (14)} \quad (16h)$$

where Z is a sufficiently large positive constant. Optimization problem (16) slightly abuses the notation, and uses $\mu(z^o)$ and $\tau(z^a)$ to represent the probabilities the grid operator applies z^o and the adversary applies z^a, respectively. Constraints (16b) and (16c) ensures that μ is a well-defined mixed strategy. Constraints (16d) and (16e) capture the fact that the adversary computes a pure strategy as its best response. Constraints (16f) and (16g) quantify the optimal power flow disruption r that the adversary can cause. By Eq. (16f), we have that if the adversary plays its best response ($\tau(z^a) = 1$), then it can achieve r amount of power flow disruption. For $\tau(z^a) = 0$, constraint (16f) is satisfied trivially. Constraint (16h) guarantees that the strategies are proper.

Optimization problem (16) is a mixed integer nonlinear program (MINLP). The nonlinearity can be mitigated by defining a new variable $u_{z^o z^a}$, which is defined as $u_{z^o z^a} = \mu(z^o)\tau(z^a)$ for all z^o, z^a satisfying Eq. (16h) and $u_{z^o z^a} = 0$ otherwise. The constraints defined on $u_{z^o z^a}$ are

$$u_{z^o z^a} \in [0,1], \ \forall z^o \in \mathcal{Z}^o, \forall z^a \in \mathcal{Z}^a, \ 0 \leq \sum_{z^a \in \mathcal{Z}^a} u_{z^o z^a} \leq 1, \ \forall z^o \in \mathcal{Z}^o \tag{17a}$$

$$\sum_{z^o \in \mathcal{Z}^o} \sum_{z^a \in \mathcal{Z}^a} u_{z^o z^a} = 1. \tag{17b}$$

Using $u_{z^o z^a}$, MINLP (16) is converted to a mixed integer linear program (MILP):

$$\min_{u, \tau, r} \sum_{z^o \in \mathcal{Z}^o} \sum_{z^a \in \mathcal{Z}^a} u_{z^o z^a} \sum_{(i,j) \in \mathcal{L}} \frac{1 - z^o_{i,j} z^a_{i,j}}{2}(|P_{i,j}| + |P_{j,i}|) \tag{18a}$$

subject to   Eq. (16d), (16e), (16g), and (17) \hfill (18b)

$$0 \leq r - \sum_{z^o \in \mathcal{Z}^o} \left[\sum_{(i,j) \in \mathcal{L}} \frac{1 - z^o_{i,j} z^a_{i,j}}{2}(|P_{i,j}| + |P_{j,i}|) \right] \left[\sum_{\bar{z}^a \in \mathcal{Z}^a} u_{z^o \bar{z}^a} \right]$$
$$\leq (1 - \mathbb{P}(z^a))Z, \ \forall z^a \in \mathcal{Z}^a \tag{18c}$$

Similar techniques for converting MINLP to MILP have been used in [23]. The equivalence between MILP (18) and MINLP (16) is presented as follows.

Lemma 3. *The MINLP (16) is equivalent to the MILP (18).*

Proof. We first prove that the objective functions of MINLP (16) and MILP (18) are identical. We then show that a feasible solution to Eq. (16) is also feasible to Eq. (18), and vice versa. The equivalence between (16a) and (18a) holds by the construction of $u_{z^o z^a}$.

Let μ, τ, and r be feasible solutions to Eq. (16). Let $u_{z^o z^a} = \mu(z^o)\tau(z^a)$. We have that $u_{z^o z^a} \in [0,1]$ holds by the construction of $u_{z^o z^a}$. By the definition of $u_{z^o z^a}$, we have that $\sum_{z^o \in \mathcal{Z}^o} \sum_{z^a \in \mathcal{Z}^a} u_{z^o z^a} = 1$ holds by constraints (16b) and (16e). Inequality $0 \leq \sum_{z^a \in \mathcal{Z}^a} u_{z^o z^a} \leq 1$ holds by Eq. (16d) and the definition of $u_{z^o z^a}$. Constraint (18c) follows by substituting $u_{z^o z^a}$ into Eq. (16f).

Let u, τ, and r be feasible to Eq. (18). We prove that μ, τ, and r are feasible solutions to Eq. (16), where $\mu(z^o) = \sum_{z^a} u_{z^o z^a}$. Since $\mu(z^o) = \sum_{z^a} u_{z^o z^a}$ and $\tau(z^a) \in \{0,1\}$, we have that constraint $\sum_{z^o \in \mathcal{Z}^o} \sum_{z^a \in \mathcal{Z}^a} u_{z^o z^a} = 1$ implies that constraint (16b) holds. Using $\mu(z^o) = \sum_{z^a} u_{z^o z^a}$, constraint $0 \leq \sum_{z^a \in \mathcal{Z}^a} u_{z^o z^a} \leq 1$ can be rewritten as $0 \leq \mu(z^o) \leq 1$, i.e., constraint (16c). Similarly, the equivalence between constraints (18c) and (16f) follows by $\mu(z^o) = \sum_{z^a \in \mathcal{Z}^a} u_{z^o z^a}$. $\square$

Consider line 5 of Algorithm 1. This corresponds to Eq. (15a) to (15b) when the strategy of the adversary is fixed. Given any feasible (y, z^a) for the adversary, the grid operator solves the following optimization problem:

$$\min_{w,x,z^o,f,\tilde{P},g,\theta} \sum_{(i,j)\in\mathcal{L}} (1 - z_{i,j}^o z_{i,j}^a)\frac{|P_{i,j}| + |P_{j,i}|}{2} \tag{19a}$$

$$\text{subject to Eq. (8) to Eq. (14)} \tag{19b}$$

Equation (19) is an MILP and can be solved using commercial solvers. Note that optimization problem (19) computes a pure strategy (z^o, g) for the grid operator.

In the following, we present an MILP for line 7 of Algorithm 1, which corresponds to solving Eq. (15c) to (15d) when the strategy of the grid operator is given. Since the grid operator plays a mixed strategy, the goal of the adversary then becomes maximizing the expected power flow disruption, where the expectation is taken over mixed strategy μ. With a slight abuse of notation, we denote the probability that the grid operator trips the transmission lines corresponding to z^o as $\mu(z^o)$. The MILP corresponding to line 7 of Algorithm 1 is given as

$$\max_{y,z^a} \sum_{z^o \in \mathcal{Z}^o} \mu(z^o) \sum_{(i,j)\in\mathcal{L}} (1 - z_{i,j}^o z_{i,j}^a)\frac{|P_{i,j}| + |P_{j,i}|}{2} \tag{20a}$$

$$\text{subject to Eq. (6) to Eq. (7)} \tag{20b}$$

In the following, we show that the optimization problem (20) can be mapped to a submodular maximization problem subject to a cardinality constraint. As a consequence, a greedy algorithm is presented to solve for a pure strategy for the adversary. We relax optimization problem (20) as

$$\max_{\hat{\mathcal{B}}} \sum_{z^o \in \mathcal{Z}^o} \mu(z^o) \left[\sum_{(i,j)\in\hat{\mathcal{L}}} \frac{|P_{i,j}| + |P_{j,i}|}{2} + \sum_{(i,j)\in\tilde{\mathcal{L}}} \frac{|P_{i,j}| + |P_{j,i}|}{2} \right] \tag{21a}$$

$$\text{subject to } \hat{\mathcal{L}} = \{(i,j) \in \mathcal{L} : i \in \hat{\mathcal{B}} \text{ or } j \in \hat{\mathcal{B}}\} \tag{21b}$$

$$|\hat{\mathcal{B}}| \leq C \tag{21c}$$

where $\tilde{\mathcal{L}} \subset \mathcal{L}$ is the set of transmission lines tripped by the grid operator when taking action z^o. We characterize the relation between optimization problem (20) and (21) using the following lemma.

Lemma 4. *Given the strategy of the grid operator, the optimal solution to optimization problem (21) is identical to that of optimization problem (20).*

Proof. We omit the proof due to space constraint.   □

We now map optimization problem (21) to a problem of maximizing a submodular function subject to a cardinality constraint. We define $\chi_{i,j}(\hat{\mathcal{B}})$ as

$$\chi_{i,j}(\hat{\mathcal{B}}) = \begin{cases} 1 & \text{if } i \in \hat{\mathcal{B}} \text{ or } j \in \hat{\mathcal{B}} \\ 0 & \text{otherwise} \end{cases} \tag{22}$$

Using the definition of $\chi_{i,j}(\hat{\mathcal{B}})$, optimization problem (21) can be rewritten as

$$\max_{\hat{\mathcal{B}}} \sum_{z^o \in \mathcal{Z}^o} \mu(z^o) \sum_{(i,j) \in \mathcal{L}} \chi_{i,j}(\hat{\mathcal{B}}) \frac{|P_{i,j}| + |P_{j,i}|}{2} \tag{23a}$$

$$\text{subject to } |\hat{\mathcal{B}}| \leq C \tag{23b}$$

We have the following result.

Proposition 1. *Objective function (23a) is submodular and nondecreasing with respect to $\hat{\mathcal{B}}$.*

Proof. We first prove Eq. (23a) is submodular with respect to $\hat{\mathcal{B}}$ using the definition of submodularity. Let $\hat{\mathcal{B}}_2 \subseteq \hat{\mathcal{B}}_1 \subset \mathcal{B}$. By Eq. (22), we have that

$$\chi_{i,j}(\hat{\mathcal{B}} \cup \{h\}) - \chi_{i,j}(\hat{\mathcal{B}}) = \begin{cases} 1 & \text{if } h = i \text{ or } h = j \text{ and } i, j \notin \hat{\mathcal{B}} \\ 0 & \text{otherwise} \end{cases}, \forall \hat{\mathcal{B}} \subset \mathcal{B} \tag{24}$$

Suppose that $\chi_{i,j}(\hat{\mathcal{B}}_1 \cup \{h\}) - \chi_{i,j}(\hat{\mathcal{B}}_1) = 1$. Since $\hat{\mathcal{B}}_2 \subseteq \hat{\mathcal{B}}_1$, we have that $h = i$ or $h = j$ and $i, j \notin \hat{\mathcal{B}}_2$. Then we have that $\chi_{i,j}(\hat{\mathcal{B}}_2 \cup \{h\}) - \chi_{i,j}(\hat{\mathcal{B}}_2) = 1$. Therefore, we have that $\chi_{i,j}(\hat{\mathcal{B}}_2 \cup \{h\}) - \chi_{i,j}(\hat{\mathcal{B}}_2) \geq \chi_{i,j}(\hat{\mathcal{B}}_1 \cup \{h\}) - \chi_{i,j}(\hat{\mathcal{B}}_1)$ holds for all $\hat{\mathcal{B}}_2 \subseteq \hat{\mathcal{B}}_1 \subset \hat{\mathcal{B}}$, which implies that Eq. (22) is submodular with respect to $\hat{\mathcal{B}}$.

Consider $\hat{\mathcal{B}}_2 \subset \hat{\mathcal{B}}_1$. Then there must exist some $i \in \hat{\mathcal{B}}_1$ while $i \notin \hat{\mathcal{B}}_2$. Let $j \in \mathcal{B}$ be a substation satisfying $j \notin \hat{\mathcal{B}}_1$. Using Eq. (22), we have that $\chi_{i,j}(\hat{\mathcal{B}}_2) = 0 \leq \chi_{i,j}(\hat{\mathcal{B}}_1) = 1$. Let $j \in \mathcal{B}$ be a substation satisfying $j \in \hat{\mathcal{B}}_2$. Then we have that $\chi_{i,j}(\hat{\mathcal{B}}_2) = \chi_{i,j}(\hat{\mathcal{B}}_1) = 0$. If $j \in \hat{\mathcal{B}}_1$ holds while $j \notin \hat{\mathcal{B}}_2$ does not hold. Then we have that $\chi_{i,j}(\hat{\mathcal{B}}_2) = 0 \leq \chi_{i,j}(\hat{\mathcal{B}}_1) = 1$. Summarizing the arguments above, we have that Eq. (22) is nondecreasing with respect to $\hat{\mathcal{B}}$.

Combining the arguments above, we have that Eq. (23a) is a summation of non-negative submodular and nondecreasing functions. Therefore, Eq. (23a) is a submodular and nondecreasing function with respect to $\hat{\mathcal{B}}$. □

According to Proposition 1, optimization problem (20) is equivalent to a submodular maximization problem with cardinality constraint. Optimization problem (23) can be solved using a greedy algorithm in polynomial time [15]. It has been shown that the greedy algorithm achieves $1 - \frac{1}{e}$ optimality guarantee [15].

We conclude this section by giving the convergence and optimality of double oracle algorithm [19]. We state the result in the following lemma.

Lemma 5. *Algorithm 1 converges to the Stackelberg equilibrium within finitely many iterations if the best responses in line 5 and line 7 are calculated exactly.*

6   Numerical Evaluations

This section presents our simulation setup and numerical results. We use IEEE 9-bus, 14-bus, 30-bus, 39-bus, 57-bus, and 118-bus power systems in our evaluations [1]. All the experiments are implemented using MATLAB R2020a on a workstation with Intel(R) Xeon(R) W-2145 CPU with 3.70 GHz processor and 128 GB memory. Simulation codes can be found at [27].

Table 1. First three columns show IEEE power system case study data used in the numerical evaluations. Last two columns present the maximum number of iterations and maximum run time that Algorithm 1 takes to converge. The maximum values in the last two columns are found across a set of experiments where the adversary budget (C) is increased from $C = 1$ until adversarial actions cause the power system to fail.

IEEE dataset	Reference generators	Coherent generator groups (using bus indices)	Maximum # of iterations	Maximum run time
9-Bus	1; 3	{1,2}, {3}	1	0.07 s
14-Bus	1; 6	{1:3}, {6,8}	7	0.31 s
30-Bus	1; 13; 22	{1,2}, {13}, {22,23,27}	6	0.43 s
39-Bus	30; 31; 37	{30}, {31:36}, {37:39}	9	1.11 s
57-Bus	1; 6; 9	{1:3}, {6, 8}, {9, 10}	21	5.23 s
118-Bus	10; 46; 49; 87	{10, 12, 25, 26, 31}, {46}, {49, 54, 59, 61, 65, 66, 69, 80}, {87, 89, 100, 103, 111}	16	62.70 s

6.1 Simulation Setup

We extract the topology of power system, transmission line susceptance, load demands, generator capacities, transmission line capacities, and voltage angle bounds from the IEEE case study datasets [1]. The power flow in the system at the initial operating point is computed using Matpower [36]. The reference generators and generator coherent groups are chosen as in Table 1.

We initialize Algorithm 1 using adversary *pure* strategies that result in the four largest DC power flow disruptions to the system, a grid operator *pure* islanding strategy in the absence of any adversary (solution to optimization problem in Eq. (19) with $z_{i,j}^a = 1$ for all $(i, j) \in \mathcal{L}$) and corresponding grid operator and adversary best responses, respectively.

We evaluate the performance of our approach by comparing the DC power flow disruption resulting from Algorithm 1 and a baseline case. A grid operator in the baseline case computes an islanding strategy without considering the presence of an adversary, i.e., the grid operator solves Eq. (19) with $z_{i,j}^a = 1$ for all $(i, j) \in \mathcal{L}$. The adversary in baseline observes the islanding strategy computed by the grid operator, and computes its best response by solving Eq. (4). Let $\mathcal{S}_{\mathbf{S}}$ and $\mathcal{S}_{\mathbf{B}}$ denote the transmission lines tripped in the proposed model (Algorithm 1) and baseline case, respectively. We denote the DC power flow disruption corresponding to Algorithm 1 and baseline as $R(\mathcal{S}_{\mathbf{S}})$ and $R(\mathcal{S}_{\mathbf{B}})$, respectively.

6.2 Case Study Results

Figure 1 illustrates the grid operator islanding strategy and adversary strategy obtained using Algorithm 1 on IEEE 39-bus data for adversary budget, $C = 8$. The grid operator performs islanding strategy 1 with probability (w.p.) 0.27 and islanding strategy 2 w.p. 0.73. In this case study we obtain $R(\mathcal{S}_{\mathbf{B}}) \approx 10.04$ GW

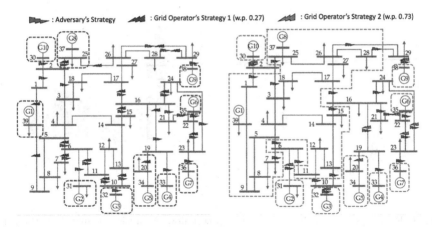

Fig. 1. Grid operator and adversary strategies obtained using Algorithm 1 on IEEE 39-bus data for adversary budget, $C = 8$. The islands induced by the grid operator and adversary strategies are marked by the dotted lines.

and $R(\mathcal{S_S}) \approx 10.22$ GW. Hence, by committing to the islanding strategy given by Algorithm 1, the grid operator incurs ~180 MW less DC power flow disruption.

Figure 2-(a) plots the reduced DC power flow disruption achieved by the grid operator via committing to an islanding strategy given by Algorithm 1 (i.e., $R(\mathcal{S_B})$ - $R(\mathcal{S_S})$) for different values of adversary budget, C, under each test case given in Table 1. We construct a set of *attack scenarios* by increasing the values of C from $C = 1$ until the value of C breaks down the grid (i.e., all the generators are isolated into individual islands). The results show that the grid operator achieves a better performance by committing to a strategy of Algorithm 1 under some attack scenarios and in other scenarios the grid operator achieves the same performance as committing to a baseline strategy. Algorithm 1 and the baseline achieve same performance when equilibrium strategies of the adversary and the grid operator do not contain any common set of transmission lines.

Figure 2-(b) shows the percentage of attack scenarios where the grid operator is able to achieve lower DC power flow disruption by committing to a strategy given by Algorithm 1. We only consider the attack scenarios that does not break down the grid when computing the related percentage values. The results suggest that on average grid operator is able to perform better in 44% of the attack scenarios and save 12.27 MW when committing to a strategy of Algorithm 1.

Last two columns of Table 1 present the maximum number of iterations and maximum run time of Algorithm 1 to converge across the attack scenarios considered under each case study. The results show that Algorithm 1 takes less than 21 iterations to converge for the cases analyzed. Also, run time to converge is less than 63 seconds in Algorithm 1 for the largest dataset (IEEE-118 bus) analyzed. For other cases, Algorithm 1 finds the optimal strategies in less than 5.23 seconds. Note that the worst-case number of iterations Algorithm 1 can take to converge is $(2^L - 1)$, (i.e., worst-case computation time is exponential in L).

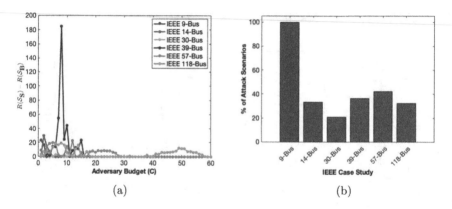

Fig. 2. Figure-(a) shows the reduced DC power flow disruption achieved by the grid operator via committing to an islanding strategy given by Algorithm 1 ($R(\mathcal{S_B})$) compared to a baseline case ($R(\mathcal{S_S})$). Figure-(b) shows the percentage of attack scenarios where the grid operator performs better by committing to a strategy given by Algorithm 1.

Therefore, the results suggest that Algorithm 1 converges with substantially less number of iterations compared with the worst-case bound.

7   Conclusion

In this paper, we studied the problem of controlled islanding of a power system in the presence of a malicious adversary. We formulated the interaction between the grid operator and adversary as a Stackelberg game. The grid operator first synthesizes a mixed strategy for controlled islanding, as well as the power generation for the post-islanding system. The adversary observes the islanding strategy of the grid operator. The adversary then compromises a subset of substations in the power system and trips the transmission lines that are connected with the compromised substations. We formulated an MINLP to compute the Stackelberg equilibrium of the game. To mitigate the computational challenge incurred by solving MINLP, we proposed a double oracle algorithm based approach to solve for the equilibrium strategies. The proposed approach solved a sequence of MILPs that model the best responses for both players. Additionally, we proved that the adversary's best response can be formulated as a submodular maximization problem under a cardinality constraint. We compared the proposed approach with a baseline, where the grid operator computes an islanding strategy by minimizing the power flow disruption without taking into account the adversary's response, using IEEE 9-bus, 14-bus, 30-bus, 39-bus, 57-bus, and 118-bus systems. The proposed approach outperformed the baseline in about 44% of test cases and saved about 12.27 MW power flow disruption on average.

References

1. Illinois center for a smarter electric grid (ICSEG). https://icseg.iti.illinois.edu/power-cases/
2. Abur, A., Exposito, A.G.: Power System State Estimation: Theory and Implementation. CRC Press (2004)
3. Bosansky, B., Kiekintveld, C., Lisy, V., Pechoucek, M.: An exact double-oracle algorithm for zero-sum extensive-form games with imperfect information. J. Artif. Intell. Res. **51**, 829–866 (2014)
4. Chow, J.H.: Time-Scale Modeling of Dynamic Networks with Applications to Power Systems, vol. 46. Springer, Heidelberg (1982). https://doi.org/10.1007/BFb0044327
5. Conitzer, V.: On stackelberg mixed strategies. Synthese **193**(3), 689–703 (2016)
6. Delgadillo, A., Arroyo, J.M., Alguacil, N.: Analysis of electric grid interdiction with line switching. IEEE Trans. Power Syst. **25**(2), 633–641 (2009)
7. Demetriou, P., Asprou, M., Kyriakides, E.: A real-time controlled islanding and restoration scheme based on estimated states. IEEE Trans. Power Syst. **34**(1), 606–615 (2018)
8. Deng, R., Xiao, G., Lu, R.: Defending against false data injection attacks on power system state estimation. IEEE Trans. Ind. Inf. **13**(1), 198–207 (2015)
9. Ding, L., Gonzalez-Longatt, F.M., Wall, P., Terzija, V.: Two-step spectral clustering controlled islanding algorithm. IEEE Trans. Power Syst. **28**(1), 75–84 (2012)
10. Haque, M., Rahim, A.: Identification of coherent generators using energy function. In: IEE Proceedings C (Generation, Transmission and Distribution), vol. 137, pp. 255–260. IET (1990)
11. Hasan, S., Ghafouri, A., Dubey, A., Karsai, G., Koutsoukos, X.: Vulnerability analysis of power systems based on cyber-attack and defense models. In: 2018 IEEE Power & Energy Society Innovative Smart Grid Technologies Conference, pp. 1–5. IEEE (2018)
12. Henner, V.: A network separation scheme for emergency control. Int. J. Electr. Power Energy Syst. **2**(2), 109–114 (1980)
13. Jain, M., Korzhyk, D., Vaněk, O., Conitzer, V., Pěchouček, M., Tambe, M.: A double oracle algorithm for zero-sum security games on graphs. In: The 10th International Conference on Autonomous Agents and Multiagent Systems, vol. 1, pp. 327–334 (2011)
14. Karwowski, J., Mańdziuk, J.: Double-oracle sampling method for Stackelberg equilibrium approximation in general-sum extensive-form games. In: Proceedings of the AAAI Conference on Artificial Intelligence, vol. 34, pp. 2054–2061 (2020)
15. Krause, A., Golovin, D.: Submodular function maximization. Tractability **3**, 71–104 (2014)
16. Lee, M.R., Assante, J.M., Conway, T.: Analysis of the cyber attack on the Ukrainian power grid. https://www.eisac.com/cartella/Asset/00006542/TLP_WHITE_E-ISAC_SANS_Ukraine_DUC_6_Modular_ICS_Malware%20Final.pdf?parent=64412
17. Liu, J., Xiao, Y., Li, S., Liang, W., Chen, C.P.: Cyber security and privacy issues in smart grids. IEEE Commun. Surv. Tutor. **14**(4), 981–997 (2012)
18. Liu, Z., Clark, A., Bushnell, L., Kirschen, D.S., Poovendran, R.: Controlled islanding via weak submodularity. IEEE Trans. Power Syst. **34**(3), 1858–1868 (2018)
19. McMahan, H.B., Gordon, G.J., Blum, A.: Planning in the presence of cost functions controlled by an adversary. In: Proceedings of the 20th International Conference on Machine Learning, pp. 536–543 (2003)

250   L. Niu et al.

20. Mo, Y., et al.: Cyber-physical security of a smart grid infrastructure. Proc. IEEE **100**(1), 195–209 (2011)
21. Muir, A., Lopatto, J.: Final report on the August 14, 2003 blackout in the United States and Canada: causes and recommendations (2004)
22. Nedic, D.P., Dobson, I., Kirschen, D.S., Carreras, B.A., Lynch, V.E.: Criticality in a cascading failure blackout model. Int. J. Electr. Power Energy Syst. **28**(9), 627–633 (2006)
23. Paruchuri, P., Kraus, S., Pearce, J.P., Marecki, J., Tambe, M., Ordonez, F.: Playing games for security: An efficient exact algorithm for solving Bayesian Stackelberg games. In: International Foundation for Autonomous Agents and Multiagent Systems (2008)
24. Patsakis, G., Rajan, D., Aravena, I., Oren, S.: Strong mixed-integer formulations for power system islanding and restoration. IEEE Trans. Power Syst. **34**(6), 4880–4888 (2019)
25. Peiravi, A., Ildarabadi, R.: A fast algorithm for intentional islanding of power systems using the multilevel kernel k-means approach. J. Appl. Sci. **9**(12), 2247–2255 (2009)
26. Pita, J., et al.: Using game theory for Los Angeles airport security. AI Mag. **30**(1), 43 (2009)
27. Sahabandu, D.: Controlled islanding code. https://github.com/sdinuka/Controlled-Islanding-Code
28. Sun, K., Zheng, D.Z., Lu, Q.: Splitting strategies for islanding operation of large-scale power systems using OBDD-based methods. IEEE Trans. Power Syst. **18**(2), 912–923 (2003)
29. Wang, W., Lu, Z.: Cyber security in the smart grid: survey and challenges. Comput. Netw. **57**(5), 1344–1371 (2013)
30. Yang, B., Vittal, V., Heydt, G.T., Sen, A.: A novel slow coherency based graph theoretic islanding strategy. In: 2007 IEEE Power Engineering Society General Meeting, pp. 1–7. IEEE (2007)
31. Yang, Q., Yang, J., Yu, W., An, D., Zhang, N., Zhao, W.: On false data-injection attacks against power system state estimation: Modeling and countermeasures. IEEE Trans. Parallel Distrib. Syst. **25**(3), 717–729 (2013)
32. Yardley, J., Harris, G.: 2nd day of power failures cripples wide swath of India. https://www.nytimes.com/2012/08/01/world/asia/power-outages-hit-600-million-in-india.html
33. You, H., Vittal, V., Wang, X.: Slow coherency-based islanding. IEEE Trans. Power Syst. **19**(1), 483–491 (2004)
34. Zhao, Q., Sun, K., Zheng, D.Z., Ma, J., Lu, Q.: A study of system splitting strategies for island operation of power system: a two-phase method based on OBDDs. IEEE Trans. Power Syst. **18**(4), 1556–1565 (2003)
35. Zhu, Y., Yan, J., Sun, Y., He, H.: Revealing cascading failure vulnerability in power grids using risk-graph. IEEE Trans. Parallel Distrib. Syst. **25**(12), 3274–3284 (2014)
36. Zimmerman, R.D., Murillo-Sánchez, C.E., Thomas, R.J.: MATPOWER: steady-state operations, planning, and analysis tools for power systems research and education. IEEE Trans. Power Syst. **26**(1), 12–19 (2010)

Game Theoretic Hardware Trojan Testing Under Cost Considerations

Swastik Brahma[1(✉)], Laurent Njilla[2(✉)], and Satyaki Nan[1(✉)]

[1] Department of Computer Science, Tennessee State University, Nashville, TN, USA
{sbrahma,snan}@tnstate.edu
[2] Cyber Assurance Branch, Air Force Research Laboratory, Rome, NY, USA
laurent.njilla@us.af.mil

Abstract. In this paper, we consider the problem of testing integrated circuits (ICs) to check for the presence of hardware Trojans from a game theoretic perspective. Under consideration of complex cost structures involved in the testing process, the paper analytically characterizes the Nash Equilibrium (NE) strategy of a malicious manufacturer for inserting a hardware Trojan into a manufactured IC and that of a defender for testing the acquired IC to check for the presence of Trojans. The paper first considers the defender, who incurs testing costs, to be capable of testing one Trojan type and analytically characterizes the NE of such a scenario. The paper also considers the scenario where the defender can test an IC to check for the presence of multiple types of Trojans under a cost budget constraint and analytically characterizes the NE of such a game. Numerous numerical results are presented in the paper that provide important insights into the game theoretic strategies presented.

Keywords: Game Theory · Hardware Trojans · Security

1 Introduction

A hardware Trojan is a malicious alteration of the circuitry of an integrated circuit (IC) [7]. The presence of hardware Trojans in ICs can lead to disastrous consequences [7,12,15], including leakage of confidential information from a system, derangement of system operation, and even complete system failure. For example, the failure of a Syrian radar system to warn about an incoming assault has been largely attributed to the presence of malicious circuitry in the system's components [1]. Such attacks have become a serious threat to the semiconductor industry and to modern cyber systems with the outsourcing trends of manufacturing processes in today's economy exacerbating integrity concerns regarding manufactured ICs.

This work was supported in part by the NSF under Award Number HRD 1912414 and in part by the Air Force under PIA FA8750-19-3-1000.
DISTRIBUTION A. Approved for public release. Distribution unlimited. Case Number AFRL-2021-3034. Dated 08 Sep 2021.

B. Bošanský et al. (Eds.): GameSec 2021, LNCS 13061, pp. 251–270, 2021.
https://doi.org/10.1007/978-3-030-90370-1_14

The primary technique that past work [2–5,7,8,16–18] has focused on for mitigating threats from hardware Trojans is the development of testing strategies that can check for the presence of Trojans in acquired ICs. For example, in [2], the authors have used random sequences of test patterns that can generate noticeable differences between the power profile of a genuine IC and its Trojan counterpart for the detection of Trojans, but the effectiveness of the proposed scheme is limited in terms of the manufacturing processes, behavior and the size of the inserted Trojans. In [3], the authors propose a method that seeks to detect and estimate the locations of hardware Trojans in ICs using region-based partitioning. Again, in [8], the authors propose a technique, referred to as MERO (Multiple Excitation of Rare Occurence), that maximizes the probability of detecting an inserted Trojan using statistical methods. Since exhaustive testing of all possible Trojan types can be prohibitive, the works in [6,10,11,13,14] develop game theoretic [9] hardware Trojan testing strategies that can intelligently determine which Trojan types should an IC be tested for against a strategic malicious manufacturer. Specifically, the work in [10] presents a two-person Trojan detection game, but limits investigation of the equilibrium to an example scenario of the model. The works in [11,13,14] limit themselves to the use of software-based techniques for analyzing game theoretic testing strategies. In [6], the authors characterize equilibrium strategies for performing testing while, however, ignoring the costs incurred in the testing process.

In contrast to the aforementioned works on developing testing strategies using game theory, in this paper, we investigate game theoretic hardware Trojan testing under consideration of the costs incurred in the testing process and analytically characterize the Nash Equilibrium (NE) strategies as closed-form expressions. It should be noted that, to the best of our knowledge, analytical characterization of NE strategies in closed-forms under testing cost considerations remains an unsolved problem in past work. Specifically, the main contributions of the paper are as follows:

– We present game theoretic models that consider the costs incurred by a defender (i.e., the buyer of an IC) to perform testing and analytically characterize the NE strategies for Trojan insertion (from the perspective of a malicious manufacturer) and testing (from the perspective of the defender) in closed-forms.
– We first consider the scenario where the defender, who incurs costs for performing testing, is capable of testing the acquired IC for one Trojan type and analytically characterize the NE of such a game, which provide important insights into the impact of testing costs on the equilibrium solution.
– We also consider the general scenario where the defender can choose to test the acquired IC against multiple Trojan types under a cost budget constraint and analytically characterize the NE of such a Trojan insertion-testing game under consideration of the availability of various amounts of the defender's cost budget.
– Numerous numerical results are presented to gain important insights into the game theoretic strategies presented in the paper.

The rest of the paper is organized as follows. Section 2 presents our game theoretic model and results where the defender is capable of testing one Trojan type under consideration of the costs incurred for performing testing. Section 3 presents our game theoretic model and results where the defender can select multiple Trojan types for testing under a cost budget constraint. Section 4 presents numerical results that provide important insights into the game theoretic strategies presented. Finally, Sect. 5 concludes the paper.

2   Game Theoretic Trojan Testing Under Cost Considerations

In this section, we consider the problem of performing game theoretic hardware Trojan testing where a defender D (who corresponds to the buyer of an IC) can test the acquired IC to check for the presence of one Trojan type and a malicious manufacturer (referred to as the attacker (A)) can insert a single Trojan type into a manufactured IC. We investigate the game where the defender can choose to test an IC against multiple types of Trojans under a cost budget constraint in Sect. 3.

Consider that there are N types of Trojans, viz. $\{1, \cdots, N\}$. Also, consider that the attacker (A) chooses to insert Trojan type $i \in \{1, \cdots, N\}$ with a probability q_i into a manufactured IC (such that $0 \leq \sum_{i=1}^{N} q_i \leq 1$) and that the defender D tests the IC to check for the presence of Trojan type i with a probability p_i (such that $0 \leq \sum_{i=1}^{N} p_i \leq 1$). Note that we consider that the attacker does not insert any Trojan with a probability $q_0 = 1 - \sum_{i=1}^{N} q_i$, in which case the defender obtains a benefit B^S from putting the IC to desired use. Also, note that we allow the defender in our model to not test the acquired IC to check for the presence of any Trojan with a probability $p_0 = 1 - \sum_{i=1}^{N} p_i$. Further, we consider that the defender incurs a cost c_i to test the IC for the presence of Trojan type $i \in \{1, \cdots, N\}$ and that if the defender tests the IC against the inserted Trojan type, the Trojan is detected, and the malicious manufacturer is imposed a fine F. However, if the defender tests the IC for the presence of a Trojan type which was not inserted by the attacker, or chooses not to test the IC, the inserted Trojan (if the attacker chose to insert one) remains undetected and we consider that an undetected Trojan of type $i \in \{1, \cdots, N\}$ causes the defender to incur damage V_i (and provides a benefit V_i to the attacker). The strategic interactions between the defender and the attacker, in this paper, is modeled as a zero-sum game. Note that in our model we consider the testing costs incurred by the defender to positively impact the attacker's utility reflecting the 'satisfaction' the attacker derives from making the defender incur costs for defending against attacks.

For illustration, the payoff matrix of the game when $N = 2$ is shown in Table 1. As can be seen from the table, the strategy of the attacker not inserting any Trojan is a strictly dominated strategy (i.e., we have $\sum_{i=1}^{N} q_i = 1$ at NE). The NE of the game, as can be seen from the table, depends on the relationships among cost structures of the game. Specifically, the game can have pure strategy

Table 1. Payoff matrix of the game when $N = 2$.

Defender\Attacker	$Don't\ insert\ Trojan$	$Insert\ Trojan\ type\ 1$	$Insert\ Trojan\ type\ 2$
$Don't\ test\ IC$	$B^S, -B^S$	$-V_1, V_1$	$-V_2, V_2$
$Test\ Trojan\ type\ 1$	$B^S - c_1, c_1 - B^S$	$F - c_1, c_1 - F$	$-V_2 - c_1, V_2 + c_1$
$Test\ Trojan\ type\ 2$	$B^S - c_2, c_2 - B^S$	$-V_1 - c_2, V_1 + c_2$	$F - c_2, c_2 - F$

Nash equilibria which corresponds to the attacker inserting any Trojan type $i \in \{1, \cdots, N\}$ for which $V_i = \max_{j \in \{1, \cdots, N\}} V_j$ and $F \leq c_i - V_i$, and the defender choosing not to test the IC for the presence of any Trojan. It is easy to show that there does not exist any profitable unilateral deviation from such a strategy profile. However, with the attacker's strategy of not inserting a Trojan being strictly dominated (and therefore never adopted by the attacker) as noted above, if $F > c_i - V_i \ \forall i \in \{1, \cdots, N\}$, the defender's strategy of not testing the IC becomes strictly dominated and the game no longer has a pure strategy NE. We provide the mixed strategy NE in this scenario in the next theorem.

Theorem 1. *At NE,*

- *the defender, for any chosen $i \in \{1, \cdots, N\}$, tests the acquired IC to check for the presence of Trojan type i with a probability $p_i = \dfrac{1 - \sum_{j=1, j \neq i}^{N} \frac{(V_j - V_i)}{F + V_j}}{1 + \sum_{j=1, j \neq i}^{N} \frac{F + V_i}{F + V_j}}$ and tests the IC for the presence of Trojan type j with a probability $p_j = \dfrac{(V_j - V_i)}{F + V_j} + \dfrac{p_i(F + V_i)}{F + V_j}, \forall j \in \{1, \cdots, N\}, j \neq i$, and*
- *the attacker, for any chosen $i \in \{1, \cdots, N\}$, inserts Trojan type i into the manufactured IC with a probability $q_i = \dfrac{1 - \sum_{j=1, j \neq i}^{N} \frac{c_i - c_j}{F + V_j}}{1 + \sum_{j=1, j \neq i}^{N} \frac{F + V_j}{F + V_i}}$ and inserts Trojan type j with a probability $q_j = \dfrac{q_i(F + V_i)}{F + V_j} + \dfrac{c_j - c_i}{F + V_j}, \forall j \in \{1, \cdots, N\}, j \neq i$.*

Proof. The expected utility (say, E_D^i) of the defender D from testing the acquired IC to check for the presence of Trojan type $i \in \{1, \cdots, N\}$ is

$$E_D^i = (F - c_i)q_i + \sum_{j=1, j \neq i}^{N} (-V_j - c_i)q_j \qquad (1)$$

At the mixed strategy NE, since the defender must become indifferent over its undominated strategy space, we must have $E_D^1 = E_D^2 = \cdots = E_D^N$. Now, for $i, j \in \{1, \cdots, N\}, i \neq j$, equating $E_D^i = E_D^j$, after some simplifications, we get

$$q_j = \frac{q_i(F + V_i)}{F + V_j} + \frac{c_j - c_i}{F + V_j} \qquad (2)$$

Further, since not inserting a Trojan is a strictly dominated strategy for the attacker, in the attacker's adopted strategy, for any $i \in \{1, \cdots, N\}$, we have

$$q_i + \sum_{j=1,j\neq i}^{N} q_j = 1 \tag{3}$$

$$\Rightarrow q_i + \sum_{j=1,j\neq i}^{N} \frac{q_i(F+V_i)}{F+V_j} + \frac{c_j - c_i}{F+V_j} = 1 \quad \text{(using (2))}$$

$$\Rightarrow q_i = \frac{1 - \sum_{j=1,j\neq i}^{N} \frac{c_i - c_j}{F+V_i}}{1 + \sum_{j=1,j\neq i}^{N} \frac{F+V_j}{F+V_i}} \tag{4}$$

Clearly, from the above, if the attacker, for any chosen $i \in \{1, \cdots, N\}$, chooses q_i as given in (4) and q_j, $\forall j \in \{1, \cdots, N\}, j \neq i$, as given in (2), the defender becomes indifferent over its undominated strategy space making any strategy of defender (such that $\sum_{i=1}^{N} p_i = 1$) to become a best response against the attacker's strategy (as well as it is ensured that $\sum_{i=1}^{N} q_i = 1$, which is needed since the attacker's strategy of not inserting any Trojan is a strictly dominated strategy).

Now, the expected utility (say, E_A^i) of the attacker A from choosing to insert Trojan type $i \in \{1, \cdots, N\}$ into the manufactured IC is

$$E_A^i = (c_i - F)p_i + \sum_{j=1,j\neq i}^{N} (V_i + c_j)p_j \tag{5}$$

At the mixed strategy NE, since the attacker must also become indifferent over its undominated strategy space, we must have $E_A^1 = E_A^2 = \cdots = E_A^N$. Now, for $i,j \in \{1, \cdots, N\}, i \neq j$, equating $E_A^i = E_A^j$, after some simplifications, we get

$$p_j = \frac{(V_j - V_i)}{F+V_j} + \frac{p_i(F+V_i)}{F+V_j} \tag{6}$$

Further, when $F > c_i - V_i \ \forall i \in \{1, \cdots, N\}$, since the defender's strategy of not testing the IC becomes strictly dominated, in the defender's adopted strategy, for any $i \in \{1, \cdots, N\}$, we have

$$p_i + \sum_{j=1,j\neq i}^{N} p_j = 1 \tag{7}$$

$$\Rightarrow p_i + \sum_{j=1,j\neq i}^{N} \frac{(V_j - V_i)}{F+V_j} + \frac{p_i(F+V_i)}{F+V_j} = 1 \quad \text{(using (6))}$$

$$\Rightarrow p_i = \frac{1 - \sum_{j=1,j\neq i}^{N} \frac{(V_j - V_i)}{F+V_j}}{1 + \sum_{j=1,j\neq i}^{N} \frac{F+V_i}{F+V_j}} \tag{8}$$

Clearly, if the defender, for any chosen $i \in \{1, \cdots, N\}$, chooses p_i as given in (8) and p_j, $\forall j \in \{1, \cdots, N\}, j \neq i$ as given in (6), the attacker becomes indifferent over its undominated strategy space making any strategy of the attacker (such that $\sum_{i=1}^{N} q_i = 1$) to become a best response against the defender's strategy (as well as it is ensured that $\sum_{i=1}^{N} p_i = 1$, which is needed since the defender's strategy of not testing the IC is a strictly dominated strategy).

Thus, in summary, if the attacker, for any chosen $i \in \{1, \cdots, N\}$, chooses q_i as given in (4) and $q_j, \forall j \in \{1, \cdots, N\}, j \neq i$ as given in (2) and if the defender, for any chosen $i \in \{1, \cdots, N\}$, chooses p_i as given in (8) and $p_j, \forall j \in \{1, \cdots, N\}$, $j \neq i$ as given in (6), both the defender and the attacker would be playing their best responses against each other. This proves the theorem.

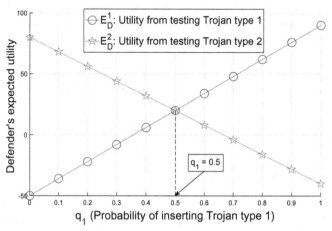

(a) Defender's expected utility versus the attacker's strategies.

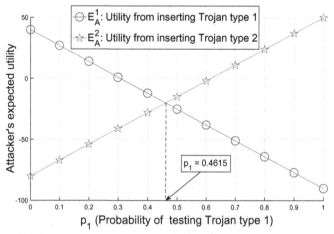

(b) Attacker's expected utility versus the defender's strategies.

Fig. 1. Expected utilities of the defender and the attacker versus their opponents' strategies.

We now provide numerical results to corroborate Theorem 1. In Fig. 1, we show the expected utilities of the defender and the attacker versus their opponents' strategies. For the figure, we consider two Trojan types, viz. $\{1, 2\}$, with $V_1 = 20$, $V_2 = 40$, $F = 100$, $c_1 = 10$, and $c_2 = 20$. In Fig. 1(a), we show the defender's expected utility versus the probability (q_1) with which the attacker inserts Trojan type 1 into the manufactured IC (considering $q_2 = 1 - q_1$). Using (1), the blue line represents the defender's expected utility (E_D^1) from testing the acquired IC to check for the presence of Trojan type 1 and the red line represents the defender's expected utility (E_D^2) from testing the IC to check for the presence of Trojan type 2. The point where the two lines intersect makes the defender's expected utility obtained from testing the IC against Trojan type 1 to be equal to that obtained from testing against Trojan type 2 (as needed at the mixed strategy NE), which, as can be seen from the figure, occurs at $q_1 = 0.5$ (with $q_2 = 1 - 0.5 = 0.5$). It can be verified that the mixed strategy NE of the attacker obtained from Theorem 1 is also $q_1 = 0.5$ and $q_2 = 0.5$.

In Fig. 1(b), we show the attacker's expected utility versus the probability (p_1) with which the defender tests an acquired IC to check for the presence of Trojan type 1 (considering $p_2 = 1 - p_1$). Using (5), the blue line represents the attacker's expected utility (E_A^1) from inserting Trojan type 1 into the manufactured IC and the red line represents the attacker's expected utility (E_A^2) from inserting Trojan type 2. The point where the two lines intersect makes the attacker's expected utility obtained from inserting Trojan type 1 to be equal to that obtained from inserting Trojan type 2 (as needed at the mixed strategy NE), which, as can be seen from the figure, occurs at $p_1 = 0.4615$ (with $p_2 = 1 - 0.4615 = 0.5385$). It can be verified that the mixed strategy NE of the defender obtained from Theorem 1 is also $p_1 = 0.4615$ and $p_2 = 0.5385$. This corroborates Theorem 1.

3   Game Theoretic Trojan Testing Under a Cost Budget Constraint

In this section, we consider that the defender can test for the presence of multiple types of Trojans under a cost budget constraint in a game theoretic context. Similar to Sect. 2, we consider that there are N types of Trojans, viz., $\{1, \cdots, N\}$, with the attacker's strategy denoted as $\mathbf{q} = (q_1, \cdots, q_N)$, where q_i is the probability of the attacker inserting Trojan type $i \in \{1, \cdots, N\}$ into the manufactured IC such that $0 \leq \sum_{i=1}^{N} q_i \leq 1$. We denote the defender's strategy as $\mathbf{p} = (p_1, \cdots, p_N)$, where p_i is the probability with which the defender tests the acquired IC to check for the presence of Trojan type $i \in \{1, \cdots, N\}$, and consider that the defender incurs a cost c_i for testing the IC against Trojan type i. In this section, we allow the defender to test the IC against multiple Trojan types without exceeding a cost budget C such that $\sum_{i=1}^{N} p_i c_i \leq C$. If the set of Trojan types tested by the defender contains the Trojan type inserted by the attacker, the inserted Trojan is considered to be detected and the malicious manufacturer in such a case is imposed a fine F. However, if the set of Trojan types tested by the defender does not contain the Trojan type inserted by the attacker, the inserted Trojan remains undetected and we consider that an undetected Trojan of type $i \in \{1, \cdots, N\}$ makes the defender incur damage V_i. In case the attacker does not insert any Trojan into the manufactured IC, the defender is considered to obtain a benefit B^S from putting the IC to desired use. The expected utility of the defender in such a game is

$$E_D(\mathbf{p}, \mathbf{q}) = B^S \Big(1 - \sum_{i=1}^{N} q_i\Big) + \sum_{i=1}^{N} \big[p_i q_i F - (1 - p_i) q_i V_i \big] \tag{9}$$

Denoting

$$\gamma_i(p_i) = p_i F - (1 - p_i) V_i - B^S \tag{10}$$

we can rewrite (9) as

$$E_D(\mathbf{p}, \mathbf{q}) = B^S + \sum_{i=1}^{N} \gamma_i(p_i) q_i \tag{11}$$

From a game theoretic perspective, the goal of the *defender* is to choose $\mathbf{p} = (p_1, \cdots, p_N)$ such that (11) is maximized (under consideration of the attacker optimizing against the defender's strategy) and that of the *attacker* is to choose $\mathbf{q} = (q_1, \cdots, q_N)$ such that (11) is minimized (under consideration of the defender optimizing against the attacker's strategy). The game is clearly a zero-sum game. Therefore, the NE of the game (which would coincide with its saddle point) corresponds to choosing $(\mathbf{p}, \mathbf{q})$ that solves the following optimization problem:

$$\max_{\mathbf{p}} \min_{\mathbf{q}} E_D(\mathbf{p}, \mathbf{q}) = \min_{\mathbf{q}} \max_{\mathbf{p}} E_D(\mathbf{p}, \mathbf{q}) \tag{P1}$$

$$\text{subject to: } \sum_{i=1}^{N} p_i c_i \leq C$$

$$\sum_{i=1}^{N} q_i \leq 1$$

To characterize $(\mathbf{p}, \mathbf{q})$ in the above game, we first prove some properties of $\gamma_i(p_i)$ (10).

Lemma 1. $\gamma_i(p_i)$ *as defined in* (10) *is a strictly increasing function of* p_i *having the slope* $F + V_i$, *with* $\gamma_i(p_i) = 0$ *when* $p_i = \frac{B^S + V_i}{F + V_i}$.

Proof. Clearly, $\frac{d(\gamma_i(p_i))}{dp_i} = F + V_i > 0$. Again, equating $\gamma_i(p_i) = 0$ yields $p_i = \frac{B^S + V_i}{F + V_i}$.

In the following, we characterize $(\mathbf{p}, \mathbf{q})$ at NE in the game described above by considering three possible cases in terms of the available cost budget (C) of the defender, viz., $C > \sum_{i=1}^{N} \frac{B^S + V_i}{F + V_i} c_i$, $C = \sum_{i=1}^{N} \frac{B^S + V_i}{F + V_i} c_i$, and $C < \sum_{i=1}^{N} \frac{B^S + V_i}{F + V_i} c_i$.

Now, note that, in the case where $C > \sum_{i=1}^{N} \frac{B^S+V_i}{F+V_i} c_i$, there exists $p_i > \frac{B^S+V_i}{F+V_i} \forall i \in \{1, \cdots, N\}$ such that $\sum_{i=1}^{N} p_i c_i \leq C$. Thus, the NE in this case corresponds to the defender testing the acquired IC to check for the presence of every Trojan type $i \in \{1, \cdots, N\}$ with a probability $p_i > \frac{B^S+V_i}{F+V_i}$ (while satisfying the cost budget constraint) and the attacker not inserting any Trojan into the manufactured IC (i.e., choosing $q_i = 0, \forall i \in \{1, \cdots, N\}$). Clearly, against the defender's strategy of choosing every $p_i > \frac{B^S+V_i}{F+V_i}$ (which makes every $\gamma_i(p_i) > 0$ following Lemma 1), the attacker's best response becomes choosing every $q_i = 0$ (since the attacker seeks to minimize (11)). Again, against the attacker's strategy of choosing every $q_i = 0$, clearly there does not exist any profitable unilateral deviation for the defender from its aforementioned strategy, which proves the above NE.

Next, we characterize the NE for the case where $C = \sum_{i=1}^{N} \frac{B^S+V_i}{F+V_i} c_i$, in which case we say that the defender has a *sufficient cost budget*.

3.1 NE Under Sufficient Cost Budget of the Defender

As mentioned above, we say that the defender has a sufficient cost budget when $C = \sum_{i=1}^{N} \frac{B^S+V_i}{F+V_i} c_i$. In the next lemma, we provide the property that characterizes the defender's strategy at NE in this case.

Lemma 2. When $C = \sum_{i=1}^{N} \frac{B^S+V_i}{F+V_i} c_i$, the defender's strategy $\mathbf{p} = (p_1, \cdots, p_N)$ at NE is such that

$$\gamma_i(p_i) = 0, \forall i \in \{1, \cdots, N\} \tag{12}$$

Proof. Consider a strategy profile $\mathbf{p} = (p_1, \cdots, p_N)$ of the defender such that $\sum_{i=1}^{N} p_i c_i \leq C$. Denote $\underline{g} = \min_{i \in \{1, \cdots, N\}} \gamma_i(p_i)$, $\overline{g} = \max_{i \in \{1, \cdots, N\}} \gamma_i(p_i)$, where $\gamma_i(p_i)$ is defined in (10), and suppose that $\underline{g} < \overline{g}^1$. Moreover, define the set $\underline{G} = \{i | i \in \{1, \cdots, N\} \text{ and } \gamma_i(p_i) = \underline{g}\}$, the set $\overline{G} = \{i | i \in \{1, \cdots, N\} \text{ and } \gamma_i(p_i) = \overline{g}\}$, and the set $\underline{G}' = \{1, \cdots, N\} - \underline{G}$ (it can be noted that $|\underline{G}'| > 0$ necessarily holds when $\underline{g} < \overline{g}$). In such a scenario, to satisfy the cost budget constraint, it can be noted that we must have $\underline{g} < 0$. This is because, otherwise (if $\underline{g} \geq 0$), following Lemma 1, $\forall j \in \overline{G}$ we would have $p_j > \frac{B^S+V_j}{F+V_j}$ (i.e., $\gamma_j(p_j) > 0$) and $\forall i \in \{1, \cdots, N\} - \overline{G}$ we would have $p_i \geq \frac{B^S+V_i}{F+V_i}$ (i.e., $\gamma_i(p_i) \geq 0$), which would imply that $\sum_{i=1}^{N} p_i c_i > C$ (i.e., would violate the cost budget constraint).

Now, having noted that $\underline{g} < 0$, it should be further noted that, since the attacker aims to minimize (11), the best response of the attacker against the strategy $\mathbf{p}$ of the defender defined above is to adopt a strategy $\mathbf{q} = (q_1, \cdots, q_N)$ such that $\sum_{i \in \underline{G}} q_i = 1$. Consider now the following two possible cases.

- Case-I ($\overline{g} \leq 0$): In this case, following Lemma 1, $\forall i \in \underline{G}$ we have $p_i < \frac{B^S+V_i}{F+V_i}$ and $\forall j \in \underline{G}'$ we have $p_j \leq \frac{B^S+V_j}{F+V_j}$, which implies that $\sum_{i=1}^{N} p_i c_i < C$.

---

[1] In other words, for such a strategy profile, there exists $i, j \in \{1, \cdots, N\}$ for which $\gamma_i(p_i) \neq \gamma_j(p_j)$.

Consider now $w \in \underline{G}$ for which $q_w > 0$ (as follows from the aforementioned attacker's best response $\mathbf{q}$, such a w is guaranteed to exist) and consider changing the strategy of the defender from $\mathbf{p} = (p_w, p_{-w})$ to $\mathbf{p}' = (p_w + \delta, p_{-w})$, where p_{-w} denotes the vector of probabilities used by the defender to test all Trojan types except Trojan type w and $\delta \in (0, \frac{B^S + V_w}{F + V_w} - p_w]$. Clearly, $(p_w + \delta)c_w + \sum_{i \in \{1, \cdots, N\}, i \neq w} p_i c_i \leq C$ (i.e., $\mathbf{p}'$ satisfies the cost budget constraint). Moreover, we have $\gamma_w(p_w + \delta) > \gamma_w(p_w)$ (which follows from Lemma 1) implying that $E_D(\mathbf{p}', \mathbf{q}) > E_D(\mathbf{p}, \mathbf{q})$ showing that there exists a profitable unilateral deviation for the defender from the strategy profile $(\mathbf{p}, \mathbf{q})$ (where $\mathbf{q}$, as described earlier, forms a best response of the attacker against $\mathbf{p}$).

– Case-II ($\bar{g} > 0$): In this case, following Lemma 1, $\forall i \in \underline{G}$ we have $p_i < \frac{B^S + V_i}{F + V_i}$ and $\forall j \in \overline{G}$ we have $p_j > \frac{B^S + V_j}{F + V_j}$ (with $\sum_{i=1}^{N} p_i c_i \leq C$). Consider now $w \in \underline{G}$ for which $q_w > 0$ and any $z \in \overline{G}$ (note, as follows from the aforementioned attacker's best response strategy $\mathbf{q}$ against $\mathbf{p}$, $q_z = 0, \forall z \in \overline{G}$) and consider changing the strategy of the defender from $\mathbf{p} = (p_w, p_z, p_{-wz})$ to $\mathbf{p}' = (p_w + \delta_w, p_z - \delta_z, p_{-wz})$, where p_{-wz} denotes the vector of probabilities with which the defender tests all Trojan types except Trojan types w and z, while ensuring[2] $\delta_w c_w \leq \delta_z c_z$ to have the strategy $\mathbf{p}'$ satisfy the cost budget constraint. Now, we have $\gamma_w(p_w + \delta_w) > \gamma_w(p_w)$ (which follows from Lemma 1) implying that $E_D(\mathbf{p}', \mathbf{q}) > E_D(\mathbf{p}, \mathbf{q})$ showing that there again exists a profitable unilateral deviation for the defender from the strategy profile $(\mathbf{p}, \mathbf{q})$ (where $\mathbf{q}$, as described earlier, forms a best response of the attacker against $\mathbf{p}$).

From the above, clearly there always exists a profitable unilateral deviation for the defender from a strategy profile $(\mathbf{p}, \mathbf{q})$ where $\mathbf{p}$ is such that $\underline{g} \neq \bar{g}$ and $\mathbf{q}$ forms a best response of the attacker against $\mathbf{p}$. Thus, at NE, we must have $\underline{g} = \bar{g}$, which implies that $\gamma_i(p_i) = \alpha$ at NE $\forall i \in \{1, \cdots, N\}$, where α is a constant.

We next prove that $\alpha = 0$ at NE. When $\alpha < 0$, the best response of the attacker becomes adopting a strategy $\mathbf{q} = (q_1, \cdots, q_N)$ such that $\sum_{i \in \{1, \cdots, N\}} q_i = 1$ (which would make the utility of the defender (11) to be $E_D(\mathbf{p}, \mathbf{q}) < B^S$). Against such a strategy of the attacker, using arguments similar to Case-I in this proof, it can be shown that there exists profitable unilateral deviations for the defender from any strategy $\mathbf{p}$ for which $\alpha < 0$. Again, $\alpha > 0$ would require $p_i > \frac{B^S + V_i}{F + V_i}, \forall i \in \{1, \cdots, N\}$, which would violate the cost budget constraint. From the above, clearly at NE we must have $\alpha = 0$, which proves the lemma.

Next, using Lemma 1 and Lemma 2, we characterize the NE for the sufficient cost budget case in Theorem 2.

---

[2] Note that in the strategy $\mathbf{p}'$, $\delta_w c_w$ is the additional cost incurred by the defender due to the increase in the probability of testing Trojan type w and $\delta_z c_z$ is the decrease in cost incurred due to the decrease in the probability of testing Trojan type z.

Theorem 2. *When $C = \sum_{i=1}^{N} \frac{B^S+V_i}{F+V_i} c_i$, at NE, the defender's strategy corresponds to testing the acquired IC to check for the presence of every Trojan type $i \in \{1, \cdots, N\}$ with a probability $p_i = \frac{B^S+V_i}{F+V_i}$ and the attacker's strategy corresponds to, for any chosen $i \in \{1, \cdots, N\}$, inserting Trojan type i into the manufactured IC with a probability $q_i = \frac{k}{\frac{F+V_i}{c_i} \sum_{j=1}^{N} \frac{c_j}{F+V_j}}, k \in [0,1]$, and inserting Trojan type j with a probability $q_j = q_i \frac{c_j}{c_i} \frac{F+V_i}{F+V_j}, \forall j \in \{1, \cdots, N\}, j \neq i.$*

Proof. Using Lemma 2, at NE, the defender's strategy $\mathbf{p} = (p_1, \cdots, p_N)$ must be such that $\gamma_i(p_i) = 0, \forall i \in \{1, \cdots, N\}$, implying that $p_i = \frac{B^S+V_i}{F+V_i}, \forall i \in \{1, \cdots, N\}$ at NE (using Lemma 1). Against such a strategy of the defender, it should be noted that any strategy $\mathbf{q} = (q_1, \cdots, q_N)$ (such that $0 \leq \sum_{i=1}^{N} q_i \leq 1$) forms a best response for the attacker. However, not all such strategies of the attacker result in a NE since some may allow profitable unilateral deviations to exist for the defender from the strategy $\mathbf{p}$ defined above. Consider now the deviation of the defender from the strategy $\mathbf{p} = (p_i, p_j, p_{-ij})$ at NE defined above to a strategy $\mathbf{p}' = (p_i + \delta_i, p_j - \delta_j, p_{-ij})$, where p_{-ij} denotes the vector of probabilities with which the defender tests all Trojan types except Trojan types i and j. To have $\mathbf{p}'$ satisfy the cost budget constraint, we must have[3]

$$\left(\frac{B^S + V_i}{F + V_i} + \delta_i \right) c_i + \left(\frac{B^S + V_j}{F + V_j} - \delta_j \right) c_j + \sum_{z=1, z \neq i, z \neq j}^{N} \frac{B^S + V_z}{F + V_z} c_z = C \quad (13)$$

which implies $\delta_i c_i - \delta_j c_j = 0$ in (13), which yields

$$\delta_j = \delta_i \frac{c_i}{c_j} \quad (14)$$

Now, recalling from Lemma 1 that $\frac{d(\gamma_x(p_x))}{dp_x} = F + V_x$ and from Lemma 2 that $\gamma_x(p_x) = 0 \ \forall x \in \{1, \cdots, N\}$ in the strategy $\mathbf{p}$ of the defender at NE defined earlier, in the strategy $\mathbf{p}'$ defined above we have $\gamma_i(p_i + \delta_i) = (F + V_i)\delta_i$ and $\gamma_j(p_j - \delta_j) = -(F + V_j)\delta_j$. Thus, to prevent a profitable unilateral deviation of the defender from the strategy $\mathbf{p}$ to the strategy $\mathbf{p}'$, the strategy $\mathbf{q} = (q_1, \cdots, q_N)$ of the attacker must be such that, $\forall i, j \in \{1, \cdots, N\}, i \neq j, |\gamma_i(p_i + \delta_i)|q_i = |\gamma_j(p_j - \delta_j)|q_j$, i.e.,

$$(F + V_i)\delta_i q_i = (F + V_j)\delta_j q_j \quad (15)$$

which implies, using (14),

$$q_j = q_i \frac{c_j}{c_i} \frac{F + V_i}{F + V_j}, \ \forall i, j \in \{1, \cdots, N\}, i \neq j \quad (16)$$

---

[3] Note, it is easy to show that, for strategies $\grave{\mathbf{p}} = (\grave{p}_1, \cdots, \grave{p}_N)$ (where $\sum_{i=1}^{N} \grave{p}_i c_i < C$) and $\acute{\mathbf{p}} = (\acute{p}_1, \cdots, \acute{p}_N)$ (where $\sum_{i=1}^{N} \acute{p}_i c_i = C$) of the defender, it always holds true that $E_D(\acute{\mathbf{p}}, \mathbf{q}) \geq E_D(\grave{\mathbf{p}}, \mathbf{q})$ for any attacker's strategy $\mathbf{q}$, implying that $\acute{\mathbf{p}}$ dominates $\grave{\mathbf{p}}$.

Now, it is easy to show that, for any chosen $i \in \{1, \cdots, N\}$, having $q_j = q_i \frac{c_j}{c_i} \frac{F+V_i}{F+V_j}, \forall j \in \{1, \cdots, N\}, j \neq i$, implies $q_j = q_i \frac{c_j}{c_i} \frac{F+V_i}{F+V_j}, \forall i, j \in \{1, \cdots, N\}, j \neq i$. Moreover, as noted earlier, any strategy $\mathbf{q}$ of the attacker forms a best response against the strategy $\mathbf{p}$ of the defender at NE defined earlier. Thus, we have $\sum_{i=1}^{N} q_i = k$ at NE (where k can be any value in $[0,1]$), which can be expressed for any chosen $i \in \{1, \cdots, N\}$ as

$$q_i + \sum_{j=1, j \neq i}^{N} q_j = k$$

$$\Rightarrow q_i + \sum_{j=1, j \neq i}^{N} q_i \frac{c_j}{c_i} \frac{F+V_i}{F+V_j} = k \quad \text{(using (16))}$$

$$\Rightarrow \sum_{j=1}^{N} q_i \frac{c_j}{c_i} \frac{F+V_i}{F+V_j} = k$$

$$\Rightarrow q_i = \frac{k}{\frac{F+V_i}{c_i} \sum_{j=1}^{N} \frac{c_j}{F+V_j}} \tag{17}$$

Clearly, from the above, if the attacker, for any chosen $i \in \{1, \cdots, N\}$ and any $k \in [0,1]$, chooses q_i as given in (17) and $q_j, \forall j \in \{1, \cdots, N\}, j \neq i$, as given in (16), the attacker would be playing its best response against the strategy $\mathbf{p}$ of the defender defined earlier (which, recall, comprises of $p_i = \frac{B^S + V_i}{F + V_i} \forall i \in \{1, \cdots, N\}$) without the defender having any profitable unilateral deviations from the strategy $\mathbf{p}$. This proves the theorem.

Next, we provide numerical results in Fig. 2 to corroborate Theorem 2 considering two Trojan types, viz. $\{1, 2\}$, with $B^S = 80$, $V_1 = 20$, $V_2 = 40$, $F = 150$, $c_1 = c_2 = 30$, and $C = \frac{B^S + V_1}{F + V_1} c_1 + \frac{B^S + V_2}{F + V_2} c_2 = 36.5944$. In Fig. 2(a), considering $\mathbf{p} = (p_1, p_2)$ and $\mathbf{q} = (q_1, q_2)$, we present a 3-D plot of $E_D(\mathbf{p}, \mathbf{q})$ (11) versus the probability (p_1) with which the defender tests an acquired IC to check for the presence of Trojan type 1 (with $p_2 = \frac{C - p_1 c_1}{c_2}$ so that $p_1 c_1 + p_2 c_2 = C$) and the probability (q_1) with which the attacker inserts Trojan type 1 into the manufactured IC (with $q_2 = 1 - q_1$). In Fig. 2(b), we depict the contours and the gradient plot for $E_D(\mathbf{p}, \mathbf{q})$ in the $p_1 - q_1$ plane. From the figures, we observe that there exists a saddle point whose coordinates are $(p_1, q_1) = (0.5882, 0.5278)$. Specifically, from Fig. 2(b), it can be seen that the gradient arrows point toward the point $(0.5882, 0.5278)$ in one direction and point outward from the point $(0.5882, 0.5278)$ in the perpendicular direction, implying that $(p_1, q_1) = (0.5882, 0.5278)$, with $(p_2, q_2) = (\frac{C - p_1 c_1}{c_2}, 1 - q_1) = (0.6316, 0.4722)$, is a saddle point (and hence the NE). It can be verified that the NE obtained from Theorem 2, considering $k = 1$ for the attacker, is also $(p_1, p_2) = (0.5882, 0.6316)$ and $(q_1, q_2) = (0.5278, 0.4722)$, which corroborates the theorem.

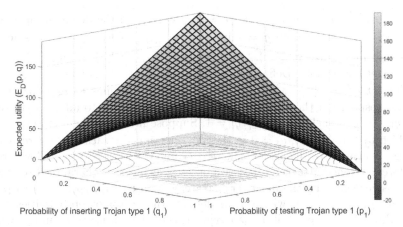

(a) Expected utility ($E_D(\mathbf{p}, \mathbf{q})$) versus the defender's strategy (p_1) and the attacker's strategy (q_1).

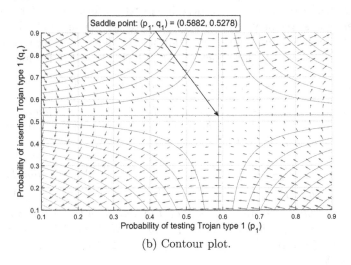

(b) Contour plot.

Fig. 2. Expected utility ($E_D(\mathbf{p}, \mathbf{q})$) versus the defender's and the attacker's strategies for the sufficient cost budget case.

3.2 NE Under Insufficient Cost Budget of the Defender

We now consider the scenario when $C < \sum_{i=1}^{N} \frac{B^S + V_i}{F + V_i} c_i$, which we refer to as the defender having an *insufficient cost budget*. Without loss of generality, consider $V_1 \leq V_2 \leq \cdots \leq V_N$ for the analysis of this scenario. In the next lemma, we provide the property that characterizes the defender's NE strategy in this case.

Lemma 3. *When* $C < \sum_{i=1}^{N} \frac{B^S + V_i}{F + V_i} c_i$, *the defender's strategy* $\mathbf{p} = (p_1, \cdots, p_N)$ *at NE is such that*

$$\gamma_j(p_j) = \min_{i \in \{1, \cdots, N\}} \gamma_i(p_i), \ if \ p_j > 0 \tag{18}$$

Proof. Consider a strategy profile $\mathbf{p} = (p_1, \cdots, p_N)$ of the defender such that $\sum_{i=1}^{N} p_i c_i \leq C$ and denote $\underline{g} = \min_{i \in \{1, \cdots, N\}} \gamma_i(p_i)$. Clearly, $\underline{g} < 0$ (since, if $\underline{g} \geq 0$, we must have $p_i \geq \frac{B^S + V_i}{F + V_i}, \forall i \in \{1, \cdots, N\}$, which would violate the cost budget constraint). Define the set $\underline{G} = \{i | i \in \{1, \cdots, N\}$ and $\gamma_i(p_i) = \underline{g}\}$ and the set $\underline{G}' = \{1, \cdots, N\} - \underline{G}$. Since the attacker aims to minimize (11), the best response of the attacker against the strategy $\mathbf{p}$ is to adopt a strategy $\mathbf{q} = (q_1, \cdots, q_N)$ such that $\sum_{i \in \underline{G}} q_i = 1$. Suppose now that there exists $j \in \underline{G}'$ for which $p_j > 0$ (clearly, $q_j = 0$ in the aforementioned attacker's best response strategy $\mathbf{q}$ against $\mathbf{p}$). Consider now $w \in \underline{G}$ for which $q_w > 0$ (as follows from the aforementioned attacker's best response $\mathbf{q}$, such a w is guaranteed to exist) and consider changing the defender's strategy from $\mathbf{p} = (p_w, p_j, p_{-wj})$ to $\mathbf{p}' = (p_w + \delta_w, p_j - \delta_j, p_{-wj})$, where p_{-wj} denotes the vector of probabilities with which the defender tests all Trojan types except Trojan types w and j, while ensuring $\delta_w c_w \leq \delta_j c_j$ (to ensure that $\mathbf{p}'$ satisfies the cost budget constraint). Now, we have $\gamma_w(p_w + \delta_w) > \gamma_w(p_w)$ (which follows from Lemma 1) implying that $E_D(\mathbf{p}', \mathbf{q}) > E_D(\mathbf{p}, \mathbf{q})$, where $\mathbf{q}$ (as described earlier) forms a best response of the attacker against $\mathbf{p}$, showing that, with the attacker playing its best response, there exists a profitable unilateral deviation for the defender from any strategy $\mathbf{p}$ where there exists $j \in \underline{G}'$ for which $p_j > 0$, which proves the lemma.

We next present two important remarks based on Lemma 3.

Remark 1. Since, as discussed in the proof of Lemma 3, in the defender's strategy $\mathbf{p} = (p_1, \cdots, p_N)$ at NE, we must have $p_i = 0 \ \forall i \in \underline{G}'$ (and $\underline{g} < 0$), it follows using Lemma 1 that at NE $\gamma_j(p_j) < 0, \forall j \in \{1, \cdots, N\}$.

Remark 2. Since $\frac{d}{dV_i} \frac{B^S + V_i}{F + V_i} \geq 0$ for $B^S \leq F$ (i.e., $\frac{B^S + V_i}{F + V_i}$ is a non-decreasing function of V_i when $B^S \leq F$) and since $\frac{d(\gamma_i(p_i))}{dp_i} \leq \frac{d(\gamma_j(p_j))}{dp_j}$ if $V_i \leq V_j$ (which follows from Lemma 1), it can be noted that it follows from Lemma 3, considering $V_1 \leq V_2 \leq \cdots \leq V_N$ without loss of generality, that the NE strategy of the defender has the form $\mathbf{p} = (p_1 = 0, \cdots, p_{k-1} = 0, p_k > 0, p_{k+1} > 0, \cdots, p_N > 0)$, where $k \in [1, N]$.

Next, using Lemma 3, Remark 1, and Remark 2, we present the NE of the insufficient cost budget case in Theorem 3.

Theorem 3. *When $C < \sum_{i=1}^{N} \frac{B^S + V_i}{F + V_i} c_i$, at NE,*

- *the defender's strategy corresponds to $\mathbf{p} = (p_1 = 0, \cdots, p_{k-1} = 0, p_k = \frac{B^S + V_k}{F + V_k} - \delta_k, p_{k+1} = \frac{B^S + V_{k+1}}{F + V_{k+1}} - \delta_{k+1} \cdots, p_N = \frac{B^S + V_N}{F + V_N} - \delta_N)$, where, $\delta_k = \frac{\sum_{i=k}^{N} \left(\frac{B^S + V_i}{F + V_i} \right) c_i - C}{(F + V_k) \sum_{i=k}^{N} \frac{c_i}{F + V_i}}$, $\delta_i = \frac{F + V_k}{F + V_i} \delta_k, \forall i \in [k+1, N]$, and $k \in [1, N]$ is the least value that satisfies $\delta_k = \frac{\sum_{i=k}^{N} \left(\frac{B^S + V_i}{F + V_i} \right) c_i - C}{(F + V_k) \sum_{i=k}^{N} \frac{c_i}{F + V_i}} < \frac{B^S + V_k}{F + V_k}$, and*

- *the attacker's strategy corresponds to, for any chosen $i \in \underline{G}$, where $\underline{G} = \{i | i \in \{1, \cdots, N\}$ and $\gamma_i(p_i) = \min_{i \in \{1, \cdots, N\}} \gamma_i(p_i)\}$ with p_i being the defender's*

strategy of testing against Trojan type i at NE, choosing $q_i = \frac{1}{\frac{F+V_i}{c_i} \sum_{j=1}^{N} \frac{c_j}{F+V_j}}$
and $q_j = q_i \frac{c_j}{c_i} \frac{F+V_i}{F+V_j}$, $\forall j \in \underline{G}$, $j \neq i$.

Proof. Using Remark 1 and Remark 2, let us represent the NE strategy of the defender as $\mathbf{p} = (p_1 = 0, \cdots, p_{k-1} = 0, p_k = \frac{B^S + V_k}{F + V_k} - \delta_k, p_{k+1} = \frac{B^S + V_{k+1}}{F + V_{k+1}} - \delta_{k+1}, \cdots, p_N = \frac{B^S + V_N}{F + V_N} - \delta_N)$ for $k \in [1, N]$ and $\delta_i \in (0, \frac{B^S + V_i}{F + V_i})$ for $i \in [k, N]$. Now, to have $\mathbf{p}$ satisfy the cost budget constraint, we must have

$$\sum_{i=1}^{k-1} (0 \cdot c_i) + \sum_{i=k}^{N} \left(\frac{B^S + V_i}{F + V_i} - \delta_i \right) \cdot c_i = C$$

$$\Rightarrow \sum_{i=k}^{N} \delta_i c_i = \sum_{i=k}^{N} \left(\frac{B^S + V_i}{F + V_i} \right) c_i - C \qquad (19)$$

Now, recalling from Lemma 1 that $\frac{d\gamma_x(p_x)}{dp_x} = F + V_x$ and that $\gamma_x(\frac{B^S + V_x}{F + V_x}) = 0$, $x \in \{1, \cdots, N\}$, and noting that Lemma 3 implies that in the defender's NE strategy we have $\gamma_k(p_k) = \gamma_{k+1}(p_{k+1}) = \cdots = \gamma_N(p_N)$, we conclude that in the strategy $\mathbf{p}$ of the defender at NE we have

$$(F + V_k)\delta_k = (F + V_{k+1})\delta_{k+1} = \cdots = (F + V_N)\delta_N \qquad (20)$$

which implies that

$$\delta_i = \frac{F + V_k}{F + V_i} \delta_k, \forall i \in [k+1, N] \qquad (21)$$

Substituting (21) into (19), we get

$$\sum_{i=k}^{N} \delta_k \frac{F + V_k}{F + V_i} c_i = \sum_{i=k}^{N} \left(\frac{B^S + V_i}{F + V_i} \right) c_i - C$$

$$\Rightarrow \delta_k = \frac{\sum_{i=k}^{N} \left(\frac{B^S + V_i}{F + V_i} \right) c_i - C}{(F + V_k) \sum_{i=k}^{N} \frac{c_i}{F + V_i}} \qquad (22)$$

Now, it is easy to show that higher the value of k chosen (while having $\gamma_k(p_k) = \cdots = \gamma_N(p_N)$ and satisfying the cost budget constraint), lower would be $\min_{i \in \{1, \cdots, N\}} \gamma_i(p_i)$, which implies that lower would be the expected utility of the defender against a strategic attacker. Thus, in the strategy $\mathbf{p} = (p_1 = 0, \cdots, p_{k-1} = 0, p_k = \frac{B^S + V_k}{F + V_k} - \delta_k, p_{k+1} = \frac{B^S + V_{k+1}}{F + V_{k+1}} - \delta_{k+1}, \cdots, p_N = \frac{B^S + V_N}{F + V_N} - \delta_N)$ of the defender at NE, to have $\frac{B^S + V_i}{F + V_i} - \delta_i > 0$, $i \in [k, N]$, the defender must choose the least value of $k \in [1, N]$ such that δ_k (22) satisfies

$$\delta_k = \frac{\sum_{i=k}^{N} \left(\frac{B^S + V_i}{F + V_i} \right) c_i - C}{(F + V_k) \sum_{i=k}^{N} \frac{c_i}{F + V_i}} < \frac{B^S + V_k}{F + V_k} \qquad (23)$$

with δ_i, $\forall i \in [k+1, N]$, chosen as given in (21), which proves the defender's NE strategy as given in the theorem. Against such a strategy $\mathbf{p}$ of the defender, since the attacker seeks to minimize (11), the best response of the attacker becomes adopting a strategy $\mathbf{q} = (q_1, \cdots, q_N)$ such that $\sum_{i \in \underline{G}} q_i = 1$, where $\underline{G} = \{i | i \in \{1, \cdots, N\}$ and $\gamma_i(p_i) = \min_{i \in \{1, \cdots, N\}} \gamma_i(p_i)\}$. However, not all such strategies of the attacker comprise a NE. It can be shown, using an approach similar to the proof of Theorem 2, which we omit for brevity, that the NE strategy of the attacker consists of, for any chosen $i \in \underline{G}$, inserting Trojan type i into the manufactured IC with a probability $q_i = \frac{1}{\frac{F+V_i}{c_i} \sum_{j=1}^{N} \frac{c_j}{F+V_j}}$ and inserting Trojan type j with a probability $q_j = q_i \frac{c_j}{c_i} \frac{F+V_i}{F+V_j}$, $\forall j \in \underline{G}$, $j \neq i$. This proves the theorem.

Next, we provide numerical results in Fig. 3 to corroborate Theorem 3 considering two Trojan types, viz. $\{1, 2\}$, with $B^S = 80$, $V_1 = 20$, $V_2 = 40$, $F = 150$, $c_1 = c_2 = 30$, and $C = 35$. In Fig. 3(a), considering $\mathbf{p} = (p_1, p_2)$ and $\mathbf{q} = (q_1, q_2)$,

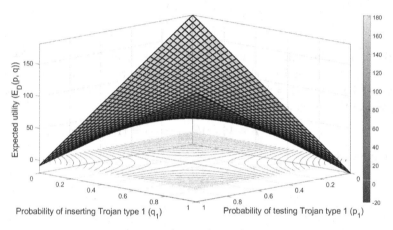

(a) Expected utility ($E_D(\mathbf{p}, \mathbf{q})$) versus the defender's strategy (p_1) and the attacker's strategy (q_1).

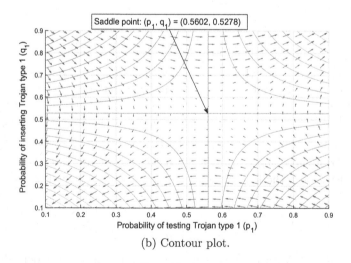

(b) Contour plot.

Fig. 3. Expected utility ($E_D(\mathbf{p}, \mathbf{q})$) versus the defender's and the attacker's strategies for the insufficient cost budget case.

we present a 3-D plot of $E_D(\mathbf{p}, \mathbf{q})$ (11) versus the probability (p_1) with which the defender tests an acquired IC to check for the presence of Trojan type 1 (with $p_2 = \frac{C - p_1 c_1}{c_2}$ so that $p_1 c_1 + p_2 c_2 = C$) and the probability (q_1) with which the attacker inserts Trojan type 1 into the manufactured IC (with $q_2 = 1 - q_1$). In Fig. 3(b), we depict the contours and the gradient plot for $E_D(\mathbf{p}, \mathbf{q})$ in the $p_1 - q_1$ plane. From the figures, we observe that there exists a saddle point whose coordinates are $(p_1, q_1) = (0.5602, 0.5278)$. Specifically, from Fig. 3(b), it can be seen that the gradient arrows point toward the point $(0.5602, 0.5278)$ in one direction and point outward from the point $(0.5602, 0.5278)$ in the perpendicular direction, implying that $(p_1, q_1) = (0.5602, 0.5278)$, with $(p_2, q_2) = (\frac{C - p_1 c_1}{c_2}, 1 - q_1) = (0.6065, 0.4722)$, is a saddle point (and hence the NE). It can be verified that the NE obtained from Theorem 3 is also $(p_1, p_2) = (0.5602, 0.6065)$ and $(q_1, q_2) = (0.5278, 0.4722)$, which corroborates the theorem.

4   Numerical Results

In this section, we provide numerical results to provide important insights into our developed game theoretic Trojan testing strategies. In Fig. 4, we show the impact of the fine (F) on the strategies of the attacker and the defender and on their expected utilities at NE for the insufficient cost budget case. For the figure, we consider four types of Trojans, viz. $\{1, 2, 3, 4\}$, with $B^S = 100$, $V_1 = 20$, $V_2 = 40$, $V_3 = 60$, $V_4 = 80$, $c_1 = c_2 = c_3 = c_4 = 40$, and $C = 50$. The NE strategies for the figure have been computed using Theorem 3. As can be seen from Fig. 4(a), as F increases, at NE, the attacker increases its probability of inserting a Trojan which is relatively more damaging in nature (which corresponds to Trojan types 3 and 4 having $V_3 = 60$ and $V_4 = 80$, respectively) while decreasing its probability of inserting a Trojan which is relatively less damaging (which corresponds to Trojan types 1 and 2 having $V_1 = 20$ and $V_2 = 40$, respectively). This can be attributed to the fact that, since F negatively impacts the attacker's utility, increasing the probability of inserting a more damaging Trojan as F increases helps the attacker counteract the negative impact of having to pay a heftier fine upon the defender correctly detecting an inserted Trojan. For the defender's strategy at NE, with increasing F, it can be noted from Fig. 4(b) that the defender increases its probabilities of testing the acquired IC to check for the presence of relatively less damaging Trojans (which correspond to Trojan types 1 and 2) and decreases its probabilities of testing the IC against more damaging Trojans (which correspond to Trojan types 3 and 4).

Further, from Fig. 4(b) it can be observed that, as is intuitive, for any given F, at NE, the defender tests an acquired IC against a more damaging Trojan with a higher probability than that of testing against a less damaging one while, as can be seen from Fig. 4(a), the attacker exhibits the reverse trend. As can be seen from Fig. 4(c), the expected utility of the defender at NE increases with F, and accordingly the attacker's expected utility decreases with F, indicating the advantage that charging a higher fine has on enhancing the defender's utility against strategic insertion of hardware Trojans by malicious manufacturers.

In Fig. 5, we show the expected utilities of the defender and the attacker at NE (computed using Theorem 3) versus the cost budget (C) available for performing

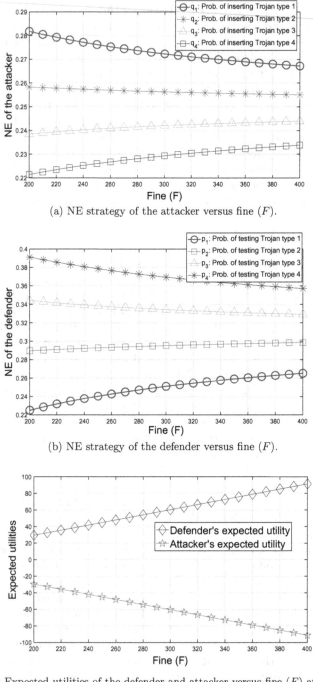

(a) NE strategy of the attacker versus fine (F).

(b) NE strategy of the defender versus fine (F).

(c) Expected utilities of the defender and attacker versus fine (F) at NE.

Fig. 4. Impact of fine (F) on the defender's and the attacker's strategies and on their expected utilities at NE.

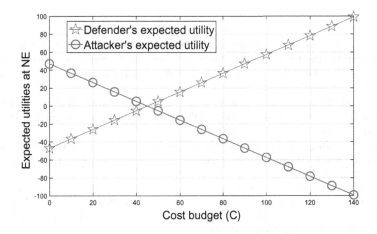

Fig. 5. Expected utilities of the defender and the attacker at NE versus the cost budget (C).

testing (considering C taken in the figure to satisfy the insufficient cost budget case). For the figure, we consider four Trojan types, viz. $\{1, 2, 3, 4\}$, with $B^S = 100$, $F = 120$, $V_1 = 20$, $V_2 = 40$, $V_3 = 60$, $V_4 = 80$, and $c_1 = c_2 = c_3 = c_4 = 40$. As can be seen from the figure, the expected utility of the defender at NE increases as the cost budget (C) of the defender for performing testing increases. This is because, with increasing C, the capability of the defender to test more types of Trojans increases which enhances its ability to correctly determine whether the acquired IC contains a Trojan which, in turn, enhances the defender's capability to avoid the damage caused by an inserted Trojan and impose a fine on the malicious manufacturer (both of which positively impact the defender's utility). As can also be seen from the figure, as expected, the attacker's expected utility decreases with increasing C. Such trends in the expected utilities show the ability of our characterized NE strategies to tactfully exploit the cost budget available for performing testing to enhance the utility of the defender against a strategic attacker.

5   Conclusion

This paper investigated the problem of game theoretic hardware Trojan testing and analytically characterized NE strategies for inserting a Trojan (from the perspective of a malicious manufacturer) and testing a Trojan (from the perspective of a defender) in closed-forms under consideration of testing costs incurred by the defender. The paper first characterized the NE for the case where the defender, who incurs costs for performing testing, is capable of testing an acquired IC against one Trojan type. The paper also characterized the NE for the case where the defender can test the acquired IC against multiple types of Trojans under a cost budget constraint. Numerical results were presented to gain important insights into the NE strategies characterized in the paper.

References

1. Adee, S.: The hunt for the kill switch. IEEE Spectr. **45**(5), 34–39 (2008)
2. Agrawal, D., Baktir, S., Karakoyunlu, D., Rohatgi, P., Sunar, B.: Trojan detection using IC fingerprinting. In: 2007 IEEE Symposium on Security and Privacy (SP 2007), pp. 296–310. IEEE (2007)
3. Banga, M., Hsiao, M.S.: A region based approach for the identification of hardware trojans. In: 2008 IEEE International Workshop on Hardware-Oriented Security and Trust, pp. 40–47. IEEE (2008)
4. Bhasin, S., Regazzoni, F.: A survey on hardware trojan detection techniques. In: 2015 IEEE International Symposium on Circuits and Systems (ISCAS), pp. 2021–2024. IEEE (2015)
5. Bhunia, S., Hsiao, M.S., Banga, M., Narasimhan, S.: Hardware trojan attacks: threat analysis and countermeasures. Proc. IEEE **102**(8), 1229–1247 (2014)
6. Brahma, S., Nan, S., Njilla, L.: Strategic hardware trojan testing with hierarchical trojan types. In: 2021 55th Annual Conference on Information Sciences and Systems (CISS), pp. 1–6 (2021)
7. Chakraborty, R.S., Narasimhan, S., Bhunia, S.: Hardware trojan: threats and emerging solutions. In: 2009 IEEE International High Level Design Validation and Test Workshop, pp. 166–171. IEEE (2009)
8. Chakraborty, R.S., Wolff, F., Paul, S., Papachristou, C., Bhunia, S.: MERO: a statistical approach for hardware trojan detection. In: Clavier, C., Gaj, K. (eds.) CHES 2009. LNCS, vol. 5747, pp. 396–410. Springer, Heidelberg (2009). https://doi.org/10.1007/978-3-642-04138-9_28
9. Fudenberg, D., Tirole, J.: Game Theory. MIT Press, Cambridge (1991)
10. Graf, J.: Trust games: how game theory can guide the development of hardware trojan detection methods. In: 2016 IEEE International Symposium on Hardware Oriented Security and Trust (HOST), pp. 91–96. IEEE (2016)
11. Graf, J., Batchelor, W., Harper, S., Marlow, R., Carlisle, E., Athanas, P.: A practical application of game theory to optimize selection of hardware trojan detection strategies. J. Hardw. Syst. Secur. **4**(2), 98–119 (2020)
12. Hu, N., Ye, M., Wei, S.: Surviving information leakage hardware trojan attacks using hardware isolation. IEEE Trans. Emerg. Top. Comput. **7**(2), 253–261 (2017)
13. Kamhoua, C.A., Zhao, H., Rodriguez, M., Kwiat, K.A.: A game-theoretic approach for testing for hardware trojans. IEEE Trans. Multi-Scale Comput. Syst. **2**(3), 199–210 (2016)
14. Kwiat, K., Born, F.: Strategically managing the risk of hardware trojans through augmented testing. In: 13th Annual Symposium on Information Assurance (ASIA), pp. 20–24 (2018)
15. Nagarajan, K., De, A., Khan, M.N.I., Ghosh, S.: TrappeD: DRAM trojan designs for information leakage and fault injection attacks. arXiv preprint arXiv:2001.00856 (2020)
16. Rajendran, J., Gavas, E., Jimenez, J., Padman, V., Karri, R.: Towards a comprehensive and systematic classification of hardware trojans. In: Proceedings of 2010 IEEE International Symposium on Circuits and Systems, pp. 1871–1874. IEEE (2010)
17. Salmani, H., Tehranipoor, M., Plusquellic, J.: New design strategy for improving hardware trojan detection and reducing trojan activation time. In: 2009 IEEE International Workshop on Hardware-Oriented Security and Trust, pp. 66–73. IEEE (2009)
18. Schulze, T.E., Kwiat, K., Kamhoua, C., Chang, S.C., Shi, Y.: RECORD: temporarily randomized encoding of combinational logic for resistance to data leakage from hardware trojan. In: 2016 IEEE Asian Hardware-Oriented Security and Trust (AsianHOST), pp. 1–6. IEEE (2016)

Strategic Remote Attestation: Testbed for Internet-of-Things Devices and Stackelberg Security Game for Optimal Strategies

Shanto Roy[1]($^{(\boxtimes)}$), Salah Uddin Kadir[1], Yevgeniy Vorobeychik[2], and Aron Laszka[1]

[1] University of Houston, Houston, TX, USA
shantoroy@ieee.org
[2] Washington University in St. Louis, St. Louis, MO, USA

Abstract. Internet of Things (IoT) devices and applications can have significant vulnerabilities, which may be exploited by adversaries to cause considerable harm. An important approach for mitigating this threat is *remote attestation*, which enables the defender to remotely verify the integrity of devices and their software. There are a number of approaches for remote attestation, and each has its unique advantages and disadvantages in terms of detection accuracy and computational cost. Further, an attestation method may be applied in multiple ways, such as various levels of software coverage. Therefore, to minimize both security risks and computational overhead, defenders need to decide strategically which attestation methods to apply and how to apply them, depending on the characteristic of the devices and the potential losses.

To answer these questions, we first develop a *testbed for remote attestation of IoT devices*, which enables us to measure the detection accuracy and performance overhead of various attestation methods. Our testbed integrates two example IoT applications, memory-checksum based attestation, and a variety of software vulnerabilities that allow adversaries to inject arbitrary code into running applications. Second, we model the problem of finding an optimal strategy for applying remote attestation as a *Stackelberg security game* between a defender and an adversary. We characterize the defender's optimal attestation strategy in a variety of special cases. Finally, building on experimental results from our testbed, we evaluate our model and show that optimal strategic attestation can lead to significantly lower losses than naïve baseline strategies.

Keywords: Remote attestation · Stackelberg security game · Internet of Things · Security testbed · Software security

1 Introduction

With the growing number of Internet of Things (IoT) devices around the world, security has been a significant concern for researchers in the last decade. Due to

© Springer Nature Switzerland AG 2021
B. Bošanský et al. (Eds.): GameSec 2021, LNCS 13061, pp. 271–290, 2021.
https://doi.org/10.1007/978-3-030-90370-1_15

more exposure in a resource-limited environment, IoT devices often do not have access to the latest security primitives, and a number of security issues including various software vulnerabilities (e.g., stack and heap-based buffer overflows, format-string vulnerabilities) exist due to the usage of unsafe languages like C/C++ and vulnerable functions [11,17,21]. Adversaries can exploit these vulnerabilities to compromise devices by altering the software code or the control flow. Therefore, from a defensive point of view, device attestation that allows an organization to verify integrity remotely is a powerful tool [17].

IoT devices are a preferable target for adversaries these days, and organizations are implementing various methods to mitigate these attacks. However, security measures for IoT devices are different from those for servers, since IoT devices usually have low-power resource-limited configurations and are often placed in unknown or unsafe locations. To detect and mitigate attacks, a defender may employ remote attestation methods to verify the integrity of a program.

While remote attestation methods can be effective at detecting compromised devices, running attestation can also incur significant computational cost, which may present a prohibitively high overhead on resource-limited IoT devices. There are a number of approaches for remote attestation, and each has its unique advantages and disadvantages in terms of detection accuracy and computational cost. Further, an attestation method may be applied in multiple ways, such as various levels of software coverage. Therefore, to minimize both security risks and computational overhead, defenders need to decide strategically which attestation methods to apply and how to apply them, depending on the characteristic of the devices and the potential losses.

In this paper, we address these questions by (1) implementing an IoT testbed for measuring the detection accuracy and performance overhead of remote-attestation methods and by (2) introducing and solving a game-theoretic model for finding optimal remote-attestation strategies. Specifically, we formulate and answer the following research questions.

Q1. Testbed Development: How to develop an IoT security testbed that can simulate software vulnerability exploitation and evaluate remote attestation?

Q2. Remote Attestation Methods: What is the trade-off between the detection rate and computational cost of various remote attestation methods?

Q3. Optimal Attestation Strategies: How to model the strategic conflict between a defender and an adversary, and how to find optimal attestation strategies for the defender?

We answer the first question by describing the design and development of our security testbed for IoT device attestation (Sect. 3). We discuss the architecture of our testbed as well as the development of major components, such as vulnerability exploits and attestation methods. Our testbed enables us to experiment with software vulnerabilities and exploits and to rigorously evaluate various attestation methods in terms of computational cost and detection rate.

We answer the second question by studying the detection rate and computational cost of memory-checksum based remote attestation (Sect. 6). We implement and evaluate memory-checksum based attestation in our testbed for two example IoT applications. We characterize the trade-off between computational cost and detection rate, which we then use to develop the assumptions of our game-theoretic model.

We answer the third question by developing a Stackelberg security game to model the strategic conflict between a defender and an adversary (Sect. 4). We formulate the defender's optimal remote-attestation strategy assuming an adversary who always mounts a best-response attack. We show how to compute an optimal strategy in various special cases, and we demonstrate through numerical examples that optimal strategies can attain significantly lower losses than naïve baselines. To the best of our knowledge, our model and analysis constitute the first effort to provide optimal remote-attestation strategies.

Organization. The rest of the paper is organized as follows: Sect. 2 provides necessary background information. Section 3 discusses the design and development details of our IoT security testbed. Section 4 introduces the attacker-defender model based on Stackelberg security games. Section 5 provides analytical results characterizing the defender's optimal attestation strategy. Section 6 presents experimental results from our testbed as well as numerical results on the optimal attestation strategies. Section 7 gives a brief overview of related work followed by our concluding remarks and future directions in Sect. 8.

2   Background

ARM processors are very widely used in IoT platforms. Therefore, we develop an ARM-based IoT security testbed to experiment with exploitation and remote attestation on ARM devices. Here, we provide a brief overview of IoT device vulnerabilities, remote attestation methods, and the Stackelberg game model.

2.1   Software Vulnerabilities and Exploitation in IoT Devices

Adversaries can take control of an IoT device by hijacking the code execution flow of an application and injecting arbitrary executable code into its memory space. For example, an attacker can use stack- or heap-based *buffer overflow* or *format string vulnerabilities* to inject malicious executable code into a process. By injecting executable code, the adversary can alter the functionality of an application (e.g., providing a backdoor to the adversary or causing harm directly). While the mitigation for these attacks may be well established in the server and desktop environment, the unique design characteristics of resource-constrained embedded devices makes it challenging to adapt the same defenses techniques. For example, many deeply embedded devices often do not support virtual memory, which is essential for address space layout randomization (ASLR).

2.2   IoT Remote Attestation

Remote attestation establishes trust in a device by remotely verifying the state of the device via checking the integrity of the software running on it. Remote attestation methods can be divided into two main categories: hardware and software based. Hardware-based attestation requires additional dedicated hardware (e.g., Trusted Platform Module) on the device [1]. Deploying dedicated hardware can incur additional cost in terms of hardware cost and power consumption, which are often prohibitive for inexpensive or low-power devices. In contrast, software-based attestation requires a *software prover* on the device, which performs specific computations (e.g., memory- or time-based checksum [13,14]) and returns the result to the verifier. Note that there are also hardware-software co-design hybrid platforms for remote attestation [10]. In this paper, we focus on software-based remote attestation.

Steiner et al. categorized checksum-based memory attestation in terms of evidence acquisition (software-based, hardware-based, or hybrid), integrity measurement (static or dynamic), timing (loose or strict), memory traversal (sequential or cell/block-based pseudo random), attestation routine (embedded or on-the-fly), program memory (unfilled or filled), data memory (unverified, verified, or erased), and interaction pattern (one-to-one, one-to-many, or many-to-one) [17]. Memory checksums can be generated based on *sequential* or *pseudo-random* traversal. In sequential traversal, each program memory cell is accessed in a sequential order. In contrast, in pseudo-random traversal, memory is accessed in a random cell-by-cell or block-by-block order. The effectiveness of pseudo-random traversal depends on the probability that each cell has been accessed at least once.

2.3 Stackelberg Security Games

A Stackelberg security game (SSG) is a game-theoretic model, where typically a defending player acts as the leader, and the adversarial player acts as the follower. The leader has the advantage of making the first move, while the follower has the advantage of responding strategically to the leader's move. Stackelberg security games have been successfully applied to finding optimal defensive strategies in a variety of settings, both in the cyber and physical domain [16]. For example, SSG have helped researchers and practitioners to address a security issues such as security-resource allocation at airports, biodiversity protection, randomized inspections, road safety, border patrol, and so on [5,7,19,24].

Game theory can model attacker-defender interactions and characterize optimal strategies given the players' strategy spaces and objectives. In our game-theoretic model of remote attestation, the defender acts as the leader by deciding how often to perform remote attestation, and the adversary acts as the follower by deciding which devices to attack. We provide detailed definitions of the environment, the player's strategy spaces, and their objectives in Sect. 4.

3 Testbed Design and Development

In our testbed, multiple IoT applications are running on multiple IoT devices. We implement and enable various software vulnerabilities (e.g., heap-based buffer overflow) in these applications so that adversaries can remotely compromise the devices by exploiting these vulnerabilities. As a result, adversaries can modify the code of processes without crashing or restarting them. We also integrate memory checksum-based attestation method in the applications. Therefore, a verifier can remotely verify the integrity of the vulnerable processes.

3.1 Testbed Components

A typical IoT testbed consists of several IoT devices running various IoT server applications. Our testbed also includes two other types of nodes to mount attacks (e.g., code injection) against the IoT devices and to detect the attacks using remote attestation. The architecture of our testbed is presented in Fig. 1.

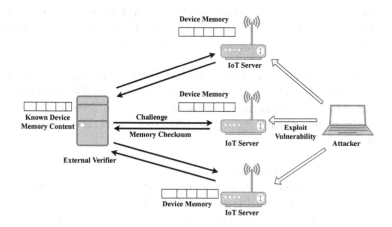

Fig. 1. Remote attestation testbed architecture.

IoT Server Node. We set up various IoT server applications on these nodes, add vulnerable code snippets to the applications, and debug them to find exploitation opportunities that can be used to perform code-injection attacks. Then, we incorporate a memory-checksum generator that can calculate a checksum whenever the application receives a challenge from an external verifier node.

Attacker Node. The attacker is a client node that can interact with the IoT application servers and execute various exploits (e.g., stack- or heap-based buffer overflow). The attacker's purpose is to inject or alter the software code of vulnerable applications without crashing the processes.

External Verifier Node. The verifier is responsible for performing memory-checksum based attestation of the potentially compromised application servers. For checksum-based attestation, the verifier sends a challenge along with a random seed to the potentially compromised server node and records the response in return to verify.

3.2 Testbed Development

To experiment with various remote attestation strategies, we implement the following features in the testbed: start or terminate various IoT applications, exploit these applications from an attacker node, and generate challenge-response for remote attestation.

Testbed Setup. Our testbed uses five Raspberry Pi 3 Model B+ devices (two IoT application servers, an attacker, and two nodes for the verifier). All devices run Raspbian Linux. We incorporate two example IoT applications: an irrigation server[1] and a smart home[2].

Enabling Vulnerabilities. We disable certain security features of the Linux kernel and the compiler to enable stack- and heap-overflow based exploitation. To enable these vulnerabilities, we disable the ASLR and stack protection; and enable code execution while compiling the applications.

Exploitation Simulation. We debug all of the applications on the application server nodes to find stack- and heap-based vulnerabilities. Then, we create corresponding exploit payloads on the attacker node. The attacker node sends a request to the server, which triggers the vulnerability and thereby injects a shellcode into the process.

Integrity Verification Simulation. In our testbed, we implement memory-checksum (sequential- and random-order checksum) as remote attestation strategies, which require an external trusted verifier. The verifier can attest a potentially compromised device by sending the same challenge to the target device and an identical isolated device, and compare their responses.

4 Game-Theoretic Model of Remote Attestation

Remote attestation enables a defender to detect compromised devices remotely. However, the effectiveness and computational cost of attestation depends on strategies, such as when to attest a device and what method of attestation to employ. As IoT devices are resource-limited and attestation incurs computational cost, some devices should not be verified frequently (e.g., devices with low value for an adversary). On the other hand, some devices (e.g., ones with high value for the adversary) may need frequent attestation.

To find optimal strategies for remote attestation, we propose a game-theoretic model. Our model is a *two-player, general-sum Stackelberg security game*, where the defender is the leader and the adversary is the follower (i.e., defender first selects its attestation strategy to defend its IoT devices, and then the adversary chooses which devices to attack considering the defender's attestation strategy).

---

[1] https://github.com/NamedP1ayer/IrrigationServer.
[2] https://github.com/renair/smarthome.

We assume that the defender chooses for each device and for each attestation method the probability of applying that method to that device; the adversary chooses for each device whether to attack it or not.

Table 1 summarizes the notation of our game-theoretic model.

4.1 Environment and Players

There is a set of IoT devices $\mathcal{D}$ in the environment, where each individual device $\delta \in \mathcal{D}$ runs various IoT applications and services. As different devices may have different software stacks, we divide the devices into disjoint classes. These device classes are denoted $\mathcal{E}_1, \mathcal{E}_2, \ldots, \mathcal{E}_n$, where we have $i \neq j \rightarrow \mathcal{E}_i \cap \mathcal{E}_j = \emptyset$ and $\bigcup_i \mathcal{E}_i = \mathcal{D}$. Devices belonging to the same class have the same vulnerabilities and may be attacked using the same exploits.

In our Stackelberg game model, there are two players: a defender (leader) and an attacker (follower). The defender tries to minimize the security risks of the IoT devices by detecting compromises, while the attacker tries to compromise the devices but avoid detection. To detect compromised devices, the defender uses various attestation methods (e.g., memory checksum, control-flow integrity). We let $\mathcal{M}$ denote the set of attestation methods, where each attestation method is an $m \in \mathcal{M}$. If the defender detects a compromised device, the defender resets the device back to its secure state.

4.2 Strategy Spaces

Knowing the defender's strategy (i.e., probability of attesting each device using each method), the attacker chooses which devices to attack. We assume that the attacker follows a deterministic strategy and chooses for each device whether to attack it or not. Note that in an SSG, restricting the follower (i.e., the attacker) to deterministic strategies is without loss of generality. We let the attacker's strategy be represented as a vector $\boldsymbol{a} = \langle a_\delta \rangle_{\delta \in \mathcal{D}}$, where $a_\delta = 1$ means attacking device $\delta \in \mathcal{D}$, and $a_\delta = 0$ means not attacking device δ. Therefore, the attacker's strategy space is

$$\boldsymbol{a} \in \{0,1\}^{|\mathcal{D}|}.$$

On the other hand, the defender can choose a randomized strategy, i.e., for each device $\delta \in \mathcal{D}$ and attestation method $m \in \mathcal{M}$, the defender chooses the probability $p_\delta^m \in [0,1]$ of running attestation method m on device δ. We let the defender's strategy be represented as a vector $\boldsymbol{p} = \langle p_\delta^m \rangle_{\delta \in \mathcal{D}, m \in \mathcal{M}}$, where $p_\delta^m = 0$ means never running method $m \in \mathcal{M}$ on device $\delta \in \mathcal{D}$, and $p_\delta^m = 1$ means always running method m on device δ. Therefore, the defender's strategy space is

$$\boldsymbol{p} \in [0,1]^{|\mathcal{D} \times \mathcal{M}|}.$$

4.3 Utility Functions

Next, we formalize the players' objectives by defining their utility functions.

Table 1. List of symbols

Symbol	Description
Constants	
$\mathcal{D}$	Set of devices
$\mathcal{M}$	Set of attestation method
$\mathcal{E}_i$	A set of devices that share common vulnerabilities, where $\mathcal{E}_i \subseteq \mathcal{D}$
μ^m	Detection probability of attestation method $m \in \mathcal{M}$ when executed on a compromised device
C_D^m	Defender's cost to run attestation method $m \in \mathcal{M}$
C_A^δ	Attacker's cost to compromise device $\delta \in \mathcal{D}$
$C_A^\mathcal{E}$	Attacker's cost to develop an exploit for a device class $\mathcal{E} \subseteq \mathcal{D}$
G_D^δ, G_A^δ	Defender's/attacker's gain for compromised device $\delta \in \mathcal{D}$
L_D^δ, L_A^δ	Defender's/attacker's loss for compromised device $\delta \in \mathcal{D}$ (represented as negative values)
Variables	
$\boldsymbol{p}$	Defender's strategy vector
$\boldsymbol{a}$	Attacker's strategy vector
a_δ	Attacker's action (i.e., attack or not) against device $\delta \in \mathcal{D}$
p_δ^m	Probability of running attestation method $m \in \mathcal{M}$ on device $\delta \in \mathcal{D}$
Functions	
$P_\delta(\boldsymbol{p})$	Conditional probability of defender detecting with strategy $\boldsymbol{p}$ that device $\delta \in \mathcal{D}$ is compromised (given that it is actually compromised)
$C_D^T(\boldsymbol{p})$	Defender's total cost for strategy $\boldsymbol{p}$
$C_A^T(\boldsymbol{a})$	Attacker's total cost For strategy $\boldsymbol{p}$
$U_D(\boldsymbol{p}, \boldsymbol{a})$	Defender's expected utility for strategy profile $(\boldsymbol{p}, \boldsymbol{a})$
$U_A(\boldsymbol{p}, \boldsymbol{a})$	Attacker's expected utility for strategy profile $(\boldsymbol{p}, \boldsymbol{a})$
$U_D^\delta(p_\delta^m, a_\delta)$	Defender's expected utility from device $\delta \in \mathcal{D}$
$U_A^\delta(p_\delta^m, a_\delta)$	Attacker's expected utility from device $\delta \in \mathcal{D}$
$\mathcal{F}_A(\boldsymbol{p})$	Attacker's best response against defender strategy $\boldsymbol{p}$

Defender's Utility. Different attestation methods can have different detection rates (i.e., different probability of detecting an attack when the method is run on a compromised device). For each attestation method $m \in \mathcal{M}$, we let μ^m denote the probability that method m detects that the device is compromised.

However, the defender can run multiple attestation methods on the same device, and any one of these may detect the compromise. Therefore, the probability $P_\delta(\boldsymbol{p})$ of detecting that device $\delta \in \mathcal{D}$ is compromised when the defender uses attestation strategy $\boldsymbol{p}$ is

$$P_\delta(\boldsymbol{p}) = 1 - \prod_{m \in \mathcal{M}} (1 - \mu^m \cdot p_\delta^m). \tag{1}$$

Each attestation method also has a computational cost, which the defender incurs for running the method on a device. For each attestation method $m \in \mathcal{M}$, we let C_D^m be the cost of running method m on a device. Then, the defender's expected total cost $C_D^T(\boldsymbol{p})$ for running attestation following strategy $\boldsymbol{p}$ is

$$C_D^T(\boldsymbol{p}) = \sum_{\delta \in \mathcal{D}} \sum_{m \in \mathcal{M}} C_D^m \cdot p_\delta^m. \qquad (2)$$

Note that the expected total cost of attestation $C_D^T(\boldsymbol{p})$ depends on the probability of running attestation (higher the probability p_δ^m, higher the expected cost for device δ and method m).

Next, we let G_D^δ be the defender's gain when the attacker chooses to attack device $\delta \in \mathcal{D}$ and the defender detects that the device is compromised. On the other hand, let L_D^δ be the defender's loss when the attacker chooses to attack device δ and the defender does not detect that the device is compromised. Then, we can express the defender's expected utility $U_D(\boldsymbol{p}, \boldsymbol{a})$ when the defender uses attestation strategy $\boldsymbol{p}$ and the attacker uses attack strategy $\boldsymbol{a}$ as

$$U_D(\boldsymbol{p}, \boldsymbol{a}) = \sum_{\delta \in \mathcal{D}} \left[G_D^\delta \cdot P_\delta(\boldsymbol{p}) + L_D^\delta \cdot (1 - P_\delta(\boldsymbol{p})) \right] \cdot a_\delta - C_D^T(\boldsymbol{p}). \qquad (3)$$

Attacker's Utility. Let $C_A^{\mathcal{E}}$ be the cost of developing an exploit for device class $\mathcal{E}$, and let C_A^δ be the cost of attacking a particular device $\delta \in \mathcal{D}$. For any attack strategy $\boldsymbol{a}$, the set of device classes that the adversary attacks can be expressed as $\{\mathcal{E} \mid \exists \delta \in \mathcal{E} \, (a_\delta = 1)\}$. Then, we can express the adversary's total cost $C_A^T(\boldsymbol{a})$ for attack strategy $\boldsymbol{a}$ as

$$C_A^T(\boldsymbol{a}) = \sum_{\mathcal{E}} \left(C_A^{\mathcal{E}} \cdot 1_{\{\exists \delta \in \mathcal{E}(a_\delta = 1)\}} + \sum_{\delta \in \mathcal{E}} C_A^\delta \cdot a_\delta \right). \qquad (4)$$

Note that the attacker incurs cost for both developing an exploit for each class that it targets as well as for each individual device.

Similar to the defender, we let attacker's gain and loss for attacking a device $\delta \in \mathcal{D}$ be G_A^δ and L_A^δ when the compromise is not detected and detected, respectively. Then, we can express the adversary's expected utility $U_A(\boldsymbol{p}, \boldsymbol{a})$ when the defender uses attestation strategy $\boldsymbol{p}$ and the attacker uses attack strategy $\boldsymbol{a}$ as

$$U_A(\boldsymbol{p}, \boldsymbol{a}) = \sum_{\delta \in \mathcal{D}} \left[L_A^\delta \cdot P_\delta(\boldsymbol{p}) + G_A^\delta \cdot (1 - P_\delta(\boldsymbol{p})) \right] \cdot a_\delta - C_A^T(\boldsymbol{a}). \qquad (5)$$

For the sake of simplicity, we assume that with respect to gains and losses from compromises, the players' utilities are zero sum, that is, $G_D^\delta = -L_A^\delta$ and $L_D^\delta = -G_A^\delta$. Note that the game is not zero sum due to the players' asymmetric costs $C_D^T(\boldsymbol{p})$ and $C_A^T(\boldsymbol{a})$.

4.4   Solution Concept

We assume that both the defender and attacker aim to maximize their expected utilities. To formulate the optimal attestation strategy for the defender, we first define the attacker's best-response strategy.

In response to a defender's strategy p, the attacker always chooses an attack strategy a that maximizes the attacker's expected utility $U_A(p, a)$. Therefore, we can define the attacker's best response as follows.

Definition 1 (Attacker's best response). *Against a defender strategy* p, *the attacker's* best-response strategy $\mathcal{F}_A(p)$ *is*

$$\mathcal{F}_A(p) = \text{argmax}_a \, U_A(p, a). \tag{6}$$

Note that the best response is not necessarily unique (i.e., $\mathcal{F}_A$ may be a set of more than one strategies). Hence, as is usual in the literature, we will assume tie-breaking in favor of the defender to formulate the optimal attestation strategy.

Since the defender's objective is to choose an attestation strategy p that maximizes its expected utility $U_D(p, a)$ anticipating that the attacker will choose a best-response strategy from $\mathcal{F}(p)$, we can define the defender's optimal strategy as follows.

Definition 2 (Defender's optimal strategy). *The defender's* optimal attestation strategy p^* *is*

$$p^* = \text{argmax}_{p, \, a \in \mathcal{F}_A(p)} \, U_D(p, a) \tag{7}$$

5   Analysis of Optimal Attestation Strategies

Here, we present analytical results on our game-theoretic model, characterizing the defender's optimal strategy in important special cases. For ease of exposition, we present these special cases in increasing generality. Due to lack of space, we omit proofs and details of the analysis in this document. The proofs and details are available in the extended online version [12].

5.1   Case 1: Single Device and Single Attestation Method

First, we assume that there exists only one device δ and one attestation method m.

Attacker's Best-Response Strategy. Whether the attacker's best response is to attack or not depends on the defender's strategy p_δ^m. Further, it is easy to see that if attacking is a best response for some p_δ^m, then it must also be a best response for any $\hat{p}_\delta^m < p_\delta^m$. Therefore, there must exist a threshold value τ_δ of the defender's probability p_δ^m that determines the attacker's best response.

Lemma 1. *The attacker's best-response strategy $\mathcal{F}(\boldsymbol{p})$ is*

$$\mathcal{F}(\boldsymbol{p}) = \begin{cases} \{1\} & \text{if } p_\delta^m < \tau_\delta \\ \{0,1\} & \text{if } p_\delta^m = \tau_\delta \\ \{0\} & \text{otherwise,} \end{cases} \tag{8}$$

where

$$\tau_\delta = \frac{1}{\mu^m} \cdot \frac{C_A^\mathcal{E} + C_A^\delta - G_A^\delta}{L_A^\delta - G_A^\delta}. \tag{9}$$

In other words, it is a best response for the attacker to attack if the defender's attestation probability p_δ^m is lower than the threshold τ_δ; and it is a best response not to attack if the probability p_δ^m is higher than the threshold τ_δ.

Defender's Optimal Strategy. The defender may pursue one of two approaches for maximizing its own expected utility: selecting an attestation probability that is high enough to deter the attacker from attacking (i.e., to eliminate losses by ensuring that not attacking is a best response for the attacker); or selecting an attestation probability that strikes a balance between risk and cost, accepting that the adversary might attack.

First, from Eqs. (2) and (8), it is clear that the lowest-cost strategy for deterring the attacker is $p_\delta^m = \tau_\delta$. Second, if the defender does not deter the attacker, then it must choose a probability p_δ^m from the range $[0, \tau_\delta]$ that maximizes $U_D(p_\delta^m, 1)$. Then, it follows from Eq. (3) that the optimal probability is either $p_\delta^m = 0$ or τ_δ, depending on the constants μ^m, C_D^m, G_D^δ, and L_D^δ.

Proposition 1. *The defender's optimal attestation strategy p^{*m}_δ is*

$$p^{*m}_\delta = \begin{cases} 0 & \text{if } C_D^m \geq (G_D^\delta - L_D^\delta) \cdot \mu^m \text{ and } \tau_\delta \geq \frac{L_D^\delta}{-C_D^m} \\ \tau_\delta & \text{otherwise.} \end{cases} \tag{10}$$

Note that the first case corresponds to when deterrence is not necessarily better than non-deterrence (first condition), and for non-deterrence strategies, minimizing risks over costs is not better (second condition).

5.2 Case 2: Multiple Devices and Single Device Class

Next, we generalize our analysis by allowing multiple devices $\mathcal{D}$, but assuming a single device class $\mathcal{E} = \mathcal{D}$ and single attestation method m.

Attacker's Best-Response Strategy. First, the attacker needs to decide whether it will attack at all: if the attacker does not attack at all, it attains $U_A(\boldsymbol{p}, \boldsymbol{0}) = 0$ utility; if the attacker does attack some devices, it incurs the cost $C_A^\mathcal{E}$ of attacking the class once, and it will need to make decisions for each individual device $\delta \in \mathcal{D}$ without considering this cost $C_A^\mathcal{E}$. The latter is very similar to *Case 1* since for each individual device δ, the decision must be based on a threshold value τ_δ of the attestation probability p_δ^m; however, this threshold must now ignore $C_A^\mathcal{E}$.

Lemma 2. *The attacker's best-response strategy $\mathcal{F}(p)$ is*

$$\mathcal{F}(p) = \begin{cases} \{a^*\} & \text{if } U_A(p, a^*) > 0 \\ \{a^*, 0\} & \text{if } U_A(p, a^*) = 0 \\ \{0\} & \text{otherwise,} \end{cases} \qquad (11)$$

where

$$a_\delta^* = \begin{cases} 1 & \text{if } p_\delta^m < \overline{\tau}_\delta \\ 0 & \text{otherwise,} \end{cases} \qquad (12)$$

and

$$\overline{\tau}_\delta = \frac{1}{\mu^m} \cdot \frac{C_A^\delta - G_A^\delta}{L_A^\delta - G_A^\delta}. \qquad (13)$$

Note that strategy a^* is a utility-maximizing strategy for the attacker assuming that it has already paid the cost $C_A^{\mathcal{E}}$ for attacking the class. Hence, the decision between attacking (in which case a^* is optimal) and not attacking at all ($a = 0$) can is based on the utility $U_A(p, a^*)$ obtained from strategy a^* and the utility $U_A(p, 0) = 0$ obtained from not attacking at all.

Defender's Optimal Strategy. Again, the defender must choose between deterrence and acceptance (i.e., deterring the adversary from attacking or accepting that the adversary might attack). However, in contrast to *Case 1*, the defender now has the choice between completely deterring the adversary from attacking (i.e., adversary is not willing to incur cost $C_A^{\mathcal{E}}$ and hence attacks no devices at all) and deterring the adversary only from attacking some devices (i.e., adversary incurs cost $C_A^{\mathcal{E}}$ and attacks some devices, but it is deterred from attacking other devices).

Proposition 2. *The defender's optimal attestation strategy p^* is*

$$p^* = \begin{cases} \{p^{ND}\} & \text{if } U_D(p^{ND}, a^*) > U_D(p^D, 0) \\ \{p^{ND}, p^D\} & \text{if } U_D(p^{ND}, a^*) = U_D(p^D, 0) \\ \{p^D\} & \text{otherwise,} \end{cases} \qquad (14)$$

where

$$(p^{ND})_\delta^m = \begin{cases} 0 & \text{if } C_D^m \geq (G_D^\delta - L_D^\delta) \cdot \mu^m \text{ and } \overline{\tau}_\delta \geq \frac{L_D^\delta}{-C_D^m} \\ \overline{\tau}_\delta & \text{otherwise,} \end{cases} \qquad (15)$$

a^* *is as defined in Eq.* (12) *with* $p = p^{ND}$, *and*

$$p^D = \text{argmin}_{\{p:\, U_A(p,1) \leq 0 \,\wedge\, \forall \delta (p_\delta^m \in [0, \tau_\delta])\}} \sum_{\delta \in \mathcal{D}} C_D^m \cdot p_\delta^m. \qquad (16)$$

Note that p^{ND} is the optimal attestation strategy if the defender does not completely deter the adversary from attacking, calculated similarly to *Case 1*; p^D is the optimal attestation strategy if the defender completely deters the adversary from attacking, which may be computed by solving a simple linear optimization (Eq. 16).

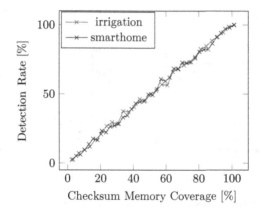

Fig. 2. Detection rate of pseudo-random memory checksum as a function of memory coverage.

5.3   Case 3: Multiple Devices and Multiple Device Classes

Next, we consider multiple device classes $\mathcal{E}_1, \mathcal{E}_2, \ldots, \mathcal{E}_n$. We generalize our previous results by observing that both the attacker's and defender's decisions for each class of devices are independent of other classes.

Lemma 3. *For each device class $\mathcal{E}_i$, let a_i be a best response as given by Lemma 2. Then, $\langle a_1, a_2, \ldots, a_n \rangle$ is a best-response attack strategy.*

Proposition 3. *For each device class $\mathcal{E}_i$, let p_i^* be an optimal attestation strategy as given by Proposition 2. Then, $\langle p_1^*, p_2^*, \ldots, p_n^* \rangle$ is an optimal attestation strategy.*

6   Numerical Results

Here, we present experimental results from our testbed, which confirm our modeling assumptions, as well as numerical results on our game-theoretic model.

6.1   Experimental Results from the Remote Attestation Testbed

We consider an experimental setup with two test applications, an irrigation and a smarthome application. We implement sequential and pseudo-random memory checksum as exemplary software-based remote attestation methods. Software-based attestation incurs various costs; in this section, we study checksum-based remote attestation in terms of memory and computational overhead. We also evaluate checksum-based attestation in terms of detection rate.

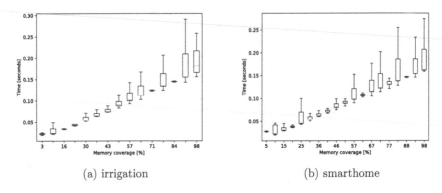

(a) irrigation   (b) smarthome

Fig. 3. Running time of checksum calculation as a function of memory coverage.

Detection Rate of Pseudo-random Memory Checksum. In this experiment, we study the efficacy of pseudo-random memory checksum in terms of detecting changes to the code of a running application. We use a block-based pseudo-random technique, where each block is 500 bytes. We start our experiment with checking 200 blocks, which are selected pseudo-randomly based on a seed value. Then, we increase the number of blocks by 200 in iterations to measure the impact of increasing memory coverage. In each iteration, we run the pseudo-random memory checksum 500 times, using a different random seed each time, to reliably measure the detection rate for a certain number of blocks.

Figure 2 shows the detection rate of pseudo-random memory checksum as a function of the fraction of memory covered by the checksum calculation, for our two test applications. Note that we express the fraction of memory covered as a percentage. Specifically, we calculate the ratio as (number of blocks × block size × 100)/total memory size of the program. We find that detection rate increases roughly proportionally with memory coverage, ranging from 0% to 100%, which supports our modeling choices.

Running Time of Pseudo-Random Memory Checksum. Next, we study the running time of calculating pseudo-random memory checksum with memory coverage ranging from 3% to 98%. For each memory-coverage level, we run the checksum calculation 500 times to obtain reliable running-time measurements. Figure 3 shows the distribution of running time for various memory-coverage level for our two test applications. We find that similar to detection rate, the average of running time also increases proportionally with memory coverage, which supports our modeling choices.

6.2 Evaluation of Game-Theoretic Model and Optimal Strategies

To evaluate our model and optimal strategies, we consider an example environment consisting of $|\mathcal{D}| = 50$ IoT devices from 5 different classes (10 devices in each class $\mathcal{E}_i$), and for simplicity, we consider a single attestation method m

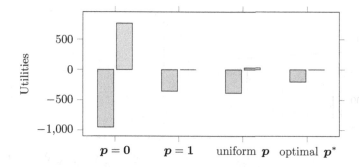

Fig. 4. Comparison between optimal and naïve defender strategies based on the defender's utility (blue ▮) and the attacker's utility (red ▮), assuming that the attacker chooses its best response.

implemented in these devices. For each device δ, we choose both the defender's and the attacker's gain values G_D^δ and G_A^δ uniformly at random from $[20, 40]$. We assume that the game is zero-sum with respect to gains and losses; that is, we let the players' losses (L_D^δ, L_A^δ) be $G_D^\delta = -L_A^\delta$ and $L_D^\delta = -G_A^\delta$. Finally, we choose the detection probability of the attestation method μ uniformly at randomly from $[0.5, 0.9]$, the attestation cost C_D from $[0, 10]$, the exploit development cost $C_A^\mathcal{E}$ from $[15, 40]$, and the device attack costs C_A^δ from $[1, 3]$ for each device δ.

Comparison to Naïve Baselines. We compare the defender's optimal attestation strategy p^* to three naïve baseline strategies: $p = 0$, $p = 1$, and an optimal uniform p (i.e., same probability p_δ^m for all devices δ, but this probability is chosen to maximize the defender's utility given that the adversary always chooses its best response). Figure 4 shows the players' utilities for the optimal and naïve defender strategies, assuming that the adversary chooses its best response in each case. We see that the optimal strategy outperforms the naïve baselines in terms of the defender's utility. Specifically, it outperforms $p = 0$ and optimal uniform p by deterring the adversary from attacking, which these naïve baselines fail to achieve; and it outperforms $p = 1$ by achieving deterrence at a lower cost.

Detailed Comparison to Naïve Baselines. Figure 5 provides a more detailed comparison between the optimal attestation strategy p^* and the three naïve baselines. In contrast to Fig. 4, this figure shows utilities both in the case when the adversary decides to attack (Fig. 5a) and in the case when it decides to not attack at all (Fig. 5b). In Fig. 5a, we see that the adversary can obtain a positive utility from attacking against $p = 0$ and the optimal uniform p. Therefore, these strategies do not deter the adversary from attacking. In contrast, the adversary's utility is negative against both $p = 1$ and the optimal strategy p^*. In Fig. 5b, we see that the defender incurs higher computational cost with $p = 1$ than with the optimal strategy p^*, making the latter the better choice.

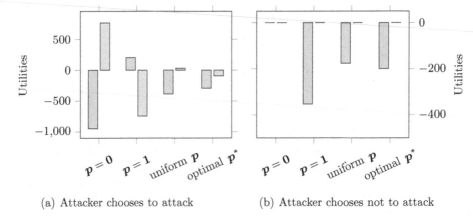

(a) Attacker chooses to attack   (b) Attacker chooses not to attack

Fig. 5. Detailed comparison between optimal and naïve defender strategies based on the defender's utility (blue ▯) and the attacker's utility (red ▯).

Comparison of Strategy Profiles. To better understand how the optimal attestation strategy outperforms the other strategies, we now take a closer look at the players' utilities in specific strategy profiles. For the defender, we consider two strategies: optimal strategy given that the defender does not completely deter the attacker (p^{ND}, see Proposition 2) and optimal strategy that completely deters the attacker (p^D, which is the optimal attestation strategy in this problem instance). For the adversary, we also consider two strategies: attacking every device ($a = 1$, which is a best response against p^{ND} in this problem instance) and not attacking at all ($a = 0$, which is always a best response against p^D).

Figure 6 shows the players' utilities in the four strategy profiles formed by the above strategies. We observe that the defender's utility is highest when it does not completely deter the adversary from attacking and the adversary does not attack at all (p^{ND} vs. $a = 0$) since the defender incurs minimal computational cost and suffers no security losses in this case. However, this is not an equilibrium since the adversary can attain higher utility by attacking every device (see p^{ND} vs. $a = 1$), which results in the best utility for the adversary and worst for the defender. To avoid such catastrophic losses, the defender can use the strategy of complete deterrence, in which case the adversary will be indifferent between attacking and not attacking (p^D vs. $a = 0$ and $a = 1$). Note that since the defender's utility is higher if the adversary does not attack, the defender can opt to tip the balance in favor of not attacking through an infinitesimal change.

7   Related Work

In this section, first we discuss the pros and cons of different IoT testbeds in the existing literature. Then we discuss existing works related to hardware- or software-based IoT remote attestation. Finally, we present a few SSG works and how our approach is different from theirs.

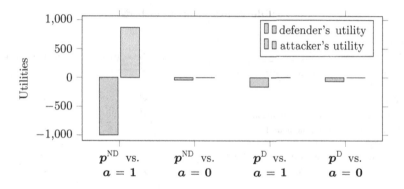

Fig. 6. Players' utilities in various strategy profiles: not deter vs. attack (p^{ND} vs. $a = 1$), not deter vs. not attack (p^{ND} vs. $a = 0$), deter vs. attack (p^{D} vs. $a = 1$), deter vs. not attack (p^{D} vs. $a = 0$).

7.1 IoT Security Testbeds

General application- or hardware-oriented IoT testbeds are widely used for research works. The primary concern for these testbeds are to find ideal configurations or set up in different types of environments [2,4]. Several IoT security testbeds are available to test different security and reliability issues. For example, Siboni et al. proposed an IoT security testbed framework, arguing that an ideal testbed should ensure reliability, anti-forensics, and adaptivity [15]. In another work, Arseni et al. developed a heterogeneous IoT testbed named *Pass-IoT*, consisting of three different architectures (MCU, SDSoC, traditional CPU) that can test, optimize, and develop lightweight cryptographic algorithms [3].

Nowadays, the number of IoT applications is rising, and so are associated security concerns for these applications. Therefore, Tekeoglu et al. developed a security testbed that can perform privacy analysis of IoT devices, including HDMI sticks, IP cameras, smartwatches, and drones [18]. The testbed enables identifying insecure protocol versions, authentication issues, and privacy violations.

We find the existing IoT security testbeds offering general security concerns related to cryptographic development, secure protocol implementations, and data privacy issues. Our remote attestation testbed offers testing application vulnerabilities, developing associated exploits, and evaluating mitigation measures through software-oriented remote attestation. Table 2 presents a comparative analysis between our work and the existing IoT security testbeds.

7.2 Remote Attestation

Checksum-based remote attestation has been widely used to secure IoT devices for a long time. Earlier, Seshadri et al. proposed a cell-based pseudo-random traversal approach in their software-based attestation scheme entitled *SWATT* [14]. The authors developed the 8-bit micro-controller architecture

Table 2. IoT security testbeds

Features	Works		
	Arseni et al., 2016	Tekeoglu et al., 2016	Our work
Lightweight encryption algorithms development	✓	X	X
Vulnerability scans	X	✓	✓
Authentication, privacy violations	X	✓	X
Exploitation development and analysis	X	X	✓
Mitigation measures testing	X	X	✓
Remote attestation experiments	X	X	✓

scheme to generate random addresses to checksum using an RC4 stream cipher. Yang et al. proposed a distributed software-based attestation scheme for WSN to verify the integrity of code in a distributed fashion [23]. The works led to later works in terms of cell- and block-based pseudo-random checksum, respectively.

A few recent works include hardware-assisted remote runtime attestation [8] that addresses runtime attack detection, a low-cost checksum-based remote memory attestation for smart grid [22], lightweight remote attestation in distributed wireless sensor networks where all nodes validate each other's data [9], and so on. Survey papers on attestation, for example, Steiner et al. presented a more comprehensive overview on checksum-based attestation [17].

7.3 Stackelberg Security Games

SSGs have been successfully applied to security problems in resource-limited domains such as airport security, biodiversity protection, randomized inspections, border patrols, cyber security, and so on [5,7,19]. To the best of our knowledge, our work is the first to apply game theory in the area of remote attestation.

While there is no prior work within the intersection of game theory and remote attestation, a number of research efforts have applied SSGs to other detection problems that resemble ours. For example, Wahab et al. developed a Bayesian Stackelberg game that helps the defender to determine optimal detection load distribution strategy among virtual machines within a cloud environment [20]. As another example, Chen et al. develops an SSG model that detects adversarial outbreak in an IoT environment through determining strategic dynamic scheduling of intrusion detection systems [6].

8   Conclusion and Future Work

IoT device exploitation has been a significant issue lately, and organizations are investing significant resources and effort into managing these security risks. An important approach for mitigating this threat is remote attestation, which enables the defender to remotely verify the integrity of devices and their software. In this work, we developed a testbed that offers research opportunities to explore and analyze IoT vulnerabilities and exploitation and to conduct experiments with varous remote attestation methods.

So far, we have developed attack strategies mostly for when kernel and compiler-based security measures are disabled. In future work, we plan to include exploitation with security features enabled in the resource-limited IoT environment. Additionally, in this paper, we evaluated software-based attestation methods (sequential and random memory-based checksum). We intend to include some other variants of attestation methods (e.g., hybrid checksum) in the testbed and to conduct experiments with control-flow integrity.

Further, we have showed how to optimize remote-attestation strategies by formulating and studying a Stackelberg security game model. Our analytical results provide algorithmic solutions for finding optimal attestation strategies in a variety of settings. These results can provide guidance to practitioners on how to protect IoT devices using remote attestation in resource-limited environments.

In this work we discussed optimal strategies for one attestation method ($|\mathcal{M}| = 1$). In future, we plan to provide analytical solutions for more general cases of multiple devices ($|\mathcal{D}| > 1$), multiple classes ($|\mathcal{E}| > 1$), and multiple attestation methods ($|\mathcal{M}| > 1$) as well. Additionally, we intend to refine our model and find optimal strategies in a more complex environment using machine learning algorithms (e.g., reinforcement learning).

Acknowledgments. This material is based upon work supported by the National Science Foundation under Grant No. CNS-1850510, IIS-1905558, and ECCS-2020289 and by the Army Research Office under Grant No. W911NF1910241 and W911NF1810208.

References

1. Abera, T., et al.: Things, trouble, trust: on building trust in IoT systems. In: Proceedings of the 53rd Annual Design Automation Conference, pp. 1–6 (2016)
2. Adjih, C., et al.: FIT IoT-LAB: a large scale open experimental IoT testbed. In: 2015 IEEE 2nd World Forum on Internet of Things (WF-IoT), pp. 459–464. IEEE (2015)
3. Arseni, Ş.C., Miţoi, M., Vulpe, A.: Pass-IoT: a platform for studying security, privacy and trust in IoT. In: 2016 International Conference on Communications (COMM), pp. 261–266. IEEE (2016)
4. Belli, L., et al.: Design and deployment of an IoT application-oriented testbed. Computer **48**(9), 32–40 (2015)
5. Bucarey, V., Casorrán, C., Figueroa, Ó., Rosas, K., Navarrete, H., Ordóñez, F.: Building real Stackelberg security games for border patrols. In: Rass, S., An, B., Kiekintveld, C., Fang, F., Schauer, S. (eds.) GameSec 2017. LNCS, vol. 10575, pp. 193–212. Springer, Cham (2017). https://doi.org/10.1007/978-3-319-68711-7_11
6. Chen, L., Wang, Z., Li, F., Guo, Y., Geng, K.: A stackelberg security game for adversarial outbreak detection in the internet of things. Sensors **20**(3), 804 (2020)
7. Gan, J., Elkind, E., Wooldridge, M.: Stackelberg security games with multiple uncoordinated defenders. In: Proceedings of the 17th International Conference on Autonomous Agents and MultiAgent Systems, pp. 703–711 (2018)

8. Geden, M., Rasmussen, K.: Hardware-assisted remote runtime attestation for critical embedded systems. In: 2019 17th International Conference on Privacy, Security and Trust (PST), pp. 1–10. IEEE (2019)

9. Kiyomoto, S., Miyake, Y.: Lightweight attestation scheme for wireless sensor network. Int. J. Secur. Appl. **8**(2), 25–40 (2014)

10. Nunes, I.D.O., Eldefrawy, K., Rattanavipanon, N., Steiner, M., Tsudik, G.: VRASED: a verified hardware/software co-design for remote attestation. In: 28th USENIX Security Symposium (USENIX Security 2019), pp. 1429–1446 (2019)

11. Parikh, V., Mateti, P.: ASLR and ROP attack mitigations for arm-based android devices. In: Thampi, S.M., Martínez Pérez, G., Westphall, C.B., Hu, J., Fan, C.I., Gómez Mármol, F. (eds.) SSCC 2017. CCIS, vol. 746, pp. 350–363. Springer, Singapore (2017). https://doi.org/10.1007/978-981-10-6898-0_29

12. Roy, S., Kadir, S.U., Vorobeychik, Y., Laszka, A.: Strategic remote attestation: testbed for Internet-of-Things devices and Stackelberg security game for optimal strategies. arXiv preprint arXiv:2109.07724 (2021)

13. Seshadri, A., Luk, M., Shi, E., Perrig, A., Van Doorn, L., Khosla, P.: Pioneer: verifying integrity and guaranteeing execution of code on legacy platforms. In: Proceedings of ACM Symposium on Operating Systems Principles (SOSP), vol. 173, pp. 10–1145 (2005)

14. Seshadri, A., Perrig, A., Van Doorn, L., Khosla, P.: SWATT: software-based attestation for embedded devices. In: 2004 Proceedings of IEEE Symposium on Security and Privacy, pp. 272–282. IEEE (2004)

15. Siboni, S., et al.: Security testbed for internet-of-things devices. IEEE Trans. Reliab. **68**(1), 23–44 (2019)

16. Sinha, A., Fang, F., An, B., Kiekintveld, C., Tambe, M.: Stackelberg security games: looking beyond a decade of success. In: Proceedings of the 27th International Joint Conference on Artificial Intelligence. IJCAI (2018)

17. Steiner, R.V., Lupu, E.: Attestation in wireless sensor networks: a survey. ACM Comput. Surv. (CSUR) **49**(3), 1–31 (2016)

18. Tekeoglu, A., Tosun, A.Ş.: A testbed for security and privacy analysis of IoT devices. In: 2016 IEEE 13th International Conference on Mobile Ad Hoc and Sensor Systems (MASS), pp. 343–348. IEEE (2016)

19. Trejo, K.K., Clempner, J.B., Poznyak, A.S.: Adapting strategies to dynamic environments in controllable Stackelberg security games. In: 2016 IEEE 55th Conference on Decision and Control (CDC), pp. 5484–5489. IEEE (2016)

20. Wahab, O.A., Bentahar, J., Otrok, H., Mourad, A.: Resource-aware detection and defense system against multi-type attacks in the cloud: repeated Bayesian stackelberg game. IEEE Trans. Dependable Secure Comput. **18**(2), 605–622 (2019)

21. Xu, B., et al.: A security design for the detecting of buffer overflow attacks in IoT device. IEEE Access **6**, 72862–72869 (2018)

22. Yang, X., et al.: Towards a low-cost remote memory attestation for the smart grid. Sensors **15**(8), 20799–20824 (2015)

23. Yang, Y., Wang, X., Zhu, S., Cao, G.: Distributed software-based attestation for node compromise detection in sensor networks. In: 26th IEEE International Symposium on Reliable Distributed Systems (SRDS 2007), pp. 219–230. IEEE (2007)

24. Yin, Z., Korzhyk, D., Kiekintveld, C., Conitzer, V., Tambe, M.: Stackelberg vs. nash in security games: interchangeability, equivalence, and uniqueness. In: Proceedings of the 9th International Conference on Autonomous Agents and Multiagent Systems, vol. 1, pp. 1139–1146 (2010)

Innovations in Attacks and Defenses

Bet and Attack: Incentive Compatible Collaborative Attacks Using Smart Contracts

Zahra Motaqy[1]([✉]), Ghada Almashaqbeh[1], Behnam Bahrak[2],
and Naser Yazdani[2]

[1] University of Connecticut, Storrs, USA
{raha,ghada.almashaqbeh}@uconn.edu
[2] University of Tehran, Tehran, Iran
{bahrak,yazdani}@ut.ac.ir

Abstract. Smart contract-enabled blockchains allow building decentralized applications in which mutually-distrusted parties can work together. Recently, oracle services emerged to provide these applications with real-world data feeds. Unfortunately, these capabilities have been used for malicious purposes under what is called criminal smart contracts. A few works explored this dark side and showed a variety of such attacks. However, none of them considered collaborative attacks against targets that reside outside the blockchain ecosystem.

In this paper, we bridge this gap and introduce a smart contract-based framework that allows a sponsor to orchestrate a collaborative attack among (pseudo)anonymous attackers and reward them for that. While all previous works required a technique to quantify an attacker's individual contribution, which could be infeasible with respect to real-world targets, our framework avoids that. This is done by developing a novel scheme for trustless collaboration through betting. That is, attackers bet on an event (i.e., the attack takes place) and then work on making that event happen (i.e., perform the attack). By taking DDoS as a usecase, we formulate attackers' interaction as a game, and formally prove that these attackers will collaborate in proportion to the amount of their bets in the game's unique equilibrium. We also model our framework and its reward function as an incentive mechanism and prove that it is a strategy-proof and budget-balanced one. Finally, we conduct numerical simulations to demonstrate the equilibrium behavior of our framework.

Keywords: Collaborative attacks · Mechanism design · Criminal smart contracts · Blockchain model

1 Introduction

Cryptocurrencies and blockchain technology continue to build innovative computing models and economic tools that can reshape the services and systems

---

Z. Motaqy—Most work done while at University of Tehran.

B. Bošanský et al. (Eds.): GameSec 2021, LNCS 13061, pp. 293–313, 2021.
https://doi.org/10.1007/978-3-030-90370-1_16

around us. Fueled by the huge interest this technology received, researchers and practitioners alike are racing to build new applications and improve existing ones. Smart contracts facilitate this process; individuals can deploy arbitrary code on a blockchain, allowing for trustless collaboration between participants under terms enforced by the contract execution. More recently, and to achieve the quest of allowing blockchain to react to real-world events, the concept of oracles has been introduced [1,3,9]. These are external services that supplement a smart contract with information about specific real-world events.

However, these new capabilities have been used for malicious purposes as well. This falls under what is called criminal smart contracts (CSCs), a term that was first coined by Juels et al. [17]. They showed that CSCs can be used for cryptographic key theft, leakage of confidential information, and real-world crimes such as murder. Since then, several studies have proposed new smart contract-based attacks mainly related to bribery to disrupt the mining process [12,15,18,25]. Nonetheless, these works were limited to (collaborative) attacks on the cryptocurrency/blockchain itself rather than outsider real-world targets. Juels et al. [17] considered real-world targets, but only for solo attackers.

Collaborative attacks are known to be more devastating [4–6,19,26,27,29]. This raises the question of whether CSCs can facilitate such attacks in the real world. Addressing this question is challenging; (pseudo)anonymity of blockchain users leads to incomplete information about the attackers. Also, dealing with attackers in the real world makes it hard to measure and verify their contribution. Attackers are represented by random-looking public keys in a CSC who tend to hide their involvement in a given attack to avoid legal consequences. This is different from attacks with targets within the blockchain ecosystem itself, where usually cryptographic primitives comes for the rescue to prove a claimed contribution [15]. This is even easier in the context of a solo attacker; the fact that an attack took place at the promised time/location implies that the work has been done [17]. Verifying contribution is essential to ensure that self-interested parties cannot collect their rewards without doing the required work.

Contributions. In this paper, we bridge this gap by showing how smart contracts can be used to perform collaborative attacks against real-world targets. We develop an incentive compatible framework that allows a sponsor to orchestrate a collaborative attack among (pseudo)anonymous attackers and reward them for that. Our framework mitigates the requirement of quantifying attackers' individual contributions by introducing a betting-based technique to allow trustless collaboration. In particular, attackers bet on an event (i.e., the attack takes place) and then work on making that event happen (i.e., perform the attack). By designing an incentive-compatible reward mechanism, these attackers will be motivated to deliver the work represented by the value of their bets, and hence, obtain their rewards. To the best of our knowledge, our work is the first generic CSC-based collaborative attack framework against real-work targets.

As a use case, we consider distributed denial of service (DDoS) attacks.[1] We design a smart contract to perform this attack, and we formulate attackers' inter-

---

[1] We note that [22] dealt with smart contract-based DDoS, but the work is very high level and lacks many important details, making it hard to assess its feasibility.

action as a game. Then we formally prove that these attackers will collaborate in proportion to the amount of their bets in the game's unique equilibrium. We also model our framework and its reward function as an incentive mechanism and prove that it is strategy-proof (i.e., attackers will not misrepresent the amounts of their bets) and that it is budget-balanced (i.e., the total rewards allocated to the attackers doesn't exceed the deposited attack rewards). Through numerical simulations, we study the impact of several parameters, including the reward function, total amount of bets, and attack cost, on the attack outcome. We show that in a typical scenario, the proposed incentive mechanism provides individual rationality and fairness for the collaborating attackers.

We argue that showing feasibility of collaborative attacks using CSCs is essential to identifying such threats, and devising secure countermeasures. Moreover, and although our focus is on attacks in this paper, we believe that our framework can facilitate benign collaboration between users. For example, it can be employed in blockchain-based decentralized systems offering digital services, such as content delivery [8] and file storage [7], to incentivize peers to act honestly while serving others. Such a feature has a huge impact on system efficiency. That is, incentive compatibility mechanisms (when applicable) can be used to defend against potential threats instead of (usually computationally-heavy) cryptographic mechanisms.

Related Work. Many incidents were reported on cybercriminals collaboration in the context of malware and massive DDoS attacks [4–6,19]. Attackers trade goods, services, and money through the phishing marketplace and even advertise their demands [10]. Moreover, botnets can be even rented for spam campaigns and DDoS attacks [2].

Usually these attacks involve some trust assumption that a sponsor will reward attackers for participation. CSCs can replace such assumption by providing an automated and transparent way for coordination and sponsorship [11,17,20]. As mentioned before, this observation was first investigated by Juel et al. [17]. They proved how the CSCs they developed can be commission fair, meaning that neither the sponsor nor the attackers can cheat. Another work that considered real world targets is [14] who proposed a semi-autonomous (file) ransomware architecture using CSCs. Their scheme allows paying for individual files or reimbursing the victim if decryption is invalid. Despite handling real-world targets, these works focused only on solo attackers.

Another line of work on CSCs focused on bribery to attack the cryptocurrency or blockchain itself. [25] showed an attack to allow a mining pool manager to destroy competing mining pools, and [15,18] showed how a sponsor can bribe miners to pursue a mining strategy that benefits him (e.g., to allow him to revert a transaction or to double spend). CSC-based attacks on mining have been systematically analyzed in [16] under the umbrella of algorithmic incentive manipulation attacks. On the game theoretic front, Chen et al. [12] introduced a game modeling of a bribery contract. They showed that in any Nash equilibrium, a sponsor cannot win the majority of the votes unless he/she controls more than 20% of the total bribing budget. Although the aforementioned bribery attacks consider collaborative attackers, their target is the blockchain/cryptocurrency itself. Also, these works implement techniques to enable attackers to provide cryptographic proofs that the desired mining strategy has been performed. As we mentioned before, such aspect is hard to achieve when the target resides outside the blockchain ecosystem. Our work handles these issues by showing the feasibility of CSC-based collaborative attacks against real-world targets without measuring the individual contribution of attackers.

2   A Model for a CSC-Based Collaborative Attack

In this section, we present the blockchain and threat models we adopt in this work, along with a security notion for CSCs. After that, we introduce the proposed CSC-based collaborative attack model with DDoS attacks as a usecase.

2.1   Blockchain Model

We deal with permissionless public blockchains that support smart contracts, such as Ethereum [28]. Hence, the code of the smart contract, its state, and all messages (or transactions) sent to this contract are logged in the clear on the blockchain. Any party needs an account in order to interact with a smart contract, referred to as externally owned account (EOA) in Ethereum. This account is identified by the public key of its owner, and has a public state that is mainly concerned with the account currency balance. Anyone can create any number of EOAs and participate in a CSC, and no real identities are required. Although we consider Ethereum in our CSC model, any other smart contract infrastructure can be used given that its scripting language can represent the CSC functionality.

We require the blockchain to have access to oracles that provide authenticated real-world data feeds. A popular example of such oracle services is Provable [9]. In the context of a CSC, the attack sponsor (who is also the CSC creator) will specify the metrics that the CSC will query from the oracle that will quantify the outcome of the attack. For example, in our DDoS usecase, we use the response delay as the attack outcome metric, where excessive delays means an overwhelmed (or a down) server. Provable can measure this metric by sending http requests to the target server and report the response to the CSC for which parameters like delay can be measured.

2.2   Threat Model

We adopt the following threat model in this paper:

- The blockchain is secure in the sense that the majority of the mining power is honest. So the confirmed state of the blockchain contains only valid transactions, and that any attempt to rewrite the blockchain will fail with over-whelming probability. We also assume liveness, meaning that messages cannot be blocked or delayed beyond some bounded duration, and availability in the sense that the blockchain records are accessible at anytime.

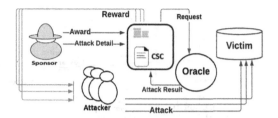

Fig. 1. A model for a CSC-based collaborative attack.

- The oracle service is secure (i.e., provide valid digitally signed data), always available, and capable of measuring the attack result in terms of some predefined metrics.[2]
- No trusted party of any type exists. Also, attackers involved in any CSC are mutually-distrusted and rational so they will act based on what maximizes their individual profits. Moreover, these attackers are regarded as independent risk-neutral decision-makers; they will be interested in maximizing the expected value of their utility.[3]

A *fully successful attack* in our model is defined as meeting the desired attack result set by the CSC sponsor. The difference between the actual and desired attack result denote the success level of an attack. It should be noted that in some attacks such success level is not applicable; it is either the attack has been done or not (e.g., steal a cryptographic key).

For security, we adopt the notions of *correctness* and *commission-fairness* proposed in [17]. A correct CSC is one that implements the attack protocol as designed by the sponsor. And a commission-fair CSC is one that guarantees that neither the sponsor nor the perpetrator of the crime can cheat; attack sponsor cannot avoid paying attackers for the work they have done, and attackers cannot collect rewards for work they have not done. Note that *work* here refers to pursuing the attack as per the sponsor's desired metrics.

2.3 Attack Model

At a high level, and as shown in Fig. 1, a CSC-based collaborative attack is composed of three phases: a CSC design and deployment phase, an attack phase, and a reward allocation phase. In order to make the discussion easier to follow, we present these phases with a running example. In particular, we consider one of the devastating cybersecurity attacks, namely, DDoS attacks. The sequence diagram of this attack is captured by Fig. 2, while the following paragraphs elaborate on the attack protocol according to our framework phases.

---

[2] It is the responsibility of the attack sponsor to pick metrics for which there is a secure oracle service that cam measure and report them.

[3] While it is true that attackers are not always risk-neutral, we assume that is the case here for simplicity. For an analysis of non-risk neutral attackers, see [21].

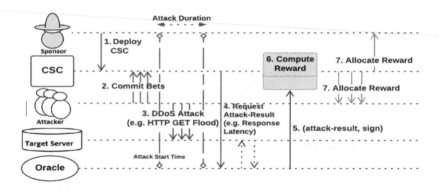

Fig. 2. Sequence diagram for a DDoS attack using CSC

Phase 1. Design and Deployment of CSC. In this phase, an attack sponsor designs the CSC functionality. This includes defining all APIs and methods needed to orchestrate the attack and distribute the rewards. This in addition to attack parameters such as attack target, duration (measured in rounds, where a round is the time needed to mine a block on the blockchain), the metrics used to measure the attack result, and the reward allocation function. For DDoS, the target can be a specific server, and the metric that we use is response delay. The oracle service Provable can measure such quantity by simply sending HTTP requests to the specified target and report the response back to the CSC for which parameters like delay can be measured [9].

The sponsor then creates a smart contract implementing the CSC functionality and publishes it on the Ethereum blockchain. He will also deposit an award for the attackers in the CSC account. Once published, and since the contract code is public on the blockchain, interested attackers can evaluate the terms and assess if it is feasible for them to participate in the attack. For example, they check their availability during the attack duration and whether they have the resources required to achieve the attack goal. If feasible, each attacker will submit a bet to the CSC's account during the betting period. This period starts when the contract is confirmed on the blockchain until the attack starting time.

In terms of DDoS, an attacker checks if he can reaches the target server, and that he can afford sending traffic to overwhelm the server. In this context, this attacker can, for example, rent botnets to achieve that [2]. Based on the amount of traffic this attacker can afford, which represents his amount of contribution in the attack, the attacker will choose his bet value and deposit in the DDoS CSC.

Phase 2. The Attack. The second phase of our framework is the attack phase. Once the deposits are made by both the sponsor and the attackers, and the attack period starts, these attackers will launch the attack. Each attacker may choose any strategy given that it achieves the attack goal set by the sponsor. For DDoS, an attacker sends appropriate traffic to overwhelm the target.[4] Since all

---

[4] While it is common that the target defends itself by identifying and filtering the attack traffic, for simplicity we assume that attackers generate effective attack traffic (traffic that passes the defense walls and gets to the target server).

attackers are sending traffic during this period, and although they do not know and do not trust each other, they are collaborating against the same target. CSC allows this automated collaboration coordination without placing trust in anyone. The attack phase continue until the end of the attack period specified in the contract.

Phase 3. Reward Allocation. In the third phase, the CSC queries the oracle to obtain the attack result. This can be done by having the sponsor send a transaction to invoke a function in CSC that sends a request to the oracle. The oracle then fetches the attack result and return it by executing a callback function in CSC. Based on the attack goal, this can happen either when the specified attack duration is over (e.g., check that the target server is down) or during that period (i.e., check that the server response delay is long enough). If multiple measures are reported, then the average, minimum or maximum can be computed (recall this is part of the terms that the sponsor specifies).

After that, the CSC computes the total currency value of the sponsor award and the attackers' bets. Then, it distributes this amount among the sponsor and the attackers based on the reward allocation function and the attack result. If the attack is fully successful, the total currency will be distributed among the attackers. If the attack is unsuccessful, then this currency will go to the sponsor (i.e., attackers are punished by taking away their bets). For attacks where there is a success level some where in between, as in DDoS, both attackers and sponsors will get part of the total currency. The distribution of this amount will be based on a reward allocation function that the sponsor chooses. In Sects. 3 and 4 we thoroughly discuss the details of the reward allocation mechanism.

At the end, the CSC sends payment transactions to the sponsor and/or attackers' accounts (these accounts are defined by the attackers public keys used when registering the bets).

We note that despite advances in devising countermeasures against DDoS [23], these attacks cannot be fully prevented. Nonetheless, it is important to point out that given that the CSC is public on the blockchain, the target could be aware of the attack (assuming he is inspecting the blockchain regularly). Hence, the target can employ defense strategies during the specified attack period. This will increase the cost of performing the attack as we will show in Sect. 5.

The Contract. The CSC contract for the above collaborative DDoS attack is outlined in Fig. 3. We model a data feed (oracle) as a sequence of pairs (m, σ). Where m is the attack result reported by the oracle, and σ is the oracle's digital signature over m. Thus, the oracle has an private/public key pair (pk_O, sk_O) used to sign/verify signatures. In the figure, $bal[X]$ denotes the balance of users' account X on the blockchain.

3   Game Theoretic Model and Analysis

Dealing with self-interested attackers is problematic; they do not care about the sponsor's goals, and they would lie to collect more rewards if they can. Attacking

---

Upon Deploying CSC by an Attack Sponsor S

Init: $award$, $target\_server_{url}$, $start\_time$, $attack\_duration$, bet_{min}, $Sponsor_{address} := [S]$, pk_O
Create:

- Profile of each attacker: Struct $Attacker$ {$account$, bet, $reward$}
- List of all bets placed: $Attacker$ [ ] public $Bets$

Deposit Award:
Assert $bal[S] \geq award$
Transfer $award$ coins from S to CSC's account

Upon Submitting a Bet by an Attacker $\mathcal{A}$

Input: $bet = msg.value$
Description:
If: $(current\_time < start\_time)$ and $(bet > bet_{min})$
Then:
Assert $bal[\mathcal{A}] \geq bet$
Transfer bet coins from $\mathcal{A}$ to CSC's account
$Bets$.push(

- $Attacker.account$: $msg.sender$,
- $Attacker.bet$: bet,
- $Attacker.reward$: 0)

Upon End of Attack Duration

Description:
Assert $current\_time > start\_time + attack\_duration$
$(m, \sigma) :=$ **requestMeasure**$(oracle, target\_server_{url})$
Assert **sigVer**(pk_O, m, σ)
* Update the $Attacker.reward$ property for all attackers in $Betts$ list based on the reward allocation function *\
ComputePayments$(award, Bets, m)$
* Pay attackers their reward and transfer the rest of the deposited money, if any, to the sponsor's account *\
TransferPayments$(Bets, Sponsor_{address})$

Fig. 3. CSC pseudocode

real world targets complicates the problem since attackers will tend to hide such information to avoid any legal consequences. This raises the question of how a CSC can measure the individual contribution of each attacker. Our goal is to identify and analyze factors that influence the attacker's behavior and use that to configure incentives properly and encourage faithful collaboration. Towards this goal, in this section, we formulate our framework for CSC-based collaborative attacks as an incomplete information game, and we show that it has a strong dominant strategy equilibrium. For simplicity, we present this modeling and analysis in the context of DDoS attack, but it can be generalized to any other attack type using the proper metrics.

3.1 Attackers Contribution

Our solution utilizes betting to avoid direct measuring of individual contributions. The attack sponsor places an initial award and each attacker places a bet, all deposited in the CSC account. An attacker is supposed to contribute in the attack in proportion to his bet value. Based on how successful the attack is (as reported by the oracle), the total amount of currency in the CSC account will be distributed among the attackers and/or the sponsor (the sponsor gets a refund only if the attack is not fully successful).

Recall that all CSC information is public on the blockchain as part of the CSC code and state. However, and given that attackers are known only by their random-looking public keys, we cannot guarantee that each attacker will place only one bet. In fact, an attacker may use that to gain privacy, as well as increase his utility (if possible), by dividing the bet into multiple smaller bets, then post these bets using several accounts all controlled by this attacker. Thus, each attacker privately knows his true bet (consisted of several smaller bets), even though all the transactions are public.

Therefore, in our framework, attackers have to decide on two actions. First, before the attack phase starts, they should decide on a betting strategy: each attacker can submit multiple bets that sum to his true bet or one bet that is equal to his true bet. We call the latter *truthful betting*. Afterward, in the attack phase, each attacker should decide on the amount of contribution to the attack.

Later in this section, we show that each attacker's relative contribution is independent of others' contributions and bets and is a function of his own bet value. In the next section, we also show that truthful betting is the best strategy for an attacker.

3.2 Interdependent Attackers Game (IAG)

We study the interaction among a set of interdependent strategic attackers as a game with independent private values and strict incomplete information. Independent private values means the utility of an attacker depends entirely on his own private information. Strict incomplete information means we have no probabilistic information in the model, i.e., we consider a worst-case scenario for missing information.

In this game, let N represent the attackers set such that $|N| = n$, ω_S be the award of the sponsor, bet_i be the true bet value of the ith attacker such that $0 < bet_i < \omega_S$, and $t_i = \frac{bet_i}{\omega_S}$ be the private information that this attacker has and it represents his type.[5] Let e_{th} represent an estimation of the total traffic

---

[5] We assume dealing with homogeneous agents in terms of the cost of contributing to the attack (all have same α in Eq. 3). Also, we show later that an attacker's bet value represents his actual contribution in the attack, and hence, his cost.

needed to satisfy the desired DDoS attack result set by the sponsor, and e_i be the relative contribution of the ith attacker in this amount, i.e., $0 \leq e_i \leq 1$. Thus, if attacker i is a free-rider and makes no effort to contribute in the attack, then $e_i = 0$. While if $e_i = 1$, this means that attacker i has launched a fully successful attack on his own. Let T denote the set of all type profiles $\hat{t} = (t_1, \ldots, t_n)$ and E denote the set of all action profile $\hat{e} = (e_1, \ldots, e_n)$. Based on his type t_i, attacker i chooses the action $e_i \in [0, 1]$. The strategy function $S : T \to E$ maps each attacker type to an action e_i. Rational attackers will select a strategy that will maximize their own utility as possible.

The reward allocation function is one of the mechanism rules that has a significant impact on the attacker's preferred strategies and attack result. In our framework, the sponsor defines the reward allocation function $R : [0, 1] \times [0, 1] \to \mathbb{R}$ in the smart contract. We propose a simple allocation function that allots reward to attackers according to the amount of their bets and the their total relative contributions in the attack denoted as e_{tot}, i.e., $e_{tot} = \sum_{i \in N} e_i$.[6] Let M be the total money amount deposited in the CSC's account, so $M = \omega_S + \sum_{i \in N} bet_i$. After the attack phase ends, the CSC distributes M among the attackers and the sponsor, and automatically generate payment transactions to transfer the allocated rewards to their accounts.

We consider the following reward allocation function (where $bet_{tot} = \sum_{i \in N} bet_i$):

$$R(bet_i, e_{tot}) = M \cdot e_{tot} \cdot \frac{bet_i}{bet_{tot}} \qquad (1)$$

That is, the share of each attacker from M is proportional to his bet value. As noted, if $e_{tot} < 1$, meaning that the attack is not fully successful, then the residual of M will go back to the sponsor. For our analysis, we want the formulation of R to depend on the attacker type t_i. As such, Eq. 1 can be converted into an equivalent formulation as follows:

$$R(t_i, e_{tot}) = M \cdot t_i \cdot e_{tot} \cdot \left(\frac{bet_{tot}}{\omega_S} \right)^{-1} \qquad (2)$$

In order to compute the utility of an attacker, we need also to characterize the cost of preforming an attack. Let $C : [0, 1] \to \mathbb{R}^+$ be a cost function that maps a value e_i to the cost expended in achieving the attack contribution profile e_i. We assume that C is strictly increasing and convex on its domain. In particular, we use the following general form cost function:

$$C(e_i) = \alpha \cdot \frac{\exp(e_i) - 1}{e_{max} - e_i} \qquad \forall i = 1, \ldots, n \qquad (3)$$

---

[6] Note that in reality we cannot compute e_i. Hence, e_{tot} is computed by using a suitable function to convert the delay reported by the oracle into the proper total traffic relative value. For example, if the measured delay meets the desired value, i.e., fully successful attack, then $e_{tot} = 1$. If it is 50% the value of the desired attack result, then $e_{tot} = 0.5$, and so on.

where e_{max} is the max possible attack traffic (the one beyond any attacker capability), such that the cost of generating attack traffic will approach infinity when e_i approaches e_{max}. And α is the average cost factor for generating attack traffic, where its value depends on the type of attack, the target's defensive power, and attackers' resources. The resulting utility function $U : [0,1] \times [0,1] \to \mathbb{R}$ for the ith attacker can be computed as $U(bet_i, e_i, e_{tot}) = R(t_i, e_{tot}) - C(e_i) - bet_i$, which again we convert in terms of t_i as follows:

$$U(t_i, e_i, e_{tot}) = R(t_i, e_{tot}) - C(e_i) - t_i \cdot \omega_S \tag{4}$$

Let $\hat{e}_{-i}$ denotes the vector components consisting of elements of $\hat{e}$ other than the ith element, so $e_i + \hat{e}_{-i} = e_{tot}$. Based on that, we can write the utility function as $U(t_i, e_i, \hat{e}_{-i})$, which emphasizes that the ith attacker only has control over his own attack effort, e_i. A static strict incomplete information game is then defined by a tuple $IAG = <N,\ E,\ T,\ U>$. In the IAG, each attacker (aka player) maximizes its own utility in a distributed fashion. Formally, the non-cooperative IAG is expressed as:

$$\max_{e_i \in [0,1]} U(t_i, e_i,\ \hat{e}_{-i}) \quad \forall i \in N \tag{5}$$

3.3 Equilibrium Analysis

It is necessary to characterize a set of attack efforts where each player is satisfied with the utility he receives (which maximizes his utility), given the attack efforts of other players. Such an operating point is called an equilibrium. The equilibrium concept offers a predictable, stable outcome of a game where multiple players with conflicting interests compete through self-optimization and reach a point where no player wishes to deviate. The condition for stability we aim for here is that of strong dominant strategy equilibrium. Note that rules of the game, including the utilities of all players, are public knowledge but not their private information, namely, t_i and e_i.

First, we derive the best-response strategy of a player in IAG. Then we prove that the described game among attackers in this setting has a dominant strategy equilibrium. The ith attacker's best response strategy $S^*(t_i, \hat{e}_{-i})$ to a given strategy profile $\hat{e}_{-i}$ is given as the unconstrained maximizer of his utility, where AW, bet_{tot} and e_{th} are fixed:

$$S^*(t_i, \hat{e}_{-i}) = \arg\max_{e_i \in [0,1]} U(t_i, e_i,\ \hat{e}_{-i}) \tag{6}$$

To find the maximizing $S^*(t_i)$, we take the first derivative of U with respect to e_i and equate it to 0:

$$-\alpha \cdot \frac{\exp(e_i)}{e_{max} - e_i} - c \cdot \frac{\exp(e_i) - 1}{(e_{max} - e_i)^2} + \frac{\omega_S \cdot t_i \cdot (\omega_S + bet_{tot})}{bet_{tot}} = 0 \tag{7}$$

So, the best response strategy $S^*(t_i, \hat{e}_{-i})$ of the ith player (with a value denoted as e_i^*) does not depend on the attack efforts of the other players $\hat{e}_{-i}$.

Therefore, we can represent the best response strategy function by $S^*(t_i)$. Furthermore, the only parameters (other than t_i) that determine $S^*(t_i) = e_i^*$ are the cost of the required attack traffic α and the quantity $\frac{bet_{tot}}{w_S}$.

Definition 1. *Given an incomplete information game $\Gamma = <N, E, T, U>$, a strategy $S^*(t_i)$ is a strongly dominant strategy, if for every t_i we have that the strategy $S^*(t_i)$ is a strongly dominant strategy in the full information game defined by t_i. Formally, for all t_i, all $\hat{e}_{-i}$, and all possible values for e_i (denoted as e_i') such that $e_i' \neq S^*(t_i)$, we have*

$$U(t_i, S^*(t_i), \hat{e}_{-i}) > U(t_i, e_i', \hat{e}_{-i}) \tag{8}$$

Definition 2. *Given an incomplete information game $\Gamma = <N, E, T, U>$, a strong dominant strategy equilibrium is an action profile $\hat{e}^* = (S^*(t_1), \ldots, S^*(t_n))$ in which each $S^*(t_i)$ is a strongly dominant strategy. The notion of strongly dominant strategy requires that $S^*(t_i)$ is the unique best response to all possible $\hat{e}_{-i}$, i.e., without knowing anything about $\hat{t}_{-i}$ (the type of other attackers).*

Theorem 1. *IAG defined above has a strong dominant strategy equilibrium.*

Proof. For each player i and for fixed t_i and e_{-i}, the reward function $R : T \times E \to \mathbb{R}$ is linear, and cost function $C : E \to \mathbb{R}$ is convex with respect to e_i. So $U(t_i, e_i, \hat{e}_{-i})$ is concave and has a unique maximum. $S^*(t_i)$ is the unique maximizer of $U(t_i, e_i, \hat{e}_{-i})$[7] and is a strongly dominant strategy that is the best response regardless of $\hat{e}_{-i}$. So for any $i \in N$ and all t_i, all $\hat{e}_{-i}$ and all e_i', we have $U(t_i, S^*(t_i), \hat{e}_{-i}) > U(t_i, e_i', \hat{e}_{-i})$ and strategy profile $\hat{e} = (S^*(t_1), \ldots, S^*(t_n))$ is the strong dominant strategy equilibrium of the game.   □

4   Exploring Incentive Compatibility

As discussed earlier, due to the anonymity characteristic of blockchain users, we can not determine the number of attackers n and the amount of their individual bets bet_i. In fact, knowing these bets allows predicting the attack result in the equilibrium of the game, i.e., $\sum_{i \in N} S^*(t_i) = e_{tot}^*$. In this section, we model the rules that govern the interactions in the CSC as a mechanism. By applying mechanism design theory, we prove that despite private information and pure selfish behavior, we can predict the attack result and the conditions that impact it. In addition, we show that under certain reasonable conditions, our mechanism satisfies the necessary constraints of mechanism design, namely, incentive compatibility, individual rationality, budget balance, and fairness.

---

[7] Note that the utility function is increasing at $e_i = 0$ and decreasing at $e_i = 1$, so the maximum can not occur at end points.

4.1   Mechanism Formulation

As we showed in the previous section, the IAG game modeling players' interactions in a CSC has a strong dominant strategy equilibrium. As such, in equilibrium, the contribution of the ith attacker with type t_i will be $S^*(t_i) = e_i^*$, and it is independent of other attackers' types and strategies. Based on that, for an attacker type profile $\hat{t} \in T$, we define the attack result function $AR : T \to E$ as:

$$AR(\hat{t}) = \sum_{i \in N} S^*(t_i) = \sum_{i \in N} e_i^* = e_{tot}^* \qquad (9)$$

We consider the ith attacker's bet bet_i as his payment to CSC, and the reward $R(t_i, AR(\hat{t}))$ is what the mechanism pays him. Accordingly, this attacker receives a payment amount p_i, or makes it if p_i is negative, expressed as (note that $t_i \cdot \omega_S = bet_i$):

$$p_i(\hat{t}) = R(t_i, AR(\hat{t})) - t_i \cdot \omega_S \qquad (10)$$

Let $G(\hat{t}) = (S(\hat{t}), P(\hat{t}))$ be the outcome function that maps each type profile $\hat{t} \in T$ to an outcome $o = (e_{tot}^*, \hat{p})$ where the payment rule $P(.)$ defines a profile of attackers' payments $\hat{p} = (p_0, p_1, \ldots, p_n)$, and the set of possible outcomes is denoted by O.

The attack result e_{tot}^* is the non-monetary part in the outcome. To monetize it, we introduce a valuation function $V : \mathbb{R}^+ \times T \to \mathbb{R}$ (in terms of some currency) to represent an attackers' preference for a given attack result. In other words, the valuation function expresses the cost that an attacker is willing to tolerate when contributing to the attack (based on his dominant strategy), in addition to the transaction fee paid to post his bets on the CSC (i.e., fees for Ethereum miners). So, if this attacker post his true bet in k small bets, each of which will require δ transaction fee (since each will be sent in a separate transaction), the total fee will be $k \cdot \delta$. Based on that, V can be expressed as follows:

$$V(e_{tot}^*, t_i) = -(C(S^*(t_i)) + k \cdot \delta), \quad \forall i \in N, \forall t_i \in [0, 1] \qquad (11)$$

Recall that attacker i's contribution depends only on his type t_i, and so is the valuation function shown in Eq. 11. Thus, we can express it as $V(e_{tot}^*, t_i) = V(t_i)$. As a result, this valuation function can be used to represent the type of attacker, and announcing a type is similar to reporting the attacker's valuation function.

Since we have money/incentive transfer between agents (aka attackers), we work in quasi-linear setting. Each agent has a utility that is the motivating factor behind the selection of his strategy. The preference of attacker i can be captured using his utility function that can be redefined as follows (this is equivalent to the one defined in Eq. 4):

$$U(t_i, o) = V(t_i) + p_i \qquad (12)$$

We formalize the incentive mechanism for strategic attackers in the proposed collaborative attack as a direct mechanism.[8] In this setup, each attacker i

---

[8] This mechanism suits our model since we have the space of possible actions is equal to the space of possible types, so an attacker type (which is defined when he bets) is the same as his act (the amount of attack contribution).

announces a type t_i' to the mechanism, which is not necessarily equal to his true type $t_i \in [0,1]$, such that it will lead to an outcome that maximizes his utility. We also have a social choice function $F : T \to O$ that maps each agents' type profile to an optimal outcome, which is the same as the outcome function.

Definition 3. *A direct mechanism in a quasi-linear setting is defined by $D = (T, G(\hat{t}))$. The mechanism defines the set of allowable types T that each agent can choose and an outcome function G which specifies an outcome o for each possible type profile $\hat{t} = (t_1, \ldots, t_n) \in T$.*

4.2 Incentive Compatible Property

Direct mechanisms extract information from agents by motivating them to *tell the truth*. If the best response for all attackers to report their private information truthfully to the CSC-driven mechanism, we say the contract is incentive compatible. Here we prove that the proposed mechanism is cheat-proof, which means that all attackers are motivated to submit their bet truthfully, and any deviation will lead to a utility loss.

Definition 4. *The social choice function $F(\cdot)$ is a dominant strategy incentive compatible (DSIC) (aka strategy-proof or cheat-proof) if and only if*

$$U(t_i, o) \geq U(t_i', o') \quad \forall i \in N, \ \forall \hat{t} \in T, \ \forall t_i' \in [0,1] \tag{13}$$

where $o = G(t_i, \hat{t}_{-i})$ and $o' = G(t_i', \hat{t}_{-i})$.

Thus, if the SCF is DSIC, then the best response for agent i is to bet truthfully, i.e., $bet_i = t_i \cdot \omega_S$, regardless of other attackers' bets. By calling a direct mechanism DSIC or strategy-proof, we mean that the mechanism implements an incentive-compatible or strategy-proof social choice function.

Theorem 2. *The proposed direct mechanism (or social choice function) modeling our CSC-based collaborative attacks is DSIC.*

Proof. We need to show that the utility of attacker i, is maximized when he bet truthfully. We use proof by contradiction. Without loss of generality, assume that the true type of attacker i is t_i, but he tries to misrepresent his type and submit his bet with two distinct blockchain addresses in two transactions ($k = 2$) containing two bets $bet_{i,1}$ and $bet_{i,2}$, such that $bet_{i,1} + bet_{i,2} = bet_i$ and $bet_i = t_i \cdot \omega_S$. We denote the incorrect types by $t_{i,1}$ and $t_{i,2}$, so we have $t_i = t_{i,1} + t_{i,2}$. We assume that he benefits from this untruthful act which means $\exists t_{i,1}, t_{i,2} \in T$, where $t_i = t_{i,1} + t_{i,2}$, and $\exists \hat{t}_{-i} \in T^{n-1}$ such that

$$U(o', t_{i,1}) + U(o', t_{i,2}) > U(o, t_i) \tag{14}$$

where $G(t_{i,1} + t_{i,2}, \hat{t}_{-i})$ and $G(t_i, \hat{t}_{-i})$ are the values of o' and o, respectively.

Note that, from each attacker i's perspective, his dominant strategy $S^*(t_i)$ is a function of his true type t_i, which he knows, and so he can calculate his dominant strategy as $S^*(t_i) = S^*(t_{i,1} + t_{i,2})$. Thus:

$$AR(t_{i,1} + t_{i,2}, \hat{t}_{-i}) = S^*(t_{i,1} + t_{i,2}) + \sum_{j \in N, i \neq j} S^*(t_j) \tag{15}$$

$$= S^*(t_i) + \sum_{j \in N, i \neq j} S^*(t_j) = AR(t_i, \hat{t}_{-i})$$

And for the rewards, we have:

$$R(t_{i,1}, e_{tot}) + R(t_{i,2}, e_{tot}) = (t_{i,1} + t_{i,2}) \cdot (bet_{tot} + \omega_S) \cdot \left(\frac{bet_{tot}}{\omega_S}\right)^{-1} \cdot e_{tot} \tag{16}$$

$$= t_i \cdot (bet_{tot} + \omega_S) \cdot \left(\frac{bet_{tot}}{\omega_S}\right)^{-1} \cdot e_{tot} = R(t_i, e_{tot})$$

So the attacker's reward does not increase by hiding his type (i.e., hiding his bet). Therefore, from the mechanism point of view, the payments are the same as if the attacker would announce his true type, so:

$$p_i(t_i, \hat{t}_{-i}) = p_i(t_{i,1}, \hat{t}_{-i}) + p_i(t_{i,2}, \hat{t}_{-i}) \tag{17}$$

As we see, rewards and payments are identical in both cases. So the only way for an attacker to obtain a higher utility when lying, is to have a higher valuation than the one for the betting truthfully. This means that we have:

$$V(t_{i,1}) + V(t_{i,2}) > V(t_i) \tag{18}$$

Which means that:

$$C(S^*(t_i)) + 2\delta < C(S^*(t_i)) + \delta \tag{19}$$

This inequality cannot hold since this means that a transaction fee δ is negative, which is not the case. Thus, we a get a contradiction, meaning that an attacker will not get a higher utility by submitting multiple bets instead of the a single one (i.e., his true bet).   □

Note that we assumed attackers do not trust each other, so each attacker at least needs one transaction to submit his bet or he can submit multiple bets that sum to his true bet. However, let's assume that two attackers do trust each other and want to collude and fool the mechanism to increase their profit. The only possible misbehavior is to submit one bet that its amount is equal to the sum of their bets. In this case, the mechanism considers them as one identity (i.e., one attacker) and based on the proposed reward allocation function, this will not increase their reward. The only effect of this collusion is that the actual attack result would be higher than the pre-calculated attack result. This is because the same amount of contribution costs less for two attackers than one attacker (recall that the cost function is convex) and when two attackers assumed as one, their contribution will be considered less.

4.3   Budget Constraint

To be economically feasible, an incentive mechanism must be budget constrained. In our framework, the total rewards allocated to the attackers should not exceed $M = \sum_{i \in N} bet_i + \omega_S$, which is the total deposit made to the CSC account. In terms of payments, this means that the total attackers payment should not exceed the sponsor award ω_S.

Definition 5. *(Budget Constraint for CSC). A reward mechanism is budget constrained if for $\forall \hat{t} \in T$ we have $\sum_{i \in N} p_i(\hat{t}) \leq \omega_S$.*

Theorem 3. *The proposed direct mechanism is budget constrained.*

Proof. The total attackers payments can be expressed as:

$$
\sum_{i \in N} p_i(\hat{t}) = \sum_{i \in N} \left(R(t_i, S(\hat{t})) - t_i \cdot \omega_S \right)
$$

$$
= \sum_{i \in N} \left((bet_{tot} + \omega_S) \cdot t_i \cdot \left(\frac{bet_{tot}}{\omega_S} \right)^{-1} \cdot S(\hat{t}) - t_i \cdot \omega_S \right) \tag{20}
$$

$$
= (bet_{tot} + \omega_S) \cdot AR(\hat{t}) - bet_{tot}
$$

where $AR : T \to E$ is as given in Eq. 9 and $E = [0, 1]$. So for any type profile $\hat{t} \in T$ we have:

$$
- bet_{tot} \leq (bet_{tot} + \omega_S) \cdot S(\hat{t}) - bet_{tot} \leq \omega_S \tag{21}
$$

From Eqs. 20 and 21, we get $\sum_{i \in N} p_i(\hat{t}) \leq \omega_S$, completing the proof.   □

4.4   Voluntary Participation Constraint

Individual rationality or voluntary participation property of a social choice function means that each attacker gains a non-negative utility by participating in the mechanism that implements the social choice function. There are two stages at which individual rationality can be examined. First, when the amount of bet (types) of other attackers $\hat{t}_{-i}$ is unknown to attacker i, and therefore predicting attack result (i.e. outcome) is impossible. Second, when before the attack phase (ex-post stage), a choice to withdraw from the mechanism is given to all attackers. That is when all the attackers have announced their bet, and an attack result can be calculated. Note that a truthful attacker who submits his bet in one transaction incurs two transaction fees, 2δ, to withdraw from the mechanism (and if an attacker submits k smaller bets, his cost to withdraw will $2k\delta$). This property of *ex-post individual rationality* is stated as follows.

Definition 6. *(Ex-post Individual Rationality). The utility an attacker i with type t_i receives by withdrawing from a CSC is equal to $-2k\delta$. To ensure attacker i's participation when withdrawal is allowed at the ex-post stage, we must satisfy the following ex-post Individual Rationality (or participation) constraint*

$$
U(G(\hat{t}), t_i) \geq -2k\delta \qquad \forall \hat{t} \in T \tag{22}
$$

A mechanism satisfies ex-post individual rationality if it implements a social choice function that satisfies ex-post individual rationality. In the next section, through numerical analysis, we show that under mild conditions the proposed mechanism satisfies this constraint. Note that these conditions can be encoded as rules in CSC by the sponsor. For instance, he can condition the attack on a specified amount of total bets, or he can restrict attackers' type by specifying upper bound and lower bound on acceptable bets.

4.5   Fairness

Different definitions for fairness have been proposed in the literature including proportional fairness, max-min fairness, $\alpha-$fairness [24]. To measure the fairness of the proposed incentive mechanism, we need a metric that captures how close the payment obtained by this mechanism is to fair payment. By fair payment, we mean reward allocation based on the contribution of attackers (instead of the amount of their bets). In other words, if attackers could prove their contribution, then the reward allocation function would simply be a function of their contribution and the attack result.

We denote the fair payment by p_i' and can be computed as:

$$p_i'(\hat{e}) = \omega_S \cdot e_i \cdot e_{tot} \tag{23}$$

Similar to [13], we consider a metric, which we call the fairness-score, based on the root mean square (RMS) of the difference between the mechanism payment and the fair payment. The fairness-score is defined as

$$D_{rms} = \sqrt{\frac{1}{n} \sum_{i \in N} (p_i(\hat{t}) - p_i'(\hat{e}))^2} \tag{24}$$

where $p_i(\hat{t})$ is given by Eq. 10. A value of zero for D_{rms} indicates that the mechanism payment equals to the fair payment, which discourages free-riders and rewards contributors. As the value increases, the fairness of the reward allocation function decreases. In the next section, using numerical simulation for two reward functions, we show that under some mild conditions, the fairness score drops for both rewarding schemes after hitting the desired attack result.

5   Numerical Simulations and Discussion

Based on our game model, there are four key parameters that impact the attack outcome (in terms of payment and attack result). These factors are bet_{tot}, ω_S, $C(e_{th})$, and type profile $\hat{t} = (t_1, \ldots, t_n)$. Furthermore, the reward allocation function has a significant impact on the attack result and other properties, such as fairness and individual rationality.

In this section, we conduct simulations for a typical DDoS scenario to analyze how various system parameters impact attack outcome. The parameter values

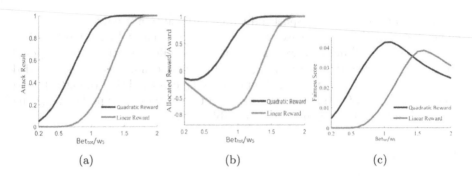

Fig. 4. The impact of increasing θ for fixed $\gamma = 0.35$ on (a) attack result (b) proportion of allocated award to attackers, and (c) fairness-score of payment.

used in this study are $n = 30$, $\frac{bet_{max}}{bet_{min}} = \frac{1}{10}$, $bet_i \sim Uniform(bet_{min}, bet_{max})$, and the results are averaged over 50 randomly chosen attackers' bets. In our simulations, we consider two reward allocation functions: linear and quadratic (in the bet amount). The former is the one given by Eq. 2 and denoted by R, while the latter is expressed as:[9]

$$R'(\hat{t}, e_{tot}) = M \cdot e_{tot} \cdot \frac{t_i^2}{\sum_{i \in N} t_i^2} \qquad (25)$$

As for the attack result, it will have an upper bound based on the contract terms. That is, putting more effort beyond what is needed to reach the desired attack result will not increase the rewards for the attackers. Thus, rational attacker will stop when the measured attack result reaches the desired value.

We define two parameters: $\theta = \frac{bet_{tot}}{w_S}$, and $\gamma = \frac{C(e_{th})}{w_S}$. Here, θ gives an indication of the total amount of bets with respect to the sponsor award, and γ is an indicator of the cost of performing the attack with respect to this award. We use these parameters in our simulations to study the impact of total bet and cost on the attack result.

Comparing the impact of reward allocation functions, as Fig. 4(a) shows the quadratic scheme attracts significantly more contribution than the linear reward scheme with the same value of θ. In this scheme, having $\theta = 1$, one can estimate that the expected attack result e_{tot}^* would be around 90% of the desired attack result e_{th}. On the other hand, we observe that the linear reward allocation function takes $\theta \approx 1.7$ to attract such contribution however this scheme allocate the rewards fairer compared to the quadratic scheme. Moreover, Fig. 4(b) shows that at that point the quadratic reward scheme pays 75% of the considered award while it costs attackers around 80% of the total cost of a successful attack. The remaining 25% of the award will be paid for reaching the desired attack result e_{th}. As expected, the attack result, the allocated reward to award ratio, and fairness

---

[9] Note that the theoretical (game and mechanism) analysis conducted for R holds for R', too.

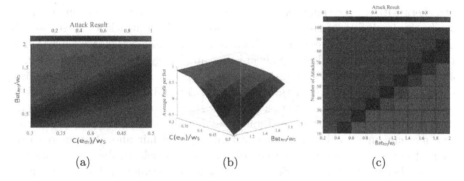

Fig. 5. The impact of θ and γ on (a) the attack-result, and (b) ratio of average profit over average bet size, with fixed number of attackers $n = 30$. (c) the impact of θ and number of attackers on attack result ($\gamma = 0.35$)

score increase with the increase of θ. Therefore, the attack sponsor can condition the attack on a minimum amount of total bet to ensure the success of the attack and a given fairness score. Also, Fig. 4(c) demonstrates that after hitting the desired attack result, in both rewarding schemes, the fairness-score drops which means after this point, the more the total bet, the fairer the allocation will be.

As Fig. 5(a) shows, the required θ for providing the incentive of launching a successful attack increases as the cost factor γ increases. Therefore, as the attack cost goes higher, a larger value of bet_{tot} is needed to provide the required incentives to launch a successful attack. Accordingly, knowing the total amount of the bets, the number of attackers, and the award, the target server can estimate and change the attack result through increasing the cost of that attack (be deploying proper defenses against DDoS).

As discussed in Sect. 4.4, attackers are incentivized to participate when a non-negative utility is expected. Figure 5(b) shows that under some mild conditions, in terms of θ and γ, the proposed mechanism satisfies the desirable property of individual rationality. The red region denotes the situations that the average attackers' profit is positive. That is knowing the cost of the desired attack and the minimum total bet, the attack sponsor or the attack target can adjust the award or the cost to incentivize or deincentivize attackers to participate.

As shown in Fig. 5(c), the larger the number of attackers the larger bet_{tot} required for launching a successful attack. In other words, increasing the number of attackers alone would not lead to more collaboration rather they should be incentivized enough to collaborate. Therefore accepting small bets decreases the attack result and a rule of minimum acceptable bet in the CSC can be helpful.

6   Conclusion

In this paper, we introduced a framework for employing CSCs to orchestrate real-world targeted attacks. These attacks are launched by several collaborating attackers without any knowledge of each other or any trust between them. To study the feasibility of this idea, we considered DDoS attack as a usecase. By using thorough game theoretic analysis and mechanism design, we showed that the attack sponsor can design a cheat-proof and budget-balanced mechanism to encourage collaboration of selfish rational attackers. Furthermore, the sponsor can predict and adapt the attack result, i.e., determine under what conditions attackers will participate in the attack. Simulation results show that, under some mild conditions on the attack cost and total amount of bets, the proposed incentive mechanism provides individual rationality and fair allocation of rewards. Being the first to study CSC-based collaborative attacks against real-work targets, we believe that our work will contribute in promoting the foundational understanding of these attacks, an important step towards developing effective countermeasures.

References

1. Aeternity oracles. https://aeternity.com/documentation-hub/protocol/oracles/oracles/
2. Botnet economy runs wild. https://www.networkworld.com. Accessed 18 Sept 2020
3. Chainlink. https://chain.link/
4. Cyber criminal collaboration intensifies. https://www.computerweekly.com. Accessed 18 Sept 2020
5. Cybercriminals are increasing efficiency with coordinated attacks. https://www.enisa.europa.eu. Accessed 18 Sept 2020
6. Evidence found of malware families collaborating. http://www.darkreading.com. Accessed 18 Sept 2020
7. Filecoin. https://filecoin.io/
8. Noia. https://noia.network/
9. Provable. https://provable.xyz/
10. Abad, C.: The economy of phishing: a survey of the operations of the phishing market. First Monday **10**(9), 1–11 (2005)
11. Brunoni, L., Beaudet-Labrecque, O.: Smart contracts and cybercrime: a game changer. Math. Struct. Model. **4**, 136–142 (2017)
12. Chen, L., et al.: The game among bribers in a smart contract system. In: Zohar, A. (ed.) FC 2018. LNCS, vol. 10958, pp. 294–307. Springer, Heidelberg (2019). https://doi.org/10.1007/978-3-662-58820-8_20
13. Da, B., Ko, C.C.: Resource allocation in downlink MIMO-OFDMA with proportional fairness. J. Commun. **4**(1), 8–13 (2009)
14. Delgado-Mohatar, O., Sierra-Cámara, J.M., Anguiano, E.: Blockchain-based semi-autonomous ransomware. Future Gener. Comput. Syst. **112**, 589–603 (2020)
15. Judmayer, A., et al.: Pay to win: cheap, crowdfundable, cross-chain algorithmic incentive manipulation attacks on pow cryptocurrencies. In: Workshop on Trusted Smart Contracts (2021)
16. Judmayer, A., et al.: SoK: algorithmic incentive manipulation attacks on permissionless pow cryptocurrencies. In: Workshop on Trusted Smart Contracts (2021)
17. Juels, A., Kosba, A., Shi, E.: The ring of gyges: investigating the future of criminal smart contracts. In: ACM CCS, pp. 283–295 (2016)

18. McCorry, P., Hicks, A., Meiklejohn, S., et al.: Smart contracts for bribing miners. In: Zohar, A. (ed.) FC 2018. LNCS, vol. 10958, pp. 3–18. Springer, Heidelberg (2019). https://doi.org/10.1007/978-3-662-58820-8_1

19. Nazario, J.: Politically motivated denial of service attacks. In: The Virtual Battlefield: Perspectives on Cyber Warfare, pp. 163–181 (2009)

20. O'hara, K.: Smart contracts - dumb idea. Internet Comput. 21(2), 97–101 (2017)

21. Qian, Y., Haskell, W.B., Tambe, M.: Robust strategy against unknown risk-averse attackers in security games. In: AAMAS (2015)

22. Rodrigues, B., Trendafilov, S., Scheid, E., Stiller, B.: SC-FLARE: Cooperative DDoS signaling based on smart contracts. In: IEEE ICBC, pp. 1–3 (2020)

23. Zargar, S.T., Joshi, J.: A survey of defense mechanisms against distributed denial of service (DDoS) flooding attacks. EEE Commun. Surv. Tutor. 15(4), 2046–2069 (2013)

24. Trichakis, N.K.: Fairness in operations: from theory to practice. Ph.D. thesis, Massachusetts Institute of Technology (2011)

25. Velner, Y., Teutsch, J., Luu, L., et al.: Smart contracts make bitcoin mining pools vulnerable. In: Brenner, M. (ed.) FC 2017. LNCS, vol. 10323, pp. 298–316. Springer, Cham (2017). https://doi.org/10.1007/978-3-319-70278-0_19

26. Vogt, R., Aycock, J.: Attack of the 50 foot botnet. Technical report, Department of Computer Science, University of Calgary (2006)

27. Vogt, R., Aycock, J., Jacobson Jr., M.J.: Army of botnets. In: NDSS (2007)

28. Wood, G.: Ethereum: a secure decentralised generalised transaction ledger (2014)

29. Xu, S.: Collaborative attack vs. collaborative defense. In: Bertino, E., Joshi, J.B.D. (eds.) CollaborateCom 2008. LNICST, vol. 10, pp. 217–228. Springer, Heidelberg (2009). https://doi.org/10.1007/978-3-642-03354-4_17

Combating Informational Denial-of-Service (IDoS) Attacks: Modeling and Mitigation of Attentional Human Vulnerability

Linan Huang[✉] and Quanyan Zhu

Department of Electrical and Computer Engineering, New York University,
2 MetroTech Center, Brooklyn, NY 11201, USA
{lh2328,qz494}@nyu.edu

Abstract. This work proposes a new class of proactive attacks called the Informational Denial-of-Service (IDoS) attacks that exploit the attentional human vulnerability. By generating a large volume of feints, IDoS attacks deplete the cognitive resources of human operators to prevent humans from identifying the real attacks hidden among feints. This work aims to formally define IDoS attacks, quantify their consequences, and develop human-assistive security technologies to mitigate the severity level and risks of IDoS attacks. To this end, we use the semi-Markov process to model the sequential arrivals of feints and real attacks with category labels attached in the associated alerts. The assistive technology strategically manages human attention by highlighting selective alerts periodically to prevent the distraction of other alerts. A data-driven approach is applied to evaluate human performance under different Attention Management (AM) strategies. Under a representative special case, we establish the computational equivalency between two dynamic programming representations to reduce the computation complexity and enable online learning with samples of reduced size and zero delays. A case study corroborates the effectiveness of the learning framework. The numerical results illustrate how AM strategies can alleviate the severity level and the risk of IDoS attacks. Furthermore, the results show that the minimum risk is achieved with a proper level of intentional inattention to alerts, which we refer to as the *law of rational risk-reduction inattention*.

Keywords: Human vulnerability · Alert fatigue · Cyber feint attack ·
Temporal-difference learning · Risk analysis · Attention management ·
Cognitive load

1 Introduction

Human is the weakest link in cybersecurity due to their innate vulnerabilities, including bounded rationality and limited attention. These human vulnerabilities are difficult to mitigate through short-term training, rules, and incentives. As a result, sophisticated

Q. Zhu—This work is partially supported by grants SES-1541164, ECCS-1847056, CNS-2027884, and BCS-2122060 from National Science Foundation (NSF), and grant W911NF-19-1-0041 from Army Research Office (ARO).

© Springer Nature Switzerland AG 2021
B. Bošanský et al. (Eds.): GameSec 2021, LNCS 13061, pp. 314–333, 2021.
https://doi.org/10.1007/978-3-030-90370-1_17

attacks, such as Advanced Persistent Threats (APTs) and supply-chain attacks, commonly exploit them to breach data and damage critical infrastructures. Attentional vulnerabilities have been exploited by adversaries to create visual blindspots or misperceptions that can lead to erroneous outcomes. One way to exploit the attentional vulnerabilities is to stealthily evade the attention of human users or operators as we have seen in many cases of social engineering and phishing attacks. It is a passive approach where the attacker does not change the attention patterns of the human operators and intends to exploit the inattention to evade the detection. In contrast, a proactive attacker can strategically influence attention patterns. For example, an attacker can overload the attention of human operators with a large volume of feints and hide real attacks among them [1]. This class of proactive attacks aims to increase the perceptual and cognitive load of human operators to delay defensive responses and reduce detection accuracy. We refer to this class of attacks as the Informational Denial-of-Service (IDoS) attacks.

IDoS is no stranger to us in this age of information explosion. We are commonly overloaded with terabytes of unprocessed data or manipulated information on online media. However, the targeted IDoS attacks on specific groups of people, e.g., security guards, operators at the nuclear power plant, and network administrators, can pose serious threats to lifeline infrastructures and systems. The attacker customizes attack strategies to targeted individuals or organizations to quickly and maximally deplete their human cognitive resources. As a result, common methods (e.g., set tiered alert priorities) to mitigate alert fatigue are insufficient under these targeted and intelligent attacks that generate massive feints strategically. There is a need to understand this phenomenon, quantify its consequence and risks, and develop new mitigation methods. In this work, we establish a probabilistic model to formalize the definition of IDoS attacks, evaluate their severity levels, and assess the induced cyber risks. The model captures the interaction among attackers, human operators, and assistive technologies as highlighted by the orange, green, and blue backgrounds, respectively, in Fig. 1.

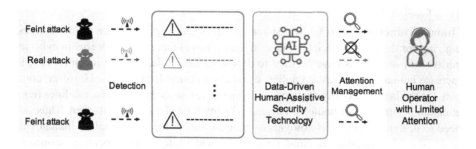

Fig. 1. Interaction among IDoS attacks, human operators, and assistive technologies.

Attackers generate feints and real attacks that trigger alerts of detection systems. Due to the detection imperfectness, human operators need to inspect these alerts in detail to determine the attacks' types, i.e., feint or real, and take responsive security decisions. The accuracy of the security decisions depends on the inspection time and the operator's sustained attention without distractions. The large volume of feints exerts an additional cognitive load on each human operator and makes it hard to focus on each alert, which can significantly decrease the accuracy of his security decisions and increase cyber risks. Accepting the innate human vulnerability, we aim to develop assistive technologies to compensate for the human attention limitation. Evidence from the cognitive load theory [2] has shown that divided attention to multiple stimuli can degrade the performance and cost more time than responding to these stimuli in sequence. Hence, we design the *Attention Management* (AM) strategies to intentionally make some alerts inconspicuous so that the human operator can focus on the other alerts and finish the inspection with less time and higher accuracy. We further define risk measures to evaluate the inspection results, which serves as the stepping stone to designing adaptive AM strategies to mitigate attacks induced by human vulnerabilities.

Due to the unpredictability and complexity of human behaviors, cognition, and reasoning, it is challenging to create an exact human model of the IDoS attack response. Therefore, we provide a probabilistic characterization of human decisions concerning AM strategies and other observable features from the alerts. By assuming a sequential arrival of attacks with semi-Markov state transitions, we conduct a data-driven approach to evaluate the inspection results in real-time. Under a mild assumption, we prove the *computational equivalency* between two Dynamic Programming (DP) representations to simplify the value iteration and the Temporal-Difference (TD) learning process. Numerical results corroborate the effectiveness of learning by showing the convergence of the estimated value to the theoretical value. Without an AM strategy, we show that both the severity level and the risk of IDoS attacks increase with the product of the arrival rate and the detection threshold. With the assistance of AM strategies, we illustrate how different AM strategies can alleviate the severity level of IDoS attacks. Concerning the IDoS risks, we illustrate the tradeoff between the quantity and quality of the inspection, which leads to a meta-principle referred to as the *law of rational risk-reduction inattention*.

1.1 Related Works

Human Vulnerability in Cyber Space. Attacks that exploit human vulnerabilities, e.g., insider threats and social engineering, have raised increasing concerns in cybersecurity. Previous works have focused to design security rules [3] and incentives [4] to increase human employees' compliance and elicit desirable behaviors. However, compared to the lack of security awareness and incentives, some human vulnerabilities (e.g., attention limitation and bounded rationality) cannot be altered or controlled. Thus, we need to design assistive technologies to compensate for the 'unpatchable' human vulnerabilities. In [5], adaptive attention enhancement strategies have been developed to engage users' attention and maximize the rate of phishing recognition. Compared to [5] that defends against stealthy attacks and the exploitation of inattention, this work combats proactive attackers that overload human attention.

Data-Driven Approach for Security and Resilience. As more data becomes available, data-driven approaches have been widely used to create cyber situational awareness and enhance network security and resilience [6], e.g., Bayesian learning for parameter uncertainty [7,8] and Q-learning for honeypot engagement [9]. The authors in

[10] have studied the detection of feint attacks by a few-shot deep learning algorithm. However, they have modeled feints as multi-stage attacks and focused on detecting the revised causal relationship. Here, we focus on how feints affect human operators' cognitive resources and the consequent security decisions. The TD learning method helps address the long-standing challenge of human modeling and further enables us to evaluate human performance efficiently and robustly.

1.2 Notations and Organization of the Paper

We summarize notations in Table 1. The rest of the paper is organized as follows. Section 2 introduces the system modeling for IDoS attacks, alert generations, and the inspections of human operators. Based on the system model, we present a Semi-Markov Process (SMP) model in Sect. 3 to evaluate human performance, the severity level, and the risks of IDoS attacks. We present a case study in Sect. 4 to corroborate our results and Sect. 5 concludes the paper.

Table 1. Summary of variables and their meanings.

Variable	Meaning
$t^k \in [0, \infty)$	Arrival time of the k-th attack
$\tau^k = t^{k+1} - t^k \in [0, \infty)$	Time duration between k-th and $(k+1)$-th attack
$\tau_{IN}^{h,m} := \sum_{k'=hm}^{hm+m-1} \tau^{k'}$	Inspection time at inspection stage $h \in \mathbb{Z}^{0+}$
$w^k \in \mathcal{W} := \{w_{FE}, w_{RE}, w_{UN}\}$	Security decision at attack stages $k \in \mathbb{Z}^{0+}$
$a_m \in \mathcal{A}$	Attention management strategy of period $m \in \mathbb{Z}^+$
$\theta^k \in \Theta := \{\theta_{FE}, \theta_{RE}\}$	Attack's type at attack stages $k \in \mathbb{Z}^{0+}$
$\bar{\theta}^h := [\theta^{hm}, \cdots, \theta^{hm+m-1}]$	Consolidated type at inspection stage $h \in \mathbb{Z}^{0+}$
$s^k \in \mathcal{S}$	Alert's category label at attack stages $k \in \mathbb{Z}^{0+}$
$x^h := [s^{hm}, \cdots, s^{hm+m-1}]$	Consolidated state at inspection stage $h \in \mathbb{Z}^{0+}$
$\mathrm{Tr}(s^{k+1}|s^k; \theta^k)$	Transition probability from s^k to s^{k+1} under attack type θ^k
$\bar{T}r(x^{h+1}|x^h; \bar{\theta}^h)$	Transition function of the consolidated state

2 System Modeling of Informational Denial-of-Service Attacks

In Sect. 2.1, we present a high-level structure of the Informational Denial-of-Service (IDoS) attacks and use a motivating example to illustrate their causes, consequences, and mitigation methods. Then, we introduce the system modeling of sequential arrivals of alerts that are triggered by feints and real attacks in Sect. 2.2. The manual inspection and the attention management strategies are introduced in Sect. 2.3. Human operators inspect each alert in real-time to determine the associated attack's hidden type. Meanwhile, the assistive technology automatically designs and implements the optimal attention management strategy to compensate for human attention limitations.

2.1 High-Level Abstraction and Motivating Example

As shown in Fig. 2, there is an analogy between the Denial-of-Service (DoS) attacks in communication networks and the Informational Denial-of-Service (IDoS) attacks in the human-in-the-loop systems. Both of them achieve their attack goals by exhausting the limited resources. DoS attacks happen when the attacker generates a large number of superfluous requests to deplete the computing resource of the targeted machine and prevent the fulfillment of legitimate services. Analogously, IDoS attacks create a large amount of unprocessed information to deplete cognitive resources of human operators and prevent them from acquiring the knowledge contained in the information. We list

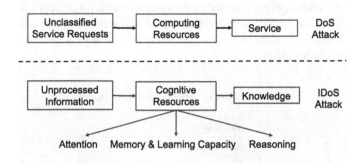

Fig. 2. The service request fulfillment process under DoS attacks and the information processing flows under IDoS attacks in green and blue backgrounds, respectively.

several assailable cognitive resources under IDoS attacks as follows.

- **Attention**: Paying sustained attention to acquire proper information is costly. From an economic perspective, inattention occurs when the cost of information acquisition is lower than the attention cost measured by the information entropy [11]. IDoS attacks generate feints to distract the human from the right information. An excessive number of feints prohibit the human from process any information.
- **Memory and Learning Capacity**: Humans have limited memory and learning capacity. Humans cannot remember the details or learn new things if there is an information overload [2].
- **Reasoning**: Human decision-making consumes a large amount of energy, which is one of the reasons why we have two modes of thought [12] ('system 1' thinking is fast, instinctive, and emotional; while 'system 2' thinking is slower and more logical). IDoS attacks can exert a heavy cognitive load to prevent humans from deliberative decisions that use the 'system 2' thinking. Moreover, evidence shows the *paradox of choice* [13]; i.e., rich choices can bring anxiety and prevent humans from making any decisions.

When these cognitive resources are exhausted, the information cannot be processed correctly and timely and serves as noise that leads to *alert fatigue* [14]. We use operators in the control room of nuclear power plants as a stylized example to illustrate

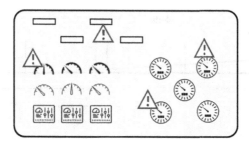

Fig. 3. A stylized example of the monitor screen for operators in the control room of nuclear power plants. The red triangles represent warnings and security messages.

the consequences of IDoS attacks and motivate the need for the security technology to assist human operators against IDoS attacks. In Fig. 3, a monitor screen contains meters that show the real-time readings of the temperature, pressure, and flow rate in a nuclear power plant. Based on the pre-defined generation rules, warnings and messages pop up at different locations. Due to the complexity of the nuclear control system, the inspection of these alerts consumes the operator's time and cognitive resources. The attempt to inspect all alerts and the constant switching among them can lead to missed detection and erroneous behaviors. If the alerts are generated strategically by attacks, they may further mislead humans to take actions in the attacker's favor; e.g., focusing on feints and ignoring the real attacks that hide among feints.

One way to mitigate IDoS attacks is to train the operators or human users to deal with the information overload and remain vigilant and productive under a heavy cognitive load. However, attentional training can be time-consuming and the effectiveness is not guaranteed. The second method is to recruit more human operators to share the information load. It would require the coordination of the operator team and can incur additional costs of human resources. The third method is to develop assistive technologies to rank and filter the information to alleviate the cognitive load of human operators. It would leverage past experiences and data analytics to pinpoint and prioritize critical alerts for human operators to process. The first two methods aim to increase the capacity or the volume of the cognitive resources in Fig. 2. The third method pre-processes the information so that it adapts to the capacity and characteristics of cognitive resources.

2.2 Sequential Arrivals of Alerts Triggered by Feints and Real Attacks

In this work, we focus on the temporal aspect of the alerts (i.e., the frequency and duration of their arrivals). The future work will incorporate their spatial locations on the monitor screen as shown in Fig. 3. As highlighted by the orange background in Fig. 4, attacks arrive sequentially at time $t^k, k \in \mathbb{Z}^{0+}$ where $t^0 = 0$. Let $\tau^k := t^{k+1} - t^k \in [0, \infty)$ be the inter-arrival time between the $(k+1)$-th attack and the k-th attack for all $k \in \mathbb{Z}^{0+}$. We refer to the k-th attack equivalently as the one at *attack stage* $k \in \mathbb{Z}^{0+}$.

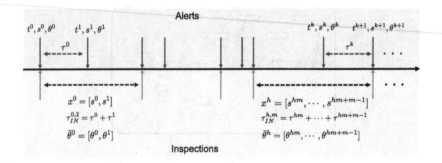

Fig. 4. The sequential arrival of alerts at *attack stage* $k \in \mathbb{Z}^{0+}$ and the periodic manual inspections at *inspection stage* $h \in \mathbb{Z}^{0+}$ under AM strategy $a_m \in \mathscr{A}$ where $m = 2$.

Each attack can be either a feint (denoted by θ_{FE}) or a real attack (denoted by θ_{RE}) with probability $b_{FE} \in [0, 1]$ and $b_{RE} \in [0, 1]$, respectively, where $b_{FE} + b_{RE} = 1$. We assume that both types of attacks trigger alerts with the same time delay. Thus, there is a one-to-one mapping between the sequence of attacks and alerts, and we can consider the zero delay time without loss of generality. The alerts cannot reflect the *attack's type* denoted by $\theta^k \in \Theta := \{\theta_{FE}, \theta_{RE}\}$ at all attack stages $k \in \mathbb{Z}^{0+}$. However, the alerts can provide human operators with a *category label* from a finite set $\mathscr{S}$ based on observable features or traces of the associated attacks, e.g., the attack locations as shown in Sect. 4. We denote the alert's category label at attack stage $k \in \mathbb{Z}^{0+}$ as $s^k \in \mathscr{S}$.

2.3 Manual Inspection and Attention Management

Since an alert does not directly reflect whether the attack is feint or real, human operators need to inspect the alert to determine the hidden type, which leads to three *security decisions*: the attack is feint (denoted by w_{FE}), the attack is real (denoted by w_{RE}), or the attack's type is unknown (denoted by w_{UN}). We use $w^k \in \mathscr{W} := \{w_{FE}, w_{RE}, w_{UN}\}$ to denote the human operator's security decision of the k-th alert. Each human operator has limited attention and cannot inspect multiple alerts simultaneously. Moreover, the human operator requires sustained attention on an alert to make an accurate security decision. Frequent alert pop-ups can distract humans from the current alert inspection and result in *alert fatigue* and the *paradox of choice* as illustrated in Sect. 2.1. To compensate for the human's attention limitation, we can intentionally make some alerts less noticeable, e.g., without sounds or in a light color. Then, the human can pay sustained attention to the alert currently under inspection. These inconspicuous alerts can be assigned to other available inspectors with an additional cost of human resources. If these alerts are time-insensitive, they can also be queued and inspected later by the same operator at his convenience. However, in practice, the number of alerts usually far exceeds the number of available inspectors, and the alerts cannot tolerate delay. Then, these alerts are dismissed as a tradeoff for the timely and accurate inspection of the other highlighted alerts. In this case, these inconspicuous alerts are not inspected and automatically assigned the security decision w_{UN}.

In this paper, we focus on the class of *Attention Management (AM) strategies*, denoted by $\mathscr{A} := \{a_m\}_{m \in \mathbb{Z}^+}$, that highlight alerts periodically to engage operators in the alert inspection. We assume that the human operator can only notice and inspect an alert when it is highlighted. Then, AM strategy $a_m \in \mathscr{A}$ means that the human operator inspects the alerts at attack stages $k = hm, h \in \mathbb{Z}^{0+}$. We refer to the attack stages during the h-th inspection as the *inspection stage* $h \in \mathbb{Z}^{0+}$. Then, under AM strategy $a_m \in \mathscr{A}$, each inspection stage contains m attack stages as shown in the blue background of Fig. 4. The h-th inspection has a duration of $\tau_{IN}^{h,k'} := \sum_{k'=hm}^{hm+m-1} \tau^{k'}$ for all $h \in \mathbb{Z}^{0+}$.

Decision Probability with N Thresholds. The human operator's security decision depends on the attack's type, the category label, and the AM strategy. We refer to $\Pr(w^k | s^k, a_m; \theta^k)$ as the *decision probability*; i.e., the probability of human making decision $w^k \in \mathscr{W}$ when the attack's type is $\theta^k \in \Theta$, the category label is $s^k \in \mathscr{S}$, and the AM strategy is $a_m \in \mathscr{A}$. As a probability measure, the decision probability satisfies $\sum_{w^k \in \mathscr{W}} \Pr(w^k | s^k, a_m; \theta^k) = 1, \forall \theta^k \in \Theta, \forall s^k \in \mathscr{S}, \forall a_m \in \mathscr{A}$.

At attack stages where alerts are inconspicuous, i.e., for all $k \neq hm, h \in \mathbb{Z}^{0+}$, the security decision w^k is w_{UN} with probability 1; i.e., for any given inspection policy $a_m \in \mathscr{A}$, we have $\Pr(w^k | s^k, a_m; \theta^k) = \mathbf{1}_{\{w^k = w_{UN}\}}, \forall s^k \in \mathscr{S}, \forall w^k \in \mathscr{W}, \forall \theta^k \in \Theta, \forall k \neq hm, h \in \mathbb{Z}^{0+}$. At attack stages of highlighted alerts, i.e., for all $k = hm, h \in \mathbb{Z}^{0+}$, the human operator inspects the h-th alert for a duration of $\tau_{IN}^{h,m}$. At each inspection stage h, a longer period length m induces a longer inspection time $\tau_{IN}^{h,m} = \sum_{k'=hm}^{hm+m-1} \tau^{k'}$. Based on the IDoS model in Sect. 2, different AM strategies only affect the inspection time. Thus, we can rewrite the decision probability $\Pr(w^k | s^k, a_m; \theta^k)$ as $\Pr(w^k | s^k, \tau_{IN}^{h,m}; \theta^k)$ at attack stages $k = hm, h \in \mathbb{Z}^{0+}$.

Adequate inspection time $\tau_{IN}^{h,m}$ leads to an accurate security decision. In this work, we assume that the probability of correct decision-making can be approximated by an increasing step function of the inspection time as shown in Fig. 5. That is, $N+1$ thresholds divide the support of the random variable $\tau_{IN}^{h,m}$, i.e., $[0, \infty)$, into N regions where the probability of correct security decisions increases. We can increase the number of thresholds, i.e., the value of N, to improve the accuracy of the approximation. For each $s^k \in \mathscr{S}$ and $\theta^k \in \Theta$, we denote the corresponding N thresholds as $\bar{\tau}_n(s^k, \theta^k) \in \mathscr{N}(s^k, \theta^k), n \in \{0, 1, \cdots, N\}$, where $\mathscr{N}(s^k, \theta^k)$ is a finite set, $\bar{\tau}_0(s^k, \theta^k) = 0$, $\bar{\tau}_N(s^k, \theta^k) = \infty$, and $\bar{\tau}_0(s^k, \theta^k) < \bar{\tau}_N(s^k, \theta^k) < \bar{\tau}_2(s^k, \theta^k) < \cdots < \bar{\tau}_N(s^k, \theta^k)$. If $\tau_{IN}^{h,m}$ belongs to the region $n \in \{0, 1, \cdots, N\}$, i.e., $\bar{\tau}_{n-1}(s^k, \theta^k) < \tau_{IN}^{h,m} < \bar{\tau}_n(s^k, \theta^k)$, then the decision probabilities under θ_{FE} and θ_{RE} are represented as (1) and (2), respectively,

$$\Pr(w^k | s^k, \tau_{IN}^{h,m}; \theta_{FE}) = \begin{cases} \bar{p}_{CD}^{n-1}(s^k, \theta_{FE}) \in [0, 1] & \text{if } w^k = w_{FE} \\ \bar{p}_{ID}^{n-1}(s^k, \theta_{FE}) \in [0, 1] & \text{if } w^k = w_{RE} \\ 1 - \bar{p}_{CD}^{n-1}(s^k, \theta_{FE}) - \bar{p}_{ID}^{n-1}(s^k, \theta_{FE}) & \text{if } w^k = w_{UN} \end{cases} \quad (1)$$

and

$$\Pr(w^k | s^k, \tau_{IN}^{h,m}; \theta_{RE}) = \begin{cases} \bar{p}_{CD}^{n-1}(s^k, \theta_{RE}) \in [0, 1] & \text{if } w^k = w_{RE} \\ \bar{p}_{ID}^{n-1}(s^k, \theta_{RE}) \in [0, 1] & \text{if } w^k = w_{FE} \\ 1 - \bar{p}_{CD}^{n-1}(s^k, \theta_{RE}) - \bar{p}_{ID}^{n-1}(s^k, \theta_{RE}) & \text{if } w^k = w_{UN} \end{cases} \quad (2)$$

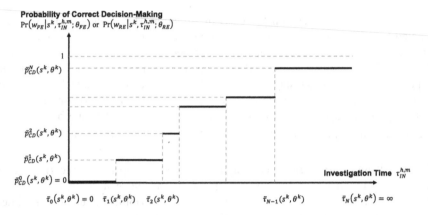

Fig. 5. The probability of the human operator making correct security decisions, i.e., $\Pr(w_{FE}|s^k, \tau_{IN}^{h,m}; \theta_{FE})$ and $\Pr(w_{RE}|s^k, \tau_{IN}^{h,m}; \theta_{RE})$, is approximated as an increasing step function of the inspection time $\tau_{IN}^{h,m}$ at inspection stage $h \in \mathbb{Z}^{0+}$.

In both (1) and (2), the first and second cases represent the probability of making correct and incorrect security decisions, respectively. The third case represents the probability that the human operator is uncertain about the attack's type and needs more time to inspect. A longer inspection time has two impacts:

- Increases the probability of making correct security decisions, i.e., $0 = \bar{p}_{CD}^0(s^k, \theta^k) \leq \bar{p}_{CD}^1(s^k, \theta^k) \leq \cdots \leq \bar{p}_{CD}^N(s^k, \theta^k) \leq 1$, for any given $s^k \in \mathscr{S}$ and $\theta^k \in \Theta$.
- Decreases the probability of incorrect security decisions, i.e., $0 \leq \bar{p}_{ID}^N(s^k, \theta^k) \leq \bar{p}_{ID}^{N-1}(s^k, \theta^k) \leq \cdots \leq \bar{p}_{ID}^0(s^k, \theta^k) \leq 1$, for any given $s^k \in \mathscr{S}$ and $\theta^k \in \Theta$.

3   Semi-Markov Process Model for Performance Evaluation

We assume that the category label of the sequential attacks follows a semi-Markov process based on the attack's type where $\mathrm{Tr}(s^{k+1}|s^k; \theta^k)$ represents the *transition probability* from $s^k \in \mathscr{S}$ to $s^{k+1} \in \mathscr{S}$ when the attack's type is $\theta^k \in \Theta$ at attack stage $k \in \mathbb{Z}^{0+}$. As a probability measure, the transition probability satisfies $\sum_{s^{k+1} \in \mathscr{S}} \mathrm{Tr}(s^{k+1}|s^k; \theta^k) = 1, \forall s^k \in \mathscr{S}, \forall \theta^k \in \Theta$. The inter-arrival time τ^k is a continuous random variable with a Probability Density Function (PDF) denoted by $z(\cdot|s^k; \theta^k)$.

3.1   Consolidated State and Consolidated Cost

Since the inspection is made every m attack stages, we define the *consolidated state* $x^h := [s^{hm}, \cdots, s^{hm+m-1}] \in \mathscr{X} := \mathscr{S}^m$ that consists of the category labels of m successive alerts at inspection stage $h \in \mathbb{Z}^{0+}$. Analogously, we define the *consolidated type* $\bar{\theta}^h := [\theta^{hm}, \cdots, \theta^{hm+m-1}] \in \bar{\Theta} := \Theta^m$. Then, we denote the transition function of the consolidated state as $\bar{T}r(x^{h+1}|x^h; \bar{\theta}^h)$, which is also Markov as shown below.

$$\Pr(x^{h+1}|x^h,\cdots,x^1;\bar{\theta}^h,\cdots,\bar{\theta}^1) = \frac{\Pr(x^{h+1},x^h,\cdots,x^1;\bar{\theta}^h,\cdots,\bar{\theta}^1)}{\Pr(x^h,\cdots,x^1;\bar{\theta}^h,\cdots,\bar{\theta}^1)}$$

$$= \frac{\Pr(s^{(h+2)m-1}|s^{(h+2)m-2};\theta^{(h+2)m-2})\Pr(s^{(h+2)m-2}|s^{(h+2)m-3};\theta^{(h+2)m-3})\cdots\Pr(s^1 s^0;\theta^0)}{\Pr(s^{(h+1)m-1}|s^{(h+1)m-2};\theta^{(h+1)m-2})\Pr(s^{(h+1)m-2}|s^{(h+1)m-3};\theta^{(h+1)m-3})\cdots\Pr(s^1 s^0;\theta^0)}$$

$$= \Pr(s^{(h+2)m-1}|s^{(h+2)m-2};\theta^{(h+2)m-2})\cdots\Pr(s^{(h+1)m-1}|s^{(h+1)m-2};\theta^{(h+1)m-2})$$

$$= \bar{T}r(x^{h+1}|x^h;\bar{\theta}^h).$$

$$(3)$$

The *inspection time* $\tau_{IN}^{h,m} = \sum_{k'=hm}^{hm+m-1}\tau^{k'}$ at inspection stage $h \in \mathbb{Z}^{0+}$ is a continuous random variable with support $[0,\infty)$ whose PDF $\bar{z}(\cdot|x^h;\bar{\theta}^h)$ can be computed based on the PDF z. Based on $\bar{z}$ and $\Pr(w^{hm}|s^{hm},\tau_{IN}^{h,m};\theta^{hm})$ in (1) and (2), we can compute the probability of security decision w^{hm} at inspection stage $h \in \mathbb{Z}^{0+}$ given x^h and $\bar{\theta}^h$, i.e.,

$$\Pr(w^{hm}|x^h,a_m;\bar{\theta}^h) = \int_0^\infty \Pr(w^{hm},\tau_{IN}^{h,m}|x^h;\bar{\theta}^h)d(\tau_{IN}^{h,m})$$

$$= \int_0^\infty \Pr(w^{hm}|s^{hm},\tau_{IN}^{h,m};\theta^{hm})\bar{z}(\tau_{IN}^{h,m}|x^h,\bar{\theta}^h)d(\tau_{IN}^{h,m}). \quad (4)$$

Let $\Pr(w^{hm}|x^h,a_m;\theta^{hm})$ be the shorthand notation for $\mathbb{E}_{\theta^l\sim[b_{FE},b_{RE}],l\in\{hm+1,\cdots,hm+m-1\}}$ $[\Pr(w^{hm}|x^h,a_m;\bar{\theta}^h)], \forall\theta^{hm} \in \Theta$. We define the probability of the human operator making correct security decisions at inspection stage $h \in \mathbb{Z}^{0+}$ as

$$\hat{p}_{CD}(x^h,a_m) := b_{FE}\Pr(w_{FE}|x^h,a_m;\theta_{FE}) + b_{RE}\Pr(w_{RE}|x^h,a_m;\theta_{RE}), \forall x^h \in \mathcal{X}, \quad (5)$$

which leads to the *consolidated severity level* of IDoS attacks in Definition 1.

Definition 1 (Consolidated Severity Level). *We define* $1 - \hat{p}_{CD}(x^h,a_m)$ *as the consolidated severity level of IDoS attacks under the consolidated state* $x^h \in \mathcal{X}$ *and AM strategy* $a_m \in \mathcal{A}$.

We denote $c(w^k,s^k;\theta^k)$ as the operator's cost at attack stage $k \in \mathbb{Z}^{0+}$ when the alert's category label is $s^k \in \mathcal{S}$, the attack's type is $\theta^k \in \Theta$, and the security decision is $w^k \in \mathcal{W}$. At attack stages where alerts are inconspicuous, i.e., for all $k \neq hm, h \in \mathbb{Z}^{0+}$, the security decision is w_{UN} without manual inspection, which incurs an *uncertainty cost* $c_{UN} > 0$. At attack stages of highlighted alerts, i.e., for all $k = hm, h \in \mathbb{Z}^{0+}$, the human operator obtains a reward (resp. cost), denoted by $c_{CD}(s^k;\theta^k) < 0$ (resp. $c_{ID}(s^k;\theta^k) > 0$), for correct (resp. incorrect) security decisions. If the human operator remains uncertain about the attack's type after the inspection time $\tau_{IN}^{h,m}$, i.e., $w^{hm} = w_{UN}$, there is the uncertainty cost c_{UN}. We define the human operator's *consolidated cost* at inspection stage $h \in \mathbb{Z}^{0+}$ as

$$\bar{c}(x^h,a_m;\bar{\theta}^h) := (m-1)c_{UN} + \sum_{w^{hm}\in\mathcal{W}} \Pr(w^{hm}|x^h,a_m;\bar{\theta}^h)c(w^{hm},s^{hm};\theta^{hm}). \quad (6)$$

3.2 Long-Term Risk Measures for IDoS Attacks

In this section, we define four long-term risk measures whose relations are shown in Fig. 6. The *Cumulative Cost (CC)* and *Expected Cumulative Cost (ECC)* on the left directly follow from the discounted summation of the consolidated cost $\bar{c}$ in (6). Since CC and ECC depend on the consolidated state x^h and the consolidated type $\bar{\theta}^h$, it is of high dimension and thus difficult to store and compute. By taking an expectation over $s^{hm+1}, \cdots, s^{hm+m-1} \in \mathscr{S}$, we reduce the dimension and obtain the Aggregated Cumulative Cost (ACC) and Expected Aggregated Cumulative Cost (EACC) on the right of the figure. The DP representations for CC (resp. ECC) and ACC (resp. EACC) are generally not equivalent. We identify the condition under which two DP representations are equivalent in Sect. 3.3. The two risk learning schemes are introduced in Sect. 3.4. Since the consolidated risk learning is based on ECC, it has to wait for the realization of the consolidated state $x^h := [s^{hm}, \cdots, s^{hm+m-1}]$ to evaluate the inspection performance. On the contrary, the EACC-based aggregated risk learning just needs s^{hm} to evaluate the inspection performance, which reduces the dimension of the samples and enables evaluations with no delay.

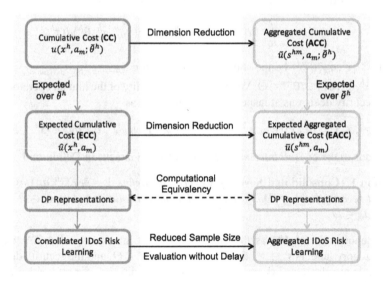

Fig. 6. Relations among four long-term risk measures, their DP representations, and two risk learning schemes.

Cumulative Cost and Expected Cumulative Cost. With discounted factor $\gamma \in (0,1)$, we define the *Cumulative Cost (CC)* under x^{h_0}, $\bar{\theta}^{h_0}$, and action a_m as $u(x^{h_0}, a_m; \bar{\theta}^{h_0}) := \mathbb{E}[\sum_{h=h_0}^{\infty} (\gamma)^h \cdot \bar{c}(x^h, a_m; \bar{\theta}^h)]$, where the expectation is taken over x^{h_0+n} and $\theta^{h_0 m+n}$ for all $n \in \{1, 2, \cdots, \infty\}$. By Dynamic Programming (DP), we represent u in the following iterative form, i.e., for all $x^h \in \mathscr{X}$, $\bar{\theta}^h \in \bar{\Theta}$, and $h \in \mathbb{Z}^{0+}$,

$$u(x^h, a_m; \bar{\theta}^h) = \bar{c}(x^h, a_m; \bar{\theta}^h) + \gamma \sum_{x^{h+1} \in \mathscr{X}} \bar{T}r(x^{h+1} | x^h; \bar{\theta}^h) \mathbb{E}_{\bar{\theta}^{h+1}} [u(x^{h+1}, a_m; \bar{\theta}^{h+1})]. \quad (7)$$

Denote $u^l(x^h, a_m; \bar{\theta}^h), l \in \mathbb{Z}^{0+}$, as the estimated value of $u(x^h, a_m; \bar{\theta}^h)$ at the l-th iteration, we can compute (7) by the following value iteration algorithm in Algorithm 1. It can be shown that $u^{\infty}(x^h, a_m; \bar{\theta}^h)$ converges to $u(x^h, a_m; \bar{\theta}^h)$ and the following lemma holds [15].

Algorithm 1: Value Iteration

---

1 **Initialize** a stopping threshold $\varepsilon > 0$, $l = 0$, and $u^0(x^h, a_m; \bar{\theta}^h) = 0, \forall x^h \in \mathcal{X}, \bar{\theta}^h \in \bar{\Theta}$;
2 **while** $\max_{x^h \in \mathcal{X}, \bar{\theta}^h \in \bar{\Theta}} [u^{l+1}(x^h, a_m; \bar{\theta}^h) - u^l(x^h, a_m; \bar{\theta}^h)] \geq \varepsilon$ **do**
3   **for** $x^h \in \mathcal{X}$ and $\bar{\theta}^h \in \bar{\Theta}$ **do**
4   Update estimated value $u^{l+1}(x^h, a_m; \bar{\theta}^h) =$
         $\bar{c}(x^h, a_m; \bar{\theta}^h) + \gamma \sum_{x^{h+1} \in \mathcal{X}} \bar{T}r(x^{h+1}|x^h; \bar{\theta}^h) \mathbb{E}_{\bar{\theta}^{h+1}} [u^l(x^{h+1}, a_m; \bar{\theta}^{h+1})]$;
5   **end**
6      $l \leftarrow l+1$;
7 **end**
8 **Return** $u^{l+1}(x^h, a_m; \bar{\theta}^h)$;

Lemma 1 (Monotonicity Lemma). *Let* $u'(x^{h_0}, a_m; \bar{\theta}^{h_0}) := \mathbb{E}[\sum_{h=h_0}^{\infty} (\gamma)^h \cdot \bar{c}'(x^h, a_m; \bar{\theta}^h)]$. *If* $\bar{c}(x^h, a_m; \bar{\theta}^h) > \bar{c}'(x^h, a_m; \bar{\theta}^h), \forall x^h \in \mathcal{X}, \bar{\theta}^h \in \bar{\Theta}$, *then* $u(x^h, a_m; \bar{\theta}^h) > u'(x^h, a_m; \bar{\theta}^h)$ *for all* $x^h \in \mathcal{X}, \bar{\theta}^h \in \bar{\Theta}$.

We define the *Expected Cumulative Cost (ECC)* as $\hat{u}(x^h, a_m) := \mathbb{E}_{\bar{\theta}^h}[u(x^h, a_m; \bar{\theta}^h)]$, $\forall x^h \in \mathcal{X}$, and write the DP representation of $\hat{u}$ in (8) by taking expectation over $\bar{\theta}^h$ in (7).

$$\hat{u}(x^h, a_m) = \mathbb{E}_{\bar{\theta}^h}[\bar{c}(x^h, a_m; \bar{\theta}^h)] + \gamma \sum_{x^{h+1} \in \mathcal{X}} \mathbb{E}_{\bar{\theta}^h}[\bar{T}r(x^{h+1}|x^h; \bar{\theta}^h)]\hat{u}(x^{h+1}, a_m). \quad (8)$$

Aggregated Cumulative Cost and Expected Aggregated Cumulative Cost. We define the *Aggregated Cumulative Cost (ACC)* as

$$\bar{u}(s^{hm}, a_m; \bar{\theta}^h) := \sum_{s^{hm+1}, \cdots, s^{hm+m-1} \in \mathcal{S}} \left[\Pr(s^{hm+1}, \cdots, s^{hm+m-1}|s^{hm}; \bar{\theta}^h) \right.$$

$$\left. \cdot u([s^{hm}, \cdots, s^{hm+m-1}], a_m; \bar{\theta}^h) \right], \quad (9)$$

and the *Expected Aggregated Cumulative Cost (EACC)* as

$$\bar{u}(s^{hm}, a_m) := \mathbb{E}_{\theta^l \sim [b_{FE}, b_{RE}], l \in \{hm, \cdots, hm+m-1\}} [\bar{u}(s^{hm}, a_m; \bar{\theta}^h)], \forall s^{hm} \in \mathcal{S}. \quad (10)$$

Both ECC $\hat{u}(x^0, a_m)$ and EACC $\bar{u}^0(s^0, a_m)$ evaluate the long-term performance of the AM strategy $a_m \in \mathcal{A}$ on average as defined in Definition 2. However, EACC depends on s^{hm} but not on $s^{hm+1}, \cdots, s^{hm+m-1}$.

Definition 2 (Consolidated and Aggregated IDoS risks). *We define ECC* $\hat{u}(x^h, a_m)$ *(resp. EACC* $\bar{u}(s^{hm}, a_m)$) *as the consolidated (resp. aggregated) risk of the IDoS attack under* $x^h \in \mathcal{X}$ *(resp.* $s^{hm} \in \mathcal{S}$) *and attention strategy* $a_m \in \mathcal{A}$.

3.3 Inter-arrival Time with Independent PDF

In Sect. 3.3, we consider the special case where PDF z is independent of s^k and θ^k, which reduces the dependency of $\hat{p}_{CD}$ and $\bar{c}$ from x^h to s^{hm} as shown in Lemma 2. Moreover, we can obtain DP representations for ACC $\tilde{u}$ and EACC $\bar{u}$ as shown in Theorem 1. Value iteration in Algorithm 1 can be revised accordingly to solve these two DP representations.

Lemma 2. *If PDF z is independent of s^k and θ^k, then $\hat{p}_{CD}(x^h, a_m)$ in (5) can be rewritten as $\hat{p}_{CD}(s^{hm}, a_m)$ and the consolidated cost $\bar{c}(x^h, a_m; \bar{\theta}^h)$ in (6) can be rewritten as $\bar{c}(s^{hm}, a_m; \theta^{hm})$ without loss of generality.*

Proof. If z is independent of s^k, θ^k, then $\bar{z}$ is independent of $x^h, \bar{\theta}^h$, and $\Pr(w^{hm} | x^h, a_m; \bar{\theta}^h)$ in (4) only depends on s^{hm} and θ^{hm}. Thus, $\hat{p}_{CD}$ becomes a function of s^{hm}, a_m, and the consolidated cost $\bar{c}$ in (6) becomes a function of s^{hm}, θ^{hm}, and a_m.   □

Theorem 1. *If PDF z is independent of s^k and θ^k, then we have the following DP representation in (11) for the ACC*

$$\tilde{u}(s^{hm}, a_m; \bar{\theta}^h) = \bar{c}(s^{hm}, a_m; \theta^{hm})$$
$$+ \gamma \sum_{s^{(h+1)m} \in \mathscr{X}} \Pr(s^{(h+1)m} | s^{hm}; \bar{\theta}^h) \mathbb{E}_{\bar{\theta}^{h+1}} [\tilde{u}(s^{(h+1)m}, a_m; \bar{\theta}^{h+1})], \quad (11)$$

and the following DP representation in (12) for the EACC

$$\bar{u}(s^{hm}, a_m) = \mathbb{E}_{\theta^{hm}} [\bar{c}(s^{hm}, a_m; \theta^{hm})]$$
$$+ \gamma \sum_{s^{(h+1)m} \in \mathscr{X}} \mathbb{E}_{\bar{\theta}^h} [\Pr(s^{(h+1)m} | s^{hm}; \bar{\theta}^h)] \cdot \bar{u}(s^{(h+1)m}, a_m), \quad (12)$$

where

$$\mathbb{E}_{\bar{\theta}^h} [\Pr(s^{(h+1)m} | s^{hm}; \bar{\theta}^h)] = \sum_{s^{hm+1}, \cdots, s^{hm+m-1} \in \mathscr{S}} \prod_{l=hm}^{(h+1)m} \mathbb{E}_{\theta^l \sim [b_{FE}, b_{RE}]} [Tr(s^{l+1} | s^l; \theta^l)]. \quad (13)$$

Proof. First, for all $\bar{\theta}^h \in \bar{\Theta}$, we have

$$\sum_{s^{hm+1}, \cdots, s^{hm+m-1} \in \mathscr{S}} \Pr(s^{hm+1}, \cdots, s^{hm+m-1} | s^{hm}; \bar{\theta}^h) \cdot \bar{c}(s^{hm}, a_m; \theta^{hm}) \equiv \bar{c}(s^{hm}, a_m; \theta^{hm}).$$

Second, since

$$\bar{T}r(x^{h+1} | x^h; \bar{\theta}^h) = \Pr(s^{(h+1)m}, \cdots, s^{(h+2)m-1} | s^{hm+m-1}; \bar{\theta}^h)$$
$$= \Pr(s^{(h+1)m+1}, \cdots, s^{(h+2)m-1} | s^{(h+1)m}; \bar{\theta}^h) Tr(s^{(h+1)m} | s^{hm+m-1}; \theta^{hm+m-1})$$

as shown in (3), we have

$$
\sum_{s^{hm+1},\cdots,s^{hm+m-1}\in\mathscr{S}} \Pr(s^{hm+1},\cdots,s^{hm+m-1}|s^{hm};\bar{\theta}^{h})
$$
$$
\cdot \sum_{x^{h+1}\in\mathscr{X}} \bar{T}r(x^{h+1}|x^{h};\bar{\theta}^{h})\mathbb{E}_{\bar{\theta}^{h+1}}[u(x^{h+1},a_{m};\bar{\theta}^{h+1})]
$$
$$
= \sum_{s^{hm+1},\cdots,s^{hm+m-1}\in\mathscr{S}} \Pr(s^{hm+1},\cdots,s^{hm+m-1}|s^{hm};\bar{\theta}^{h})
$$
$$
\cdot \sum_{s^{(h+1)m}\in\mathscr{S}} Tr(s^{(h+1)m}|s^{hm+m-1};\theta^{hm+m-1})\cdot\mathbb{E}_{\bar{\theta}^{h+1}}[\tilde{u}(s^{(h+1)m},a_{m};\bar{\theta}^{h+1})].
$$

Based on the Markov property, we have

$$
\sum_{s^{hm+1},\cdots,s^{hm+m-1}\in\mathscr{S}} \Pr(s^{hm+1},\cdots,s^{hm+m-1}|s^{hm};\bar{\theta}^{h})Tr(s^{(h+1)m}|s^{hm+m-1};\theta^{hm+m-1})
$$
$$
= \Pr(s^{(h+1)m}|s^{hm};\bar{\theta}^{h}).
$$

Therefore, we obtain (11) by plugging (7) into the definition of ACC in (9). We obtain (12) by taking expectation over $\bar{\theta}^{h}$ and using the definition of EACC in (10). Based on (13), we can compute $\mathbb{E}_{\bar{\theta}^{h}}[\Pr(s^{(h+1)m}|s^{hm};\bar{\theta}^{h})]$ directly from the transition probability Tr by the forward Kolmogorov equation.   □

*Remark 1 **(Computational Equivalency)**.* To compute $\tilde{u}$, we generally need to first compute u via (7) and then take expectation over $s^{hm+1},\cdots,s^{hm+m-1}$. This computation is of high temporal and spatial complexity as u depends on x^{h}. However, for the special case where z is independent of s^{k} and θ^{k}, we can compute $\tilde{u}$ directly based on (11) and reduce the computational complexity. Thus, Theorem 1 establishes a computational equivalence between the two DP representations in (7) and (11), which contributes to a lightweight computation scheme. Analogously, we also establish a computational equivalence between the two DP representations in (8) and (12) by taking expectations of (7) and (11) with respect to $\bar{\theta}^{h}$.

3.4 Data-Driven Assessment

In practice, we do not know the parameters of the SMP model, including the transition probability Tr, the PDF z, the threshold set $\mathcal{N}(s^{k},\theta^{k})$, and the set of probability of making correct (resp. incorrect) decisions $\bar{p}^{n}_{CD}$ (resp. $\bar{p}^{n}_{ID}$), $n \in \{0,1\cdots,N\}$. Therefore, we use Temporal-Difference (TD) learning [15] to evaluate the performance of the AM strategy $a_{m} \in \mathscr{A}$ based on the inspection results in real-time.

Consolidated IDoS Risk Learning. Letting $v^{h}(x^{h},a_{m})$ be the estimated value of $\hat{u}(x^{h},a_{m})$ at the inspection stage $h \in \mathbb{Z}^{0+}$, we have the following recursive update in real-time as shown in (14).

$$
v^{h+1}(\hat{x}^{h},a_{m}) = (1-\alpha^{h}(\hat{x}^{h}))v^{h}(\hat{x}^{h},a_{m}) + \alpha^{h}(\hat{x}^{h})(\hat{c}^{h}+\gamma v^{h}(\hat{x}^{h+1},a_{m})), \quad (14)
$$

where $\hat{x}^{h}$ (resp. $\hat{x}^{h+1}$) is the observed state value at the current inspection stage h (resp. the next inspection stage $h+1$), $\alpha^{h}(\hat{x}^{h}) \in (0,1)$ is the learning rate, and $\hat{c}^{h}$ is the observed cost at stage $h \in \mathbb{Z}^{0+}$. To guarantee that v^{∞} convergences to $\hat{u}$, we require $\sum_{h=0}^{\infty} \alpha^h(x^h) = \infty$ and $\sum_{h=0}^{\infty} (\alpha^h(x^h))^2 < \infty$ for all $x^h \in \mathscr{X}$.

Aggregated IDoS Risk Learning. For the special case where PDF z is independent of s^k and θ^k, we can use TD learning to directly estimate EACC $\bar{u}(s^{hm}, a_m)$ based on (12). Letting $\bar{v}^h(x^h, a_m)$ be the estimated value of $\bar{u}(s^{hm}, a_m)$ at the inspection stage $h \in \mathbb{Z}^{0+}$, we have the following recursive update in real-time as shown in (15).

$$\bar{v}^{h+1}(\hat{s}^{hm}, a_m) = (1 - \bar{\alpha}^h(\hat{s}^{hm}))v^h(\hat{s}^{hm}, a_m) + \bar{\alpha}^h(\hat{s}^{hm})(\hat{c}^h + \gamma \bar{v}^h(\hat{s}^{(h+1)m}, a_m)), \quad (15)$$

where $\hat{s}^{hm}$ (resp. $\hat{s}^{(h+1)m}$) is the observed state value at the current inspection stage h (resp. the next inspection stage $h+1$), $\bar{\alpha}^h(\hat{s}^{hm}) \in (0,1)$ is the learning rate, and $\hat{c}^h$ is the observed cost at stage $h \in \mathbb{Z}^{0+}$. To guarantee that $\bar{v}^{\infty}$ convergences to $\bar{u}$, we require $\sum_{h=0}^{\infty} \bar{\alpha}^h(\hat{s}^{hm}) = \infty$ and $\sum_{h=0}^{\infty} (\bar{\alpha}^h(\hat{s}^{hm}))^2 < \infty$ for all $s^{hm} \in \mathscr{S}$.

4   Numerical Experiments and Analysis

We provide a numerical case study in this section to corroborate the results. Let the set of category label $\mathscr{S} = \{s_{AL}, s_{NL}, s_{PL}\}$ be the location of the attacks where s_{AL}, s_{NL}, and s_{PL} represent the application layer, network layer, and physical layer, respectively. We consider the special case where $\tau^k, \forall k \in \mathbb{Z}^{0+}$, is an exponential random variable with a constant rate $\beta > 0$, i.e., $z(\tau | s^k, \theta^k) = \beta e^{-\beta \tau}, \forall s^k \in \mathscr{S}, \theta^k \in \Theta, \tau \in [0, \infty)$. Figure 7 illustrates an exemplary sequential attack where the vertical dashed lines represent the attack stages $k \in \mathbb{Z}^{0+}$. The length of the rectangles between the k-th and $(k+1)$-th vertical dash lines represents the k-th attack's duration τ^k. The height of each square distinguishes the attack's type; i.e., tall and short rectangles represent feints and real attacks, respectively.

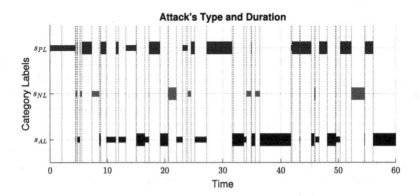

Fig. 7. The sequential arrival of feints and real attacks with different category labels.

The inspection time $\tau_{IN}^{h,m}$, as the summation of m i.i.d. exponential random variables, is an Erlang distribution with shape m and and rate $\beta > 0$, i.e., $\bar{z}(\tau | x^h; \bar{\theta}^h) = \frac{\beta^m \tau^{m-1} e^{-\beta \tau}}{(m-1)!}, \forall x^h \in \mathcal{X}, \forall \bar{\theta}^h, \tau \in [0, \infty)$. Consider a single threshold $N = 1$ and $\mathcal{N} = \{\bar{\tau}_0(s^k, \theta^k), \bar{\tau}_N(s^k, \theta^k)\}$. Then, $Pr(w^{hm} | x^h, a_m; \bar{\theta}^h)$ in (4) has the following closed form in (16) for correct decisions, i.e., $\theta^{hm} = \theta_{FE}, w^{hm} = w_{FE}$ or $\theta^{hm} = \theta_{RE}, w^{hm} = w_{RE}$.

$$Pr(w^{hm} | s^{hm}, a_m; \theta^{hm}) = \int_{\bar{\tau}_N(s^{hm}, \theta^{hm})}^{\infty} \bar{p}_{CD}^N(s^{hm}, \theta^{hm}) \frac{\beta^m \tau^{m-1} e^{-\beta \tau}}{(m-1)!} d\tau$$
$$= \bar{p}_{CD}^N(s^{hm}, \theta^{hm})(1 - CDF(\bar{\tau}_N(s^{hm}, \theta^{hm}))), \qquad (16)$$

where the Cumulative Distribution Function (CDF) of the random variable $\tau_{IN}^{h,m}$ is

$$CDF(\bar{\tau}_N(s^{hm}, \theta^{hm})) = 1 - \sum_{n=0}^{m-1} \frac{1}{n!} e^{-\beta \bar{\tau}_N(s^{hm}, \theta^{hm})} (\beta \bar{\tau}_N(s^{hm}, \theta^{hm}))^n. \qquad (17)$$

4.1 Value Iteration and TD Learning

Since PDF z is independent of s^k and θ^k, we can compute EACC in (12) by value iteration. As shown in Fig. 8a, the estimated values of EACC under three different category labels, i.e., $\bar{u}(s_{AL}, a_m)$, $\bar{u}(s_{NL}, a_m)$, and $\bar{u}(s_{PL}, a_m)$ in black, red, and blue, respectively, all converge within 40 iterations. When the exact model is unknown, we use TD learning in (15) to estimate EACC $\bar{u}(s^{hm, a_m})$. In particular, we choose $\bar{\alpha}^h(s^{hm}) = \frac{k_c}{k_{TI}(s^{hm}) - 1 + k_c}$ as the learning rate where $k_c \in (0, \infty)$ is a constant parameter and $k_{TI}(s^{hm}) \in \mathbb{Z}^{0+}$ is the number of visits to $s^{hm} \in \mathcal{S}$ up to stage $h \in \mathbb{Z}^{0+}$. We illustrate the convergence of TD learning in Fig. 8b with $k_c = 6$. Since the number of visits to s_{AL}, s_{NL}, and s_{PL} depends on the transition probability $\bar{T}r$, the learning stages for three category labels are of different lengths.

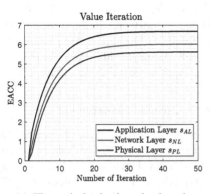
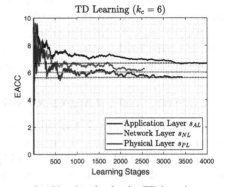

(a) Theoretical value by value iteration.   (b) Simulated value by TD learning.

Fig. 8. Computation and learning of EACC.

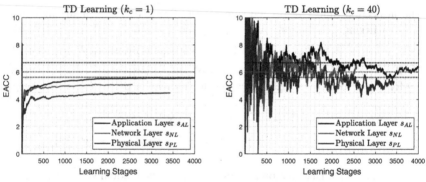

(a) Learning rate decreases too fast $k_c = 1$.   (b) Learning rate decreases too slow $k_c = 40$.

Fig. 9. Improper values of k_c lead to unsatisfactory learning performances in finite steps.

If k_c is too small as shown in Fig. 9a, the learning rate decreases so fast that new observed samples hardly update the estimated value. Then, it takes longer learning stages to learn the correct value. On the contrary, if k_c is too large as shown in Fig. 9b, the learning rate decreases so slow that new samples contribute significantly to the current estimated value, which causes a large variation and a slow convergence.

4.2 Severity Level and Aggregated Risk Without Attention Management

When there are no AM strategies, i.e., $m = 1$, the human operator switches attention whenever a new attack arrives. Then, (17) can be simplified as $CDF(\bar{\tau}_N(s^{hm}, \theta^{hm})) = 1 - e^{-\beta \bar{\tau}_N(s^{hm}, \theta^{hm})}, \forall s^{hm} \in \mathscr{S}, \theta^{hm} \in \Theta$, which is an exponential function of the product of the rate $\beta > 0$ and the threshold $\bar{\tau}_N(s^{hm}, \theta^{hm}) > 0$. Thus, $\hat{p}_{CD}(x^h, a_m)$ in (5) decreases monotonously as the value of the product $\beta \bar{\tau}_N(s^{hm}, \theta^{hm})$ increases. Based on Lemma 2, we can write the consolidated severity level as $1 - \hat{p}_{CD}(s^{hm}, a_m)$ without loss of generality. Let $\bar{\tau}_N(s_{AL}, \theta^{hm}) \geq \bar{\tau}_N(s_{NL}, \theta^{hm}) \geq \bar{\tau}_N(s_{PL}, \theta^{hm})$, we plot the severity level, i.e., $1 - \hat{p}_{CD}(s^{hm}, a_m)$, for different values of rate $\beta \in (0,5)$ in Fig. 10a. We illustrate the aggregated IDoS risk versus $\beta \in (0,5)$ in Fig. 10b. As magnified by two insert boxes, the aggregated IDoS risk under s_{AL}, s_{NL}, and s_{PL} can change orders for different β.

4.3 Severity Level and Aggregated Risk with Attention Management

We illustrate how different AM strategies affect the severity level and the aggregated risk of IDoS attacks in Fig. 11 and Fig. 12, respectively, where $\bar{p}_{CD}^N(s^{hm}, \theta_{FE}) = 1$ and $\bar{p}_{CD}^N(s^{hm}, \theta_{RE}) = 0.9$ for all $s^{hm} \in \mathscr{S}$, and $b_{FE} = 0.6$. As shown in Fig. 11, the severity level strictly decreases to 0.04 as m increases regardless of different values of β. We choose a small arrival rate $\beta = 1$ in Fig. 11a and a large rate $\beta = 3$ in Fig. 11b. For a given $m \in \mathbb{Z}^+$, a larger arrival rate results in a higher severity level, and more alerts need to be made inconspicuous to reduce the severity level.

We choose $\beta = 1$ and observe the linear increase of the aggregated IDoS risk when m is sufficiently large in Fig. 11. We investigate how high and low uncertainty costs

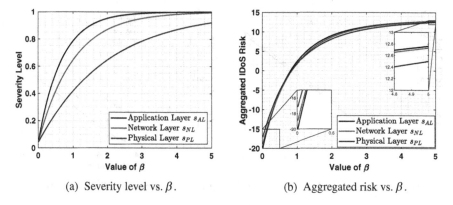

(a) Severity level vs. β.   (b) Aggregated risk vs. β.

Fig. 10. Severity level and aggregated risk of IDoS attacks under s_{AL}, s_{NL}, and s_{PL} in black, red, and blue, respectively. The insert boxes magnify the selected areas. (Color figure online)

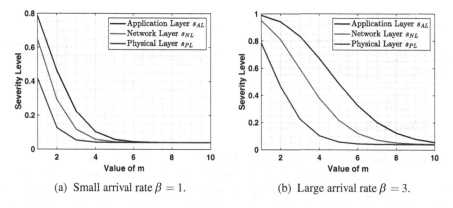

(a) Small arrival rate $\beta = 1$.   (b) Large arrival rate $\beta = 3$.

Fig. 11. Severity levels of IDoS attacks under s_{AL}, s_{NL}, and s_{PL} in black, red, and blue. (Color figure online)

c_{UN} affect the aggregated IDoS risk in Fig. 12a and Fig. 12b, respectively. If the uncertainty cost is much higher than the expected reward of correct decision-making, then the detailed inspection and correct security decisions are not of priority. As a result, the 'spray and pray' strategy should be adopted; i.e., let the operator inspect as many alerts as possible and use the high quantity to compensate for the low quality of these inspections. Under this scenario, $\bar{u}(s^{hm}, a_m)$ increases with $m \in \mathbb{Z}^+$ for all $s^{hm} \in \mathcal{S}$ as shown in Fig. 12a. If the uncertainty cost is of the same order as the inspection reward on average, then increasing m in a certain range (e.g., $m \in \{1, 2, 3, 4, \}$ in Fig. 12b) can increase the probability of correct decision-making and reduce the aggregated IDoS risk. The loss of alert omissions outweighs the gain of detailed inspection when m is beyond that range.

Remark 2 (**Rational Risk-Reduction Inattention**). In Fig. 12b, a small m represents a coarse inspection with a large number of alerts while a large m represents a fine

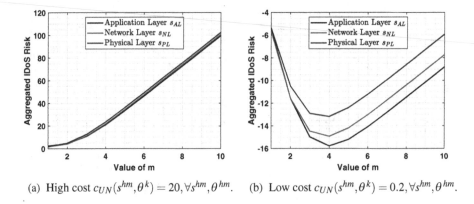

(a) High cost $c_{UN}(s^{hm}, \theta^k) = 20, \forall s^{hm}, \theta^{hm}$.   (b) Low cost $c_{UN}(s^{hm}, \theta^k) = 0.2, \forall s^{hm}, \theta^{hm}$.

Fig. 12. Aggregated IDoS risks under s_{AL}, s_{NL}, and s_{PL} in black, red, and blue. (Color figure online)

inspection of a small number of alerts. The U-shape curve reflects that the minimum risk is achieved with a proper level of *intentional inattention* to alerts, which we refer to as the *law of rational risk-reduction inattention*.

5 Conclusion

Attentional human vulnerability can be exploited by attackers and leads to a new class of advanced attacks called the Informational Denial-of-Service (IDoS) attacks. IDoS attacks intensify the shortage of human operators' cognitive resources in this age of information explosion by generating a large number of feint attacks. These feints distract operators from detailed inspections of the alerts, which significantly decrease the accuracy of their security decisions and undermine cybersecurity. We have formally introduced the IDoS attacks and established a quantitative framework that provides a theoretic underpinning to the IDoS attacks under limited attention resources. We have developed human-assistive security technologies that intentionally make selected alerts inconspicuous so that human operators can pay sustained attention to critical alerts.

We have modeled the sequential arrival of IDoS attacks as a semi-Markov process and the probability of correct decision-making as an increasing step function concerning the inspection time. Dynamic Programming (DP) and Temporal-Difference (TD) learning have been used to represent long-term costs and evaluate human performance in real-time, respectively. We have established the *computational equivalency* between the DP representation of the Cumulative Cost (CC) (resp. Expected Cumulative Cost (ECC)) and the Aggregated Cumulative Cost (ACC) (resp. Expected Aggregated Cumulative Cost (EACC)). This equivalency has reduced the dimension of the state space and the computational complexity of the value iteration and online learning algorithms.

From the case study, we have validated that both the severity level and the aggregated risk of IDoS attacks increase exponentially with the product of the attack's arrival rate and the operator's inspection efficiency. When Attention Management (AM) strategies are applied, we have observed that the severity level strictly decreases with the inspection time. We have arrived at the 'less is more' security principle in cases where correctly identifying the real and feint attacks is of high priority. It has been shown that inspecting a small number of selected alerts with sustained attention outperforms dividing the limited attention to inspect all alerts.

The future work would focus on coordinating multiple human operators to share the cognition load. Based on the literature of cognitive science and existing results of human experiments, we would develop detailed models of human attention, reasoning, and risk-perceiving to better characterize human factors in cybersecurity. Finally, we would extend the periodic AM strategies to adaptive ones that use the feedback of the alerts' category labels and the operator's current cognition status reflected by biosensors.

References

1. Hitzel, B.: The art of cyber war and cyber battle: deception operations (2019). https://www.networkdefenseblog.com/post/art-of-cyber-war-deception
2. Wickens, C.D., Hollands, J.G., Banbury, S., Parasuraman, R.: Engineering Psychology and Human Performance. Psychology Press, London (2015)
3. Casey, W., Morales, J.A., Wright, E., Zhu, Q., Mishra, B.: Compliance signaling games: toward modeling the deterrence of insider threats. Comput. Math. Organ. Theory **22**(3), 318–349 (2016). https://doi.org/10.1007/s10588-016-9221-5
4. Huang, L., Zhu, Q.: Duplicity games for deception design with an application to insider threat mitigation. IEEE Trans. Inf. Forensics Secur., arXiv preprint arXiv:2006.07942 (2021). https://doi.org/10.1109/TIFS.2021.3118886
5. Huang, L., Zhu, Q.: INADVERT: an interactive and adaptive counterdeception platform for attention enhancement and phishing prevention, arXiv preprint arXiv:2106.06907 (2021)
6. Huang, Y., Huang, L., Zhu, Q.: Reinforcement learning for feedback-enabled cyber resilience, arXiv preprint arXiv:2107.00783 (2021)
7. Huang, L., Zhu, Q.: A dynamic games approach to proactive defense strategies against advanced persistent threats in cyber-physical systems. Comput. Secur. **89**, 101660 (2020)
8. Huang, L., Zhu, Q.: A dynamic game framework for rational and persistent robot deception with an application to deceptive pursuit-evasion. IEEE Trans. Autom. Sci. Eng., 1–15 (2021). https://doi.org/10.1109/TASE.2021.3097286
9. Huang, L., Zhu, Q.: Adaptive honeypot engagement through reinforcement learning of semi-Markov decision processes. In: Alpcan, T., Vorobeychik, Y., Baras, J.S., Dán, G. (eds.) GameSec 2019. LNCS, vol. 11836, pp. 196–216. Springer, Cham (2019). https://doi.org/10.1007/978-3-030-32430-8_13
10. Zhao, D., et al.: Bidirectional RNN-based few-shot training for detecting multi-stage attack, arXiv preprint arXiv:1905.03454 (2019)
11. Sims, C.A.: Implications of rational inattention. J. Monet. Econ. **50**(3), 665–690 (2003)
12. Kahneman, D.: Thinking, Fast and Slow. Macmillan, London (2011)
13. Schwartz, B.: The Paradox of Choice: Why More is Less. Ecco, New York (2004)
14. Ban, T., Samuel, N., Takahashi, T., Inoue, D.: Combat security alert fatigue with AI-assisted techniques. In: Cyber Security Experimentation and Test Workshop, pp. 9–16 (2021)
15. Bertsekas, D., Tsitsiklis, J.: Neuro-Dynamic Programming, vol. 27 (1996)

Password Strength Signaling: A Counter-Intuitive Defense Against Password Cracking

Wenjie Bai, Jeremiah Blocki$^{(\boxtimes)}$, and Ben Harsha

Department of Computer Science, Purdue University, West Lafayette, IN, USA
{bai104,jblock,bharsha}@purdue.edu

Abstract. We introduce password strength signaling as a potential defense against password cracking. Recent breaches have exposed billions of user passwords to the dangerous threat of offline password cracking attacks. An offline attacker can quickly check millions (or sometimes billions/trillions) of password guesses by comparing a candidate password's hash value with a stolen hash from a breached authentication server. The attacker is limited only by the resources he is willing to invest. We explore the feasibility of applying ideas from Bayesian Persuasion to password authentication. Our key idea is to have the authentication server store a (noisy) signal about the strength of each user password for an offline attacker to find. Surprisingly, we show that the noise distribution for the signal can often be tuned so that a rational (profit-maximizing) attacker will crack *fewer* passwords. The signaling scheme exploits the fact that password cracking is not a zero-sum game i.e., it is possible for an attacker to increase their profit in a way that also reduces the number of cracked passwords. Thus, a well-defined signaling strategy will encourage the attacker to reduce his guessing costs by cracking fewer passwords. We use an evolutionary algorithm to compute the optimal signaling scheme for the defender. We evaluate our mechanism on several password datasets and show that it can reduce the total number of cracked passwords by up to 12% (resp. 5%) of all users in defending against offline (resp. online) attacks. While the results of our empirical analysis are positive we stress that we view the current solution as a proof-of-concept as there are important societal concerns that would need to be considered before adopting our password strength signaling solution.

Keywords: Bayesian Persuasion · Password authentication · Stackelberg game

1 Introduction

In the last decade, large scale data-breaches have exposed billions of user passwords to the dangerous threat of offline password cracking. An offline

© Springer Nature Switzerland AG 2021
B. Bošanský et al. (Eds.): GameSec 2021, LNCS 13061, pp. 334–353, 2021.
https://doi.org/10.1007/978-3-030-90370-1_18

attacker who has obtained the salt and cryptographic hash $((h_u, salt_u) = (H(salt_u, pw_u), salt_u))$ of a user u's password (pw_u) can attempt to crack the password by comparing this hash value with the hashes of likely password guesses i.e., by checking if $h'_u = H(salt_u, pw')$ for each pw'. The attacker can check as many guesses as he wants offline—without interacting with the authentication server. The only limit is the resources that the attacker is willing to invest in trying to crack the password. A rational password cracker [9,12] will choose the number of guesses that maximizes his utility.

Password hashing serves as a last line of defense against an offline password attacker. A good password hash function H should be moderately expensive to compute so that it becomes prohibitively expensive to check millions or billions of password guesses. However, we cannot make H too expensive to compute as the honest authentication server needs to evaluate H every time a user authenticates. In this paper, we explore a highly counter-intuitive[1] defense against rational attackers which does not impact hashing costs: password strength signaling! In particular, we apply Bayesian Persuasion [30] to password authentication. Specifically, we propose to have the authentication server store a (noisy) signal sig_u which is correlated with the strength of the user's password.

Traditionally, an authentication server stores the tuple $(u, salt_u, h_u)$ for each user u where $salt_u$ is a random salt value and $h_u = H(salt_u, pw_u)$ is the salted hash. We propose to have the authentication server instead store the tuple $(u, salt_u, sig_u, h_u)$, where the (noisy) signal sig_u is sampled based on the strength of the user's password pw_u. The signal sig_u is simply recorded for an offline attacker to find if the authentication server is breached. In fact, the authentication server never even uses sig_u when the user u authenticates[2]. The attacker will only use the signal sig_u if it is beneficial—at minimum the attacker could always choose to ignore the signal.

It is natural, but incorrect, to imagine that password cracking is a zero-sum game i.e., the attacker's gain is directly proportional to the defender's loss. In a zero-sum game there would be no benefit from information signaling [59] e.g., in a zero-sum game like rock-paper-scissors there is no benefit to leaking information about your action. However, we stress that password cracking is *not* a zero-sum game. The defender's (the sender of strength signal) utility is inversely proportional to the fraction of user passwords that are cracked. By contrast, it is possible that the attacker's utility is marginal even when he cracks a password i.e., when guessing costs offset the reward. In particular, the attacker's utility is given by the (expected) value of all of the cracked passwords minus his (expected) guessing costs. Thus, it is possible that password strength signaling would persuade the attacker to crack fewer passwords to reduce guessing costs. Indeed, we show that the signal distribution can be tuned so that a rational (profit-maximizing) attacker will crack *fewer* passwords.

---

[1] The propose may be less counter-intuitive to those familiar with prior work in the area of Bayesian Persuasion [30].

[2] If a user u attempts to login with password pw' the authentication server will lookup $salt_u$ and h_u and accept pw' if and only if $h_u = H(salt_u, pw')$.

To provide some intuition of why password strength signaling might be beneficial, we give two examples.

Example 1. Suppose that we add a signal $sig_u = 1$ to indicate that user u's password pw_u is uncrackable (e.g., the entropy of the password is over 60-bits) and we add the signal $sig_u = 0$ otherwise. In this case, the attacker will simply choose to ignore accounts with $sig_u = 1$ to reduce his total guessing cost. However, the number of cracked user passwords stays unchanged.

Example 2. Suppose that we modify the signaling scheme above so that even when the user's password pw_u is *not* deemed to be uncrackable we still signal $sig_u = 1$ with probability ϵ and $sig_u = 0$ otherwise. If the user's password is uncrackable we always signal $sig_u = 1$. Assuming that ϵ is not too large a rational attacker might still choose to ignore any account with $sig_u = 1$ i.e., the attacker's expected reward will decrease slightly, but the attacker's guessing costs will also be reduced. In this example, the fraction of cracked user passwords is reduced by up to ϵ i.e., any lucky user u with $sig_u = 1$ will not have their password cracked.

In this work, we explore the following questions: Can password strength signaling be used to protect passwords against rational attackers? If so, how can we compute the optimal signaling strategy?

1.1 Contributions

We introduce password information signaling as a novel, counter-intuitive, defense against rational password attackers. We adapt a Stackelberg game-theoretic model of Blocki and Datta [9] to characterize the behavior of a rational password adversary and the optimal signaling strategy for an authentication server (defender). We analyze the performance of password information signaling using several large password datasets: Bfield, Brazzers, Clixsense, CSDN, Neopets, 000webhost, RockYou, Yahoo! [10,14], and LinkedIn [8]. We analyze our mechanism both in the idealistic setting, where the defender has perfect knowledge of the user password distribution $\mathcal{P}$ and the attacker's value v for each cracked password, as well as in a more realistic setting where the defender only is given approximations of $\mathcal{P}$ and v. In our experiments, we analyze the fraction $x_{sig}(v)$ (resp. $x_{no-sig}(v)$) of passwords that a rational attacker would crack if the authentication server uses (resp. does not use) password information signaling. We find that the reduction in the number of cracked passwords can be substantial e.g., $x_{no-sig}(v) - x_{sig}(v) \approx 8\%$ under empirical distribution and 13% under Monte Carlo distribution. We also show that password strength signaling can be used to help deter online attacks when CAPTCHAs are used for throttling.

An additional advantage of our password strength signaling method is that it is independent of the password hashing method and requires no additional hashing work. Implementation involves some determination of which signal to attach to a certain account, but beyond that, any future authentication attempts are handled exactly as they were before i.e. the signal information is ignored.

We conclude by discussing several societal and ethical issues that would need to be addressed before password strength signaling is used. While password strength signaling decreases the total number of compromised accounts, there may be a few users whose accounts are cracked *because* they were assigned an "unlucky" signal. One possible solution might be to allow users to opt-in (resp. opt-out). Another approach might try to constrain the solution space to ensure that there are no "unlucky" users.

1.2 Related Work

The human tendency to pick weaker passwords has been well documented e.g., [14]. Convincing users to select stronger passwords is a difficult task [16,28,33, 47–49]. One line of research uses password strength meters to nudge users to select strong passwords [17,32,52] though a common finding is that users were not persuaded to select a stronger password [17,52]. Another approach is to require users to follow stringent guidelines when they create their password. However it has been shown that these methods also suffer from usability issues [3,24,28,50], and in some cases can even lead to users selecting weaker passwords [13,33].

Offline password cracking attacks have been around for decades [38]. There is a large body of research on password cracking techniques. State of the art cracking methods employ methods like Probabilistic Context-Free Grammars [31,55,58], Markov models [19,20,36,53], and neural networks [37]. Further work [35] has described methods of retrieving guessing numbers from commonly used tools like Hashcat [1] and John the Ripper [23].

Blocki and Datta [9] used a Stackelberg game to model the behavior of a rational (profit-motivated) attacker against a cost-asymmetric secure hashing (CASH) scheme. However, the CASH mechanism is not easily integrated with modern memory-hard functions. By contrast, password strength signaling does not require any changes to the password hashing algorithm.

A large body of research has focused on alternatives to text passwords. Alternatives have included one time passwords [25,34,41], challenge-response constructions [21,29], hardware tokens [40,46], and biometrics [4,22,45]. While all of these offer possible alternatives to traditional passwords it has been noted that none of these strategies outperforms passwords in all areas [15]. Furthermore, it has been noted that despite the shortcomings of passwords they remain the dominant method of authentication even today, and research should acknowledge this fact and seek to better understand traditional password use [27].

Password strength signaling is closely related to the literature on Bayesian Persuasion. Kamenica and Gentzkow [30] first introduced the notion of Bayesian Persuasion where a person (sender) chooses a signal to reveal to a receiver in an attempt to convince the receiver to take an action that positively impacts the welfare of both parties. There are a few prior results applying Bayesian Persuasion in security contexts, e.g., patrols [18], honeypots [43], with the sender (resp. receiver) playing the roles of defender (resp. attacker). To the best of our knowledge Bayesian Persuasion has never been applied in the context of password authentication. Most prior works use linear programming to find (or approximate) the sender's optimal signaling strategy. We stress that there are several unique challenges in the context of password authentication: (1) the action space of the receiver (attacker) is exponential in the size of (the support of) the password distribution, and (2) the sender's objective function is non-linear.

2 Preliminaries

We use $\mathbb{P}$ to denote the set of all passwords that a user might select and use $\mathcal{P}$ to denote a distribution over user-selected passwords i.e., a new user will select the password $pw \in \mathbb{P}$ with probability $\Pr_{x \sim \mathcal{P}}[x = pw]$—we typically write $\Pr[pw]$ for notational simplicity.

Password Datasets. Given a set of N users $\mathcal{U} = \{u_1, \ldots, u_N\}$ the corresponding password dataset D_u is given by the multiset $D_u = \{pw_{u_1}, \ldots, pw_{u_N}\}$ where pw_{u_i} denotes the password selected by user u_i. Fixing a password dataset D we let f_i denote the number of users who selected the ith most popular password in the dataset. We note that $f_1 \geq f_2 \geq \ldots$ and that $\sum_i f_i = N$ gives the total number N of users in the original dataset.

Empirical Password Distribution. Viewing our dataset D as N independent samples from the (unknown) distribution $\mathcal{P}$, we use f_i/N as an empirical estimate of the probability of the ith most common password pw_i and $D_f = (f_1, f_2, \ldots)$ as the corresponding frequency list. In addition, $\mathcal{D}_e$ is used to denoted the corresponding empirical distribution i.e., $\Pr_{x \sim \mathcal{D}_e}[x = pw_i] = f_i/N$. Because the real distribution $\mathcal{P}$ is unknown we will typically work with the empirical distribution $\mathcal{D}_e$. We remark that when $f_i \gg 1$ the empirical estimate will be close to the actual distribution i.e., $\Pr[pw_i] \approx f_i/N$, but when f_i is small the empirical estimate will likely diverge from the true probability value. Thus, while the empirical distribution is useful to analyze the performance of password strength signaling when the password value v is small, this analysis will be less accurate for larger values of v i.e., once the rational attacker has an incentive to start cracking passwords with lower frequency.

Monte Carlo Password Distribution. Following [5] we also use the Monte Carlo Password Distribution $\mathcal{D}_m$ to evaluate the performance of our password signaling mechanism when v is large. The Monte Carlo distributions is derived by subsampling passwords from our dataset D, generating guessing numbers from state-of-the-art password cracking models, and fitting a distribution to the resulting guessing curve. Due to the length limits, we omit discussion and experiment results for Monte Carlo Password Distribution. See more details in the full version of this paper [6].

3   Strength Signaling and Password Storage

In this section, we overview our basic signaling mechanism deferring until later how to optimally tune the parameters of the mechanism to minimize the number of cracked passwords.

3.1   Account Creation and Signaling

When users create their accounts they provide a user name u and password pw_u. First, the server runs canonical password storage procedure—randomly selecting a salt value $salt_u$ and calculating the hash value $h_u = H(salt_u, pw_u)$. Next, the server calculates the (estimated) strength $str_u \leftarrow$ getStrength(pw_u) of password pw_u and samples the signal $sig_u \overset{\$}{\leftarrow}$ getSignal(st_u). Finally, the server stores the tuple $(u, salt_u, sig_u, h_u)$—later if the user u attempts to login with a password pw' the authentication server will accept pw' if and only if $h_u = H(salt_u, pw')$. The account creation process is formally presented in Algorithm 1.

Algorithm 1. Signaling during Account Creation

Input: u, pw_u, L, d

1: $salt_u \overset{\$}{\leftarrow} \{0,1\}^L$
2: $h_u \leftarrow H(salt_u, pw_u)$
3: $str_u \leftarrow$ getStrength(pw_u)
4: $sig_u \overset{\$}{\leftarrow}$ getSignal(str_u)
5: StoreRecord$(u, salt_u, sig_u, h_u)$

A traditional password hashing solution would simply store the tuple $(u, salt_u, h_u)$ i.e., excluding the signal sig_u. Our mechanism requires two additionally subroutines getStrength() and getSignal() to generate this signal. The first algorithm is deterministic. It takes the user's password pw_u as input and outputs str_u—(an estimate of) the password strength. The second randomized algorithm takes the (estimated) strength parameter str_u and outputs a signal sig_u. The whole signaling algorithm is the composition of these two subroutines i.e., $\mathcal{A} =$ getSignal(getStrength(pw)). We use $s_{i,j}$ to denote the probability of observing the signal $sig_u = j$ given that the estimated strength level was $str_u = i$. Thus, getSignal() can be encoded using a signaling matrix $\mathbf{S}$ of dimension $a \times b$,

$$\begin{bmatrix} s_{0,0} & s_{0,1} & \cdots & s_{0,b-1} \\ s_{1,0} & s_{1,1} & \cdots & s_{1,b-1} \\ \vdots & \vdots & \ddots & \vdots \\ s_{a-1,0} & s_{a-1,1} & \cdots & s_{a-1,b-1} \end{bmatrix},$$

where a is the number of strength levels that passwords can be labeled, b is the number of signals the server can generate and $\mathbf{S}[i,j] = s_{i,j}$.

We remark that if $\mathbf{S}[i,0] = 1$ for all i[3] then the actual signal sig_u is *uncorrelated* with the password pw_u. In this case our mechanism is equivalent to the traditional (salted) password storage mechanism where getSignal() is replaced with a constant/null function. getStrength() is password strength oracle that outputs the actual/estimated strength of a password. We discuss ways that getStrength() could be implemented in full version of this paper [6].

3.2 Generating Signals

We use $[a] = \{0, 1, \ldots, a-1\}$ (resp. $[b] = \{0, 1, \ldots, b-1\}$) to denote the range of getStrength() (resp. getSignal()). For example, if $[a] = \{0, 1, 2\}$ then 0 would correspond to weak passwords, 2 would correspond to strong passwords and 1 would correspond to medium strength passwords. To generate signal for pw_u, the server first invokes subroutine getStrength(pw_u) to get strength level $str_u = i \in [a]$ of pw_u, then signals $sig_u = j \in [b]$ with probability $\Pr[\text{getSignal}(pw_u) = j \mid \text{getStrength}(pw_u) = i] = \mathbf{S}[i,j] = s_{i,j}$.

Bayesian Update. An attacker who breaks into the authentication server will be able to observe the signal sig_u and $\mathbf{S}$. After observing the signal $sig_u = y$ and $\mathbf{S}$ the attacker can perform a Bayesian update. In particular, given any password $pw \in \mathbb{P}$ with strength $i = \text{getStrength}(pw)$ we have

$$
\begin{aligned}
\Pr[pw \mid y] &= \frac{\Pr[pw]\mathbf{S}[i,y]}{\sum_{pw' \in \mathbb{P}} \Pr[\text{getSignal}(\text{getStrength}(pw'))] \cdot \Pr[pw']} \\
&= \frac{\Pr[pw]\mathbf{S}[i,y]}{\sum_{i' \in [a]} \Pr_{pw' \sim \mathcal{P}}[\text{getStrength}(pw') = i'] \cdot \mathbf{S}[i',y]}
\end{aligned}
\tag{1}
$$

If the attacker knew the original password distribution $\mathcal{P}$ then s/he can update posterior distribution $\mathcal{P}_y$ with $\Pr_{x \sim \mathcal{P}_y}[x = pw] := \Pr[pw \mid y]$. We extend our notation, let $\lambda(\pi, B; y) = \sum_{i=1}^{B} \Pr[pw_i^\pi \mid y]$ where pw_i^π is the ith password in the ordering π. Intuitively, $\lambda(\pi, B; y)$ is the conditional probability of cracking the user's password by checking the first B guesses in permutation π after observing signal y.

3.3 Delayed Signaling

In some instances, the authentication server might implement the password strength oracle getStrength() by training a (differentially private) Count-Sketch based on the user-selected passwords $pw_u \sim \mathcal{P}$, detailed discussion about use of count-sketch in password strength signaling can be found in full version of this paper [6]. The strength estimation will not be accurate until a larger number N of users have registered. In this case, the authentication server may want to delay signaling until after the Count-Sketch has been initialized. In particular, the authentication server will store the tuple $(u, salt_u, sig_u = \perp, h_u)$ when users first register their accounts. After the count-sketch has been initialized, the server can update $sig_u = \text{getSignal}(\text{getStrength}(pw_u))$ upon users' next successful login.

---

[3] The index of matrix elements start from 0.

4   Adversary Model

We adapt the economic model of [9] to capture the behavior of a rational attacker. We also make several assumptions: (1) there is a value v_u for each password pw_u that the attacker cracks; (2) the attacker is untargeted and that the value $v_u = v$ for each user $u \in U$; (3) by Kerckhoffs's principle, the password distribution $\mathcal{P}$ and the signaling matrix are known to the attacker.

Value/Cost Estimates. One can derive a range of estimates for v based on black market studies e.g., Symantec reported that passwords generally sell for \$4–\$30 [26] and [51] reported that Yahoo! e-mail passwords sold for ≈\$1. Similarly, we assume that the attacker pays a cost k each time he evaluates the hash function H to check a password guess. We remark that one can estimate $k \approx \$1 \times 10^{-7}$ if we use a memory-hard function[4].

4.1   Adversary Utility: No Signaling

We first discuss how a rational adversary would behave when no signal is available (traditional hashing). We defer the discussion of how the adversary would update his strategy after observing a signal y to the next section. In the no-signaling case, the attacker's strategy (π, B) is given by an ordering π over passwords $\mathbb{P}$ and a threshold B. Intuitively, this means that the attacker will check the first B guesses in π and then give up. The expected reward for the attacker is given by the simple formula $v \times \lambda(\pi, B)$, i.e., the probability that the password is cracked times the value v. Similarly, the expected guessing cost of the attacker is

$$C(k, \pi, B) = k \sum_{i=1}^{B} (1 - \lambda(\pi, i - 1)), \tag{2}$$

Intuitively, $(1 - \lambda(\pi, i - 1))$ denotes the probability that the adversary actually has to check the ith password guess at cost k. With probability $\lambda(\pi, i - 1)$ the attacker will find the password in the first $i - 1$ guesses and will not have to check the ith password guess pw_i^{π}. Specially, we define $\lambda(\pi, 0) = 0$. The adversary's expected utility is the difference of expected gain and expected cost, namely,

$$U_{adv}(v, k, \pi, B) = v \cdot \lambda(\pi, B) - C(k, \pi, B). \tag{3}$$

Sometimes we omit parameters in the parenthesis and just write U_{adv} for short when the v, k and B are clear from context.

---

[4] The energy cost of transferring 1 GB of memory between RAM and cache is approximately 0.3 J [44], which translates to an energy cost of ≈\$3 × 10⁻⁸ per evaluation. Similarly, if we assume that our MHF can be evaluated in 1 s [7,11] then evaluating the hash function 6.3×10^7 times will tie up a 1 GB RAM chip for 2 years. If it costs \$5 to rent a 1 GB RAM chip for 2 years (equivalently purchase the RAM chip which lasts for 2 years for \$5) then the capital cost is ≈\$8 × 10⁻⁸. Thus, our total cost would be around \$10⁻⁷ per password guess.

4.2   Optimal Attacker Strategy: No Signaling

A rational adversary would choose $(\pi^*, B^*) \in \arg\max U_{adv}(v, k, \pi, B)$. It is easy to verify that the optimal ordering π^* is always to check passwords in descending order of probability. The probability that a random user's account is cracked is

$$P_{adv} = \lambda(\pi^*, B^*). \qquad (4)$$

We remark that in practice $\arg\max U_{adv}(v, k, \pi, B)$ usually returns a singleton set (π^*, B^*). If instead the set contains multiple strategies then we break ties adversarially i.e.,

$$P_{adv} = \max_{(\pi^*, B^*) \in \arg\max U_{adv}(v,k,\pi,B)} \lambda(\pi^*, B^*).$$

5   Information Signaling as a Stackelberg Game

We model the interaction between the authentication server (leader) and the adversary (follower) as a two-stage Stackelberg game. In a Stackelberg game, the leader moves first and then the follower may select its action after observing the action of the leader.

In our setting the action of the defender is to commit to a signaling matrix $\mathbf{S}$ as well as the implementation of getStrength() which maps passwords to strength levels. The attacker responds by selecting a cracking strategy $(\vec{\pi}, \vec{B}) = \{(\pi_0, B_0), \ldots, (\pi_{b-1}, B_{b-1})\}$. Intuitively, this strategy means that whenever the attacker observes a signal y he will check the top B_y guesses according to the ordering π_y.

5.1   Attacker Utility

If the attacker checks the top B_y guesses according to the order π_y then the attacker will crack the password with probability $\lambda(\pi_y, B_y; y)$. Recall that $\lambda(\pi_y, B_y; y)$ denotes the probability of the first B_y passwords in π_y according to the posterior distribution $\mathcal{P}_y$ obtained by applying Bayes Law after observing a signal y. Extrapolating from no signal case, the expected utility of adversary conditioned on observing the signal y is

$$U_{adv}(v, k, \pi_y, B_y; \mathbf{S}, y) = v \cdot \lambda(\pi_y, B_y; y) - \sum_{i=1}^{B_y} k \cdot (1 - \lambda(\pi_y, i - 1; y)), \qquad (5)$$

where B_y and π_y are now both functions of the signal y. Intuitively, $(1 - \lambda(\pi_y, i - 1; y))$ denotes the probability that the attacker has to pay cost k to make the ith guess. We use $U_{adv}^s\left(v, k, \{\mathbf{S}, (\vec{\pi}, \vec{B})\}\right)$ to denote the expected utility of the adversary with password strength signaling,

$$U_{adv}^s\left(v, k, \{\mathbf{S}, (\vec{\pi}, \vec{B})\}\right) = \sum_{y \in [b]} \Pr[Sig = y] U_{adv}(v, k, \pi_y, B_y; \mathbf{S}, y), \qquad (6)$$

where
$$Pr[Sig = y] = \sum_{i \in [b]} \Pr_{pw \sim \mathcal{P}}[\text{getStrength}(pw) = i] \cdot S[i, y].$$

5.2 Optimal Attacker Strategy

Now we discuss how to find the optimal strategy $(\vec{\pi}^*, \vec{B}^*)$. Since the attacker's strategies in response to different signals are independent. It suffices to find $(\pi_y^*, B_y^*) \in \arg\max_{B_y, \pi_y} U_{adv}(v, k, \pi_y, B_y; y)$ for each signal y. We first remark that the adversary can obtain the optimal checking sequence π_y^* for pw_u associated with signal y by sorting all $pw \in \mathcal{P}$ in descending order of posterior probability according to the posterior distribution $\mathcal{P}_y$.

Given the optimal guessing order π_y^*, the adversary can determine the optimal budget B_y^* for signal y such that $B_y^* = \arg\max_{B_y} U_{adv}(v, k, \pi_y^*, B_y; y)$. Each of the password distributions we analyze has a compact representation allowing us to apply techniques from [5] to further speed up the computation of the attacker's optimal strategy π_y^* and B_y^*.

We observe that an adversary who sets $\pi_y = \pi$ and $B_y = B$ for all $y \in [b]$ is effectively ignoring the signal and is equivalent to an adversary in the no signal case. Thus,

$$\max_{\vec{\pi}, \vec{B}} U_{adv}^s \left(v, k, \{\mathbf{S}, (\vec{\pi}, \vec{B})\} \right) \geq \max_{\pi, B} U_{adv}(v, k, \pi, B), \ \forall \mathbf{S}, \qquad (7)$$

implying that adversary's expected utility will never decrease by adapting its strategy according to the signal.

5.3 Optimal Signaling Strategy

Once the function getStrength() is fixed we want to find the optimal signaling matrix $\mathbf{S}$. We begin by introducing the defender's utility function. Intuitively, the defender wants to minimize the total number of cracked passwords.

Let $P_{adv}^s(v, k, \mathbf{S})$ denote the expected adversary success rate with password strength signaling when playing with his/her optimal strategy, then

$$P_{adv}^s(v, k, \mathbf{S}) = \sum_{y \in SL} \Pr[Sig = y]\lambda(\pi_y^*, B_y^*; \mathbf{S}, y), \qquad (8)$$

where (π_y^*, B_y^*) is the optimal strategy of the adversary when receiving signal y, namely,
$$(\pi_y^*, B_y^*) = \arg\max_{\pi_y, B_y} U_{adv}(v, k, \pi_y, B_y; \mathbf{S}, y).$$

If $\arg\max_{\pi_y, B_y} U_{adv}(v, k, \pi_y, B_y; y)$ returns a set, we break ties adversarially.

The objective of the server is to minimize $P_{adv}^s(v, k, \mathbf{S})$, therefore we define

$$U_{ser}^s \left(v, k, \{\mathbf{S}, (\vec{\pi}^*, \vec{B}^*)\} \right) = -P_{adv}^s(v, k, \mathbf{S}). \qquad (9)$$

Our focus of this paper is to find the optimal signaling strategy, namely, the signaling matrix $\mathbf{S}^*$ such that $\mathbf{S}^* = \arg\min_{\mathbf{S}} P_{adv}^s(v, k, \mathbf{S})$. Finding the optimal signaling matrix $\mathbf{S}^*$ is equivalent to solving the mixed strategy Subgame Perfect Equilibrium (SPE) of the Stackelberg game. At SPE no player has the incentive to derivate from his/her strategy. Namely,

$$\begin{cases} U_{ser}^s\left(v, k, \{\mathbf{S}^*, (\vec{\pi}^*, \vec{B}^*)\}\right) \geq U_{ser}^s\left(v, k, \{\mathbf{S}, (\vec{\pi}^*, \vec{B}^*)\}\right), \forall \mathbf{S}, \\ U_{adv}^s\left(v, k, \{\mathbf{S}^*, (\vec{\pi}^*, \vec{B}^*)\}\right) \geq U_{adv}^s\left(v, k, \{\mathbf{S}^*, (\vec{\pi}, \vec{B})\}\right), \forall(\vec{\pi}, \vec{B}). \end{cases} \quad (10)$$

Notice that a signaling matrix of dimension $a \times b$ can be fully specified by $a(b-1)$ variables since the elements in each row sum up to 1. Fixing v and k, we define $f : \mathbb{R}^{a(b-1)} \to \mathbb{R}$ to be the map from $\mathbf{S}$ to $P_{adv}^s(v, k, \mathbf{S})$. Then we can formulate the optimization problem as

$$\begin{aligned} \min_{\mathbf{S}} \quad & f\big(s_{0,0}, \ldots s_{0,(b-2)}, \ldots, s_{(a-1),0}, s_{(a-1),(b-2)}\big) \\ \text{s.t.} \quad & 0 \leq s_{i,j} \leq 1, \ \forall 0 \leq i \leq a-1, \ 0 \leq j \leq b-2 \\ & \sum_{j=0}^{b-2} s_{i,j} \leq 1, \ \forall 0 \leq i \leq a-1. \end{aligned} \quad (11)$$

The feasible region is a $a(b-1)$-dimensional probability simplex. Notice that in 2-D ($a = b = 2$), the second constraint would be equivalent to the first constraint. In our experiments we will treat f as a black box and use derivative-free optimization methods to find good signaling matrices $\mathbf{S}^*$.

6   Experimental Design

We now describe our empirical experiments to evaluate the performance of password strength signaling. Fixing the parameters v, k, a, b, a password distribution $\mathcal{D}$ and the strength oracle getStrength($\cdot$) we define a procedure $\mathbf{S}^* \leftarrow$ genSigMat($v, k, a, b, \mathcal{D}$) which uses derivate-free optimization to solve the optimization problem defined in Eq. (11) and find a good signaling matrix $\mathbf{S}^*$ of dimension $a \times b$. Similarly, given a signaling matrix $\mathbf{S}^*$ we define a procedure evaluate($v, k, a, b, \mathbf{S}^*, \mathcal{D}$) which returns the percentage of passwords that a rational adversary will crack given that the value of a cracked password is v, the cost of checking each password is k. To simulate settings where the defender has imperfect knowledge of the password distribution we use different distributions $\mathcal{D}_1$ (training) and $\mathcal{D}_2$ (evaluation) to generate the signaling matrix $\mathbf{S}^* \leftarrow$ genSigMat($v, k, a, b, \mathcal{D}_1$) and evaluate the success rate of a rational attacker evaluate($v, k, a, b, \mathbf{S}^*, \mathcal{D}_2$). We can also set $\mathcal{D}_1 = \mathcal{D}_2$ to evaluate our mechanism under the idealized setting in which defender has perfect knowledge of the distribution.

Password Distribution. We evaluate the performance of our information signaling mechanism using 9 password datasets: Bfield (0.54 million), Brazzers

($N = 0.93$ million), Clixsense (2.2 million), CSDN (6.4 million), LinkedIn (174 million), Neopets (68.3 million), RockYou (32.6 million), 000webhost (153 million) and Yahoo! (69.3 million). The Yahoo! frequency corpus ($N \approx 7 \times 10^7$) was collected and released with permission from Yahoo! using differential privacy [10] and other privacy-preserving measures [14]. All the other datasets come from server breaches.

Differentially Private Count-Sketch. When using the empirical distribution $\mathcal{D}_e$ for evaluation we evaluate the performance of an imperfect knowledge defender who trains a differentially private Count-Mean-Min-Sketch. As users register their accounts, the server can feed passwords into a Count-Mean-Min-Sketch initialized with Laplace noise to ensure differential privacy (we briefly introduce count sketch and discuss the use of it to guarantee differential privacy in the full version of this paper [6]). After the Count-Sketch has been trained, the server can query the sketch about the estimated frequency for new users' passwords. Thus we can obtain a differentially private password frequency list D^{dp}.

When working with empirical distributions in an imperfect knowledge setting we split the original dataset D in half to obtain D_1 and D_2. Our noise-initialized Count-Mean-Min-Sketch is trained with D_1. We then use this count sketch along with D_2 to extract a noisy distribution $\mathcal{D}_{train}$. In particular, for every $pw \in D_2$ we query the count sketch to get $\tilde{f}_{pw}$, a noisy estimate of the frequency of pw in D_2 and set $\Pr_{\mathcal{D}_{train}}[pw] \doteq \frac{\tilde{f}_{pw}}{\sum_{w \in D_2} \tilde{f}_w}$. We also use the Count-Mean-Min Sketch as a frequency oracle in our implementation of getStrength(). $\mathcal{D}_{train}$ is used to derive frequency thresholds for getStrength() and to generate the signaling matrix $\mathbf{S}^* \leftarrow$ genSigMat($v, k, a, b, \mathcal{D}_{train}$). Finally we evaluate results on the original empirical distribution $\mathcal{D}_e$ for the original dataset D i.e., $P^s_{adv} \leftarrow$ evaluate($v, k, a, b, \mathbf{S}^*, \mathcal{D}_e$).

Derivative-Free Optimization. Given a value v and hash cost k we want to find a signaling matrix which optimizes the defenders utility. Recall that this is equivalent to minimizing the function $f(\mathbf{S}) =$ evaluate($v, k, a, b, \mathbf{S}, \mathcal{D}$) subject to the constraints that $\mathbf{S}$ is a valid signaling matrix.

In experiment we will treat f as a black box and use BITmask Evolution OPTimization [54] (BITEOPT) with 10^4 iterations to generate signaling matrix $\mathbf{S}^*$ for each different v/C_{max} ratio, where C_{max} is server's maximum authentication cost satisfying $k \leq C_{max}$.

7 Empirical Analysis

We describe the results of our experiments. In the first batch of experiments, we evaluate the performance of password strength signaling against an offline and an online attacker where the ratio v/C_{max} is typically much smaller.

7.1 Password Strength Signaling Against Offline Attacks

We consider four scenarios using the empirical/Monte Carlo distribution in a setting where the defender has perfect/imperfect knowledge of the distribution.

Empirical Distribution. From each password dataset we derived an empirical distribution $\mathcal{D}_e$ and set $\mathcal{D}_{eval} = \mathcal{D}_e$. In the perfect knowledge setting we also set $\mathcal{D}_{train} = \mathcal{D}_e$ while in the imperfect knowledge setting we used a Count-Min-Mean Sketch to derive $\mathcal{D}_{train}$ (see details in the previous section).

We fix dimension of signaling matrix to be 11 by 3 (the server issues 3 signals for 11 password strength levels) and compute attacker's success rate for different value-to-cost ratios $v/C_{max} \in \{i \times 10^j : 1 \le i \le 9, 3 \le j \le 7\} \cup \{(i+0.5) \times 10^j : 1 \le i \le 9, 6 \le j \le 7\}$. In particular, for each value-to-cost ratio v/C_{max} we run $\mathbf{S}^* \leftarrow$ genSigMat$(v, k, a, b, \mathcal{D}_e)$ to generate a signaling matrix and then run evaluate$(v, k, a, b, \mathbf{S}^*, \mathcal{D}_e)$ to get the attacker's success rate. The same experiment is repeated for all 9 password datasets. We plot the attacker's success rate vs. v/C_{max} in Fig. 1. Due to space limitations Fig. 1 only shows results for 2 datasets—additional plots can be found in full version of this paper [6].

We follow the approach of [5], highlighting the uncertain regions of the plot where the cumulative density function of the empirical distribution might diverge from the real distribution. In particular, the red (resp. yellow) region indicates $E > 0.1$ (resp. $E > 0.01$) where E can be interpreted as an upper bound on the difference between the two CDFs.

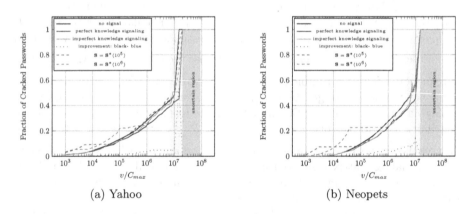

(a) Yahoo   (b) Neopets

Fig. 1. Adversary success rate vs v/C_{max} for empirical distributions the red (resp. yellow) shaded areas denote unconfident regions where the empirical distribution might diverge from the real distribution $E \ge 0.1$ (resp. $E \ge 0.01$). (Color figure online)

Figure 1 demonstrates that information signaling reduces the fraction of cracked passwords. The mechanism performs best when the defender has perfect knowledge of the distribution (blue curve), but even with imperfect knowledge, there is still a large advantage. For example, for the Neopets dataset when $v/C_{max} = 5 \times 10^6$ the percentage of cracked passwords is reduced from 44.6% to 36.9% (resp. 39.1%) when the defender has perfect (resp. imperfect) knowledge of the password distribution. Similar results hold for other datasets. The green curve (signaling with imperfect knowledge) curve generally lies in between the black curve (no signaling) and the blue curve (signaling with perfect knowledge), but sometimes has an adverse effect when v/C_{max} is large. This is because the noisy distribution will be less accurate for stronger passwords that were sampled only once.

We also use guessing numbers generated by state-of-the-art password cracking models (neural network, Markov model, PCFG) to fit a distribution, which we call Monte Carlo distribution. Monte Carlo distributions are useful in evaluating the performance of strength signaling when v/C_{max} is large. Experiments show that the reduction in the percentage of cracked passwords is up to 12% for Neopets, results can be found in the full version of this paper [6].

Which Accounts Are Cracked? As Fig. 1 demonstrates password strength signaling can substantially reduce the overall fraction of cracked passwords i.e., many previously cracked passwords are now protected. It is natural to ask whether there are any unlucky users u whose password is cracked after signaling *even though* their account was safe before signaling. Let X_u (resp. L_u) denote the event that user u is unlucky (resp. lucky) i.e., a rational attacker would originally not crack pw_u, but after password strength signaling the account is cracked. We measure $E[X_u]$ and $E[L_u]$ (see Fig. 2) for various v/C_{max} values under each dataset. Generally, we find that the fraction of unlucky users $E[X_u]$ is small in most cases e.g. ≤ 0.04. For example, when $v/k = 2 \times 10^7$ we have that $E[X_u] \approx 0.09\%$ and $E[L_u] \approx 5\%$ for Neopets. In all instances the net advantage $E[L_u] - E[X_u]$ remains positive.

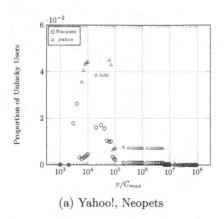

(a) Yahoo!, Neopets

Fig. 2. Proportion of unlucky users for various datasets ($E[X_u]$)

We remark that the reduction in cracked passwords does not necessarily come from persuading the attacker to crack weak passwords, but rather through the attacker shifting his attention towards certain signals. A utility-maximizing attacker will be interested in passwords whose signals suggest the attacker will not need to spend as much effort to crack them. However, because of the noisy nature of the signaling scheme, this is only similar to, but not quite the same, as attacking only the weakest passwords in a set. Some weak passwords may be "saved" when they are signaled as being in a higher strength category than their true strength merits. By contrast, without signaling we expect that a rational attacker will crack all of the weak passwords.

Robustness. We also evaluated the robustness of the signaling matrix when the defender's estimate of the ratio v/C_{max} is inaccurate. In particular, for each dataset we generated the signaling matrix $\mathbf{S}(10^5)$ (resp. $\mathbf{S}(10^6)$) which was optimized with respect to the ratio $v/C_{max} = 10^5$ (resp. $v/C_{max} = 10^6$) and evaluated the performance of both signaling matrices against an attacker with different v/C_{max} ratios. We find that password signaling is tolerant even if our estimate of v/k is off by a small multiplicative constant factor e.g., 2. For example, in Fig. 1b the signaling matrix $\mathbf{S}(10^6)$ outperforms the no-signaling case even when the real v/C_{max} ratio is as large as 2×10^6. In the "downhill" direction, even if the estimation of v/k deviates from its true value up to 5×10^5 at anchor point 10^6 it is still advantageous for the server to deploy password signaling.

7.2   Password Strength Signaling Against Online Attacks

We can extend the experiment from password signaling with perfect knowledge to an online attack scenario. One common way to throttle online attackers is to require the attacker to solve a CAPTCHA challenge [56], or provide some other proof of work (PoW), after each incorrect login attempt [42]. One advantage of this approach is that a malicious attacker cannot lockout an honest user by repeatedly submitting incorrect passwords [2]. However, the solution also allows an attacker to continue trying to crack the password as long as s/he is willing to continue paying the cost to solve the CAPTCHA/PoW challenges. Thus, password strength signaling could be a useful tool to mitigate the risk of online attacks.

When modeling a rational online password we will assume that $v/C_{max} \leq 10^5$ since the cost to pay a human to solve a CAPTCHA challenge (e.g., 10^{-3} to 10^2 [39]) is typically much larger than the cost to evaluate a memory-hard cryptographic hash function (e.g., 10^{-7}). Since $v/C_{max} \leq 10^5$ we use the empirical distribution to evaluate the performance of signaling against an online attacker. In the previous subsection, we found that the uncertain regions of the curve started when $v/C_{max} \gg 10^5$ so the empirical distribution is guaranteed to closely match the real one.

Since an online attacker will be primarily focused on the most common passwords (e.g., top 10^3 to 10^4) we modify getStrength() accordingly. We consider two modifications of getStrength() which split passwords in the top 10^3 (resp. 10^4) passwords into 11 strength levels. By contrast, our prior implementation of getStrength() would have placed most of the top 10^3 passwords in the bottom two strength levels. As before we fix the signaling matrix dimension to be 11×3. Our results are shown in Fig. 3. Plots for other datasets can be found in the full version of this paper [6].

Our results demonstrate that password strength signaling can be an effective defense against online attackers as well. For example, in Fig. 3a, when $v/C_{max} =$

9×10^4, our mechanism reduces the fraction of cracked passwords from 12.7% to just 9.6%. Similarly, observations hold true for other datasets. We observe that the red curve (partitioning the top 10^3 passwords into 11 strength levels) performs better than the blue curve (partitioning the top 10^3 passwords into 11 strength levels) when v/k is small e.g., $v/C_{max} < 2 \times 10^4$ in Fig. 3a). The blue curve performs better when v/C_{max} is larger. Intuitively, this is because we want to have a fine-grained partition for the weaker (top 10^3) passwords that the adversary might target when v/C_{max} is small.

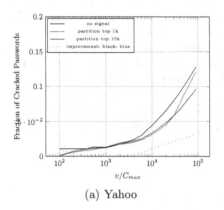
(a) Yahoo

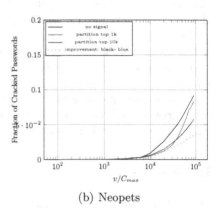
(b) Neopets

Fig. 3. Adversary success rate vs v/C_{max} in defense of online attacks (Color figure online)

7.3 Discussion

- While password strength signaling reduced the total number of cracked passwords a few unlucky users might be harmed i.e., instead of being deterred the unlucky signal helps the rational attacker to crack a password that they would not otherwise have cracked. The usage of password signaling raises important ethical and societal questions. How would users react to such a solution knowing that they could be one of the unlucky users? One possible way to address these concerns would be to allow users to opt-in/out of password strength signaling. However, each user u would need to make this decision without observing their signal. Otherwise, the decision to opt-in/out might be strongly correlated with the signal allowing the attacker to perform another Bayesian update. Another possible way to address these concerns would be to modify the objective function (Eq. (11)) to penalize solutions with unlucky users.
- Can we analyze the behavior of rational targeted attackers? We only consider an untargeted attacker. In some settings, an attacker might place a higher value on some passwords e.g., celebrity accounts. Can we predict how

a targeted attacker would behave if the value v_u varied from user to user? Similarly, a targeted adversary could exploit demographic and/or biographical knowledge to improve password guessing attacks e.g., see [57].

8 Conclusions

We introduce password strength signaling as a novel, yet counter-intuitive defense against rational password attackers. We use Stackelberg game to model the interaction between the defender and attacker, and present an algorithm for the server to optimize its signaling matrix. We ran experiments to empirically evaluate the effectiveness of password strength signaling on 9 password datasets. When testing on the empirical (resp. Monte Carlo) password distribution we find that password strength signaling reduces the number of passwords that would have been cracked by up to 8% (resp. 12%). Additionally, we find that password strength signaling can help to dissuade an online attacker by saving 5% of all user accounts. We view our positive experimental results as a proof of concept which motivates further exploration of password strength signaling.

References

1. Hashcast: advanced password recovery. https://hashcat.net/hashcat/
2. Hackers find new way to bilk eBay users - CNET (2019). https://www.cnet.com/news/hackers-find-new-way-to-bilk-ebay-users/
3. Adams, A., Sasse, M.A.: Users are not the enemy. Commun. ACM **42**(12), 40–46 (1999)
4. Aleksic, P.S., Katsaggelos, A.K.: Audio-visual biometrics. Proc. IEEE **94**(11), 2025–2044 (2006)
5. Bai, W., Blocki, J.: DAHash: distribution aware tuning of password hashing costs. In: Borisov, N., Diaz, C. (eds.) International Financial Cryptography Association 2021, FC 2021. LNCS 12675, pp. 1–24 (2021). https://doi.org/10.1007/978-3-662-64331-0_20
6. Bai, W., Blocki, J., Harsha, B.: Password strength signaling: a counter-intuitive defense against password cracking (2021)
7. Biryukov, A., Dinu, D., Khovratovich, D.: Argon2: new generation of memory-hard functions for password hashing and other applications. In: 2016 IEEE European Symposium on Security and Privacy (EuroS&P), pp. 292–302. IEEE (2016)
8. Blocki, J., Harsha, B.: Linkedin password frequency corpus (2019). https://figshare.com/articles/linkedin_files_zip/7350287
9. Blocki, J., Datta, A.: CASH: a cost asymmetric secure hash algorithm for optimal password protection. In: IEEE 29th Computer Security Foundations Symposium, pp. 371–386 (2016)
10. Blocki, J., Datta, A., Bonneau, J.: Differentially private password frequency lists. In: NDSS 2016. The Internet Society, February 2016
11. Blocki, J., Harsha, B., Kang, S., Lee, S., Xing, L., Zhou, S.: Data-independent memory hard functions: new attacks and stronger constructions. Cryptology ePrint Archive, Report 2018/944 (2018). https://eprint.iacr.org/2018/944

12. Blocki, J., Harsha, B., Zhou, S.: On the economics of offline password cracking. In: 2018 IEEE Symposium on Security and Privacy, pp. 853–871. IEEE Computer Society Press, May 2018. https://doi.org/10.1109/SP.2018.00009
13. Blocki, J., Komanduri, S., Procaccia, A., Sheffet, O.: Optimizing password composition policies. In: Proceedings of the Fourteenth ACM Conference on Electronic Commerce, pp. 105–122. ACM (2013)
14. Bonneau, J.: The science of guessing: analyzing an anonymized corpus of 70 million passwords. In: 2012 IEEE Symposium on Security and Privacy, pp. 538–552. IEEE Computer Society Press, May 2012. https://doi.org/10.1109/SP.2012.49
15. Bonneau, J., Herley, C., van Oorschot, P.C., Stajano, F.: The quest to replace passwords: a framework for comparative evaluation of web authentication schemes. In: 2012 IEEE Symposium on Security and Privacy, pp. 553–567. IEEE Computer Society Press, May 2012. https://doi.org/10.1109/SP.2012.44
16. Campbell, J., Ma, W., Kleeman, D.: Impact of restrictive composition policy on user password choices. Behav. Inf. Technol. **30**(3), 379–388 (2011)
17. Carnavalet, X., Mannan, M.: From very weak to very strong: analyzing password-strength meters. In: NDSS 2014. The Internet Society, February 2014
18. Carroll, T.E., Grosu, D.: A game theoretic investigation of deception in network security. In: 2009 Proceedings of 18th International Conference on Computer Communications and Networks, pp. 1–6 (2009). https://doi.org/10.1109/ICCCN.2009.5235344
19. Castelluccia, C., Chaabane, A., Dürmuth, M., Perito, D.: When privacy meets security: leveraging personal information for password cracking. arXiv preprint arXiv:1304.6584 (2013)
20. Castelluccia, C., Dürmuth, M., Perito, D.: Adaptive password-strength meters from Markov models. In: NDSS 2012. The Internet Society, February 2012
21. Chiasson, S., van Oorschot, P.C., Biddle, R.: Graphical password authentication using cued click points. In: Biskup, J., López, J. (eds.) ESORICS 2007. LNCS, vol. 4734, pp. 359–374. Springer, Heidelberg (2007). https://doi.org/10.1007/978-3-540-74835-9_24
22. Daugman, J.: How iris recognition works. In: The Essential Guide to Image Processing, pp. 715–739. Elsevier (2009)
23. Software Designer: John the ripper password cracker (2006)
24. Florêncio, D., Herley, C., Van Oorschot, P.C.: An administrator's guide to Internet password research. In: Proceedings of the 28th USENIX Conference on Large Installation System Administration, LISA 2014, pp. 35–52 (2014)
25. Florêncio, D., Herley, C.: One-time password access to any server without changing the server. In: Wu, T.-C., Lei, C.-L., Rijmen, V., Lee, D.-T. (eds.) ISC 2008. LNCS, vol. 5222, pp. 401–420. Springer, Heidelberg (2008). https://doi.org/10.1007/978-3-540-85886-7_28
26. Fossi, M., et al.: Symantec report on the underground economy, November 2008. Accessed 1 Aug 2013
27. Herley, C., Van Oorschot, P.: A research agenda acknowledging the persistence of passwords. IEEE Secur. Priv. **10**(1), 28–36 (2011)
28. Inglesant, P.G., Sasse, M.A.: The true cost of unusable password policies: password use in the wild. In: Proceedings of the SIGCHI Conference on Human Factors in Computing Systems, CHI 2010, New York, NY, USA, pp. 383–392. ACM (2010). https://doi.org/10.1145/1753326.1753384
29. Jhawar, R., Inglesant, P., Courtois, N., Sasse, M.A.: Make mine a quadruple: strengthening the security of graphical one-time pin authentication. In: 2011 5th International Conference on Network and System Security, pp. 81–88. IEEE (2011)

30. Kamenica, E., Gentzkow, M.: Bayesian persuasion. Am. Econ. Rev. **101**(6), 2590–2615 (2011)

31. Kelley, P.G., et al.: Guess again (and again and again): measuring password strength by simulating password-cracking algorithms. In: 2012 IEEE Symposium on Security and Privacy, pp. 523–537. IEEE Computer Society Press, May 2012. https://doi.org/10.1109/SP.2012.38

32. Komanduri, S., Shay, R., Cranor, L.F., Herley, C., Schechter, S.: Telepathwords: preventing weak passwords by reading users' minds. In: 23rd USENIX Security Symposium (USENIX Security 2014), San Diego, CA, pp. 591–606. USENIX Association, August 2014. https://www.usenix.org/conference/usenixsecurity14/technical-sessions/presentation/komanduri

33. Komanduri, S., et al.: Of passwords and people: measuring the effect of password-composition policies. In: CHI, pp. 2595–2604 (2011). http://dl.acm.org/citation.cfm?id=1979321

34. Kuhn, M.: OTPW–a one-time password login package (1998)

35. Liu, E., Nakanishi, A., Golla, M., Cash, D., Ur, B.: Reasoning analytically about password-cracking software. In: 2019 IEEE Symposium on Security and Privacy (SP), pp. 380–397. IEEE (2019)

36. Ma, J., Yang, W., Luo, M., Li, N.: A study of probabilistic password models. In: 2014 IEEE Symposium on Security and Privacy, pp. 689–704. IEEE Computer Society Press, May 2014. https://doi.org/10.1109/SP.2014.50

37. Melicher, W., et al.: Fast, lean, and accurate: modeling password guessability using neural networks. In: Holz, T., Savage, S. (eds.) USENIX Security 2016, pp. 175–191. USENIX Association, August 2016

38. Morris, R., Thompson, K.: Password security: a case history. Commun. ACM **22**(11), 594–597 (1979)

39. Motoyama, M., Levchenko, K., Kanich, C., McCoy, D., Voelker, G.M., Savage, S.: Re: CAPTCHAs-understanding CAPTCHA-solving services in an economic context. In: USENIX Security 2010, pp. 435–462. USENIX Association, August 2010

40. Parno, B., Kuo, C., Perrig, A.: Phoolproof phishing prevention. In: Di Crescenzo, G., Rubin, A. (eds.) FC 2006. LNCS, vol. 4107, pp. 1–19. Springer, Heidelberg (2006). https://doi.org/10.1007/11889663_1

41. Pashalidis, A., Mitchell, C.J.: Impostor: a single sign-on system for use from untrusted devices. In: IEEE Global Telecommunications Conference, GLOBECOM 2004, vol. 4, pp. 2191–2195. IEEE (2004)

42. Pinkas, B., Sander, T.: Securing passwords against dictionary attacks. In: Atluri, V. (ed.) ACM CCS 2002, pp. 161–170. ACM Press, November 2002. https://doi.org/10.1145/586110.586133

43. Rabinovich, Z., Jiang, A.X., Jain, M., Xu, H.: Information disclosure as a means to security. In: Proceedings of the 2015 International Conference on Autonomous Agents and Multiagent Systems, AAMAS 2015, Richland, SC, pp. 645–653. International Foundation for Autonomous Agents and Multiagent Systems (2015)

44. Ren, L., Devadas, S.: Bandwidth hard functions for ASIC resistance. In: Kalai, Y., Reyzin, L. (eds.) TCC 2017. LNCS, vol. 10677, pp. 466–492. Springer, Cham (2017). https://doi.org/10.1007/978-3-319-70500-2_16

45. Ross, A., Shah, J., Jain, A.K.: From template to image: reconstructing fingerprints from minutiae points. IEEE Trans. Pattern Anal. Mach. Intell. **29**(4), 544–560 (2007)

46. RSA: RSA SecurID® 6100 USB Token (2003)

47. Shay, R., et al.: Can long passwords be secure and usable? In: Proceedings of the SIGCHI Conference on Human Factors in Computing Systems, CHI 2014, New York, NY, USA, pp. 2927–2936. ACM (2014). https://doi.org/10.1145/2556288. 2557377

48. Shay, R., et al.: Encountering stronger password requirements: user attitudes and behaviors. In: Proceedings of the Sixth Symposium on Usable Privacy and Security, SOUPS 2010, New York, NY, USA, pp. 2:1–2:20. ACM (2010). https://doi.org/10.1145/1837110.1837113

49. Stanton, J.M., Stam, K.R., Mastrangelo, P., Jolton, J.: Analysis of end user security behaviors. Comput. Secur. **24**(2), 124–133 (2005)

50. Steves, M., Chisnell, D., Sasse, A., Krol, K., Theofanos, M., Wald, H.: Report: authentication diary study. Technical report, NISTIR 7983, National Institute of Standards and Technology (NIST) (2014)

51. Stockley, M.: What your hacked account is worth on the dark web, August 2016. https://nakedsecurity.sophos.com/2016/08/09/what-your-hacked-account-is-worth-on-the-dark-web/

52. Ur, B., et al.: How does your password measure up? The effect of strength meters on password creation. In: Proceedings of USENIX Security Symposium (2012)

53. Ur, B., et al.: Measuring real-world accuracies and biases in modeling password guessability. In: Jung, J., Holz, T. (eds.) USENIX Security 2015, pp. 463–481. USENIX Association, August 2015

54. Vaneev, A.: BITEOPT - derivative-free optimization method (2021). https://github.com/avaneev/biteopt. C++ source code, with description and examples

55. Veras, R., Collins, C., Thorpe, J.: On semantic patterns of passwords and their security impact. In: NDSS 2014. The Internet Society, February 2014

56. von Ahn, L., Blum, M., Hopper, N.J., Langford, J.: CAPTCHA: using hard AI problems for security. In: Biham, E. (ed.) EUROCRYPT 2003. LNCS, vol. 2656, pp. 294–311. Springer, Heidelberg (2003). https://doi.org/10.1007/3-540-39200-9_18

57. Wang, D., Zhang, Z., Wang, P., Yan, J., Huang, X.: Targeted online password guessing: an underestimated threat. In: Weippl, E.R., Katzenbeisser, S., Kruegel, C., Myers, A.C., Halevi, S. (eds.) ACM CCS 2016, pp. 1242–1254. ACM Press, October 2016. https://doi.org/10.1145/2976749.2978339

58. Weir, M., Aggarwal, S., de Medeiros, B., Glodek, B.: Password cracking using probabilistic context-free grammars. In: 2009 IEEE Symposium on Security and Privacy, pp. 391–405. IEEE Computer Society Press, May 2009. https://doi.org/10.1109/SP.2009.8

59. Xu, H., Freeman, R.: Signaling in Bayesian Stackelberg games. In: Proceedings of the 15th International Conference on Autonomous Agents and Multiagent Systems (2016)

Evaluating Attacker Risk Behavior in an Internet of Things Ecosystem

Erick Galinkin$^{(\boxtimes)}$ ⓘ, John Carter ⓘ, and Spiros Mancoridis ⓘ

Drexel University, Philadelphia, PA 19104, USA
eg657@drexel.edu

Abstract. In cybersecurity, attackers range from brash, unsophisticated script kiddies and cybercriminals to stealthy, patient advanced persistent threats. When modeling these attackers, we can observe that they demonstrate different risk-seeking and risk-averse behaviors. This work explores how an attacker's risk seeking or risk averse behavior affects their operations against detection-optimizing defenders in an Internet of Things ecosystem. Using an evaluation framework which uses real, parametrizable malware, we develop a game that is played by a defender against attackers with a suite of malware that is parameterized to be more aggressive and more stealthy. These results are evaluated under a framework of exponential utility according to their willingness to accept risk. We find that against a defender who must choose a single strategy up front, risk-seeking attackers gain more actual utility than risk-averse attackers, particularly in cases where the defender is better equipped than the two attackers anticipate. Additionally, we empirically confirm that high-risk, high-reward scenarios are more beneficial to risk-seeking attackers like cybercriminals, while low-risk, low-reward scenarios are more beneficial to risk-averse attackers like advanced persistent threats.

Keywords: Game theory · Security · Malware · Internet of Things

1 Introduction

As a discipline, Cybersecurity has had the privilege of borrowing tools from economics, risk analysis, and even psychology [2], one of which has been the use of game theory in the context of attack-defense modeling. However, many of these game theoretic models deal with perfectly rational actors or even an actor who makes no decisions at all, such as a worm – a self-propagating malware. Despite the popularity of these models, the majority of real-world attacks are not defenders operating against worms, but rather defenders taking actions against a human attacker. Our work aims to describe the relationship between attacker strategies and risk-seeking behavior, leverage an Internet of Things (IoT) ecosystem to

Funded by the Auerbach Berger Chair in Cybersecurity held by Spiros Mancoridis, at Drexel University.

B. Bošanský et al. (Eds.): GameSec 2021, LNCS 13061, pp. 354–364, 2021.
https://doi.org/10.1007/978-3-030-90370-1_19

create and detect actual malware, and analyze the potential effects of varying risk acceptance.

In recent years, smart home and smart office devices have become more widely available – smart locks, smart thermostats, smart fridges, and even smart oven ranges have cropped up. Consequently, the Internet of Things has become a fresh battleground for security. Malware like the Mirai botnet [3] has turned thousands of largely insecure, simple devices into a widely distributed, mass of unwitting soldiers. To that end, considerable work has been done to attempt to secure IoT systems, such as those in healthcare [1], where adaptive approaches have proven useful.

We note however, that definitions of IoT vary widely, as IoT are typically associated with consumer-grade products, and correspondingly are often over-looked by corporate information technology and security teams [10]. This lack of clarity makes it quite difficult for defenders to know what the best defensive technologies are, and in cases where any security technology is deployed, often results in an approach to IoT devices that fails to mitigate the entirety of the threat. This ultimately leads to an environment ripe for attackers to exploit.

In security game theoretic literature, attacker-specific strategies and decision making remains an under explored element of security game and decision theory that often necessitates significant amounts of uncertainty modeling [8]. Many factors go into an attacker's decision making: the available exploits and pay-loads, the systems in the environment that are vulnerable to their exploits, what attackers know about the defender's strategy, and risk-seeking or risk-averseness of attackers. Risk aversion and incentives have been studied extensively since the seminal work of Holt and Laury [11], showing the incentive effects of different payoffs. This is most often used in financial modeling, showing where risk seeking bidders fare well versus risk averse bidders, and establishing strategies based on portfolio simulations. We aim to apply a similar framework to one facet of security games, enabling more thoughtful modeling of attacker behavior.

2   Background

Though our data is collected from an IoT ecosystem, our primary focus is on attacker strategies. As a result, the works most closely related to ours are two papers by Chatterjee et al. [8,9]. In their work on quantifying attacker payoffs, Chatterjee et al. leverage a leader-follower security game to compute a range of possible payoffs for an attacker. This builds off of the attacker response function developed by Kiekintveld et al. [12], that generates probabilities of attack for various targets.

Chatterjee et al.'s other work on propagating uncertainties evaluates the uncertainties in attacker payoffs and leverages Monte Carlo sampling and bound analysis to estimate attacker payoffs in partially observable security games. These works acknowledge the problem of describing and dealing with the large number of potential attackers and our inability to know what exploits and pay-loads are available to those attackers. Our work veers away from this probabilistic approach and deals instead with data generated by real malware in a real IoT ecosystem.

We define risk aversion as a utility function that is concave and strictly increasing. Risk seeking, then, is a utility function which is convex and strictly increasing. Example plots of risk-seeking, risk-averse, and risk-neutral utility are shown in Fig. 1. This relationship to risk has been used in behavioral game theory [5] to describe investor behavior. From a security perspective, this corresponds to the dichotomy between cybercriminals – threat actors who seek to quickly maximize their profits and engage in risk-seeking behavior, and advanced persistent threats – threat actors who are willing to wait long periods and want to minimize their chances for detection.

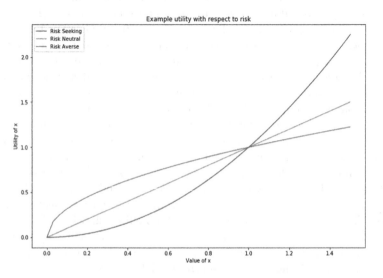

Fig. 1. Example plot of risk-seeking, risk-averse, and risk-neutral utility, $u(x)$, derived from a good of value x

Risk aversion has also been tied to uncertainty aversion [4], building on early experiments [6] in the subjective beliefs of actors in an environment. The expected utility model does not fully capture uncertainty aversion, but this is a first step in the space. In the context of security games, attackers and defenders both leverage their beliefs about the capabilities of their adversary, but there is significant uncertainty about the interplay between attacker capabilities and defender capabilities. Kiekintveld *et al.* [12] acknowledge the significant challenges faced about both attacker capabilities and the efficacy of defender responses against attacks. Our work leverages the idea that human operators will choose their tools not only based on what is available to them and what is likely to help them accomplish their objectives, but also their perception of value relative to the probability of success.

3   Methods

Leveraging a simple IoT ecosystem with parameterizable malware living on an infected router, we compute the probability of detection for each detection strategy and each malware family with default parameters. Our ecosystem is comprised of an IP camera, an infected router, and an attacker laptop which is exfiltrating data from the infected router. In our ecosystem, there are three different families of malware: ransomware, keylogger, and cryptominer. Each of these malware has customizable parameters that control the rate of their operation and the size of data that is sent to the malware command and control. By default, the ransomware will communicate with its command and control server every 15 s; the keylogger will exfiltrate 2 keypresses every 0.1 s; and the cryptominer will communicate with its command and control server every 0.1 s. These rates can be adjusted up and down or modified to change at each communication interval to create an unlimited number of variants (Fig. 2).

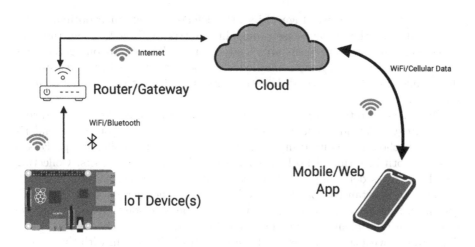

Fig. 2. An Example IoT Ecosystem

Detection strategies consist of three support vector machine (SVM) malware detectors. These three SVMs differ in terms of the data that they leverage to conclude whether or not malware is present. One leverages system call (syscall) data from the endpoint and a bag-of-n-grams approach to create feature vectors; the second leverages features from network packets; and the third merges the syscall data and the packet data. We refer to these three detectors by the name of the data that they use: syscall, packets, and merged.

In order to establish a baseline for the various defensive capabilities, we generate 15 malware samples per malware family using the default parameters. Each sample is run over a 7-min window in which each of the three detection strategies are able to observe the environment's behavior and estimate a probability that malicious activity is present in the ecosystem. If the malware detector crosses the threshold for maliciousness, it sets an alert and the malware is considered caught. If the detector does not cross the threshold, the malware is not detected and is considered to have successfully accomplished its task. We average these detection rates over our 15 trials per combination of malware and detector to compute a probability of detection for each detector.

These baseline probabilities for each detection strategy to find each family of malware establish a detection probability matrix that allows defenders to select the strategy with the highest probability of detecting malicious activity in general. Having committed to their strategy, we simulate attackers with different willingness to accept risk based on their expected payoffs for their malware. These attackers will target our defender, and the efficacy of their attacks informs our analysis in Sect. 5.

4 Defining the Game

Our game proceeds in two stages. First, the defender selects their optimal strategy based upon the average-case probability matrix in Table 1, where the malware family names have been abbreviated for readability. In our game, this probability matrix is common knowledge for both players – in the real-world, this is analagous to advertised detection rates by different commercial security solutions.

Defenders are often budget constrained, so attackers cannot know what defensive strategy a defender will choose but can be confident that once a defender's strategy is chosen, it is fixed in the short-term. In general, collecting packets is low-cost both in terms of both deployment and maintenance costs. Collecting syscalls involves deploying agents to endpoints and licensing software for each endpoint, a substantial cost to many businesses. The merged data uses both syscall and packet data, making it the most expensive solution to deploy. We assume that our defender is not constrained by resources and chooses the detection strategy with the best average detection rates – the system with the merged detections, which has an average detection rate across all 3 malware families of 98.01%.

Table 1. Probability of attacker detection

		Defender		
		Syscall	Packets	Merged
	Keylog	96.53%	88.76%	96.35%
Attacker	Mine	96.14%	96.54%	97.76%
	Ransom	99.92%	99.38%	99.91%

In this case, an attacker will consider three different malware families: keyloggers, cryptominers, and ransomware. Our three families of malware have different potential payoffs for successful attackers. The keylogger collects keystrokes and may collect usernames and passwords, or other sensitive data which can be sold. Overall, the keylogger is of middling value. A cryptominer can remain resident on a system for quite some time, mining cryptocurrency like bitcoin. However, it may require a significant amount of time for a block to be mined and for the miner to yield a payoff, so it has a low value. Ransomware hits quite quickly and offers a significant payoff – assuming that a victim pays – giving it the highest value for successful attacks. Thus, for successful attacks:

$$v_{ransomware} \succ v_{keylogger} \succ v_{cryptominer}$$

We assume that all attackers are seeking to maximize their utility over their set of attacks. Each attacker has a utility function $u(v_i)$, which asserts the utility they gain from the value of a successful attack, defined as an attack which goes unnoticed. Their expected utility for attack i is then $(1-p_i) \cdot u(v_i)$, where p_i is the average probability of detection for the attack from Table 1. Given the detection rates, the probability of detecting cryptominers is higher than that of detecting keyloggers, and keylogger utility is greater than that of cryptominers. Therefore, no rational attacker would choose the cryptominer, and so the remainder of our analysis concerns only ransomware and keyloggers.

We leverage exponential utility for the attackers, defining our $u(v_i)$:

$$u(v_i) = \begin{cases} \frac{1-e^{-\alpha v_i}}{\alpha} & \alpha \neq 0 \\ v_i & \alpha = 0 \end{cases} \tag{1}$$

Exponential utility has been well studied in behavioral economics [7] and implies constant absolute risk aversion (CARA) with a risk aversion coefficient equal to the constant α such that for valuation v_i:

$$\alpha = \frac{-u''(v_i)}{u'(v_i)}$$

Where $u'(v_i)$ and $u''(v_i)$ are the first and second derivatives of the utility function, respectively. This provides a parameter α such that $\alpha = 0$ for risk-neutral attackers, $\alpha > 0$ for risk-averse attackers, and $\alpha < 0$ for risk-seeking attackers.

The factor that will determine the strategy of the attacker then, is a function of the risk behavior of the attacker and the value ratio between our two rational malware choices – keyloggers and ransomware. Figure 3 shows that there is a relationship between the relative value of the ransomware versus the keylogger and the risk seeking behavior of the attacker. The blue-shaded areas are the regions where a keylogger is preferential, while the orange-shaded areas are the regions where ransomware is preferable.

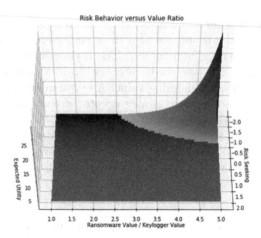

Fig. 3. 3d plot showing the relationship between risk seeking behavior and the relative value of ransomware over a keylogger

We conclude that given the higher value of ransomware coupled with a higher probability of detection, an attacker's propensity to use ransomware or a keylogger is directly tied to their constant of risk aversion. Specifically, more negative CARA corresponds to a greater propensity to use ransomware and more positive CARA corresponds to a greater propensity to use keyloggers. Based on the data collected from our environment, risk-neutral attackers with $\alpha = 0$ will tend to use keyloggers.

Empirically, a rational, risk-averse attacker will still choose ransomware in the case where their expected utility is higher than that of a keylogger. As an example, let the attacker be risk-averse with $\alpha = 0.04$ and let the keylogger valuation $v_k = 1$. Using the detection probabilities in Table 1, we find that the expected utility for v_k is 0.059992158. This means that $u(v_r) > u(v_k)$ only for $v_r \geq 64.08456v_k$, which yields expected utility 0.059992159 as we can observe in Fig. 4.

Therefore, the risk-averse attacker will choose ransomware only when the value of ransomware, v_r is more than 64 times as large. These conclusions assume that these malware values and detection rates are static. However, the customization capabilities of the malware ecosystem allows a risk-seeking attacker to attempt to increase the value of their malware variants and allows a risk-averse attacker to attempt to decrease the detection rates of their malware variants. In this case, the attacker may manipulate the parameters in such a way that they believe they can improve their expected utility.

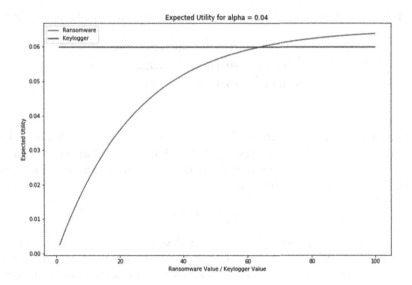

Fig. 4. Expected utility for $\alpha = 0.04$

5   Evaluation

The defender aims to minimize the threat by choosing the strategy with the highest probability of stopping an arbitrary attack and so chooses the merged detection system. Our attackers, not knowing the malware parameters used to generate the probabilities in Table 1, may choose their own parameters for the malware. As an illustrative example, we define a risk-seeking attacker with $\alpha = -0.04$, and a risk-averse attacker with $\alpha = 0.04$, who parameterize a suite of malware to be more aggressive and more stealthy as follows:

1. Aggressive ransomware: Exfiltration every 2 s
2. Aggressive keylogger: Exfiltration every 0.05 s
3. Stealthy ransomware: Exfiltration every 45 s
4. Stealthy keylogger: Exfiltration every 2 s

These malware parameters can be viewed as impacting the value of successful attack, v_i. A more aggressive ransomware variant will complete encryption more quickly, reducing the time a defender can take to interrupt the operation. Meanwhile, a more aggressive keylogger variant is likely to exfiltrate greater amounts of data, leading to more potential income. The stealthier variants space out exfiltration, a technique which is commonly assumed to result in lower detection rates. These variants are evaluated against the defender's chosen detection strategy, with the common expectation being that a risk-seeking attacker will find more value in aggressive variants while a risk-averse attacker would favor stealthy variants.

Table 2. Detection results for risk-seeking and risk-averse malware variant

	Ransomware	Keylogger
Aggressive	99.958%	100%
Stealthy	99.956%	99.72%

The variants described above are detected at the rates depicted in Table 2. We find that these detection rates are higher than expected in the average case across variants. Given the actual rates of detection, we compute the attacker's actual derived utility by computing:

$$(1 - p)u(x)$$

Where p is the actual rate of detection and $u(x)$ is the same utility function defined by Eq. 1. We set $x = 1$ for default parameters on each malware variant to compare results within a malware family. To establish the value of aggressive and stealthy variants, we use the ratio of the default and modified exfiltration rate to establish the value. For readability, the utility values shown are scaled by a factor of 1000.

Table 3. Aggressive, stealthy, and expected utilities for attackers across malware variants, scaled by 1000

	Ransomware			Keylogger		
	Aggressive	Stealthy	Expected	Aggressive	Stealthy	Expected
Risk-Seeking	3.674	0.148	2.653	0.0	0.140	62.440
Risk-Averse	2.721	0.146	2.549	0.0	0.140	59.992

We observe from the results in Table 3 that across malware families, risk-averse attackers gain lower nominal actual utility in all cases – a function of the very high probability of being detected. Although the aggressive ransomware had the highest detection rate, it conferred the most actual utility relative to expectations for both attacker types. This is largely due to the high value it received, $v = 15/2$ compared with the stealthy variant $v = 15/45$ and the stealthy keylogger $v = 0.1/2$ and the fact that all detection rates exceeded their expected rate.

A rational actor will choose whatever option *a priori* offers the highest expected value. By assumption in Sect. 4, the value of ransomware is greater than that of keyloggers by some unknown amount. To incentivize ransomware use, this value must exceed 64 times the value of a keylogger for risk-averse attackers and exceed 16 times the value of a keylogger for risk-seeking attackers given the detection rates in Table 1. This fact stems from three dimensional analysis of the value ratio and risk sensitivity, visualized in Fig. 3.

On observation, the actual utility of the aggressive ransomware variant is 26.24 times the actual utility of the stealthy keylogger for risk-seeking attackers and 19.44 times the actual utility of the stealthy keylogger for risk-averse attackers. If attackers used either of these values *a priori* to compute the expected value of ransomware, the risk-seeking attacker would choose ransomware, but the risk-averse attacker would choose a keylogger. In this case, the risk-seeking attacker would be satisfied with their outcome relative to expectations, while the risk-averse attacker would be unsatisfied relative to expectations.

6 Conclusion

This work has explored how under the framework of exponential utility, a well-studied case of expected utility theory satisfying CARA, attackers who are operating against an unknown defender will choose their attack strategy based on the combination of their risk appetite and the expected value of the available strategies. We conclude that in environments where detection rates are higher than expected, risk-seeking attackers are more satisfied with their *a priori* best choice, while risk-averse attackers are less satisfied. This suggests that risk-averse attackers may seek environments that are more vulnerable and less well-guarded, while risk-seeking attackers are less swayed by a defender's strategy.

Crucially, our work makes a step forward in empirically evaluating attacker strategies using real, parameterizable malware families. This has long been a difficult task, as valuations and utility functions are highly subjective. This work demonstrates that given a fairly small set of assumptions, we can test expected utility models and their efficacy. In future work, we will explore the intricate relationships between attacker risk attitudes and past successes, leveraging a Bayesian model to set the expected value for a successful attack.

From a defender's perspective, we would like to deal directly with the different risk attitudes toward gains and losses. Different defensive strategies have different costs and different attacks can result in more or less damage to systems. Using Tversky and Kahneman's cumulative prospect theory [14], we can frame the risk of loss differently from that of retaining existing resources or gaining more capital. Using a cumulative prospect theory model would also allow for better generalization to unknown attacks, since we can consider arbitrary outcome distributions.

Our defensive parameters and malware parameters are also highly configurable and have a continuous range, allowing for unlimited configurations of both offensive and defensive strategies. The specific parameterization will alter both our detection rates and valuations in ways which are difficult to predict. In future work, we seek to expand on the limited number of offensive and defensive strategies considered in this paper and instead seek to understand how these parameters can be chosen as a function of the risk appetites of both attackers and defenders. We will do this by finding optimal parameter settings for both attackers and defenders and developing a significant way of directly relating parameterization with value, using the framework of Dempster-Shafer theory [13] to better capture the uncertainty of the players. This extension of our current work would help frame the relationship between attackers and defenders and their risk appetites in a way that captures the overwhelming number of malware variants and defensive architectures that exist in the real world.

References

1. Abie, H., Balasingham, I.: Risk-based adaptive security for smart IoT in eHealth. In: Proceedings of the 7th International Conference on Body Area Networks, pp. 269–275 (2012)
2. Anderson, R.: Security Engineering: A Guide to Building Dependable Distributed Systems. Wiley, Hoboken (2020)
3. Antonakakis, M., et al.: Understanding the mirai botnet. In: 26th USENIX Security Symposium (USENIX Security 17), pp. 1093–1110. USENIX Association, Vancouver, August 2017. https://www.usenix.org/conference/usenixsecurity17/technical-sessions/presentation/antonakakis
4. Calford, E.M.: Uncertainty aversion in game theory: experimental evidence. J. Econ. Behav. Organ. **176**, 720–734 (2020)
5. Camerer, C.F.: Behavioural game theory. In: Durlauf, S.N., Blume, L.E. (eds.) Behavioural and Experimental Economics. TNPEC, pp. 42–50. Palgrave Macmillan UK, London (2010). https://doi.org/10.1057/9780230280786_6
6. Camerer, C.F., Karjalainen, R.: Ambiguity-aversion and non-additive beliefs in non-cooperative games: experimental evidence. In: Munier, B., Machina, M.J. (eds.) Models and Experiments in Risk and Rationality. Theory and Decision Library (Series B: Mathematical and Statistical Methods), vol. 29, pp. 325–358. Springer, Dordrecht (1994). https://doi.org/10.1007/978-94-017-2298-8_17
7. Camerer, C.F., Loewenstein, G., Rabin, M.: Advances in Behavioral Economics. Princeton University Press, Princeton (2004)
8. Chatterjee, S., Halappanavar, M., Tipireddy, R., Oster, M.: Quantifying mixed uncertainties in cyber attacker payoffs. In: IEEE International Symposium on Technologies for Homeland Security. IEEE (2015)
9. Chatterjee, S., Tipireddy, R., Oster, M., Halappanavar, M.: Propagating mixed uncertainties in cyber attacker payoffs : exploration of two-phase Monte Carlo sampling and probability bounds analysis. In: IEEE International Symposium on Technologies for Homeland Security. IEEE (2016)
10. Heiland, D.: Iot security and risk: what is it, where is it heading, and how do we embrace it? (2019). https://www.rapid7.com/blog/post/2019/11/12/iot-security-and-risk-what-is-it-where-is-it-heading-and-how-do-we-embrace-it/
11. Holt, C.A., Laury, S.K.: Risk aversion and incentive effects. Am. Econ. Rev. **92**(5), 1644–1655 (2002)
12. Kiekintveld, C., Marecki, J., Tambe, M.: Approximation methods for infinite Bayesian Stackelberg games: modeling distributional payoff uncertainty. In: The 10th International Conference on Autonomous Agents and Multiagent Systems-Volume 3, pp. 1005–1012 (2011)
13. Shafer, G.: Dempster-Shafer theory. Encycl. Artif. Intell. **1**, 330–331 (1992)
14. Tversky, A., Kahneman, D.: Advances in prospect theory: cumulative representation of uncertainty. J. Risk Uncertain. **5**(4), 297–323 (1992). https://doi.org/10.1007/BF00122574

Paying Firms to Share Cyber Threat Intelligence

Brandon Collins$^{(\boxtimes)}$, Shouhuai Xu, and Philip N. Brown

University of Colorado Colorado Springs, Colorado Springs, CO 80918, USA
{bcollin3,sxu,pbrown2}@uccs.edu

Abstract. Effective cyber defense requires stakeholders to collaborate with each other and share cyber threat intelligence. Sharing such intelligence can improve the community's cybersecurity posture, preventing others from being hacked or compromised. However, intelligence sharing is still relatively uncommon due in part to the associated costs as well as other legitimate concerns. In this paper, we ask how a central authority could employ monetary incentives to promote intelligence sharing among competitive firms. We propose a novel game-theoretic model of intelligence sharing and derive the minimal incentive payments which ensure that firms profitably share with their competitors. We investigate the value of being able to differentiate incentives among firms (i.e., paying a different amount to each firm), and show formally that the ability to differentiate is the most valuable when the network among firms is highly heterogeneous. Finally, we show that our results are sharp in an important sense: if the authority offers less than the minimal incentive to every firm, this can render no-sharing as the unique Nash equilibrium.

Keywords: Cyber threat intelligence sharing · Incentive design · Game theory · Cooperative cyber defense · Cybersecurity risk management

1 Introduction

Cyberspace is a large complex system not only because of the large number of interconnected devices, but also because of the interdependence and interaction between the devices. A challenging dimension of this interconnection is the "fragmentation" of cyberspace, namely that it is comprised of many networks which are managed by different authorities. This lack of centralized authority can make it extremely challenging to effectively defend and manage cyberspace.

Ideally, these disparate decisionmakers would cooperate with each other to ensure effective cyber defense. For example, when a firm is hacked or compromised, it would be valuable for the firm to share with others why it was hacked, how it was hacked, and what could have been done to prevent it from having been

---

This work was supported in part by NSF Grants #2122631, #2115134 and #ECCS-2013779, ARO Grant #W911NF-17-1-0566, and Colorado State Bill 18-086.

B. Bošanský et al. (Eds.): GameSec 2021, LNCS 13061, pp. 365–377, 2021.
https://doi.org/10.1007/978-3-030-90370-1_20

hacked; this information would enable other firms to harden their own networks to avoid future attacks of the same kind [1]. In this paper, we use the term cyber threat intelligence, or intelligence for short, to represent a wide range of information that can be shared by one firm and used by others to harden their networks or cybersecurity posture. In practice, this information is often not shared among firms for a number of reasons [16,23] including confidentiality concerns and overhead costs associated with establishing sharing protocols [8].

To address this shortfall of intelligence sharing, there have been initiatives and legislation geared toward encouraging intelligence sharing [5,10]. However, since effective sharing is still rare in practice, the question remains: which incentive policies would be most cost-effective in promoting intelligence sharing among firms? What information would a regulatory body require to implement such incentives effectively? To address these questions, this paper proposes a novel mathematical model of intelligence sharing among firms and uses game-theoretic tools design financial incentives to promote sharing. Before summarizing our contributions, we briefly review relevant literature.

There are many studies on modeling cybersecurity problems using game theory; we refer to [2,12,15,17] for surveys on this topic, including [22] for a survey of cyber threat intelligence sharing topics. Earlier studies [6,7,9,20] focus on intelligence sharing between two firms, whereas our work considers the more realistic setting of intelligence sharing between many firms connected by an arbitrary graph. Intelligence sharing between many firms has been investigated in [18], which however assumes the presence of a central repository for shared intelligence; in contrast, we allow firms fine control of whom they share with.

In the setting of sharing other kinds of cybersecurity information, Luiijf and Klaver [14] present a cybersecurity information sharing framework to accommodate both strategic level policies and tactical/operational level techniques, as well as legal issues. The sharing of software vulnerability information is studied in [11,21]. Ezhei and Ladani [3] study information sharing games when privacy is also a concern (i.e., information will not be shared when the gain outweighs the risk to privacy). Layfield et at. [13] conduct an evolutionary game-theoretic study on incentive and trust issues in assured information sharing [4,24]. Thakkar et al. [19] investigate how to incentivize participants to share cybersecurity information in the presence of malicious participants. In contrast, we consider a higher level of abstraction by focusing on network-wide policy-making, while explicitly modeling the impact of the graph structure without requiring a centralized party.

In this paper, we propose a novel game-theoretic model to describe how firms make intelligence sharing decisions in response to financial incentives from an authority or policy-maker (i.e., decentralized sharing but centralized incentive management because the authority is only involved in managing incentives but not involved in the routine intelligence sharing practice). Our model also applies in a second scenario when a centralized information sharing organization already exists that all firms participate in, however firms control who their sensitive intelligence is shared with. Business relationships between firms are described by a graph, and each firm can choose to make intelligence available to any or all of its graph neighbors. A firm incurs some cost by choosing to share intelligence, but hopes to "recoup" this cost when its neighboring firms reciprocate and share their own intelligence in return. Finally, firms are hesitant to share intelligence due to confidentiality concerns or a reluctance to assist competitors. In order to promote intelligence sharing, the authority offers monetary incentives to firms. Under this model, we ask: What is the minimal amount of incentives that must be paid to the firms to ensure they can all profitably share, and how valuable is the ability to differentiate payments across firms? Finally, if the authority cannot afford differentiated payments to all firms, can *any* sharing be guaranteed if only a subset of the firms are paid?

We consider two incentive scenarios for an authority: (i) a differentiated incentive setting where the authority can pay each firm an individualized amount; (ii) a uniform case where the authority must pay all firms an identical amount. In Proposition 1, we characterize the minimal incentive payments for both the differentiated and uniform cases such that the all-sharing state is a Nash equilibrium; critically, these incentive payments can be computed in polynomial time. Intuitively, Proposition 1 shows that a highly capable authority (i.e., one that has the information required to employ differentiated incentives) pays no more than a low-capability authority (i.e., one that can only employ uniform incentives), hinting at the potential value of heterogeneous incentives. This can be explained as follows: The firm which possesses the highest-quality intelligence will not benefit from uniform incentives because it receives little reward from the lower-quality intelligence received by its neighbors.

We then explore the role of graph structure on this value of differentiation. Proposition 2 characterizes the graphs and game parameters which maximize the value of differentiated prices; specifically, it shows that differentiated prices are most valuable when the firm with the highest-quality intelligence is poorly connected to other firms, confirming the value of heterogeneous incentives.

Finally, we conclude with Proposition 3 which illustrates that if an authority attempts to pay firms less than the minimal incentive derived above, this can lead to a behavior cascade which makes no-sharing the unique Nash equilibrium.

2 Model

2.1 Cyber Threat Intelligence Sharing Game

We consider n firms (i.e., enterprises or entities under different cybersecurity management jurisdictions). We model the business network among the firms with an undirected graph $G = (V, E)$, where $V = \{1, \ldots, n\}$ (e.g., each firm is represented as a node or vertex) and E is the edge set. An undirected edge $(i, j) \in E$ means that firms i and j have some preexisting business relationship (e.g., they operate in a similar industry) and that their cyber threat intelligence is mutually relevant (i.e., the firms use similar technology stacks). Thus, $(i, j) \in E$ means that firms i and j may share intelligence with each other if they choose to do so. Note that this graph is generally different from the underlying communication network connecting the firms.

Each firm i has cyber threat intelligence worth value $r_i \geq 0$, and experiences a cost of $c_i \geq 0$ if the firm chooses to make its intelligence available to other firms. This cost is incurred once-for-all; that is, it represents an investment in preparing intelligence for sharing, for example by hiring new employees or extending the existing infrastructure. We write $r = (r_1, r_2, \ldots, r_n)$ and $c = (c_1, c_2, \ldots, c_n)$ to concisely represent the firms' values and costs, respectively.

We write the set of *neighbors* of firm i as $\mathcal{N}_i := \{j \in V \mid (i, j) \in E\}$. If firm i chooses to make its intelligence available to neighbor $j \in \mathcal{N}_i$, we say that firm i *shares with* j. However, intelligence is only exchanged between the firms if the choice to share is mutual: if firm i shares with j and j shares with i, then intelligence is *exchanged*. This reciprocity requirement is justified by the notion that no firm is willing to share without receiving something in return. Formally, we represent firm i's decision to share with its neighbors with binary tuple $A_i = \{0, 1\}^{|\mathcal{N}_i|}$, where $a_{ij} = 1$ indicates that firm i shares with firm j, and $a_{ij} = 0$ indicates that firm i does not share with firm j. Thus, intelligence is exchanged between firms i and j if and only if $a_{ij} a_{ji} = 1$; i.e., both i and j choose to share with each other. The firms' joint action space is given by $A = A_1 \times A_2 \times \cdots \times A_n$ and we denote an action profile as $a \in A$. We frequently write A_{-i} to denote the action space of all firms other than i, and $a_{-i} \in A_{-i}$ to denote a specific action choice of every firm other than i.

When intelligence is exchanged between firms i and j, each firm benefits from the other's intelligence; i.e., i receives a benefit of r_j and firm j receives a benefit of r_i. Finally, firms may be reluctant to share intelligence with competitors or may have confidentiality concerns associated with making intelligence available. To model this, when intelligence is exchanged between firm i and a neighbor, firm i experiences an additional cost of αr_i, where $\alpha \in [0, 1]$ is a penalty factor. That is, firm i views its intelligence in the hands of a neighbor as a cost.

It is easy to see that without external incentives, the no-sharing action profile is a Nash equilibrium; that is, if no other firm is sharing, each individual firm cannot benefit by choosing to share unilaterally due to the setup cost c_i. Accordingly, to study the problem of incentive design to promote sharing among firms, we assume that there is an authority (or policy-maker) who selects incentive vector $\vec{p} = (\vec{p}_1, \ldots, \vec{p}_n) \in \mathbb{R}^n_+$, where firm i is paid a monetary amount $\vec{p}_i$ for each neighbor with whom i shares intelligence.

Combining all the above, we have that firm i makes its sharing choice a_i, given the choices of other firms a_{-i} and incentive vector $\vec{p}$ to maximize utility function given by

$$u_i(a_i, a_{-i}; \vec{p}) = -c_i \mathbb{1}\left(\sum_j a_{ij} > 0\right) + \sum_{j \in \mathcal{N}_i} (a_{ij} a_{ji}(r_j - \alpha r_i) + a_{ij} \vec{p}_i) \quad (1)$$

where $\mathbb{1}(P) = 1$ if logical proposition P is true and $\mathbb{1}(P) = 0$ otherwise.

If all elements of $\vec{p}$ are equal, i.e., $\vec{p}_i = \vec{p}_j$ for all $i, j \in V$, we call $\vec{p}$ *uniform*. When discussing uniform incentive vectors, we typically write p and omit the vector arrow. If $\vec{p}$ is not uniform, we call it *differentiated*. We compactly write

$g = (G, c, r, \alpha, \vec{p})$ to denote an instance of the game described above and $\mathcal{G}$ to denote the space of all such games.

2.2   Research Questions

The core research problem is to investigate how the authority should optimally incentivize the firms, and how constraints on the authority impact the cost of incentive payments. We consider a cybersecurity-oriented authority who desires to maximize the amount of cyber threat intelligence sharing among the firms. This means that the optimal action profile is the one where every firm shares with each of its neighbors. We denote this profile by $\vec{1} := \left((1)_{j=1}^{|\mathcal{N}_i|} \right)_{i=1}^{n}$. The authority wishes to derive an incentive vector $\vec{p}$ such that the firms profitably select $\vec{1}$; formally, we seek to characterize incentive vectors such that $\vec{1}$ is a *Nash equilibrium* of the game. An action profile $a \in A$ is a Nash equilibrium under incentives $\vec{p}$ if for all $i \in V$ it holds that $u_i(a_i, a_{-i}; \vec{p}) \geq u_i(a_i', a_{-i}; \vec{p})$, where $a_i' \in A_i$ is any unilateral deviation by firm i. For any game $g \in \mathcal{G}$, we write $\mathrm{NE}(g)$ to denote the set of Nash equilibria of g.

Our first research question is: *How can the authority minimize its incentive payments while still ensuring that $\vec{1}$ is a Nash equilibrium?* To formalize the notion of minimal, we measure the total incentive payments by $C : \mathbb{R}^n \to \mathbb{R}$ in the all-sharing action profile $\vec{1}$; naturally, we have $C(\vec{p}) = \sum_{i \in V} \sum_{j \in \mathcal{N}_i} p_i$.

Since the authority wishes to minimize its total payments, we define the *minimal* uniform incentive payment p^* as

$$p^* \in \arg\min_{p \in \mathbb{R}_+^n} \{ C(p) \mid \vec{1} \in \mathrm{NE}(g(p)), \text{ and } p_i = p_j \forall i, j \in V \} \tag{2}$$

where for brevity we write $g(p) := (G, c, r, \alpha, p)$, and the minimal differentiated incentive payment $\vec{p}^*$ as

$$\vec{p}^* \in \arg\min_{\vec{p} \in \mathbb{R}_+^n} \{ C(\vec{p}) \mid \vec{1} \in \mathrm{NE}(g(\vec{p})) \} \tag{3}$$

where for brevity we write $g(\vec{p}) := (G, c, r, \alpha, \vec{p})$.

The second research question is: *Which game structures render differentiated incentives the most valuable relative to uniform incentives?* That is, we wish to understand which game features allow the authority to realize a cost savings by implementing differentiated incentives. Formally, for any fixed graph G we characterize the worst-case cost and value vectors c, r such that the difference $C(p^*) - C(\vec{p}^*)$ is maximized.

The third research question is: *If the authority pays less than the minimal incentives, can any sharing be guaranteed in the game's resulting equilibria?* Here, we consider a scenario in which the authority cannot afford to pay the minimal incentives to each firm, so decides to pay only a lower uniform incentive. Via a specific case study, we show that underpaying only one firm can lead to a behavior cascade which renders the no-sharing state as a unique Nash equilibrium.

3 Results

3.1 Minimal Payments

We begin by characterizing minimal incentives for both the uniform and differentiated incentive cases. We present both vectors in closed form.

Proposition 1. *Let $\vec{g} = (G, c, v, \alpha, \vec{p}^*) \in \mathcal{G}$ where G is connected. The minimal differentiated incentive vector such that the all-sharing state is a Nash equilibrium is given by*

$$\bar{p}_i^* = \max\left\{\frac{c_i + \sum_{j \in \mathcal{N}_i} \alpha r_i - r_j}{|\mathcal{N}_i|}\right\} \cup \{\alpha r_i - r_j \mid j \in \mathcal{N}_i\} \cup \{0\}. \qquad (4)$$

Further, in the uniform incentive case $g = (G, c, v, \alpha, p^*)$ where p^* is defined as

$$p_i^* = \max\left\{\frac{c_i + \sum_{j \in \mathcal{N}_i} \alpha r_i - r_j}{|\mathcal{N}_i|} \;\middle|\; i \in V\right\} \cup \{\alpha r_i - r_j \mid i \in V, j \in \mathcal{N}_i\} \cup \{0\}, \quad (5)$$

p^* is the minimal uniform incentive vector such that the all-sharing state is a Nash equilibrium.

Before presenting the proof we provide some intuition behind the sets featured in (4), (5). Note in the proceeding discussion that $p_i^* = \max_j \bar{p}_j^*$ for all $i \in V$, which is formally shown in the proof. That is, under the minimal uniform incentive vector p^*, all firms are paid the maximum incentive paid to any single firm under the minimal differentiated incentive vector $\bar{p}^*$. The first set on the right-hand of (4), (5) represents the condition that if all other firms are sharing intelligence, then any single firm will maximize its utility by sharing with all of its neighbors. This set contains the maximum when a firm either has a high cost c_i or a high-quality intelligence value r_i which in either case leads to firm i requiring a large incentive to share with all of its neighbors. The second set on the right hand of (4), (5) ensures that firms can profitably share on every individual link on G. This set contains the maximum if there exists some pair i, j with highly unbalanced r_i, r_j. That is, if the difference $\alpha r_i - r_j$ is large then firm i requires a large incentive to share on that link. The third set in (4), (5) ensures $\bar{p}_i^*, p_i^*$ is nonnegative.

Proof. Let $\vec{g} = (G, c, r, \alpha, \vec{p}^*) \in \mathcal{G}$, with G being connected and $\vec{p}^*$ be defined according to (4). We show that no firm can unilaterally deviate from $\vec{1}$ and increase its utility. We do this in two cases. In the first case, firm i selects some nonempty set $S \subset \mathcal{N}_i$ such that $a_{is} = 0$ for $s \in S$ and $a_{ij} = 1$ for $j \notin S$. Evaluating the difference in utility resulting from deviating, we have

$$
\begin{aligned}
u_i(\vec{1}; \vec{p}^*) - u_i(a_i, \vec{1}_{-i}; \vec{p}_i^*) &= \sum_{j \in \mathcal{N}_i} (r_j - \alpha r_i + \bar{p}_i^*) - \sum_{j \in \mathcal{N}_i \setminus S} (r_j - \alpha r_i + \bar{p}_i^*) \\
&= \sum_{j \in S} (r_j - \alpha r_i + \bar{p}_i^*) \geq 0,
\end{aligned}
\qquad (6)
$$

where the inequality follows by the definition of $\vec{p}^*$ in (4); specifically the second set ensures this property. In the second case, i deviates to sharing with none of its neighbors. That is, $a_{ij} = 0$ for all $j \in \mathcal{N}_i$. Evaluating the difference in utility,

$$u_i(\vec{1}; \vec{p}^*) - u(a_i, \vec{1}_{-i}; \vec{p}^*) = -c_i + \sum_{j \in \mathcal{N}_i} (r_j - \alpha r_i + \vec{p}_i^*) - 0$$

$$= -c_i + |\mathcal{N}_i|\vec{p}_i^* + \sum_{j \in \mathcal{N}_i} (r_j - \alpha r_i) \geq 0, \qquad (7)$$

where the inequality again follows by the left set of (4). Therefore no firm may profitably deviate from $\vec{1}$ and it is by definition a Nash equilibrium in $\vec{g}$.

Secondly, we show that $\vec{p}^*$ is minimal. Specifically, we show that for any $\vec{p} \in \mathbb{R}_+^n$ with $C(\vec{p}) < C(\vec{p}^*)$ then $\vec{1}$ is not a Nash equilibrium in game $g' = (G, c, r, \alpha, \vec{p})$ in three cases on $\vec{p}^*$. In the first case, let $\vec{p} \in \mathbb{R}_+^n$ with $C(\vec{p}) < C(\vec{p}^*)$. It can be seen that $C(\vec{p}) < C(\vec{p}^*)$ gives that there exists $i \in V$ such that $\vec{p}_i < \vec{p}_i^*$, and let i denote that firm. We now take cases on $\vec{p}^*$, starting with the case $\vec{p}^* = \alpha r_i - r_k$ for some $k \in \mathcal{N}_i$; that is, the maximum is achieved on the middle set of (4). Consider action profile a such that $a_{ik} = 0$, and $a_{ij} = 1$ for all $j \in \mathcal{N}_i \setminus \{k\}$. Evaluating a_i as a unilateral deviation from $\vec{1}$ in g',

$$u_i(\vec{1}; \vec{p}) - u_i(a_i, \vec{1}_{-i}; \vec{p}) = -c_i + \sum_{j \in \mathcal{N}_i} (r_j - \alpha r_i + \vec{p}_i) + c_i - \sum_{j \neq k} (r_j - \alpha r_i + \vec{p}_i)$$

$$= (r_k - \alpha r_i + \vec{p}_i) < 0 \qquad (8)$$

where the inequality follows by hypothesis. Because the difference is negative, firm i may unilaterally increase their utility by deviating via a_i, and therefore $\vec{1}$ is not a Nash equilibrium in g'. In the second case, let $\vec{p}_i^* = \frac{c_i + \sum_{j \in \mathcal{N}_i} \alpha r_j - r_i}{|\mathcal{N}_i|}$, meaning that the maximum in (4) is achieved in the first set. Let a_i such that $a_{ij} = 0$ for all $j \in \mathcal{N}_i$ and consider firm i's utility as they unilaterally deviate from $\vec{1}_i$ to a_i under incentive $\vec{p}$,

$$u_i(\vec{1}; \vec{p}) - u_i(a_i, \vec{1}_{-i}; \vec{p}) = -c_i + |\mathcal{N}_i|\vec{p} + \sum_{j \in \mathcal{N}_i} (r_j - \alpha r_i) < 0 \qquad (9)$$

where the inequality can be seen from via an algebraic manipulation of (4) similar to the one used in (7). Again, firm i can profitably unilaterally deviate from $\vec{1}$ under $\vec{p}$ meaning it is not a Nash equilibrium by definition. In the third case, there exists no i such that the first two cases hold. Then $\vec{p}_i^* = 0$ as it must be defined via the third set in (4). It is trivial to see that $\vec{p}_i$ must be nonnegative so that no $\vec{p}_i < \vec{p}_i^*$ is feasible. This concludes all cases on $\vec{p}^*$ and in all of them no $C(\vec{p}) < C(\vec{p}^*)$ exists such that $\vec{1}$ is a Nash equilibrium under $\vec{p}$. Therefore $\vec{p}^*$ must be the minimal incentive vector such that $\vec{1}$ is a Nash equilibrium.

Now we consider the uniform case. Let $g = (G, c, r, \alpha, p^*)$ where p^* is defined in (5). We begin by observing that p^* may be alternately defined in terms of $\vec{p}_i^*$, particularly $p_i^* = \max_j \bar{p}_j^*$ for all $i \in V$. This holds because every element in the union of sets in (5) appears in the union of sets in (4) for some $j \in V$. Note that $\vec{1} \in NE(g)$ can be verified via the same calculations in (6), (7) for any $i \in V$ under incentive p_i^*. However, we omit the calculations because $p_i^* = \max_j \bar{p}_j^*$ yields $p_i^* \geq \bar{p}_i^*$, and it is easy to see the same inequalities in (6), (7) hold in this case. Further, we show minimality of p^* by considering some $p' \in \mathbb{R}_+^n$ such that $p_i' = p_j'$ for all $i, j \in V$ and $C(p') < C(p^*)$ or equivalently $p_i' < p_i^*$ for all $i \in V$. Similar to the minimality arguments on $\bar{p}^*$, it can be shown using three cases on p^*. The same calculations used in (8), (9) can be applied this time considering firm i such that $\bar{p}_i^* = p_i^*$, concluding the proof.   □

3.2   The Importance of Differentiated Incentives

Given the characterization of minimal incentive vectors $\bar{p}^*, p^*$ given in Proposition 1, we now investigate when c, r make $C(\bar{p}^*) - C(p^*)$ large. That is, in what scenarios is it particularly cost-effective for the authority to differentiate incentives? Since $p^* = \max_j \bar{p}_j^*$, a single firm i requiring a high incentive causes all other firms $j \neq i$ to receive the same high incentive, effectively overpaying them when compared with the differentiated case. Note that as per (5), a large c_i or r_i can cause this effect. Following with the intuition that a single firm with large c_i, r_i causes the difference in costs between the uniform and differentiated incentive cases, we provide a characterization of the worst case c, r such that the difference between $C(p^*) - C(\bar{p}^*)$ is maximized on arbitrary graphs. For clarity we will specify $p^*(c, r), \bar{p}^*(c, r)$ as a function of c, r while noting that dependence on G, α is implicit.

Proposition 2. *Consider a class of games where $c_i \in [0, \bar{c}]$ $r_i \in [0, \bar{r}]$ for all $i \in V$ with $\bar{c}, \bar{r} > 0$. Let G be a connected graph and node indices be ordered such that $|\mathcal{N}_1| \leq |\mathcal{N}_2| \leq \cdots \leq |\mathcal{N}_n|$. If $c^* = (\bar{c}, 0, 0, \ldots, 0)$ and $r^* = (\bar{r}, 0, 0, \ldots, 0)$ then*

$$c^*, r^* \in \underset{c \in [0, \bar{c}]^n, r \in [0, \bar{r}]^n}{\arg\max} C(p^*(c, r)) - \vec{C}(\bar{p}^*(c, r)). \tag{10}$$

That is, c^*, r^* represents the scenario where the most savings are available to an authority by being able to differentiate incentives.

Proof. Let G be a connected graph and with V ordered by degree such that $|\mathcal{N}_1| \leq |\mathcal{N}_2| \leq \cdots \leq |\mathcal{N}_n|$ and let $\alpha \in [0, 1]$. For convenience, define $\Delta C(c, r) := C(p^*(c, r)) - \vec{C}(\bar{p}^*(c, r))$ and let $c^* = (\bar{c}, 0, 0, \ldots, 0)$, $r^* = (\bar{r}, 0, 0, \ldots, 0)$. We begin by evaluating $\Delta C(c^*, r^*)$:

$$\Delta C(c^*, r^*) = |E| p_1^*(c^*, r^*) - \sum_{i \in V} \sum_{j \in \mathcal{N}_i} \bar{p}_i^*(c^*, r^*)$$

$$= |E| p_1^*(\bar{c}, \bar{r}) - \sum_{j \in \mathcal{N}_1} \bar{p}_i^*(\bar{c}, \bar{r}) = (|E| - |\mathcal{N}_1|) \left(\frac{\bar{c}}{|\mathcal{N}_1|} + \alpha \bar{r} \right), \tag{11}$$

noting that since $p_i^* = p_j^*$ for all i, j, p_1^* is taken as an arbitrary index and the second equality follows as $\bar{p}_j^* = 0$ for all $j \neq 1$.

We show (10) by taking cases on $p^*(c,r)$. In the first case, consider $c \in [0,\bar{c}]^n, r \in [0,\bar{r}]^n$ such that $p_1^*(c,r) = 0$. Trivially, $\Delta C(c,r) = 0$ but $\Delta C(c^*,r^*) > 0$ therefore such c, r can not contradict (10). In a second case, consider $c \in [0,\bar{c}]^n, r \in [0,\bar{r}]^n$ such that $p_1^*(c,r) = \alpha r_y - r_z$ for some $y \in V, z \in \mathcal{N}_y$. We show $\Delta C(c,r)$ is a strict lower bound of $\Delta C(c^*,r^*)$,

$$\Delta C(c,r) = |E|p_1^*(c,r) - \sum_{i \in V} \sum_{j \in \mathcal{N}_i} \bar{p}_i^*(c,r)$$

$$\leq |E|p_1^*(c,r) - \sum_{j \in \mathcal{N}_y} \bar{p}_y^*(c,r)$$

$$< (|E| - |\mathcal{N}_1|)(\frac{\bar{c}}{|\mathcal{N}_1|} + \alpha\bar{r}) = \Delta C(c^*,r^*). \tag{12}$$

thus if c, r induces the maximum of (5) to be obtained by middle set then c, r does not have $\Delta C(c,r) < \Delta C(c^*,r^*)$. In the third case, we have $c \in [0,\bar{c}]^n, r \in [0,\bar{r}]^n$ such that $p_1^*(c,r) = \frac{c_y + \sum_{j \in \mathcal{N}_y} \alpha r_y - r_j}{|\mathcal{N}_y|}$ for some $y \in V$. Again we show $\Delta C(c,r)$ lower bounds $C(c^*,r^*)$,

$$\Delta C(c,r) \leq |E|\frac{c_y + \sum_{j \in \mathcal{N}_y} \alpha r_y - r_j}{|\mathcal{N}_y|} - \sum_{j \in \mathcal{N}_y} \bar{p}_y^*(c,r)$$

$$= |E|\frac{c_y + \sum_{j \in \mathcal{N}_y} \alpha r_y - r_j}{|\mathcal{N}_y|} - |\mathcal{N}_y|\frac{c_y + \sum_{j \in \mathcal{N}_y} \alpha r_y - r_j}{|\mathcal{N}_y|}$$

$$\leq (|E| - |\mathcal{N}_1|)(\bar{c}/|\mathcal{N}_1| + \alpha r_y) = \Delta C(c^*,r^*). \tag{13}$$

Thus no c, r can make $\Delta C(c,r) > \Delta C(c^*,r^*)$. Since this property holds for any (c,r), (c^*,r^*) must maximize the desired difference as provided by (10). □

3.3   Case Study: A Cascading Failure on Regular Graphs

We examine a case on regular graphs where the authority with budgetary constraints or limited information attempts to save money by ignoring the heterogeneity of firms. Let G be a connected k-regular graph with $r = (\bar{r}, \bar{r}, \ldots, \bar{r})$ for $\bar{r} > 0$ and $c = (\bar{c}, k\bar{r}, k\bar{r}, \ldots, k\bar{r})$ where $0 < k\bar{r} < \bar{c}$. Letting $\alpha \in [0,1)$ denote this game by $\bar{g}(\bar{p}) = (G, c, r, \alpha, \bar{p})$.

We begin by showing that $C(p^*(c,r)) - C(\bar{p}^*(c,r))$ depends solely on the size of the graph and the difference between firm 1's cost and other firms, $x = \bar{c} - k\bar{r}$. To calculate $C(p^*(c,r)) - C(\bar{p}^*(c,r))$ we first calculate $p^*(c,r), \bar{p}^*(c,r)$, and it can be seen that

$$p^*(c,r) = \frac{\bar{c} + \sum_{j \in \mathcal{N}_1} \alpha\bar{r} - \bar{r}}{|\mathcal{N}_1|} = \alpha\bar{r} + \frac{x}{k}, \text{ and} \tag{14}$$

$$\bar{p}_i^*(c,r) = \frac{k\bar{r} + \sum_{j \in \mathcal{N}_1} \alpha\bar{r} - \bar{r}}{|\mathcal{N}_i|} = \alpha\bar{r}, \tag{15}$$

for any $i \in V \setminus \{1\}$ while noting that $\bar{p}_1^*(c,r) = p^*(c,r)$. Now we have

$$C(p^*(c,r)) - C(\bar{p}^*(c,r)) = |E|p^*(c,r) - \sum_{i \in V} \sum_{j \in \mathcal{N}_i} \bar{p}_i^*(c,r)$$

$$= kn(\alpha\bar{r} + \frac{x}{k}) - k(\alpha\bar{r} + \frac{x}{k}) - (n-1)k\alpha\bar{r}$$

$$= (n-1)x.$$

That is, the cost to the authority for not being able to differentially incentivize firms in a regular graph depends linearly both on the size of the graph and the difference in costs between firm 1 and all other firms.

With this potentially large difference in mind, suppose the authority naively tries to cut costs. From (15) it can be seen that for all $i \neq 1$, $\bar{p}_i^*$ is the same. What happens if the authority opts to incentivize all firms, including firm 1, at this rate? Formally, let $p_i'(c,v) = \bar{p}_j^*(c,v)$ for any $i \in V, j \neq 1$ and we omit the arguments (c,v) for simplicity. Besides naiveté, there are other reasons why an authority might reasonably select uniform incentives of p'. Consider the scenario where the authority cannot observe each firm's c_i, r_i. If firm 1 is not observed then the authority would compute $p_1^* = p_i'$. In a second scenario consider the case where the authority can only compute an average of $\bar{p}^*$. As the graph grows large the average of $\bar{p}^*$ approaches p'. We now provide a characterization of the equilibria under p', particularly that the no sharing state $\vec{0} \in A$ such that $\vec{0}_{ij} = 0$ for all $i \in V, j \in \mathcal{N}_i$ is the sole Nash equilibrium.

Proposition 3. *Let G be a connected k-regular graph with $r = (\bar{r}, \bar{r}, \ldots, \bar{r})$ for $\bar{r} > 0$ and $c = (\bar{c}, k\bar{r}, k\bar{r}, \ldots, k\bar{r})$ where $0 < k\bar{r} < \bar{c}$ with $\alpha \in [0,1)$. If $p'(c,r)$ is given by $p_i'(c,r) = \alpha\bar{r}$ for all $i \in V$ then in $g' = (G, c, r, \alpha, p'(c,r))$, $\vec{0}$ is the unique Nash equilibrium.*

Proof. Let G be a connected k-regular graph with $r = (\bar{r}, \bar{r}, \ldots, \bar{r})$ for $\bar{r} > 0$ and $c = (\bar{c}, k\bar{r}, k\bar{r}, \ldots, k\bar{r})$ where $0 < k\bar{r} < \bar{c}$ with $\alpha \in [0,1)$. Let $p'(c,v) = \alpha\bar{r}$ then and denote the game by $g = (G, c, r, \alpha, p'(c,r))$. The proof proceeds by developing a necessary condition for $a \in A$ to be a Nash equilibrium. Consider some $a \in A$ such that $a_{1j} = 1$ for some j and consider the utility difference of Firm 1 deviating from a_i to a_i' where $a_{ij}' = 0$ for all $j \in \mathcal{N}_1$,

$$u_1(a; p') - u_1(a_1', a_{-1}; p') = -c_1 + \sum_{j:a_{1j}=1} (r_j - \alpha r_1 + p') - 0$$

$$= -\bar{c} + |\{j \mid a_{1j} = 1\}|(\bar{r} - \alpha\bar{r} + \alpha\bar{r})$$

$$\leq -\bar{c} + k\bar{r} < 0, \tag{16}$$

meaning that firm 1 may profitably deviate to not sharing from any profile a_i that features sharing. This yields desired condition that if $a \in NE(g)$ then $a_1 = (0)^{|\mathcal{N}_1|}$. Now consider $i \in \mathcal{N}_1$ with $a \in A$ such that $a_{1j} = 0$ for all neighbors j and there exists $k \in \mathcal{N}_i$ such that $a_{ik} = 1$. We evaluate i's utility from deviating from a_i to a_i' where $a_{ij}' = 0$ for all neighbors j,

$$u_i(a; p') - u_i(a_i', a_{-i}; p') = -c_1 + \sum_{j:a_{1j}=1} (a_{ji}(r_j - \alpha r_1) + p') - 0$$
$$\leq -k\bar{r} + (k-1)(\bar{r} - \alpha\bar{r}) + k\alpha\bar{r}$$
$$= -\bar{r} + \alpha\bar{r} < 0,$$

again meaning that if firm 1 has $a_1 = (0)^{|\mathcal{N}_1|}$ then any of its neighbors may always deviate to $a_i = (0)^{|\mathcal{N}_i|}$. Note that the last inequality holds because $\alpha \neq 1$. Combining this result with the above necessary condition, if $a \in NE(g)$ then we have $a_i = (0)^{|\mathcal{N}_i|}$ for $i \in \{1\} \cup \mathcal{N}_1$. Further, it can be seen that because all firms have the same r_i and c_i as firm $i \in \mathcal{N}_1$, the above calculation applies to any firm with a single neighbor j that has $a_j = (0)^{|\mathcal{N}_j|}$. By connectivity of G it can be seen that the condition will cascade to all firms and yields that if $a \in NE(g)$, then $a = \vec{0}$.

To complete the proof we show the converse, giving that $\vec{0}$ is indeed an equilibrium in $g(p')$. Consider some firm $i \in V \setminus \{1\}$'s arbitrary unilateral deviation from $\vec{0}$, $a_i \in A_i \setminus \{\vec{0}_i\}$,

$$u_i(\vec{0}; p') - u_i(a_i, \vec{0}_{-i}; p') = 0 - \left(-c_i + \sum_{j:a_{ij}=1} a_{ji}(r_j - \alpha r_i) + p' \right)$$
$$\geq k\bar{r} - k\alpha\bar{r} > 0$$

meaning any firm besides 1 strictly prefers to play $\vec{0}_i$ if other firms play $\vec{0}_{-i}$ under incentive p'. This property is given for firm 1 under any a_{-1} under p' in (16). Taking the special case that $a_{-1} = \vec{0}_{-1}$, $\vec{0}$ satisfies the definition of Nash equilibrium. □

4   Conclusion

This paper initiates a study on incentive design for cyber threat intelligence sharing among firms, and in particular investigates the value of differentiating incentives across firms. We show that the ability to differentiate incentives is most valuable to an authority when the least-connected firm possesses the most valuable intelligence; this is justifiable because a uniform incentive would incur too much cost to the particular firm which receives little reward from the intelligence shared by its neighbors. Furthermore, we illustrate that failing to pay such a firm a sufficiently-high incentive can lead to a behavior cascade which leads all firms to cease sharing intelligence.

Acknowledgement. We thank the reviewers for their useful comments.

References

1. Brown, S., Gommers, J., Serrano, O.S.: From cyber security information sharing to threat management. In: Proceedings of the 2nd ACM WISCS 2015, Denver, Colorado, USA, 12 October 2015, pp. 43–49 (2015)
2. Do, C.T., et al.: Game theory for cyber security and privacy. ACM Comput. Surv. **50**(2), 30:1–30:37 (2017)
3. Ezhei, M., Ladani, B.T.: Information sharing vs. privacy: a game theoretic analysis. Expert Syst. Appl. **88**, 327–337 (2017)
4. Finin, T., et al.: Assured information sharing life cycle. In: IEEE ISI 2009, Dallas, Texas, USA, 8–11 June 2009, Proceedings, pp. 307–309 (2009)
5. Fischer, E., Liu, E., Rollins, J., Theohary, C.: The 2013 cybersecurity executive order: Overview and considerations for congress, 15 December 2014
6. Gao, X., Zhong, W.: A differential game approach to security investment and information sharing in a competitive environment. IIE Trans. **48**(6), 511–526 (2016)
7. Gao, X., Zhong, W., Mei, S.: A game-theoretic analysis of information sharing and security investment for complementary firms. J. Oper. Res. Soc. **65**(11), 1682–1691 (2014)
8. Garrido-Pelaz, R., González-Manzano, L., Pastrana, S.: Shall we collaborate?: a model to analyse the benefits of information sharing. In: Proceedings of WISCS 2016, Vienna, Austria, 24–28 October 2016, pp. 15–24 (2016)
9. Hausken, K.: Information sharing among firms and cyber attacks. J. Account. Pub. Policy **26**(6), 639–688 (2007)
10. Johnson, C., Badger, L., Waltermire, D., Snyder, J., Skorupka, C.: The NIST guide to cyber threat information sharing (NIST special publication 800–150), October 2016
11. Khouzani, M.H.R., Pham, V., Cid, C.: Strategic discovery and sharing of vulnerabilities in competitive environments. In: Poovendran, R., Saad, W. (eds.) Decision and Game Theory for Security. GameSec 2014, Los Angeles, CA, USA, 6–7 November 2014. Proceedings. LNCS, vol. 8840, pp. 59–78. Springer, Cham (2014). https://doi.org/10.1007/978-3-319-12601-2_4
12. Kiennert, C., Ismail, Z., Debar, H., Leneutre, J.: A survey on game-theoretic approaches for intrusion detection and response optimization. ACM Comput. Surv. (CSUR) **51**(5), 1–31 (2018)
13. Layfield, R., Kantarcioglu, M., Thuraisingham, B.: Incentive and trust issues in assured information sharing. In: Bertino, E., Joshi, J.B.D. (eds.) Collaborative Computing: Networking, Applications and Worksharing, CollaborateCom 2008. LNICST, vol. 10, pp. 113–125. Springer, Heidelberg (2009). https://doi.org/10.1007/978-3-642-03354-4_10
14. Luiijf, E., Klaver, M.: On the sharing of cyber security information. In: Rice, M., Shenoi, S. (eds.) Critical Infrastructure Protection IX, pp. 29–46. Springer International Publishing, Cham (2015). https://doi.org/10.1007/978-3-319-26567-4_3
15. Manshaei, M.H., Zhu, Q., Alpcan, T., Basar, T., Hubaux, J.: Game theory meets network security and privacy. ACM Comput. Surv. **45**(3), 25:1–25:39 (2013)
16. Mermoud, A., Keupp, M.M., Huguenin, K., Palmié, M., David, D.P.: To share or not to share: a behavioral perspective on human participation in security information sharing. J. Cybersecurity **5**(1), tyz006 (2019)
17. Pawlick, J., Zhu, Q.: Game Theory for Cyber Deception: From Theory to Applications. Springer Nature (2021)

18. Solak, S., Zhuo, Y.: Optimal policies for information sharing in information system security. Eur. J. Oper. Res. **284**(3), 934–950 (2020)
19. Thakkar, A., Badsha, S., Sengupta, S.: Game theoretic approach applied in cyber-security information exchange framework. In: IEEE CCNC 2020, Las Vegas, NV, USA, 10–13 January 2020, pp. 1–7 (2020)
20. Tosh, D.K., Sengupta, S., Kamhoua, C.A., Kwiat, K.A., Martin, A.P.: An evolutionary game-theoretic framework for cyber-threat information sharing. In: 2015 IEEE ICC 2015, London, United Kingdom, 8–12 June 2015, pp. 7341–7346 (2015)
21. Vakilinia, I., Sengupta, S.: A coalitional game theory approach for cybersecurity information sharing. In: 2017 IEEE MILCOM 2017, Baltimore, MD, USA, 23–25 October 2017, pp. 237–242 (2017)
22. Wagner, T.D., Mahbub, K., Palomar, E., Abdallah, A.E.: Cyber threat intelligence sharing: survey and research directions. Comput. Secur. **87**, 101589 (2019)
23. Webster, G.D., Harris, R.L., Hanif, Z.D., Hembree, B.A., Grossklags, J., Eckert, C.: Sharing is caring: collaborative analysis and real-time enquiry for security analytics. In: 2018 iThings, IEEE GreenCom, IEEE Cyber, CPSCom and IEEE Smart-Data, pp. 1402–1409. IEEE (2018)
24. Xu, S., Sandhu, R., Bertino, E.: TIUPAM: a framework for trustworthiness-centric information sharing. In: Ferrari, E., Li, N., Bertino, E., Karabulut, Y. (eds.) Trust Management III , IFIPTM 2009. IAICT, vol. 300, pp. 164–175. Springer, Heidelberg (2009). https://doi.org/10.1007/978-3-642-02056-8_11

Author Index

Printed in the United States
by Baker & Taylor Publisher Services

THE FRONTIERS COLLECTION

Series Editors:
A.C. Elitzur M.P. Silverman J. Tuszynski R. Vaas H.D. Zeh

The books in this collection are devoted to challenging and open problems at the forefront of modern science, including related philosophical debates. In contrast to typical research monographs, however, they strive to present their topics in a manner accessible also to scientifically literate non-specialists wishing to gain insight into the deeper implications and fascinating questions involved. Taken as a whole, the series reflects the need for a fundamental and interdisciplinary approach to modern science. Furthermore, it is intended to encourage active scientists in all areas to ponder over important and perhaps controversial issues beyond their own speciality. Extending from quantum physics and relativity to entropy, consciousness and complex systems – the Frontiers Collection will inspire readers to push back the frontiers of their own knowledge.